CAUSAL CONCEPTS IN PSYCHOPATHOLOGY

Causality extends across many areas of psychiatry, from the purely conceptual and philosophical to the interpretation of genetic, epidemiological, and neurobiological work. This book offers new, interdisciplinary perspectives on causation in psychopathology, exploring it in relation to the latest scientific and philosophical advances as well as through psychiatric research and practice. It features contributions from many internationally known psychologists, clinical researchers, and philosophers of science. The chapters are organized into four parts: The Causes Themselves; Causes, Genes, and Neuroscience; Causality and Nosology; and Causality and Phenomenology. Each main chapter is preceded by a brief introduction written by the editors and a commentary by another author in this volume. By taking a multidisciplinary approach spanning psychiatry, philosophy, and psychology, the book is written to be accessible for members of all three disciplines.

KENNETH S. KENDLER has been publishing actively in psychiatric genetics and psychiatric nosology for 35 years and is the recipient of many honors and awards. He has written extensively on topics at the interface between psychiatry, philosophy, and history.

JOSEF PARNAS has dedicated the past 25 years to writing about the philosophy of psychopathology and applying it to psychiatric diagnosis and classification. He is a cofounder of the interdisciplinary theoretical institute, The Center for Subjectivity Research at the University of Copenhagen.

PETER ZACHAR is Professor in the Department of Psychology at Auburn University at Montgomery and a Fellow in the Association for Psychological Science. His primary area of scholarship is philosophical issues in psychiatric classification, with notable works including *A Metaphysics of Psychopathology* (2014, Japanese trans. 2018).

CAUSAL CONCEPTS IN PSYCHOPATHOLOGY

Multidisciplinary Perspectives

EDITED BY

KENNETH S. KENDLER

Virginia Commonwealth University

JOSEF PARNAS

University of Copenhagen

PETER ZACHAR

Auburn University at Montgomery

CAMBRIDGE
UNIVERSITY PRESS

CAMBRIDGE
UNIVERSITY PRESS

Shaftesbury Road, Cambridge CB2 8EA, United Kingdom

One Liberty Plaza, 20th Floor, New York, NY 10006, USA

477 Williamstown Road, Port Melbourne, VIC 3207, Australia

314–321, 3rd Floor, Plot 3, Splendor Forum, Jasola District Centre, New Delhi – 110025, India

Cambridge University Press is part of Cambridge University Press & Assessment, a department of the University of Cambridge.

We share the University's mission to contribute to society through the pursuit of education, learning and research at the highest international levels of excellence.

www.cambridge.org
Information on this title: www.cambridge.org/9781009390637

DOI: 10.1017/9781009390620

When citing this work, please include a reference to the DOI 10.1017/9781009390620

First published 2026

Cover image: Layne Kennedy / Corbis Documentary via Getty Images.

A catalogue record for this publication is available from the British Library

A Cataloging-in-Publication data record for this book is available from the Library of Congress

ISBN 978-1-009-39063-7 Hardback

Contents

PART III CAUSALITY AND NOSOLOGY

Figures

Tables

Contributors

Editors and Contributors

Kenneth S. Kendler, MD
(Chapters 1, 8, 11, 13, 16, 24, 25, 28, 31)
Virginia Commonwealth University
Virginia Institute for Psychiatric and Behavioral Genetics
Department of Psychiatry
Richmond, VA
Josef Parnas, MD, Dr. Med
(Chapters 36, 41)
University of Copenhagen, Faculty of Medicine and Health Sciences and Faculty of Humanities,
Center for Subjectivity Research
Copenhagen, Denmark
Peter Zachar, PhD
(Chapters 4, 7, 9, 10, 19, 22, 32, 34, 37, 40)
Department of Psychology, Auburn University at Montgomery
Montgomery, AL

Contributors

Denny Borsboom, PhD
(Chapters 26, 30)
Department of Psychology
University of Amsterdam
Amsterdam, the Netherlands
Erica Busch, BA
(Chapter 35)
Department of Psychology
Yale University

New Haven, CT
John Campbell, DPhil
(Chapters 3, 29)
University of California, Berkeley
Berkeley, CA
Carl F. Craver, PhD
(Chapters 18, 20)
Washington University
St. Louis, MO
Shaun Gallagher, PhD
(Chapters 38, 42)
The University of Memphis
Memphis, TN
Stephan Heckers, MD
(Chapters 6, 17)
Department of Psychiatry
Vanderbilt University
Nashville, TN
Steven E. Hyman, MD
(Chapters 15, 23)
Department of Stem Cell and Regenerative Biology
Harvard University
Cambridge, MA
Jonathan Kaplan, PhD
(Chapter 14)
Oregon State University
Corvallis, OR
Adina L. Roskies, PhD
(Chapters 35, 39)
Department of Philosophy
University of California, Santa Barbara
Santa Barbara, CA
Lauren N. Ross, PhD
(Chapters 8, 21)
Department of Logic and Philosophy of Science
University of California, Irvine
Irvine, CA
Federica Russo, PhD
(Chapters 5, 12)
Freudenthal Institute
Utrecht University

Utrecht, the Netherlands
Eric Turkheimer, PhD
(Chapters 14, 27)
Department of Psychology
University of Virginia
Charlottesville, VA
Dingmar van Eck, PhD
(Chapter 5)
University of Amsterdam
Amsterdam, the Netherlands
Ashley Walton, PhD
(Chapter 35)
Massachusetts General Hospital Brain Modulation Lab
Boston, MA
James Woodward, PhD
(Chapters 2, 33)
Department of History and Philosophy of Science
University of Pittsburgh
Pittsburgh, PA
Maja Zandersen, PhD
(Chapter 41)
Mental Health Centre Glostrup, Institute of Clinical Medicine
University Hospital of Copenhagen
Center for Subjectivity Research
Copenhagen, Denmark

General Introduction

Peter Zachar and Kenneth S. Kendler

There may be nothing of such obvious importance to human knowledge that is more elusive than the concept of causation. It sits as the crossroads of many disciplines, including philosophy, statistics, epidemiology, psychology, and clinical medicine. Causal theories in psychiatry trace back to the very beginning of the discipline and have often been speculative – and incorrect. These include the humoral theories of the Galenists from Roman times, ideas about vibrating nerves and intestinal vapors in the 18th century, degeneration theory the 19th century, Oedipal conflicts in the middle of the 20th century, and the dopamine theory of schizophrenia and other rudimentary "chemical imbalance" perspectives of the late 20th century.

Ironically, nearly every one of these perspectives was formulated using a causal framework that remains relevant today. This is the notion that people differ in their degree of vulnerability to illness, some are more and others less likely to become ill, but life events both random and systematic – and how those events are interpreted – play an important role in the generation and maintenance of illness (and health). In other words, although causal theory after causal theory from the past has been abandoned, one of the oldest theories – a broad framework including predisposing and precipitating factors – is still considered accurate.

In this book we examine causation as it applies to the origins of psychiatric disorders and related distress and dysfunction utilizing a multidisciplinary framework, from the perspectives of psychiatry, philosophy, and psychological science. Although members of all three disciplines discuss many of the same problems, they do not always share the same framework for studying those problems. This can lead them to focus on different features of the shared causal issues.

There is of course variation within each discipline – also evident in these chapters – making it misleading to lump all members of a discipline together. Nevertheless, different training, histories, and types of expertise establish disciplinary identities that can influence perspectives, including perspectives on causation. The issue is not the identity of disciplines themselves, but what a discipline is more likely to emphasize in contrast to other related disciplines. Our articulation of these perspectives, we contend, highlights some relevant differences that can be gleaned in this volume as members of the different disciplines interact with perspectives from the other disciplines.

For psychiatrists, causal theorizing had one great success, now rarely discussed: the discovery that general paresis of the insane was a late-stage manifestation of syphilis. This discovery, combined with the introduction of a range of treatments and eventually antibiotics, resulted in the disappearance of one of the most prevalent institutionalized mental disorders of the 19th century. For psychiatry the core elements of causation include etiology (what initiated an illness) and the pathological process that constitutes the disorder in question. For many psychiatrists it is nearly canonical that establishing the etiopathological validity for psychiatric disorders would increase the discipline's medical respectability and, most importantly, lead to better therapeutic success. Even for thinkers who do not favor reductive accounts, and in proportion to how strongly they identify with medicine, etiopathological validity is not something they want to abandon.

For philosophers (especially philosophers of science), as briefly described by Lauren Ross in Chapter 21, the issue of causation is entwined with the nature of scientific explanation. In the 18th century, following the work of David Hume, scientifically minded philosophers viewed the very idea of causation to be speculative metaphysics – and not an appropriate candidate for being a defining feature of scientific explanation. Alternative candidates not directly based on causation included laws of nature, relationships of probability, and unifying theoretical frameworks (like the Newtonian model in physics).

However, aside from Darwin's theory of evolution, laws of nature and grand unifying theories are not prevalent in the life sciences, so causal approaches to explanation have become more important for philosophers who study those sciences. These approaches include causal pathway accounts, mechanistic accounts, interventionist accounts, and cascade accounts. Many of these approaches emphasize how causal claims are understood and validated in the sciences. Such accounts, however, do not just trail the sciences but dig deeper. For example, a psychiatrist may talk loosely about endophenotypes or biomarkers as "mechanistic," but a philosopher would point out that endophenotypes may be a part of a mechanism but are not mechanisms. Philosophers will have detailed accounts of what mechanisms in science are and will also distinguish them from other kinds of causal accounts.

To characterize psychological scientists, we will contrast them with what we said about psychiatry and philosophy of science. With respect to psychiatry, neuroscience and genetics are an increasingly important part of training in psychology, but developmental psychology, personality and social psychology, and cognitive psychology are still core subjects. In trying to put this all together, the resulting notion of complex psychological states makes it less likely for psychologists to prioritize etiopathological validity. Psychometric construct validity would typically be front and center in psychological science.

With respect to questions about the nature of scientific explanation and causation, psychologists are unlikely to dig down as deeply as do the philosophers of science. Especially in clinical psychological science, the questions that would be of direct interest in philosophy either take a back seat to or are viewed by psychological scientists as entangled with issues relating to measurement, quantification, and scientific methodology.

This book is the sixth volume in a series documenting philosophical issues in psychiatry conferences that have been held in Copenhagen, Denmark. The first conference was in 2006. The meeting for the current volume occurred May 15–17, 2023. Although these books have been described as being based on the Copenhagen conferences, over time we have come to see that description as inaccurate. A better description is that we selected a book topic and invited specific people to contribute chapters. The initial drafts of these chapters were presented at the meeting in Copenhagen.

The conference was co-sponsored by the University of Copenhagen Center for Subjectivity Research. The funding for the conference, including travel and accommodations for all presenters, was generously provided by the Lundbeck Foundation. The conference itself was free and open to the public.

Although presenters were invited based on the quality and relevance of their prior work, everyone was free to select their own topic related to the issue of causation. Once the specific topics coalesced, we organized them into four different sections: The Causes Themselves; Causes, Genes, and Neuroscience; Causality and Nosology; and Causality and Phenomenology. A key feature of the conference phase of the book is that every main presentation is followed by a commentary by another presenter, a brief response to the commentary, and then a general discussion with questions taken from anyone in the audience. The interaction between presenter and commentator is designed to continue after the conference as final versions of the chapters are written.

Each presentation–commentary section in the book is preceded by a brief introduction by one of the editors. These introductions were shared with the section authors, who provided suggestions for improvement. The purpose of the brief introductions is to increase the accessibility of the chapters to those from multiple disciplines.

We have no better summary of this meeting than the final comments Kenneth Kendler gave at the formal close of the conference phase of the book:

> This now brings the first phase of our joint venture to a close. Our three days together has well demonstrated the richness of the issues involved in causality for the multilevel field of psychiatry.
>
> We explored the benefits and potential limitations of counterfactual methods, especially the interventionist approach of Woodward. We debated about the nature of mechanisms, from sketches at a high psychosocial level to worked-out biological pathways and large-effect molecular variants. We pondered the boundaries between mechanisms and the more generic concept of causal pathways and examined the possible contribution of network approaches. We examined the notion that our measurements index disorders versus constituting them, looking that what implication a constituting relation might have for causal models.
>
> We looked at how meaning and explanation aided understanding. We explored how phenomenological approaches should be integrated into our causal approach, how to clarify the sometime confusing division into so-called proximal and distal causes, and had a peek into how we might learn about the key feature of agency from deep-brain-stimulation studies. We debated whether optimism about the reductionist molecular approach is warranted. We examined in some detail how brain-based imaging, molecular genetics, and molecular neuroscience approaches to the etiology of psychiatry disorders could clarify causal pathways.
>
> For us, the best return on our organization effort would be for new collaborations to spring up among the participants (or expansions of prior work). Most of all, the speakers engaged with energy the topics they selected. We had some good-spirited discussions that, for me, were the epitome of our academic mission – the pursuit of truth in the company of friends. It doesn't get much better.

Preface

This book is the sixth volume stemming from conferences focused on various philosophical issues in psychiatry that have been held in Copenhagen, Denmark since 2006. The meeting for the current volume occurred May 15–17, 2023 and was organized by the editors of this volume: Kenneth S. Kendler, Peter Zachar, and Josef Parnas. Although these books have been traditionally described as being based on the Copenhagen conferences, over time we have come to see them differently. A better description is that we selected a book topic and invited specific people to contribute chapters. The initial drafts of these chapters were presented at the meetings in Copenhagen.

The conference was co-sponsored by the University of Copenhagen, Institute of Clinical Medicine. The funding for the conference, including travel and accommodation for all presenters, was generously provided by the Lundbeck Foundation. The conference itself was free and open to the public.

As in years past, each talk was followed by a formal commentary from another participant and then an open give-and-take with the audience and other speakers, who were rarely shy in posing challenging questions. Sometimes spirited discussions followed. Therefore, each speaker who came to the meeting agreed to present a paper of their own, comment formally on another paper, and to write up both for publication.

As with the five prior volumes, we have tried to capture the interactive nature of the meeting through the organization of this volume. Each individual chapter has an introduction (written by one of the volume editors) and a discussion. Our hope is that this format will provide the reader with a sense of the give-and-take of the actual meeting.

In working on a contributed volume of this kind, the editing team has accumulated a number of debts. Most importantly, our thanks go to the contributors to the volume. Their interest and willingness to take on their conceptually challenging topics, and often work across disciplinary boundaries, were critical to the success of this project. As in past meetings, we received many compliments during the three days and later about the quality of individual contributions and the stimulating nature of the entire experience. These comments were, as you might expert, heartwarming to us.

As in previous years, we owe a special thanks to Jill Opalesky for her superb organizational skills and her enduring good nature and sense of calm. Her participation was vital to all aspects of this project, including the invitation of the speakers, the establishing of the schedule, the actual hands-on running of the meeting, and especially keeping straight all the chapters, comments, and introductions through their multiple revisions and chasing down some of our contributors to get their material to us at least approximately on time. It was through her persistent but polite efforts that we were able to deliver this volume to the publishers on time. We also want to express our appreciation to Caroline Imelda Sørensen, Dr. Rasmus Handest, and Lisbeth Jensen for their invaluable managerial and administrative assistance.

In each prior volume in this series, we have concluded our preface with these words, which describe our experience of organizing the conference and editing the volume: "This project was, to use the philosophical term, emergent – in the end, the sum was much more than the individual parts." We are happy to say that once again this applies. We hope you, the readers, will agree with us as you read through this volume.

REFERENCES

Kendler, K. S., & Parnas, J. (2008). *Philosophical issues in psychiatry: Explanation, phenomenology and nosology.* Johns Hopkins University Press.

(2012). *Philosophical issues in psychiatry II: Nosology.* Oxford University Press.

(2015). *Philosophical issues in psychiatry III: The nature and sources of historical change.* Oxford University Press.

(2017). *Philosophical issues in psychiatry IV: Classification of psychiatric illness.* Oxford University Press.

Kendler, K. S., Parnas, J., & Zachar, P. (2020). *Levels of analysis in psychopathology: Cross-disciplinary perspectives.* Cambridge University Press.

PART I

The Causes Themselves

Section 1

CHAPTER 1

Introduction to Woodward's "Reflections on Some Strategies for Causal Inference in Psychiatry"

Kenneth S. Kendler

Jim Woodward has, for a number of years, been a leading philosophical theorist of causation, playing a particularly prominent role in the articulation of the influential theory of interventionism as outlined in his book, *Making Things Happen* (Woodward, 2003). Readers are therefore in for a treat in this essay (Chapter 2) in which he reviews his current thinking about causation as it applies to psychiatric research and more particularly to the clarification of the impact of environmental risk factors by epidemiological methods. In this introduction, I will seek only to expand on a modest number of points among the many he covers in this review. Most of my points are focused on one relatively well researched risk factor for psychiatric disorders – childhood sexual abuse.

First, most of the important questions about environmental exposures that influence risk of psychiatric or substance use disorders are not, for practical and/or ethical reasons, amenable to randomized controlled trial designs. Indeed, many are quite messy and likely to contain several "active ingredients" that determine the overall level of experienced stress. Woodward notes one such example: the common risk factor of low socioeconomic status. Let me provide an additional, rather striking example. After obtaining approval from our cohort, we conducted a detailed study of childhood sexual abuse (CSA) in a large sample of female twins whom we followed for more than a decade (Kendler et al., 2000). As expected, we found a large increase in risk for a range of psychiatric disorders for those who reported CSA. For example, in the most severe form – repeated sexual intercourse – the risk for major depression was increased 2.8-fold – from a population-based rate of about 12–13% to 50%. We asked a lot of background questions about the nature of the abuse, such as threats of violence, number of perpetrators, and the like (Bulik et al., 2001). One pair of questions turned out to be unexpectedly potent. We asked whether they told anyone about the abuse, and if so, what happened after. For those who told someone (typically a parent) and the result was that the abuse stopped, the odds ratio for major depression was 0.35 – meaning a 65% reduction (Bulik et al., 2001). A little algebra will show that for major depression, the increased risk associated with severe CSA almost entirely disappears in these situations. In addition to the psychological and physical trauma of the forced intercourse itself, our results suggest that a substantial part of the pathogenic effect of CSA is the feeling of not being protected by one's loved ones, which has a magnifying effect on the feelings of shame and worthlessness associated with the CSA. To give these statistical figures a more human form, one of our interviewers describe the story told by one such twin. The abuser was a next-door neighbor and friend of her parents who had said he would kill her parents if she ever told. Finally, after years of abuse, she broke down and told her mother. On hearing the news, her mother immediately got on the phone and called the police; within a few minutes, sirens were wailing. Her mother took her by the hand and walked her out onto the porch in time to see several policemen escorting the handcuffed neighbor into the police car. The twin then spoke of the fears of telling her mother, that her mother would blame her and not understand the terrible isolation and shame she had experienced. Standing by her mother on the porch, she understood that she had been wrong. She was loved, it wasn't her fault, and her parents would protect her when they had the needed information. I tell this to illustrate the subtlety of causal pathways of risks for psychiatric illness.

Second, as Woodward and previous authors (Ohlsson & Kendler, 2020) have pointed out, it is important to distinguish between potential confounders that are known and those that are unknown. Only if the main confounders are known and are in your dataset can you have reasonable confidence in the typical first level approach to causal inference – regression with control of confounders. Take as an example the large literature showing that peer deviance is strongly associated with problematic alcohol and drug use (Hoeben et al., 2016). Many confounds might influence these results, including association of deviant peer groups with poor academic performance, low socioeconomic status, and levels of parent education and self-selection, as genetic factors influence the choice of deviant peers (Kendler et al., 2007). These associations suggest that we should be skeptical of standard regression-based causal models, as that requires that you have good measures of all significant confounders – an unlikely scenario. A relatively definitive approach to determining the nature of the causal effect of peer deviance on substance abuse would likely need to control both for unknown and known confounders such as an instrumental variable or co-relative design.

Third, Woodward is skeptical of the often emphasized importance of causal specificity. I concur. While there are some environmental stressors that appear to have some diagnostic specificity in psychiatry, such as the relationship between loss and depression (Brown et al., 1995) and danger and anxiety disorders (Kendler et al., 2003), CSA increases risk for nearly every major form of psychiatric and substance use disorders (Kendler et al., 2000). The wide breadth of the impact of CSA does not, in and of itself, provide an argument of much power against it causal impact, which is supported by co-twin control and structural equation analyses (Kendler & Aggen, 2013; Kendler et al., 2000).

Fourth, Woodward comments that few studies of psychiatric environmental risk factors for psychiatric disorders can examine a "dose–response" relationship, which has been suggested as another possible index of causal effects. However, in developing a widely used scale for CSA, Martin et al. (1993) proposed three levels of severity: "no genital contact," "genital contact but no intercourse," and "sexual intercourse." In many subsequent studies, including our own (Kendler et al., 2000), the risk for both psychiatric and substance use disorders increased monotonically with the increasing severity of CSA. So sometimes this method can be applied to strengthen causal claims.

Finally, Woodward reviews the criterion of stability of a putative causal effect, which I also consider an important criterion that reflects the degree to which the risk factors for psychiatric illness are sensitive to the personal and cultural context in which it occurs. My work with CSA provided a good opportunity to test its cross-cultural stability. When we began the large-scale molecular genetic study of depression in women in China – the CONVERGE project – our Chinese collaborators were quite very skeptical of our efforts to assess CSA given its strong associated with cultural taboos. Our effort was further complicated by concerns of large cultural effects on depression in China that might make it a different kind of entity to that assessed in Western culture (Kleinman, 1986). However, we persisted in our efforts and, with a quite large sample of depressed and control women of Han Chinese ancestry, robustly replicated both the overall magnitude of the CSA–depression association and the previously seen dose–response relationship (Chen et al., 2014).

In closing, I want to emphasize further another point raised by Woodward – the importance of triangulation (Munafo & Davey-Smith, 2018). Many scientists are exposed to repeated emphases on the importance of replication. In observational sciences, such as psychiatric epidemiology, however, specific methods can have unknown biases, and a replication in a different sample my suffer from the same bias. By contrast, a study in a different sample using an *entirely different method* would be of greater value, as it controls both for sample difference and potential biases in the original method.

REFERENCES

Brown, G. W., Harris, T. O., & Hepworth, C. (1995). Loss, humiliation and entrapment among women developing depression: a patient and non-patient comparison. *Psychological Medicine, 25*(1), 7–21. http://www.ncbi.nlm.nih.gov/pubmed/7792364

Bulik, C. M., Prescott, C. A., & Kendler, K. S. (2001). Features of childhood sexual abuse and the development of psychiatric and substance use disorders. *British Journal of Psychiatry, 179*, 444–449.

Chen, J., Cai, Y., Cong, E., Liu, Y., Gao, J., Li, Y., Tao, M., Zhang, K., Wang, X., Gao, C., Yang, L., Li, K., Shi, J., Wang, G., Liu, L., Zhang, J., Du, B., Jiang, G., Shen, J., . . . Flint, J. (2014). Childhood sexual abuse and the development of recurrent major depression in Chinese women. *PloS One, 9*(1), e87569. https://doi.org/10.1371/journal.pone.0087569

Hoeben, E. M., Meldrum, R. C., Walker, D. A., & Young, J. T. (2016). The role of peer delinquency and unstructured socializing in explaining delinquency and substance use: A state-of-the-art review. *Journal of Criminal Justice, 47*, 108–122.

Kendler, K. S., & Aggen, S. H. (2013). Clarifying the causal relationship in women between childhood sexual abuse and lifetime major depression. *Psychology and Medicine, 13*, 1–9. https://doi.org/S0033291713001797

Kendler, K. S., Bulik, C. M., Silberg, J., Hettema, J. M., Myers, J., & Prescott, C. A. (2000). Childhood sexual abuse and adult psychiatric and substance use disorders in women: An epidemiological and cotwin control analysis. *Archives of General Psychiatry, 57*(10), 953–959.

Kendler, K. S., Hettema, J. M., Butera, F., Gardner, C. O., & Prescott, C. A. (2003). Life event dimensions of loss, humiliation, entrapment, and danger in the prediction of onsets of major depression and generalized anxiety. *Archives of General Psychiatry, 60*(8), 789–796.

Kendler, K. S., Jacobson, K. C., Gardner, C. O., Gillespie, N. A., Aggen, S. H., & Prescott, C. A. (2007). Creating a social world: A developmental study of peer deviance. *Archives of General Psychiatry, 64*(8), 958–965.

Kleinman, A. (1986). *Social origins of distress and disease: Depression, neurasthenia, and pain in modern China.* Yale University Press.

Martin, J., Anderson, J., Romans, S., Mullen, P., & O'Shea, M. (1993). Asking about child sexual abuse: Methodological implications of a two-stage survey. *Child Abuse and Neglect, 17*, 383–392.

Munafo, M. R., & Davey-Smith, G. (2018). Robust research needs many lines of evidence. *Nature, 553*(7689), 399–401. https://doi.org/d41586-018-01023-3

Ohlsson, H., & Kendler, K. S. (2020). Applying causal inference methods in psychiatric epidemiology: A review. *Journal of American Medical Association: Psychiatry, 77*(6), 637–644. https://doi.org/10.1001/jamapsychiatry.2019.3758

Woodward, J. (2003). *Making things happen* (P. Humphreys, Ed.). Oxford University Press.

CHAPTER 2

Reflections on Some Strategies for Causal Inference in Psychiatry

James Woodward

2.1 Introduction

This chapter discusses some widely used strategies (not just in psychiatry but elsewhere) for inferring causal relations, including randomized controlled trials (RCTs) and instrumental variables. In psychiatry, these seem to be most useful in identifying environmental factors that may play a causal role in mental illness, or drugs or therapies that may be used in treating mental illness; it is less obvious (at least to me) how these techniques might be used in any particularly direct way to make inferences about the causal role of genetic factors or neural functioning in mental illness. Hence my focus will be on the use of these strategies in identifying environmental causes. I will discuss both the advantages and limitations of the strategies.

2.2 Causation in General

2.2.1 *Necessity*

A common feature of many accounts is that causation should be understood in terms of some mixture of necessity and sufficiency. In modern treatments, necessity is generally understood in terms of the idea that a cause is something that, under the right conditions, makes a difference to whether an effect occurs, so that there is a relation of dependence between the cause and the effect. The qualifying phrase "under the right conditions" is required because, for example, *C1* might cause *E* but the difference-making role of *C1* may be masked by the presence of another cause, *C2* of *E*. In such cases, the difference-making role of *C1* may be recovered by removing or inactivating *C2*, thus revealing the dependence of *E* on *C1*, as in the example involving the discovery of path-specific effects discussed later in the chapter. The idea that causes are difference makers in this sense is highlighted in "counterfactual" accounts of causation, including the potential outcomes framework associated with Rubin and prominent in statistics and econometrics as well as the interventionist account described later.

2.2.2 *Sufficiency*

The sufficiency aspect of causation is more subtle. Both in ordinary life and in the biomedical and behavioral sciences, virtually none of the variables we describe as causes are literally sufficient for their effects in the sense that the effects always follow when the causes are present. Smoking causes lung cancer, but not always, and even when it does, other conditions must be present – for example, failure of DNA repair or tumor suppression mechanisms. I suggest later here that a natural way of capturing what is right about the sufficiency idea is that causal relationships (or at least the sorts of causal relationships we value and would like to discover) are expected to be at least somewhat *stable* or *invariant*, in the sense that we expect that they will continue to operate across a range of different circumstances. Thus, smoking does not always cause lung cancer, but it does for different demographic groups, environmental conditions, and so on.

Although the necessity aspect of causation is well captured by counterfactual and interventionist accounts of the sort described in the sections that follow, I have come to believe (in agreement with recent criticisms from others, e.g., Deaton & Cartwright, 2018) that such accounts tend to somewhat underplay the importance of the sufficiency or stability aspect of causation. I will explore some of the consequences of this for causal inference later in the chapter, arguing that a number of standard inferential techniques also underplay the sufficiency aspect.

2.3 Interventionism

In what follows, I assume a broadly interventionist account of causation. Because I have discussed this account elsewhere (e.g., Woodward, 2003) and in order to save space, I will describe just the bare bones. The basic idea is that if you were to perform the right kind of manipulation of C (an "intervention") and E changes, then C causes E. "Right kind" means that the manipulation of C should be such that any change in E resulting from this manipulation should occur "through" C and not in some other way. Put more simply, the manipulation should be unconfounded. At a population level, when the target causal notion is the estimation of an average causal effect, randomized control experiments are one widely recognized way of implementing interventions. However, many – arguably most – experimental manipulations in sciences such as physics, chemistry, and even biology that establish the existence of causal effects do *not* involve randomization, although they do make use of interventions in the sense characterized earlier. When Michael Faraday established that moving a conductor through a magnetic field induced a current in the conductor, he did not employ randomization. The most famous experiments in molecular biology do not make use of randomization. As discussed in the later sections of this chapter, randomization is a rational response to a very particular set of inferential problems that can arise in portions of the biomedical and behavioral sciences – problems that arise less often in other areas of science.

2.4 Distinctions among Causal Concepts

So far, I have been talking about causation in a rather generic way. But one of the attractions of interventionist approaches to causation is that they allow for a more fine-grained characterization of a number of distinct causal notions, corresponding to different questions in which we may be interested.

2.4.1 Total or Net Effects

This has to do with overall total causal impact of a change in one variable on another.

2.4.2 Causal Contribution along a Path

An important contrasting notion is of a causal contribution along a path. Consider the causal structure presented in Figure 2.1.

Assuming the relationships are linear, the total effect of X on Z is the sum of the effects of X along the two paths, one direct and one going through Y – and hence given by the coefficient $a + bc$. The causal contribution of X to Z along the direct path is captured by the coefficient a, and the contribution of X to Z along the indirect path is given by bc. Breaking total causal effects into contributions made along distinct paths (rather than just representing the total effect) is often desirable, perhaps particularly in the biomedical sciences and psychiatry. For example, a gene

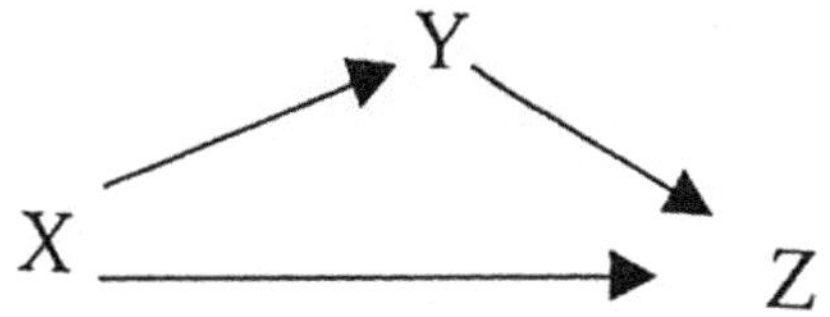

Figure 2.1 *X* directly causes *Y*, *Y* directly causes *Z*, and *X* directly causes *Z*. *X* causally contributes to *Z* along two distinct paths: the $X \rightarrow Y \rightarrow Z$ path and the $X \rightarrow Z$ path. Assuming that the causal relations are linear, the total effect of X on Z is the sum of its effects on these two distinct paths.

G might contribute to depression *D* via an "inside-the-skin" pathway directly affecting brain chemistry but also via a distinct, outside-the-skin pathway in which *G* contributes to behavior *B*, which creates stressful situations *S*, which also contribute to depression. I take it that part of what is involved in the discovery of mechanisms is often the decomposition of total effects into effects along distinct pathways, with distinct mediating variables.

In many (but not all) cases, we can capture this notion of a cause making a contribution to an effect along a path by considering *combinations* of interventions rather than single interventions as in the characterization of a total effect. In the above example, if we were to intervene to fix the value of one of the mediating variables *B* or *S* at the off position (e.g., by teaching a patient to avoid behavior that causes stressful situations) and, independently of this, intervene to change *G* or its downstream but inside-the-skin effects, this would (if the postulated causal structure is correct) lead to a change in *D*, thus revealing the role of the inside-the-skin causal path from *G* to *D* . Similarly, if we could somehow interfere with the inside-the-skin path from *G* to *D* (while leaving the outside-the-skin path through *B* unaffected) while changing *G*, this would reveal the existence of the outside-the-skin path. As this example brings out, one of several reasons why the decomposition of total causal relations into path-specific causal relationships is important is that distinct paths can offer distinct points or variables for intervention, and sometimes it may be easier (or more beneficial) to intervene on these than on a total cause. In the example above, an intervention that takes the form of a change in variable *B* may ameliorate the effects of *G* even if we cannot intervene on *G* itself. In psychiatry and psychology, "mediation analysis" is sometimes employed in an effort to achieve this sort of decomposition into paths when one has only observational and not intervention-based information concerning the relation between a candidate mediator and other variables. I discuss this briefly in what follows, noting that it requires very strong assumptions to be reliable.

2.4.3 *Average Causal Effect*

A third notion of causation (or at least of causal effect) that deserves mention is the notion of average causal effect (ACE) or average treatment effect (ATE). Here an intervention fixes a value for a putative cause for some individuals in a population (the treatment group) and withholds the treatment from other individuals (the control group). If allocation of treatment is randomized (and other well-known conditions such as the stable unit treatment value assumption [SUTVA][1] are satisfied), any "statistically significant" difference in average value for an effect variable between the treatment and control group is taken to support an inference to the average causal effect of the treatment. Average causal effect qualifies as a notion of causation that belongs in the interventionist family because, if the RCT is reliable, it tells us how an intervention that changes the average value of the treatment variable will change the expected value of the effect variable for the population and circumstances the RCT represents.

2.5 Stability

The interventionist conditions for the various causal notions just described can be regarded as *minimal* conditions for causation – that is, they are conditions that must be satisfied if a relationship is to count as causal at all, as opposed to being a relationship of noncausal association. However, there are further distinctions we may draw among causal relations. I will focus on two of these: here, the aforementioned *stability* (or invariance) and, later, *specificity*. These are among the "aspects" of causation that Bradford Hill (1965) discusses, so I will be picking up on some of Hill's ideas about causal inference.

Suppose that a relationship satisfies the minimal condition for causation in the sense that it correctly describes how a variable or its expected value

[1] SUTVA requires that the response of each unit in the population should not depend on the treatment assigned to other units. This requirement is violated when there is interference or "spillover" between units, as when a drug delivered to one patient affects the health of other patients in the population who are not treated.

will respond to interventions on the individuals within a population in some circumstances. The stability of that causal relationship has to do with the extent to which it continues to hold in other circumstances or populations – whether it generalizes or "ports." As noted earlier, the smoking → lung cancer causal relation is stable in the sense that it holds across many different circumstances and populations – among different demographic groups, people with different diets and life circumstances, and so on. (Note that this is not the same as the requirement that the relationship be "strong" in the sense that, say, the correlation between smoking and lung cancer be "large"; the correlation might be modest but hold across a variety of circumstances.) As I understand stability, it is not an all-or-nothing matter, but rather one of degree: A causal relationship can be more or less stable, and stable across some changes in circumstances but not others. We can make a causal claim more precise by specifying this additional information.

Stability is related to what Hill called consistency:

> Has [the relationship] been repeatedly observed by different persons, in different places, circumstances and times? (Hill, 1965, p. 296)

However, my notion of stability is somewhat different from and stronger than this. It's not just with whether an *association* generalizes to different circumstances but whether a *causal relationship*, holding in some local circumstances, also holds in others. It isn't just that smoking and lung cancer are associated in many different circumstances; in addition, smoking *causes* lung cancer in many different circumstances. It is entirely possible for an association to hold in many different circumstances but not be causal. This can happen when the association is the consequence of a confounding structure that is very pervasive. As noted later, socioeconomic status (SES) is just such a pervasive potential confounder in the case of many medical and social outcomes.

Hill seems to think of stability of association largely in terms of its evidential significance: It is one possible kind of evidence that an association can be interpreted causally. In what follows I argue that there is something right about this, but that stability is most evidentially informative when an association holds not just in different circumstances but in circumstances that are sufficiently different that they are likely to involve different confounding structures. Of course, stability is not just of interest in its role of dealing with confounders; causal relations that are stable are valuable for many additional reasons having to do with manipulation, control, and explanation.

2.5.1 Stability and Mechanisms

What is the relationship between information about stability and information about mechanisms? The two are different though not unrelated. It is certainly possible to discover a stable causal relationship between *C* and *E* without knowing what mechanism connects *C* to *E*, as examples like smoking → lung cancer and the aspirin → headache relief illustrate. And knowing the mechanism connecting *C* to *E* may lead us to conclude that the *C* → *E* relation is unstable/will not generalize well to a variety of circumstances if the mechanism is "special" and unlikely to be found in other circumstances. In addition, we may identify a mechanism connecting *C* to *E* in some circumstances and not know whether that mechanism is operative in other circumstances – a mechanism found in mice may or may not be present and operative in the same way in humans. (Think of mouse models of neurodegenerative diseases.) On the other hand, when we have evidence that *C* causes *E* in one set of circumstances and are wondering whether that relation generalizes to other circumstances, information about the mechanism operative in the first set of circumstances can sometimes help provide evidence (including evidence of a negative sort) about generalizability. To take an example discussed later in the chapter, if the mechanism underlying the causal relation between poverty and children's mental illnesses has to do with the increased time more affluent parents have for child supervision, increases in parental income that are the result of both parents working more than full time (as opposed to income increases from a stipend) would not be expected to benefit offspring mental health.

2.5.2 Stability in Relation to the Minimal Conditions for Causation

My discussion so far has adopted an analytical separation between whether a causal relationship holds at all in certain local circumstances (whether it satisfies the minimal condition for causation) and whether it generalizes to other circumstances (stability). Such a separation is assumed, either explicitly or implicitly, in many discussions of causal inference. For example, it is assumed in the contrast frequently drawn between internal and external validity: An RCT might establish that a causal relation holds between *X* and *Y* in a particular experiment (or perhaps in a population if the subjects are representative of the population), and thus that the experiment is internally valid in the sense of establishing causality in that particular context. However, it is taken to be a further question, not settled by the experiment, whether *X* will cause *Y* in other circumstances – whether and to what extent the experimental result is "externally valid." A similar contrast holds for other causal inference techniques such as the use of instrumental variables. Here current practice generally assumes that such inferences can establish (at best) only locally valid causal conclusions, holding for specific populations or even subpopulations, as in talk of "local average treatment effects," which are taken to hold only for those members of a population whose behavior is changed by the treatment (e.g., Imbens & Angrist, 1994). The extent to which such conclusions generalize is a distinct issue.

A related set of assumptions, perhaps not so frequently discussed, concerns trade-offs among different kinds of mistakes. The internal/external separation just discussed can be motivated by (something like) the assumption that it is better to avoid mistakenly claiming that a causal relationship exists when it does not than to fail to discover a causal relationship that does exist. In particular, if the kinds of causal inferences that are most reliable are those (such as RCTs) that establish only local causal conclusions, it might be argued that it is preferable to employ these even if they don't yield results about the extent to which causal claims generalize to other contexts. The latter, it may be thought, are inevitably more risky and more likely to be erroneous.

This contrast between whether a causal relationship holds locally and the extent to which it generalizes is certainly defensible in some respects. With techniques like RCTs and instrumental variables, we have analytical results that establish that if the various conditions required for their correct implementation hold, claims about local causal conclusions (or more precisely claims about their expected error rates) follow deductively. Of course, we may mistakenly think that the required conditions hold when they do not, and this may lead to invalid inferences, but in such cases it can be argued that we have known sources of inductive risk. By contrast, generalization to other circumstances appears to raise other unknown and less controllable forms of inductive risk. Moreover, the contrast seems to track (to at least some extent) what might be described as one natural order of causal discovery, at least in portions of biomedicine and the behavioral and social sciences: First, one establishes that a causal relationship holds locally; then (in a further step), one explores to what extent that relationship holds in other circumstances. If one does not have good reason to suppose that the relationship holds in some local circumstances, it seems pointless to worry about the extent to which it generalizes.

Nonetheless, the common assumption that the two steps (internal versus external validity, etc.) are not just analytically separable but can be carried out completely independently of one another can be misleading and methodologically detrimental, as has become apparent in recent discussions of RCTs and instrumental variables. One basic problem is that a purely local result about causation, even if apparently internally valid, can be scientifically uninteresting and difficult to interpret unless accompanied by at least some information about stability or generalizability. Put in terms of our earlier discussion, too much focus on internal validity puts too much weight on the dependency aspect of causation (attempting to establish that *C* is a difference maker for *E* in specific, local circumstances) to the neglect of the sufficiency or stability aspect. A closely related point is that sometimes evidence relevant to establishing a local causal claim can come from information about the apparent stability or generalizability of that claim to other circumstances, so that at the level of evidential reasoning the internal and external aspects of validity are not always sharply separable. I will provide illustrations of these points in the following sections.

2.6 Causal Inference: Design-Based versus Non-design-Based

So far I have focused on distinctions among several causal concepts and some other features causal relations may possess. I turn now to a discussion of some strategies for causal inference. Given an interventionist account, a natural way of conceptualizing problems of causal inference follows. First, in some (ideal) cases we may be able to carry out an intervention experiment of the very sort that is involved in our characterization of the relevant causal notion. For example, if we are interested in whether *C* is a net cause of *E*, we may intervene to change the value of *C*, observe a change in the value of *E*, and conclude that *C* causes *E*, this inference being straightforwardly warranted because of the connection between intervention and causation. If we are interested in the average causal effect of a drug, we may be able to perform a randomized experiment. As the later discussion will show, even in these cases we may be able to conclude much less than we would like to know, but the connection to the causal conclusion is transparent.

Suppose, however, as is very often the case (both in psychiatry and elsewhere), we don't have data that are the result of a deliberate experiment; instead, we have "observational" data consisting of associations or correlations among various measured variables. Within an interventionist

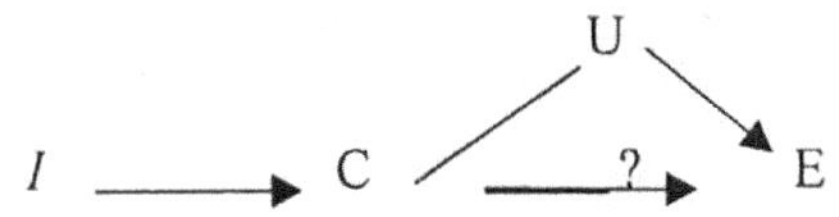

Figure 2.2 The undirected edge involving *C* and *U* indicates that *C* and *U* are correlated, and hence that the possible *C/E* causal relation is confounded (at least to some extent) by unobserved *U*. Adopting the Rubin-style counterfactual notation according to which E_c stands for the value *E* would have if $C = c$, *I* will be a valid instrument if (i) *I* _|_ E_c and (ii) I _/|_ C where _|_ stands for independence and _/|_ for dependence.

framework, a natural way of conceptualizing the inferential problem we face in these circumstances is that we are trying to figure out what the results of some relevant intervention experiment would be were we to perform it but without actually doing the experiment. This suggests (I don't say that it establishes) that we should look for data produced in a way that is "close to" or "emulates" data that would be produced by an intervention experiment (that is, data produced by an intervention-like process), the idea being that to the extent we can find such data, it is more likely to lead to reliable causal inferences than data not (known to be) produced in a way that emulates an intervention-like experiment.

There are several inferential strategies that have this general feature, to a greater or lesser degree. For example, in the case of instrumental variables, the idea is to find a naturally occurring variable *X* that is related to some candidate cause *C* for *E* in the so-called soft-intervention-like way illustrated in Figure 2.2: if (i) *X* is correlated with or known to affect *C* (ii) in such a way that any variation in *E* that it causes occurs only through variation in *C* and not in some other way (known as the *exclusion restriction*), and an association between *C* and *E* is observed, we may conclude that *C* causes *E*. Importantly, this conclusion can be warranted even if there is an unobserved or unknown confounder *U* of *C* and *E*.

Other designs that can emulate interventions to a greater or lesser degree include regression discontinuity and differences-in-differences designs. In these designs too, the idea is to look for processes involved in the production of data that are intervention-like and to exploit this fact in causal inference. In these designs the result is virtually always a causal conclusion that is "local" in the sense that (just as is the case when one conducts an experiment) the upshot is a claim about the existence (or quantitative estimate) of a causal relation between a variable and an effect in some particular set of circumstances.

The strategies just described contrast with alternative strategies that are more global in the sense that they involve using the associations between a large number of observed variables to estimate causal relations among all of these at once, rather than focusing, as with the previous designs, on observations involving intervention-like designs that have as their target whether some particular causal relationship holds between two candidate variables. Typically, this second strategy involves trying to measure various potential confounders for causal relationships and then to eliminate their influence by statistical means, for example by conditioning on them. Accordingly, I will call these conditioning strategies. These might be carried out by various statistical packages or machine learning algorithms. The result typically takes the form of a set of structural equations and/or a directed graph. Path diagrams such as the multilevel diagram representing causes of depression in Kendler and Prescott, 2006 are one example of this.

For both approaches – conditioning and intervention-emulation based – control of confounders is crucial. However, the two approaches employ different strategies for accomplishing this. The intervention-emulating strategies are *design based.* This may be illustrated by a (rather idealized) physics example. Suppose one wishes to determine whether a certain particle *X* exists. When this particle is present, it produces a certain characteristic "signature" in a detector. Unfortunately, there are other particles *Y* that may also be present and can produce the same signature, making it unclear whether the signature in question is really due to the *X*s . So we have to control in some way for the presence of the *Y*s. Consider two possible strategies for doing this. One consists of trying to measure how many *Y*s are present or perhaps constructing a model that estimates how many are present and then using this to correct for possible confounding. A different strategy is to build a large shield around the apparatus that blocks all incoming *Y*s. Assuming that there are good reasons to think the shield is effective, there are obvious reasons for thinking that the second strategy is likely to be more reliable. The first strategy is subject to the worry that we may fail to detect all of the *Y*s or we may have the wrong model of their behavior. The second strategy does not require that we are able to detect the *Y*s or have the correct model of their behavior; the physical design of the experiment eliminates the possibility that they will be present. (Of course, we may be mistaken in thinking that the shield is effective, but there will be independent ways of checking this, for example by turning off the experiment and seeing if, in the presence of the shield, there is any evidence for *Y*s.) In this sense the second strategy is design based and the first one isn't; the first tries to achieve by measurement and calculation what the second achieves by the physical structure of the experiment.

A similar contrast applies to the two approaches to causal inference described earlier. In a randomized experiment, the physical design of the experiment itself – the fact that there is random assignment – can, when correctly implemented and additional assumptions are satisfied, ensure that the treatment and control group are equivalent in expectation with respect to other factors that might influence the outcome.[2] Carrying out the randomization does not require one to know what these potentially confounding factors are or that one can measure them or correct for them by statistical means – just as is the case with the physics experiment with the shield. A similar point holds for the instrumental variable strategy: again, one does not have to know whether the potential confounder U in Figure 2.2 exists, or be able to measure it, to be able to use this design to estimate the effect of X on Y.

By contrast, in the more global, non-designed-based approach we follow a strategy like that in the first physics experiment: measuring the confounding factors and somehow correcting for their influence by calculation. There are various ways this can go wrong, the most obvious being that we fail to measure and correct for all of the confounders. But there are also more subtle problems with this strategy, including conditioning on the wrong variables (as opposed to failing to condition on the right ones).[3] In many cases, even on very optimistic background assumptions, such strategies will return at most an equivalence class of causal structures rather than a single unique structure.

These remarks are intended to supply some insight into why one might think that the results of the design-based approach are often more reliable than the results of the non-designed-based approach. But as mentioned earlier, I take them to be at best suggestive: as I see it, the choice between the two approaches is ultimately an empirical one: which approach gives more reliable results in the sense of correctly identifying which causal relationships are present. Such empirical assessments can be accomplished in a variety of ways, including determining the ability of the different strategies to recover causal relations that are known on other grounds (a calibration strategy), and the use of "triangulation" in which different

[2] Of course, as frequently pointed out, expectation in equivalence does not guarantee that in any particular randomized experiment this equivalence will indeed be present.

[3] For example, if one is trying to determine whether X causes Y and conditions on a third variable Z, which is an effect of X and Y (entirely possible if one does not know the correct causal structure), this will induce a conditional association between X and Y, making it look as though there is a direct causal relation between them.

strategies are assessed based on whether they yield coherent or consistent results (see a discussion later in the chapter).

The recent literature seems to have largely settled on the conclusion that, as an empirical matter, the design-based approaches tend to produce more reliable results than the conditioning strategy. When the latter strategies are compared with the design-based ones, there is very often evidence that the former have not been successful in correcting for all confounders, different design-based strategies commonly yield more consistent results than the non- design-based strategies, and so on. Randomized experiments often yield different results from purely observational studies, as do designs employing various instrumental variable studies (Davey Smith & Hemani, 2014; Lalonde, 1986). In econometrics and statistics, the increasing preference for design-based strategies is often described as the "credibility revolution," on the assumption that earlier, non-designed-based causal inferences were in many cases simply not credible and design-based inferences are at least more credible. In what follows I am going to accept this conclusion about the superior reliability of design-based approaches (in comparison with the alternative just based on conditioning) and for this reason will mainly focus on them. Having said this, however, let me also emphasize, as will become apparent from the following discussion, that non-design-based sources of information can also play an important role in securing reliable causal inference. Indeed, in many cases, the most convincing support for a causal claim will involve a process of triangulation in which mutually reinforcing evidence from a variety of different sources is brought to bear.

2.6.1 An Evidence Hierarchy?

Readers will no doubt be familiar with the notion in evidence-based medicine (EBM) of an "evidence hierarchy" with (in some formulations) RCTs functioning as the "gold standard" at the top of this hierarchy. Like a number of other commentators, I don't find this picture entirely satisfactory, at least for the kinds of issues addressed in this essay. As suggested previously, RCTs have a number of virtues, but they are certainly not the only source of information that legitimately can be used in causal inference. This is fortunate, since there are many causal questions that cannot be addressed by RCTs, both for ethical and other (e.g., practical) reasons. The hierarchy picture also seems to inadequately stress the role of triangulation of evidence from different sources and theory elaboration discussed later here. I do think, however, that there is something right about EBM's discussion of different sorts of evidence: different inferential strategies are subject to different sorts of errors and, relatedly, are good at providing certain kinds of causal information and not others. It is a good idea to be cognizant of these differences, even if they don't translate into a hierarchy.

2.7 Randomized Controlled Experiments and Their Limitations

As suggested earlier, although design-based inferences are generally more reliable than a pure conditionalizing strategy, they nonetheless have several important limitations. I turn now to a discussion of these, beginning with RCTs.

As I understand RCTs, they are designed for a particular kind of problem situation, although one that is common in parts of the biomedical and behavioral sciences. The situation is this: one has a candidate cause *C* and effect *E*, but it is also known that the units or systems to which *C* may be applied differ among themselves in all sorts of other unmeasured ways that may be causally relevant to *E*. In particular, the units may be causally heterogeneous, and features of the units may be differentially correlated with causal factors besides *C* that affect *E*. Randomization attempts to address this problem by creating two groups that do not differ in expectation with respect to *E*, except for the fact that one group receives *C* and the other does not. As remarked previously, there are many experiments in which this is not necessary; one may be confident one is dealing with homogenous units or one may be able to remove the "in addition to *C*" influences on *E* by other means such as shielding, preparing pure samples, and so on. Randomization is what one does when these other strategies are not available. It does deal with unknown confounders, at least in expectation, but its use comes with costs.

Of course, it is also true that an RCT can be badly designed – for example, there may be failure of double-blind conditions as when subjects can tell that they have received the active drug and not a placebo, employment of a defective outcome measure, failure to account for noncompliance, violations of the stable unit treatment value assumption (SUTVA), and so on – but let's put these possibilities aside and consider what can be learned from a well-designed RCT that does not have these sorts of defects. Even in this case some important limitations remain, many of which have to do with the fact that RCTs do not provide evidence for the stability of causal claims, in several different senses of stability.

2.7.1 *What Is the Active Ingredient?*

Consider the following hypothetical randomized experiment drawn from Esterling et al. (2025). Researchers induced the Riverside County (California) Superior Court to mail postcards with an official government seal to residents who have received a jury summons, randomizing so that half receive a standard reminder postcard and the other half a postcard informing recipients that failure to appear can result in fines and imprisonment. This second "enforcement condition" results in a statistically significant increase in turnout in comparison with those in the control condition. The researchers conclude that enforcement messages cause increases in jury turnout. Next, they repeat this experiment in Orange County (a nearby but more affluent location). To their disappointment, in this sample there is no effect of the enforcement message. In an effort to figure out what is going on, the researchers resolve to repeat their original experiment in Riverside County. This time, however, they do not have the cooperation of the Riverside court, so they send out randomized postcards with the same enforcement message but without the official court seal. Again, there is no treatment effect.

Let's stipulate (what may not be warranted) that the original RCT produced a valid result in the sense that it captures the ACE of the original manipulation performed on the Riverside population. One way of putting the problem posed by this example is that while the researchers can conclude that in the first experiment they performed a manipulation that had the observed effect, their result does not tell them what was the "causally active ingredient" in that manipulation. That is, they don't know what features of their manipulation were causally relevant to the outcome they observed and which were irrelevant in the sense that these could have been omitted and the same result would have ensued. Another way of conceptualizing the problem is that what is actually known to be manipulated in the Riverside experiment (whether or not subjects receive a certain message with the official seal of the Riverside superior court about penalties for failure to appear for a jury summons) is not the same as what is assumed to be manipulated when the results of the experiment are described in terms of the generalization "enforcement messages increase jury turnout." The former (the message from the Riverside Superior Court) is (at best) a particular way of operationalizing the more general category of "enforcement message," which the generalization takes to be the relevant causally active ingredient. Given the Orange County results and the second Riverside experiment, the original Riverside result does not support this more general claim about the effects of "enforcement messages." The latter is a claim about what is stable in the Riverside result (i.e., the presence of an enforcement message per se stably increases turnout). Even though the original Riverside experiment apparently found an ACE, this experiment does not tell us anything about the stability of that result, and this failure is sufficiently acute that it makes the experiment difficult to interpret.

In some cases in which an RCT is performed, one has background knowledge or good grounds for belief, coming from theory or some other source about the active element in the manipulation, if there is one. If the treatment involves ingestion of a pill, and there is adequate control for placebo effects, one may have good grounds for assuming that it is the material in the pill that is causally relevant to any observed outcome rather than, say, variations in the manner of swallowing. (Of course, it is possible to be wrong about this, and even here the RCT by itself will not establish exactly what in the pill was relevant to the outcome.) The (or one) problem we face in the jury summons example is that we don't have anything analogous to even the weak background knowledge we have in the pill example. As a consequence, the RCT is difficult to interpret and of limited usefulness. As this example illustrates, although part of the appeal of an RCT is that it requires very limited theory or background knowledge, it does require some to be useful.

2.7.2 *Ambiguous Interventions/Heterogeneous Effects*

I turn next to a second illustration of a limitation of RCTs, related to but not the same as the first. This involves a much discussed example in the causal modeling literature due to Spirtes and Scheines (2004). Following them, I'm going to distort the history and relevant science a bit to make the illustration more salient. Assume that total cholesterol (TC) is simply the sum of high-density lipoprotein (HDL) and low-density lipoprotein (LDL). Initially these two forms of cholesterol were not distinguished and were measured by TC, which was taken to causally contribute to heart disease (HD). It was subsequently discovered that HDL was protective for heart disease while LDL had an opposite, deleterious impact.

Now consider a randomized experiment in which TC is set to different levels in a treatment and a control group. The association between TC and HD will depend on the precise mix of HDL and LDL that realizes TC in this particular experiment. If the imposed TC is mainly made up of HDL, the impact of TC on heart health will seem to be positive for greater levels of TC. If the TC is mainly made up of LDL, the impact will seem to be negative. If the mixture of HDL and LDL realizing TC across different experiments varies, the association between TC and HD across different experiments (and hence its apparent causal impact) will be variable or unstable and, arguably, not well defined.

Intuitively, the problem with TC is that is not a causally homogenous variable; instead, it is a mixture of two different variables with very different causal effects. At an abstract level this is another example of not knowing what one is manipulating. However, it has a different structure from the Riverside example. Conducting a single RCT with TC will not tell us that this heterogeneity is present, although if a number of RCTs are conducted with different mixtures of TC, the resulting instability of the results may be suggestive of heterogeneity.

In the jury summons example, we were not sure what the active ingredient was, but we assumed, perhaps wrongly, that anything that was manipulated that did not contribute to the observed result was neutral or irrelevant to it. In the TC example, the problem is that there are two ingredients in the overtly manipulated variable that have "opposite" effects. In both cases, however, the problem is that we lack the right sort of information about what it is that we are manipulating. As these examples illustrate, causal inference, even when design based, can lead us astray when we have the "wrong" variables.

To what extent do candidates for causal variables in psychiatry exhibit problems of the sort described in the preceding paragraphs? I'm not competent to provide a general answer to this question, but one obvious case in which similar problems arise has to do with RCTs that attempt to evaluate various forms of psychotherapy. There are a well-known number of methodological problems that arise in the use of RCTs for this purpose, but one issue is this: the RCT needs to specify a protocol for treatment that (one hopes) will be followed uniformly by all therapists in the treatment arm of the experiment. In such cases, even if there is an apparent positive average causal effect, the RCT may leave it unclear which features of the protocol causally contributed to the beneficial result and which were causally irrelevant, in analogy with the problem with the social science experiment discussed earlier.[4] This of course creates problems for

[4] A more alarming possibility is that some elements of the protocol are deleterious for mental health, but their effects are often masked by advantageous elements, in analogy with the total cholesterol example. Perhaps, though, it can be assumed that usually the inactive elements are causally irrelevant.

generalizability to other contexts, particularly since it is unlikely (very difficult to ensure) that the protocol will be exactly repeated in those contexts. Again, this might in principle be addressed by additional RCTs that vary features of the protocol, but this may be difficult and expensive. One might hope that over some range of variations in the protocol the beneficial effect will be roughly the same (or will at least have the same sign in the sense of being at least somewhat beneficial), but whether this is so is of course an empirical question.[5] This issue is discussed by Shrout (2011), who considers the use of mediation analysis to identify the active ingredients in cognitive behavioral therapy (CBT), one of the most popular and well-studied forms of psychotherapy. I will say a bit more about this in what follows.

Next consider that many of the environmental variables thought to influence mental illness (whether these are analyzed through design-based inferences or in some other way) may be subject to varying degrees to the problems described earlier. Low SES is associated with increased risk of many mental illnesses, and it seems plausible that there are specific ingredients in low SES that are causal for these outcomes. On the other hand, depending on how it is measured, SES will be a mixture of many different, more specific variables having to do with income, education, cultural capital, and much else. Some of these may be more causally relevant to mental health than others (and different mixes of these may be present in different subjects with same SES), and this may affect the generalizability of results. Moreover, the various components vary in the extent to which they can in fact be manipulated or even whether such manipulation makes clear sense. Income can be manipulated, hence it can be a treatment in an RCT and might be identified as a cause of some mental disorders in an instrumental variable analysis, as in the Smokey Mountain study described later here, but it is less clear what might be involved in an intervention on cultural capital or, for that matter, education.[6] Moreover, a skeptic might wonder whether even income is a causally homogeneous variable on the grounds that income derived from a grant, or a lottery may have different causal effects than "earned" income; again see the Smokey Mountain

[5] One might think of this as a kind of "monotonicity" assumption: if individuals respond to the treatment at all, they will respond in a "positive" way or their probability of a positive response will be boosted rather than diminished. This may be a reasonable assumption in many cases, but course its warrant is ultimately empirical.

[6] "Assigning" subjects different educational levels is morally objectionable and in any case is very different from observing subject's educational levels, when these reflect subject choices, the resources they have available, and so on.

study. In general, when the value of a variable is somewhat under individual control or reflects individual choices, one might wonder whether it has the same causal properties as a value of that variable that is exogenously imposed. (In addition to receiving a stipend versus earned income, contrast chosen with imposed school attendance, or mandated psychotherapy with voluntarily chosen psychotherapy.) To the extent this is so, it will be a complication in the interpretation of intervention-like designs.

2.7.3 Relativity

So far, I have focused on the fact that experimenters may not know what it is about their manipulation that is relevant to the outcome they observe. (The same is true for other designed-based strategies, as noted in the later discussion.) However, there is another problem that at least in practice is difficult to separate from the first. Specifically, as previously mentioned, the notion of an ACE (which again is the upshot of an RCT and many other design-based inferences) is population relative, and even if the subjects in such an experiment are randomly sampled from some clearly defined population, the RCT, strictly speaking, will provide information only about that population.[7] For example, it might be that the reason why the original jury summons experiment (performed in Riverside) failed to replicate in Orange County doesn't have to do with the variation in enforcement message employed, but rather occurs because the residents of the latter are, on average, causally different in some way from the former: for example, the latter are more affluent than the former, and more affluent people are less affected by enforcement messages. The problem is that we can't tell from the failure of replication in Orange County whether this results from a causal difference in the two populations, the variations in the manipulation performed in the two experiments, or both.

2.7.4 The Significance of Individual Variability

In the total cholesterol example, TC had different "effects" (arguably not well defined at all), depending on the mix of LDL and HDL. We did not,

[7] The issue of whether there is random assignment in an experiment is of course distinct from whether the participants are a random sample from some population. In some (perhaps even many) cases the participants in an RCT represent a sample of convenience that is not randomly drawn from any well-defined population. For example, drug company–run RCTs are typically unrepresentative of patient populations. This raises additional problems of generalizability.

however, consider the possibility that different subjects might have different responses to LDL and HDL; instead, we assumed that the level of these had the same constant effect on each subject. However, another possibility is that the treatment variable in an RCT has different effects on different subjects in a way that cannot be captured in a constant effect representation.[8] The result of an RCT is an estimate of an average effect, which is consistent with substantial variability in individual response. Of course, such variability is very often observed in both the treatment and control group, and the RCT by itself provides no insight into why this variability occurs. A particularly disturbing possibility in biomedical contexts is that although the average effect of the treatment across the entire treatment group may be positive, some subjects may be harmed by the treatment while a larger group benefits. Rothwell (1995) describes a study of the results of carotid endarterectomy (a surgical procedure that removes plaque from the carotid artery). Although this procedure reduces the risk of stroke for many patients, it can also increase the risk of stroke by dislodging plaque that can contribute to arterial blockage. Rothwell employed a "prospective" model that accurately predicted stroke risk in the patients studied. He found from this that surgery reduced the risk of stroke in those patients at high risk of stroke but appeared to increase the risk of stroke among low-risk patients.

Of course, there is also a great deal of variability in the responses of patients with mental illness to various drugs and therapies. The sources of this variability are in many cases not well understood and, as noted earlier, are not addressed by standard RCTs or other designed-based strategies, which also just provide information about average causal effects. In the study described earlier, Rothwell had an empirically supported model that allows him to distinguish among patients according to the degree of stroke risk they faced. My impression is that in psychiatry, finding markers that allow for the prospective classification of patients into subtypes depending on how they are likely to respond to a treatment has turned out to be difficult, although I assume genotyping or the use of polygenetic risk scores

[8] A standard way of modeling individual variation in an RCT represents this, as due to the distribution of an additive error term U around a constant effect: $Y = f(T) + U$, where T is the treatment with constant effect given by $f(T)$ and individual variability is due to different individuals having different values of U. Note that this does not seem to capture what is going on in the stroke treatment example immediately following, where there is nothing corresponding to this constant effect. In many – if not most – cases in which there is variability of individual response to treatment according to differences in individual "type" this is not captured by an additive error term.

may afford some possibilities.[9] Conducting retrospective analyses in which one looks for distinguishing characteristics among patients who have responded differently to a treatment carries obvious risks of overfitting. Understanding variability is of course beneficial for individual patients but also bears on issues of stability and generalizability: if different types of subjects respond differently to treatment and these types are distributed differently across different populations and circumstances, then even average effects will be unstable.

Note also that the problems described so far (lack of information about the active ingredient, population relativity, subject heterogeneity) are not problems of "confounding" in the ordinary sense. (Again, I take confounding to arise when there is a noncausal association between *X* and *Y* that is due to, e.g., some omitted variable and that we mistakenly interpret as causal.) Instead, the problems are best conceptualized as arising from lack of stability/invariance in the identified causal relationship or an inappropriate choice of variables. These problems illustrate the point that RCTs and other design-based inferences can address problems having to do with "local" confounding, at least in principle, but they do not address the other problems discussed earlier in the chapter.

2.8 Total versus Path-Specific Effects Again

I now turn to another limitation of an ordinary RCT (and other intervention-emulation experiments). Even if otherwise unimpeachable by themselves, designs of this nature tell us at most about the total effect of the candidate cause and do not provide information about distinct paths by which this cause may influence the effect. Recall our earlier example of a gene *G* that affects an outcome *T* via an inside-the-skin pathway involving neural processing but also via a mediating outside-the-skin pathway that goes through the external environment and the subject's behavior *B*, as when *G* also causes a tendency to explore intellectually rich environments or, in the case of depression, a tendency to behave in a way that elicits negative events contributing to depression. In such cases a single experimental manipulation of *G* will reflect its total effect on *T* summed over both these paths. Of course, if we know where to look for the outside-the-skin variable, we could in principle perform a second intervention that

[9] There have been a number of studies that attempt to do this, but Kenneth Kendler notes that "progress in pharmacogenetics has been slower than expected – better at predicting side effects such as weight gain, than therapeutic effects" (personal communication).

fixes the value of that variable while at the same time manipulating *G*. This would separate the two paths and reveal the portion of the impact of *G* on *T* that is direct or inside the skin.

2.8.1 Mediation Analysis

In psychiatry and psychology, the much more common case is (at best) one in which there is randomization of / intervention on the treatment variable but no intervention on or independent randomization of any candidate-mediating variable (i.e., a variable that is on a path in between the treatment and its putative effect) that might be used to distinguish different paths. Instead, the value of any candidate-mediating variable (and its association with the treatment and candidate effect) is merely observed. In this situation, *mediation analysis* is sometimes performed to attempt to understand the causal role, if any, of the mediator. Without going into a lot of statistical detail, consider an early version of this idea developed by Baron and Kenny (1986). Suppose *X* has a net or total effect on *Y* and that this may be at least partially mediated through an intermediate variable *M* where both *Y* and *M* have additional sources of variation – U_M and U_Y – and all of the relationships are linear. Suppose (very optimistically) that U_M and U_Y are uncorrelated. Suppose also (1) *X* is related to *Y* via coefficient *c*, (2) *M* can be measured and is found to be associated with *X* via coefficient *a*, and (3) after controlling for *X*, *M* is related to *Y* by coefficient *b*. (We estimate these coefficients by ordinary regression analysis.) We then proceed by estimating the "direct" effect c^* of *X* on *Y*, controlling for *M*. If $c^* < c$, this shows the relationship between *X* and *Y* is at least partially mediated by *M* (Figure 2.3).

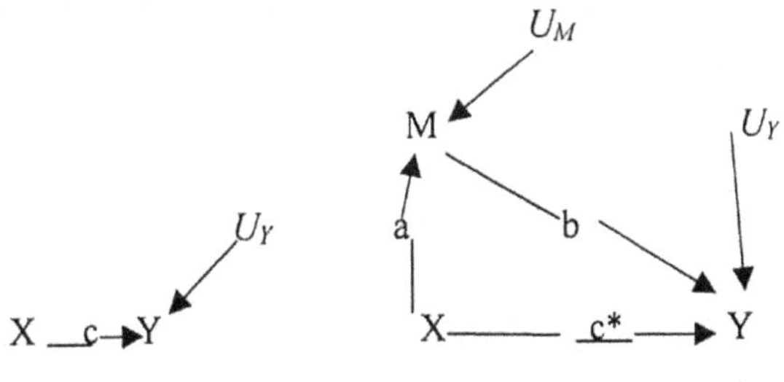

Figure 2.3 (Left) *X* has a total effect on *Y* described by coefficient *c*. *Uy* is an uncorrelated "error" term. (Right) Conditions (described in more detail in the text) that must be satisfied for the identification of a (partially) mediating variable *M* between *X* and *Y*.

Although this design can, under the aforementioned assumptions, lead to the identification of a mediating variable (a mechanism or part of a mechanism?) linking *X* to *Y*, the assumptions are highly restrictive and are likely often violated. In particular (and even putting aside the assumption of linearity), since *M* is not randomized or the result of an intervention, the design does not exclude the possibility that the relation between *M* and *Y* is confounded (due to a correlation between U_M and U_Y), resulting in a biased estimate for the indirect effect. More recent work has shown how to relax the assumptions about linearity, but it remains the case that an accurate decomposition into path effects requires strong assumptions that are often not satisfied. A recent meta-analysis (Stuart et al., 2021) showed that the majority of papers included did not satisfy the assumptions required for reliable mediation analysis.

Putting aside these statistical issues, mediation analysis can in principle be helpful not just with decomposition of total effects into path specific effects but also with the problem of identifying active ingredients described earlier. Shrout (2011) draws attention to a randomized controlled experiment conducted by Freedland et al. (2009), which found that CBT is associated with reduced symptoms of depression *D* among patients who have experienced coronary artery bypass surgery – reduced in comparison with an alternative treatment for depression or no treatment at all. As Shrout observes, one might wonder what "component" ("active ingredient") of CBT was responsible for this effect: control of distressing automatic thoughts (*T*) or control of dysfunctional attitudes (*A*). (Assume that there are theoretical considerations that support the claim that *T* and *A* are distinct and that these are the two most likely mediators.) If we could measure *T* and *A* and their association with whether subjects received CBT, and the incidence of depression and the relevant requirements were satisfied, we could use mediation analysis to determine whether *T* or *A* was a mediating variable. This in turn might help improve the efficacy of CBT and its generalizability as a treatment for depression in other circumstances.

2.9 Instrumental Variables

Kendler et al. (2018) provide an interesting and in my view convincing example of the use of instrumental variable analysis in a psychiatric context. Poor academic achievement (*AA*) has long been known to be associated with drug abuse (*DA*). However, this association could arise from several potential confounders; for example, family background might act as a common cause of both *AA* and *DA*. Kendler et al. used a complete population cohort of Swedish students aged 15 to 20 years to investigate a possible causal relationship between *AA* and *DA*. Like many other countries, Sweden has a cutoff date for school enrollment, with students who are born in the same year placed in the same class; thus students in the same class can differ in age by as much as 12 months. Unsurprisingly, the younger students in a given class tend to do less well in terms of *AA*. Kendler et al. used student month of birth (MOB) as an instrument. Their assumption was that MOB affects *AA* (again there was considerable independent evidence for this) and that it affects *DA*, if at all, only through *AA*. Without going into all of the statistical details, their instrumental variable analysis found a significant association between *AA* and *DA* underage-associated variation in *AA*, thus supporting the claim that *AA* has a causal effect on *DA*. They also found, reassuringly, that conditioning on *AA*, there was no association between month of birth and *DA*, thus supporting the claim that any influence of month of birth on *DA* occurred through *AA*. Although the authors do not make this observation, it is also relevant that if the direction of causation was instead from *DA* to *AA*, conditioning on *AA* should induce a conditional dependence between *AA* and month of birth, and this was not observed.

The authors also employed a co-relative design, exploring the association between low *AA* and *DA* in first cousins, full sibling, and monozygotic twins who were discordant for *AA*. This provided varying degrees of control for genetic factors and family environment. They again found results that were consistent with their model of the influence of *AA* on *DA*: that is, among monozygotic twins who are discordant for *AA*, the twin with lower *AA* was more at risk for *DA*, and a similar pattern was found among other relatives. *AA* is a variable that might be intervened on, and the authors also cite a meta-analysis showing that programs in the United States and elsewhere aimed at improving *AA* in targeted students were also associated with decreased drug use, consistent with the authors' causal hypothesis. It is plausible that these alternative designs – instrumental variables and co-relatives as well as direct interventions on *AA* – have different possible sources of confounding. If the association between *AA* and *DA* is noncausal, different kinds of confounding would have to be present in each of the three designs that are "coordinated" in such a way that they happen to produce this consistent association between *AA* and *DA*. There is no reason to expect this. The convergence of the different designs on the same conclusion thus strengthens support for this conclusion. I will say more later about the benefits of this "triangulation" strategy.

As I said, my assessment is that these results provide good evidence that *AA* causally influences *DA* at least in some circumstances. But if we focus just on the instrumental variable part of the Kendler et al. study, there are obvious worries one might raise about the stability and generalizability of the result, again illustrating our general theme about the local character of the results of design-based inferences. In particular, as far as the instrumental variable part of the study goes, even if one accepts that the results support a causal claim about the population of Swedish students studied (i.e., that this causal claim is internally valid), one might be inclined to suspend judgment about the extent to which the claimed causal connection holds in other populations or circumstances. (Of course, the meta-analysis involving intervention experiments helps address this worry.) More radically, one might conclude that we know only that the results hold for the particular cohort studied. Even more radically, some might think that we are entitled to conclude only that the $AA \rightarrow DA$ result holds for students whose *AA* is affected by their age, rather than for all students. (If this seems unduly skeptical, similar claims have been made by prominent econometricians in interpreting the results of instrumental variable analyses.)[10]

In addition, although the study is framed in terms of the causal influence of *AA*, one might wonder about what the causally active ingredients of *AA* are. The authors measured *AA* by grade point average, but they noted that "our measure of AA does not perfectly reflect the way this construct is typically defined in the education literature, which includes students' attitudes about their teachers, their commitment to school, their educational aspirations, and their level of truancy" (p. 1186).

Strictly speaking, the study might thus be taken to show only that grade point average influences *DA*, since that is the measured variable. On the other hand, there are good reasons for wanting to know whether other previously described elements of *AA* influence *DA*. For example, in some cases it may be easier to intervene to affect student attitudes and truancy than their grade point averages.

2.10 An Additional Role for Stability

I noted earlier that sufficiently radical failures of stability in a putative "local" causal relation can undermine its interpretability. But stability

[10] One might also wonder whether month of birth satisfies the exclusion restriction. Suppose that younger students are more socially immature *S* and that *S* influences *DA*, either positively or negatively, via a path that does not go through *AA*.

considerations can be important in another, more positive way: as a device for detecting when confounders are present and providing some support for claims that they are absent. The underlying intuition is that if a putative causal relation seems to continue to hold across (what are plausibly regarded as) different potential confounding structures, this supports the claim that the relationship is genuinely causal. By contrast, if the relation fails to hold across different potential confounding structures or if it changes considerably in strength, this may undermine the claim that it is causal. In employing this form of argument, it is important that the potential confounding structures are genuinely different. As observed earlier, it is a very real possibility that an association might continue to hold across what seem to be "different" circumstances but nonetheless be noncausal – the association instead holding because it is generated by an underlying confounding structure present across all those circumstances. In biomedicine and behavioral sciences, confounding structures, due to pervasive and entrenched variables like SES, can have this feature.

An illustration of this strategy is provided by an investigation into the effects of maternal smoking on children's outcomes. In previous studies, maternal smoking was found to be robustly associated with conduct and cognitive problems, and hyperactivity as well as low birth weight (LBW). Sellers et al. (2020) compared the association of maternal smoking with outcomes in two different UK cohorts, one born in 1958 and the other in 2000–2001. The authors found the association with LBW was relatively stable across these two cohorts. By contrast, the association with conduct disorder and the like was considerably stronger in the 2000–2001cohort than in the earlier cohort. At the same time smoking in general decreased from 1958 to 2000–2001 and became much more strongly associated with low SES and social disadvantage. This suggests, even if does not conclusively establish, that the association between maternal smoking and conduct disorder is confounded by SES effects.[11] The contrasting stability of the relation between maternal smoking and LBW across these demographic changes makes it more plausible that this is a genuine effect – perhaps especially because the effect, if present, is plausibly understood to be the result of biological processes that operate independently of social

[11] Kenneth Kendler has remined me that this issue has also been studied using co-relative analyses and mothers who smoked in one pregnancy and not the other – another example of triangulation. Both approaches suggest that the association between smoking during pregnancy and attention deficit hyperactivity disorder (ADHD) in offspring is not causal; see, e.g., Skoglund et al. (2014).

circumstances.[12] Results from other studies support this conclusion via triangulation arguments. For example, behavioral and cognitive problems in offspring but not LBW are associated with paternal smoking, again suggesting that social disadvantage is casually contributing to these problems, with paternal smoking being correlated with social disadvantage. The absence of a correlation between paternal smoking and LBW is what one would expect if maternal smoking was genuinely causal for LBW. In other studies involving monozygotic female twins who are discordant for smoking, LBW of offspring is observed in the smoking twin in comparison with the nonsmoker, suggesting that this effect is not entirely due to genetic or shared family background. Other possible analyses might compare the birth weights of siblings whose mother smoked during one pregnancy but not the other; again, if the effect is causal, one would expect a difference in birth weights across the two cases. Yet another technique appeals to Mendelian randomization, using as an instrument a genetic variant associated with greater cigarette consumption among those who smoke. Mothers who have the variant and smoke had offspring with LBWs than nonsmokers with the variant. Here the variant acts as an independent, random source of variation in smoking behavior; finding an association between this variation in smoking and LBW strengthens the claim that this association is causal.

2.11 A Role for Causal Specificity

Presumably no one doubts that it is desirable to discover stable causal relationships when they exist. The notion of causal specificity has a different status; many have thought that whether a cause is specific has no special significance for reliable causal inference. As I noted earlier, Bradford Hill did not agree. He lists specificity as one of the "aspects" of causation that is relevant to establishing a causal conclusion. He illustrates the notion in the context of diseases associated with working in certain industries[13]:

[12] This involves an assumption about a likely mechanism, but note its *conditional* form: if a certain generic sort of mechanism is present, we would expect a certain pattern of results. This is different from establishing that such a mechanism exists and then using it to support a causal conclusion. An additional discussion follows later in the chapter.

[13] Hill's running example is cancers among nickel refiners. Immediately after introducing the characterization of specificity quoted above, he writes: "We must not, however, over-emphasise the importance of the characteristic. Even in my present example there is a cause-and-effect relationship with two different sites of cancer – the lung and the nose. Milk as a carrier of infection and, in that sense, the cause of disease can produce such a disparate galaxy as scarlet

> If, as here, the association is limited to specific workers and to particular sites and types of disease and there is no association between the work and other modes of dying, then clearly that is a strong argument in favour of causation. (Hill, 1965, p. 297)

This suggests the following general characterization: a causal relation involving a cause *C* is specific to the extent that *C* is associated with a single kind of effect or a small number of kinds rather than many different kinds of effect.[14] That is, *C* is nonspecific to the extent that it causes (or appears to cause) not only E_1 but also the different kinds of effects E_2, E_3, and so on. In Hill's example, an exposure associated with working in a certain industry will be specific if it is associated only with a particular kind of cancer (or a small number of such kinds) and less specific if is associated with death from many other diseases.

Although Hill clearly thought that the specificity of an association was relevant to whether it was causal, he noted that some genuine causal relationships can be relatively nonspecific: for example, smoking causes many different diseases. More recently, a number of epidemiologists have completely dismissed the role of specificity in causal inference. For example, Rothman and Greenland (2005) describe specificity as a "wholly invalid" consideration.

Against this, I follow several recent discussions (e.g., Blanchard, 2022) in holding that specificity-like considerations can be relevant to the reliability of causal inference. Basically, this is because specificity in a causal relationship can sometimes support claims about the absence of confounding, and lack of specificity can suggest that confounding may be present. Weiss (2002) gives the following example. Suppose a lower rate of head injury is observed in cyclists who wear helmets as opposed to those who do not. One interpretation is that the helmets protect against head injury. However, there are possible confounds: perhaps those who wear helmets are more careful in general and thus less prone to head injury. In this case if the protection is specific to head injury – that is, if there is no association between wearing a helmet and injury to other parts of the body – this

fever, diphtheria, tuberculosis, undulant fever, sore throat, dysentery and typhoid fever." (1965, 297).

Similarly, cigarette smoking causes many kinds of cancers, but this does not undermine its status as a cause of each of these. Thus, as Hill goes on to remark, while the presence of specificity suggests (although does not conclusively establish) the presence of a causal relationship, its absence need not undermine the claim that a relationship is causal. As I observe later, one way of thinking about this is that the presence of specificity suggests the absence of confounding.

[14] What is it for effects to represent "different kinds" rather than a single kind? This seems to involve context-specific judgments of various sorts that I will not try to elucidate.

counts against the operation of a confounder of the sort described. On the other hand, if helmet wearers are also less likely to suffer non-head injuries, this suggests that it may be general carefulness, rather than their helmets, that is responsible for their lower rate of head injury. Note that as far as this second possibility goes, it is not (on the reconstruction offered earlier) the mere fact of nonspecificity that is relevant, but rather that the nonspecificity is of such a character as to suggest confounding. To compare this example with the case of smoking, one might think it plausible that smoking causes several different kinds of cancers (of the lung, esophagus, etc.), perhaps because all of these organs are exposed to smoke, as well as heart disease, so finding this sort of nonspecificity would not necessarily suggest confounding, in agreement with Hill's assessment.

It is worth noting that the helmet example might also be understood in terms of a mechanism-based reasoning: if helmets protect against head injury, the mechanism by which they do so involves covering portions of the head but not other parts of the body, and this has implications of the sort described in the preceding paragraph. However, it is not clear that mechanistic information figures in the aforementioned inference in quite the way that proponents of a role for mechanism in causal inference sometimes suggest. These proponents suggest that to establish a causal relationship one must show that an association is present and, independently, identify a mechanism that accounts for the association or, more weakly, at least provide evidence that such a mechanism exists. However, in the example just described, it is not known whether helmets are a mechanism that protects against head injury or even that a head injury–protecting mechanism exists that explains the observed association; instead, this is what one is trying to find out. The logic of the reasoning is rather conditional: *if* helmets are a mechanism that protects against head injury, one expects one pattern of association; if they are not, one expects another pattern of association. Put differently, the role of the possible mechanism is to suggest additional predictions if the original causal claim is correct – what is sometimes called "theory elaboration," as I note later.

Another illustration of the use of specificity in assessing whether confounders may be present is provided by the notion of "negative controls." Smoking has been robustly associated with suicide in several observational studies. This might be thought to support a causal connection. However, as shown by Davey Smith et al. (1992), smoking is equally strongly associated with homicide: that is, smokers are more likely to be homicide victims than nonsmokers. Even if we suppose that there is some mechanism by which smoking causes suicide, it is very hard to see why this same mechanism should also lead from smoking to homicide victimhood. Instead, it is far more likely that the smoking–homicide association is due to demographic/environmental factors (people with lower SESs are more likely to smoke and also more likely to live in more dangerous neighborhoods) or other uncontrolled confounders. Since we have strong evidence that the smoking–homicide association does not control for such factors, it is arguable that this should undermine our confidence that such factors have been adequately controlled for in connection with the smoking–suicide association. Note that here too the reasoning is conditional insofar as it involves an inference about "mechanisms."

I remarked earlier that the mere fact that an association between observed variables is found in a number of different studies or background circumstances is not a very strong reason for taking that relation to be causal. The association may instead be due to a common cause or confounding structure present in all of these circumstances – a possibility that is by no means unlikely when, for example, the confounding structure involves entrenched socioeconomic or cultural factors. The smoking–homicide example illustrates this.[15]

2.12 Elaboration of Cause–Effect Relations and Dose–Response Relations

As I see it, the aforementioned role for specificity is an instance of a more general strategy that can be employed in causal inference: that of *elaborating* a putative cause–effect relation. Suppose there is an association between C and E, and one wonders whether it is causal. Often one has additional information or grounds for belief about what that relation would be like *if* it were causal. (This information may be vague and qualitative, as illustrated later here.) One can then sometimes use this additional information to help assess whether confounders are present that render the association noncausal.

[15] There is another role for specificity. Earlier we noted that when an instrumental variable is employed in causal inference, it is crucial that it satisfy an exclusion restriction: the instrument should affect the putative effect E only through the putative cause C and not via some other route that does not go through C. To the extent that an instrumental variable (or, for that matter, an ordinary intervention variable) is relatively specific, this provides some support for the claim that the exclusion restriction is likely to be satisfied. By contrast, if a purported instrument is highly nonspecific, with many different effects, this raises a concern that at least one of these involves a path that does not go through C and yet affects E.

A simple illustration is provided by the existence of a dose–response relation – another of Hill's "aspects" of causation. Suppose one observes an association between smoking and lung cancer. A commonsense thought is that if this relation is causal, it must involve the passage of some material from the smoke into the lungs; hence it would not be surprising if the incidence of lung cancer increases for those who smoke more heavily or for a longer period of time or who report inhaling more deeply. In fact, these relationships are observed. But a conclusion that smoking causes lung cancer does not rely just on the fact that this hypothesis predicts what is observed. The observed dose–response relations have another role as well: they can help make it implausible that the smoking–lung cancer association is entirely due to confounding. The reason for this is that for some confounding hypothesis to account for the observed associations, including the dose–response relationships, the confounders would need to take a very specific form or be distributed in a very precise way that we have no reason to expect. For example, if there is a common cause *X* of smoking and lung cancer (e.g., some genetic factor as suggested by Fisher), then *X* would need to be such that variations in it cause variations in how much people smoke and for how long and how deeply they inhale that are precisely matched to variations in their probability of lung cancer. This is not impossible, but it arguably makes the hypothesis of complete confounding less plausible.

Note that in arguing this way we are *not* assuming that for a relationship to be causal there *must* be a dose–response relation. (Hill is sometimes mistakenly interpreted as claiming this.) Rather, the argument is that (1) it can be plausible to expect such a relation in some specific cases (which is consistent with its not being present in others); (2) one can observe whether such a relation is present; and (3) if it is present, one can appeal to this to help render implausible certain hypotheses about confounding. A dose–response relation, if present, is just one way of elaborating or developing a hypothesis about a causal relationship in a way that may help exclude alternative hypotheses about confounding.

I am not aware of appeals to a dose–response relation being widely used in causal inference in psychiatry, but there do seem to be some examples, and this is a strategy that might be more widely used. For example, Costello et al. (2003) report the results of a study (the Great Smokey Mountains Study) of a population of rural children, a quarter of whom were Native American and the remainder white. The opening of a casino gave each Native American an annual income supplement. Consistently with findings from other populations, children whose families received the supplements showed reduced risk for problems such as conduct disorders. Moreover, younger children who were exposed to this increase in family income over a longer period of time showed a reduced risk in comparison with older children who benefited from the supplement for a shorter period of time. In other words, a stronger exposure to the putative cause was associated with a stronger response in the form of reduced conduct problems. As argued earlier, this makes it at least somewhat less plausible that the observed association is due to confounding; any confounders would have to be distributed in such a way as to be associated with both additional income and reduced conduct disorders in a way that reproduces the dose–response relation between the two.

The role of poverty and family income in children's mental health problems also provides additional illustrations of many themes in this chapter. Costello et al. (2003) report the results of tests of a number of possible mediators of the connection between poverty and mental health, including traumatic life events (e.g., parent separation or divorce, sexual or other physical abuse, unplanned pregnancy), neglect, harsh or inconsistent parenting, overprotective or intrusive parenting, lax supervision, and maternal depression. Of these only one met the requirements described earlier by Baron and Kenny for full mediation: failure of parents to provide adequate supervision, which accounted for 77% of the effect of changing poverty level on symptoms. As previously noted, the effect of poverty was strong for conduct disorders; there was little evidence of an effect on outcomes like depression and social anxiety. Moreover, a similar pattern held for non–Native American participants in the study who did not receive stipends. Consistently with this, ex-poor families in both groups (i.e., those who had moved out of poverty) reported an increase in time available for supervision (because both parents no longer needed to work full time). The resulting picture is thus fairly coherent: it makes sense (in terms of our folk-psychological assumptions) that increased parental supervision should affect conduct disorders, but there is less reason to expect it will affect outcomes like depression, and this is what is found. (Note the role of specificity here.) It also makes sense that increased income that reduces the necessity of both parents working full (or more) time should increase parental supervision. Note, however, that this also seems to suggest that the increased income per se may not be the active ingredient in reducing conduct disorder. If family income increases only because both parents work more, this will not contribute to a reduction in conduct disorder if the "mechanism" by which income affects disorder is as previously specified. By contrast, an increase in income due to a stipend will work through the previously described mechanism. This is thus an argument for the use of stipends/income supplementation.

2.13 Summary and Conclusion

This chapter has explored some of the strengths and limitations of various strategies for inferring causal relations involving mainly environmental variables in psychiatry. I have emphasized the advantages of design-based strategies such as RCTs and instrumental variables over more traditional strategies based on identifying and conditioning on possible confounders. However, these strategies can come with costs, including failures of generalizability and intepretability, as well as inattention to patient heterogeneity. The role of such considerations as stability and specificity in controlling for possible confounders, as well as the benefits of triangulation strategies, was also emphasized.

Acknowledgment

Many thanks to Ken Kendler for very helpful comments on an earlier draft.

REFERENCES

Baron, R. M., & Kenny, D. A. (1986). The moderator-mediator variable distinction in social psychological research: Conceptual, strategic, and statistical considerations. *Journal of Personality and Social Psychology, 51*(6), 1173–1182.

Blanchard, T. (2022). Specificity of association in epidemiology. *Synthese, 200*, 482.

Costello, E., Compton, S., Keeler, G., & Angold, A. (2003). Relationships between poverty and psychopathology: A natural experiment. *Journal of the American Medical Association, 290*(15), 2023–2029.

Davey Smith, G., Phillips, A., & Neaton, J. (1992). Smoking as "independent" risk factor for suicide: Illustration of an artifact from observational epidemiology? *The Lancet, 340*, 709–712.

Davey Smith, G., & Hemani, G. (2014). Mendelian randomization: Genetic anchors for causal inference in epidemiological studies. *Human Molecular Genetics, 23*(R1), R89–R98.

Deaton, A., & Cartwright, N. (2018). Understanding and misunderstanding randomized controlled trials. *Social Science and Medicine, 210*, 2–21.

Esterling, K.., Brady, D., & Schwitzgebel, E. (2025) The necessity of construct and external validity for generalized causal claims. *Journal of Causal Inference, 13*. https://doi.org/10.1515/jci-2024-0002

Freedland, K., Skala, J., & Carney, R. (2009). Treatment of depression after coronary artery bypass surgery: A randomized controlled trial. *Archives of General Psychiatry, 66*(4), 387–396.

Hill, A. (1965). The environment and disease: Association or causation? *Proceedings of the Royal Society of Medicine, 58*(5), 295–300.

Imbens, G., & Angrist, J. (1994). Identification and estimation of local average treatment effects. *Econometrica, 62*(2), 467–475.

Kendler, K., Ohlsson, H., Fagan, A., Lictenstein, P., Sundquist, J., & Sundquist, K. (2018). Academic achievement and drug abuse risk assessed using instrumental variable analysis and co-relative designs. *American Medical Association: Psychiatry, 75*(11), 1182–1188.

Kendler, K., & Prescott, C. (2006). *Genes, environment and psychopathology*. The Guilford Press.

Lalonde, R. (1986). Evaluating the econometric evaluations of training programs with experimental data. *The American Economic Review, 76*, 604–620.

Rothman, K. J., & Greenland, S. (2005). Causation and causal inference in epidemiology. *American Journal of Public Health, 95*, S144–S150.

Rothwell, P. (1995). Can overall results of clinical trials be applied to all patients? *Lancet, 345*(8965), m1616–m1619.

Sellers, R., Warne, N., Rice, F., Langley, K., Maughan, B., & Pickles, A. (2020). Using a cross-cohort comparison design to test the role of maternal smoking in pregnancy in child mental health and learning: Evidence from two UK cohorts born four decades apart. *International Journal of Epidemiology, 49*, 390–399.

Shrout, P. (2011). Integrating causal analysis into psychopathology research. In P. Shrout, K. Keyes, & K. Kendler (Eds.). *Causality and psychopathology* (pp. 3–24). Oxford University Press.

Skoglund, C., Chen, Q., D'Onofrio, B. M., Lichtenstein, P., & Larsson, H. (2014). Familial confounding of the association between maternal smoking during pregnancy and ADHD in offspring. *Journal of Child Psychology and Psychiatry, 55*(1), 61–68.

Spirtes, P., & Scheines, R. (2004). Causal inference of ambiguous manipulations. *Philosophy of Science, 71*(5), 833–845.

Stuart, E., Schmid, I., Nguyen, T., Sarker, E., Pittman, A., Benke, K., Rudolph, K., Badillo-Goicoechea, E., & Leoutsakos, J.-M. (2021). Assumptions not often assessed or satisfied in published mediation analyses in psychology and psychiatry. *Epidemiologic Reviews, 43*, 48–52,

Weiss, N. (2002). Can the "specificity" of an association be rehabilitated as a basis for supporting a causal hypothesis? *Epidemiology, 13*, 6–8.

Woodward, J. (2003). *Making things happen*. Oxford University Press.

CHAPTER 3

Commentary on Woodward's "Reflections on Some Strategies for Causal Inference in Psychiatry"

John Campbell

3.1 Introduction

It is a pleasure to be commenting on James Woodward's characteristically magisterial chapter. I'll remark on three topics: (1) where things stand now with what Woodward calls "the interventionist framework" for discussing causation; (2) whether the idea of stability has any role in establishing causal relations, particularly in psychiatry; and (3) whether the strategies Woodward outlines in his chapter have any place for one kind of causal thinking that seems essential to psychiatric practice, that of the therapist achieving an understanding of the origin of the content of the patient's delusions.

Just to provide some orientation, let me anticipate the main points:

1. Woodward has previously suggested that there is a special place for the idea of an intervention in the analysis of causation. In the present chapter, however, some of the force of that idea seems to have been lost. Interventions now seem to provide merely one among many possible types of evidence for a causal claim, without any special role in an account of what causation is.
2. The idea that a genuinely causal relation should be "stable" across contexts needs to be treated with special caution in psychiatry; there seems, for example, to be no a priori presumption that a causal relation that holds between psychiatric phenomena in one culture should also hold in another culture.
3. Perhaps the most striking feature of causation in psychiatry is the extraordinary diversity of the phenomena. In particular, it's natural to be struck by the wide variation in the contents of the delusions people can have. It's natural to think of the development of a disorder in a patient on the model of a causal variable plus an error variable, the causal variable highlighting something that is in common to many

psychotic patients, the error variable mopping up the various contents of the various delusions.

The trouble with this picture, however, is that it suggests that the details of the patient's delusions are outside the scope of causal understanding. We can have causal understanding only when there is a causal variable generating an outcome. The contents of the error variable are not themselves causally explained.

It is, however, commonplace that in a psychiatric interview, the therapist may try to recover the patient's train of thought and feeling, recovering "from the inside," the same way the patient's delusions were produced. The details of the contents of the individual patient's delusions seem basic to this kind of causal understanding. Yet although this kind of reasoning is commonplace in psychiatry, it does not seem to fall under any of the strategies Woodward describes.

3.2 Interventionism

Woodward has argued in a number of places that the notion of an intervention has some special role to play in the analysis of causation. This is an attractive idea. It helps make explicit a connection between our understanding of causation and our capacities for manipulation and instrumental observation. We can think of manipulation as exploiting knowledge of what happens under interventions, and we can think of instrumentation as involving external phenomena intervening on our instruments. To give a sense of the analysis, we might say, "X causes Y if and only if (potential) interventions on X are correlated with changes in the value of Y." Woodward makes use of the idea of an intervention in giving analyses of various more specialized causal notions, such as average causal effect versus causation along a pathway, or the interpretation of structural equations.

The natural challenge to this view is to acknowledge that facts about interventions can provide strong evidence for causal conclusions, but that the truth of causal claims is not constituted by facts about interventions. This seems to be a general lesson from much of 20th-century philosophy: attempts to analyze one type of claim or another in terms of the ways in which we find evidence for the claims is perennially tempting, but often what we find is a Quinean web in which its difficult to separate out any one method of verification as particularly central.

Does "interventionism," considered as an analysis of causation, have any implications for psychiatric practice, and in particular for the discovery of environmental risk factors for disorders? Are experimental manipulations somehow more central to the discovery of causation in psychiatry than the mere observation of correlations between phenomena, and the measurement of potential confounders? Suppose, for example, we have a hypothesis that one cause of eating disorders is being teased or bullied about one's weight. Is there some sense in which an intervention is the preferred way of establishing this hypothesis? Couldn't we make a conclusive case that bullying is a cause of the disorder without ever having to do an experimental intervention on whether people are bullied?

In the case of causation, as Woodward remarks, there is a lot that can be discovered without relying on interventions. He distinguishes what he calls "conditioning" strategies for controlling for the effect of confounders on an outcome, from "design-based" strategies. Suppose we're trying to determine whether a particle X exists, and there's a particular signature that Xs produce in a detector. There are also Y particles that produce the same signature at the detector, so we have to control for these confounds. One way is to measure how many Y particles are present. Another way is to build a shield around the detector that blocks Ys, so that only Xs can be affecting the reading at the detector. In this kind of approach, there is no need to measure the potential confounders. This second type of experiment includes randomized controlled trials.

So why should we think that there is something more basic about the connection between causation and design-based, or interventionist, strategies than there is about the connection between causation and conditioning strategies for finding causation? Isn't there, as Quine might have put it, just a web of design-based and conditioning strategies, with many cases using elements of both types of strategy, as well as other considerations, such as derivations from previous causal knowledge based on physical theory? These may all be ways of finding out about causation, but no one can be singled out as canonical.

I really can't find anything in Woodward's chapter that would explain why interventions, rather than conditioning strategies, should be seized on as central to the analysis of causation. He remarks that "the recent literature seems to have largely settled on the conclusion that, as an empirical matter, the design-based approaches tend to produce more reliable results than the conditioning strategy" (p. XX). As Woodward also remarks, though, "non-design-based sources of information can also play an important role in securing reliable causal inference. Indeed, in many cases, the most convincing support for a causal claim will involve a process of triangulation in which mutually reinforcing evidence from a variety of different sources is brought to bear" (p. XX). It is, of course, true that in a particular case an intervention, such as a randomized controlled trial, may provide reliable evidence of causation. But there are going to be other cases where we can be confident about a causal conclusion without ever having carried out an intervention. In any case, it is difficult to see that reliability is the key notion here. It isn't in general true that if S1 is a more reliable way than S2 of finding out about X, then X can be analyzed in terms of S1.

Woodward also remarks that, "In many cases, even on very optimistic background assumptions, [non-design-based] strategies will return at most an equivalence class of causal structures rather than a single unique structure" (p. XX). This remark stands against an attempt to explain causality exclusively in terms of conditioning strategies. Where there is a single unique causal structure to be found, our analysis of causation should respect that, even if conditioning strategies alone could not find that causal structure. But it isn't yet clear what is wrong with the picture on which both design-based and conditioning strategies are merely provisional parts of the great web of evidence we currently use to establish and refute causal claims, rather than being any part of an analysis of what causation is. If we want to explain causation in terms of the methods by which we verify causal claims, there is no evident reason to focus on interventions and design-based approaches rather than conditioning approaches.

Even if we abandon the attempt to explain causation in interventionist terms, there is still a lot of value in the approach. The analysis of "intervention" itself is a valuable contribution to our understanding of the epistemics of causal claims. The framework of variables, causal pathways, and linkages between conditional and unconditional probability claims on the one hand and causal propositions on the other seems likely to be of lasting value. But it's not clear what would be left of "the interventionist framework" if the claim to be providing an analysis of causation is dropped. (For a picture that has some resonances with this reaction, see Glymour, 2004.)

3.3 Stability

Woodward says that his notion of stability "has to do not just with whether an *association* generalizes to different circumstances but whether a *causal relationship*, holding in some local circumstances, also holds in others" (p. XX). The stability of a causal relationship has to do with "the extent to which it holds in other circumstances or populations – whether it generalizes or 'ports'" (p. XX). He further states, "stability is most evidentially informative when an association holds not just in different circumstances but in circumstances that are sufficiently different that they are likely to involve different confounding structures" (p. XX).

One way Woodward suggests of thinking of stability is in terms of a contrast between external and internal validity for randomized controlled trials. One "internal" question is whether the trial succeeded in eliminating possible confounders. The "external" question is whether the population sample used in the trial is representative of a larger group. One way of thinking of this is that an experiment with internal validity can establish what Woodward calls "local causation," but whether a causal relation holds in the larger population is a further question, dependent on the "external validity" of the sample.

Woodward, however, challenges this way of putting things: "One basic problem is that a purely local result about causation, even if apparently internally valid, can be scientifically uninteresting and difficult to interpret unless accompanied by at least some information about stability or generalizability" (p. XX).

Suppose we find a treatment for an eating disorder that seems to work. Perhaps it is a family intervention that tries to provide a restructuring of the dynamics of a family with an adolescent who has anorexia. Suppose that the treatment is found to be effective in many studies of American patients, across the country. It seems to me that, by looking at American studies alone, one could develop a strong case that the family restructuring is causing remission of illness. But what about the demand for stability? This requires that the causal relation between the treatment and the remission should hold in many other places too: perhaps in China, or Africa. Woodward says that if the demand for stability is not met, the results may be "scientifically uninteresting and difficult to interpret" (p. XX). We can contrast our hypothetical family intervention with the relation between smoking and cancer. Woodward says, "the smoking → lung cancer causal relation is stable in the sense that it holds among many different circumstances and populations – among different demographic groups, people with different diets and life circumstances and so on" (p. XX). Now it seems evident that there will be many such physical causal connections that hold for any group of humans, whatever their local culture. But s strong condition of stability does not seem so reasonable for psychiatry. The authors of DSM-IV wrote that, "[a]lthough presentations conforming to the major DSM-IV categories can be found throughout the world, the particular symptoms, course, and social response are very often influenced by local cultural factors" (American Psychiatric Association, 2000, p. 898). The cultural dependency of the symptoms and course of the disorder may mean that there are causal connections between, for example, particular interventions on family dynamics and remission from illness that do not work across cultures. The familial interventions that work in Atlanta just may not work in Southeast Asia.

You might argue that for a connection between family therapy and remission of an eating disorder to have been established across the United States already requires some stability; people with anorexia in rural Alabama should be viewed in a different context to fishermen with anorexia in New England. And maybe geographical categories are not the right ones to be looking at anyway; it may be that we should be looking at socioeconomic status, ethnicity, or something else. But it seems hard to believe that establishing a causal connection in psychiatry really requires stability (perhaps as a result of multiple studies across different subjects). There may be causal connections that exist only in a particular cultural context.

At one extreme, there is what Ian Hacking called "transient mental illness": "an illness that appears at a time and in a place, and later fades away. It may spread from place to place and reappear from time to time. It may be selective for social class or gender, preferring poor women or rich men" (Hacking, 1998, p. 1). When we encounter this kind of thing, as with Hacking's "mad travelers," it surely is possible to run studies and find out about causal relations between various elements of the disorder. But Hacking's idea was that there may be no question of being able to generalize, or "port," causal findings from one circumstance to another, for the disorder may be intrinsically local. Moreover, as in the case of the major DSM categories, there may be significant local variation in what affects what.

Why does Woodward think that causal findings without stability can be "scientifically uninteresting and difficult to interpret"? Suppose we have an "internally valid" result to the effect that having X rather than not-X increases the probability of a patient getting an eating disorder. Woodward's point is that there may be something more to find out about what the "causally active ingredient" is: it may be that there is a further factor, Y, and it's only in the context of Y being present that the value of X affects outcome. So, for example, we may find out that our familial intervention only works in the context of a traditional nuclear family.

In other domestic configurations, maybe the familial intervention makes no difference. So we might make a mistake about this. Maybe we think it's the familial intervention only that's the key thing, so we try to apply this intervention even to communities that are not organized around nuclear families, communities where children grow up in the context of large extended families. And then we find it's only in combination with the background of a nuclear family that the familial intervention can make a difference. This was the point of Woodward's example about the idea that "enforcement messages increase jury turnout" (p. XX). Perhaps the enforcement messages only work in the context of an official court seal (p. XX).

This argument seems overstretched to me. After all, in the context of an official court seal, enforcement messages *do* make a difference. In our psychiatric example, the conclusion – that in our original studies of adolescents in nuclear families, familial interventions make a difference – is still correct. It's true that we may not know *which* features of the cultural context are playing a background role here. But that should lead us to be cautious about overgeneralizing, about supposing our initial result is "stable" in Woodward's sense, and applicable to human communities generally, when it may hold only in the culture studied. I do not see that a case has been made for supposing that there is anything uninteresting or difficult to interpret about such a finding.

The thrust of Woodward's account is to insist on the demand that causal generalizations be stable, and that causal generalizations should be treated with suspicion if they are not stable. I think this doesn't sound right for psychiatry. Of course, it is reassuring to find some rough similarities across the earth in psychiatric phenomena. But I do not see that findings of causation in psychiatry need to be based on cross-cultural work.

3.4 Diversity in Psychiatry

The enormous diversity in patients' delusions is one of the perennially astonishing facts about psychiatry. For example, people try to find risk factors for schizophrenia, along with generalizations about the effects of schizophrenia on the patient. But there may be massive individual variation in the contents of the delusions of individual patients. Why do an individual patient's delusions take the form they do? Why do one patient's delusions focus entirely on Satan whereas another patient's are all about Catherine the Great? Presumably there are causal answers to these questions, and presumably they will involve environmental factors. Do any of

Woodward's "strategies for causal inference" tell us how to probe the causality here?

On the one hand, a natural reaction is that perhaps we can find patterns here, but that it will take an enormous amount of research to find just how the specific contents of peoples' delusions can be predicted on the basis of their environments and backgrounds. I think that this reaction is what Woodward has in mind when he says:

> A standard way of modeling individual variation in an RCT represents this as due to the distribution of an additive error term U around a constant effect: $Y = f(T) + U$, where T is the treatment with constant effect given by $f(T)$ and individual variability is due to different individuals having different values of U . . . In many if not most cases in which there is variability of individual response to treatment according to differences in individual 'type' this is not captured by an additive error term. (p. XX, fn. 8)

Woodward gives the example of plaque removal from the carotid artery. At first there seems to be a great deal of individual variation in whether the procedure raises or lowers the risk of stroke. We could try to capture this by an error term. But it would be more illuminating to find a further variable, or variables, which would explain why the procedure sometimes increases and sometimes decreases risk (p. XX).

If we apply this approach to the individual variation in the contents of delusions, then it appears that the only way to causally explain the contents of a patient's delusions would be to find the further variables that explain why one individual's delusions are all about Satan whereas another individual's delusions are all about Catherine the Great. Insofar as we have only an error variable mopping up the variety in the contents of delusions, we do not have an explanation of the contents of the delusions. We have explanations only to the extent that we can find variables correlated under interventions with the outcome.

The trouble with this is that the therapist interviewing a patient will typically not be, as it were, finding generalizations governing the contents of the patient's delusions. The therapist will not, for example, be trying to find a variable that partitions off those who have delusions about Catherine the Great from those who have delusions about other things. Yet, in the course of ordinary human contact with the patient, the therapist will not simply be collecting a few static snapshots about what the patient now believes. The therapist will, typically, be trying to follow the development of the patient's thoughts and feelings over a period of time – perhaps from well before the therapy began, and certainly over the course of the therapy. So the therapist might go from the patient's earliest memories of mother, another Catherine, through their learning about Russian history and to their fascination with the Empress Catherine, and how that played into the course of the patient's delusions after the death of both their parents. The therapist forming such a picture of the origin and elaboration of the patient's delusions certainly seems to be giving a causal story. This does not seem, on the face of it, to be a matter of the psychiatrist finding the right variables to measure. It seems to be a kind of humanistic understanding that is as central to psychiatry as the clinical interview. And it is also a matter of finding out what caused what.

REFERENCES

American Psychiatric Association. (2000). *Diagnostic and statistical manual of mental disorders* (4th ed., text rev.). APA.

Glymour, C. (2004). Critical notice of James Woodward, *Making Things Happen: A Theory of Causal Explanation*. *British Journal for the Philosophy of Science*, 55, 779–790.

Hacking, I. (1998). *Mad travelers*. University Press of Virginia.

Section 2

CHAPTER 4

Introduction to Russo and van Eck's "Charting the Explanatory Potential of Network Models in Psychopathology"

Peter Zachar

In their chapter, Federica Russo and Dingmar van Eck offer a novel approach to the network theory of mental disorders. According to the network theory, a syndrome such as depression occurs when the symptoms of depression become organized into an integrated causal network that remains stable over time. Rather than explaining the occurrence of depression with respect to hidden, underlying causes, the network theory emphasizes direct casual relationships between the symptoms themselves. According to this view, symptoms are not manifestations of an underlying common cause, but parts of the disorder. The organizational structure of the symptoms, therefore, constitutes the disorder. Russo and van Eck also suggest that as an alternative to the underlying cause model, the explanatory resources of the network model are underdeveloped. The purpose of their chapter is to expand on the explanatory potential of network models.

They begin by describing a recently proposed network-based, computational model of panic attack and panic disorder offered by Robinaugh and colleagues. This model is composed three feedback loops: a physiological arousal and perceived threat loop, a perceived threat and escape behavior loop, and a panic attack and a worry about panic attacks loop. In this chapter they look primarily at the first loop, which is important for panic attacks. They present two equations, one of which says physiological arousal will rapidly increase if the perceived threat is greater than the current level of arousal and decrease if the level of arousal is greater than the perceived threat. According to the second equation, a slight change in arousal will not raise the level of perceived threat until a threshold is crossed, upon which the perceived threat will start to rise steeply.

Although one could conclude that in rejecting underlying disease mechanisms that explain disorders, the network models are nonmechanistic, Russo and van Eck claim that symptom networks can be considered qualified mechanistic models in conformity with *minimal mechanism.* According to minimal mechanism, any model of entities/parts whose interactions are organized to produce and maintain a phenomenon is mechanistic. Certainly, viewing symptoms as parts of disorders and seeing a disorder as coming into being when an integrated symptom network is established and then maintained overtime fits with minimal mechanism. This is doubly true if network models are used to *explain* disorders.

One reason Russo and van Eck advocate for this mechanistic perspective on network models is they believe that such models have unexplored explanatory potential. In their view, the formal specification of relations such as *arousal will rapidly increase if the perceived threat is greater than the current level of arousal* is consistent with Woodward's notion of causation that defines cause in terms of counterfactual dependencies using a *what if things had been different* approach. So, if perceived threat was not greater than the corresponding level of arousal, arousal would not have increased, thus perceived threat was a (difference-making) cause. Russo and van Eck, however, diverge from Woodward in examining not just relations between individual variables; they also examine network structures as a whole because the target variables are causally connected to other parts of the network. For example, there is also a dependency relationship between perceived threat and escape behavior. If escaping reduces threat, it will also reduce arousal.

A second reason they advocate for a mechanistic perspective on network models is that they believe that network models offer valuable heuristics. For example, they can be a heuristic for the description of symptom networks at the level of individual cases. This makes sense, as an individual case will include more details than a generic model, but a generic model can be used to dig into individual cases and generate hypotheses about additional dependencies. Over time, the findings can be used to modify the generic model. Russo and van Eck also note that this perspective is consistent with one of the philosophical premises of network models, the mechanistic property cluster model. This is a nonessentialist model that emphasizes variation among cases of the same kind rather than possession of features shared equally by all.

A third reason Russo and van Eck advocate for a mechanistic perspective on network models of psychopathology is that these kinds of models can reshape how we think about the boundaries of causal systems. In brief, symptoms are the "parts" that constitute causal networks in psychopathology. These networks are nonessentialist and dynamic so the "parts" can vary across persons and over time. Russo and van Eck observe that this notion contradicts an important tenet of the new mechanism in the philosophy of sciences, *constitutive relevance*, which posits that the boundaries of a mechanism are best defined by distinguishing between the parts, processes, and organizational features that constitute the mechanism and those that do not. According to this view, if a part is an actual constituent of a mechanism, (what the mechanism is made of), then the macro and the micro are tightly coupled so that altering a part alters the whole, and vice versa. In contrast, Russo and van Eck claim that in psychopathology, more explanatory mechanist models have to accommodate alterations in parts, processes, and organizational features over time, and thus variation in the boundaries of a mechanism.

In his commentary Stephen Heckers elaborates on Russo and van Eck's description of panic attacks and panic disorder, adding features to the model. He also observes that only a small percentage of people who experience panic attacks will develop panic disorder. Panic attacks are also transdiagnostic, being features of posttraumatic stress disorder, agoraphobia, and so on (and, I add, are sometimes transient without being part of a "disorder"). A more ecologically comprehensive model of panic attacks, he notes, would also accommodate other broad systems such as agoraphobia.

CHAPTER 5

Charting the Explanatory Potential of Network Models in Psychopathology

Federica Russo and Dingmar van Eck

5.1 Introduction

The network approach to psychopathology is gaining momentum in psychiatry and clinical psychology. The network theory of mental disorders – the theoretical core of this burgeoning approach – conceptualizes mental disorders in terms of networks of causally connected symptoms. Mental disorders are understood as stable, dysfunctional states in which such networks can get locked. This conceptualization departs significantly from latent variable or common cause models of mental disorders in which symptoms are understood as arising from latent variables (i.e., underlying common causes) (Aristodemou et al., 2024). Similarly, it departs from the related idea that latent variables or common causes are to be understood as (proxies for) common disease mechanisms or pathogenic pathways. According to the advocates of the network approach, very few (if any) of such common disease mechanisms for mental disorders exist (Borsboom et al., 2019).

Network theorists thus assert that attempts at explaining the occurrence and persistence of mental disorders by reference to underlying common causes will, by and large, not succeed and propose an alternative explanatory strategy (Borsboom et al., 2019). Yet the current methodological literature, we argue, is underdeveloped with regard to explicating what this alternative explanatory strategy precisely entails and what network theorists exactly have in mind when speaking about "explanation" (cf. de Boer et al., 2021). Hence there is room for offering an account that clarifies what kind of alternative to common cause explanations is exactly being offered by the network approach. In this chapter we aim to chart the explanatory potential of network models in psychopathology, thereby contributing to one of the main aims that the network approach has set itself for the decade to come, namely developing formal theories for explaining mental disorders, and thus offering an explanatory alternative to reductionist/common cause models for explaining psychopathologies.

We chart the explanatory potential of network models in psychopathology by relating our discussion to a recently developed (computational, dynamical) network model of panic disorder (Robinaugh et al., 2019), philosophical work on (counterfactual) explanation, heuristics, and (mechanistic) modeling (Poliseli et al., 2022), and the mechanistic property cluster interpretation of psychiatric kinds/disorders (Kendler et al., 2011). A key insight that we elaborate is that network models enable evaluating difference-making relations among variables in a way that is akin to tracking relationships of counterfactual dependencies as in Woordward's (2003) approach to (causal) explanation, but with some important differences. In Woodward's approach, formulating and answering *what-if-things-had-been different questions* (what-if questions) enables one to track counterfactual dependency relations and thus identify difference making relations. These dependency relations are assessed between specific variables. Our analysis shows that asking what-if questions is also key to chart the explanatory potential of network models of mental disorders; however, the relevant dependency relations here concern (and are assessed by evaluating) how changes in specific variables affect others *in the context of the whole network structure*. This insight also informs our view that network models are heuristic devices for hypothesis testing (*heuristics*) and that the boundaries of networks are fluid across time and bound to vary from case to case (*system demarcation*). We also take our analysis to show that network model builders can resist the possible criticism that their models merely offer descriptions rather than explanations of phenomena, a theme heavily discussed in the philosophical literature on explanation (Craver, 2016; Kaplan & Bechtel, 2011; van Eck, 2018).

The chapter is organized as follows. We start with a brief reconstruction of network theory and network modeling in psychopathology and illustrate core ideas with a recently developed network model for explaining panic attacks and panic disorder (Robinaugh et al., 2019). We continue by charting the *explanatory potential* of network models of mental disorders. We then discuss our *heuristic* interpretation of network models. Afterwards, we briefly connect this interpretation to issues about *system demarcation* and end the chapter with a concluding section.

5.2 Network Theory and Network Modeling in Psychopathology

The network theory of mental disorders conceptualizes mental disorders in terms of networks of causally connected symptoms. Mental disorders are understood as stable, dysfunctional states in which such networks can get locked (Borsboom, 2017). A key idea of this network theory is that symptoms are not to be understood as indicators or manifestations of an underlying mental disorder, but rather that the symptoms are part of and compose a given disorder. According to network theory, mental disorders are networks of casually connected symptoms. Borsboom (2017) lists five key principles of this network theory:

1. *Complexity* (interaction between different components in a network);
2. *System-component correspondence* (components are symptoms);
3. *Direct causal connections* (network structures are patterns of causal connections between symptoms);
4. *Mental disorders follow network structure* (symptoms are causally connected/grouped in specific ways);
5. *Hysteresis* (networks are self-sustaining: causal connections persist when the triggers have vanished).

Consider a simplified explanation of the network model approach:

> For instance, if one thinks that other people can read one's mind (delusion), this may generate extreme suspicion (paranoia); this paranoia can lead one to avoid other people (social isolation), which, because one is no longer exposed to corrective actions of the social environment, may serve to sustain and exacerbate the relevant delusions. In this way, symptoms may form feedback loops that lead the person to spiral down into the state of prolonged symptom activation that we phenomenologically recognize as a mental disorder. (Borsboom, 2017, pp. 5–6)

One major aim of network theory is to (statistically) estimate such networks based on data and build *computational* network models of mental disorders. We briefly discuss a recently developed computational network model of panic attack and panic disorder, serving as motivation and illustration of our ideas about the explanatory value of network models of mental disorders (see Section 5.3).

Informed by a rich literature from clinical psychology on panic attacks and panic disorders, Robinaugh et al. (2019) identified three key components of panic attack: (autonomic) *physiological arousal*, *perceived threat*, and *escape behavior*. They identified two additional key components of panic disorder: *persistent concern* (about panic attacks) and *avoidance behavior*.

In their proposed model of panic attack and panic disorders, these components are organized – informed by findings from the psychological literature – in three feedback loops that jointly make up panic attack and panic disorder: a loop between physiological arousal and perceived threat; a

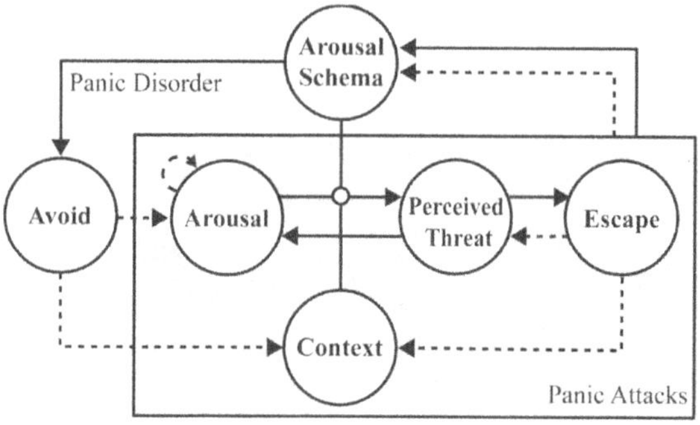

Figure 5.1 The model of panic attacks and panic disorders.

loop between perceived threat and escape behavior; and a loop between panic attacks and belief formation about the dangers of arousal. The specifics of the learning effect/belief formation (i.e., arousal is dangerous versus arousal is not dangerous) in the third loop (thus strengthening or lessening persistent concern/worry about panic attacks) is dependent on whether escape behavior is manifested or not. The first two loops compose panic attack, and the three loops conjointly make up panic disorder. This model is graphically depicted in Figure 5.1 (the term "arousal schema" is used by Robinaugh et al. [2019] to depict [the strengthening or weakening of] "persistent concern").

Robinaugh et al. (2019) mathematically elaborate on the relationships between these components (understood as variables or parameters), thus offering a computational model of panic attacks and panic disorder that they take to enable procuring explanations of specific characteristics of the phenomena of panic attacks and panic disorder. We briefly discuss some of the mathematical specifications of the variables, parameters, and their relations – that is, some of the feedback loops – providing the basis for our discussion of the explanatory value of such models. We take these issues in turn, focusing on the first feedback loop (from perceived threat to physiological arousal, and vice versa).

5.2.1 The Perceived Threat–Physiological Arousal Feedback Loop

Arousal (A) concerns all bodily activity related to arousal and is treated as a continuous variable. Arousal changes over time. The change in arousal over time is specified as $\frac{dA}{dt}$. Change in arousal over time depends on current levels of arousal (*A*) and perceived threat (*T*). These dependencies are specified as follows:

$$\frac{dA}{dt} = \alpha\,(vT - A)$$

where α is a parameter representing the intrinsic rate at which arousal may change and ν is a parameter representing "the strength of the effect of perceived threat on arousal" (Robinaugh et al., 2019, p. 15). Arousal (i.e., $\frac{dA}{dt}$) will increase if νT is greater than A and decrease if A is greater than νT. Say, a large growling dog that is not on a leash and is approaching rapidly may elicit in persons that are (extremely) fearful of dogs quick transitions from current levels of perceived threat (*T*) to elevated levels of perceived threat, thereby rapidly strengthening the effect of perceived threat on arousal (v), with the effect that current levels of arousal (*A*) also quickly transition to elevated levels of arousal ($\frac{dA}{dt}$ will increase). In turn, the level of arousal ($\frac{dA}{dt}$) may decrease again when the owner of the dog leashes the dog and walks away, which leads the current level of perceived threat (*T*) to decrease – back again to average levels – thereby diminishing the effect of perceived threat on arousal (v), thus resulting in the transition of the current level of arousal (*A*) to a decreased level of arousal – back again to average levels ($\frac{dA}{dt}$ will decrease). In short, this equation gives a mathematical specification of the effect of *T* on *A (T —> A)*.

5.2.2 The Physiological Arousal–Perceived Threat Feedback Loop

Perceived threat (*T*) is about the "perceived severity, proximity, and probability of a perceived threat" (Robinaugh et al., 2019, p. 15). Like *A*, *T* is treated as a continuous variable. The change in perceived threat over time is specified as $\frac{dT}{dt}$. Change in perceived threat over time depends on current levels of perceived threat (*T*) and on current levels of arousal (*A*). These dependencies are specified as follows:

$$\frac{dT}{dt} = \gamma \left(\frac{A^{\mu}}{A^{\mu} + \lambda^{\mu}} - T \right)$$

where γ is a parameter representing the intrinsic rate at which perceived threat may change and μ and λ represent "the effect of arousal on perceived threat" (Robinaugh et al., 2019, p. 16). This effect is taken to be S-shaped (sigmoidal), since low-level variation in arousal does not elicit perceived threat, but above a threshold does start to elicit perceived threat, and the strength of this effect will increase with increasing levels of arousal until a maximum level of perceived threat is reached. Two parameters are used to capture this sigmodal effect. Perceived threat will increase (i.e., $\frac{dT}{dt}$ will increase) if $\frac{A^{\mu}}{A^{\mu}+\lambda^{\mu}}$ is greater than T and decrease if T is greater than $\frac{A^{\mu}}{A^{\mu}+\lambda^{\mu}}$. In short, this equation gives a mathematical specification of the effect of A on T $(A \rightarrow T)$.

In the next section we clarify how such mathematical specifications of dependency relations enable formulating and answering what-if questions and argue that the explanatory potential of network models resides in this capacity. Before doing so, we start the next session by arguing for what perhaps may sound as a surprising claim to some mechanist authors and perhaps to some network theorists as well: *network models are mechanistic models*, albeit in a qualified fashion. Our analysis of network models enriches the mechanist program of explanation in philosophy, *inter alia* by supporting the Ubiquity Thesis on mechanistic explanation, which states that mechanistic explanations are widespread across the sciences (Glennan et al., 2022); we will not elaborate further on this issue here, but we take our approach to be in line with Craver's (2007), Glennan's (2017), and Glennan, Illari, and Weber's (2022) reconstructions of the philosophy of mechanisms program. We will approach questions about heuristics (Section 5.4) and of systems demarcation (Section 5.5) precisely from this viewpoint.

5.3 Charting the Explanatory Potential of Network Models

5.3.1 Network Models as Qualified Mechanistic Models

The psychometrics literature on network models of mental disorder is replete with mechanistic commitments. Here is an example of how reference to "mechanisms" is made: "At the heart of the theory lies the notion that symptoms of psychopathology [represented in network models as causally connected nodes] are causally connected through myriads of biological, psychological and societal mechanisms" (Borsboom 2017, p. 5). These commitments are also evident when considering a philosophical foundation underpinning the network theory of mental disorders, namely the understanding of mental disorders as *mechanistic property clusters* (MPC) (Kendler et al., 2011; Robinaugh et al., 2020). On the MCP view, mental disorders are understood as clusters of causally connected (and, hence, co-occurring) properties that are produced and sustained by underlying causal mechanisms. Network models offer one kind of MPC model (Kendler et al., 2011; Robinaugh et al., 2020): symptoms ("properties") connected through causal relations, locked in stable, dysfunctional states.

While network theorists connect their approach to mechanisms, the literature on network models can sometimes be read as supporting the view that network models are not mechanistic. For instance,

> Because the network model is not tied to a particular level of explanation (e.g., biological, psychological or environmental), and *does not single out particular mechanisms that generate the network structure*, it is perhaps best interpreted as an organizing framework – an explanatory scheme with broad use across sub-domains of psychopathology ... [T]he network theory of psychopathology yields broad explanatory principles (e.g., hyperconnectivity in symptom networks yields alternative stable states that correspond to disorders), without specifying, in advance, the realization or implementation of these principles. This is an advantage, because it means that the network theory offers a framework for the integration of different levels of explanation (i.e., biological, psychological, sociological). (Borsboom 2017, p. 11, emphasis added)

This quote might be read as supporting a nonmechanistic view given the claim that network models do "not single out particular mechanisms." We, however, think that network models are plausibly interpreted as mechanistic. We agree that network models embody such "broad explanatory principles," but we also see points for arguing that network models are mechanistic models, albeit a *qualified* kind of *mechanistic models.* Let us elaborate.

Philosophical analysis of mechanisms and mechanistic explanation is ongoing for more than two decades, and while a variety of definitions of mechanisms have been put forward in the literature over the years, more recently one can also find efforts to define mechanisms in such a way that the definition embodies commonly held assumptions. This consensus definition is called *minimal mechanism,* as proposed by Glennan (2017) and Glennan and Illari (2018) and reiterated in Glennan, Illari, and Weber (2022):

> a mechanism for a phenomenon consists of entities (or parts) whose activities and interactions are organized so as to be responsible for the phenomenon. (Glennan et al., 2022, p. 145)

Discovery, description, and explanation of the working of mechanisms require scientists to construct models of mechanisms (Glennan et al. 2022). Models of mechanisms are "inevitably partial, abstract, idealized, and plural" (Glennan et al. 2022, p. 147); as is any scientific model, such is the nature of the modeling endeavor. Modeling mechanisms, furthermore, as any modeling endeavor, commits modelers to include relevant details in their models and exclude irrelevant ones (relative to the purposes for which models are constructed and used). In light of these insights on mechanisms and models thereof, paired with the claim made by network theory that few (if any) common disease mechanisms or pathogenic pathways underlying mental disorders exist, we understand network models of mental disorders to be a *qualified* kind of *mechanistic models* (see also the six theses advanced by Glennan, Illari, and Weber [2022], specifically the *representation thesis* and the *ubiquity thesis*).

In light of *minimal mechanism* and the related view on the modeling of mechanisms, we take network models to be mechanistic, since they articulate (dysfunctional, harmful, or disrupted) *activities* that *interact* by being *organized* in specific ways and, through their interactions, also *change organization* in specific ways, and these (changing) ways in which activities are arranged *constitute* (changing) behaviors that we phenomenologically recognize as mental disorders. Differently put, we take network models to be mechanistic for their *explanatory structure*. In turn, the explanation pertains to a given phenomenon (here, a mental disorder, e.g., panic disorder), through the *network* (i.e., organization) of causally connected symptoms. All this is also codified in the five principles of network theory, mentioned in Section 5.2. So we have key elements of mechanisms and mechanistic models thereof:

- (descriptions of) activities;
- interactions;
- causal and temporal organization;
- constitution.

Furthermore, we also have descriptions of entities, if one is willing (as we are) to count certain variables as descriptions of entities (that produce interactions or activities), such as sleep, appetite, weight gain or loss, circadian rhythms, legal regulations, socioeconomic conditions, dietary routines, cortisol concentrations, or physiological arousal, to name but a few (see also Borsboom et al., 2019). The idea that entities need not be token individuals but can also be variables in a model has been argued for by Wunsch, Mouchart, and Russo (2014) and Mouchart and Russo (2011), in which structural equation models in social sciences are interpreted to be mechanistic for their explanatory structure, as well as by Levy and Bechtel (2013), in which models in biology that articulate organizational relations, rather than concrete entities, are interpreted as mechanistic for their explanatory structure.

While we hasten to add that nothing in our account of explanatory potential hinges on interpreting network models as *mechanistic* models – also without this label, network models afford answering relevant what-if questions and thus have explanatory potential, as we will argue in Section 5.3.2 – we consider, however, the mechanistic interpretation of network models we offer here to be a plausible one and, importantly, also a *fruitful* one for extending and enriching the philosophy of mechanisms and mechanistic explanation. If one subscribes to our mechanistic interpretation, philosophical analysis of network models offers relevant new angles for thinking about and enriching the toolbox of (fallible) heuristics for mechanism discovery (see Section 5.4), and for broadening our thinking about system–mechanism boundaries and demarcation (see Section 5.5). One insight into system–mechanism boundaries that we unpack is that the relevance of (testing and evidence for) constitutive relevance is context relative. In the context of network models, testing for constitutive relevance is irrelevant. We take up these issues in Sections 5.4 (heuristics) and 5.5 (system boundaries). First, we chart the explanatory potential of network models.

5.3.2 Network Models Track Difference-Making Relations at the Mechanistic Network Structure Level

With network models of mental disorders, modelers afford explaining the covariation between two or more symptoms by clarifying when a symptom is (and when it isn't) a difference maker for the occurrence of another symptom – for example, how a change in physiological arousal affects (a change in) perceived threat – and afford explaining changes in the strength of such causal symptom–symptom relations – for example, how a change in arousal schema affects the strength of the impact of physiological arousal on perceived threat (see Figure 5.1). Mathematical specifications of these dependencies allow one to offer precise answers to what-if questions about such dependency relations. For example, the strength of the effect of physiological arousal on perceived threat will increase with increasing levels of arousal until a maximum level of perceived threat is reached; this strength of effect and changes therein can be tracked in quantitative fashion by assigning values to the parameters in the equation specifying the impact of physiological arousal on perceived threat, namely $\frac{dT}{dt} = \gamma \left(\frac{A^{\mu}}{A^{\mu} + \lambda^{\mu}} - T \right)$.

Importantly, however, to assess these changes adequately – that is, to understand the occurrence and persistence of mental disorders and their changing nature – one needs to take into account how these changes affect *the whole network structure*, or their impact on the mental disorder as a whole. This is a salient difference with how the tracking of dependency relations works in Woodward's (2003) account of (causal) explanation, which conceptually inspired our account. In Woodward's approach, formulating and answering *what-if-things-had-been-different questions* (what-if questions) enables you to track counterfactual dependency relations and thus identify difference-making relations. These dependency relations are assessed *between specific variables*. Asking what-if questions is also key to chart the explanatory potential of network models of mental disorders; however, the relevant dependency relations here concern (and are assessed by evaluating) how changes in specific variables affect others *in the context of the whole network structure*. Examples of such questions are: "How would the impact of arousal on perceived threat change if one's beliefs and learned associations about arousal (i.e., one's appraisal of arousal) had been different?"; "How would the impact of arousal on perceived threat change if the situational context were to change that predisposes an individual to panic attacks?" Answers to such questions, in our view, need to take into account how these changes impact other variables and thus the network structure *as a whole* if one wants to understand the role and relevance of such difference-making relations in the occurrence, persistence, and undoing of mental disorders. For instance, a change (decrease) in the perception of threat can only be adequately assessed by, for example, looking at the way escape behavior undergoes changes as well; which, in turn, may lead to changes in arousal and appraisals thereof; which, in turn, may affect the perception of threat. In short, tracking such changes in other parts of the network structure is key to understanding the relevance of specific dependency relations between variables for the whole network structure. Consider that across individuals or across time intervals, a change in a specific dependency relation may impact other dependency relations in different ways. For example, while in one case a decrease in perceived threat produced by a decrease in physiological arousal may have little effect on decreasing escape behavior (perhaps because of robust mental associations between specific contexts and escape behavior), it may have a major effect on decreasing escape behavior in another case (perhaps because mental associations between specific contexts and escape behavior are more fragile). Or perhaps, in yet another case, when stressors are removed or absent, there are no resulting decreases in physiological arousal and perceived threat and escape behavior, but instead the difference-making relations are persisting. That is, the causal connections and feedback loops are persisting even though the triggers have vanished (hysteresis). Understanding the dynamics of such a persisting or self-sustaining system state also requires that one tracks how changes in specific variables affect others in the context of the whole network structure – that is, how the self-sustaining network is brough about. Such understanding then may also (ideally) lead to thinking about and identifying other interventions that may break hysteresis. This contrastive scenario shows that the role and relevance of specific dependency relations (e.g., between physiological arousal and perceived threat) should be assessed in the context *of the whole network*. This contextual perspective gives (improved) understanding of the mental disorder as a whole. It also shows that the tracking and understanding (of the role and relevance) of dependency relations in network models of mental disorders is a less straightforward and hence more challenging affair than in Woodward's apparatus. This observation leads us to discuss the status of network models as *heuristic tools* in the next section.

5.4 Network Models as Heuristics for Hypothesis Testing

In Section 5.3 we learned that network models do aim to be explanatory, and that the explanation locates at the level *of the system*: what-if questions about (relations between) single symptoms help reason about (connections between symptoms and changes therein at the level of) *the system*. Here we briefly elaborate a related insight, namely that network models also enable us to *generate hypotheses* about which symptom–symptom relations or configurations of symptoms in the model to scrutinize and test further in individual therapeutic settings. The idea is to use generic network models by inquiring into how patients and clinicians view the relations articulated in a generic model, possibly identifying new relations and questioning the relevance of other relations, thereby testing and possibly refining the generic model. In this sense, we claim, network models are (in addition to explanatory models) *heuristic tools* too.

Heuristics are not to be understood as some kind of algorithmic approach to modeling, but as (sets of) epistemic tools that we use to gather understanding of a given phenomenon, and at various levels. This insight is illustrated in recent work by Poliseli et al. (2022), who describe practices in ecological modeling and show that mechanistic models – or, better said, *various aspects and elements* of mechanistic modeling – provide a *heuristic set* that contributes to producing knowledge about a phenomenon of interest: "a rule of thumb for model building and other epistemic actions used to grasp a phenomenon and the processes generating it" (p. 21). The work of Poliseli et al. (2022) is useful for our purposes because it also lends support to the qualified interpretation of network models as *mechanistic* models: a model is not mechanistic because it pins down, unequivocally, what the real mechanism of phenomenon X is (assuming that such a thing exists), but because it is related to various explanatory practices performed by modelers, and said practices hinge and rely on various aspects of mechanisms (say, decomposition, organization, etc.) at different moments. We submit that the arguments provided by Poliseli et al. (2022) for ecological modeling hold (some) similarity with modeling mental disorders using network models. For our purposes, however, the main idea we retain from Poliseli et al. (2022) is that of a heuristic set, which is based on characteristics of mechanisms.

The heuristic perspective we have in mind goes two ways: from a generic model to specific individuals (e.g., to partly inform therapy) and from specific individuals to a generic model (e.g., to explore other connections or measurement). We take this heuristic interpretation to be in line with work mentioned by Robinaugh et al., (2020). They cite an alternative method for network estimation, in addition to statistics, which they consider promising but has been "underutilized" thus far – asking patients and clinicians their views on relationships between symptoms (p. 358). Generic network models, we thus suggest, are a useful tool for this, and this application may inform adjustments to generic models as well.

We take it that our heuristics perspective is also in line with the mentioned philosophical foundation underpinning the network theory of mental disorders, namely the understanding of mental disorders as *mechanistic property clusters* (MPC) (Kendler et al., 2011; Robinaugh et al., 2020). The MCP view has several important characteristics for our purposes. First, the MPC view acknowledges and predicts some cross-individual variation at both the level of MPCs and the level of underlying mechanisms. The *symptom/property space* is expected to be occupied by prototypical cases (individuals who share often occurring clusters of causally connected symptoms) and a variety of less frequently occurring cases (individuals who share, in varying ways, some but not all of the causally connected symptoms observed in the prototypical cases) (see Kendler et al., 2011). This implies that the causal structures articulated in network models may vary to some extent from case to case. In turn, this implies that whenever it is possible to construct plausible explanatory models of underlying mechanisms, these may vary to some extent as well. This variation at the level of models of mechanisms plays out in different fashion as well: "the MPC view allows that the same cluster of symptoms might arise from different etiological, underlying or sustaining mechanisms in different cases" (Kendler et al., 2011, p. 1148). So, both variation in causal structures depicted in network models and multiple realizability give rise to variation in models of mechanisms. Second, the MPC view acknowledges that these "etiological, underlying or sustaining mechanisms" may be of different kinds, ranging from evolutionary to social mechanisms and quite a few other kinds of mechanism in between. To be sure, all these characteristics are also acknowledged in the network literature (Borsboom, 2017; Borsboom et al., 2019; Robinaugh et al., 2020).

Our heuristics perspective agrees with this picture and gives it a methodological orientation: prototypical/generic models may enable charting symptom–symptom relations in specific cases/individuals, in turn informing network estimation further by exploring how individual cases/individuals may align or deviate from generic/prototypical models. In the latter case, when insights about novel connections between symptoms indeed emerge, cases deviating from the prototypical ones in the symptom/property space can be regimented further. This symptom–symptom charting is also quite specific to modeling mental disorders, and thus adds to the library of heuristics that Poliseli et al. (2022) have first charted.

There is a further lesson to draw from this heuristic interpretation: system boundaries of networks of causally related symptoms and of underlying mechanisms are fluid, not fixed or rigid. We explore this in the next section.

5.5 Shaping and Reshaping Fluid System Boundaries

So far, we have discussed the explanatory potential and heuristic functions of network models. A further issue that we briefly consider, given the mechanistic commitments of MPC and network theory and *our interpretation of network models as qualified mechanistic models*, concerns whether explanations informed by network theory should be constructed and evaluated on the basis of what the philosophical literature on mechanisms takes to be a key explanatory norm for mechanistic discovery and explanation, namely *constitutive relevance* (Craver, 2007; Craver, Glennan, & Povich, 2021).

According to mechanistic accounts of explanation, macro-level behaviors or capacities of systems are explained (mechanistically) by specifying the micro-level mechanisms that constitute those behaviors or capacities (Craver, 2007; Machamer et al., 2000). Hence, a crucial aspect of mechanistic explanation is to identify those spatiotemporal parts or components – that is, organized entities and activities – of mechanisms that are constitutively relevant to the macro-level behavior or capacity targeted for explanation. Now, a key constraint on establishing constitutive relevance is that the coupling between micro and macro levels cannot be broken: only when extensive testing indicates that changes on the macro level are always accompanied by changes in specific spatiotemporal parts or components does one obtain abductive, fallible evidence that those specific parts or components are constitutively relevant to the mechanism's macro-level behavior (Baumgartner & Casini, 2017). In other words, system boundaries of mechanisms and models thereof are thought to be rigid/robust configurations. Our claim is that *things are exactly the opposite in the case of network models* (understood as qualified mechanistic models). In the case of network models, *causal structures may change (to some extent) from case to case.*

As we saw, mental disorders are changing, evolving, and constituted by their own symptoms/components (and not results of hidden, common-cause variables). That is, causal network structures (described in network models), *and thus system boundaries* of networks (described in network models), are dynamic and prone to change. The point of network modeling is to identify the relevant symptoms/components and to clarify how they may change as conditions change, or to clarify how these symptoms/components and their relations differ across cases. Revisiting our example of panic attack and disorder, this would involve clarifying how the impact of arousal on perceived threat is different across cases in light of different beliefs about the threat of a specific stressor (e.g., a growling dog) and/or different appraisals of arousal levels across cases. In this example, the components composing the causal structures differ across cases, specifically different beliefs and/or different appraisals. Thus, establishing the robustness of the system boundary – the configuration of the symptoms/components – as a proxy for explanatory power of the network model runs counter to explanatory purposes in the case of network modeling. If anything, the contrary is the case: *the more a network model is able to adapt and shape explanations across different configurations, the higher its explanatory power.* Given the dynamic, changing nature of causal structures articulated in network models and hence of system boundaries, attempts to identify rigid or robust system boundaries by testing for constitutive relevance, as advertised in the philosophical literature on mechanistic explanation, are misguided.

What we may call "robustness constraint" of constitutive relevance, which is widely endorsed in the literature on mechanistic discovery and explanation, does not apply in the case of network models for mental disorders. This is a salient difference, and one that calls for alternative analyses of system boundaries and measures of explanatory power of network models in psychopathology. The ubiquity thesis of mechanistic explanation that tells us that mechanistic explanations are widespread across the sciences goes hand in glove with the *Discovery Pluralism Thesis* (Glennan et al., 2022), according to which "the diversity of kinds of mechanisms requires and explains the diversity of tools, strategies and heuristics for mechanism discovery" (p. 153). Our analysis underwrites these theses, and we thus present our heuristics perspective as an alternative tool both to chart changing system boundaries and to rethink explanatory power assessments. We present our heuristics perspective as an alternative measure of explanatory power to the "robustness constraint" of constitutive relevance. We offer some additional considerations in support of our alternative measure of explanatory power in the following discussion.

First, as we saw, there currently is preciously little known about mechanisms underlying the causal symptom–symptom relations articulated in network models. Without knowledge of micro and macro levels, hypotheses about constitutive relevance cannot be articulated and tested in the first place. Second, we also have seen that this does not mean that network models lack explanatory potential. While from one perspective the relation between a network structure and a model of a mechanism can be viewed as a relation between explanandum and explanans, respectively, from another stance network structures can be conceptualized as providing both explanation-seeking questions and answers. That is, network structures can be used to explain how specific symptoms are brough about by others, how contextual factors affect the strength of such relationships in a given environment, and how changes in dependency/difference-making relations between variables (may) induce changes to the network structure as a whole. By enabling the tracking of such dependency/difference-making relationships at the level of the whole network, they do meet another key explanatory norm discussed in the philosophical literature on explanation, namely that network models afford posing and answering *what-if questions* (Woodward, 2003; see Section 5.3). The heuristics perspective we advocate is one (underdeveloped) strategy for exploring dependency/difference-making relations and, we hope, can provide, when implemented in practice, an epistemic pointer to *relevant* dependency relations and what-if questions, specifically those that inform therapeutic interventions and ideally contribute to transitioning network structures from dysfunctional into functional states. But these relevant dependency relations are bound to differ from case to case (within and across individuals) given the variation in network structures and the dynamic, changing nature of network structures.

5.6 Outlook and Conclusions

In this chapter, we explored network models of mental disorders. A salient feature of these models is that they offer an alternative to the still dominant approach that sees mental disorders as the result of underlying mechanisms or pathogenic pathways. Contrary to this, network modelers see mental disorders as networks of causally connected symptoms and emphasize the relevance of *network structures*. While this literature clearly aims at *explaining* mental disorders, there is room to provide a more in-depth account of what such explanations amount to. We took up this opportunity and proposed that network models have to be interpreted as *mechanistic models*.

These models qualify as mechanistic, in our view, because they embody/have/express a mechanistic explanatory structure, and this structure helps us tackle what-if questions at the level of the whole system. They also function as heuristic tools for the generation of hypotheses (both generic hypothesis and for therapy). Finally, an analysis of their explanatory potential shows that boundaries of mechanisms are in this context very fluid and, hence, that adaptable explanatory schema enjoy higher explanatory power.

While our analysis contributes – or so we hope – to developing the philosophical underpinnings of the network modeling approach, we think that much more needs to be done. In particular, we hope that our contributions will fuel further conversations with network modelers about the implications that a mechanistic interpretation of this modeling approach has for developing protocols for data collection and for informing therapy. These are both pressing questions to be addressed, and having clarity about what and how network models do or can explain will clearly influence how we design protocols for data collection and for therapy.

REFERENCES

Aristodemou, M. E., Kievit, R. A., Murray, A. L., Eisner, M., Ribeaud, D., & Fried, E. I. (2024). Common cause versus dynamic mutualism: An empirical comparison of two theories of psychopathology in two large longitudinal cohorts. *Clinical Psychological Science, 12*(3), 380–402.

Baumgartner, M., & Casini, L. (2017). An abductive theory of constitution. *Philosophy of Science, 84*(2), 214–233.

Borsboom, D. (2017). A network theory of mental disorders. *World Psychiatry, 16*, 5–13.

Borsboom, D., Cramer, A. O. J., & Kalis, A. (2019). Brain disorders? Not really: Why network structures block reductionism in psychopathology research. *Behavioral and Brain Sciences, 42*, 1–63.

Craver, C. (2007). *Explaining the brain: Mechanisms and the mosaic unity of neuroscience*. Oxford University Press.

(2016). The explanatory power of network models. *Philosophy of Science, 83*, 698–709.

Craver, C., Glennan, S., & Povich, M. (2021). Constitutive relevance and mutual manipulability revisited. *Synthese, 199*, 8807–8828.

De Boer, N. S., de Bruin, L. C., Geurts, J. J. G., & Glas, G. (2021). The network theory of psychiatric disorders: A critical assessment of the inclusion of environmental factors. *Frontiers in Psychology, 12*, 1–13.

Glennan, S. (2017). *The new mechanical philosophy*. Oxford University Press.

Glennan, S., & Illari, P. (2018). Varieties of mechanisms. In S. Glennan & P. Illari (Eds.), *The Routledge handbook of mechanism and mechanical philosophy* (pp. 91–103). Routledge.

Glennan, S., Illari, P., & Weber, E. (2022). Six theses on mechanisms and mechanistic science. *Journal for General Philosophy of Science, 53*, 143–161.

Kaplan, D. M., & Bechtel, W. (2011). Dynamical models: An alternative or complement to mechanistic explanations? *Topics in Cognitive Science, 3*, 438–444.

Kendler, K. S., Zachar, P., & Craver, C. (2011). What kinds of things are psychiatric disorders? *Psychological Medicine, 41*, 1143–1150.

Levy, A., & Bechtel, W. (2013). Abstraction and the organization of mechanisms. *Philosophy of Science, 80*, 241–261.

Machamer, P. K., Darden, L., & Craver, C. F. (2000). Thinking about mechanisms. *Philosophy of Science, 57*, 1–25.

Mouchart, M., & Russo, F. (2011). Causal explanation: Recursive decompositions and mechanisms. In I. P. McKay, F. Russo, & J. Williamson (Eds.), *Causality in the sciences* (pp. 317–337). Oxford University Press.

Poliseli, L., Coutinho, J., Viana, B., Russo, F., & El-Hani, C. (2022). Philosophy of science in practice in ecological model building. *Biology and Philosophy, 37*, 21. https://doi.org/10.1007/s10539-022-09851-4

Robinaugh, D. J., Haslbeck, J. M. B., Waldorp, L. J., Kossakowski, J. J., Fried, E. I., Millner, A. J., McNally, R. J., van Nes, E. H., Scheffer, M., Kendler, K. S., & Borsboom D. (2019). Advancing the network theory of mental disorders: A computational model of panic disorder. *PsyArXiv* preprint.

Robinaugh, D. J., Hoekstra, R., Toner, E., & Borsboom, D. (2020). The network approach to psychopathology: A review of the literature 2008–2018 and an agenda for future research. *Psychological Medicine, 50*(3), 353–366.

Van Eck, D. (2018). Rethinking the explanatory power of dynamical models in cognitive science. *Philosophical Psychology, 31*, 1131–1161.

Woodward, J. (2003). *Making things happen*. Oxford University Press.

Wunsch, G., Mouchart, M., & Russo, F. (2014). Functions and mechanisms in structural explanations. *Journal for General Philosophy of Science, 45*(1), 187–208.

CHAPTER 6

Commentary on Russo and van Eck's "Charting the Explanatory Potential of Network Models in Psychopathology"

Stephan Heckers

Psychopathology is the scientific exploration of abnormal mental states and behavior. The phenomena under consideration are first-person (i.e., lived) experiences and third-person clinical descriptions, which can be studied and explained in two different ways. On the one hand, descriptive psychopathology aims to capture these phenomena without any preconceived notions of cause or mechanism (Häfner, 2015). On the other hand, theoretical psychopathology explores the etiology of abnormal mental states, applying methods ranging from the social sciences to neurobiology and genetics (Schultze-Lutter et al., 2018). Here I will focus on the descriptive and theoretical psychopathology of panic disorder given that Russo and van Eck use it as the paradigmatic psychiatric illness in their chapter, "Charting the Explanatory Potential of Network Models in Psychopathology."

The symptoms of panic disorder, described since the 1830s, had initially been recognized along separate medical or psychological axes (condition) (Angst, 1998). Accordingly, physicians described "irritable heart" or "hyperventilation syndrome," whereas psychologists and psychiatrists diagnosed "neurasthenia" or "anxiety syndrome." Klein's (1964) observation that newly available antidepressants are effective in treating panic states led to a unification of the medical and psychological approaches and, in 1980, to the inclusion of panic disorder as a new diagnosis in the DSM-III.

Panic disorder is one of five major anxiety disorders recognized in the current version of the DSM: specific phobia, social anxiety disorder (social phobia), panic disorder, agoraphobia, and generalized anxiety disorder (American Psychiatric Association, 2022). Panic disorder is defined as panic attacks that are both recurrent and unexpected (i.e., not triggered by or associated with a specific situation). A panic attack is defined as "an abrupt surge of intense fear or intense discomfort that reaches a peak within minutes" during which 4 or more of 13 criteria A occur:

A1. Palpitations, pounding heart, or accelerated heart rate.
A2. Sweating.
A3. Trembling or shaking.
A4. Sensations of shortness of breath or smothering.
A5. Feelings of choking.
A6. Chest pain or discomfort.
A7. Nausea or abdominal distress.
A8. Feeling dizzy, unsteady, light-headed, or faint.
A9. Chills or heat sensations.
A10. Paresthesias (numbness or tingling sensations).
A11. Derealization (feelings of unreality) or depersonalization (being detached from oneself).
A12. Fear of losing control or "going crazy."
A13. Fear of dying.

In addition to meeting criterion A, a person given the diagnosis panic disorder must also meet criterion B, which includes

B1. Persistent concern or worry about additional panic attacks or
B2. Change in behavior (such as avoidance), following at least one of the panic attacks.

An item response theory analysis of panic attack symptoms in both ICD-10 and DSM-IV revealed that #1 palpitation, the most frequently reported panic attack symptom, discriminates well between cases and non-cases at low level of panic attack severity (Ietsugu et al., 2007). In contrast, #10 paresthesia, #5 choking, and #13 fear of dying are good indicators of severe panic attacks. Of interest, "dry mouth," recognized in ICD-10 but not DSM-IV as a panic attack symptom, was found not to be an efficient marker in diagnosing panic attacks (Ietsugu et al., 2007). It was removed as a diagnostic criterion in ICD-11 (Kogan et al., 2016).

How do we make sense of the various physical symptoms and mental states experienced during a panic attack? For example, why are some symptoms more prevalent than others? Similarly, why are some experienced in mild attacks, whereas others are more likely to occur during severe attacks? These are questions for the descriptive psychopathology, epidemiology, and nosology of panic disorder.

At a mechanistic level, do some experiences trigger others? For example, is there a predictable pattern of symptoms during the course of a panic attack (Wilhelm & Roth, 2001)? Ultimately, can we identify a functional neuroanatomy of panic attacks (Gorman et al., 2000)? These are questions for the theoretical psychopathology and neurobiology of panic disorder.

Russo and van Eck critically discuss a recent computational model of panic disorder (Robinaugh et al., 2019), which is built on the theoretical framework of network theory (Borsboom, 2017). Network theory conceptualizes mental disorders as systems of mutually reinforcing symptoms. In short, the phenomena (i.e., first-person experiences and third-person clinical descriptions) are statistically analyzed in such a way that causal relationship between them can be explored.

The model by Robinaugh et al. posits that panic disorder arises from three interlocking feedback loops among panic attack symptoms. At the core are an amplifying feedback loop between arousal and perceived threat and a dampening feedback loop among perceived threat, escape behavior, and context. These two feedback loops operate on a time scale of minutes, specifically during the experience of a panic attack.

In addition, Robinaugh et al. propose a third feedback loop, operating on a time scale of days, which slowly amplifies between arousal schema, escape schema, and avoidance behavior.

To build the model, Robinaugh et al distill the previously listed panic disorder symptoms into just two clinical features: arousal and perceived threat. However, they do not provide a crosswalk between those two and the DSM criteria. It is likely that they consider the somatic symptoms captured in DSM criteria A1 to A10 to represent arousal and criteria A11 to A13 to represent perceived threat. It is conceivable that criterion B1, on a time scale beyond an individual panic attack, also presents perceived threat.

At the core of the computational model is a bidirectional, amplifying relationship between arousal (A) and perceived threat (T): the experience of arousal is interpreted as threat, which increases arousal, which in turn is interpreted as even greater threat. This creates a vicious cycle of T → A, A → T, T → A at the core of the panic attack. Robinaugh and colleagues define the arrows (→) as causal relationships. In biological terms, they interpret the vicious cycle as abnormal interoception – that is, an incorrect detection or interpretation of signals from the body (Van Diest, 2019).

While the T → A → T cycle drives panic, escape behavior slows panic. In the diagnostic criteria for panic disorder, escape behavior is defined as "behaviors designed to avoid having panic attacks, such as avoidance of exercise or unfamiliar situations" (American Psychiatric Association, 2022).

In their critique of Robinaugh's computational model of panic disorder, Russo and van Eck make the claim that network models are mechanistic models, albeit in a qualified fashion. They consider network models to be mechanistic because they include relevant dependency relations: changes in specific variables (e.g., the severity or duration of arousal changes) affect others in the context of the whole network structure. They rightfully point out that much of the computational work presented by Robinaugh et al. focuses on the T → A → T cycle but does not consider the relevant dependency relations for the whole network. Without such a comprehensive approach, they conclude, the arrows between T and A do not meet the stringent criteria of causal explanations proposed by Woodward's (2003) interventionist account of explanation. For example, do arousal and perceived threat capture all the relevant clinical features of a panic attack? If so, how can the somatic (e.g., palpitations), cognitive (e.g., fear of dying), and meta-cognitive (e.g., persistent worry) symptoms be accurately captured for each person, at any level of severity or duration of a panic attack?

In addition, a computational model of panic attacks needs to explain the occurrence of panic attacks beyond the diagnostic category panic disorder. As stated earlier, panic disorder is defined as recurrent and unexpected (i.e., not triggered by or associated with a specific situation) panic attacks. While the lifetime risk to experience at least one panic attack is about 40%, less than 5% of persons will meet the criteria for panic disorder. Many patients diagnosed with other psychiatric conditions, especially agoraphobia and post-traumatic stress disorder, also present with recurrent panic attacks. For example, panic disorder may be antecedent to PTSD or may develop as a sequela of PTSD (Berenz et al., 2019). In such conditions, the T → A → T cycle is included in a larger network of life experiences, memories, and adaptive behaviors. Any network model of panic attacks needs to accommodate such variables.

Russo and van Eck consider network models to be mechanistic, but they point out that they lack an important feature of mechanistic explanations, specifically constitutive relevance. Mechanistic explanations of behavior identify spatiotemporal parts of mechanisms that are constitutively relevant to the macro level, the coupling of which cannot be broken. Specifically, only when one can show that changes at the macro level are always accompanied by changes in specific spatiotemporal parts is there evidence for constitutive relevance. Russo and van Eck claim that things are exactly the opposite in the case of network models: "the more a network model is able to adapt and shape explanations across different configurations, the higher its explanatory power."

They conclude that network models can serve as heuristics for hypothesis testing in psychopathology. For example, the relationships between perceived threat, arousal, and escape behavior can be used for the selection of various pharmacological and psychotherapeutic treatments. In addition, the open structure of a network allows for the addition of new data, such as the first-person (lived) experience of panic attack, including experience sampling and momentary assessment (Walz et al., 2014).

I would like to add here that additional data may also come from network models based on neuroimaging data (Bassett & Sporns, 2017). Recent examples of purely neurobiological network models of panic disorder have focused on white matter connections (Jiang et al., 2023) or activation patterns of the amygdala (Brehl et al., 2020). However, it is likely that reductionist biological models of panic disorder will capture neither the clinical complexity nor the causal mechanism. In contrast, integration of biological, environmental, and cultural factors is possible within network theory, which "yields broad explanatory principles, without specifying, in advance, the realization or implementation of these principles" (Borsboom, 2017, p. 11).

An impactful theoretical psychopathology of panic disorder requires the capture of the first-person experience, a flexible model of the dynamics between the clinical and biological features, and, ultimately, the application of mechanistic explanations in the selection and application of interventions.

REFERENCES

American Psychiatric Association. (2022). *Diagnostic and statistical manual of mental disorders* (5th ed., text rev.). American Psychiatric Publishing. https://doi.org/https://doi.org/10.1176/appi.books.9780890425787

Angst, J. (1998). Panic disorder: History and epidemiology. *European Psychiatry, 13*(S2), 51s–55s. https://doi.org/10.1016/S0924-9338(98)80014-X

Bassett, D. S., & Sporns, O. (2017). Network neuroscience. *Nature Neuroscience, 20*(3), 353–364. https://doi.org/10.1038/nn.4502

Berenz, E. C., York, T. P., Bing-Canar, H., Amstadter, A. B., Mezuk, B., Gardner, C. O., & Roberson-Nay, R. (2019). Time course of panic disorder and posttraumatic stress disorder onsets. *Social Psychiatry and Psychiatric Epidemiology, 54*(5), 639–647. https://doi.org/10.1007/s00127-018-1559-1

Borsboom, D. (2017). A network theory of mental disorders. *World Psychiatry, 16*(1), 5–13. https://doi.org/10.1002/wps.20375

Brehl, A. K., Kohn, N., Schene, A. H., & Fernandez, G. (2020). A mechanistic model for individualised treatment of anxiety disorders based on predictive neural biomarkers. *Psychology Medicine, 50*(5), 727–736. https://doi.org/10.1017/S0033291720000410

Gorman, J. M., Kent, J. M., Sullivan, G. M., & Coplan, J. D. (2000). Neuroanatomical hypothesis of panic disorder, revised. *American Journal of Psychiatry, 157*(4), 493–505.

Häfner, H. (2015). Descriptive psychopathology, phenomenology, and the legacy of Karl Jaspers. *Dialogues in Clinical Neuroscience, 17*(1), 19–29. https://doi.org/10.31887/DCNS.2015.17.1/hhaefner

Ietsugu, T., Sukigara, M., & Furukawa, T. A. (2007). Evaluation of diagnostic criteria for panic attack using item response theory: Findings from the National Comorbidity Survey in USA. *Journal of Affective Disorders, 104*(1–3), 197–201. https://doi.org/10.1016/j.jad.2007.03.005

Jiang, M., Zhang, P., Yang, X., Yu, A., Zhang, J., Xu, X., & Li, Z. (2023). Altered white matter network topology in panic disorder. *Journal of Personalized Medicine, 13*(2), 227. https://doi.org/10.3390/jpm13020227

Klein, D. F. (1964). Delineation of two drug-responsive anxiety syndromes. *Psychopharmacologia, 5*, 397–408. https://doi.org/10.1007/bf02193476

Kogan, C. S., Stein, D. J., Maj, M., First, M. B., Emmelkamp, P. M., & Reed, G. M. (2016). The classification of anxiety and fear-related disorders in the ICD-11. *Depression and Anxiety, 33*(12), 1141–1154. https://doi.org/10.1002/da.22530

Robinaugh, D. J., Haslbeck, J. M. B., Waldorp, L. J., Kossakowski, J. J., Fried, E. I., Millner, A. J., NMcNally, R. J., Ryan, O., de Ron, J., van der Maas, H. J. L., van Nes, E. H., Scheffer, M., Kendler, K. S., & Borsboom, D. (2019). Advancing the network theory of mental disorders: A computational model of panic disorder. PsyArXiv Preprints. https://doi.org/https://doi.org/10.31234/osf.io/km37w

Schultze-Lutter, F., Schmidt, S. J., & Theodoridou, A. (2018). Psychopathology: A precision tool in need of re-sharpening [perspective]. *Frontiers in Psychiatry, 9*. https://doi.org/10.3389/fpsyt.2018.00446

Van Diest, I. (2019). Interoception, conditioning, and fear: The panic threesome. *Psychophysiology, 56*(8), e13421. https://doi.org/10.1111/psyp.13421

Walz, L. C., Nauta, M. H., & Aan Het Rot, M. (2014). Experience sampling and ecological momentary assessment for studying the daily lives of patients with anxiety disorders: a systematic review. *Journal of Anxiety Disorder, 28*(8), 925–937. https://doi.org/10.1016/j.janxdis.2014.09.022

Wilhelm, F. H., & Roth, W. T. (2001). The somatic symptom paradox in DSM-IV anxiety disorders: Suggestions for a clinical focus in psychophysiology. *Biological Psychology, 57*(1–3), 105–140. https://doi.org/10.1016/s0301-0511(01)00091-6

Woodward, J. (2003). *Making things happen: A theory of causal explanation.* Oxford University Press.

Section 3

CHAPTER 7

Introduction to Ross and Kendler's "Proximal and Distal Causes in Medicine"

Peter Zachar

After a brief overview, Lauren N. Ross and Kenenth S. Kendler begin their chapter reviewing the history of the proximal versus distal cause distinction in public health and epidemiology. Its purpose is to provide a framework for understanding how social and biological causes jointly impact the development of disease and health outcomes. This distinction traditionally utilizes a causal pathway model in which, for example, upstream, social factors such as organizational policies for remote work influence downstream, direct biological factors such as infection.

One long-standing problem in medicine is understanding how macro-level social factors causally get under the skin to influence both health and disease. For example, how does a social event such as divorce or the death of a loved one cause depression? The typical causal pathway framework addresses this issue by introducing intermediate causes that connect remote events at the beginning of a causal chain with the outcomes at the end. Although the remote event does not directly cause the outcome, it causes something else that causes something next, and next, and next, until the outcome is produced – in other words, a connected process account of causation.

While the proximal–distal model is commonly found in public health, epidemiology, and other medical contexts, it has also received significant criticism. For example, Nancy Krieger (2008) claims that proximal causes are not always more powerful and explanatory than distal causes. To illustrate, in the United States, political decisions in Washington, DC can have powerful effects in places far away, and for a long time. Causes that are closer in space and time to an effect may not be more powerful. Krieger cites these and other features to argue that reference to proximal and distal causes should be eliminated, as they fail to accurately capture such causal scenarios and, thus, mislead.

Unlike Krieger, Ross and Kendler are not willing to abandon the proximal-versus-distal distinction because it calls attention to the importance of social causes and their potential to have explanatory priority over biological causes. In particular, Ross and Kendler introduce three distinct causal scenarios that capture the role of social and biological causes of health and disease. The first pattern is most similar to standard proximal–distal models of social and biological causes, while the other two patterns show how social and biological causes can interact in other ways. These three scenarios involve social factors as distal causes, parallel causes, and proximal causes.

In the first pattern, social causes are distal to biological causes. Their example is the distribution of disease. For example, people with white collar jobs whose organization could both afford the technology for and accommodate remote work would have reduced exposure to an infectious disease compared with those in service industry jobs, where the work requires in-person contact. In this case, social factors, although distal, better explain the distribution of a disease, and intervening on distal factors can be a more effective way to alter outcomes on a large scale than intervening on proximal factors. Thus, Ross and Kendler claim, it would be a mistake to totally abandon the proximal-versus-distal distinction.

In the second pattern, social and biological causes operate in parallel. Their example is drawn from cancer research. Two factors important in increasing the risk of stomach cancer are one's genetic profile and one's dietary habits (described as environmental). Genetically one can have a low, intermediate, or high risk of developing stomach cancer. The extent to which one consumes processed meat can also put one at lower or higher risk. Neither of these factors is upstream to the other. Variations in diet can modify risk irrespective of genetics, and genetic differences can modify risk irrespective of diet. I would note that even if there is an interaction effect in which high genetic risk magnifies the causal power of diet, these factors are still operating in parallel. Ross and Kender also point out that this example nicely illustrates the fact that occurring earlier in time (genetic endowment precedes dietary habits) does not mean the earlier event is causally upstream to the later one.

In the third pattern, social causes are more proximal than biological causes. Their example is based on the concept of genetic nurturance. The idea is that the environments we select and/or create for ourselves are genetically influenced. Someone with intellectual interests will preferentially seek out and create for themselves intellectually stimulating environments. Along these lines, parental proclivities will also influence the environments they create for their children. A child immersed in an intellectually stimulating environment may be more likely to have higher educational attainment. Even if the relevant parental genotype is not transmitted to the child, it can influence the child's phenotype. Thus, the effect of parental genetics can be indirect and distal, mediated by the more proximal environmental niche. Ross and Kendler note that in this case, the proximal causes do offer better targets for intervention, but those targets are now social, not biological.

Ross and Kendler rely on an interventionist model of causation wherein "the cause" refers to an event that, when manipulated, alters the effect. This approach to causation does not require a fully mapped out connected process account – which, as noted, refers to accounts in which the causal relationship is based on physical connections between cause and effect, sometimes direct and at other times via intermediate steps. Indeed, on the interventionist account, detailed information about intermediate steps between cause and effect is not necessary for successful causal reasoning – thereby removing some of the mystery about how macro-level social factors can be causes. Furthermore, they argue, the counterfactual reasoning used in an interventionist model can readily accommodate absences such as lack of social support as causes in a way that connected process accounts cannot.

In my commentary I expand on the notion of causal pluralism and call into question a tendency in psychiatry to afford metaphysical priority to only one variety of causation, specifically proximal biological causation. I then offer further examples from contemporary psychopathology of the relevance of the proximal-versus-distal distinction, specifically psychosis risk and attenuated psychosis syndrome, alcoholism, and the pharmacological treatment of depression. I conclude by showing that causal pluralism is also relevant for connected process accounts.

REFERENCES

Krieger, N. (2008). Proximal, distal, and the politics of causation: What's level got to do with it? *American Journal of Public Health,* 98(2), 221–230. https://doi.org/10.2105/ajph.2007.111278

CHAPTER 8

Proximal and Distal Causes in Medicine

Lauren N. Ross and Kenneth S. Kendler

8.1 Introduction

In modern medicine, it is common to find claims that diseases are multicausal. According to these views, diseases are produced by many interacting causes as opposed to single, main causal factors. While earlier disease frameworks accommodated monocausal diseases – such as germ theory (tuberculosis), vitamin deficiencies (scurvy), and genetic conditions (Tay Sachs) – modern perspectives view such frameworks as a limited oversimplification (Kendler, 2019; Ross, 2018b). Motivation for these multicausal views comes in part from a growing appreciation for social causes and efforts to capture how social and biological causes interact to produce disease outcomes. Social causes include stressful life events, socioeconomic status, and social structures (such as material resources, education, public policies, and so on). Biological causes, on the other hand, include genetic, immunologic, hormonal, and other factors. While biomedicine overemphasizes the role of biological causes, public health and epidemiology fare better in appreciating social factors that influence health and disease (Braveman & Gottlieb, 2014; Engel, 1980). Attention to social factors has increased across each of these perspectives, but challenges remain for understanding their influence, importance, and interaction with other causes. In particular, it has proven difficult to clarify how macro-scale social factors "get under the skin" to cause disease and how they integrate with lower-level biological mechanisms in producing these outcomes (Caspi & Moffitt, 2006; Gehlert et al., 2008).

One conceptual framework that has emerged to address these challenges is the proximal–distal model of disease causation (Gehlert et al., 2008; Graham, 2004; Krieger, 2011; World Health Organization, 2010). This model is commonly found in public health and epidemiology contexts, particularly in discussions of the role of social causes – often called "social determinants of health" – in human health and disease. This model organizes causes into linear chains, in which upstream (distal) social factors influence downstream (proximal) biological factors, directly causing disease. This model provides an account of how social and biological causes interact, specifies the role social causes play in health outcomes, and captures how social causes may be prioritized in serving as the "root" causes that initiate a sequence of domino effects.

While the proximal–distal framework is common in these fields, it is not without drawbacks. In influential work, Krieger (2008) criticizes this "problematic" framework for failing to capture the complexities of disease and health causation. She claims that this model fails to capture the causal impact of social factors on disease and health, that "proximal–distal" language confuses multifactorial thinking, and that work in this area conflates the notions of causal "space," "time," and "strength" (Krieger, 2008). Due to these issues, she recommends that we "abandon the deeply confused language of the terms proximal and distal" by omitting them from medical discussions (Krieger, 2008, p. 227). This is not the first time that causal language has come under fire. Her suggestion resembles Russell's famous call for the "complete extrusion" of the word "cause" from our language because, according to him, it was used in incompatible, confused, and misleading ways (Russell, 1912). Even closer to home, consider the strict guidelines for publishing in the *Journal of the American Medical Association* (*JAMA*), which advises that "causal language (including use of terms such as effect and efficacy) should be used only for randomized clinical trials" (*Journal of the American Medical Association*, 2023). When other methods are used, the results "should be described in terms of association or correlation and should avoid cause-and-effect wording" (*Journal of the American Medical Association*, 2023). According to Krieger, after omitting these causal terms, she recommends that we shift to the language of "levels, pathways, and power," which she claims offer a solution to the noted issues (Krieger, 2008).

This chapter provides an analysis of the proximal–distal model, motivated by Krieger's (2008) insights. We agree with many of Krieger's criticisms, but we examine different weaknesses of this model and argue that it has important strengths. In the first part of this work, we clarify key features and assumptions of the proximal–distal model. These include the model's emphasis on the position of causes along linear pathways and the assumption that proximal causes are often more explanatory, causally relevant, and "intervenable" than distal ones. After clarifying these aspects of the model, we argue that the proximal–distal model adequately captures some causal scenarios, but that it does not apply universally. We examine three causal scenarios to show how social and biological causes interrelate in many different ways, which are only partly captured by this model. In particular, we show how social factors can play three types of causal roles: they can be *distal* causes, *parallel* causes, and *proximal* causes. We clarify these three causal scenarios, their implications for the explanatory status of social causes, and how they relate to the traditional proximal–distal framework.

This work shows that social factors can play various causal roles in producing disease and that different justifications exist for privileging them in explanations. Instead of following Krieger's suggestion of eliminating "proximal" and "distal" causal terminology, we argue that accurate use of these terms is not only possible, but that it is instrumental in capturing the diverse ways that social causes influence health and disease. Instead of omitting causal language (and reference to proximal and distal causes), we call for more clarity and precision in the communication of causality and important causal distinctions in medical science.

8.2 The Proximal–Distal Model: What Is It?

Medical communities use a rich, colorful, and varied causal terminology to capture the causal nature of human disease. Hippocratic medicine distinguished environmental causes from constitutional causes; 18th- and 19th-century medicine separated predisposing from exciting causes; and in many modern sciences, remote causes are distinguished from proximate causes (Kendler, 2020; Ross, 2018b; Ross & Woodward, 2016). A large number of other causal distinctions exist in modern medicine, including causal mechanisms, pathways, and cascades producing disease; the genetic drivers of a phenotype versus mere passenger genes; multicausal disease models in contrast to monocausal frameworks; and various causal topologies (bowtie, feedforward loop, feedback loop, and so on) in network models of systems medicine (Haber & Settleman, 2007; Ross, 2018a, 2021a, 2021b). An interest in proximal and distal causes is found in many other fields as well. This is evident in evolutionary biology with Mayr's (1961) ultimate–proximate cause distinction and in legal settings, which place importance on the "proximate causes" of outcomes (Hart & Honore, 1985).

The proximal–distal model of disease in the 21st century is a conceptual framework originating in public health and epidemiology. A main goal of this model is to capture the impact of social causes on human health and disease (see Figure 8.1; Gehlert et al., 2008; Graham, 2004; Krieger, 2011;

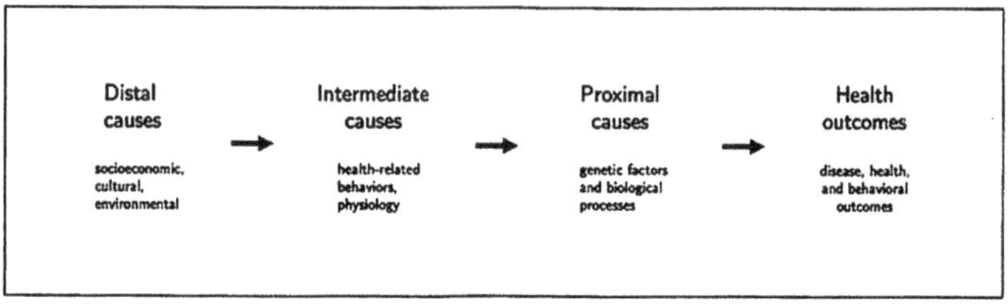

Figure 8.1 The proximal–distal model of disease causation and health outcomes. Causal factors relevant to a final health outcome are organized along a causal pathway. This framework represents the causal location of various factors – in terms of a more distal (upstream) and a more proximal (downstream) position – with respect to the final outcome of interest.

World Health Organization, 2010). Social causes are macro-level factors that are part of an individual's environment and, in some cases, the social structures around them. Material resources are a type of social factor that influences health outcomes – for example, limited access to clean water and "healthy" foods influences rates of infectious disease, diabetes, and obesity. Stressful life events are another social factor that impacts health – these are environmental stresses that can influence major depression, generalized anxiety, and substance use disorders (Kendler et al., 1995, 2003, 2011, 2012). As noted earlier, the influence of these factors on the health of individuals had led many to refer to them as "social determinants of health" (Braveman & Gottlieb, 2014; Marmot & Bell, 2019).

While evidence suggests that these social and environmental factors causally contribute to health outcomes, various questions have been raised regarding these claims. One main challenge is that it is not clear how higher-scale, macro-social factors causally impact disease phenotypes at the lower scales of biology and neuroscience. Caspi and Moffit (2006, p. 583) refer to this as the "biggest mystery of human psychopathology," namely "how does an environmental factor, external to the person, get inside the nervous system and alter its elements to generate the symptoms of a disordered mind?" This worry is driven by expectations that causation involves physically connected "mechanisms," and their progression from the social to the biological is not always obvious (Ross, 2018b). These debates are further complicated by the fact that social structure is often viewed as a vague and mysterious factor, with explanatory influence that is unclear (Little, 1991).

The proximal–distal model aims to address these issues by providing a conceptual framework for disease causation. This model relies on a linear causal chain or pathway to represent the causal order of factors that lead to disease, as shown in Figure 8.1 (Krieger, 2008; World Health Organization, 2010). In this model, social factors are located in the distal or upstream position of the causal pathway while biological factors are downstream, proximal causes of disease. In this manner, social factors represent the "root causes," "starting points," and "beginnings" of disease outcomes (Graham 2004; World Health Organization, 2010). The causal impact of these factors is "mediated through" biological mechanisms, which are the "direct," "proximal" causes of disease. Consider a description of this from the World Health Organization (WHO):

> The social determinants of health inequities are causally antecedent to ... intermediary determinants, which are linked, on the other side, to a set of individual-level influences, including health-related behaviors and physiological factors ... At the most proximal point in the models, genetic and biological processes are emphasized, mediating the health effects of social determinants. (World Health Organization, 2010)

As this and other descriptions suggest (see Table 8.1; Gehlert et al. 2008; Graham 2004; National Institute of Health, 2020; National Institute of Mental Health, 2021), the causal order inherent to this model implies that upstream causes regulate downstream causes, which lead to disease.[1]

This model supports various assumptions that are important to highlight. First, it presupposes that disease causation is appropriately understood with a linear "pathway" model of sequentially ordered causes. Second, it maintains that social factors are always distal in this sequence and that biological factors are always proximal. This is used to suggest that upstream social factors causally determine downstream outcomes.

Third, this model is used to justify various claims regarding the priority of social and biological causes. Interestingly, while this model was developed to highlight the "causal priority" of social factors, it can "unwittingly reinforce" a preference for biological causes (Link & Phelan, 1995). This is seen in claims that proximal causes are more causally relevant, explanatorily powerful, and "intervenable" for control. For example, it is claimed that as we move further upstream, our inferences are "less secure" and our interventions are "less efficient" and "less effective" (Rothman et al., 1998). Furthermore, this model can seem to imply that if biological factors are a funnel through which all other upstream causes operate, then biological interventions alone could control and explain whatever health outcome follows.

[1] However, as noted in Section 8.3, it also suggests that proximal causes can be targeted to potentially stop the influence of distal causal factors.

Table 8.1 *Selected quotations relevant to the proximal–distal framework.*

Author, Year	Relevant Text
World Health Organization (WHO)	The structural determinants operate through a series of what we will term intermediary social factors or social determinants of health. The social determinants of health inequities are causally antecedent to these intermediary determinants, which are linked, on the other side, to a set of individual-level influences, including health-related behaviors and physiological factors. . .At the most proximal point in the models, genetic and biological processes are emphasized, mediated the health effects of social determinants. The main categories of intermediary determinants of health are: material circumstances; psychosocial circumstances; behavioral and/or biological factors; and the health system itself as a social determinant (p. 36–37)
Graham, H.	The most distal factor is the social structure of society, variously labeled general socioeconomic, cultural, and environmental conditions, social structure, social context, and social, economic, and cultural characteristics of a society. . .Radiating out from this societal level, the models contain a set of intermediate social factors: social position and its attendant working and living conditions, and the social networks of family and community. The intermediate social factors are ranged above a set of individual-level influences, including health-related behaviors and physiological factors. At the most proximal point in the models, genetic and biological processes are emphasized, mediating the health effects of social determinants (p. 106)
Gehlert, S. et al.	In these frameworks, upstream determinants are defined as features of the social environment, such as socioeconomic status and discrimination, that influence individual behavior, disease, and health status. Viewing health disparities though a lens that incorporates social/environmental conditions as upstream factors in multilevel models better allows us to design and implement interventions targeted at levels downstream from those conditions (p. 340)
National Institute of Mental Health (NIMH)	What the NIMH lists as social determinants of health "social determinants of health (e.g., education, economic stability, quality of housing, access to health care, experience of discrimination). . .Of particular priority is research that identifies mechanisms contributing to the persistence of mental health disparities

Table 8.1 (*cont.*)

Author, Year	Relevant Text
National Institutes of Health (NIH)	The set of factors that impact health beyond individual-level characteristics are often referred to as "upstream factors" or more commonly, social determinants of health. Social determinants of health (SDOH) are sometimes loosely defined as the conditions in the places where people live, learn, work, and play that can affect a wide range of health risks and outcomes. Some examples include access to healthy foods, access to quality health care, reliable transportation, stable housing, and economic stability. Societal or macro-level influences, including structural racism, discrimination, and certain policies can result in inequities observed in these determinants

8.3 Krieger on the Proximal–Distal Divide

Krieger's analysis of the proximal–distal model highlights some of the already mentioned points but also provides more historical context. She examines early uses of "proximal" and "distal" in medicine, which often referred to spatial distance in anatomical contexts. When considering the location of anatomical structures – such as the bones, blood vessels, or nerves in the forearm – those structures closer to the center of the body are more proximal (the elbow), while those that are farther away are more distal (the wrist). In this usage, the center of the body is a point of reference that helps capture differences in spatial location. This language was extended to temporal dimensions in various sciences, such as geology, in which it captured the position of events along a timeline (closer to or farther from some point of interest).

According to Krieger, the link between causation and these proximal–distal concepts was formed when views in physics (such as the inverse square law) suggested that closer proximity implies increased causal power. She suggests that the assumption that "'proximal' causes remain most potent" continues to this day and is present across the life and physical sciences (Krieger, 2008, p. 223). We see this in cases where biological causes are emphasized over social causes, when bodily causes are privileged over remote environmental causes, and in cases where local physiological causes are prioritized over distant evolutionary causes.

Krieger rightly notes two issues with the aforementioned developments, specifically that (1) causal order is not the same as spatial or temporal order and that (2) proximal causes are not always more powerful, explanatory, or potent than distal ones are. With respect to the second, very spatially distant causes can provide powerful explanations, while creeping further along a causal chain to some effect does not always identify stronger or more explanatorily relevant causes. For example, remote decisions in Washington, DC can be a main explanatory and causal factor for far-reaching effects in the country (such as access to health care). Additionally, when biological causes such as genes explain disease outcomes, we do not always view more proximal causal intermediates (such as damaged proteins) as more potent causes. And concerning the first point, when temporal or spatial order is confused with causal order – in other words, how causal factors and their influence are organized in relation to each other – it seems important to point out this confusion and the different meanings these orderings involve.

These issues with the proximal–distal model lead Krieger to suggest abandoning the language of proximal and distal causation and replacing it with concepts of levels, pathways, and power. If these terms are to help, this will need to be supported and established in future work, as Krieger does not discuss this replacement process in detail. There are clear formulations of the "pathway" concept, which clarify its meaning, and we rely on this concept in our following analysis (Ross, 2021). However, one complication with her suggestion is that many view the notion of "levels" in science as highly ambiguous and imprecise, much more so than the notions of proximal and distal causation (Potochnik, 2021). Until "levels" and "power" receive a clear treatment that can advance these discussions, whether they provide clarity in these contexts remains an open question.

What we focus on instead are ways of understanding, clarifying, and specifying a principled use of the proximal–distal model. While this model may mistakenly emphasize biological causes in some situations, it is often used to capture the importance of social causes and their explanatory priority over biological causes. This is a main goal of many analyses of social determinants of health. Explicit reference to these distal factors as "root causes" and "the causes of the causes" is intended to capture their critical causal influence. Insofar as these frameworks may capture important principles that follow from causal order and can be used to assess causal relevance, we suggest that it is worth examining their claims and reasoning. Even if proximal and distal causal relationships are confused in the literature, they may still represent a distinction that is principled, ripe for clarification, and important in capturing important explanatory distinctions.[2]

8.4 Locating the Causes of Health and Disease

We provide an analysis that clarifies the notions of proximal and distal causation, primarily their use in medical contexts. We examine three scenarios that clarify distinct ways that social and biological causes relate to each other, in leading to a health outcome of interest. These cases aim to clarify the notions of proximal and distal causes, including assessments of when and why such causes differ in explanatory power.

8.4.1 Disease Distribution: Social as a Distal Cause

We describe a first causal scenario to show that, in some cases, it is perfectly reasonable to view social causes as distal to biological ones, as suggested by the proximal–distal model. However, in these cases, other assumptions commonly associated with this model do not always hold.

A main explanatory target in public health and epidemiology is disease distribution in populations (Krieger, 2011). In some cases, infectious diseases – such as cholera or COVID-19 – are more common in lower socioeconomic groups compared to higher ones (Patel et al., 2020). In these situations, social factors (such as access to clean water, ability to work remotely, etc.) are upstream, as they control exposure to downstream biological contagions that produce disease. The difference in exposure explains the population-wide disease pattern, as social factors "shape distribution of main risk factors" (Marmot & Bell, 2019, p. 10). A central concept in these examples are causal pathways or "pathways of action" that connect upstream, social factors to downstream, biological intermediates. In these situations, social factors are considered the "causes of the causes," as they causally influence biological factors that are the proximal causes of disease (Marmot & Bell, 2019).

Biological factors are, of course, "part" of these explanations; they are intermediates along the causal pathway from exposure to disease. However, for this explanatory target, social factors are more explanatory because they can account for much of the population-wide disease

[2] In fact, if confusions exist in the literature, you might think that setting the record straight and clarifying language is fruitful (while outlawing language is less realistic).

distribution, which is lost at the lower levels of biology. For this reason, these outcomes are referred to as "socially structured patterns of disease" (Metzl & Hansen, 2014, p. 129).

This causal scenario reveals several important points. First, social causes can be distal to biological causes, consistent with the proximal–distal model. Notice that while these social factors are distal to some biological causes (contagion-triggered immune reaction, cellular damage, etc.), they are not distal to others such as genetic profile, which have the potential to moderate disease susceptibility. This indicates that while some biological causes are intermediates along socially triggered pathways to disease, these intermediates are not always genetic, as suggested by standard representations of the proximal–distal model. We consider this situation further in the next subsection.

A second lesson from this example is that the elevated status of proximal causes within the proximal–distal framework is not always justified. In contrast with the assumptions of this framework, distal causes are sometimes better targets for explanation, causal relevance, and control. We see this in the ability of social causes to explain disease distribution and in the fact that they can provide better targets for intervention. Policies that change social conditions can be more effective than genetic, cellular-level, and individual treatments. For example, in efforts to reduce alcoholism, higher-level policies (such as restrictions on marketing, availability, and screenings for drunk drivers) remain more effective than individual treatments (Babor et al., 2010). Social factors can also be easier to intervene on for technological and practical reasons: in some cases interventions on genetic and cellular causes are not available, while interventions on social causes are. Additionally, social causes can involve a single main point of intervention, in contrast to targeting the multitude of biological factors they initiate. Public policies that target smoking cessation are fewer in number than interventions fine-tuned to the distinct carcinogens, various mutagenic effects, and heterogeneous cellular pathologies leading to lung cancer. This is not to say that social interventions are not without challenges or that they are always better. The suggestion is that social factors are sometimes better locations for control despite being upstream, distal causes to their effects. Finally, if they address social needs like access to clean water and safe working conditions, they result in many positive effects.

The proximal–distal model represents these causal scenarios well, but this representation requires appreciating the unique explanatory target in these cases, namely disease distribution. Insofar as disease distribution is a central explanatory target for public health and epidemiology, much would be lost in discarding this model and the language of proximal–distal causation. Epidemiology is not the only context in which use of the proximal–distal model is principled, although distribution cases provide one example. The medical sciences contain various types of explanatory targets, while different targets pick out different factors as more or less causally relevant.

This suggests that the proximal–distal model has some utility; but does it provide a comprehensive picture of how social factors influence health and disease? We explore two further case studies to identify situations in which this model does not apply but that capture alternative ways that social factors have causal influence.

8.4.2 Genes and Environment: Social as a Parallel Cause

The proximal–distal model applies to some cases but not others. One set of examples it does not capture are situations in which social and biological factors are "parallel" causes of a disease outcome. In these cases, social and biological causes operate without either upstream cause operating "through" the other.

Examples of this are found in models of how genetic and environmental factors cause disease. In modern research, many different methods are used to quantify the causal influence of genetic and environmental factors on disease. These include path analysis, heritability studies, multivariate analyses in various populations (including twin and adoption samples), and gene intervention experiments in animal models (Caspi & Moffitt, 2006; Kendler & Eaves, 1986).

Many of these studies use statistical methods that support causal claims, although these methods do not reveal fine-grained causal details of the biological process itself (Kendler & Gardner, 2010). A number of these methods distinguish two main ways that genes and environment interrelate statistically: their interrelations can be additive or multiplicative (Kendler & Gardner, 2010; Kendler et al., 1995). In the additive model, the impact of one factor on the outcome is the same with or without the other. In the multiplicative model, the magnitude of the impact of each factor on the outcome depends on the other.

Consider a causal scenario discussed by Kendler and Eaves (1986), which is captured by the additive model. In this example, the disease outcome is depression and the candidate causes are genetic risk profile and environment. The genetic risk profile captures two genetic profiles, which are a resilient (R) or sensitive (S) disposition to stress. The other cause is an environmental factor, which is an environment that is either high stress (H) or low stress (L). This example shows how both factors have causal influence, where the influence of one factor is not mediated by the other and where the status of both factors is needed to explain the outcome. If an individual has a resilient genetic profile, this might protect against depression, but switching the environment from one of low to high stress can overwhelm this and cause the depressive state. Alternatively, a low-stress environment can also protect against stress, but the genetic profile still matters here because a sensitive profile can result in depression. This represents a "commonsense" model for how environment and genetics influence disease risk as independent factors with additive influence. These factors are independent in the sense that no matter what the patient's genetic profile, changes to diet influence disease risk. Similarly, no matter what the patient's dietary status, differences in their genetic profile alter disease risk.

When this statistical model is interpreted causally, each factor acts as a "parallel cause," as they operate concurrently without one being upstream to the other. This is evident by the fact that when one cause is held "fixed," changes to the other still provide causal control over the outcome. Both factors explain the risk of stomach cancer: both causally impact the outcome, without one being causally upstream of the other.[3]

Appreciating that social-environmental factors can be parallel causes is important for many reasons. First, this shows that social causes are not always distal to biological factors, as they can operate concurrently with them. This reveals a helpful role of targeting social causes: they can alter the likelihood of disease without operating through genes. This also shows how both are individually important causes and should be equally prioritized in our explanations.

It should be noted that one of Krieger's concerns rings true in this context, specifically the worry of conflating causal location with temporal location. In some of this literature, causes that present earlier in time (e.g., genes) are referred to as "distal," while causes triggered closer in time to the outcome (e.g., environmental stressors) are "proximal" (van Heeringen, 2012). These temporal differences relate to the distinction between

[3] Another example (and way of illustrating) parallel causes include cases in which two causes act conjunctively to produce an outcome (Lucas et al., 2014). These are cases of interacting causes, in which both causes control the outcome, and the control they each have is dependent on the other (Ross, 2018a; Spirtes et al., 2000).

"predisposing" and "exciting" causes, as the earlier causes predispose to disease while the later ones trigger or excite it (Kendler, 2020). Care should be taken to distinguish these different uses of "proximal" and "distal" terminology. Just because a cause takes place earlier in time does not mean it is upstream on a causal pathway leading to the other cause. Both causes can still operate in parallel, even if one is set at an earlier point in time. Maintaining the utility, clarity, and meaning of "proximal" and "distal" terminology requires specifying whether it is used to capture a distinction that is causal, temporal, or of some other nature.

This parallel causal framework shows how social and biological causes can interrelate in more complex ways than is captured by the standard proximal–distal model. While this framework captures a basic relationship between these causes, ways in which they interrelate and depend on each other can be (and often are) far more complex.

8.4.3 Social Genomics: Social as a Proximal Cause

In a final causal scenario, the locations of social and biological causes are switched relative to the standard proximal–distal model. In this case, biological causes are distal while social causes are proximal.

One example of this scenario is when genetic factors work "through" the environment to influence behavioral outcomes (Bates et al., 2018; Rietveld et al., 2013; Stefansson et al., 2018). As an illustration of this, consider explanations of educational attainment in children. Standard explanations cite combinations of the child's genetic profile and environment, which are both causal factors present during the child's lifespan. In recent work, an alternative "intergenerational" explanation is provided, sometimes called "genetic nurture," which includes gene variants of the parents (Bates et al., 2018). In these studies, evidence suggests that the parent's gene variants have influence over the "environmental niche" they create for a child (for example, the degree to which they provide intellectual stimulation for their children through challenging dinner table discussions, taking them to museums, etc.), which influences the child's educational attainment (Bates et al., 2018). (The parental gene variants in these studies are not transmitted to the child and thus rule out their direct influence on educational attainment by being present in children.)

In this manner, the causal pathway of interest runs from genes, to environment, to outcome, namely from parental genetics, to environmental niche, to educational attainment, respectively (Bates et al., 2018). As genes work through an "environmental route," they have an "indirect" influence on the outcome (Bates et al., 2018; Stefansson et al., 2018). Other studies support a similar causal intermediate role of environment for other health outcomes (Thorgeirsson, 2008).

This research is associated with a social genomics perspective, in which genetic factors are included in a social science approach to health outcomes (Harden and Koellinger, 2020). Whereas studying genetic causes is often viewed as distinct from (if not in conflict with) a social science approach, this perspective brings both together. Instead of competing, advances in genetics are viewed as a helpful "toolbox" for social scientists to use in clarifying the complex role of social and biological factors on health outcomes (Harden and Koellinger, 2020).

This causal scenario shows, first, that the causal positions of social and biological factors can be switched. Social factors can influence health outcomes as proximate causes through which biology operates. This matters because it reveals how the proximate cause can be a better intervention point in overriding the influence of upstream genes. If genes and environment worked in parallel, as discussed in Section 8.3.2, this would not be the case. Furthermore, intervening on this social cause can be easier, more effective, and more practical than interventions on upstream biology. In contrast to standard assumptions, privileging proximal causes sometimes means privileging social factors.

Second, this case shows that, in contrast to Krieger's suggestions, we should not want to remove "proximal" and "distal" terminology from our lexicon. This causal language is crucial for capturing the accurate causal location of these factors, their relation to the outcome, and their difference in causal influence. The problem is not with using these terms but with using them in a way that is principled, clear, and accurate.

Finally, this case and others can help resolve puzzles regarding the causal influence of macro-level social factors. These puzzles are tied to connected process accounts of causation, which can influence expectations about social causes. Connected process accounts maintain that causes are physically connected to their effects – a view related to identifying detailed "mechanisms" or intermediates from causes to effects (Ross, 2024; Woodward, 2003). This perspective can make social causes seem mysterious, as there are often no clear physical connections from public policies, social resources, and environments to the downstream health outcomes they impact. The problem here is that connected process accounts are misleading and poor guides to successful causal reasoning in scientific contexts. For example, many absences (deleted genes, lack of resources, etc.) are causally relevant to outcomes, despite lacking a physical connection to these outcomes.

A better account of causation is an interventionist one, which more accurately captures causal reasoning in science (Kendler & Campbell, 2009; Woodward, 2003). On this account, causes are factors that provide control over their effects; intervening and changing the cause leads to a change in the effect (Woodward, 2003). While extra detail about intermediates can be useful, it is not necessary for identifying causal relationships, and these relationships need not involve physical connection. This is consistent with the methods and reasoning used by social scientists (and scientists in many other fields) used to understand, study, and describe causation (Morgan & Winship, 2015).

In the three models discussed in this section, social factors are causal in the sense that if they were intervened upon and changed, this would lead to changes in their downstream effects. These causal dependency relations can span levels and capture external causes that get "under the skin" to produce health outcomes. Proper use of "proximal" and "distal" causal conceptions requires specifying an account of causation and appreciating the many ways that social and biological causes interrelate to produce health outcomes.

8.5 Conclusion

This analysis shows that social factors can influence health outcomes in a manner outlined by the standard proximal–distal model, but in many other ways as well. Social factors can be distal causes, parallel causes, and proximal causes of disease and health. This reveals three unique ways that social factors interrelate with biology and exert causal influence. We have also shown how some assumptions of the proximal–distal model are incorrect, including assumptions about causal relevance, explanatory power, and targetable factors for control. Although this model is sometimes used to support a prioritization of proximal causes, this approach should be resisted as a universal principle. In some cases, social causes that are distal can have more explanatory power, as was seen in explanations of disease distribution.

Although the proximal–distal model is not a comprehensive conceptual framework for the influence of social causes on disease and health, this does not call for abandoning "proximal" and "distal" terminology. In fact, this language is helpful in capturing important distinctions in causal architecture and how causes interrelate in producing outcomes. Care needs to be taken in deciding when and how this model is applied to causal scenarios (if this is done accurately) and what assumptions are associated with the model's use (such as viewing proximal causes as always more explanatorily potent). One by-product of clarifying the rationale behind this model is that this identifies reasons for prioritizing social causes for some explanations. Policies that change social conditions can be more effective than genetic, cellular-level, and individual treatments. In short, there are many situations in which social causes better serve the goals of controlling, preventing, and treating health outcomes.

Examining the concepts of proximal and distal causes relates to other important causal distinctions in medicine. These include distinguishing causal mechanisms from causal pathways, predisposing from exciting causes, higher- from lower-level causes, and structuring from triggering causes (Kendler, 2020; Ross, 2018a, 2021b, 2023). It is important to clarify what these distinctions capture in science, how they should be understood, and why they matter. This requires examining the causal concepts we use in scientific settings, how they capture causal differences in the world, and specifying how these differences matter for our goals of explanation and understanding in medicine.

REFERENCES

Babor, T., Caetano, R., Casswell, S., Edwards, G., Giesbrecht, N., Graham, N., Grube, J., Hill, L., Holder, H., Livingston, M., Osterberg, E., Rehm, J., Room, R., & Rossow, I. (2010). *Alcohol: No ordinary commodity: Research and public policy.* Oxford University Press.

Bates, T. C., Maher, B. S., Medland, S. E., McAloney, K., Wright, M. J., Hansell, N. K., Kendler, K. S., Martin, N. G., & Gillespie, N. A. (2018). The nature of nurture: using a virtual-parent design to test parenting effects on children's educational attainment in genotyped families. *Twin Research and Human Genetics, 21*(2), 73–83.

Braveman, P., & Gottlieb, L. (2014). The social determinants of health: It's time to consider the causes of the causes. *Public Health Reports, 129*(Suppl. 2), 19–31.

Caspi, A., & Moffitt, T. E. (2006). Gene-environment interactions in psychiatry: joining forces with neuroscience. *Nature Reviews Neuroscience, 7*(7), 583–590.

Engel, G. L. (1980). The clinical application of the biopsychosocial model. *The American Journal of Psychiatry, 137*(5), 535–544. https://doi.org/10.117/ajp.137.5.535

Gehlert, S., Sohmer, D., Sacks, T., Mininger, C., McClintock, M., & Olopade, O. (2008). Targeting health disparities: A model linking upstream determinants to downstream interventions. *Health Affairs, 27*(2), 339–349.

Graham, H. (2004). Social determinants and their unequal distribution: Clarifying policy understandings. *The Milbank Quarterly, 82*(1), 101–124.

Haber, D. A., & Settleman, J. (2007). Studies that have provided the first unbiased, large-scale analyses of DNA mutations across an array of cancers also have lessons for the proposal to annotate the entire cancer genome. *Nature, 446*(8), 2.

Harden, K. P., & Koellinger, P. D. (2020). Using genetics for social science. *Nature Human Behaviour, 4*(6), 567–576.

Hart, H., & Honore, T. (1985). *Causation in the law*. Oxford University Press.

Journal of the American Medical Association. (2023). *Instructions for authors*. JAMA. Retrieved August 5, 2025 from https://jamanetwork.com/journals/jama/pages/instructions-for-authors

Kendler, K., & Campbell, J. (2009). Interventionist causal models in psychiatry: Repositioning the mind-body problem. *Psychological Medicine*, 39(6), 881–887. https://doi.org/10.1017/S0033291708004467

Kendler, K., & Eaves, L. (1986). Models for the joint effect of genotype and environment on liability to psychiatric illness. *The American Journal of Psychiatry*.

Kendler, K. S. (2019). From many to one to many: The search for causes of psychiatric illness. *Journal of the American Medical Association Psychiatry, 76*(10), 1085.

(2020). A prehistory of the diathesis-stress model: Predisposing and exciting causes of insanity in the 19th century. *American Journal of Psychiatry, 177*(7), 576–588.

Kendler, K. S., Aggen, S. H., Knudsen, G. P., Røysamb, E., Neale, M. C., & Reichborn-Kjennerud, T. (2011). The structure of genetic and environmental risk factors for syndromal and subsyndromal common DSM-IV Axis I and All Axis II disorders. *American Journal of Psychiatry, 168*(1), 29–39.

Kendler, K. S., & Gardner, C. O. (2010). Interpretation of interactions: Guide for the perplexed. *British Journal of Psychiatry, 197*(3), 170–171.

Kendler, K. S., Hettema, J. M., Butera, F., Gardner, C. O., & Prescott, C. A. (2003). Life event dimensions of loss, humiliation, entrapment, and danger in the prediction of onsets of major depression and generalized anxiety. *Archives of General Psychiatry, 60*(8), 789.

Kendler, K. S., Ronald, M., Kessler, C., Walters, E. E., MacLean, C., Neale, M. C., Heath, A. C., & Eaves, L. J. (1995). Stressful life events, genetic liability, and onset of an episode of major depression in women. *American Journal of Psychiatry, 152*(6), 833–842. https://doi.org/10.1176/ajp.152.6.833

Kendler, K. S., Sundquist, K., Ohlsson, H., Palm´er, K., Maes, H., Winkleby, M. A., & Sundquist, J. (2012). Genetic and familial environmental influences on the risk for drug abuse: A national Swedish adoption study. *Archives of General Psychiatry, 69*(7), 690–697. https://doi.org/10.1001/archgenpsychiatry.2011.2112

Krieger, N. (2008). Proximal, distal, and the politics of causation: What's level got to do with it? *American Journal of Public Health, 98*(2), 221–230.

(2011). *Epidemiology and the people's health*. Oxford University Press.

Link, B. G., & Phelan, J. (1995). Social conditions as fundamental causes of disease. *Journal of Health and Social Behavior, 35*, 80.

Little, D. (1991). *Varieties of social explanation.* Westview Press.

Lucas, C. G., Bridgers, S., Griffiths, T. L., & Gopnik, A. (2014). When children are better (or at least more open-minded) learners than adults: Developmental differences in learning the forms of causal relationships. *Cognition, 131*(2), 284–299.

Marmot, M., & Bell, R. (2019). Social determinants and non-communicable diseases: Time for integrated action. *British Medical Journal*, 364, l251. https://doi.org/10.1136/bmj.l251

Mayr, E. (1961). Cause and effect in biology. *Science, 134*(3489), 1501–1506. http://www.jstor.org/stable/1707986

Metzl, J. M., & Hansen, H. (2014). Structural competency: Theorizing a new medical engagement with stigma and inequality. *Social Science & Medicine, 103*, 126–133.

Morgan, S. L., & Winship, C. (2015). *Counterfactuals and causal inference* (2nd ed.). Cambridge University Press.

National Institute of Health. (2020). *Targeting upstream social determinants of health.* NIH. Retrieved September 10, 2025 from https://www.nidcr.nih.gov/grants-funding/funding-priorities/future-research-initiatives/targeting-upstream-social-determinants-health

National Institute of Mental Health. (2021). *NIMH strategic plan: Challenges and opportunities.* NIMH. Retrieved September 10, 2025 from https://www.nimh.nih.gov/about/strategic-planning-reports/progress/2021-strategic-plan-progress-report

Patel, J., Nielsen, F., Badiani, A., Assi, S., Unadkat, V., Patel, B., Ravindrane, R., & Wardle, H. (2020). Poverty, inequality and COVID-19: The forgotten vulnerable. *Public Health, 183*, 110–111.

Potochnik, A. (2021). *Levels of organization in biology.* MIT Press.

Rietveld, C. A., Medland, S. E., Derringer, J., Yang, J., Esko, T., Martin, N. W., Westra, H. J., Shakhbarov, K., Abdellaoui, A., Agrawal, A., Albrecht, E., Alizadeh, B. Z., Amin, N., Barnard, J., Baumeister, S. E., Benke, K. S., Bielak, L. F., Boatman, J. A., Boyle, P. A., et al. (2013). GWAS of 126,559 individuals identifies genetic variants associated with educational attainment. *Science, 340*(6139), 1467–1471.

Ross, L. (2023). The explanatory nature of constraints: Law-based, mathematical, and causal. *Synthese, 202*, 56. https://doi.org/10.1007/s11229-023-04281-5

(2024). What is social structural explanation? A causal account. *Nous*, 58, 163–179. https://doi.org/10.1111/nous.12446

Ross, L. N. (2018a). Causal selection and the pathway concept. *Philosophy of Science, 85*, 551–572.

(2018b). The doctrine of specific etiology. *Biology & Philosophy, 33*(37). https://doi.org/10.1007/s10539-018-9647-x

(2021a). Distinguishing topological and causal explanation. *Synthese, 198*, 9803–9820. https://doi.org/10.1007/s11229-020-02685-1

(2021b). Causal concepts in biology: How pathways differ from mechanisms and why it matters. *The British Journal for the Philosophy of Science, 72*, 131–158. https://doi.org/10.1093/bjps/axy078

Ross, L. N., & Woodward, J. F. (2016). Koch's postulates: An interventionist perspective. *Studies in History and Philosophy of Biology & Biomedical Science, 59*, 35–46.

Rothman, K. J., Adami, H.-O., & Ttichopoulos, D. (1998). Should the mission of epidemiology include the eradication of poverty? *The Lancet, 352*(9130), 810–813.

Russell, B. (1912). On the notion of cause. *Proceedings of the Aristotelian Society, 13*, 1–26. http://www.jstor.org/stable/4543833

Spirtes, P., Glymour, C., & Scheines, R. (2000). *Causation, prediction, and search* (2nd ed.). MIT Press.

Stefansson, K., Thorsteinsdottir, U., Bjornsdottir, G., Helgason, A., Gudbjartsson, D., Masson, G., Halldorsson, B., Oddsson, A., Benonisdottir, S., Thorgeirsson, T., Young, A., Vilhjalmsson, B., Frigge, M., Thorlesifsson, G., & Kong, A. (2018). The nature of nurture: Effects of parental genotypes. *Science*, 359(6374), 424–428. https://doi.org/10.1126/science.aan6877

Thorgeirsson, T. E. (2008). A variant associated with nicotine dependence, lung cancer and peripheral arterial disease. *Nature, 452*(7187), 638–642.

van Heeringen, K. (2012). Stress-diathesis model of suicidal behavior. In Y. Dwivedi (Ed.), *The neurobiological basis of suicide* (pp. 113–124). CRC Press.

Woodward, J. (2003). *Making things happen*. Oxford University Press.

World Health Organization. (2010). *A conceptual framework for action on the social determinants of health: Social determinants of health discussion paper 2*. WHO. Retrieved September 10, 2025 from https://www.afro.who.int/sites/default/files/2017-06/SDH_conceptual_framework_for_action.pdf

CHAPTER 9

Commentary on Ross and Kendler's "Proximal and Distal Causes in Medicine"

Peter Zachar

Ross and Kendler argue that despite Nancy Krieger's persuasive criticisms of the distal-versus-proximal framework, distinguishing between distal and proximal causes is still informative in medicine. They are especially concerned about viewing, by default, social causes of disease as distal and biological causes as proximal, showing that in some cases social causes occur in parallel with biological causes and in others social causes are more proximal than biological causes.

Krieger (2008) argues that the distal-versus-proximal distinction is muddled, referring alternatively to temporal relations (proximal causes and effects occur closer in time than distal causes and effects), spatial relations (proximal causes and effects occur closer in space than distal causes and effects), strength of association (proximal causes are more powerful than distal causes), and levels of organization (events in adjoining levels are more casually proximal). Krieger was particularly concerned about using ideas about causal pathways in spatial and time scales to model causal relationships between levels. For example, she claims that the 1973 US Supreme Court decision legalizing abortion (a distal event) skipped intervening levels to have an immediate effect on individual women's health on the ground and then reverberated back up through state and federal levels to have long-term effects as well.

In this commentary I will expand on some implicit metaphysical notions in the chapter. Ross and Kendler do not quite put it this way, but they also dispute the metaphysical notion that proximal causes are the "real" causes, whereas distal factors such as access to accurate information are sometimes causally relevant but rarely casually decisive in a way demanded by realism. According to this particular version of causal realism, proximal causes are real in the sense of being physically connected to their effects (and ideally producing rapid and powerful effects). Ross and Kendler term this a *connected process account* of causal pathways, which is similar to what others call production accounts, mechanistic accounts, and/or energy transfer (billiard ball) models. The physical connection may be direct, but there can also be intermediaries between the cause and the effect.

Philosophical references to causality invariably include a metaphysical dimension. In discussing the causes of nearly anything, the causes are considered real. Even when causes have constructed elements, like with centers of gravity, latent factors, or defense mechanisms, the causal part is important for being real in some sense. Realism about causes, however, does not have to be supersized – for example, supersizing proximal, biological causes of disorders as more real. Given that proximate, direct biological causes for psychiatric disorders have been difficult to discover, adopting this metaphysical perspective makes causality in psychiatry somewhat elusive.

Ross and Kendler do not feel compelled to supersize certain kinds of causes or to eliminate them from our diet either. Krieger, more abstemious, argues that the distal versus proximal distinction can distort our understanding of phenomena and should therefore be avoided. For example, in medicine, the economics of the tobacco industry would be a higher-level factor and the effects of tobacco on the body a lower-level factor. Krieger notes the economics of the tobacco industry can be classified as a distal cause of cancer and tobacco exposure can be classified as a proximal cause, but this creates an artificial separation between two co-occurring and deeply related processes. For instance, the proximal effects of tobacco on lung cancer cannot be fully understood apart from economics of raising the levels of nicotine in the tobacco that is produced. Social norms about the acceptability of smoking are also relevant factors in the degree of exposure.

Like Krieger, Ross and Kendler agree that the traditional causal pathway models deserve to be challenged, but they do not completely reject the distal-versus-proximal distinction. In their view, it is not invariably distorting. For example, distal causes such as social policies regarding remote work or the availability of masks are important factors in the distribution of a biological disease such as COVID-19. This version of the distal-versus-proximal distinction underlies the distinction between primary and tertiary prevention in community psychiatry. For example, in the early days of COVID-19, waiting for someone to become infected and then treating it could easily become more expensive and costly than preventing the infection by encouraging masking.

Nor does the distal-versus-proximal distinction need to be completely divorced from casual pathway models. Consider how a lack of shared understanding about targeting distal versus proximal causes was an important driver of the debate about whether to include a psychosis risk diagnosis in the DSM-5. Those who opposed the diagnosis were worried that a tertiary intervention, namely antipsychotic medication, would be used indiscriminately as a preventative and prescribed to young adults who were not actually going to transition to psychosis (Frances, 2009). In other words, the (inferred) proximal causes targeted by the medicine were typically not present. Those who favored the diagnosis argued that one should not use an end-stage treatment model (medication) for early-stage conditions (a risk syndrome) (Woods et al., 2010) The target was distal risk. Later in the debate those who advocated for including the diagnosis renamed it "attenuated psychosis syndrome," shifting their thinking to say they are not targeting distal risk; rather, for these young people, a decline in functioning had already occurred, and although it was not typically a psychosis prodrome, it was still associated with suffering and impairment and thus deserving of treatment in itself (Zachar et al., 2020).

Examples like this from psychopathology also show that the distal-versus-proximal distinction can be relative to one's frame of reference. For instance, in one frame of reference a disorder such as alcoholism resides in the future. In this frame, traits such as impulsivity and failure to anticipate negative consequences are distal risk factors placed early in a causal pathway. In another frame of reference, alcoholism has already developed. The impulsivity and failure to anticipate negative consequences are still operating, but now the causal pathway has contracted, and what was distal risk is concurrently maintaining the disorder. If genetic risk is also reflected functionality in impulsivity and the like, it too can be considered distal or proximal depending on one's reference frame.

Consider another example of the relativity of distinctions. In the super-sized version of biological psychiatry, medication is considered proximal. Compare, however, standard antidepressant medication to ketamine. A good rule of thumb is that the standard medication can take four to six weeks to have an effect. Ketamine infusion, however, can produce improvement in 24 hours. Relative to ketamine, standard medication is somewhat distal and likely acts through a series of intermediate steps.

It is also useful to keep in mind that spatial scales, temporal scales, and causal powers are dimensional concepts and thus matters of degree. It is not the case that spatial continuity, temporal contiguity, and causal power are always tightly integrated, as represented by Hume's billiard balls. One example of how they can vary would be two continental masses colliding and creating a mountain. There is spatial contiguity, and the cause is powerful – there is no way we can prevent the creation of a mountain – but temporally this will occur very slowly, over millions of years. There is also some choice as to what is identified as the beginning and the end of the causal pathway, and those points can occur far apart in time, yet the effect will be inevitable.

As noted, Ross and Kendler do not supersize the conventional causal metaphysics of biological psychiatry, which is usually based on a connected process view of causal pathways. Their favored alternative more accurately represents how scientists work with causation and does not require one to map out detailed causal pathways between cause and effect to understand causal relations. This alternative is an interventionist model which holds that if an intervention on a variable (*C*) is reliably followed by a change in some effect (*E*), then *C* is a cause of *E*. This account also requires the counterfactual that if the intervention on *C* does not occur, the effect will not occur. One of Ross and Kendler's examples is lung cancer. If we want to alter the prevalence of lung cancer in a population, intervening on more distal factors regarding tobacco use, such as marketing practices, taxation policies, and corporate ethics, is likely to be more effective on a larger scale than the tertiary strategy of treating lung cancer one patient at a time.

Certainly, if we can intervene on a biological factor and change outcomes, those factors are causes, but they are not the only factors on which we can intervene. For psychiatric disorders, following Fine (1986), we can say, for instance, that genetics and physiology play a causal role in the development of disorders, but given the many potential answers to the "why" question, we should not supersize those particular causes by stomping our feet, thumping our desk, and shouting out: "Genetics and physiology cause psychopathology, REALLY!"

If causes are answers to "how" and "why" questions, many different things can count as causes. Consider a connected process account such as Hume's billiard balls: for example, the cue ball knocks the 2 ball into the side pocket. In addition to spatially and temporally contiguous causes with immediate effects, in a bigger scheme of things there are many additional causal influences. These can include the density of the cue stick, someone drinking too much and forgetting that he was playing stripes and not solids, the rained-out golf game leading to being in the bar, the random meeting months ago that resulted in a weekend wedding, being born, and so on. It would be impossible to enumerate all the causes and causal patterns that can be named real, but many different options should be described and available to identify – including distal and proximal relationships

REFERENCES

Fine, A. (1986). *The shaky game: Einstein, realism, and the quantum theory*. University of Chicago Press.

Frances, A. (2009). A warning sign on the road to DSM-V: Beware of its unintended consequences. *Psychiatric Times*. Retrieved May 5, 2010 from http://www.psychiatrictimes.com/display/article/10168/1425378

Krieger, N. (2008). Proximal, distal, and the politics of causation: What's level got to do with it? *American Journal of Public Health, 98*(2), 221–230. https://doi.org/10.2105/ajph.2007.111278

Woods, S. W., Walsh, B. C., Saksa, J. R., & McGlashan, T. H. (2010). The case for including attenuated psychotic symptoms syndrome in DSM-5 as a psychosis risk syndrome. *Schizophrenia Research, 123*(2–3), 199–207. https://doi.org/10.1016/j.schres.2010.08.012

Zachar, P., First, M. B., & Kendler, K. S. (2020). The DSM-5 proposal for attenuated psychosis syndrome: A history. *Psychological Medicine, 50*, 920–926.

Section 4

CHAPTER 10

Introduction to Kendler's "A Working Scientist's View on Causality in Psychiatry"

Peter Zachar

In his chapter, Kenneth Kendler succinctly explains some difficult-to-understand philosophical concepts and then shows how they can be used to illuminate psychiatric research and practice. The concepts he explains are those relating to causality, specifically the contrast between counterfactual and mechanistic approaches.

Counterfactual approaches to causality, says Kendler, are conceptually based. If you have two conditions (or worlds) in which everything is the same except one has a certain intervention occurring whereas the other one does not, then any differences in outcome between those conditions can be attributed to the intervention. This is also called counterfactual dependence, meaning that the outcome casually depends on an intervention if we can infer the counterfactual: had the intervention not occurred, the outcome would not have occurred. These inferences also have probabilistic nature: if not X, then it is *likely* that not Y.

Mechanistic approaches to causality represent what is typically meant by causality in the physical sciences. For example, when a cue ball hits an 8 ball and the 8 ball moves, it moves because of the transfer of kinetic energy from one ball to the next. As Kendler notes, mechanistic approaches provide details about *how* effects come about. The cue ball hitting the 8 ball is also an intervention, so counterfactual reasoning applies across the board. Mechanistic approaches encompass counterfactual dependencies but go beyond them.

The difficulty with emphasizing mechanistic approaches in psychiatry is that valid models of the biological mechanisms that produce psychiatric disorders have not been discovered, despite an enormous investment of resources. Kendler argues that counterfactual reasoning has been a better strategy for advancing our causal understanding of psychopathology. For much of his career he embraced counterfactual approaches (made more tractable by the introduction of multivariate statistics) and was skeptical of overblown, reductionistic claims about mechanisms.

Currently, however, Kendler views counterfactual and mechanistic approaches to causality as complementary. On this score he has a qualified sympathy for the Russo–Williamson thesis. This thesis proposes that both counterfactual-probabilistic and mechanistic-physical approaches are necessary to validate causality claims in medicine. To explain it from his vantage point, Kendler asserts that counterfactual reasoning indexes potential causal relationships, but one should also have some scientifically plausible ideas of what the mechanistic story could be. For instance, he introduces an example in which research findings indicate that patients hospitalized for coronary problems have better outcomes if they are prayed for by people who happen to live hundreds of miles away from the hospital. How exactly could that occur? If our only answer is through divine grace, the counterfactual inference – *had these patients not been prayed for, they would have had worse outcomes* – might be what some people want to believe, but without a scientifically plausible mechanism, skepticism about the counterfactual claim is warranted.

The reason for describing Kendler as having qualified sympathy with the claim that both counterfactual and mechanistic approaches are necessary is that he diverges on the "necessary" part. He believes that mechanistic hypotheses offer more added value to counterfactual inferences where the probabilities are moderate than they do to those with higher probabilities. He continues to reject any claim that good psychiatric science must be mechanistic.

Kendler next offers three examples of how counterfactual and mechanistic approaches can work together. The first example is about academic achievement and drug abuse. In one research study, all children in a school grade were born in the same calendar year. He discovered that students in the same grade who enter school at a younger age (because they were born later in the year, e.g., November or December) have lower levels of academic achievement than those who enter at an older age (e.g., born in January of February). Furthermore, the students with lower achievement are at increased risk for drug abuse. There is a nice counterfactual here: if students had higher levels of academic achievement, they would not be at increased risk for drug abuse. When Kendler was asked *how* an intervention that raises academic achievement would lower the risk of drug abuse, he did not have a plausible mechanistic hypothesis. Working closely with experts in drug prevention programs, he learned of a plausible mechanism, namely that having positive attitudes to school facilitates prosocial attitudes. If students stay in school and are in debate clubs and intramurals rather than dropping out, the chances that they will engage in substance abuse are lower. Causal hypotheses like this make it possible to design interventions that have been shown to succeed in lowering student risk of drug abuse. Kendler's take-home message is that ideas about possible mechanisms helpfully supplement counterfactual reasoning, but those mechanisms need not be biological mechanisms.

His second example is about the genetics of schizophrenia. Findings from genome-wide association studies have detected a strong signal for the human leukocyte antigen region on chromosome 6 and increased risk for schizophrenia. Kendler then describes several supplements to this finding. For instance, some genes in this region control synaptic pruning. This is interesting because over-pruning of synapses has been suggested as a possible cause of schizophrenia. Additional studies show that the more of these pruning genes someone has, the greater the risk of schizophrenia. Furthermore, postmortem studies of brains of patients with schizophrenia show that they possessed more of these same genes. Finally, in mouse models, intervening on the expression of structurally similar genes increases synaptic pruning. Kendler's take-home message is that these studies do not achieve the reductionist goal of mapping out a detailed causal pathway from genes to disorder, but they nevertheless advance our mechanistic understanding by sketching out and filling in patchy details about a plausible pathway.

His third example is about income supplements and conduct disorder. The context for this example is the contrast between the hypothesis that people can drift down into lower levels of socioeconomic status (SES) after developing certain psychiatric disorders and the hypothesis that the stress of occupying a lower SES makes people more vulnerable to developing disorders. Research does show that, compared to those with higher SES, people with lower SES experience more psychiatric symptoms. According to the stress hypothesis, *if people were not of lower SES, they would not be at increased risk for psychiatric symptoms*. Fortuitously, another natural experiment occurred in which a group of Native American individuals in the lower SES category started receiving cash payments from a casino owned by their tribe, thus raising their SES. In those families who received cash payments, the level of psychiatric symptoms in their children was reduced, but it remained the same for those lower-SES families that did not receive payments.

Upon a closer examination, what was reduced were externalizing symptoms such as those associated with conduct disorder. In addition, a series of regression equations indicated that one predictor of the changes was increased parental supervision contingent on the parents being able to spend more time at home. Kendler's take-home message is that even when the data are correlational and statistical, counterfactual reasoning can supplement itself with mechanistic hypotheses. If those hypotheses contribute to the design of successful interventions, they can increase the potential impact of scientific findings.

In her commentary, Federica Russo compares Kendler's perspective to a tradition in the philosophy of science that she calls "philosophy of science in practice," which, according to her, engages with the practice of science. This is similar to what Carl Craver refers to as a practice-first approach in Chapter 20. Russo also notes that the philosophy of psychiatry has been disconnected from a recent development in the philosophy of medicine known as medical methodology, which has put considerable focus on evidence, causation, and explanation. What counts as a mechanism and what counts as medical are broadly construed in the study of medical methodology. Russo describes how her own thinking has developed in collaboration with others, culminating in the notion of evidence-based medicine plus (EBM+). EBM+ emphasizes the incremental validity the study of mechanisms offers to traditional randomized controlled trial approaches. She then describes various congruencies between Kendler's chapter and the ideas articulated in EBM+, arguing that a broader engagement between medical methodology and psychiatry could be fruitful.

CHAPTER 11

A Working Scientist's View on Causality in Psychiatry

Kenneth S. Kendler

11.1 Introduction

In this chapter, I will not attempt to plumb the depths of the large and daunting philosophical literature on causality as it is relevant to psychiatry. Rather, I provide here the reflections of an active psychiatric researcher whose empirical work has often touched on causality, tested a range of models in their application to observational data, and tried to read in the relevant epidemiological, statistical, and philosophical literature.

I posit two major approaches to causal inference that I will call *counterfactual* and *mechanistic*. Each has had other names. Let me define them in a commonsense manner. At its core, counterfactual approaches are conceptual/statistical. They ask "what if" questions. For me, the central thought experiment toward which all counterfactual methods strive is that of two parallel worlds. They differ, at the start of the mental experiment, in only one way: event X occurs in world 1 but not in world 2. Call this event an intervention. We then come back later and observe the difference in outcomes between the two worlds. Given that they are identical in every other way, we can, with confidence, ascribe these differences to our intervention. My worldview of this kind of causality has been substantially shaped by the works of Jim Woodward (e.g., Woodward, 2003) that I have been reading for many years. In the biomedical world, the leading experimental paradigm that tries to instantiate the counterfactual approach to causality is the randomized, double-blind, controlled trial.

The mechanistic approach to causality for me, at its core, asks "how" questions. I think of billiard balls knocking into each other on a pool table, a ball hit with velocity breaking a window, or, perhaps more relevant here, gene transcription from mRNA on a ribosome and the downstream changes through the translation of that gene into proteins. Here I have been much influenced by the work of Carl Craver and colleagues (Craver, 2007; Machamer, Darden, & Craver, 2000).

The main question I seek to address through three research examples is how these two approaches to causal inference act and interact in psychiatric research. This is a topic much discussed in other aspects of the medical sciences by Frederica Russo and collaborators (P. Illari & Russo, 2014; Russo & Williamson, 2007). But few writers have sought to focus on the relationship between these two casual approaches as it particularly applies to psychiatric research.

What brought me to this problem? My day job, which I have now pursued for more than 40 years, is a researcher in psychiatric genetics. My first major project was conducting, in the 1980s, a large case–control family study of schizophrenia and mood disorders in Roscommon County, Ireland (Kendler et al., 1993). A modern family study is a somewhat convoluted example of a counterfactual experiment. Imagine I want to assess the close family members of 200 random people residing in Roscommon County. I interview them, track down their hospital records, diagnose them blindly, and so on. Then, I want to do exactly the same thing for the relatives of another 200 people who are as identical as possible to the first group (e.g., on age, sex, social class) as possible, except that they now all have schizophrenia. We can consider that the intervention – one made by nature. When this effort is completed, we compare the rates of disorders in the two groups of relatives of the matched controls. In the Roscommon Family Study, the risk for schizophrenia was 6.5% in the first-degree relatives of the schizophrenia proband and 0.5% in the relatives of controls (Kendler et al., 1993).

When this study was designed, we had no hope of trying to clarify the biological mechanisms by which the risk for schizophrenia ran in families. But fast-forward to the early 2020s. I am now involved in a series of case–control studies of a range of psychiatric disorders. But we are not interviewing relatives. Instead, we are collecting DNA and finding genetic variants that differ significantly in their frequency in cases and controls. Using rapidly expanding methods of molecular genetics and molecular neuroscience (see a more detailed discussion later in the chapter), we are now trying to understand the pathway from DNA variants to brain functioning that underlies the risk for psychiatric illness. That, in my book, is trying to understand mechanisms.

So, I practice a science that utilizes each of these causal approaches.

11.2 What Might Make Causal Issues in Psychiatry Differ from Those of Much of the Rest of Medicine?

A lot has been written on the question of causation in general medicine. I suggest two features that might make psychiatry at least somewhat different with respect to the relative role of counterfactual versus mechanistic approaches. First, the diversity of "levels" of causal explanations in psychiatry exceed that of many branches of medicine. Our major journals publish papers examining a bewildering array of fields including molecular neuroscience and genetics, systems neuroscience, cognitive, personality and social psychology, many branches of epidemiology, sociology of a variety of forms, health economics, and anthropology (Kendler, 2014). The meaning of causation, and especially of mechanistic causation across such a wide variety of disciplines, is a challenging one. While "mechanism" for much of medicine equals "biological mechanism," that definition is clearly too narrow for psychiatry.

Second, we really do not know, even in broad terms, the causal mechanisms for any of our major psychiatric disorders (with narcolepsy forming one possible exception). This is not true for an increasing number of medical diseases. We will review a causal "sketch" for schizophrenia in our second example in this chapter. How "sketchy" can a mechanism get and still be a form of mechanistic causation? How big can the "gaps" be in a proposed mechanism before it falls apart (Schaffner, 1980)? Schaffner has suggested that psychiatry is likely to proceed by patchy reductionism (Schaffner, 2011). Might such insights serve as the basis for causal inference?

11.3 The Hill Criteria, the Russo–Williamson Thesis, and the Efficacy of Prayer

We need to make a requisite stop at the famous 1965 Bradford Hill criteria for causation in medicine based on the struggle, in which Hill was centrally involved, to prove the causal association between smoking and lung cancer (Hill, 1965). Of current import, these criteria include some items reflecting broadly counterfactual claims, based on epidemiological findings, such as strength and consistency of the prospective and retrospective studies and evidence for a dose–response relationship. But Hill included one "mechanism-like" criterion: experimental evidence. For example, early in the smoking–lung cancer debate, cigarette tar had been painted on laboratory rabbits' ears and shown to produce cancer in the ear tissue over time. Hence, it was clear that carcinogens were present in tobacco tar.

This is a good jumping-off point for a later – and, for this essay, central – development in causal theorizing in medicine. In 2007, Federica Russo and Jon Williamson published a paper in which they made the following claim:

> We argue that the health sciences make causal claims on the basis of evidence both of physical mechanisms, and of probabilistic dependencies.

> Consequently, an analysis of causality solely in terms of physical mechanisms or solely in terms of probabilistic relationships, does not do justice to the causal claims of these sciences. (Russo & Williamson, 2007, p. 157)

This became known as the Russo–Williamson thesis (RWT), and its evaluation for psychiatry became, during my work on this project, a secondary aim.

A strategy I often find of use in my conceptual reasoning is to try to find an example at the extremes that can be used to reason back to more realistic examples. I want to apply this to what was for me one obvious use of mechanistic theories of causation vis-á-vis counterfactual evidence. Let's imagine we produce convincing evidence for an effect, such as a randomized controlled trial, showing the efficacy of remote prayer in improving outcomes of people in a coronary care unit hundreds of miles away from those who are praying. Such a study has been published in a solid medical journal (Harris et al., 1999). I am as inherently skeptical of such findings as I am of prior evidence for extrasensory perception and astrology. This skepticism, I suggest, points to a limitation of counterfactual evidence taken entirely on its own. If you, as a critical reader, can find no plausible means by which the intervention could produce the effect, are you entitled to downgrade the statistical evidence and maintain a skeptical approach.

This seems like a plausible stance, but it will sometimes be mistaken. Think of the initial rejection of continental drift or the transmission of kuru by prions. These theories, both later proved correct, were initially rejected as implausible because of the lack of any plausible mechanistic explanation. But I still suggest this has power and points to a "latent" linkage between counterfactual theories of causation and mechanistic approaches. There is, in my view, at least some justification for skepticism about even good counterfactual evidence where there appears to be no plausible mechanism by which the cause could have the described effect.

11.4 Example #1: Academic Achievement and Drug Abuse

Moving to the guts of this essay – the review of three examples of causal claims in psychiatric research – I begin with a paper I wrote with Swedish colleagues that initiated my intellectual love affair with natural experiments and instrumental variables more specifically (Kendler et al., 2018). The work on this paper began with my interest in tracing out the causal risk factors for drug abuse (as measured in several national Swedish registers), which include poor educational attainment (Kendler et al., 2017). But was this association causal or the result of what might be numerous possible confounders?

Enter the "month-of-birth effect." This is most easily described for school systems, like the one in Sweden, where, with only rare exceptions, all members of a school class are born in the same calendar year. This means that, throughout their education, members of this class can differ by as much as 364 days of age – from someone born on January 1 to someone born on December 31. A wide range of research has shown that older members of such classes (e.g., born January through March) are more likely to become successful athletes (Cobley et al., 2009) and younger members (e.g., born October to December) have higher rates of attention-deficit/hyperactivity disorder (Karlstad et al., 2017). For my purposes, most importantly, several prior studies had shown that younger members also perform less well in school (Crawford, Dearden, & Greaves, 2011; Solli, 2017).

This gave me an instrument. Indeed, using a quantitative measure of academic achievement at age 16 – roughly a grade point average – we showed a 0.25 standard deviation (SD) difference in mean academic achievement of students born in January versus the ones born in December. We showed that the other assumptions of an instrumental variable were met (e.g., no significant relationship between month of birth and risk for drug abuse when controlling for academic achievement). If we looked directly at our measure of academic achievement, it robustly predicted future risk for drug abuse in a Cox proportional model with a Hazard Ratio (HR) per SD of 2.33 with 95% CI of 2.30–2.35. The way to interpret these numbers is to say that for each SD decline in academic achievement, an individual's risk for developing drug abuse increased about 2.3-fold. In our instrumental variable analysis, the effect was only slightly weaker (HR = 2.04; 95% CI, 1.75–2.33).

I was thrilled. Using a relatively robust statistical method, I had shown direct causal effects of low academic achievement on risk for drug abuse. This effect was not largely due to confounders and could therefore be potentially used as a basis for interventions. But my excitement was short-lived. In presenting these results to some colleagues, I got asked the following question: "Great data. But how do you get from higher academic achievement to reduced risk for drug abuse?"

I hadn't considered that question in any detail. I swallowed hard and muttered something about "smart kids must be less likely to get caught up in drug abuse." But it was a weak *post hoc* suggestion, and I knew it. Applying the terminology of this chapter, I had great counterfactual evidence for the effect of interest but no mechanistic explanation to speak of.

As I was no expert in adolescent development, let alone drug prevention programs in that age group, I sought help. I contacted colleagues at the National Institute for Drug Abuse, which was funding this work, and asked for a "referral" – someone with expertise in this area who might be willing to collaborate with me in writing up this work. They were very helpful and recommended Dr. Abigail Fagan, an expert in prevention trials for drug abuse. When I showed her the results, she was excited and knew exactly where our findings fitted into prior theories and empirical studies of short-term prevention trials. Here is part of the text for our article that she wrote:

> According to both social control theory and the social development model, students who succeed academically will tend to develop strong positive attachments to school, thereby facilitating their commitment to prosocial lifestyles, which in turn reduces risk of drug abuse. By contrast, those who lack this bond are more prone to a range of deviant behaviors, including drug abuse. (Kendler et al., 2018, p. 1185)

Dr. Fagan described several short-term prevention trials based on these theories where schools were randomized. The experimental schools had a range of interventions that would include counseling teachers in how to make school more fun, setting up group meetings with parents to help them encourage their children's involvement in school, and establishing chess and debate clubs. A year or two later they would find, through surveys of students, parents, and teachers, that the students from the schools with the intervention compared to the control schools were more involved in school, were getting better grades, and – most important for us – rates of drug use, typically smoking and drinking, declined. This was exactly what the theory would have predicted. Kids who did well in school and were praised for their success by teachers and parents were more likely to do other prosocial things. Not very surprising. But those who did poorly found school less rewarding and often came to the conclusion that was dumb to do your homework, that it was only for "nerds," and it was much more fun to cut school, smoke cigarettes, and chase after possible sexual partners. Abby was very excited over our results because we had a large sample (a whole country), a longer follow-up period, and harder outcomes (i.e., drug abuse diagnoses) rather than self-reported rates of drug use.

My experience working on this paper taught me two lessons. First, did we find a "mechanism" to explain our instrumental variable findings? Did our paper meet the criteria of the RWT? If by mechanism it was meant a biochemical pathway or even the kind of evidence Hill used (rates of skin cancer in rabbits painted with cigarette tar), the answer is clearly "No." But that is simply too restrictive a model for this kind of legitimate psychiatric research. Our mechanism is in the language of developmental psychology, involving neither molecular genetics nor brain science in any traditional way. In my view, for psychiatric research, a meaningful definition of "mechanism" must be broader than biology to include psychological and sociological processes.

Second, as a working scientist, how much did this "mechanistic" information from Dr. Fagan add to the work? That is clear – a lot! I went from an abstract "statistical exercise" to getting into the meaty world of intervention trials. The reviewers felt the same way. We had upped the quality of the science quite a bit, and this was reflected in the feedback we received about our study. Our ability to articulate a putative mechanism for our effects produced a more incisive science that took our descriptive findings and showed how they could support preventative interventions.

11.5 Example 2: Schizophrenia and Genetic Variants in Complement C4 Genes

Our second example of causal research comes from a quite different part of the psychiatric research world and involves centrally statistical genetics, molecular genetics, and molecular and anatomical neuroscience. The focal article, "Schizophrenia risk from complex variation of complement component 4" (Sekar et al., 2016), is widely regarded as one of the highlights of efforts to track etiologic factors in schizophrenia through molecular genetic findings and as of June 20, 2023 had been cited 2,115 times.

This is a complex article, and I can only provide highlights. The work begins with results from a 2014 genome-wide association study (GWAS) of schizophrenia coordinated by the Schizophrenia Work Group of the Psychiatric Genetics Consortium (Consortium, 2014), which demonstrated a strong signal from the human leukocyte antigen (HLA) region of chromosome 6. As noted earlier, such a design is largely counterfactual in nature. It points out a statistical association between a genetic variant at a particular location on the genome and disease risk but is, by itself, entirely uninformative about a mechanism connecting the two.

In the HLA region, the genetic risk for schizophrenia was actually spread along a rather long section of chromosome 6. One part of that region contained genetic variants that influenced the level of one of the genes in the complement cascade: C4. While most physicians know of complement as a system for mobilizing an immune reaction to foreign antigens – coming for example from bacteria – it had been known for some time that this same system was used in the central nervous system for "synaptic pruning" – the elimination of infrequently used synaptic connections between nerve cells in the brain. This is a vital feature in the development on the human central nervous system. Too many connections are made between nerve cells during early development, and the production of an efficient brain requires the redundant connections to be "pruned." But over-pruning must be avoided for optimal future brain function.

The first step of this project was to identity four structural forms of the C4 gene present in the cases and controls of the GWAS sample. Individuals carrying one and especially two forms of the gene – termed AL – had, by current GWAS standards, a significantly increased risk for schizophrenia – an odds ratio of nearly 1.3:1. Step 2 was to show, using human postmortem brain samples, that the level of C4a expression was elevated in a pattern across the different C4 alleles (i.e., copies) that was identical to the risk they conveyed for schizophrenia. In other words, the more copies of the gene, the higher the schizophrenia risk. This was only a correlation but had the potential of representing the beginning of a mechanism of action.

The next steps involved showing elevated levels of the C4a variant in the brains of schizophrenic versus control individuals and noting that prior postmortem anatomical studies had supported the hypothesis of reduced synapse formation in individuals with schizophrenia. Finally, the investigators manipulated expression of a C4-like gene in the mouse brain and showed that it resulted in increased synaptic pruning. The authors began with a broad hypothesis:

> The association of increased C4 with schizophrenia, the presence of C4 at synapses, the involvement of other complement proteins in synapse elimination, and earlier reports of decreased synapse numbers in schizophrenia patients, together suggested that C4 might work with other components of the classical complement cascade to promote synaptic pruning. (Sekar et al., 2016, p. 180)

After the manipulation of the C4-like expression in the mouse brain, they claimed, "These data provide direct evidence that C4 mediates synaptic refinement in the developing brain" (Sekar et al., 2016, p. 181). Their abstract concludes as follows: "These results implicate excessive complement activity in the development of schizophrenia and may help explain the reduced numbers of synapses in the brains of individuals with schizophrenia" (Sekar et al., 2016, p. 177).

This is my summary of the "mechanism" the authors proposed, where an "eqtl" is evidence that the gene variant is expressed in some particular tissue – in the case, the brain:

> Large GWAS signal from HLA→ Small part of this region maps to C4 e-qtl→ # of variant haplotypes coding for C4 predicts risk for SZ and level of brain C4a expression→ Prior evidence of excess pruning of synapses in SZ → Evidence of higher C4a levels in post-mortem brains of SZ vs controls→ Evidence that genetic manipulation in mouse brains to simulate genotypes at C4 locus that produces high risk for SZ results in excess pruning of neurons.

Is this a tight mechanism with strong empirical support at every step? Clearly not. But could you then just call this a very tentative mechanistic "sketch"? Probably not – it is more than this. Is it a patchy, reductionist effort as descried by Ken Schaffner? That might be close.

The most germane question is how much these results add to the original HLA GWAS finding. Again, I think the answer is, "A lot." The paper generated substantial scientific excitement. It provided, "through a glass darkly," an outline of a gene-to-disease pathway – a result rather unprecedented in prior schizophrenia work. These results have spawned a whole host of further studies. Efforts are ongoing to see if a drug target could be developed from these findings. There has been hope that this may be a biomarker, and studies are ongoing to examine whether C4a levels in cerebrospinal fluid might predict risk for developing schizophrenia.

11.6 Example 3: Income Supplements and Childhood Conduct Disorder

Our third and final example of causal analyses in psychiatric research also relies on a natural experiment but one quite different from the "month-of-birth effect." It addresses one of the oldest topics in psychiatric epidemiology: the inverse association of rates of many forms of psychopathology and social class (Costello et al., 2003). This was first observed in one of the great classics of psychiatric epidemiology (Faris & Dunham, 1939) and debated ever since. Two main positions have emerged, most typically termed *social causation* (or stress) versus *social selection* (or drift). In the "social causation" position, the causal arrow goes the from stress to disorder risk. In the "social selection" position, the causal arrow goes the other way, from psychiatric disorder through poor social functioning to poverty.

The focal article was published in the prestigious *Journal of the American Medical Association* in 2003 under the title "Relationships between poverty and psychopathology: A natural experiment," and has been cited 1,614 times as of August 13, 2025 (Costello et al., 2003). Adrian Angold and Jane Costello conducted a longitudinal epidemiological study of children and adolescents in North Carolina (The Great Smoky Mountain Study) that oversampled low-SES households. One-quarter of their sample were of Native American ancestry. In the middle of their study, one of the Native American tribes in the area of their study opened a casino. Under the terms of the agreement under which the casino was established, all members of that tribe then began to receive profits from the casino every 6 months. Within a few years, these reached $6,000 per person per year.

From this income supplement, 14% of the study families were moved out of poverty while 53%, without the supplements, remained poor and 32% were never poor. Across the study, like many that had been done before, Angold and Costello observed a modest inverse correlation between family income and child psychiatric disorders ($r = -0.13$, $p < .001$) and number of psychiatric symptoms ($r = -0.15$, $p < .001$). These correlations did not differ for Native American and non–Native American households. As should be clear by now, the nature of the causal processes behind these correlations for this study, like most others, was initially quite murky.

The casino intervention changed that. Using their division of the families into the three aforementioned groups (never poor, formerly poor, and persistently poor), the researchers tracked the total psychiatric symptoms in the three family types before and after opening of the casino. The children of the persistently poor families had high and unchanging levels of symptoms. The never poor had, over both time periods, symptoms that were consistently 40% lower than the poor families. The formerly poor families, who status had shifted due to the income from the casino, had levels of symptoms indistinguishable from the consistently poor prior the casino opening that significantly fell – by approximately 35% – with the opening of the casino. Costello et al. (2003) summarize the results as follows: "the data supported a social causation hypothesis, demonstrating a decrease in symptoms in children whose families moved out of poverty" (p. 2026).

So, we have robust counterfactual evidence: an intervention of increased income produced a significant decline in child psychopathology as predicted by the social causation model. But so far, no mechanism. The authors addressed this through a series of follow-up analyses. First, they looked more closely at the reduction in symptoms occurring with the movement out of poverty and noted that they arose entirely from behavioral symptoms (e.g., conduct disorder) rather than from internalizing or emotional symptoms (e.g., anxiety disorders). Second, they ran a series of mediational analyses, trying to understand what changes in the formerly poor families might have sat in the causal chain from increased income to reduced childhood disruptive behavioral symptoms. Only one mediator – level of parental supervision – met their mediational criteria. In what they termed "exploratory analyses" they then tried to predict parental supervision from 26 variables, 3 of which were predictive, the most notable of which was a reduction in time demands of the index parent. From this it can be concluded that the increased income reduced the amount of time parents had to work outside the home, which appears to permit for improvements in both the quantity and quality of parent–child interactions, thereby reducing the misbehaviors associated with conduct disorder.

So, we have a natural experiment, leading to a counterfactual finding and a hypothesized mechanism, all through exploratory analyses of mediational mechanisms in the same dataset. The mechanism is operating entirely on a psychological/social level. What does the mechanism add to the counterfactual results? These latter results are not as well supported as with our month-of-birth effect described earlier, where independent trials had shown the efficacy of greater school involvement in reducing drug use. The clarification adds at least somewhat to the plausibility of the findings – but they stand quite well on their own. The greatest benefit seems to me a clarification of targets for intervention. It suggests that giving money to a family largely helps the children through improving the quality and quantity of parental supervision. Perhaps they are other, even more efficient means to reach that end. And, as we have seen in our two prior examples, the clarification of a putative mechanism simply makes the science more impactful.

11.7 What Have Mechanisms Taught Us in Our Examples?

I suggest six potential lessons learned from these three examples about the respective roles of counterfactual and mechanistic perspectives in causal inference in psychiatric research. First, while these two approaches to causality might seem very different from a philosophical and statistical perspectives, for most working scientists – and certainly for yours truly – once you have a relatively convincing counterfactual story for a causal process, if feasible, you certainly will want to understand the mechanism. It is the obvious next relevant scientific question.

Second, 10 years ago I would have been entirely in the "counterfactual" camp. My main focus was on going from correlation to causal inference. Mechanisms might have added a bit, but the counterfactual methods carried the day. This approach was understandable because of the vexing problem, especially in the field of psychiatric epidemiology, of investigators (and readers) associating correlation with cause, which is, of course, a primary sin in science (it happens a lot). However, my perspective has changed. Mechanisms can be really important.

Third, understanding a potential mechanism can add a lot to the scientific story. This is not a surprise. But it gives weight, context, and direction to moving on from the counterfactual findings. It is not a small thing. And it can provide support for potential novel interventions and steps toward them, such as the identification of drug targets.

Fourth, if you believe, as I do, in the pluralistic structure of the causes of psychiatric disorders, it just won't work to require a "billiard ball" (e.g., physical energy transfer or protein–protein interactions) mechanism to advocate for causality in psychiatry. This is well demonstrated by two of our examples. I have limited patience with the neurobiological hard reductionists in our field who suggest that all the real action in the science of psychiatry is at molecular levels and that psychological and sociological work in the psychiatric space is all "fluff." These "higher-level" fields represent important and indeed critical parts of our science.

Fifth, there are some subtle points about how counterfactual and mechanistic approaches complement each other in the process of causal inference. Given that a good mechanistic explanation adds force and plausibility to the counterfactual evidence, it stands to reason that a good mechanism provides greater assistance for causal inference to a moderately strong set of counterfactual evidence rather than to a very strong one. In the latter case, especially with multiple kinds of counterfactual evidence, there just isn't much more left to prove on causal grounds.

Sixth, for me, due in large part to contributions from philosophers like Woodward, the shape of what counts as good counterfactual evidence is quite clear. But more work is needed to define what a "good" mechanism is. When is a mechanistic sketch too "sketchy" to be useful? Given that there will always be gaps, when are there too many gaps, or when are the gaps too broad?

Where do these reflections leave me as to the RWT? I am certainly more a believer than when I started this project, but I am not completely sold. To argue that no legitimate causal claims can be made without a well-understood mechanism, given the difficulties in elucidating the etiology of psychiatric disorders buried within the extraordinarily complex mind-brain system, is just too high a bar for important parts of our field. Given counterfactual evidence, one can act on that with higher confidence based on a well-worked-out mechanism, and a "solid" mechanistic sketch can also be quite helpful. But to argue that "no mechanism equals no good cause equals no good basis of intervention" would currently be an error for our field. Clarifying mechanisms for our causes should, however, be an aspirational goal for our science and in some spaces (e.g., molecular genetics moving gene variants to molecular neuroscience) is already the core mission.

11.8 Discussion

I am not the first to have tread these paths. While this is no place for a detailed literature review, I want to highlight contributions from three prior authors who have been helpful to me in my deliberations. First, working from the perspective of the social sciences, Beach (2021) has articulated the helpful concept of "evidential pluralism." The following quote is of particular interest when he suggests that it is possible to identify at least two:

> . . . different mechanism-focused methodologies in the social sciences:
>
> 1) a minimalist position in which the underlying mechanistic claim being made is not unpacked theoretically, but instead often treated as if it is an intervening or mediating variable – "*superficial form of evidential pluralism*"
> 2) an in-depth mechanistic position that argues for unpacking mechanisms theoretically into parts composed of entities engaging in activities that are then traced empirically, an "*in-depth evidential pluralism*." (Beach, 2021, p. 8901; emphasis added)

I take Beach to be trying to differentiate between a very global mechanistic sketch (e.g., "we probably get from *A* to *C* by going through process *C*"; his "minimalist position") and the one that digs into the nitty-gritty of explanatory processes in psychological or sociological science and produces putative mechanisms that can be straightforward to test (his "in-depth" position). This usefully echoes some of our discussions earlier in the chapter.

There is a danger, in the social sciences as they apply to psychiatry, for "just-so stories" to be passed off as mechanisms. In Example 1 in this chapter, successful intervention studies vetted the theoretical predictions of the social control theory and the social development models. In Example 3, statistical analyses supported specific mediational pathways for the impact of casino funds on childhood psychopathology. So, each of our two relevant examples leaned closer to Beach's in-depth evidential pluralism, which is, in my view, of considerably more value than its superficial cousin.

Second, I found an essay by P. M. Illari (2011), who has worked closely with Russo on a key book in this area (P. Illari & Russo, 2014), to be particularly helpful. Similar to my own line of reasoning, Illari concludes that a mechanism "is not always required for causal inference if excellent difference-making evidence is available, but it is very helpful" (P. M. Illari, 2011, p. 155). In discussing mechanistic and counterfactual (or "difference-making") explanations, he notes, "Each addresses the major weakness of the other evidence" (P. M. Illari, 2011, p 146).

Third, I want to note for interested readers a wonderful illuminating historical essay by Gillies (2011) that thoughtfully probes the interactions of mechanism and counterfactual evidence in the understanding of the relationship between smoking and heart disease.

In closing, I want to come back to some final thoughts about the relationship between counterfactual and mechanistic evidence of causation, which I have tried to capture Figure 11.1.

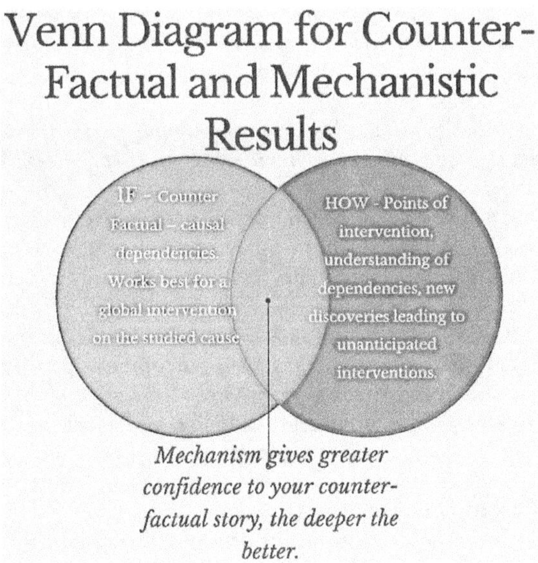

Figure 11.1 The relationship between counterfactual and mechanistic evidence of causation.

These relationships are separate but synergistic. Basically, they ask quite different questions, namely (and respectively) "What if" and "How." And from a practical interventionist perspective, counterfactual evidence is ideal for supporting interventions on the original investigated cause (think randomized controlled trials) but useless for identification of other possible (both more powerful and more proximal) interventions. That is exactly where mechanistic understanding can come in to discover unanticipated points of treatment or prevention.

REFERENCES

Beach, D. (2021). Evidential pluralism and evidence of mechanisms in the social sciences. *Synthese, 199*(3–4), 8899–8919.

Cobley, S., Baker, J., Wattie, N., & McKenna, J. (2009). Annual age-grouping and athlete development: A meta-analytical review of relative age effects in sport. *Sports Medicine, 39*, 235–256.

Consortium, S. W. G. o. t. P. G. (2014). Biological insights from 108 schizophrenia-associated genetic loci. *Nature, 511*(7510), 421–427.

Costello, E. J., Compton, S. N., Keeler, G., & Angold, A. (2003). Relationships between poverty and psychopathology: A natural experiment. *Journal of the American Medical Association, 290*(15), 2023–2029.

Craver, C. F. (2007). *Explaining the brain*. Clarendon Press.

Crawford, C., Dearden, L., & Greaves, E. (2011). *Does when you are born matter? The impact of month of birth on children's cognitive and non-cognitive skills in England.* IFS Briefing Note: BN 122. Retrieved April 1, 2023 from https://www.ifs.org.uk/bns/bn122.pdf

Faris, R. E., & Dunham, H. W. (1939). *Mental disorders in urban areas: An ecological study of schizophrenia and other psychoses.* University of Chicago Press.

Gillies, D. (2011). The Russo-Williamson thesis and the question of whether smoking causes heart disease. In P. M. Illari, F. Russo, & J. Williamson (Eds.), *Causality in the sciences* (pp. 110–125). Oxford Academic.

Harris, W. S., Gowda, M., Kolb, J. W., Strychacz, C. P., Vacek, J. L., Jones, P. G., … McCallister, B. D. (1999). A randomized, controlled trial of the effects of remote, intercessory prayer on outcomes in patients admitted to the coronary care unit. *Archives of Internal Medicine, 159*(19), 2273–2278.

Hill, A. B. (1965). The environment and disease: Association or causation? *Proceedings of the Royal Society of Medicine, 58*(4), 295–300.

Illari, P., & Russo, F. (2014). *Causality: Philosophical theory meets scientific practice.* Oxford University Press.

Illari, P. M. (2011). Mechanistic evidence: Disambiguating the Russo–Williamson thesis. *International Studies in the Philosophy of Science, 25*(2), 139–157.

Karlstad, Ø., Furu, K., Stoltenberg, C., Håberg, S. E., & Bakken, I. J. (2017). *ADHD treatment and diagnosis in relation to children's birth month: Nationwide cohort study from Norway*. Sage UK.

Kendler, K. S. (2014). The structure of psychiatric science. *American Journal of Psychiatry, 171*(9), 931–938.

Kendler, K. S., McGuire, M., Gruenberg, A. M., O'Hare, A., Spellman, M., & Walsh, D. (1993). The Roscommon Family Study. I: Methods, diagnosis of probands, and risk of schizophrenia in relatives. *Archives of General Psychiatry, 50*(7), 527–540.

Kendler, K. S., Ohlsson, H., Edwards, A. C., Sundquist, J., & Sundquist, K. (2017). A developmental etiological model for drug abuse in men. *Drug and Alcohol Dependence, 179*, 220–228. https://doi.org/10.1016/j.drugalcdep.2017.06.036

Kendler, K. S., Ohlsson, H., Fagan, A. A., Lichtenstein, P., Sundquist, J., & Sundquist, K. (2018). Academic achievement and drug abuse risk assessed using instrumental variable analysis and co-relative designs. *Journal of the American Medical Association Psychiatry, 75*(11), 1182–1188. https://doi.org/10.1001/jamapsychiatry.2018.2337

Machamer, P., Darden, L., & Craver, C. (2000). Thinking about mechanisms. *Philosophy of Science, 67*, 1–25.

Russo, F., & Williamson, J. (2007). Interpreting causality in the health sciences. *International Studies in the Philosophy of Science, 21*(2), 157–170.

Schaffner, K. F. (1980). Theory structure in the biomedical sciences. *Journal of Medical Philosophy, 5*(1), 57–97.

(2011). Reduction in biology and medicine. In F. Gifford (Ed.), *Philosophy of medicine* (pp. 137–157). Elsevier.

Sekar, A., Bialas, A. R., de, R. H., Davis, A., Hammond, T. R., Kamitaki, N., ... McCarroll, S. A. (2016). Schizophrenia risk from complex variation of complement component 4. *Nature, 530*(7589), 177–183.

Solli, I. F. (2017). Left behind by birth month. *Education Economics, 25*(4), 323–346. https://doi.org/10.1080/09645292.2017.1287881

Woodward, J. (2003). *Making things happen* (P. Humphreys, Ed.). Oxford University Press.

CHAPTER 12

Commentary on Kendler's "A Working Scientist's View on Causality in Psychiatry"

Federica Russo

In his chapter, Ken Kendler set out to explore the prospects of evidential pluralism in a field that admittedly has not been explored in the literature so far: psychiatry. I find it thoroughly impressive how Kendler has engaged with the literature on evidential pluralism, and I fully agree with his words of caution and caveats about mechanisms. In this commentary, I will try to think along with Kendler and offer pointers to other places in this broad area of evidential pluralism that might be of help to those interested in psychiatry.

Let me begin with a note on philosophical methodology. Kendler explains that he approaches this literature (1) from the perspective of scientist and (2) from the perspective of the practice (of psychiatry). This is, in my view, stepping into this literature with the right foot. The philosophy of science and of causality have changed greatly over the years, engaging with questions of practice more thoroughly and systematically than before. We can distinguish (at least) two main traditions in philosophy of science nowadays. The first I will call analytic or Anglo-American philosophy of science; the second is the so-called philosophy of science in practice. In my latest monograph (Russo 2022) I reconstruct these fields (and also philosophy of technology) and explain how they differ in terms of the way questions about science are posed and addressed. As the label suggests, philosophy of science in practice engages with the *practice* of science, and this can be done, in turn, in various ways – from carrying out ethnographic work to study science in the making to, as Kendler does, posing philosophical questions from the perspective of a working scientist. In my view, these perspectives are not mutually exclusive; instead, they are complementary to each other. What is more, philosophy of science in practice can foster (and has fostered) interdisciplinary approaches and collaborations (Poliseli & Russo, 2022; Poliseli et al., 2022). Specifically, to get a sense of how the philosophy of causality has changed over the past two decades, one could look at the publications that issued from the

Causality in the Sciences conference series,[1] which runs since 2006 and the hallmark of which has been to discuss problems and questions of causality in the practice of science. In this series (and in the publications issued from the conferences), there has been a concrete effort to establish a dialogue between philosophers and scientists – just as this History and Philosophy of Psychiatry series does. I personally cherish the deep engagement with the sciences and with the practice of the sciences. This approach is visible not only in the topics and approaches reported in published research but also in the way people have started engaging with each other's work, via conferences and workshops as well as joint publications. Clearly, this volume (and the workshop from which it stems) is an excellent example of these fruitful collaborations and exchanges. In this way of looking at the practice of science – or at the philosophical literature – there is always a lot to learn, and in my case I have learned a great deal from Kendler's presentation of the problem, from the examples he chooses, and from his way of problematizing the use and conceptualization of "mechanism" in the practice of psychiatric research. In what follows I hope to complement Kendler's argument with some clarification and nuance that come from my philosophical perspective.

The second reflection I wish to offer in the opening of my commentary concerns the scope of Kendler's argument – or, put more generally, the positioning of psychiatry with respect to medicine. For a long time, philosophy of medicine has been identified with philosophical reflection on the *ethical* aspects of medicine, often called *medical ethics*. Until 10–15 years ago, medicine has *not* been among the most popular objects of investigations by philosophers of science, with notable exceptions (see, e.g., pioneering papers by Donald Gillies [2005] or Paul Thagard [1998]). It has been a slow-growing but steady interest that philosophers of science have shown with respect to medicine, *from the perspective of its methods*. While medical methodology has been growing as a field since the early 2000s, my impression is that philosophy of psychiatry has remained rather disconnected from medical methodology, which quickly delved into questions of evidence, causation, and explanation. A large part of the debate has revolved around questions related to clinical practice and the use of randomized controlled trials (RCTs) and the rise of evidence-based medicine (EBM) as the dominant paradigm. In a chapter coauthored with Brendan Clarke (Clarke & Russo, 2017), we pleaded for a broad understanding of medicine; our idea was to understand medicine as an "umbrella

[1] https://blogs.kent.ac.uk/jonw/conferences/cits/.

term" to include (rather than exclude) as many practices as possible, from clinical medicine to epidemiology, from public health to narrative medicine. Based on this, we framed questions of causation in medicine as questions about causes and effects that may take different formulations depending on context. Given this background, I feel at ease reading and commenting on Kendler's chapter, even if I would not consider myself a specialist in psychiatry – I have in fact studied in more detailed fields such as epidemiology and public health. But I cherish this opportunity to learn about questions that are specific to psychiatry, from the perspective of "medical methodology."

As I said in the beginning, I commend Kendler for engaging so collegially and constructively with this literature – an attitude that I much appreciated also during our conversations in preparation for the workshop in Copenhagen. I would like to offer here a few clarifications on how the field came about. A large part of the debate on evidence in medicine (broadly construed) cites the paper I coauthored with Jon Williamson (Russo & Williamson, 2007). This was the first time the pluralistic thesis about evidence in medicine was formulated. Our point was that the philosophy of medicine had a number of "monistic accounts" – for instance, the probabilistic or the process-based one – but none of them, *on its own*, was able to account for the way causal claims are established in medicine. We offered an analysis of some salient episodes in medicine (the famous Semmelweis case and the discovery of *Helicobacter pylori* as the cause of gastric ulcer among them) to show that in medicine we normally make considerations (evidence) about difference making (whether a cause makes a difference to its effect) and about mechanisms (how a cause brings about an effect). Back then, however, the argument was also that even if evidence is plural, the notion of causation needs not to be if one adopts the epistemic theory of causality. I will not continue retracing here the debate around the epistemic theory of causality. Suffice it to say that, while Williamson would still endorse it, I have moved to a more radical pluralist position about causality, which I have developed with Phyllis Illari (Illari & Russo, 2014); I motivate and explain this shift in my monograph (Russo, 2022). Instead, I wish to explain what happened to the discussion on "evidence" more specifically. Donald Gillies (2011) had introduced the Russo–Williamson thesis (RWT) to refer to our claim about the need for evidence of both mechanisms and difference making.

Since then, there has been a vibrant debate, in part critical but in part also very constructive. I will focus on the constructive contributions to explain how a single coauthored paper became a research program. The contributions of Gillies (2011) and Illari (2011) helped add important qualifications to the thesis. According to Gillies, evidence of mechanisms comes "into degrees": in other words, sometimes mechanisms are well established, but sometimes they are just hypothesized. This clearly makes a difference in to the degree to which a causal claim is established. According to Illari, we should not understand evidence rigidly; RWT points to what we seek evidence *of*, and the same study could provide evidence of difference making or of mechanism, depending on how it is framed and carried out and how the results are interpreted. These two contributions led to a fruitful collaboration between the "Kent group" (Illari, Russo, Williamson) and the "UCL group" (Clarke, Gillies). We obtained funds to explore questions of evidence in medicine, and with the Arts and Humanities Research Council "Evaluating Evidence in Medicine" grant[2] the group further broadened not only in perspective (Gillies brought in a very valuable historical perspective) but also in scope, because we started collaborating with the National Institute for Health Care Excellence (via Mike Kelly) and the International Agency for Research on Cancer (via Kurt Straif), and with more junior staff bringing new case studies questions (Parkkinen, Wallmann, Wilde). We called our approach EBM+, to signal that we were not in contrast with EBM principles of evidence evaluation, but rather signaling the importance of (evidence of) mechanisms – whence the *plus*. These developments are important because there has been a genuine effort in understanding the conceptualization, use, and assessment of evidence in practice, as well as to respond to a clear need for guidelines to evaluate the quality of evidence of mechanisms in practice. I will return to this point later in the commentary.

I extend this prologue because, to me, it is important to see evidential pluralism as a methodological approach rather than as a fixed and immutable thesis about evidence. It is an approach that invites understanding specific challenges in the practice of medicine (broadly construed) and to develop a philosophy that helps address them.

Let me now turn to some specific claims Kendler makes in his chapter. I will concentrate on four of them.

First, Kendler ultimately says that mechanisms are important but their definition and role in practice of science are not easy to pin down. There is a lot to agree with; indeed, some of this can be found in the evidential pluralism literature. As I mentioned earlier, Gillies (2011) has problematized the status of "mechanism" quite some time ago, admitting a whole

[2] https://blogs.kent.ac.uk/jonw/projects/evaluating-evidence-in-medicine/.

spectrum from just plausible to well-confirmed mechanisms. This clearly makes a difference to the use of evidence, as Kendler's three examples show. In short: mechanisms are not the plug-and-play kind of thing; their usefulness (in complementarity with the counterfactual approach) depends on their status. This was precisely the goal of EBM+: not an absolute argument *for* mechanisms, but a *qualified* argument about when and how mechanisms can be useful to complement existing RCTs. Relatedly, it is worth emphasizing that the (legitimate) worries of Kendler about going down a reductionist route are de facto dissolved if one adheres to a broad and liberal understanding of mechanisms, which are not a "thing," as the "minimal definition of mechanism" indicates (Glennan & Illari, 2018; Glennan, Illari, & Weber, 2022) or as pointed out in Craver's work on levels (Craver, 2015; Povich & Craver, 2017). Conversely, including mechanisms in the practice of psychiatry is clearly more than offering "just-so stories," as it was (misleadingly) objected to in the work of Howick (2011), for example.

Second, Kendler warns the reader that mechanisms are not all the same. Indeed, we need some criteria to discriminate between better and worse descriptions (or models) of mechanisms. In part, this is what EBM+ has tried to do, but it was only an initial step. Much more is needed. So, I agree on this point as well. EBM+ made a start inventorying factors to be able to say *when* (descriptions or models of) mechanisms are of good quality and when not. One could think of this contribution as a kind of analogue of the GRADE system for the quality of methods that generate evidence of correlations (or counterfactuals, following the terminology of Kendler). EBM+ designed a series of tools (Parkkinen et al., 2018) to help different groups – for instance, those developing guidelines for medical practices or public health and social care officers – critically evaluate the existing literature and research, specifically regarding the *quality* of evidence of mechanisms, using tables and flowcharts. This is but a start, because these tools would need further development – for instance, to see whether their generality is a good feature – or instead we'd need more specific ones, depending on the medical subdomain – for instance, psychiatry may need one that tackles DSM specifically. In sum, how to evaluate evidence of mechanisms remains high on the research agenda.

Third, Kendler expresses a worry for reductionism and instead pleads for the existence of a multiplicity of causes in psychiatry. This, to rephrase it using my terminology, is a question about the nature of mechanisms. It is true that EMB+ has been implicitly talking about biochemical mechanisms of health and disease. But that was a question of priority:

the group working on the AHRC project had the urgency to convince the EBM community that we needed to complement the EBM framework with considerations about mechanisms. Simultaneously, there has been work on the need for "mixed mechanisms," specifically the idea that mechanisms are not just biological (or biochemical) but at least biosocial (and actually bio-psycho-cultural-economic-social). That health and disease are biosocial phenomena is a kind of an established mantra in sociology of medicine and social epidemiology, but the specific nature of this biosocial thing has remained elusive – or so Mike Kelly and I have argued in joint work (Kelly, Kelly, & Russo, 2014; Kelly & Russo, 2018, 2021, 2022), proposing to work with the concept of "mixed" mechanism. In the three examples examined by Kendler there are several elements that point in this direction too.

Fourth, Kendler aims to problematize the status of mechanism in explanations of health and disease. Allow me to use philosophical jargon at this point: Kendler is saying that mechanism has a more epistemic than ontic status. Epistemic here refers to the use of mechanisms for epistemic practices such as explanation or evidence generation/assessment. Ontic instead refers to what mechanisms *are*, and an ontic understanding of mechanism basically means that mechanisms are real-world objects. Since the outset of the "new mechanical philosophy," with pioneering publications of Glennan (1996) and Machamer and colleagues (2000), the status of mechanisms has been under debate. Here, the contribution of Illari (2013) stands out because she explained that we need not polarize positions; clearly, we do want to talk about mechanisms as they act in the world, but this is not independent from epistemic constraints. Vice versa, returning a faithful account of mechanistic explanatory practices also requires taking some stance about ontic boundaries or constraints. Starting from a practice approach – as Kendler does – may help prioritize questions of epistemology and methodology or of ontology, depending on specific research interest, agendas, and so forth.

Let me conclude with some reflections on where to go from here. Kendler explains where he comes from and how he approached the evidential pluralism debate from the perspective of a practitioner. What is the next step? In my view, what could be beneficial is a systematization of the needs of psychiatry as a field to complement the counterfactual approach (as he calls it) with mechanisms, *as well as* what evidential pluralism has produced that may help. I suspect that some elements are there but not fully worked out – at least, I see in his reconstruction and discussion of psychiatric research practice a fertile ground collaboration.

A large part of the contributions in "medical methodology" have not engaged with psychiatry. But Kendler clearly has paved the way for a fruitful conversation.

REFERENCES

Clarke, B., & Russo, F. (2017). Causation in medicine. In J. A. Marcum (Ed.), *The Bloomsbury companion to contemporary philosophy of medicine* (pp. 297–322). Bloomsbury Academic. https://doi.org/10.5040/9781474233033.ch-013

Craver, C. F. (2015). *Levels*. (T. Metzinger & J. M. Windt, Eds.). Open MIND. https://doi.org/10.15502/9783958570498

Gillies, D. (2005). Hempelian and Kuhnian approaches in the philosophy of medicine: The Semmelweis case. *Studies in History and Philosophy of Biological and Biomedical Sciences, 36*, 159–181.

(2011). The Russo-Williamson thesis and the question of whether smoking causes heart disease. In P. M. Illari, F. Russo, & J. Williamson (Eds.), *Causality in the sciences* (pp. 110–125). Oxford University Press.

Glennan, S. (1996). Mechanisms and the nature of causation. *Erkenntnis, 44*, 49–71.

Glennan, S., & Illari, P. (2018). Introduction: Mechanisms and mechanical philosophies. In S. Glennan & P. Illari (Eds.), *The Routledge handbook of mechanisms and mechanical philosophy* (pp. 1–10). Routledge, Taylor & Francis Group.

Glennan, S., Illari, P., & Weber, E. (2022). Six theses on mechanisms and mechanistic science. *Journal for General Philosophy of Science, 53*(2), 143–161. https://doi.org/10.1007/s10838-021-09587-x

Howick, J. H. (2011). *The philosophy of evidence-based medicine*. BMJ Books.

Illari, P. (2013). Mechanistic explanation: Integrating the ontic and epistemic. *Erkenntnis, 78*, 237–255. https://doi.org/10.1007/s10670-013-9511-y

Illari, P. M. (2011). Mechanistic evidence: Disambiguating the Russo-Williamson thesis. *International Studies in the Philosophy of Science, 25*(2), 139–157.

Illari, P. M., & Russo, F. (2014). *Causality: Philosophical theory meets scientific practice*. Oxford University Press.

Kelly, M. P., Kelly, R. S., & Russo, F. (2014). The integration of social, behavioral, and biological mechanisms in models of pathogenesis. *Perspectives in Biology and Medicine, 57*(3), 308–328. https://doi.org/10.1353/pbm.2014.0026

Kelly, M. P., & Russo, F. (2018). Causal narratives in public health: The difference between mechanisms of aetiology and mechanisms of prevention in non-communicable diseases. *Sociology of Health & Illness*, 40(1), 82–99. https://doi.org/10.1111/1467-9566.12621

(2021). The epistemic values at the basis of epidemiology and public health. *MEFISTO: Journal of Medicine, Philosophy, and History, 5*(1), 1–26.

(2022). *The 'lifeworld' of health and disease and the design of public health interventions*. Phil Sci Archive.

Machamer, P., Darden, L., & Craver, C. (2000). Thinking about mechanisms. *Philosophy of Science, 67*, 1–25.

Parkkinen, V.-P., Clarke, B., Illari, P., Kelly, M. P., Norell, C., Russo, F., Shaw, B., Wallmann, C., Wilde, M., & Williamson, J. (2018). *Evaluating evidence of mechanisms in medicine: Principles and procedures*. Springer International Publishing. https://doi.org/10.1007/978-3-319-94610-8

Poliseli, L., Coutinho, J. G. E., Viana, B., Russo, F., & El-Hani, C. N. (2022). Philosophy of science in practice in ecological model building. *Biology & Philosophy, 37*(4), 21. https://doi.org/10.1007/s10539-022-09851-4

Poliseli, L., & Russo, F. (2022). Philosophy of science in practice and weak scientism together apart. In M. Mizrahi (Ed.), *For and against scientism: Science, methodology and the future of philosophy* (pp. 105–118). Rowman & Littlefield.

Povich, M., & Craver, C. F. (2017). Mechanistic levels, reduction and emergence. In S. Glennan & P. M. Illari (Eds.), *The Routledge handbook of mechanisms and mechanical philosophy* (pp. 185–197). Routledge, Taylor & Francis Group.

Russo, F. (2022). *Techno-scientific practices: An informational approach*. Rowman & Littlefield.

Russo, F., & Williamson, J. (2007). Interpreting causality in the health sciences. *International Studies in Philosophy of Science, 21*(2), 157–170.

Thagard, P. (1998). Explaining disease: Correlations, causes, and mechanisms. *Minds and Machines, 8*, 61–78.

PART II

Causes, Genes, and Neuroscience

Section 5

CHAPTER 13

Introduction to Turkheimer and Kaplan's "Stalking the Wild Quincunx"

Kenneth S. Kendler

Since around 2010, genome-wide association studies (GWAS) have taken the field of psychiatric genetics by storm. Many of the time-honored methods – family studies, twin analyses, adoption studies – have been largely displaced by the rush toward the identification of genetic variants that could be considered *causal* of psychiatric illness. At the time of this writing in 2024, the field is awash with results. For key disorders such as schizophrenia, bipolar disorder, and major depression, hundreds of variants on the genome have been found to be associated with risk of illness. What we have learned so far is that for all psychiatric disorders investigated, many common variants in the human genome appear to reflect risk, and the effect size of all of them is small, sometimes very small. Furthermore, taken individually, most of these variants do not have any obvious biological meaning; they do not occur in the parts of the genome that codes for proteins. Often, they are just statistical signals for the block of the human genome (a "haplotype") with which they have traveled through human – and, before then, primate – evolution.

What these results mean and the degree to which it makes sense to call these variants causal remain points of considerable controversy. For several years, Erik Turkheimer, who coauthored the following chapter, has staked a claim as a hard skeptic of the explanatory claims of molecular genetics of psychiatric disorders. He has sound historical reasons for this position. Before GWAS, molecular psychiatric genetics went through two prior phases dominated by the methodologies of, respectively, linkage analysis and candidate genes. For quite different reasons, although both methods were greeted with great enthusiasm and promises of soon producing major breakthroughs in our etiologic understanding of psychiatric illness, both ended in failure.

Turkheimer and Jonathan Kaplan take us on a "simulation ride" of a GWAS in their chapter based on an intriguing little machine designed and first utilized by Francis Galton, called a quincunx. (See Chapter 14 for a description.) They grant that GWAS findings in the aggregate – for example, in polygenic risk scores – are predictive, and the evidence in favor of that for psychiatric genetics is quite strong. But the rub is whether the individual common variant findings can be converted to biological causal insights of illness. This is a form of the long-debated question of the relationship between the analysis of variance and the analysis of causes. Turkheimer and Kaplan argue – and support with their simulation results – that it is very unlikely to get from here (individual significant but very small-effect-size common single nucleotide polymorphism [SNP] findings) to there (biological pathways to illness).

In their favor are their simulation results, which do a reasonable job of recovering from the quincunx the expectations of a twin study and the aggregate results from GWAS. But when they query the predictive effect of individual SNPs, they find effects that are so small that the plausibility of this leading to a true understanding of biological causes is quite questionable.

To add flavor to their argument, Turkheimer for years has used the phenotype of divorce as a thought experiment to argue for his position. Multiple twin studies have shown that divorce has a moderate heritability in the range of that found for major depression or some anxiety disorders. Why not fund a large-scale GWAS of divorce? If we got a big enough sample, a selection of risk SNPs would surely emerge. We could then, he suggests tongue-in-cheek, use them to discover the biology of divorce, leading to risk scores used for prediction and even to developing pharmacological treatments. He regards this all, a priori, as an absurd proposition. There is no meaningful biology of divorce to be found, he would suggest. I agree.

Worthy of note, Turkheimer and I have had what is now a multiyear discussion on this topic where we have generally, if politely, disagreed. Let me continue in that tradition. There are many points of agreement. The history of human psychiatric genetics is full of false, overly optimistic promises that have been broken. To claim now, as I do, that the current situation is different could strain credulity. GWAS – which studies common variants on the human genome – has discovered variants of only small individual effects for psychiatric disorders. As discussed in Chapter 11, at least one such common variant has led to a potential biological mechanism, although the validity of that claim could not yet be considered as confirmed (Sekar et al., 2016). There are other data, however, including studying the grouping of various genetic variants and the genes they likely affect – that show statistically significant concentrations of such genes in key pre- and postsynaptic mechanisms

(Trubetskoy et al., 2022). Other investigations show the expression of such variants in particular, likely relevant brain tissues and cell types, which argues that there is a meaningful biological signal in the GWAS findings (Trubetskoy et al., 2022). Finally, there is a group of molecular variants that are much rarer and have much larger effect sizes than the common SNPs, located in protein coding genes that are much more biologically tractable than the small-effect common SNPs. More than 10 such variants for schizophrenia have been found to date (Singh et al., 2022). In response to Turkheimer's powerful divorce analogy, I fully agree that an underlying biology of divorce is implausible. However, a large enough GWAS would, I predict, find some genetic variants that influence known risk factors for divorce, such as the propensity for drug and alcohol use disorders. That would be useful causal information.

The future of psychiatric molecular genetics is uncertain. The field has a track record of overpromising. Are things different now, and will important scientific insights into disease etiology emerge from our current approaches? I would argue there is reason to consider this possibility. Turkheimer and Kaplan would be less optimistic. Reading this insightful chapter will sharpen your understanding of the issues pertaining to causal inference in one important part of psychiatric science. The lessons learned could also assist in the appreciation of many other chapters in this volume.

REFERENCES

Sekar, A., Bialas, A. R., de, R. H., Davis, A., Hammond, T. R., Kamitaki, N., Tooley, K., Presumey, J., Baum, M., Van, D., V, Genovese, G., Rose, S. A., Handsaker, R. E., Daly, M. J., Carroll, M. C., Stevens, B., & McCarroll, S. A. (2016). Schizophrenia risk from complex variation of complement component 4. *Nature, 530*(7589), 177–183. https://doi.org/nature16549

Singh, T., Poterba, T., Curtis, D., Akil, H., Al Eissa, M., Barchas, J. D., Bass, N., Bigdeli, T. B., Breen, G., Bromet, E. J., Buckley, P. F., Bunney, W. E., Bybjerg-Grauholm, J., Byerley, W. F., Chapman, S. B., Chen, W. J., Churchhouse, C., Craddock, N., Cusick, C. M., ... Daly, M. J. (2022). Rare coding variants in ten genes confer substantial risk for schizophrenia. *Nature, 604*(7906), 509–516. https://doi.org/10.1038/s41586-022-04556-w

Trubetskoy, V., Pardinas, A. F., Qi, T., Panagiotaropoulou, G., Awasthi, S., Bigdeli, T. B., Bryois, J., Chen, C. Y., Dennison, C. A., Hall, L. S., Lam, M., Watanabe, K., Frei, O., Ge, T., Harwood, J. C., Koopmans, F., Magnusson, S., Richards, A. L., Sidorenko, J., ... Schizophrenia Working Group of the Psychiatric Genomics, C. (2022). Mapping genomic loci implicates genes and synaptic biology in schizophrenia. *Nature, 604*(7906), 502–508. https://doi.org/10.1038/s41586-022-04434-5

CHAPTER 14

Stalking the Wild Quincunx

Eric Turkheimer and Jonathan Kaplan

Francis Galton's familiar "quincunx," also known as a bean board or a Galton board, is emblematic of the complex relationship between systematic causation and uncontrolled randomness in development (Figure 14.1). On the simplest level, Galton intended the quincunx as a method for illustrating what we now call the binomial theorem. Sums of random binary events, like the ball bearings bouncing left or right off pins as they descend through the device, produce normally distributed quasi-continuous outcomes with known mean and variance. The quincunx thus unifies what otherwise seem to be opposed perspectives in developmental biology: discrete and continuous, binary and normally distributed, random and deterministic, predetermined and epigenetic. In Kaplan and Turkheimer (2021), we explored how the quincunx exemplified difficult distinctions between biological causation and statistical models of variation in complex developmental outcomes. Individual pins in a quincunx are "difference makers" with regard to the bins in which balls wind up, but only in a statistical sense that applies to populations of balls, not individuals. Any individual ball does not interact with most of the pins in the quincunx as it follows its path downward, so most pins are not causally efficacious in determining the ball's destination.

In the years since we published our first paper about Francis Galton's quincunx (Kaplan & Turkheimer, 2021), Gregory Radick (2023) has published an authoritative history of the early years of theorizing about evolution and heredity, titled *Disputed Inheritance*. Radick's historical work has clarified several important points about Galton's device. Galton developed it in 1873 for a public lecture, well before he first described it in print (Galton, 1889). Radick follows the modern convention of referring to the device as a quincunx; however, Galton never used the term to refer to the device itself. Instead, the word "quincunx" refers to the pattern formed by the groups of five pins in alternating staggered rows, like the

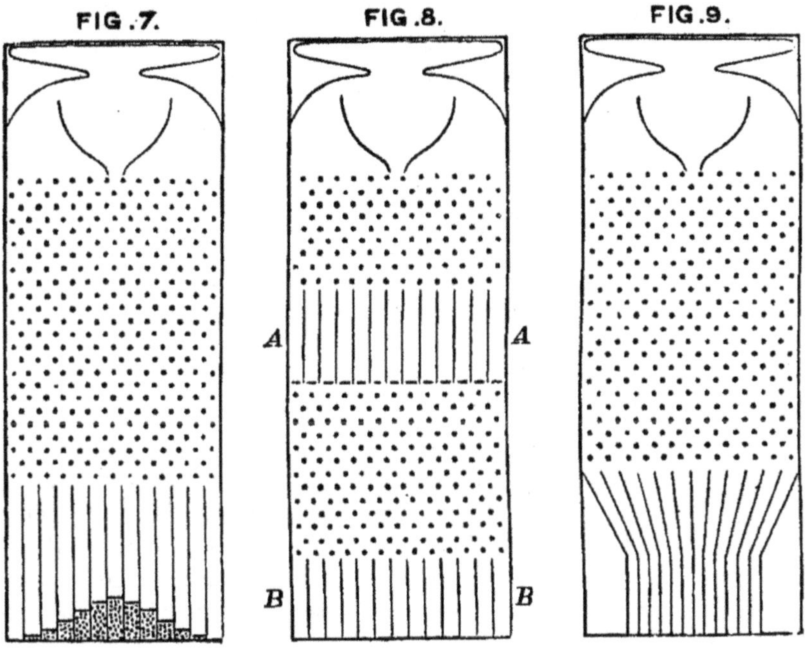

Figure 14.1 Galton's quincunx, from *Natural Inheritance* (1889).

configuration of five dots on a die. The quincunx pattern was often used in coats of arms or as a pattern for planting trees in orchards.

The full genetic significance of Galton's ingenuity did not become clear until 30 years later when R. A. Fisher (1918) formalized the application of the binomial theorem to one of the greatest scientific controversies of the last century: the debate between the so-called Mendelians, who saw genetics in terms of the discrete biological processes derived from Mendel's experiments with peas, and the biometricians, who, following Galton and Karl Pearson, were interested in the genetics of complex, normally distributed characteristics, such as height, that did not obviously conform to Mendel's laws of segregation. The modern concept of heritability followed rapidly on the heels of Fisher's insights.

With the benefit of hindsight, it is worthwhile to reflect that few of the traits we recognize as genetic reveal anything about their biological basis in meiosis and segregation. Who could derive the biology of genetics from observing the way height or schizophrenia clusters (without obvious segregation) in families? The history of genetics – especially human genetics, and most especially human behavioral and psychiatric genetics – is a fraught and very incomplete process of trying to link discrete, cause-driven biology to the variances of behavioral differences by elucidating what is called the genotype-to-phenotype pathway. The quincunx is a proof of concept that individually simple but collectively complex causal processes can have emergent properties that resemble the variation and covariation of large-scale genetic characters as we observe them. It also poses what we believe to be the core theoretical problem underlying psychiatric genetics: Do we accept the statistical devices we have conjured to model the occurrence of phenotypes in families as *causal* accounts of why those disorders occur?

Jonathan Kaplan and I explored these ideas in our 2021 "Galton's Quincunx: Probabilistic causation in developmental behavior genetics." In the article we imagined a biased quincunx in which some or all of the pins deviate from an equal probability right or left. Would it be worthwhile to consider those molar tendencies as causes of the macroscopic distributions of balls that result after many of them have tumbled down the device? The answer isn't simple and leads to an analysis of distinctions between deterministic and probabilistic causes at the individual and collective levels. On the bottom line, a scientist interested in the causes of ball placement must consider the fact that many or even most pins will have no effect at all on many or even most balls because the latter never bounce the former's way. The causal effects of biased pins can therefore only be understood in a probabilistic analysis of the properties of a population.

Radick argues that Galton's theorizing about the quincunx shows him to be less deterministically hereditarian, and more open to subtle developmental ideas, than he is usually given credit for. Radick cites the following passage from Galton (1872):

> The embryonic elements are developed into the adult person. "Development" is a word whose meaning is quite as distinct in respect to form, and as vague in respect to detail, as [can be] . . . ; it embraces the combined effects of growth and multiplication, as well as those of modification in quality and proportion, under both internal and external influences. If we were to obtain an approximate knowledge of the original elements, statistical experiences would no doubt enable us to predict the average value of the form into which they would become developed, just as a knowledge of the seeds that were sown would enable us to predict in a general way the appearance of the garden when the plant had grown up; but the individual variation of each case would of course be great, owing to the large number of variable influences concerned in the process of development. (p. 395)

Galton, of course, didn't have even an approximate "knowledge of the original elements" that underlie genetics and evolution. Today we do, to some extent. We know the pins in our biological quincunx are made of DNA. (For present purposes we aren't going to be concerned with environmental pins; the genetic part is complex enough.) It has proven to be more difficult than anyone expected to get beyond very approximate causal knowledge to something more specific, especially for human behavior. What kinds of properties do our DNA pins have that guide people to high educational attainment or mental illness? The inferential problem that Galton envisioned has taken a very particular form in modern genomics. In genome-wide association studies (GWAS) we are given information about the bins in which people have wound up and about certain characteristics of the pins that each of us has inherited. The latter information takes the form of single nucleotide polymorphisms (SNPs), the individual units of nucleotides comprised of genes and chromosomes. There are only four possible values of those nucleotides, coded as A, C, T, or G.

Presumably, each SNP is either neutral with respect to a trait or has a tendency to nudge a person either toward or away from a particular outcome. A person with an A at a particular SNP might be more likely to become depressed than a person with a G. The inferential problem is to compare the SNPs of people who have or haven't experienced depression (or, as we will conduct our simulations, to fall farther to the left or right on a continuous distribution of outcome) to infer the causal tendencies of the SNPs. The problem has turned out to be very difficult for several reasons. First, there are a great many SNPs to consider: most modern studies include more than a million. Simultaneous tests of a million SNPs require stringent statistical safeguards against random results. Second, the associations between individual SNPs and psychiatric outcomes are almost all exceedingly tiny. Any hope that GWAS would lead us to genes of more than microscopic effect was not fulfilled. The astronomical number of potential effects and the microscopic size of any one of them combine to require enormous samples to detect tiny associations at demanding levels of statistical significance. Sample sizes in the hundreds of thousands are commonplace.

For all that, GWAS has succeeded in its first-level task of discovering associations between SNPs and behavioral differences that reach genome-wide statistical significance. Although it took longer than expected to accumulate sufficiently large samples, GWAS has now reported statistically significant associations between SNPs and most psychiatric syndromes. Genome-wide statistical significance allows scientists to conclude that these associations did not occur simply because of random processes of sampling error. Significance does not, however, imply anything about the causal basis of the associations, which remains obscure, especially because the correlations are so tiny. How do we know if the correlations identified by GWAS correspond to the causal genetic processes underlying complex behavioral development? The evidence is not easy to ascertain in humans. When GWAS is conducted in corn or flies, SNP associations can be followed up with experimental procedures that might elucidate causal processes, like controlled breeding or genetic knockouts, but these cannot be conducted in humans. Suppose a value of C on SNP rs123456 (as they are designated) shows a correlation of $r = .002$ with risk for depression, $p < .05 \times 10^{-8}$ in 100,000 cases and controls. What is one to make of this? Like any correlation, SNP associations can occur for reasons meaningful or spurious, and genome-wide significance offers no assurance one way or the other.

14.1 Analysis of Variance and a Twin Study

In the current chapter, we build a computer simulation of quincunx and explore the relationships between the statistical and causal properties of the simulated device. We proceed according to the history of investigations of this kind: we start with an analysis of variance and a simple twin study, then proceed to GWAS. Figure 14.2a is a schematic representation of a simulated quincunx. The arrow at each pin represents the causal bias: in Figure 14.2a all the pins are unbiased, with a 50% chance of bouncing the ball left or right. The histogram superimposed on the quincunx is the distribution of balls that results. Figure 14.2b is a biased quincunx in

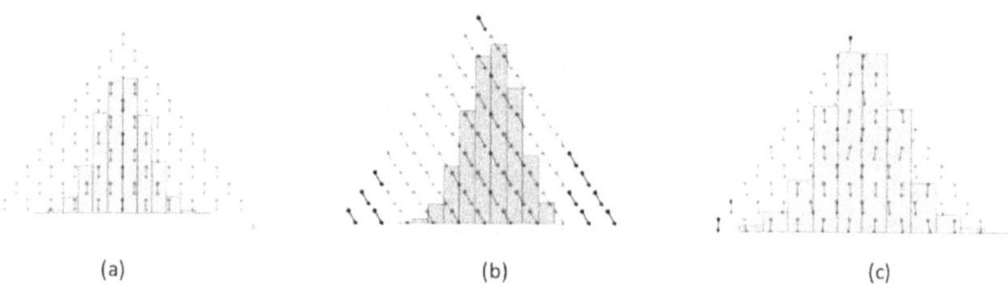

Figure 14.2 (a) An unbiased simulated quincunx; (b) a quincunx with a consistent rightward bias; (c) a quincunx with random biases. The superimposed histograms show the final locations of the simulated balls.

which all the pins tend to bounce the balls to the right. The superimposed histogram shows the effect the bias has on the outcome. Figure 14.2c is a randomly biased quincunx in which each pin has a left–right bias sampled at random. This quincunx is presumably closer in structure to the human genome, with a large set of developmental causes, each with an unobserved (and in humans, unobservable) bias to move people in one direction or the other.

As a simulation of a GWAS, the quincunx in Figure 14.2 are too small. In general, a quincunx with k rows has $\frac{k(k+1)}{2}$ pins embedded for computational reasons in a matrix with $k(2k-1)$ pins. In the example quincunx with 12 rows, there is a total of $\frac{12\times 13}{2} = 78$ pins that can possibly interact with a ball. For the analysis of variance, we created a quincunx with 50 rows, including a total of 4,950 pins. (This is, of course, much smaller than the number of SNPs analyzed in a typical genetic study, but increasing the number of rows creates computational problems and does little to change the outcome.)

The deviation of our simulation from the way quincunx are usually deployed reinforces the difficulties faced by human scientists. In a Galtonian quincunx, there is one device comprising strictly 50–50 pins, down which many balls fall into the gratifying normally distributed outcome. It is like observing a large sample of inbred mice living their lives under strictly controlled conditions. In humans, however, every genetic quincunx is different, and we only observe one ball in each of them, or in the rare case of identical twins, two. One person is bequeathed one genome, one ball, one life. Crucially, in the simulated quincunx, the biases of the pins are known both at the level of the individual pins and their mean value in the quincunx, whereas in real humans they are necessarily inferred; inferring them is the ultimate point of GWAS.

We generated populations of quincunx consisting of pins with biased deviation from a 50–50 tendency to bounce a ball left or right. The mean value of the pins in each quincunx was drawn from a normal distribution with a mean of .5 and a standard deviation of .05, so each quincunx as a whole tended to bounce balls left or right. Within each quincunx, the pin biases varied around the overall mean, also with a standard deviation of .05. Additional variability, of course, is introduced by the random bounces of the simulated balls. One simulated ball falls down each quincunx.

The simplest question to ask, mostly as a check on the functioning of the simulation, is whether the means of the biases in the quincunx are correlated with the final ball location. They are: the correlation between the average bias of the quincunx and the final ball location is $r = .57$. The

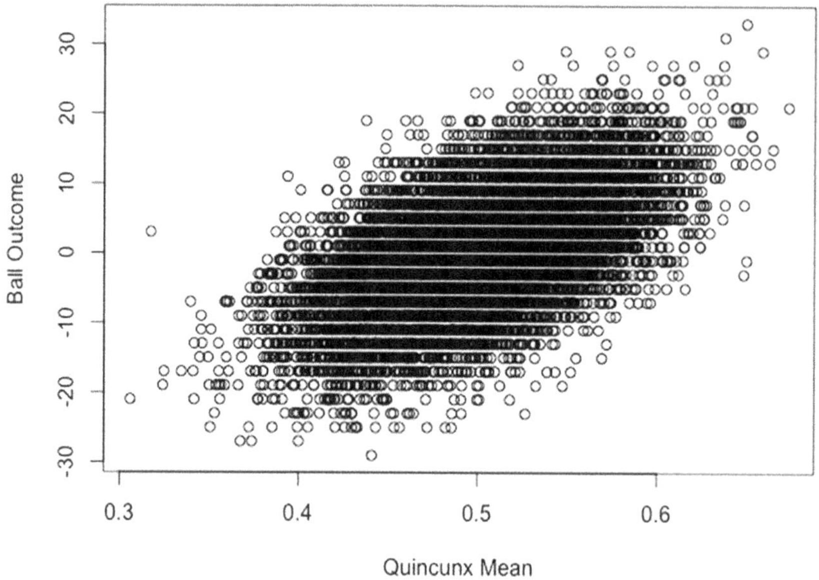

Figure 14.3 Scatterplot of relationship between mean bias of the quincunx and final location of the ball.

scatterplot is illustrated in Figure 14.3. This experiment would be impossible to conduct in humans because our genetic tendencies – the direction in which our genes are bouncing us – are unknown. A partial solution to this problem is provided by quantitative genetics in general and twin studies in particular. Even though the true genetic values of individual people are unknown, we do know that within a set of reasonable assumptions identical twins have the same value, whereas fraternal twins' values are correlated at $r = .5$. By comparing the phenotypic similarity of identical and fraternal twins, along with a set of nontrivial assumptions about environmental similarity, the proportion of outcome variance associated with genetic differences – that is, the heritability – can be estimated.

We constructed twin quincunx using the classical twin model, in which phenotypic variance is partitioned into additive genetic, shared environmental, and nonshared environmental components. (The "environmental" components were included as a way to scale the difference in similarity between identical and fraternal twins. Our goal in these simulations is to understand the relations between genetic causation and variability, not to partition genetic and environmental variance.) We constructed 10,000 pairs each of identical and fraternal twins. The quincunx pairs were

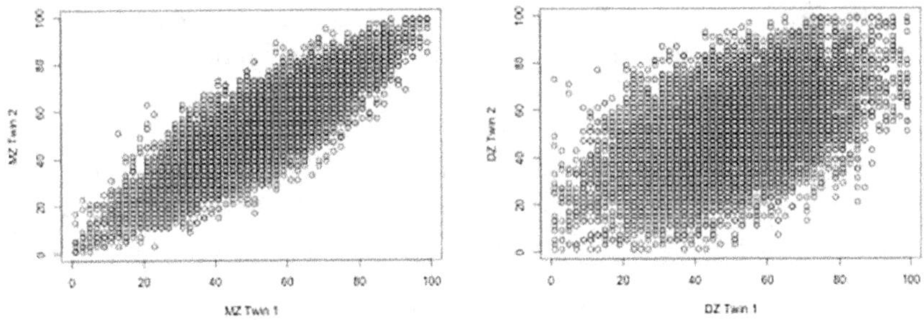

Figure 14.4 Correlation in outcome for identical (left) and fraternal (right) twin quincunx.

constructed so that the "genetic" variance in the MZ pairs was identical and in the DZ pairs was correlated .5. (We omit some of the computational details here in the interest of simplicity.) As before, one simulated ball fell down each member in each pair, and we observed the pair correlations that resulted, separately in the MZ and DZ pairs. Results are illustrated in Figure 14.4: the MZ pairs were correlated at $r = .86$ and DZ pairs at $r = .52$. According to the classical twin model, these results are equivalent to A = .68, C = .18, E = .14, typical for a complex behavioral phenotype.

14.2 GWAS

So far, the simulations have performed as would be expected according to quantitative genetics. When we assume that the average genetic values of the quincunx are known, they are correlated with phenotypic outcomes represented by left–right ball placement. When the average genetic values of the quincunx are not known, they can still be interrogated using the known similarity of identical and fraternal twin pairs. Historically, this state of affairs is analogous to the period before the completion of the Human Genome Project, when twin and family studies had demonstrated that psychiatric phenotypes are heritable, and looked forward to molecular genetic data to clarify the underlying causal basis of analysis of variance. Up to this point, we have had nothing to say about the biases in the individual pins that constitute the quincunx; we have only referred to their mean value in each device. Investigating the causal roles of the individual pins requires us to simulate the genetic properties of SNPs a little more closely.

The quincunx provides an analog of the inferential problem of GWAS. We are given an outcome describing where a person landed on a continuous dimension, and a large set of binary (A, C, T, or G) predictors describing which of the two SNPs each person inherited. The causal properties of the SNPs are unknown in GWAS but known in simulated quincunx. Can we infer the causal properties of the individual pins from the statistical associations between the binary inheritance at the pins and the outcomes in the bins?

The main task is to simulate binary SNPs. Up to now, the bias values at each pin in each quincunx were drawn at random from a continuous normal distribution. For the GWAS simulation, we generated two possible values at each pin, representing the binary inheritance at a SNP. As before, we drew the two possible bias values for each pin from a normal distribution, this time with a mean of zero (because our interest is in variation among pins, not average variation across quincunx) and a standard deviation of 0.05. Each pin in each quincunx was randomly assigned one of the two bias values for that pin. The "true causal effect" at that pin is the difference between the two bias values. For example, consider the pin at (3, −3) in Figure 14.2a, which is the leftmost pin in the third row. First, we drew at random two bias values for the pin, representing the causal consequences of having one of the two values at the SNP. Say, they were (−.03, +.06). Then, in each generated quincunx, that pin had a 50–50 chance of "inheriting" one of the two values. The true causal effect at the pin is (−.03 − .06 = −.09).

We created 50,000 unique quincunx using these procedures and dropped a single ball down each of them, recording the bin in which it landed from −50 to +50. The histogram in Figure 14.5a shows the distribution of the left–right biases in the pins, and the histogram in Figure 14.5b shows the true causal values of the pins, the difference in the biases of the two possible alleles at each pin. Both of these quantities are unknown in an actual GWAS. The resulting dataset has 50,000 rows (one for each participant) and 1,276 columns (1,275 binary SNP predictors and a single outcome for each participant). The inferential task is to use estimates of the associations between the binary SNP values at the pins and the outcome of the single ball to estimate the causal bias in the SNPs. The bin distribution of the 50,000 balls is given in Figure 14.6. (The reader is reminded that this distribution is different from the usual distribution of balls at the bottom of a single quincunx. It is the distribution of single balls dropped down unique quincunx that vary in the random assignment of biased pins.)

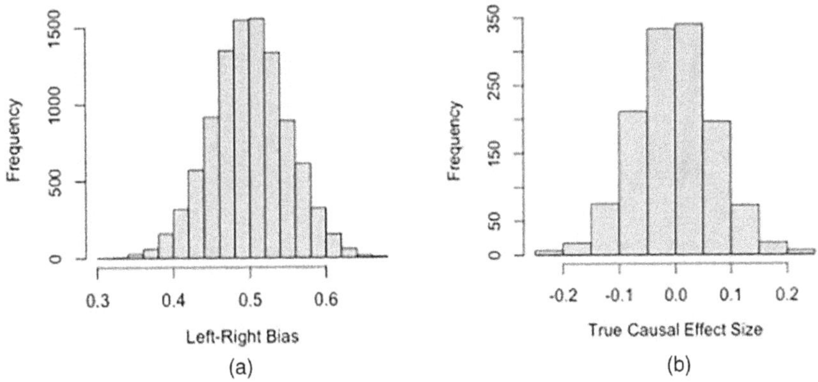

Figure 14.5 (a) Histogram of left–right biases in simulated GWAS. (b) Histogram of true causal effect sizes in simulated GWAS, calculated as the signed differences in bias between the two variants of a pin.

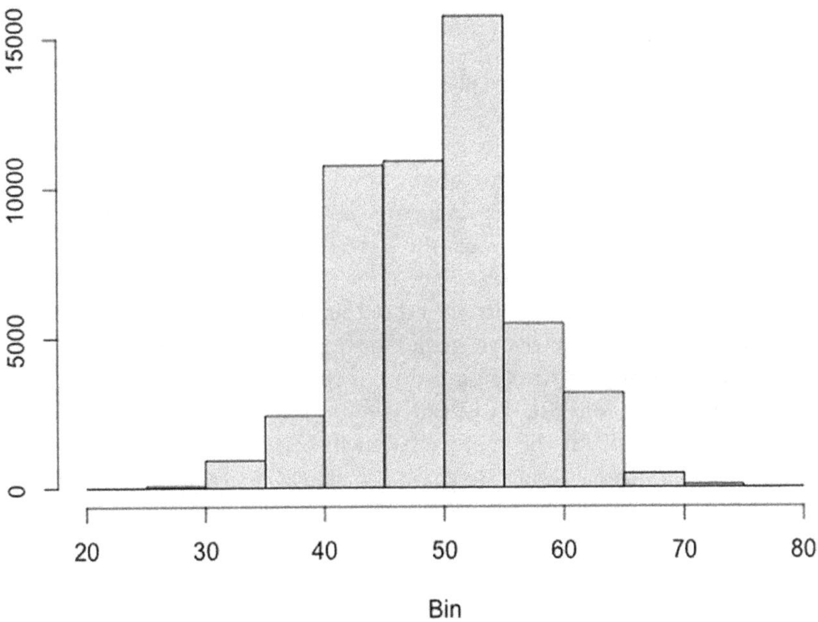

Figure 14.6 Final distribution of balls in simulated GWAS.

We now proceed to the simulated GWAS. The question is whether there is a correlation between which of the two SNPs were inherited at each pin and the bin in which the ball landed. We computed that correlation for each of the 1,275 pins in the 50,000 unique quincunx.

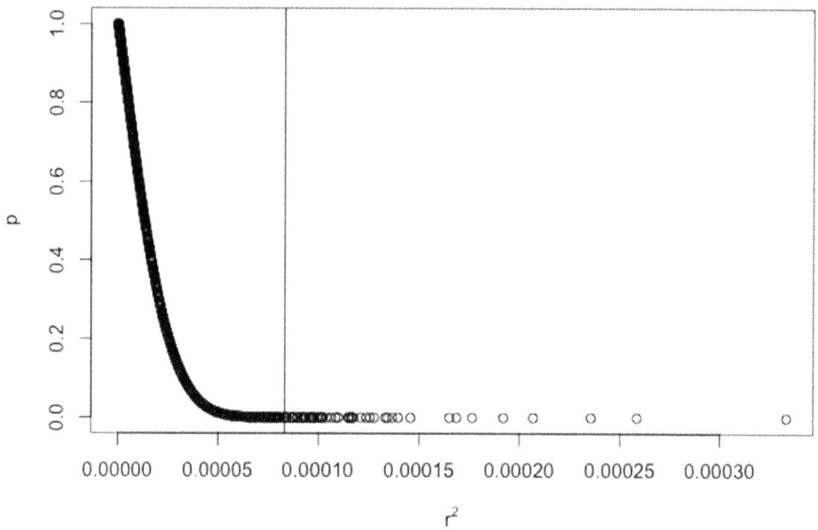

Figure 14.7 Plot of significance levels of pin associations in simulated GWAS. Points to the right of vertical line are "genome-wide" significant.

As in a real GWAS, the signs of the resulting correlations are arbitrary (depending on which SNP is designated as 1 or 2), so we report the r^2 values. The median r^2 value was 9.0×10^{-6}. The five largest values (the "top hits") were between .0002 and .0003. It is not surprising that these values are very small. They correspond to the variance explained by a single SNP in a GWAS, a quantity so small that it is not usually reported. A plot of r^2 values against statistical significance is shown in Figure 14.7. Fifty-six of the pin associations are statistically significant after using a Bonferroni correction to adjust for the 1,275 tests, as indicated by the vertical line.

Once again, these results seem like a plausible representation of an actual GWAS. The simulation allows us to proceed a step further, however. In real-world studies in humans, we can estimate the association between SNPs and outcomes as we have done here, but the actual biological actions of the SNPs remain unknown. GWAS assumes that the statistical associations reveal something about the biological properties, but that assumption can almost never be tested. In the simulation, the "biological" properties of the pins are known in terms of the left–right biases of the two possible values to which each pin is assigned. We can use this information to ask about the relationship between the statistical GWAS associations and the true causal values at the SNPs. Figure 14.8

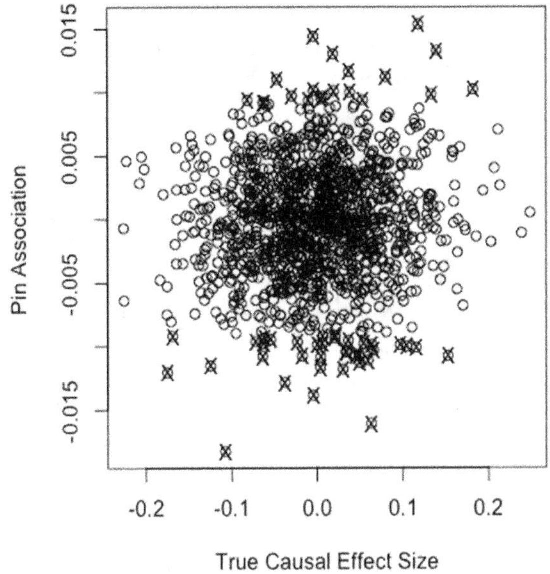

Figure 14.8 Scatterplot of relationship between true causal effect sizes and magnitude of associations with pin biases. X represents associations that were "genome-wide" statistically significant.

is a scatterplot of the true causal effect sizes of the pins and the associations between the pin values and the bin in which the ball finishes. They are correlated .07.

Although the fact that the observed pin associations are positively and significantly associated with the true causal values of the pins is an indication that the quincunx-based GWAS is not completely spurious, the magnitude of the correlation is hardly encouraging. This is the key finding of the simulation, so it bears repeating: although associations between simulated SNPs and outcomes produce statistically significant "hits," variability in the magnitude of associations across SNPs bears little relationship to the causal property it is intended to elucidate. Only 51.7% of the SNP associations are in the same direction as the causal process that underlies them. Most importantly, appeals to statistical significance are of very little help. The "X" characters in Figure 14.8 mark the statistically significant correlations. Although the associations with the pins are (by definition) larger at the 56 significant ones (median $r^2 = .0001$), and the correlation between the pin associations and the true causal values is somewhat higher ($r = .19$), more than half (31 of 56) of the pin associations are in the opposite direction than the true causal value at the pin. In other words, for more than half of the "significant" pins, the association between the pin and the left–right outcome of the ball is not in the same direction as the local tendency for the pin to bounce the ball left or right.

How could such a paradoxical result occur? The relationship between a single pin and the outcome of the ball depends on the location of the pin within the entire network of other pins. Suppose there is a pin with a slight bias to bounce the ball leftward. To the left in the next row down, however, is a pin with a *strong* tendency to bounce the ball rightward. The left-biased pin thus has the net effect of moving the ball to the right. Described in terms of quincunx results, such an explanation may seem artificial and remote, but biological development is, like a quincunx, sequential, with exposure to subsequent conditions dependent on what came before.

A natural extension of the quincunx model is to construct a polygenic score, and the results are informative. Our first approach paralleled what is usually done in genomics: for each participant, we weighted their binary SNPs with SNP effect sizes – that is, the signed correlation between each pin and the outcome – and then summed them. The result was a normally distributed score that was more highly correlated with outcome than any of the individual SNPs, at $r = .16$. We then constructed a second polygenic score (PGS) in a way that is not possible in real-world genomics: instead of weighting the binary SNPs by their correlations with outcome, we weighted them by their actual causal properties, specifically their (unknown in actual studies of humans) biased tendency to bounce the ball either left or right. We expected that knowing the causal properties would increase the validity of the PGS, but it did not; in fact, the correlation between the "causal" PGS and the outcome was essentially zero, at $r = -.01$.

The PGS results show that complex, statistically driven systems like quincunx can induce a discrepancy between causation and prediction. The more successful PGS was not based on the inner workings of the quincunx, but rather on a summary of its aggregate tendency to produce outcomes of a particular type. If one had reason to predict quincunx outcomes, and the polygenic score replicated (an interesting exercise we will not indulge here), it might be practically useful for certain purposes. But if the scientific goal was to investigate the "biology" of the quincunx, to use variation in outcome as a means for understanding its inner workings, it would fail. Conversely, using knowledge of the inner workings to predict phenotypic outcomes would be unsuccessful.

14.3 Does This Matter?

Francis Galton, one of the great tinkerers of scientific history, invented a toy in the interest of understanding the relationship between, in Lewontin's (1974) famous phrase, the analysis of variance and the analysis of causes. We simulated Galton's toy and played with it. Like all play, our simulations reflect the reality they mimic, but like all simulations, they are ultimately under the control of their creators. We did not make any effort to have the pins in our simulated toys resemble anything biological. Why should the behavior of intentionally designed virtual toys tell us anything about the properties of evolved biological systems in the real world? Simulations of complex human processes are especially valuable because we know the correct answers, and therefore can interrogate the ability of our statistical methods to infer them. The quincunx demonstrate that it is possible to detect statistically significant correlations that bear very little relation to the underlying causal processes of the device. The simulations suggest that the causal model that is presumed to be the basis for quantitative genetic models of complex behavioral phenotypes may be fundamentally incorrect.

Some time ago, Turkheimer (2011) described the relationship between biological causes and the analysis of variance as follows:

> Complex human behavior emerges out of a hyper-complex developmental network into which individual genes and individual environmental events are inputs. The systematic causal effects of any of those inputs are lost in the developmental complexity of the network. Causal explanations of complex differences among humans are therefore not going to be found in individual genes or environments any more than explanations of plate tectonics can be found in the chemical composition of individual rocks. (p. 600)

The causal properties of individual pins are difference makers in the behavior of quincunx, but those effects are "lost in the developmental complexity of the network." The aggregate causal potency of pins can be detected collectively, either in the special case of a simulation where they are known, by using twins, or, under the right circumstances, by generating a polygenic score. The goal of using analysis of variance to reveal the "biology" of the quincunx – that is, to understand the causal properties of individual pins – is, however, a lost cause. The problem is not sample size or precision of measurement: quincunx just don't work that way.

Galton and his followers, especially his disciple R. A. Fisher, were convinced that because Mendelian genetic processes had consequences for the variance–covariance structures of observed phenotypes, the converse would also turn out to be true: that one could use covariance matrices to infer the biologically causal underpinnings of complex phenotypes. The more than 100 years since Fisher (1918) represent an extended lesson in how overoptimistic this assumption was. You can see why Galton, Fisher, and those who came after them were so sorely tempted: Fisherian quantitative genetics works well in plants and animals on the farm, where many elements of the genotype–environment–phenotype covariance matrix can be zeroed out or manipulated experimentally. Even in humans, analysis of variance doesn't simply fail; in humans or quincunx, the average relationships among variation in phenotype, genotype, and environment, as quantified by the variance ratios of classical quantitative genetics, are real enough. But the hope of proceeding to the next step, from what has recently been called "thin" causal knowledge (Madole & Harden, 2022) to something meatier, remains elusive.

As distant as simulated quincunx may seem from the genesis of behavior in human beings, we contend that their structure is potentially closer to behavioral reality than models that treat the causal effects of SNPs or genes as additive. Step back a moment to an example Turkheimer (1998) has pursued for 25 years, including in previous chapters in this series (Turkheimer, 2015): How can it be that human marital status is heritable, in fact just as heritable as familiar objects of genetic scrutiny like intelligence or schizophrenia? It is insufficient to state the obvious fact that there are no divorce genes, in the literal sense that marital status is "highly polygenic." The problem runs deeper than that. To help understand the heritability of divorce, we will introduce a new distinction, between *outcome heritability* and *essence heritability*. The novel part of this distinction is outcome heritability, so we will start there.

Figure 14.9 illustrates the path that someone might follow to their eventual divorce. It is like a ball bouncing down a quincunx, turned on its side for ease of labeling. It begins at conception. Cells in the blastocyst reproduce in ways that regulate the eventual symmetry of the finished organism. Physical symmetry affects attractiveness; prenatal development can impact metabolism and preferences such as alcohol or excitement. After birth, physical appearance and relationships with family members play a role in attachment processes throughout life. As children grow into adolescents, they form different types of relationships that shape their feelings toward commitment. These experiences lead to long-term partnerships or marriages that may succeed or fail based on previous influences. Some people, at the bottom of the quincunx, wind up in the DIVORCE bin; others do not. There is no way to describe this process

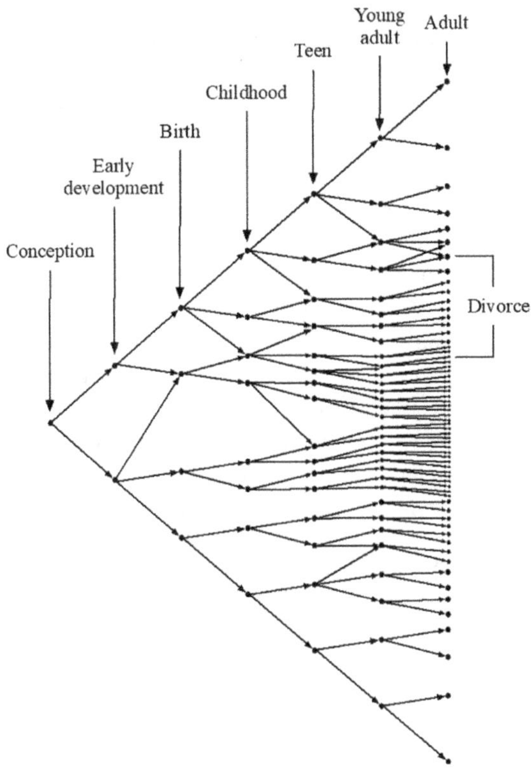

Figure 14.9 The complex developmental pathway between conception and divorce.

without simplifying it by many orders of magnitude. Characterizing it the best we know how would be to summarize the psychology and sociology of marital status, in all its nonexperimental complexity and uncertainty.

Such an uncontrolled, behaviorally driven process might seem the very opposite of what we usually think of as genetic, but consider this: throughout this complex developmental journey from blastocyst to couples therapy, genes subtly influence developmental bounces at every pin in the process, making it slightly more or less likely that a person will be nudged in the direction of an eventual divorce. Not the same genes at every pin: different genes come into play each time, for different reasons. Environmental main effects and gene-by-environment interactions complicate genetic effects at every moment of development. Probably none of the genes have anything discernable to do with the eventual outcome of interest. One might think that all this developmental complexity – different genes influencing different outcomes in different ways, in the presence of considerable randomness, with nothing pointing to our eventual interest in marital dissolution – would be sufficient to completely erase any associations between individual variants and marital outcomes, but that turns out not to be the case. Tiny, contingent, unsystematic genotype–phenotype correlations remain, enough to make marital status detectably heritable within particular populations, and enough to produce a handful of significant SNP associations if the sample is sufficiently gargantuan.

As we learned from the quincunx, a key characteristic of outcome heritability is that the association between genotypic and phenotypic variation is only detectable in the aggregate. "Aggregate" in this sense refers to both the genetic variants and the phenotypes. Individual variants that play some sort of role along the developmental pathway may retain some attenuated correlation with phenotype, but in the quincunx, the correspondence between the causal properties and the statistical associations was essentially zero, even in sign. From the phenotypic perspective, aggregate statistics tells us something about the analysis of variance in populations but nothing about analysis of causes in individuals, as explained by Lewontin (1974). This latter point applied to quincunx was the main theme of Kaplan and Turkheimer (2021).

The crucial consequence of outcome heritability for psychiatric genetics is that there is no image of divorce at a genetic level of analysis, and no collection of variants that corresponds to divorce in any way. As we noted, it is insufficient to say that marital status is "highly polygenic," as though there were many genes with small but countable and specifiable causal effects on the outcome. Instead, marital status is an emergent outcome of a developmental system in which the molar genetic units bear no straightforward causal relationship with the outcome, heritability notwithstanding. The typical human genetic distinction between "causal variants" and "noncausal variants" with which they are in linkage disequilibrium is meaningless: *there are no causal variants for divorce*. This gloomy (from the point of view of ambitious scientists) prospect will not be mitigated by massive samples or detailed phenotyping of marriages: it is built into the nature of human development and the ethical restrictions on experimental manipulation of humans that we place on ourselves.

Contrast all this with essence heritability, which is the model derived from medical genetics that scientists have been trying to force on complex behavior for the last 100 years. In previous chapters in this series, Turkheimer (2017) has discussed Huntington's disease (HD) as an example of what we are now calling essence heritability. The symptoms of HD are not an emergent property of a complex developmental system to which 4p16.3 happens to be an input. The presence of the HD variant is the first step in a causal chain, not a simple chain but a specifiable one, that results in the disorder. There *is* an image of HD at a genetic level of analysis. We can talk in meaningful ways about HD without even referring to its clinical signs and symptoms: the presence of the variant is sufficient, and an individual (of sufficient age) carrying the gene but without clinical symptoms would be an anomaly requiring explanation. Such is not the case for divorce, and the difference is not simply a matter of genetic effect size: divorce is divorce because it is defined as divorce, at the level of outcomes. There is no genetic entity, at any penetrance, that corresponds to marital status in a way that would allow scientists to use it as a genetic proxy for the phenotype.

The expectation that outcome-heritable complex phenotypes will turn out to have systematic genetic causes has a name: genetic essentialism. This returns us to Radick's history. Galton, like almost every behavioral geneticist who has come after him, was mystified by his intellectual opponents finding him objectionably hereditarian and determinist. He knew that the environment mattered. He knew that the relationship between genotype (as he understood it) and phenotype was probabilistic, not deterministic. He knew about the complexity of development. He invented the quincunx to illustrate these things. However, once again like most behavior geneticists who followed in his tradition, Galton was a genetic essentialist.

In an ironic sense, Galton's interest in eugenics (another invention of his) shielded him from the consequences of his essentialism. Ignoring for a moment the moral depravity of eugenics, among the various real-world activities in which a geneticist might engage, selective breeding can be conducted in the relative absence of any underlying genetic essence. Artificial selection for human personality traits (noting again that this is an unavoidably horrific possibility) would no doubt "work" in the limited sense that it would produce changes in the mean value of the phenotype. Darwin derived the theory of natural selection from the practice of artificial selection, which agriculturalists had been conducting for thousands of years with no scientific knowledge of genetics. But Galton was not only a eugenicist, a practitioner of the dark art of human breeding. He was also a scientist who wanted to elucidate the nature of genetic explanation, prone to make proclamations like, "I propose to show . . . that a man's natural abilities are derived by inheritance, under exactly the same limitations as are the form and physical features of the whole organic world" (1869, p. 1).

This essentialist contention is called into question by the existence of outcome heritability. Is it the case that differences in marital status are "derived by inheritance"? Can they be studied using the same scientific methods applied to "the form and physical features of the whole organic world?" Galton's opponents did not object to the notion that genetics bore some distant statistical relationship to human behavior; they objected to the idea that the genesis of complex human behaviors held the same form as the genesis of physical characteristics in lower animals. They objected to the essentialism that is required for a scientifically optimistic assessment of the likelihood that the "genetic basis" of statistically heritable human phenotypes will ever be unraveled by scientists.

Among the various domains of human behavior genetics, psychiatric genetics is particularly prone to essentialism, for understandable reasons. When medical genetics works well, it does so by discovering the genetic essences underlying disease phenotypes, which can then be analyzed scientifically and applied therapeutically. Psychiatric disease causes horrific suffering, and it is natural to hope that medical genetic essentialism will work for depression as it has worked for, say, cystic fibrosis. If psychiatric disease is an outcome, however, more like divorce than like cystic fibrosis, the future of scientific psychiatry will look more like sociology than neuropathology, and the future of psychiatric practice will consist of either post hoc tracing of paths through the quincunx in the manner of the psychotherapist, or palliative pharmaceuticals applied to symptoms after the developmental process has run its course. Neither of these possibilities is anything to be ashamed of, but they are not the kind of decisive scientific breakthroughs promised by Galtonian genetic essentialism.

Lest this chapter be read in an outdated nature–nurture sense of genes versus environment, we should be clear that isn't our point. Our designation of the quincunx pins as SNPs is, in nature–nurture terms, completely arbitrary. They might as well be individual environmental events, and the same conclusions would apply. "The environment" is detectable as an aggregate variance component, but attempts to break it down into discernable causal events have never been successful (Turkheimer & Waldron, 2000). How should one raise one's children to ensure that they have a happy marriage? There is no answer to that question: environmental essentialism fails just as certainly as genetic essentialism does. Scientists are no longer troubled by the futility of essential environmental explanations of complex outcomes, having given up on them long before the possibility of genetic explanation presented itself. Indeed, the failure of environmental social science and psychiatry to provide definitive explanations of human behavioral outcomes is a deep motivation for the undeterrable persistence of contemporary genetic (or otherwise biological) endeavors. What else is a well-meaning scientist to do?

The question posed by psychiatric genetics is not, as has been assumed since Galton, genes versus environment. It is about whether the observed heritability of psychiatric entities is the result of essential causal pathways upward from the genotype, as opposed to being an emergent property of developmental systems that cannot be reduced to genetic processes, not even incompletely. The opposite of *genetic* is *phenotypic*, not *environmental.* To make matters even more confusing, nongenetic phenotypic outcomes are "heritable" – indeed, almost universally so. The question facing psychiatric genetics is whether depression and schizophrenia are more like HD or more like divorce. This question was not resolved by twin heritabilities, and our simulations suggest that it will not be resolved by genome-wide significant SNP hits, SNP heritabilities, or polygenic scores.

Framing the question in this way leaves room for well-intended scientists to disagree about the likelihood of success of different scientific approaches applied to different psychiatric disorders. Although it is difficult to proceed from correlational observations of associations between SNPs or genes and psychiatric phenotypes, as is often the case in human behavioral science, it is not completely impossible. Scientists have used well-established understanding of gene expression and other forms of biological annotation to demonstrate that genetic variation associated with psychiatric disorders is expressed in the brain at greater than chance levels (Skene et al., 2018), and one cannot rule out the possibility that models of this kind will one day lead to knowledge of essential gene–brain–behavior pathways. Some areas of psychiatric genetics, especially involving autism and psychotic disorders, have moved on from documenting the small effects of common variants with GWAS to the identification of the larger effects of rarer variants and mutations (Howrigan et al., 2020; Sekar et al., 2016). Will understanding such rare but potent variation lead to essential biological knowledge, or even to the Holy Grail of biogenetically informed therapeutics?

The answer is: we don't know. Our goal is not to denigrate the efforts of scientists who are convinced that there are genetic explanations for why some individuals suffer from psychiatric diseases. As we have said, given the great success of medical genetics, the expectation that sooner or later the biogenetic paradigm is bound to yield results for psychiatry is easy to understand. Simulations of phenomena that lack conclusive scientific explanations cannot demonstrate that a particular approach will never yield results; they can, however, demonstrate that an approach cannot be *assumed* to be on the right path. If some psychiatric categories are more like outcomes than essences, with quincunx-like causal structures, then the obstacles to biogenetic explanation are not sample size or allelic frequency; the problem is that some behavioral constructs have no genetic representation for scientists to discover.

REFERENCES

Fisher, R. A. (1918). The correlation between relatives on the supposition of Mendelian inheritance. *Earth and Environmental Science Transactions of the Royal Society of Edinburgh, 52*(2), 399–433.

Galton, F. (1869). *Hereditary genius: An inquiry into its laws and consequences.* D. Appleton.

(1872). On blood-relationship. *Proceedings of the Royal Society of London, 20*(130–138), 394–402.

(1889). *Natural inheritance* (Vol. 42). Macmillan.

Howrigan, D. P., Rose, S. A., Samocha, K. E., Fromer, M., Cerrato, F., Chen, W. J., ... & Neale, B. M. (2020). Exome sequencing in schizophrenia-affected parent–offspring trios reveals risk conferred by protein-coding de novo mutations. *Nature Neuroscience, 23*(2), 185–193.

Kaplan, J. M., & Turkheimer, E. (2021). Galton's Quincunx: Probabilistic causation in developmental behavior genetics. *Studies in History and Philosophy of Science, 88*, 60–69.

Lewontin, R. C. (1974). Annotation: The analysis of variance and the analysis of causes. *American Journal of Human Genetics, 26*(3), 400.

Madole, J. W., & Harden, K. P. (2022). Building causal knowledge in behavior genetics. *The Behavioral and Brain Sciences, 46*, e182. https://doi.org/10.1017/S0140525X22000681.

Radick, G. (2023). *Disputed inheritance: The battle over Mendel and the future of biology.* University of Chicago Press.

Sekar, A., Bialas, A. R., De Rivera, H., Davis, A., Hammond, T. R., Kamitaki, N., ... & McCarroll, S. A. (2016). Schizophrenia risk from complex variation of complement component 4. *Nature, 530*(7589), 177–183.

Skene, N. G., Bryois, J., Bakken, T. E., Breen, G., Crowley, J. J., Gaspar, H. A., ... & Hjerling-Leffler, J. (2018). Genetic identification of brain cell types underlying schizophrenia. *Nature Genetics, 50*(6), 825–833.

Turkheimer, E. (1998). Heritability and biological explanation. *Psychological Review, 105*(4), 782.

(2011). Commentary: Variation and causation in the environment and genome. *International Journal of Epidemiology, 40*(3), 598–601.

Turkheimer E. (2015). The nature of nature. In K. S. Kendler & J. Parnas (Eds.), *Philosophical issues in psychiatry III: The nature and sources of historical change* (pp. 227–244). Oxford University Press.

(2017). The hard question in psychiatric nosology. In K. S. Kendler & J. Parnas (Eds.), *Philosophical issues in psychiatry IV: Psychiatric nosology* (pp. 27–44). Oxford University Press.

Turkheimer, E., & Waldron, M. (2000). Nonshared environment: A theoretical, methodological, and quantitative review. *Psychological Bulletin, 126*(1), 78–108.

CHAPTER 15

Commentary on Turkheimer and Kaplan's "Stalking the Wild Quincunx"

Steven E. Hyman

In their chapter, Eric Turkheimer and Jonathan Kaplan assert that Galton's quincunx "unifies discrete and continuous, binary and normally distributed, random and deterministic, predetermined and epigenetic." What starts as an anodyne recitation of antinomies, quickly raises questions about how they intend to use the quincunx model as they move from statistical couplets to the contrast of "predetermined and epigenetic." In so doing, Turkheimer and Kaplan seem to reduce epigenetics, a diverse and complex set of biological processes, into a synecdoche standing in for all nongenetic factors (stochastic and environmental) in development (the pins of the quincunx). Epigenetics refers to a complex (and variably reversible) group of biological processes that regulate gene expression. Epigenetic mechanisms are involved in gametogenesis, the earliest stages of embryonic development, and throughout life. In early development, chromatin (complexes of DNA with histones and other proteins) packages DNA and forms the basis for epigenetic regulation mediated by chemical modifications of the chromatin. Early on, epigenetics establishes cell fate and cell identities; later in development and through postnatal life, epigenetic mechanisms transduce diverse physiological signals that may originate in the body or in the environment to reversibly regulate gene expression. Epigenetic regulation of gene expression represents one of many biological mechanisms (including such important processes as learning and memory) that utilize and build on genomic information to support an organism's development, homeostasis, adaptation, and change. In so doing these processes, along with chance, increase the heterogeneity ("individuality") of organisms and significantly degrade the possibility of making precise long-term predictions from DNA sequences. From genetics alone we cannot predict with certainty whether a person will suffer from a mental illness, finish graduate school, or get divorced. Even the effects of Mendelian alleles, such as the precise age at which a carrier will develop Huntington's disease (Genetic Modifiers of Huntington's Disease

Consortium, 2015), are not deterministically predictable in the context of modifier genes, chance, and additional layers of regulation.

As a highly reductive metaphor, the quincunx does not capture these or other levels of integration and, I fear, may do a disservice to pedagogy by neglecting brain function and other aspects of biology such as learning and memory that must surely play an important role in cognition and behavioral outcomes. The complexity and heterogeneity of the human brain are staggering at each of its different scales: for example, the human brain has more than 5,000 relatively distinct cell types documented so far among its approximately 80 billion neurons and 80 billion glia, hundreds of trillions of synapses that are morphologically diverse and subject to experience dependent plasticity, and a diverse multitude of circuits that support the complex patterns of firing that underlie neural computation and thus cognition and behavior. Given this complexity across scales, it is unsurprising that emergent properties are ubiquitous within and across levels of integration. Reductionist experiments and simple model systems are necessary for progress in science by limiting the number of variables that need to be controlled for and improving intelligibility for our finite human understanding. But such experimental and explanatory simplification and reductionism are tactical; it is not a philosophical goal of neuroscience. It is widely understood by working scientists that there is no sensible epistemic framework in which reduction to elementary particles provides a useful explanation of how one fits a peg into an aptly dimensioned hole. In biology or medicine, an experimentalist in a tactically reductionist mode might add or activate chosen inputs in a well-selected model system or in a human cohort (such as a transgene inserted into a mouse genome, an optogenetic stimulus delivered to an engineered model organism, or a psychotherapy administered in a clinical trial) and then measure chosen outputs (such as anatomic differences, cellular physiology, animal behavior, or human symptom relief). Experimental or observational tools that would permit investigators to follow causation across scales – for example, from transgene to mouse behavior or from therapeutic intervention to human symptom reduction – are often lacking. Thus, intervening levels of causation are often consigned to black box status. While recognizing the need for what I have called tactical reductionism and simple model systems in science – Turkheimer and Kaplan's use of the quincunx exemplifies the use of a simplified model presumably intended as an educational aid. The recognition that stochasticity, heterogeneity, complexity, and emergence are ubiquitous features of biology means that no adequately trained biologist should try to make detailed, deterministic predictions of human outcomes from an individual's DNA sequences. It should also be clear that, given the many tens of millions of human interindividual DNA sequence differences, chance events during development (such as somatic mutations or differences in cell migration), and a seemingly infinite diversity of exposomes, attempts to place people into homogeneous, well-bounded groups or predict outcomes at the population level will always fall short of machine-like precision.

The use of essentializing heuristics characteristic of human cognition may increase processing speed (presumably in the service of survival), but at the cost of distorting the world rather than capturing it veridically (Kahneman & Tversky, 1996; Tversky & Kahneman, 1974). In short, if we need the quincunx to ward off Laplace's (1814) demon, as Turkheimer and Kaplan correctly suspect many people do, it is because we have failed as educators to overcome the essentialist distortions too often applied without correction to genetics, putative diagnostic categories of mental illness, and human groups. A currently emerging example that may illustrate Turkheimer and Kaplan's concerns while also illustrating several cognitive distortions and most importantly being deserving of moral concern is the use of polygenic scores (PGS) for both medical and nonmedical phenotypes to select embryos for implantation via in vitro fertilization. Preimplantation genetic diagnosis is in standard use to detect aneuploidy or alleles for serious monogenic disorders such as cystic fibrosis – often the reason that a family might opt for in vitro fertilization. There are now companies offering to select among embryos available for implantation using PGS for complex diseases, including schizophrenia (Capalbo, 2024; Turley et al., 2021), and for nonmedical phenotypes that have included the use of an educational attainment PGS (Turley et al., 2021). In sum, it would seem timely to improve education about genetics and biology. Perhaps one useful step would be to delay the teaching of Mendel until well after students learn about population genetics and natural variation – and then Mendelian inheritance could be taught as an exceptional limiting case.

In Turkheimer and Kaplan's zeal to quash belief that 21st-century genetics could successfully revive the credibility of deterministic prediction worthy of the 18th century (De La Mettrie, 1748; Laplace, 1814), I worry that they may have lost sight of the central goals of modern psychiatric genetics and their feasibility. From the point of view of funders and investigators, the critical goal is to provide otherwise inaccessible clues to disease mechanisms, which in turn would enable much needed advances in treatment development. Psychiatric genetics, including the PGS and related risk calculators, also have useful roles in risk prediction, but only if understood to be probabilistic – often weakly so, with current datasets – and applied in the context of other sources of information for a well-specified purpose (see Kendler et al., 2023 for an example). Such predictive applications in research, which are not yet ready for clinical application in psychiatry – albeit closer to clinical use in cardiovascular medicine (Vassy et al., 2023) – lend no support to misguided and futile attempts to make deterministic predictions about cognitive, behavioral, or mental illness phenotypes in individuals or groups. The importance of psychiatric genetics for the elucidation of disease mechanisms is highlighted by the obstacles facing other approaches to their identification. These obstacles include the fiendish complexity and extraordinary heterogeneity of human brains, both in terms of structure and function, and the challenge of relating basic neurobiology to mental illness phenotypes. An additional hurdle results from the inaccessibility of living human brain tissue in contrast to essentially all other organ pathologies, which can be biopsied to study illness (Hyman, 2012). However, the substantial contribution of DNA sequence variation to risk of mental illness signifies that clues to the mechanisms of these devastating illnesses can be found in human genomes. Given our ignorance concerning mechanisms of pathogenesis, an important scientific benefit of unbiased, large-scale genetics is that it is agnostic to biological hypotheses. Additionally, given brain complexity across scales and thus the importance of emergent properties along with the ubiquity of recurrent circuits in the brain, genetics has the scientific advantage of being proof against reverse causation. Sequence variation that is convincingly statistically associated with a phenotype can, if carefully interpreted, be considered to play a causal role, which, unlike all other biological correlates of mental disorders, cannot be the result of illness, adaptations to it, or treatment effects. As a result, genetic associations provide scientists with traction on which of many plausible biological mechanisms are causally involved in pathogenesis and thus deserving of further investigation. Without genetics, biological investigation into mental illness lacks a convincing anchor in nature, leaving the search for mechanisms and better therapeutics reliant on serendipity and speculation (Hyman, 2012, 2023).

Possible interpretations of genetic clues to disease mechanisms cannot be resolved only with genetic data. Given that most of the approximately 21,000 genes in the human genome serve multiple functions in multiple cell types, insights into disease mechanisms will require integration with other biological findings. In that context I was baffled by Turkheimer and Kaplan's claim that "few of the traits we recognize as genetic reveal anything about their biological basis in meiosis and segregation." First, referring to a trait as genetic does not seem to me a meaningful scientific term; perhaps we can think of it as folk biology. To understand the function of genes in specific biological contexts, including disease, requires that we understand the roles of their gene products (RNAs or proteins) in such contexts as biochemical pathways, molecular complexes, or cellular structures. A narrow focus on meiosis and segregation even for fully penetrant disease alleles such as identified in familial Alzheimer's disease (FAD) has led biology astray by encouraging scientists to think that they understood gene function without recognizing that they did not understand disease mechanism. Thus, amyloid beta, overproduced in FAD, has often been treated as a pathogenic molecule that should be removed from the brain at any disease stage in both FAD and late-onset AD. While the relevant mechanisms are still not well understood, amyloid beta may contribute to pathogenesis more indirectly by inducing tau (which produces neurofibrillary tangles) and neuroinflammation (which likely contributes to dementia through synapse elimination). Even the rudimentary hypothesis on the disease-related functions of amyloid cannot be gleaned from patterns of meiosis and segregation.

It is even more difficult to gain disease-relevant mechanistic insights for all common psychiatric disorders because risk is highly polygenic. Examples of success demonstrate the importance of integrating genetic and biological datasets, especially those derived from well-designed experiments performed at genomic scales, for example large-scale single-cell transcriptomic and epigenomic analyses from samples donated by affected and unaffected individuals, whether postmortem brains or peripheral blood mononuclear cells reprogrammed into induced pluripotent stem cells (iPSCs) (McCarroll, Feng, & Hyman, 2014; McCarroll & Hyman, 2013). A successful recent analysis that exemplifies integration of different experimental approaches at scale linked the polygenic risk of cardiovascular disease with cell programs in endothelial cells, which form the innermost layer of blood vessels (Schnitzler et al., 2024). The resulting dataset was based on integration of epigenetic analyses with systematic perturbation of DNA sequences within single cells. For psychiatric disorders, single-cell analyses of transcriptomes and epigenomes have been performed for millions of cells in postmortem brains with and without a history of schizophrenia, and other psychiatric disorders have provided well-used datasets. Since most postmortem samples are donated decades after onset of psychiatric disorders, with intervening years characterized by exposure to drugs and other environmental perturbations, these single-cell datasets are integrated not only with genetics but ideally with data from complementary methods. For example, it is possible to reprogram frozen mononuclear blood cells donated by affected and unaffected individuals into iPSCs and, if desired, to genetically engineer them to express or silence particular alleles. These cells can be reprogrammed into diverse neuronal or glial cell types that can then be experimentally manipulated. These technologies do not make the problem of identifying disease-relevant mechanism straightforward, but they put psychiatry shoulder to shoulder with the rest of medicine in a shared quest to turn genetic data into biological insights.

Useful biological clues often depend on the identification of causal variation within a disease-implicated genetic locus, but it is also possible to gain useful insights without such identification by observing how polygenic risk is concentrated in particular cell types or biological processes. In short, we need not reduce each common variant to a known individual "Lego block" in a pathway to exploit important clues from genetics. In a recent study using postmortem prefrontal cortex from 191 donors including people affected by schizophrenia and controls, polygenic risk for schizophrenia was found to be concentrated not in genes that define cellular identities, but in a coordinated program of gene expression between excitatory neurons and astrocytes that is required for the maintenance and plasticity of synapses. Reductions in this coordinated program in schizophrenia converges with other data showing decreased production of synaptic components in schizophrenia (Ling et al., 2024). These findings are being further investigated in a complementary experimental system that compares patient and control neurons in vitro (Pietiläinen et al., 2023).

I hope this commentary affords Turkheimer and Kaplan some happiness. Deterministic Laplacian prediction, refuted for the physical universe by the stochasticity of quantum mechanics, is equally impossible for cognition, behavior, and mental illness based on genetics because of complexity, stochasticity, and emergent properties at multiple scales. At the same time, the failure of simple mechanical determinism does not rule out the possibility of using genetics – indeed, our best hope for biological clues – to gain useful insight into biological mechanisms of psychiatric disorders. Although the path is exceedingly difficult, recent experience demonstrates that success is possible, and gives hope for biomarkers and better treatments.

REFERENCES

Capalbo, A., de Wert, G., Mertes, H., Klausner, L., Coonen, E., et al. (2024). Screening embryos for polygenic disease risk: A review of epidemiological, clinical, and ethical considerations. *Human Reproduction Update, 30*, 529–557.

De La Mettrie, J. O. (1912 [1748]). *Man a machine* (G. C. Bussey, Transl.). Open Court Press.

Genetic Modifiers of Huntington's Disease Consortium. (2015) Identification of genetic factors that modify clinical onset of Huntington's disease. *Cell, 162*, 516–526.

Hyman, S. E. (2012). Revolution stalled. *Science Translational Medicine, 4*, 1–5. https://doi.org/10.1126/scitranslmed.3003142

(2023). The biology of mental disorders: Progress at last. *Daedalus Fall, 2023*, 186–208.

Kahneman, D., & Tversky, A. (1996). On the reality of cognitive illusions. *Psychological Review, 103*, 582–591.

Kendler, K. S., Ohlsson, H., Sundquist, J., & Sundquist, K. (2023). Relationship of gamily genetic risk score with diagnostic trajectory in a Swedish nantional sample of incident cases of major depression, bipolar disorder, other non-affective psychoses, and schizophrenia. *Journal of the American Medical Association Psychiatry, 80*, 241–249.

Laplace, Pierre Simon. (1951 [1814]). *A philosophical essay on probabilities* (F. W. Truscott & F. L. Emory, Transl.). Dover.

Ling, E., Nemesh, J., Goldman, M., Kamitaki, N., Reed, N., et al. (2024). A concerted neuron-astrocyte program declines in ageing and schizophrenia. *Nature, 627*, 604–611.

McCarroll, S. A., Feng, G., & Hyman, S. E. (2014). Genome-scale neurogenetics: Methodology and meaning. *Nature Neuroscience, 17*, 746–763.

McCarroll, S. A., & Hyman, S. E. (2013). Progress in genetics of polygenic brain disorders: Significant new challenges for neurobiology. *Neuron, 80*, 578–587.

Pietiläinen, O., Trehan, A., Meyer, D., Mitchell, J., Tegtmeyer, M., et al. (2023). Astrocytic cell adhesion genes linked to schizophrenia correlate with synaptic programs in neurons. *Cell Reports, 42*, 111988.

Schnitzler, G. R., Kan, H., Fang, S., Angom, R. S., Lee-Kim, V. S., et al. (2024). Convergence of coronary artery disease genes onto endothelial cell programs. *Nature, 626*, 79–87.

Turley, P., Meyer, M. N., Wang, N., Cesarini, D., Hammonds, E., Martin, A. R., et al. (2021). Problems with using polygenic scores to select embryos. *New England Journal of Medicine, 385*, 78–86.

Tversky, A., & Kahneman, D. (1974). Judgment under uncertainty: Heuristics and biases. *Science, 18*, 1124–1131.

Vassy, J. L., Posner, D. C, Ho, Y.-L., et al. (2023). Cardiovascular disease risk assessment using traditional risk factors and polygenic risk scores in the million veteran program. *Journal of the American Medical Association Cardiology, 8*, 564–574.

Section 6

CHAPTER 16

Introduction to Heckers's "Causal Inference in Psychiatric Neuroimaging"

Kenneth S. Kendler

I recall the enthusiasm with which magnetic resonance imaging was greeted by the field of psychiatry in the 1980s, the stunning quality of the images, almost magical. This technology fed into the long desire by our field to have an innovative technology that would, in one fell swoop, solve the main problems of our field, particularly etiology and diagnosis. I recall claims such has "Now we can do neuropathology on living people," "Now we have a tool to solve the mind–body problem," and "It is now just a matter of time until we find the causes of schizophrenia." A decade or more earlier it had been monoamine neurotransmitters (serotonin, norepinephrine, and dopamine) as the revolutionary scientific breakthrough, and one or two decades later it would be molecular genetics. In each case, the "hype cycle" (Dedehayir & Steinert, 2016) produced a crest of zealous excitement (and dramatic overpromising) followed by a period of disillusionment and then some stabilization and emerging maturity. The field came to recognize that the application had merits but the problems – very hard ones – of psychiatric diagnosis and etiology were not going to yield easily. Of note, the field of psychiatric neuroimaging, although now 40-plus years old, underwent another recent round of substantial criticism about the use of underpowered sample sizes (Marek et al., 2022) and inadequate corrections for multiple testing.

In contrast to the historical ups and downs of this field, Hecker's essay is a thoughtful and sober evaluation of the field of psychiatric imaging as it approaches middle age. He advocates for a quite useful approach to the questions of causality by dividing the field into three major and largely distinct research paradigms, each of which is seeking to address a fundamentally different question: (1) establish illness markers, (2) improve neuroscience models of psychiatric disorders, and (3) map psychological events onto brain states.

The first goal is the most pragmatic: finding some index of brain pathology that might be responsible for the psychiatric presentation and require treatment. Here neuroimaging is treated like any other laboratory examination, such as obtaining blood tests for thyroid dysfunction, liver disease, or an electrolyte imbalance that might explain the disturbed mental functioning. Such tests are part of the process of "differential diagnosis" in which psychiatrists try to rule out medical or neurological causes of the mental illness they are seeing. As Heckers points out, the value of neuroimaging screening of cases of psychiatric illness is under active debate. For example, a recent report from the American College of Emergency Physicians reviewed the available literature that addressed the following question: "In the adult patient with new-onset psychosis without focal neurologic deficit, should brain imaging be obtained acutely?" (Brown et al., 2017). They concluded there was insufficient high-quality evidence to support this recommendation in contrast to the standard emergency room practice of obtaining brain imaging studies of patients presenting with an acute onset of focal neurologic signs and symptoms.

The second goal involves using imaging methods as a way to test neuroscience-based disease models of psychiatric illness – a form of etiologic research. As noted, this continues an effort dating back to the middle of the 19th century – based then almost entirely on postmortem studies – to clarify the brain basis of psychiatric disorders. Heckers notes the substantial improvement in causal inference related to methods of brain stimulation. But the progress has been slow, with persistent questions of whether the scientific "level" at which psychiatric illness originates can be well assessed by current imaging technology. Heckers illustrates this line of inquiry in his own research career investigating the role of the hippocampus in diverse psychiatric disorders.

The third goal, which expands beyond the boundaries of psychiatric science and touches on one of the great questions within philosophy is the mind–body problem. This involves the direct study of the mind–brain relationships using imaging technology. As Heckers notes, more than 20 years ago, a correlation was first noted between the subjective report of the experience of auditory hallucinations, typically among patients with schizophrenia, and increased blood flow in regions in the temporal lobe such as the superior temporal gyri, which subserve speech functions in neurotypical individuals (Lennox et al., 2000). Note that the causal interpretation of this correlation is problematic and can directly involve various theories of mind–brain function. For example, the dual-aspect theory – that mind and brain are different reflections of the same underlying phenomenon – would posit that the subjective experience of the "voices" and the increased blood flow reflecting increased neural activity would reflect the same underlying process. By contrast, an eliminative materialist perspective would argue that the brain dysfunctions are primary, and the subjective experience of voices is a "dead end" consequence of the brain processes with no causal efficacy.

We see in the following chapter the work of a psychiatric scientist who brings both extensive practical experience in this important research area and conceptual sophistication in regards to the methodological, historical, and philosophical issues involved in such research.

REFERENCES

Brown, M. D., Byyny, R., Diercks, D. B., Gemme, S. R., Gerardo, C. J., Godwin, S. A., Hahn, S. A., Hatten, B. W., Haukoos, J. S., & Ingalsbe, G. S. (2017). Clinical policy: Critical issues in the diagnosis and management of the adult psychiatric patient in the emergency department. *Annals of Emergency Medicine, 69*(4), 480–498.

Dedehayir, O., & Steinert, M. (2016). The hype cycle model: A review and future directions. *Technological Forecasting and Social Change, 108*, 28–41.

Lennox, B. R., Park, S. B. G., Medley, I., Morris, P. G., & Jones, P. B. (2000). The functional anatomy of auditory hallucinations in schizophrenia. *Psychiatry Research: Neuroimaging, 100*(1), 13–20.

Marek, S., Tervo-Clemmens, B., Calabro, F. J., Montez, D. F., Kay, B. P., Hatoum, A. S., Donohue, M. R., Foran, W., Miller, R. L., & Hendrickson, T. J. (2022). Reproducible brain-wide association studies require thousands of individuals. *Nature, 603*(7902), 654–660.

CHAPTER 17

Causal Inference in Psychiatric Neuroimaging

Stephan Heckers

Psychiatric neuroimaging is the application of in vivo structural and functional brain imaging methods in the study of persons diagnosed with a psychiatric disorder. Here I explore how these methods can be used to make causal inferences.

Clinicians and neuroscientists have long been searching for the causes of psychiatric disorders. The prospect that mental illness can be explained by abnormalities in the brain was a founding principle for academic psychiatrists, as they established themselves as an alternative to alienists, who merely managed the mentally ill in asylums (Engstrom, 2004). Much of the early brain research in psychiatry was anatomical, applying the clinicopathological model that had worked so well for the rest of medicine: clinical syndromes can be explained by findings in postmortem examinations of the body. When imaging the living human brain became possible, psychiatric researchers embraced the new technology, hoping that it could further elucidate the structural and functional neuroanatomy of psychiatric disorders.

But can neuroimaging be used to study the causes of psychiatric disorders? More specifically, can the in vivo study of brain structure and function be employed to make causal inferences about psychiatric signs and symptoms, defined as abnormalities of behavior and mental states? Do we use neuroimaging methods to study causes (at the level of the brain), or do we use them to study relationships of brain structure and function that cause psychiatric disorders?

How does neuroimaging compare to randomized clinical trials and genetic studies, which allow for strong causal inferences? Initial neuroimaging study designs were cross-sectional and provided only correlational evidence. More recently, neuroimaging methods have been used in cohorts studied over time and in the context of interventions, which have strengthened the inferences that can be drawn from brain images in persons diagnosed with a mental illness (Siddiqi et al., 2022).

The chapter has four parts. After a brief historical introduction, I first pose a question: Why do psychiatrists image the human brain at all? Clinical psychiatry is concerned with abnormal mental states, and current psychiatric nosology is not based on a mechanistic understanding of the human brain. Therefore, the value of studying brain images of persons with a mental illness needs to be defined first. Second, I will show that researchers are using neuroimaging tools to pursue three very different goals. While the techniques are similar, they aim for different – at times conflicting – inferences. Third, I will outline how the three different types of psychiatric neuroimaging studies pursue distinct aspects of causality in the study of psychiatric disorders. These aspects of causality differ in their level of explanation and in their application for clinical practice. Fourth, I will explore the evolution of causal inference testing in psychiatric neuroimaging with one example, specifically the study of the hippocampus in psychiatric disorders.

I will conclude that much of current psychiatric neuroimaging does not study the causes of psychiatric disorders. As a consequence, it has limited value in the triaging and staging of patients and is usually not included in making treatment decisions. However, the prospect of embedding neuroimaging methods in intervention trials and in the experimental dissection of behavior has the promise to reveal causal relationships between brain and abnormal behavior / mental states.

17.1 Brief History

In his 1880 lecture, “Regarding the Scientific Viewpoint in Psychiatry,” Carl Wernicke proposed that the identification and study of neural circuits are essential for a mechanistic understanding of psychiatric disorders and should become the foundation for the development of treatments (Heckers et al., 2022). Psychiatric neuroimaging is firmly in Wernicke’s tradition of localizing mental disorder to specific circuits in the human brain, primarily the cerebral cortex. In short, psychiatric neuroimaging researchers study the brain to understand the mind (Andreasen, 1997).

Initially, Wernicke’s approach was highly successful. After he had mapped clinical subtypes of aphasia to distinct lesions of a language network in the left hemisphere of the human brain, several other neurological syndromes (e.g., agnosias and apraxias) followed in short succession. They were often derived from single (or small samples of) cases and became the foundation for behavioral neurology and clinical neuropsychology (Geschwind, 1963). With the introduction of computed tomography in the 1970s and magnetic resonance imaging in the 1980s, many of these clinico-pathological correlations, established a century earlier with post-mortem studies, were confirmed and extended (Sutterer & Tranel, 2017).

In contrast to behavioral neurology, psychiatry did not have a similarly successful history of mapping abnormal mental states to the brain. In fact, within 20 years of Wernicke's 1880 lecture, most psychiatric researchers abandoned his call to translate clinical syndromes into abnormalities of neural circuits. One of his main critics, Sigmund Freud, argued that associations of thoughts and concepts cannot be localized in the brain, but need to be defined and studied as mental phenomena (Freud, 1891). Similarly, Karl Jaspers referred to Wernicke's research agenda as "brain mythology" (Hlade, 2021).

The researchers who continued to pursue neuroanatomical and neuropathological studies in psychiatry focused primarily on schizophrenia (Heckers, 1997). But the search was not fruitful, leading the neurologist Fred Plum to declare schizophrenia the "graveyard of neuropathology" (Plum, 1972).

Therefore, the introduction of structural and functional brain imaging methods changed psychiatry more fundamentally than they did neurology and neurosurgery. For the first time it became possible to associate clinical syndromes with images of the living human brain. As a result, the *broken brain* became a metaphor for mental illness (Andreasen, 1984). The 1990s were declared the "Decade of the Brain," in large part driven by the notion that brain imaging can redefine mental illness as a brain disorder.

Despite the considerable enthusiasm for psychiatric neuroimaging, almost all of the literature reviewed here comes from psychiatric neuroimaging research, not the clinical practice of psychiatric neuroimaging. The application of radiological techniques in neurology and neurosurgery resulted in the discipline of neuroradiology. Why is there no similar practice of clinical neuroimaging in psychiatry? Here I propose that one of the reasons are the divergent goals of psychiatric neuroimaging, which are not aligned, and are at times even in conflict, with the goals of clinical psychiatry. This is where I will turn next.

17.2 Goals of Psychiatric Neuroimaging

To appreciate the value of brain imaging in the study of psychiatric disorders, especially in the study of its causes, we need to appreciate the goals and values of psychiatry. There are many schools of thought in psychiatry, ranging from a reductionist view of the mind–brain problem to a humanistic exploration of the human condition (Havens, 2005).

Psychiatric training and nosology have become more standardized, but clinical case formulations, mechanistic models, and overarching theories remain poorly aligned.

The disparate views of what psychiatry is and how it should be practiced are readily apparent when reviewing the psychiatric neuroimaging literature. I have previously proposed that psychiatric neuroimaging researchers pursue three different goals (Heckers et al., 2013):

1. Find brain abnormalities in patients diagnosed with psychiatric disorders.
2. Improve neural models of psychiatric disorders.
3. Understand the person / clinical phenotype.

These goals are often pursued by separate communities of investigators. Here I will briefly outline these three goals and then map them to distinct forms of causal inference testing.

First, neuroimaging researchers aim to associate psychiatric disorder with an abnormality of brain structure or function. Here brain images are used to distinguish normal from abnormal mental states, or to differentiate types of mental illness. Imaging findings can then be used to validate an existing nosology (e.g., schizophrenia or bipolar disorder) or to define new ones (e.g., research domain criteria [Insel et al., 2010] or hierarchical taxonomy of psychopathology [Kotov et al., 2018]). This first goal of psychiatric neuroimaging can be pursued with cross-sectional samples, in longitudinal study designs, or in the context of interventions. Most findings are purely correlational and cannot be used to make causal claims.

The majority of neuroimaging researchers pursue this first goal. They hope to find brain abnormalities that can be helpful for clinical diagnosis, for staging of disease and as outcome variables for clinical trials. As such, psychiatric neuroimaging is relevant for clinical practice. For example, brain imaging can be used to diagnose a primary medical or neurological illness in a person with an acute change in mental status.

Second, brain imaging supports mechanistic models of brain dysfunction. This goal is pursued mainly by neuroscientists who want to test a mechanistic hypothesis of mental illness. The level of explanation may be at the molecular, cellular, or systems level. For example, what is the role of the dopaminergic system in the generation of symptoms in persons with schizophrenia, substance use disorders, and attention-deficit/hyperactivity disorder? Chemical tools are now available to study dopamine release in the living human brain (Post & Sulzer, 2021). It is likely that such mechanistic studies will advance our understanding of psychiatric disorders.

Even more compelling is the combination of neuromodulation and neuroimaging. For example, the effects of localized stimulation of brain circuits with repetitive transcranial magnetic stimulation (rTMS) can be measured with neuroimaging. Some have argued that such combined rTMS–neuroimaging designs can move the strength of inferences in psychiatric neuroimaging studies from purely correlational to strong causal claims (Siddiqi et al., 2022; Ward et al., 2021).

In contrast to the first aforementioned goal, this line of neuroimaging research is not constrained by current concepts of psychiatric disorders. Rather than searching for biomarkers to validate psychiatric syndromes, the researchers can explore the neural mechanisms of normal and abnormal mental states. At the same time, the findings had no impact yet on clinical psychiatry, in contrast to neurology and neurosurgery, where neuroimaging often guides the staging of disease and the selection of treatment (Ward et al., 2021).

Third, images of the brain capture the first-person experience of mental illness. Here the goal is not to separate the normal from the abnormal, but to correlate the experience of mental phenomena with activity of the human brain. The paradigmatic approach is the symptom capture study design: a person reports an experience while being scanned, and the reports are then correlated with changes in the activity of distinct brain circuits (Allen et al., 2012). Another approach is the study of brain structure and function in individuals who differ in their reports of having experienced mental phenomena not in the moment, but in the past (e.g., traumatic events).

This line of research has not reached the same prominence as the first two goals of psychiatric neuroimaging. But it has appeal for a lay audience, since it aims to map personal experiences to the brain. For example, a community of individuals with lived experience, clinicians, and researchers have embraced functional neuroimaging as a tool to study the brain of "voice listeners" (Woods et al., 2022). As the following discussion shows, the strength of causal inferences for such studies is weak.

With a better appreciation of the three goals of psychiatric neuroimaging, we can now turn to the question: How are they related to causal inference testing?

17.3 Causal Inference in Psychiatric Neuroimaging

There are many causes of mental illness, and many methods are available to study causal relations. Only some of these methods study the brain and even fewer use in vivo structural and functional neuroimaging methods.

Table 17.1 *Causal inference in psychiatric neuroimaging.*

Goals of Psychiatric Neuroimaging	Scientific Problems of Causality
Find brain abnormality	*Control*: What to do to whom?
Separate diagnostic groups	*Prediction*: What happens next?
Improve neural models of psychiatric disorders	*Inference*: What causes or maintains mental illness?
	Explanation: What level of explanation is appropriate?
Explain clinical phenotype / Understand the person	*Reasoning*: mental illness = brain disorder?
	Explanation: How does brain give rise to mind?

Here I am following Illari and Russo (2014), who define five problems of causality in science: inference, prediction, explanation, control, and reasoning.

These are some of the questions that arise when studying the causes of psychiatric disorders with neuroimaging methods:

1. *Inference*: Does a brain lesion cause a psychiatric disorder?
2. *Prediction*: Does knowing a set of risk factors (e.g., abnormal brain development) allow us to predict what will happen in the future?
3. *Explanation*: At what level (gene, cell, circuit) does a cause explain a psychiatric disorder?
4. *Control*: Where, when, and how do we intervene, at the level of the brain, to prevent, treat, or cure a psychiatric disorder?
5. *Reasoning*: What are our assumptions in searching for the causes of psychiatric disorders? How do we understand the mind–brain problem?

In Table 17.1 I have mapped the five scientific problems to the three goals of psychiatric neuroimaging. As we will see, researchers pursuing these goals ask different questions and use different concepts of causality in their effort to link brain imaging data with psychiatric disorders.

17.4 Find Brain Abnormality

The most compelling case for causal inferences derived from psychiatric neuroimaging is the triaging of a person in a psychiatric crisis. It is common practice to obtain a structural image of the brain for a person with an acute change in mental status – that is, a person who has become delirious, confused, or psychotic. The main goal for such a neuroimaging exam is the diagnosis of a brain condition that requires prompt intervention, such as a stroke or tumor. The question "What to do?" governs the use of neuroimaging in such a triage situation, and *Control* is the scientific problem of causality here.

However, the yield of neuroimaging exams in the psychiatric triage situation is low. Here I will take as an example the scenario of a first-episode psychosis (FEP) patient. A recent meta-analysis has shown that only 5% of FEP patients show an abnormality on MRI scans (Blackman et al., 2023). Even when an abnormality is found, the response to the question "What to do?" is not a simple one (Blackman et al., 2024; Dralle & Morgan, 2024; Forbes et al., 2024; Makam, 2024).

There are at least five different clinical scenarios for an abnormal finding on a neuroimaging exam.

1. The finding is incidental and not related to the acute mental status change. For example, developmental variants or white matter hyperintensities are frequently found but do not explain the patient's condition. In this case, the finding will not change the clinical management and is usually not reported to the patient.
2. The finding is incidental but there is an unclear relationship to the current mental state of the patient. For example, an old lesion, indicating an event in the distant past, might be found but cannot explain the current change in the patient's condition.
3. The finding is likely related yet does not lead to an intervention. For example, a slowly growing tumor or a vascular malformation might be causing a change in the patient's behavior yet will not lead to an intervention, but rather to a wait-and-see approach.
4. The finding is acute and requires intervention but will turn out to not be related to the patient's condition, since the mental status will not change after the intervention.
5. The finding is an acute change and leads to an intervention that normalizes the patient's previously abnormal mental state.

It is only the last of the five scenarios that, when coupled with background knowledge about likely acute causes, allows the clinician to draw strong causal inferences from the abnormal imaging finding.

In addition to the scientific problem *Control*, there are also compelling examples for the use of neuroimaging to study *Prediction*. For example, individuals in prodromal states of a psychiatric disorder can be studied prospectively and assessed for imaging findings that can predict the emergence of the illness. Compelling examples are blood oxygenation level dependent (BOLD) signal changes in individuals with mild cognitive impairment (MCI) who will go on to develop Alzheimer's disease (Bookheimer et al., 2000) and changes in cortical gray matter in adolescents and young adults who are at high risk for the development of a psychotic disorder (Pantelis et al., 2003). Such longitudinal study designs hold great promise for a future use of psychiatric neuroimaging in clinical practice. In the end, patients and clinicians want to know: What happens next?

Individuals already diagnosed with an illness can be followed with neuroimaging exams to study the progression of the illness and the risk stratification for poor outcomes. This type of imaging is crucial for the staging of psychiatric disorders and the development of treatment algorithms (McGorry & Hickie, 2019).

In sum, the majority of psychiatric neuroimaging researchers seek to find brain abnormalities in persons diagnosed with a psychiatric disorder. The vast majority of these findings are correlational and do not allow for strong inference testing (Platt, 1964). Furthermore, the hope that neuroimaging findings can validate the current nosology of psychiatric disorders has not been realized (First et al., 2018). Despite the limited impact of psychiatric neuroimaging on the clinical practice of psychiatry, the goals are ambitious, as they target two scientific problems of causality: *Control* (what to do?) and *Prediction* (what happens next?).

17.5 Improve Neural Models of Psychiatric Disorders

In neuroscience, the levels of explanation span from molecules and synapses to mental states and complex behaviors (Churchland & Sejnowski, 1988). Initially, these levels were mapped out in two dimensions (space and time), giving each of the scientific methods its proper space (Sejnowski et al., 2014). Psychiatric neuroimaging methods were located in the lower part of spatial resolution and the mid-to-long range of temporal resolution.

Recently, this traditional two-dimensional space of neuroimaging was extended by adding a causal dimension (z-axis) to the temporal (x-axis) and spatial (y-axis) dimensions (Murray & Antonakis, 2019). A third dimension was made possible by the introduction of noninvasive brain stimulation, which allows for the localized perturbation of brain activity and the acquisition of brain imaging data before and after the intervention.

This type of neuroimaging has led to the proposal of an evidence-for-causality continuum of psychiatric neuroimaging (Siddiqi et al., 2022).

Building on the Bradford–Hill criteria, six criteria were identified for appraising causality in human brain mapping studies:

1. *Counterfactual*: Modulate brain activity: YES —> behavioral change; NO —> no change.
2. *Specificity*: Stimulate brain region A —> behavior A; stimulate brain region B —> behavior B.
3. *Experimental manipulation*: Active versus Sham condition to stimulate brain region.
4. *Dose–response*: Higher-intensity stimulation results in higher-intensity behavior.
5. *Coherence*: Stimulation of region A —> behavior A; lesion of region A —> deficit of behavior A.
6. *Reversibility*: Discontinuation of brain stimulation reverses experimentally induced behavior.

Using this scale, the strength of causal inferences derived from psychiatric neuroimaging studies ranges from a total score of 1 (very weak) to a total score of 6 (very strong). Here I will review just two examples: task-based imaging and imaging during or after brain stimulation.

Task-based imaging gets a score of 2 for *counterfactual* and *specificity*. An example is the parametric modulation of memory load during the performance of a working memory task in the scanner. The experiment allows the researcher to claim that an increasing number of items to be stored in memory is causally linked to a change of blood flow in a specific brain region.

In contrast, imaging during or after targeted stimulation of a brain region with repetitive transcranial magnetic stimulation gets a score of 5. In addition to *counterfactual* and *specificity* claimed by task-based imaging, the application of a magnetic field over a specific brain region adds three more: *experimental manipulation*, *dose–response*, and *reversibility*. When one type of neuroimaging (e.g., functional magnetic resonance imaging) in such a setting is validated by another method (e.g., chemical neuroimaging), it can also assess *coherence*, for a maximum score of 6. Taken together, in such studies, *Inference* is the main scientific problem of causality.

The recent proposal of an evidence-for-causality continuum (ranging from very weak to very strong) establishes a hierarchy of methods within psychiatric neuroimaging. But not all imaging researchers will use intervention, and there is value for different types of psychiatric neuroimaging. For example, longitudinal studies of at-risk populations are at the lower end of the evidence-for-causality continuum but still provide valuable insights.

Even at the top of such a presumed hierarchy of imaging methods, some limits remain. Let us say that (1) experimental stimulation of brain region A induces behavior A (i.e., specificity), (2) increased stimulation induces greater behavioral change (i.e., dose-response), and (3) sham control and stimulation of brain region B do not lead to behavior A (i.e., counterfactual, experimental manipulation, and specificity). Despite strong evidence (a score of 5 on the suggested evidence for causality scale), it is not clear that a single brain region governs one behavior. It is likely that even a very focal stimulation of one brain region affects multiple nodes in a network and may be causally linked to more than one behavior. And it is also likely that similar behavior can be elicited by stimulating more than one node in a given network.

A recent example is the somatotopic mapping of motor behavior in the primary motor cortex (M1), located on the precentral gyrus (Gordon et al., 2023). In contrast to the standard model (known as the *motor homunculus*; Schieber, 2001), a revised model proposes that effector and inter-effector regions are both located on the precentral gyrus and, in concert, orchestrate movements and integrate movement plans, urges, somatosensory signals, and volition. Such a revised model challenges prior notions of mapping motor behavior to M1 and psychomotor behavior to regions outside of M1 (Walther & Heckers, 2024).

17.6 Explain Clinical Phenotype / Understand the Person

Studying the neural correlates of first-person experiences is still a niche area of psychiatric neuroimaging. Compared to the other two goals of psychiatric neuroimaging, it has had no impact yet on either clinical practice or treatment development. At the same time, the potential is considerable, since it has the ability to close the gap between abnormal mental phenomena (psychopathology) and brain abnormalities (neuropathology). Here I will choose the symptom capture study of auditory verbal hallucinations as an example.

Who and what is involved in imaging the experience of auditory verbal hallucinations? I submit that there are at least three aspects that deserve closer review:

1. A person reports the experience of hearing a voice.
2. At the same time, an imaging device collects data of the person's brain activity.
3. Statistical analysis of the brain activity data correlates the experience with a consistent pattern of localized brain activity.

In contrast to the other two goals, it is *Reasoning* that takes center stage for this goal of psychiatric neuroimaging. Studying the neural basis of auditory verbal hallucinations raises fundamental questions about the mind–brain problem and human consciousness (Dennett, 1991). When successful, they will aid in the *Explanation* of neural mechanisms that give rise to abnormal mental states (Barber et al., 2021; Richards et al., 2021; Zmigrod et al., 2016).

How can the very personal experience of voice hearing be related to the objective measurement of brain activity? There are several assumptions and constraints that limit the strength of inferences that can be drawn from such an approach.

First, the researcher needs to rely on the accurate reporting of the first-person experience. This is not trivial. In fact, many prospective study participants need to be excluded when such reports cannot be obtained reliably and predictably (Dierks et al., 1999).

Second, the degree of agency and ownership of the experience will vary between voice hearers. For some it might feel like an invasion, as if controlled by an alien force, resulting in great psychic pain; for others it will be experienced as under their control and as something to cherish. Consequently, some have argued that the phenomenology of auditory verbal hallucinations (or any other first-person experience of mental illness) cannot be captured adequately with neuroimaging (Woods et al., 2022).

Third, current methods of brain imaging might not reveal the relevant mechanism because of limited spatial or temporal resolution.

Finally, it is not clear whether any of the relations established by a symptom capture imaging study are causal, simply incidental, or correlational. Specifically, the activation of a brain region associated with auditory processing (e.g., Heschl's gyrus on the superior temporal gyrus) might not be causal but simply a downstream effect of an event in a different locale of the auditory processing network (Waters et al., 2012). As a corollary, activity identified in a symptom capture study does not provide sufficient evidence for intervention.

A thoughtful level of explanation approach, which maps the various aspects of the auditory verbal hallucination experience to the appropriate level (i.e., cells, circuits behaviors, beliefs), appears to be most promising (Hugdahl & Sommer, 2017).

17.7 The Example of the Hippocampus

I will finish the chapter with an example of how psychiatric neuroimaging has progressed. For the last 30 years, evidence has accumulated that the hippocampus is abnormal in psychiatric disorders, especially schizophrenia, depression, and posttraumatic stress disorder (Bartsch, 2012). Much of this evidence comes from psychiatric neuroimaging studies.

Initial evidence came from cross-sectional studies of hippocampal structure (mainly volume and shape) (Heckers, 2001). After this initial wave of imaging studies, two types of longitudinal evidence have been provided. First, hippocampal structure is already abnormal in the early stage of psychosis. Second, hippocampal structure is more significantly abnormal in individuals who progress to a poorer outcome (McHugo et al., 2020).

More recently, structural variants of the hippocampus have been defined using brain imaging (Cury et al., 2015). Such variants emerge during distinct periods of brain development in utero. Therefore, the recent finding of a greater prevalence and greater severity of such structural variants in psychotic disorders provides evidence for a neurodevelopmental etiology (Roeske et al., 2021).

Finally, interventions such as rTMS or ultrasound can modulate hippocampal activity and improve cognitive performance (Wang et al., 2014). Such interventions can be used to study causal mechanisms of psychiatric disorders and may aid in the development of treatments for psychiatric disorders (Jeong et al., 2022). Similarly, the effects of pharmacological interventions on hippocampal activity can be studied with psychiatric neuroimaging methods (Roeske et al., 2024).

In sum, neuroimaging studies have provided evidence, across multiple levels of analysis, that hippocampal structure and function are abnormal in psychiatric disorders. The initial evidence was merely correlational, but longitudinal studies and the identification of developmental variants have pointed out distinct time periods during which abnormalities appear and progress. Finally, the application of neuromodulation techniques has advanced this line of research to the top of the evidence-for-causality continuum. Ideally, several scientific problems of causality will be addressed in future studies of the hippocampus in psychiatric disorders: who is at risk, who needs an intervention, how to assess progression of illness, and how to explain cognitive deficits (e.g., associative memory impairment) with structural and functional abnormalities in the hippocampus.

17.8 Conclusion

Each of the five problems of causality in science, specifically *inference*, *prediction*, *explanation*, *control*, and *reasoning* (Illari & Russo, 2014), is relevant for the study of psychiatric disorders in general and for psychiatric neuroimaging in particular. As outlined earlier, *control* and *prediction* are the primary goals of the clinician who uses brain imaging to triage and stage patients. In contrast, neuroimaging researchers are more interested in *explanation* and the study of mechanisms of mental illness. Lastly, the general public remains intrigued by the ability to translate complex mental phenomena into an image (colored, usually) of the human brain. In the end, clinician, scientist, and layperson all share an interest in *reasoning*: How can we make sense of a person?

The ability to translate signs and symptoms of mental illness to images of the living human brain has generated considerable enthusiasm. At the same time, some critics have concluded that neuroimaging is nothing but a modern form of phrenology (Uttal, 2003). It is important to note that the community of neuroimaging researchers is acutely aware of the problems for causal inference testing in their field of research (Ramsey et al., 2010). In response, a consensus statement, recently published in *Trends in Neuroscience*, has identified important parameters for the study of causality in neuroimaging research (Barack et al., 2022). Similarly, a recent effort by the editors of *Frontiers in Neuroscience* has identified causality in neuroimaging as an important topic for further study (https://www.frontiersin.org/research-topics/30854/causality-in-neuroimaging-learning-causal-mechanisms-underlying-structure-function-and-dynamics).

To get from brain data to causes of mental illness requires reasoning. It is in the context of building and testing scientific models that Wernicke's *Scientific Viewpoint in Psychiatry* has not lost its appeal. We remain interested in the question: How does the brain give rise to abnormal mental states?

A full explanation of psychiatric disorders will require an accurate mapping of brain circuits governing complex human behavior. Tailoring the available methods of psychiatric neuroimaging to clearly defined translational goals is an important next step in this endeavor (Tervo-Clemmens et al., 2023). Only then will we have the necessary information to predict risk for and progression of disease, allowing us to intervene and prevent the burden of mental illness.

REFERENCES

Allen, P., Modinos, G., Hubl, D., Shields, G., Cachia, A., Jardri, R., Thomas, P., Woodward, T., Shotbolt, P., Plaze, M., & Hoffman, R. (2012). Neuroimaging auditory hallucinations in schizophrenia: From neuroanatomy to neurochemistry and beyond. *Schizophrenia Bulletin, 38*(4), 695–703. https://doi.org/10.1093/schbul/sbs066

Andreasen, N. C. (1984). The broken brain. Harper & Row.

(1997). Linking mind and brain in the study of mental illnesses: A project for a scientific psychopathology. *Science, 275*(5306), 1586–1593.

Barack, D. L., Miller, E. K., Moore, C. I., Packer, A. M., Pessoa, L., Ross, L. N., & Rust, N. C. (2022). A call for more clarity around causality in neuroscience. *Trends in Neuroscience, 45*(9), 654–655. https://doi.org/10.1016/j.tins.2022.06.003

Barber, L., Reniers, R., & Upthegrove, R. (2021). A review of functional and structural neuroimaging studies to investigate the inner speech model of auditory verbal hallucinations in schizophrenia. *Translational Psychiatry, 11*(1), 582. https://doi.org/10.1038/s41398-021-01670-7

Bartsch, T. (Ed.). (2012). *The clinical neurobiology of the hippocampus: An integrative view*. Oxford University Press.

Blackman, G., Kempton, M. J., & McGuire, P. (2024). Concerns regarding strength of conclusions in systematic review and meta-analysis of neuroradiological abnormalities in first-episode psychosis: Reply. *Journal of the American Medical Association Psychiatry, 81*(1), 109. https://doi.org/10.1001/jamapsychiatry.2023.4399

Blackman, G., Neri, G., Al-Doori, O., Teixeira-Dias, M., Mazumder, A., Pollak, T. A., Hird, E. J., Koutsouleris, N., Bell, V., Kempton, M. J., & McGuire, P. (2023). Prevalence of neuroradiological abnormalities in first-episode psychosis: A systematic review and meta-analysis. *Journal of the American Medical Association Psychiatry, 80*(10), 1047–1054. https://doi.org/10.1001/jamapsychiatry.2023.2225

Bookheimer, S. Y., Strojwas, M. H., Cohen, M. S., Saunders, A. M., Pericak-Vance, M. A., Mazziotta, J. C., & Small, G. W. (2000). Patterns of brain activation in people at risk for Alzheimer's disease. *New England Journal of Medicine, 343*(7), 450–456. http://www.ncbi.nlm.nih.gov/entrez/query.fcgi?cmd=Retrieve&db=PubMed&dopt=Citation&list_uids=10944562

Churchland, P. S., & Sejnowski, T. J. (1988). Perspectives on cognitive neuroscience. *Science, 242*(4879), 741–745. https://doi.org/10.1126/science.3055294

Cury, C., Toro, R., Cohen, F., Fischer, C., Mhaya, A., Samper-Gonzalez, J., Hasboun, D., Mangin, J. F., Banaschewski, T., Bokde, A. L., Bromberg, U., Buechel, C., Cattrell, A., Conrod, P., Flor, H., Gallinat, J., Garavan, H., Gowland, P., Heinz, A., . . . Consortium, I. (2015). Incomplete hippocampal inversion: A comprehensive MRI study of over 2000 subjects. *Frontiers of Neuroanatomy, 9*, 160. https://doi.org/10.3389/fnana.2015.00160

Dennett, D. C. (1991). *Consciousness explained.* Little, Brown and Company.

Dierks, T., Linden, D. E., Jandl, M., Formisano, E., Goebel, R., Lanfermann, H., & Singer, W. (1999). Activation of Heschl's gyrus during auditory hallucinations. *Neuron, 22*(3), 615–621. http://research.bmn.com/medline/search/record?uid=99211397

Dralle, B., & Morgan, R. J. (2024). Concerns regarding strength of conclusions in systematic review and meta-analysis of neuroradiological abnormalities in first-episode psychosis. *Journal of the American Medical Association Psychiatry, 81*(1), 108. https://doi.org/10.1001/jamapsychiatry.2023.4393

Engstrom, E. J. (2004). *Clinical psychiatry in imperial Germany: A history of psychiatric practice.* Cornell University Press.

First, M. B., Drevets, W. C., Carter, C., Dickstein, D. P., Kasoff, L., Kim, K. L., McConathy, J., Rauch, S., Saad, Z. S., Savitz, J., Seymour, K. E., Sheline, Y. I., & Zubieta, J. K. (2018). Clinical applications of neuroimaging in psychiatric disorders. *American Journal of Psychiatry, 175*(9), 915–916. https://doi.org/10.1176/appi.ajp.2018.1750701

Forbes, M., Stuckey, S., & Kisely, S. (2024). Concerns regarding strength of conclusions in systematic review and meta-analysis of neuroradiological abnormalities in first-episode psychosis. *Journal of the American Medical Association Psychiatry, 81*(1), 107. https://doi.org/10.1001/jamapsychiatry.2023.4390

Freud, S. (1891). Zur Auffassung der Aphasien. Eine kritische Studie. Franz Deuticke.

Geschwind, N. (1963). Carl Wernicke, the Breslau School and the history of aphasia. In E. C. Carterette (Ed.), Brain function: Speech, language, and communication (Vol. 3, pp. 1–16). University of California Press.

Gordon, E. M., Chauvin, R. J., Van, A. N., Rajesh, A., Nielsen, A., Newbold, D. J., Lynch, C. J., Seider, N. A., Krimmel, S. R., Scheidter, K. M., Monk, J., Miller, R. L., Metoki, A., Montez, D. F., Zheng, A., Elbau, I., Madison, T., Nishino, T., Myers, ... Dosenbach, N. U. F. (2023). A somato-cognitive action network alternates with effector regions in motor cortex. *Nature, 617*(7960), 351–359. https://doi.org/10.1038/s41586-023-05964-2

Havens, L. (2005). *Psychiatric movements: From sects to science.* Transaction Publishers.

Heckers, S. (1997). Neuropathology of schizophrenia: Cortex, thalamus, basal ganglia, and neurotransmitter-specific projection systems. *Schizophrenia Bulletin, 23*(3), 403–421.

(2001). Neuroimaging studies of the hippocampus in schizophrenia. *Hippocampus, 11*, 520–528.

Heckers, S., Kendler, K. S., Klee, A., & Heckers, S. (2022). "Regarding the scientific viewpoint in psychiatry", lecture by Carl Wernicke (1880). *History of Psychiatry, 33*(2), 236–255. https://doi.org/10.1177/0957154x221075240

Heckers, S., Woodward, N. D., & Ongur, D. (2013). Neuroimaging of psychotic disorders. In D. S. Charney, J. Buxbaum, P. Sklar, & E. J. Nestler (Eds.), *Neurobiology of mental illness* (pp. 256–268). Oxford University Press.

Hlade, J. (2021). Reconsidering "brain mythology". *Medicina Historica, 5*(1), e2021005. https://mattioli1885journals.com/index.php/MedHistor/article/view/10908

Hugdahl, K., & Sommer, I. E. (2017). Auditory verbal hallucinations in schizophrenia from a levels of explanation perspective. *Schizophrenia Bulletin, 44*(2), 234–241. https://doi.org/10.1093/schbul/sbx142

Illari, P., & Russo, F. (2014). *Causality: Philosophical theory meets scientific practice*. Oxford University Press.

Insel, T., Cuthbert, B., Garvey, M., Heinssen, R., Pine, D. S., Quinn, K., Sanislow, C., & Wang, P. (2010). Research domain criteria (RDoC): toward a new classification framework for research on mental disorders. *American Journal of Psychiatry, 167*(7), 748–751. https://doi.org/10.1176/appi.ajp.2010.09091379

Jeong, H., Song, I. U., Chung, Y. A., Park, J. S., Na, S. H., Im, J. J., Bikson, M., Lee, W., & Yoo, S. S. (2022). Short-term efficacy of transcranial focused ultrasound to the hippocampus in Alzheimer's disease: A preliminary study. *Journal of Personalized Medicine, 12*(2), 250. https://doi.org/10.3390/jpm12020250

Kotov, R., Krueger, R. F., & Watson, D. (2018). A paradigm shift in psychiatric classification: The Hierarchical Taxonomy Of Psychopathology (HiTOP). *World Psychiatry, 17*(1), 24–25. https://doi.org/10.1002/wps.20478

Makam, A. N. (2024). Concerns regarding strength of conclusions in systematic review and meta-analysis of neuroradiological abnormalities in first-episode psychosis. *Journal of the American Medical Association Psychiatry, 81*(1), 107–108. https://doi.org/10.1001/jamapsychiatry.2023.4396

McGorry, P. D., & Hickie, I. B. (Eds.). (2019). *Clinical staging in psychiatry: Making diagnosis work for research and treatment*. Cambridge University Press.

McHugo, M., Armstrong, K., Roeske, M. J., Woodward, N. D., Blackford, J. U., & Heckers, S. (2020). Hippocampal volume in early psychosis: A 2-year longitudinal study. *Translational Psychiatry, 10*(1), 306. https://doi.org/10.1038/s41398-020-00985-1

Murray, M. M., & Antonakis, J. (2019). An introductory guide to organizational neuroscience. *Organizational Research Methods, 22*(1), 6–16. https://doi.org/10.1177/1094428118802621

Pantelis, C., Velakoulis, D., McGorry, P. D., Wood, S. J., Suckling, J., Phillips, L. J., Yung, A. R., Bullmore, E. T., Brewer, W., Soulsby, B., Desmond, P., & McGuire, P. K. (2003). Neuroanatomical abnormalities before and after onset of psychosis: A cross-sectional and longitudinal MRI comparison. *Lancet, 361*, 281–288.

Platt, J. R. (1964). Strong inference. *Science, 146*, 347–353.

Plum, F. (1972). Prospects for research on schizophrenia. 3: Neurophysiology. Neuropathological findings. *Neuroscience Research Program Bulletin, 10*(4), 384–388. https://www.ncbi.nlm.nih.gov/pubmed/4663816

Post, M. R., & Sulzer, D. (2021). The chemical tools for imaging dopamine release. *Cellular Chemistry and Biology, 28*(6), 748–764. https://doi.org/10.1016/j.chembiol.2021.04.005

Ramsey, J. D., Hanson, S. J., Hanson, C., Halchenko, Y. O., Poldrack, R. A., & Glymour, C. (2010). Six problems for causal inference from fMRI. *Neuroimage, 49*(2), 1545–1558. https://doi.org/10.1016/j.neuroimage.2009.08.065

Richards, S. E., Hughes, M. E., Woodward, T. S., Rossell, S. L., & Carruthers, S. P. (2021). External speech processing and auditory verbal hallucinations: A systematic review of functional neuroimaging studies. *Neuroscience & Biobehavioral Reviews, 131*, 663–687. https://doi.org/https://doi.org/10.1016/j.neubiorev.2021.09.006

Roeske, M. J., McHugo, M., Rogers, B., Armstrong, K., Avery, S., Donahue, M., & Heckers, S. (2024). Modulation of hippocampal activity in schizophrenia with levetiracetam: A randomized, double-blind, cross-over, placebo-controlled trial. *Neuropsychopharmacology, 49*(4), 681–689. https://doi.org/10.1038/s41386-023-01730-0

Roeske, M. J., McHugo, M., Vandekar, S., Blackford, J. U., Woodward, N. D., & Heckers, S. (2021). Incomplete hippocampal inversion in schizophrenia: Prevalence, severity, and impact on hippocampal structure. *Molecular Psychiatry, 26*(9), 5407–5416. https://doi.org/10.1038/s41380-020-01010-z

Schieber, M. H. (2001). Constraints on somatotopic organization in the primary motor cortex. *Journal of Neurophysiology, 86*(5), 2125–2143. https://doi.org/10.1152/jn.2001.86.5.2125

Sejnowski, T. J., Churchland, P. S., & Movshon, J. A. (2014). Putting big data to good use in neuroscience. *Nature Neuroscience, 17*(11), 1440–1441. https://doi.org/10.1038/nn.3839

Siddiqi, S. H., Kording, K. P., Parvizi, J., & Fox, M. D. (2022). Causal mapping of human brain function. *Nature Reviews Neuroscience, 23*(6), 361–375. https://doi.org/10.1038/s41583-022-00583-8

Sutterer, M. J., & Tranel, D. (2017). Neuropsychology and cognitive neuroscience in the fMRI era: A recapitulation of localizationist and connectionist views. *Neuropsychology, 31*(8), 972–980. https://doi.org/10.1037/neu0000408

Tervo-Clemmens, B., Marek, S., & Barch, D. M. (2023). Tailoring psychiatric neuroimaging to translational goals. *Journal of the American Medical Association Psychiatry, 80*(8), 765–766. https://doi.org/10.1001/jamapsychiatry.2023.1416

Uttal, W. R. (2003). *The new phrenology: The limits of localizing cognitive processes in the brain*. MIT Press.

Walther, S., & Heckers, S. (2024). Mapping psychomotor behavior in the brain. *Journal of the American Medical Association Psychiatry, 81*(1), 7–8. https://doi.org/10.1001/jamapsychiatry.2023.4290

Wang, J. X., Rogers, L. M., Gross, E. Z., Ryals, A. J., Dokucu, M. E., Brandstatt, K. L., Hermiller, M. S., & Voss, J. L. (2014). Targeted enhancement of cortical-hippocampal brain networks and associative memory. *Science, 345*(6200), 1054–1057. https://doi.org/10.1126/science.1252900

Ward, H. B., Brady, Jr., R. O., & Halko, M. A. (2021). Bridging the gap: Strategies to make psychiatric neuroimaging clinically relevant. *Harvard Review Psychiatry, 29*(3), 185–187. https://doi.org/10.1097/HRP.0000000000000295

Waters, F., Allen, P., Aleman, A., Fernyhough, C., Woodward, T. S., Badcock, J. C., Barkus, E., Johns, L., Varese, F., Menon, M., Vercammen, A., & Laroi,

F. (2012). Auditory hallucinations in schizophrenia and nonschizophrenia populations: A review and integrated model of cognitive mechanisms. *Schizophrenia Bulletin, 38*(4), 683–693. https://doi.org/10.1093/schbul/sbs045

Woods, A., Alderson-Day, B., & Fernyhough, C. (Eds.). (2022). *Voices in psychosis: Interdisciplinary perspectives*. Oxford University Press.

Zmigrod, L., Garrison, J. R., Carr, J., & Simons, J. S. (2016). The neural mechanisms of hallucinations: A quantitative meta-analysis of neuroimaging studies. *Neuroscience and Biobehavior Review, 69*, 113–123. https://doi.org/10.1016/j.neubiorev.2016.05.037

CHAPTER 18

Commentary on Heckers's "Causal Inference in Psychiatric Neuroimaging"

Carl F. Craver

One of the key questions at the heart of Heckers's reflections on the uses of neuroimaging in psychiatry is whether the actual uses to which neuroimaging are being put in experimental research on the neural markers and mechanisms of psychiatric disorders have application in clinical psychiatry. He points to a mismatch in goals and methods that, it seems to me, demands further scrutiny, and scrutiny of a sort that philosophers might usefully supply. In addition to the questions of causal inference, to which I direct my attention immediately in what follows, are important questions about the difference between general truths about the brains of people with schizophrenia and truths about specific, single cases. Even if the tools of psychiatric research succeed in gleaning causal information about psychiatric disorders in general terms, there will always be an inductive leap in relating the general to the particular, in seeing the individual as properly both an example of the generalizations discovered in research on populations (and controls) and, consequently, as a fitting recipient of the predictions and explanations those generalizations deliver. This gap between the general and the particular lurks in the background of Heckers's important discussion, but perhaps could be given more of a central place, and would help us distinguish which problems attend the causal uses of neuroimaging and which attend the uniquely messy business of drawing conclusions about single-case causes on the basis of causal knowledge that holds, only for the most part, in certain conditions that we cannot fully adumbrate.

Beyond this inductive question, Heckers's discussion also provides an opportunity to reflect on the limits of the common and frequently asserted adage that neuroimaging is a correlational – that is, noncausal – methodology. Like most adages, this one contains a kernel of truth wrapped in overgeneralization. The kernel is that, in many standard applications, neuroimaging methods are not deployed in a manner that allows them to test hypotheses about the causal relevance of brain regions/processes in the most direct way: by manipulating the putative cause and detecting corresponding changes in the putative effect. The overgeneralization involves underestimating the diversity of forms that evidence about causes can take, of the various forms that causal claims can take, and of the diverse ways neuroimaging methods can be deployed against an array of background assumptions. In Heckers's essay, this shows up in the Bradford–Hill criteria, which function better as rules of thumb than as general truths about the nature of evidence about causation, as I'll try to make clear, and in the supposition that only certain kinds of evidence can be used to provide "strong" causal inferences. In general, we should avoid describing instruments and methodologies as causal or noncausal, because what makes them causal or noncausal is how they are deployed in our efforts to know the world. Furthermore, what counts as "strong" evidence depends on what else you know, what outstanding questions you have, and what assumptions you are willing to make. Evidence that might seem to be noncausal because it fails to appear, or receives a low ranking, on the Bradford–Hill criteria might be precisely what one needs to know to rule out an alternative explanation of an apparent causal relationship.

As I and most philosophers think of it, evidence for a hypothesis relative to presumed background knowledge is a finding that changes the probability of the hypothesis being true relative those background presumptions. Positive evidence increases the probability that the hypothesis is true. Negative evidence decreases it.

Two points follow from these humble beginnings that are of relevance to the Bradford-Hill criteria. First, evidence can come in degrees of strength, between entailment (the finding drives the probability of the hypothesis to 1 or 0) and something quite a bit weaker, such as when the evidence only changes the probability a tiny bit. Empirical evidence, defeasible as it is in light of future findings, never eliminates the possibility of error (unless one is willing to commit to the background knowledge that those sources of error are absent or negligible). That is, all evidence in real science falls between providing absolute falsification and absolute confirmation. It is no fault of a method if the evidence it provides is less than conclusive. Neuroimaging, it follows, can provide evidence relevant to a causal hypothesis while being nonetheless inconclusive with respect to that hypothesis. The finding that a brain region is active during the performance of a task, for example, does not tell you that the brain region's activity is causally relevant to task performance, but (as I explain later here) it should influence your assessment of that hypothesis.

The second key point here is that the assessment of the relationship between evidence and a hypothesis can be made only relative to a background of assumptions. If we change those assumptions, we can change the relationship between the evidence and the hypothesis. Compare, from Heckers's list, a case in which neuroimaging reveals a lesion that is entirely incidental to the patient's psychiatric disorder with a case in which it reveals a lesion that is actually the cause of the symptoms. Can neuroimaging help sort out these possibilities? Suppose the symptom in question is a form of declarative amnesia and that, against the backdrop of what we know in contemporary neuroscience, we find a tumor in the person's hippocampus. This finding would be very strong evidence for a causal hypothesis: the tumor is the cause of the person's memory disturbances. The evidence is purely observational, of course, but the background assumptions about likely causes strongly inclines us to the truth of this causal hypothesis in this case. This is why neuroimaging can be so important for sorting out psychiatric disorders proper from disturbances of thought and behavior that have a clear somatic cause, as Heckers emphasizes.

Before applying this further to the case at hand, a word about what it means for a hypothesis to be causal. The most common way of thinking about causal relations is in terms of efficient or etiological causation, in which a temporally antecedent occurrence (C) is the cause of a subsequent effect (E). We can present this standard form of causal claim as C—>E. But there are other important causal relationships besides this standard philosophical target. For example, X might be a (causal) component in a mechanism, M's, behavior, ψ. Here I understand ψ as a causal relationship between input (I) and output (O), which could itself be written as a causal relationship in standard form (I—> O). To say that there is a mechanism for ψ is to say that there are causal intermediaries between I and O. Let's represent a toy example like this:

I—>B—>X—>C—>D—>O.

To say that X is a component in ψ is thus to say that it is causally between I and O; in that sense, it contributes to I's making a difference to O (see Craver, Glennan, & Povich, 2021). This description should be enough to see why componency is a kind of causal relationship (X makes a causal contribution to ψ) as well as to see why it is not causal relationship of the C—>E form. X might be a cause of O and nonetheless fail to be part of how I causes O (that is, fail to be a component in ψ).

Beyond knowing merely *that* X is a component in M, we might want to know, more specifically, just *how* X contributes to M; that is, we might want to know X's *role* (or function) in M (Cummins, 1975). To answer that, we need to know more about how X is situated within M's causal organization, for example that it is a causal consequence of I and B and causally relevant to the occurrence of C, D, and O. To speak of a protein as a dopamine receptor is a shorthand way of expressing the fact that it is caused to open by the presence of dopamine and that something else happens when dopamine is present, such as the movement of ions across a membrane.

These latter kinds of causal claim ("being a component in" and "having a specific role in") are key things one seeks to learn in the process of discovering a mechanism. Although these notions are clearly causal in some respect, they do not have the (C → E) surface structure, and they are tested with rather different experimental protocols and strategies (Darden, 2006). It is arguably a shortcoming of standard philosophical accounts of causation (including Woodward's manipulationism, absent further elaboration) that it lumps these together despite their conceptual, inferential, and evidential differences from the (C → E)-type causal claim.

Let's now evaluate the common claim that neuroimaging is a noncausal method. First, let's sketch a caricature of a standard subtraction-style experiment, of the sort commonly called "purely observational" (these fall under Heckers's category of experiments designed to test mechanistic models of psychiatric disorders). A subject lies motionless in the scanner and follows the task instructions (I) in response to stimulus conditions (B). These task instructions require a behavioral output (such as a button press), which we can suppose to involve motor areas (C) and muscle contractions (D) and task solutions (O). So, we alternate tasks in which the subject gets the stimulus and the control conditions, respectively, and we compare what happens downstream. The scanner, in this situation, tells us whether the brain region of interest (C) changes its "activity" during task performance. The task performance tells us whether the subject is doing what we asked them to do. Of course, the actual structure of such an experiment is quite a bit more complex than this (see Craver, 2021), but those details only get in the way of the simple point.

If one demands that a "causal" method for testing the (C → E) relationship must wiggle C and see if E wiggles in response (which the Bradford–Hill criteria appear to emphasize), then the subtraction method doesn't do that. That is, the subtraction method does not involve intervening to change brain activity (C) and observing the consequences of that change for button pushes (E). That said, there is causal information in this signal. After all, the difference between task conditions and control conditions is an intervention on the input to the mechanism (I), and any of the other items in this caricature of a mechanism (B, C, . . . O) are putative downstream consequences of that intervention. That is, if we focus not on X → O but on I → X, then the method is, in fact, causal in precisely the sense the manipulationists defend. Such a method *can* provide precisely this putatively privileged kind of evidence, showing that one can wiggle brain activations by intervening on task conditions and stimuli. One can make the hippocampus light up in a scanner by giving people memory tasks; that's something we didn't know before we did the experiments to test it.

In the effort to find brain abnormalities in people diagnosed with psychiatric disorders, one typically does not have control over the cause of the psychiatric disorder, whether environmental or somatic. When Heckers correctly says that such findings are "mostly purely correlational and cannot be used to make causal claims," I respond only that these findings, against the right background assumptions, can be used to assess the plausibility of causal hypotheses. When Heckers claims that "most findings are purely correlational," I would say that this is true, but that correlations can be important for testing causal relationships, especially considered in contrast with the hypothesis that there would be no correlation between them whatsoever.

What is perhaps less obvious is the crucial role the causal relationship between I and C in our fictional mechanism can play in testing causal claims about X. Suppose we are interested not in whether X causes F, but rather in whether X is a component in the mechanism for ψ-ing. As noted earlier, the mechanistic component is something causally between the input (setup) and output (termination) conditions of a mechanism. This is at least partly captured by the idea of a causal mediator (Pearl, 2009, 2018; Weinberger, 2019, though the relationship between these ways of talking has yet to be clarified adequately). Such claims are frequent matters of considerable scientific controversy (Is this single nucleotide polymorphism a component in the mechanisms of schizophrenia? Is long-term potentiation a component in spatial learning in the hippocampus? Are mesosomes important contributors to metabolism?).

There are well-agreed-upon standards of evidence for establishing such things (see, e.g., Silva, Bickle, & Landreth, 2015). Establishing the following would appear to be sufficient (under further restrictions) to confirm a claim that C is a component in the mechanism:

1. That the input of the mechanism (I, in this case) is causally relevant to C.
2. That C is causally relevant to the output of the mechanism F.[1]

[1] A third, matching condition is also required to block some rather obvious counterexamples to this simple formulation. Precisely how to formulate that matching condition has been the source of some consternation, so I omit it for the present. See Craver, Povich, and Glennan (2021).

Testing claims about C's causal role also involves situating C within a causal mechanism that includes, in addition to what comes after C, a particular kind of relation to what comes before it as well. To say that C is a dopamine receptor is to say something about how, for example, it is situated between dopamine and membrane conductance. And to say that C (the hippocampus) is part of the episodic memory mechanism is to assert that stimuli we experience influence the hippocampus, and the hippocampus influences what we subsequently remember. We test that latter claim with, for example, lesion experiments or the deliverances of neuropsychology. And when we can do so, we experimentally remove or inhibit X and see if the organism can get to O in conditions I. Or we test them by stimulating X, as with an electrode, and seeing if the organism reports apparent memories (as Penfield [1952] did in the brains of people with epilepsy). And now we come to the unique contribution that neuroimaging, even the correlative sort, makes to the testing of causal claims.

Both the positive interventions (stimulating the hippocampus to action) and the negative interventions (lesioning it or blocking it somehow) face the possibility of systematic confounds: that is, there are ways these experiments could influence the organism's ability to learn about its environment even if the hippocampus (C in this case) is irrelevant to spatial learning. The lesion in the hippocampus, for example, might have distant effects on other brain regions (the process known as diaschisis), perhaps because crucial blood supply passes through the hippocampus or because the functional integrity of distant regions depends on a circuit in which the hippocampus participates. Similarly, stimulation of the hippocampus (or the medial temporal lobe) with electrical stimuli might produce apparent memories by spreading activation to other regions. These potential shortcomings for stimulation and inhibition methods are well known, and were well known at the time neuroimaging burst onto the scene. Indeed, neuroimaging was rightly seen as a corrective to these flaws.

Why? Neuroimaging, against a set of well-known background assumptions, tells us whether the brain region in question (X) is differentially active during the performance of tasks that, by our assumptions, involve ψ-ing. If X were not differentially activated during putative cases of ψ-ing, then (again, given certain assumptions) we would have less reason to think it was implicated in ψ-ing, against the backdrop of findings from lesion and stimulation experiments. Perhaps, we might reason, our lesion and stimulation experiments are in fact bringing about F via a deviant path that does not involve X, except (as it were) by accident. The initial excitement over neuroimaging as a methodology in the theoretical neurosciences was precisely because it could provide this kind of complement to the evidence coming from neuropsychology, neurology, and neurophysiology. Such evidence changes the probability of the causal hypothesis that X is a component in ψ-ing by addressing these potential confounds.

Heckers's chapter helps make clear, further, how neuroimaging can be combined with other instruments for intervening into brains to yield an experiment of the classic wiggle C → detect E variety. Combined with optogenetics, transcranial magnetic stimulation, or pharmacology, neuroimaging becomes part of a multi-technique experimental arrangement that can be used to test hypotheses about efficient causation in the most direct and obvious way. In other words, whether neuroimaging can provide evidence relevant to a causal hypothesis depends on how it is deployed, what other manipulations are in play, and what one is willing to assume about the setup.

Think about some other examples in which purely observational evidence is used to evaluate causal hypotheses:

- The dents in your car door match the swing radius of your neighbor's car door, and so you infer that it was likely their car door that put the dents in your car.
- The presence of an anatomical tract connecting area X and area Y in the brain is taken as a requirement for direct causal influence of X on Y. So diffusion tensor imaging, by revealing anatomical connectivity, can provide evidence relevant to assessing whether brain regions are or are not directly causally interacting with one another.
- The temporal correlation between the movement of your bike pedal and the clicking sounds from the drive train suggest that your crank is hitting something each time it goes around. The fact that it is coming from below rather than behind suggests it is near the front chain ring rather than something to do with the derailleur.
- Sequential firing patterns in the hippocampus seen during practice and rehearsal of a maze suggest replay of the same spatial representations in rehearsal.
- The crumbs on her lips suggest that she is the cause of the cookies' disappearance from the cookie jar.
- The presence of the tracer in the metabolites suggests that the labeled compound has been broken into these components.

One should not assume that the intervene-on-cause-and-detect-effect structure is the only kind of evidence available to test a causal hypothesis (Craver & Darden, 2013; Illari, 2011; Illari & Russo, 2014; Kaestner,

2018). And it would be an overextension of the limited purposes of the Bradrford–Hill criteria to presume a one-size-fits-all ranking of causal evidence, irrespective of what you already know and what you are trying to learn.

So, is neuroimaging purely observational, or is it causal? Heckers helps us see that this is a bad question (see Roskies, 2007, 2008). And it is bad because the answer depends on the hypothesis you are testing, the assumptions you are willing to make, and, ultimately, on the experimental context in which the scanner is deployed. We should not be tempted into thinking that the method is causal only when it is deployed in a wiggle cause → detect effect setup. There are many kinds of causal relationship besides the relation of efficient causation, specifically the related concepts of componency and causal role. Furthermore, there are many kinds of evidence relevant to establishing that relationship. The danger in the Bradford–Hill criteria (and similar list-based approaches, such as Koch's postulates) is that, if consumed uncritically as a theory of evidence rather than a set of defeasible rules of thumb for people with a distinctive practical agenda, they yield flatly false claims about the evidential value of many of the useful things scientists might discover. The measures of "strength" that animate their application seem to be matters of stipulation rather than the conclusion of a general way of thinking about evidence, even if they fit our intuitions about the kinds of knowledge we would like to have. Which evidence is important depends on what else you already know and what you are trying to figure out.

Let me close by considering perhaps the most famous experiment in the history of neuroscience: Otto Loewi's experiment with the frog heart. These experiments are generally taken as providing evidence for the causal hypothesis that nerve conduction travels chemically rather than electrically. Notice that this causal hypothesis is not like C → E, and it is not like C being a component in ψ, exactly. It is rather whether we get from I (in this case, presynaptic stimulation) to O (postsynaptic response) via a step that involves the release of a chemical substance from the presynaptic cell that then acts on the postsynaptic cell somehow. It is asking something like: What kind of component process is involved at step C?

The experiment does not have a standard wiggle C → detect E structure. You first stimulate an innervated, beating heart in a beaker full of saline solution. You then remove the first heart and dunk a second, denervated beating heart in the beaker. Compare this to what happens when you put it in a beaker of just saline. Loewi found that the heart slows down relative to the baseline and relative to the control. He concluded that there must be a chemical substance preserved in the bath. He seems to have reasoned that there were two possible options here: one chemical and one electrical. Only the former, he assumed, would last in the beaker long enough to act on the second heart.

Is the method causal? It does test whether putting a stimulated heart in the beaker makes a difference to the second heart's behavior, but that's not the point of the experiment. Rather, this surface causal hypothesis (that stimulating the heart would be able to affect the second heart's rate) is merely a tool to get at the question of how this effect is transmitted: in this case, by the secretion of a chemical substance by the nerve connected to the first heart.

As we begin to explore the diversity of the world's causal structures, we should pay attention not only to different varieties of mechanisms (cascades, feedback, feedforward, de-repression, etc.) and representations of mechanisms (pathway diagrams, network models) but also to the vast diversity of kinds of causal relations (role, contribution, component, efficient cause, background cause) and to the myriad kinds of evidence by which those features of the causal structure of the world might be revealed to us. Heckers's chapter is an important reminder of each of these features.

REFERENCES

Craver, C. F. (2007). *Explaining the brain: Mechanisms and the mosaic unity of neuroscience*. Oxford University Press.

(2021). Toward an epistemology of intervention. In J. Bickle, C. F. Craver, & A. Barwich (Eds.), *The tools of neuroscience experiment: Philosophical and scientific perspectives* (pp. 152–180). Routledge Press.

Craver, C. F., & Darden, L. (2013). *In search of mechanisms: Discoveries across the life sciences*. University of Chicago Press.

Craver, C. F., Glennan, S., & Povich, M. (2021). Constitutive relevance & mutual manipulability revisited. *Synthese*, 199: 1–22.

Cummins, R. (1975). Functional analysis. *Journal of Philosophy, 72*(20), 741–764.

Darden, L. (2006). *Reasoning in biological discoveries: Essays on mechanisms, interfield relations, and anomaly resolution*. Cambridge University Press.

Illari, P., & Russo, F. (2014). *Causality: Philosophical theory meets scientific practice*. Oxford University Press.

Illari, P. M. (2011). Mechanistic evidence: Disambiguating the Russo–Williamson thesis. *International Studies in the Philosophy of Science, 25*(2), 139–157.

Kästner, L., & Andersen, L. M. (2018). Intervening into mechanisms: Prospects and challenges. *Philosophy Compass, 13*(11), e12546.

Parkkinen, V.-P., Wallmann, C., Wilde, M., Clarke, B., Illari, P., Kelly, M. P., Norell, C., Russo, F., Shaw, B., & Williamson, J. (2018). *Evaluating evidence of mechanisms in medicine: Principles and procedures*. Springer Nature.

Pearl, J. (2009). *Causality*. Cambridge University Press.

Pearl, J., & Mackenzie, D. (2018). *The book of why: The new science of cause and effect*. Basic Books.

Penfield, W. (1952). Memory mechanisms. *Archives of Neurology & Psychiatry, 67*(2), 178–198. https://doi.org/10.1001/archneurpsyc.1952.02320140046005

Roskies, A. L. (2007). Are neuroimages like photographs of the brain? *Philosophy of Science, 74*(5), 860–872.

(2008). Neuroimaging and inferential distance. *Neuroethics, 1*(1), 19–30.

Silva, A. J., Bickle, J., & Landreth, A. (2013). *Engineering the next revolution in neuroscience: The new science of experiment planning*. Oxford University Press.

Weinberger, N. (2019). Mechanisms without mechanistic explanation. *Synthese, 196*(6), 2323–2340.

Woodward, J. (2003). *Making things happen: A theory of causal explanation*. Oxford University Press.

Section 7

CHAPTER 19

Introduction to Craver's "Mechanistic Psychiatry"

Peter Zachar

Carl Craver begins his chapter by noting that in psychiatry, mechanistic models attempt to understand the causal factors that produce, underlie, or maintain disorders. Knowledge of mechanisms, therefore, would support the goals of preventing, ameliorating, and even curing psychiatric disorders and thus represent the discipline's highest aspirations for psychiatric explanation. Some thinkers, however, are concerned that under the banner of mechanism resides a static view of phenomenon that does not bear in mind that things constantly change. Another perceived problem with a mechanistic approach is a reductionism that dismisses higher-level causal structures in favor of using new technologies designed primarily to study the smallest things. This chapter argues that such concerns are not applicable to the new mechanists in the philosophy of science.

Craver proceeds to describe two different approaches to a mechanistic philosophy: metaphysics-first and practice-first. The metaphysics-first approach begins with a conceptual analysis of things like mechanisms, causation, and levels of analysis. When complete, any subsequently developed mechanistic models must correspond to these concepts. This attempt to legislate good versus bad science is a mechanistic essentialism. Advocates for traditional mechanistic models such as Descartes, Newton, and Laplace sought such metaphysical purity for science.

In contrast, the practice-first approach does not demarcate a privileged concept of mechanism that has been shared by all mechanistic thinkers from Descartes onward. In Craver's view, a broadly mechanistic perspective has been applied to so many different and varied kinds of phenomena (including in evolution, medicine, and neuroscience) with so many different conceptions of what a mechanism is that any conceptual analysis that harkens by default to traditional mechanist accounts does not itself correspond to what the mechanistic approach has become. A practice-first approach to a mechanistic philosophy of science does not precede but follows from what occurs in science. Craver states that a practice-first approach that considers how psychiatrists are trying to explain and what they want from these explanations is better positioned to contribute to psychiatry than is a metaphysical, legislating approach.

Craver defines minimal mechanism as the view that a mechanism for a phenomenon consist of entities (or parts) whose activities are organized so as to be responsible for the phenomenon. This definition is a schematic placeholder that, for example, can accommodate a plurality of approaches to explaining a phenomenon such as alcoholism. It can encompass studying the contribution of genes that code for enzymes in the liver, the contribution of personality traits like impulsivity, or the contribution of parental modeling of drinking behavior. These would lead to substantively different notions of a mechanism. The group of mechanisms that can help explain something like alcoholism are like a mosaic and can differ in many ways, including being faster and slower, bigger and smaller, or linear and recursive.

One well-known objection to mechanistic approaches is that the world (especially a living system) is an ever-changing process rather than a container filled with entities and properties. Craver, however, points out that some of the most important successes of the mechanistic approach involve explaining biological processes. Indeed, the "activities" of minimal mechanism are processes. One specific strand of the process-oriented objection to mechanistic approaches is that that higher-level processes cannot be explained bottom-up with reference to the interaction of their parts alone because the activity of the parts cannot be understood in isolation from the higher-level process itself. With respect to this strand of criticism, Craver counters that defining what counts as a level and what it means for levels to interact has been a major focus of his and his fellow "new mechanists," including what people are talking about with top-down causation.

Another objection to a mechanistic approach is that it involves tunneling inward and downward based on the view that the more details included in one's model, the better the explanation. Craver agrees that the psychiatrists, neuroscientists, and psychologists working from a mechanistic perspective should avoid what he called an endless fascination over the smallest things and not be tempted into accepting claims such as explanations of disorders in terms of cells molecules are more scientific. The new mechanists, states Craver, are not seeking to tunnel down and describe everything in detail, but to build models. Models are abstract, analogical, idealized, schematic and so on – leaving out the details. It is important, says Craver, to not confuse the mechanism and the models.

The mechanism is some causal structure/process we want to understand. The models (genetic, molecular, psychological, etc.) are the various representation and sketches of that structure that we construct.

Craver writes that psychiatric disorders are complex. They are not fixed and unchanging but in flux, and the mosaic of causal processes that produce and maintain them spans multiple levels. The relevant casual processes can be foregrounded and backgrounded differently across vantage points. Importantly, the kind of causal model one adopts will make a difference to how we think about psychiatric disorders. Those who adopt a practice-first approach to a mechanistic philosophy of science won't stipulate which kind of models are best or more scientific or argue about what words like "mechanism" mean. The task of the practice-first approach is to study and follow the mechanistic models that are being used, emerging and otherwise, to better understand their nature, how they work, and their strengths and limitations. Hopefully, says Craver, one outcome of this kind of study and reflection is that it contributes something of relevance to psychiatry.

In her commentary, Lauren Ross applauds Craver's practice-first approach to mechanisms but resists the tendency of minimal mechanism to subsume causation-in-general under the banner of mechanistic. Stepping back, she distinguishes between explanatory scientific projects and nonexplanatory projects (such as prediction and classification). Ross notes that, especially in the life sciences, in contrast to other approaches to scientific explanation such as nomological, unifying, and probabilistic, causal approaches to scientific explanation capture the directionality of explanation and the practical importance of explanation for being able to change things (such as preventing and curing). According to Ross, minimal mechanism glosses over a contrast between causal systems that are mechanistic and those that are not. Under this generic notion, not mechanistic tends to mean noncausal. One reason Ross resists this notion is that, in her view, mechanisms depend on how we understand causation, and crediting the progress attributable to better causal understanding to mechanisms is putting the cart before the horse. Not seeing that causal explanation is broader than mechanistic explanation is problematic because discovering mechanisms has become the Holy Grail in the life sciences – but one that is loosely defined. From Ross's perspective, the narrow, traditional definition of mechanistic Carver argues against offers more conceptual clarity. What is needed, Ross contends, is a better understanding of the diversity of causal influences that exist (including but not limited to mechanisms) and discerning which influences are most relevant to psychiatric outcomes.

CHAPTER 20

Mechanistic Psychiatry
Thoughts on Commitments and Confounds

Carl F. Craver

20.1 Mechanisms in Psychiatry

Psychiatry has a core goal of understanding the mechanisms that produce, underlie, and maintain psychiatric disorders. This goal would appear to be justified on the grounds that knowledge of these mechanisms is, if not an essential component, surely a contributing cause of future developments in the ability to prevent, ameliorate, and perhaps liberate us from these sources of human suffering. Mechanistic thinking – understood here as knowing how things work and how they break, or more generally, knowing the etiological, constitutive, and contextual causal structures that produce, underlie, or maintain states of affairs or persistent processes – is explicitly baked into our collective mode of action against psychiatric disorders. If we know the mechanisms and causes, and how they have become "disordered," we can think of strategies for restoring the order by manipulating them or the contexts in which they operate. Used in this broad and encompassing sense, the term "mechanism" serves to express, if not *the* deepest, surely one of the deepest goals of science: to know how things work and to use that knowledge to solve problems. A mechanistic psychiatry, in this broad sense, (1) would be oriented toward the causal-mechanistic structures that produce, underlie, and maintain psychiatric disorders and (2) would seek to deploy that knowledge in the search for effective interventions.

Despite, and perhaps in part because of, the widespread acceptance of something like this view of what psychiatry is or should aim to be, there have been diverse pockets of resistance. Some object that to be a mechanist is to be committed to an ontology of objects or things and to neglect the fact that our world is in flux, constantly changing (Dupré, 2013; Dupré & Nicholson, 2018; Nicholson 2013). Others associate mechanism with reductionism, an obsession with details and an inability to accommodate abstract and higher-level causal structures (Batterman & Rice, 2014;

Chirimuuta, 2014; Krakauer, 2017; Levy, 2013). Others object to a one-size-fits-all ontology that fails to recognize diversity in the world's causal structure (Ross, 2021, 2022; Ross & Bassett, 2024). Finally, there is a growing sense in some corners that the call for "knowing the mechanisms" is tantamount to a demand (often in anonymous reviews) that the author must use the newest and fanciest tools to probe the smallest and least relevant things lest they fail to address the "mechanism."

Is it possible to articulate the character and scope of a mechanistic philosophy of psychiatry and to simultaneously accommodate these complaints? Can we express a general commitment to mechanism without the confounds of these historical associations? Here, I will sketch a way forward that might avoid them entirely. My aim in making this case is programmatic: to show that work on mechanisms in the philosophy of science in the last 30 years provides an important perspective on what the philosophy of psychiatry is, one that might contribute meaningfully to the aims and practices of psychiatrists (e.g., Craver, 2007; Craver, Glennan, & Povich, 2021; Craver & Kaplan, 2020; Craver, Tabery, & Illari, 2024; Glennan 2010, 2017; Illari, 2011, 2013; Kendler, Zachar, & Craver 2011; Krickel, 2014; Russo & Williamson, 2007; Steel 2007). Like all overarching frameworks of this sort, there are plusses and minuses to adopting such a mechanistic "heuristic": the search for mechanisms foregrounds some things and backgrounds others. In the following sections, I foreground some features of a thoroughly contemporary mechanism that would fit the kind of thing psychiatric researchers might plausibly hope to achieve.

20.2 Directions of Fit

How might one build a mechanistic philosophy of psychiatry? Where should one begin? In the philosophy of science more generally, folks tend to divide into two camps: metaphysics-firsters and practice-firsters. Metaphysics-firsters begin with a pre-theoretic conception of what mechanisms are and then deploy that notion to evaluate various things about science. The history of mechanistic philosophy and science is no doubt full of metaphysics-firsters. Some have in mind a clockwork universe, composed of a very few basic kinds of interaction, organized in space and time. The Aristotelian author of the *Mechanical Problems* takes circular motion as the core mechanism to which an entire family of explanations returns again and again. Descartes builds a mechanical world out of extension and conserved motion. Loeb's mechanism was fundamentally a commitment to natural law and determinism. Boyle's mechanism involved "haptic" interactions (i.e., pertaining to the sense of touch), and Du Bois Reymond's mechanistic biology would explain everything exhaustively in terms of electrostatic attraction and repulsion. The history of the mechanical philosophy is now familiar and could only be distorted in rapid retelling (see, e.g., Boas, 1952; Des Chene, 2000, 2005; Djiksterhuis, 1961; Garber & Roux, 2013; Roux, 2017; Westfall, 1977).

Against this historical backdrop, one might expect a contemporary mechanist to be strongly committed about what mechanisms are, as a matter of metaphysics, and then to use that ground floor conception to legislate good versus bad science. For example, if you want to know whether M is a good mechanistic explanation, you first work out what a mechanism must be (deterministic, contact action, sequential, linear, and/or, etc.), and then you return to M to deliver a judgment. Does it show the phenomenon to be governed by natural law? To result from contact action alone? To reduce all phenomena to attraction and repulsion? If yes, then it is a good explanation. If not, it is a bad explanation, or incomplete, or (with some irony) it is judged to be overly metaphysical in positing things beyond the few catholic admissible interactions. That there is a "history of mechanism" suggests that there must be some metaphysical essence of mechanism, and further that this essence involves a restriction on the space of possible causes.

In my view, however, the history leads to a rather different, practice-oriented take on the matter. It suggests instead that there is emphatically no single conception of mechanism that has been passed to us from Democritus through Descartes, Boyle, Helmholz, Newton, and Huygens to contemporary psychiatry. While we find across this history a complex lineage or web of influence and inspiration, we find nothing that survives across all times and places, no essence of mechanism passed from one local circumstance to the next. We find instead an idea – mechanism – changing and adapting to reflect the local concerns of different ages. The meaning of the term has evolved over the years to cover phenomena it was not originally designed to accommodate. Some of its most popular forms were concerned with the motions of planets, the trajectories of cannonballs, the nature of chemical reactions. But mechanism has since migrated to cover things like protein synthesis, reproduction, and color vision. As the term migrated to new places, it had to drop core commitments. As it adapted to face new problems, it took on altogether different forms. Coming to the history from this vantage point, those who would seek to identify first an "essence" of what it is to be a mechanism and then to use that as the starting point for one's philosophical enterprise fail to fully appreciate that the idea of mechanism is a human structure imposed on a world that would churn just the same without it. We are the ones who get to say what mechanisms ought to be. Perhaps, acknowledging upfront the historical vicissitudes of the term, we should ask first not what mechanisms are but instead what we need them to be, here and now.

This is a practice-first approach. And in fact, most people who have worked under the banner of "mechanism" in the philosophy of science have, for the most part, been practice-firsters (Craver, 2007; Darden, 2006; Glennan, 2017; Illari & Russo, 2014; Kendler, Zachar, & Craver, 2011; Russo, 2022; Williamson, 2011). A practice-firster starts with what scientists seem to be trying to do (explaining, predicting, treating, categorizing) and how they set about trying to do it (designing experiments, building models, proffering and defending and criticizing explanations, etc.). What is psychiatry attempting to achieve? And what are the current methods for attempting to achieve that end? Based on the answers to those questions, one can go on to ask: Are those reasonable aims? Are there additional, perhaps better ways to achieve those ends? How can we justify answers to these kinds of questions?

The practice-firster temperamentally approaches scientific practice with (always defeasible) intellectual charity: that what these scientists are trying to do makes some sense, that there is a more or less unified explanation for their scientific activities, for example why their experiments take this shape rather than that, why these are the appropriate controls, why these explanations are rejected. Those practices, we presume, are governed by a tacit understanding of what the world is like (at least with respect to the relevant domain) and of how it should be known. As practice-firsters, mechanists have tended to presume that the word "mechanism," so ubiquitous in scientific writing, is not merely an empty placeholder but is still doing important work *even if it does not fit some historical incarnation of the concept of mechanism.* It animates the scientific practices of experimenting, modeling, simulating, observing, inferring, and explaining.

Mechanistic approaches to the philosophy of psychiatry would benefit tremendously from a practice-first approach and will, in fact, only be hampered ineffectually trying to pin the idea of mechanism down to some overly restrictive notion designed for other purposes in a land far away.

Psychiatry is a potential beneficiary of the things the philosophy of science might have to offer by way of clarifying and justifying the aims and inferential practices of the science. It is not merely or primarily a playground for the philosopher's curiosity about the mind and its place in nature; it is a science with an important and humane project at its core.

In the effort to assist with this, one role of a mechanistic approach to the structure of psychiatry is to start with the concept of mechanism as we find it there, charitably and rationally reconstructing it, rather than imposing some pre-theoretical notion from without and judging the science by this alien standard. If we start with the problems that psychiatrists are trying to solve, we can focus our attention on problems for which the philosophy of science might in fact have something relevant to contribute.

20.3 Mechanisms and Levels: Minimal Commitments

Years of discussion over what, precisely, remains of the notion of a mechanism when it is transported from domains such as physics and chemistry to sciences such as physiology and neuroscience, genetics and evolutionary biology, geology and cognitive science has yielded a canonical schema of the minimal mechanism:

> A mechanism for a phenomenon consists of entities (or parts) whose activities and interactions are organized so as to be responsible for the phenomenon. (e.g., Glennan & Illari, 2017)

This formulation contains filler terms (*phenomenon*, *entities*, *parts*, *activities*, *interactions*, and *responsible for*) that can be made more precise for different intellectual purposes. Depending on how one fills them, one gets a substantially different notion of a mechanism.

This minimal schema contains placeholders for the sorts of things that would add content to a theoretical explanation of, for example, the etiology of alcoholism. The causes cited in the explanation here might include, for example, genes that control the production of metabolic enzymes in the liver. They might include having parental role models of drinking behavior. They might involve the failure to acquire adaptive modes of coping with anxiety, or time in a bad marriage. The entities in this sketch are of all different sorts. Some are big, some are small; some are parts of others. Some are inside people, some are outside them. Some are made of elements, and some are in the realm of experience and thought. If the notion of mechanism is going to get a grip here, it clearly must be permissive about the kinds of entities a mechanism can involve.

The activities, included alongside entities as fundamental ingredients in mechanisms, add a dynamic, processual aspect to the understanding of what a mechanism is. Activities are kinds of doing – ways of making things happen. The activities that tend to appear on the radar of psychiatrists seem typically to be themselves mechanistically explicable; that is, to say that this activity happened here (e.g., transcription or an action potential) is simply to abstract a way from details about the mechanism underlying the activity and to describe it "on its own level" (as it were), as a paragraph of change in the narrative arc of an organized and extended causal process: a mechanism.

Alcoholism is not so much a thing, like a virus or a bacterium, as it is a process that develops and evolves over time, reaches stages, and takes turns. It has a trajectory and stages of development. It is sustained, maintained, and reinforced through a variety of mechanisms spanning multiple levels of organization. Some of these involve molecules; some involve emotional development; some involve social clubs and legal cultures. The notion of mechanism appropriate to psychiatry would thus have to be one that includes the temporal organization and more processual aspects in both the characterization of alcoholism itself as well as our understanding of its parts and component processes, as they themselves evolve within a changing system.

The last major filler term I want to emphasize in this minimal statement is *organization*, a concept best articulated through examples. Spatial organization involves, for example, relative position, orientation, shape, location. Temporal organization involves, for example, order, rate, duration, frequency. More local and global motifs of organization (Alon, 2006; Levy & Bechtel, 2013) include having a feedback or feedforward, be a small world or massively connected, or be structured like a classical controller or a kind of combustion engine, or a particular kind of joint. Mechanisms can be organized in parallel, in forks, and in joins. Hierarchies of mechanisms are formed out of mechanisms within mechanisms, each defined by doing what it does in the service of a higher-level mechanism that frames our attention.

Consider a place where psychiatry is very much in the search for mechanisms: the interpretation of genome-wide association studies (GWAS). Here, the scientist discovers population-level regularities in the statistical association between genetic changes (single nucleotide polymorphisms [SNPs]) and phenotypes such as alcoholism, schizophrenia, and major depressive disorder, among others. Epidemiological data alone argue very strongly that there is a genetic contribution to each of these phenotypes, but the question of which genes contribute, and precisely how they contribute, has been of considerable intellectual importance. Once the GWAS has identified SNPs associated with the diagnosis beyond the degree one would expect if it were merely a matter of chance, the question arises: Does this difference affect occurrence (severity, onset, etc.) of this set of symptoms? And if so, how?

As we have already seen by considering the likely causal paths leading to alcoholism, there are literally no identifiable limits on the space of possible mechanisms by which a gene makes a difference to the phenotype. It might involve an enzymatic difference that leaves a person unable to process alcohol in the liver that causes the person to get sick when they drink and so decreases considerably the chance that they will ever drink enough to acquire an alcohol habit. It might involve a contribution to personality, for example to gregariousness, sociality, or risk aversion. It might involve differences to the gut lining, or alcohol receptors, or impulsivity, or the sense of smell or taste. The mind boggles at the space of possible mechanisms that might connect the many SNPs identified by GWAS as statistically associated with the diagnosis and the symptoms of the person to whom the diagnosis has been applied.

One strategy in mechanism discovery involves forward chaining: beginning with what you know and then inferring from there to future stages of the mechanism (Darden & Craver, 2013; Steel, 2007). The fact that many of the significant SNPs associated with the diagnosis of age-related macular degeneration are linked to genes involved in the human complement pathway is a potential clue that the disease is related to changes in immune function, a clue that might be of some value in thinking about how to address it pharmacologically (e.g., Fritsche et al., 2014). As this example suggests, one might attempt to forward-chain from the SNPs by looking, for example, at proteomic databases associated with the genetic regions identified as significant SNPs (Craver et al., 2020; Dozmorov, 2020; Reimers et al., 2019). One goal in forward-chaining of particular relevance in psychiatry is to identify choke points in a causal mechanism that can serve as loci for intervention. If we think of a psychiatric disorder as an assemblage of symptoms to be explained, a choke point is a place in the mechanism for a disorder from which many effects follow downstream from differences in the values of a small number of variables. A bow-tie structure, for example, might involve many SNPs feeding into a common system (the complement system), as a result of which many downstream consequences follow (the symptoms of age-related macular degeneration). There is considerable room for philosophers to think through efficient ways to search for causal mechanisms by projecting forward from genome and backward from phenotype in the effort to construct the multilevel mechanism relating them. Short of that, there is considerable room for critical reflection on the extent to which the sort of data GWAS provide are likely to deliver the kind of mechanistic knowledge they promised from the start (e.g., Turkheimer, 2012), and this is a place where a mechanistic philosophy of psychiatry might be of some benefit.

Whatever a psychiatric mechanism is, it seems from these quick examples that it should accommodate many kinds of entities, activities, and forms of organization, and that it should extend across multiple levels of organization, even looping out into the world. When psychiatrists speak of mechanism, then, we should not hear them as necessarily embracing any kind of physicalism, or a preference for cellular-molecular explanation (as embraced by Bickle, 1998, 2003), or a neglect of behavior (Krakauer, 2017). We should rather hear in this term an expression of a desire to understand the causal structures that produce, underlie, and maintain psychiatric disorders and of the causal structures that might be used for the purposes of reducing their negative impact.

20.4 Mechanisms and Processes

Some philosophers oppose mechanistic approaches from the perspective of process metaphysics. Dupré and Nicholson (2018), for example, deny that, "mechanistic explanations are capable of providing in principle a complete understanding of living systems" (p. 29). I view their position as more moderate than they perhaps intend, specifically as a corrective for overly simplistic ways of thinking about mechanisms.

It seems overblown to me to cast this criticism as an attack on mechanism itself. The history of biology is an extended argument for the idea that the search for mechanisms often delivers surprising successes where metaphysicians have asserted the necessity of defeat. Harvey's discourses on the movement of the blood showed the value of mechanistic thinking in the biological domain. Elasticity and muscular contraction, which foiled Descartes in *Le Monde*, generated numerous mechanistic theories and ultimately surrendered to actins and microfilaments. Digestion? Metabolism? Deep mysteries long ago, have surrendered to chemistry and physiology. Reproduction? Heredity? The origin of species? Animal electricity? Time and again, phenomena that were supposed to resist capture within the causal nexus, to be explicable only in terms of entelechies or life forces, have yielded to the effort to discover their antecedent, constitutive, and contextual mechanisms. One could form a reasonable inductive inference that there is value in continuing to push forward with mechanistic approaches even in the face of convincing metaphysical opposition.

Dupré and Nicholson's complaint, it turns out, is not over minimal mechanism itself, but rather over further, vaguely specified commitments about the direction of explanation possible within a multilevel mechanism, or at least within a system (or process) describable at many different "levels." Read in this way, their defense of processes provides a useful corrective to a bias one might be prone to adopt in thinking about mechanisms, namely a failure to appreciate that the mechanisms at play in many systems transgress tidy intuitions about the order of explanation. Mechanistic explanation, on their interpretation, must always work from below: "The mereological, bottom-up character of mechanistic explanations means that their deployment in a world of processes is inevitably subject to the same limits as more traditional forms of reductionism" (Dupré & Nicholson, 2018, p. 29).[1] In particular,

> The constituents of a higher-level process do not suffice to explain it, because they themselves—or, more specifically, their stability and activity—cannot be fully understood without reference to that same process, as well as to those above it. (p. 29)

To restate their objection: There are cases in which the constituents of a higher-level process do not suffice to explain that higher-level process because the stability and activity of the constituents cannot be fully understood without reference to that higher-level process itself, and perhaps also to the still-higher-level processes it partially composes. In other words, the parts cannot exist or function as they do without the whole in which they play a role, and so an ideal of the bottom-up explanation must ultimately fail; in such cases, top-down explanations are required, and so the very idea of a mechanistic explanation must be replaced with process thinking.

If mechanistic approaches quite generally eschewed the dynamic and fluid nature of things, if they ignored influences from and across levels of organization, they would have some difficulties handling things such as the progression of alcoholism. How could one build such a story without recognizing a complex dynamic interplay among factors involving human behavior (going to bars; marriage stability) alongside changes to physiology (perhaps biochemistry) that impact choices that increasingly canalize behavior along a narrow path?

In contrast to this downward-looking view of mechanism Dupré and Nicholson imagine, most philosophical mechanists have emphasized the importance of explanation across levels. Their work has been grounded in

[1] Curiously, Dupré and Nicholson cite the same mechanists that I am appealing to here in their criticisms: Bechtel (2006), Craver (2007), Craver and Darden (2013), Glennan (2002), and Machamer et al. (2000). If my reading is correct, the views of none of these authors conflict with Dupré and Nicholson's main point.

examples from cognitive neuroscience, physiology, and many areas of the biological sciences (and beyond). To fit the use in those domains, they have found it necessary time and again to emphasize the multilevel and dynamic way of thinking about mechanisms as key to the extension of the term into these domains. Machamer, Darden, and I (2000) introduced our view as "attempting to capture the healthy philosophical intuitions underlying both substantivalist and process ontologies" (p. 4) and as "explicitly dualist" (p. 4) – that is, composed of both entities and activities. Mechanisms are called on to explain "how some significant process work" (p. 2) and are themselves composed of activities, the processual, causal notion at the heart of the "dualism" (p. 2; for further exposition, see Glennan, 1996, 2009, 2010; Glennan & Illari, 2017; Krickel, 2014).

There is now a large literature on the use of dynamical models to describe the behavior of mechanisms (see Bechtel, 2013; Bechtel & Abrahamsen, 2011; Kaplan 2011; Kaplan & Bechtel, 2011; Levy & Bechtel, 2013). Organizational dynamics is part of any understanding of a causal system. Mechanisms have dynamics. They are in flux. The mechanistic world should not be opposed to a world in which, as Dupré and Nicholson describe it, everything flows. Mechanisms are how things flow.[2]

Likewise, commitment to higher-level explanations and to a working-out of the explanatory relationships among levels of explanation has in fact been one of the primary benefits of thinking about mechanism. The idea of mechanism has proved important in articulating what it means to say that things are "at different levels" (Craver, 2007; Povich & Craver, 2017) and, working within that definition, a set of claims about what it might mean to say that things at different levels interact with one another (Craver & Bechtel, 2007). Glennan (1996), likewise, has offered metaphysical arguments in favor of the existence of higher-level causes and processes, not in response to Dupré and Nicholson but entirely independently, as an

[2] Dupré and Nicholson point to the "entities" in minimal mechanism as evidence of the overly thing-like character of mechanisms. In fact, Craver and Darden (2013) discuss the criteria for something to count as an entity in a mechanistic explanation. These include metaphysical constraints, such as that it should have causal powers, and epistemic constraints, such as that it should be robustly detectable. None of these constraints turn on any strong notions of permanence, preexistence, or long-term persistence. Their view does not insist that the cells of the heart cannot be dependent on the heart's beating for the continued operation. Given that this kind of dependency is so ubiquitous and important, no notion of mechanism that started from a kind of metaphysical obstinance against such phenomena would be automatically suspect. The things that Craver and Darden discuss under the heading of entities include action potentials, spatial maps, and rats, allowing for items of different degrees of permanence and with different degrees of dependency on one another.

expression of the consequences of his view (see also Craver, 2007, chapter 6). Craver and Darden's (2013) theory of mechanism discovery is likewise driven by strategies such as asking, "what is the role of this item," looking up and out to situate an activity or part in context, a way of looking long emphasized by Bechtel (e.g., Bechtel, 2009).

Finally, Bechtel (2007) addresses the phenomenon of autopoesis, the heart of Dupré and Nicholson's objection, from a mechanistic vantage point. Autopoesis is a process that involves parts that require the continued operation of a whole to exist. Two important points stand out: (1) not all mechanisms (or even all biological mechanisms) have this kind of autopoetic dependency structure and (2) while such mechanisms require one to be careful in talking about levels and causal dependencies, they do not rule out the possibility of a mechanistic analysis. In fact, Bechtel and I tried to work out a charitable interpretation of what one could mean by top–down causation in a world of multilevel mechanisms (see Bechtel, 2007; Bechtel & Abrahamsen, 2013). The processualist might, as an exercise, see whether the contemporary mechanist's treatment of such cases is unsatisfactory in some respect before declaring the mechanical perspective on biology bankrupt.

The dialectical opposition of process and mechanism in this literature obscures the potentially important lessons the process theorist might deliver to psychiatrists about the mechanisms they seek to understand. Psychiatric disorders are not static. Their fluidity, their periodicities, their development and sustenance, their cycles of recovery and relapse – these temporal features are likely key to how these disorders are caused, maintained, and relieved. That's the key point, and it's a good one. But that is entirely consistent with every useful thing mechanists have said about the character of explanation, testing, natural kinds, and discovery, let alone about the mechanisms underlying particular psychiatric and somatic disorders.

20.5 Reduction and Detail-Orientation

A mechanical approach to psychiatry, as I have already remarked in passing, is not necessarily reductionist in its orientation, on several readings of the term "reduction." In one sense, the mechanical approach offers a different (and arguably better) way of thinking about explanation from below than did models of theory reduction embraced in the heydays of logical empiricism. In another, it emphasizes, as just remarked, the multilevel character of explanations, with dependencies that might run from big to small and whole to part.

If one is permissive about the idea of causation, as most philosophical mechanists have tended to be, one can in fact find room for mechanistic explanation wherever one finds examples of causal explanation. If one thinks of causation, for example, as a relationship that can be exploited for the purposes of controlling the effect variable by manipulating the cause variable, as many mechanists have (Craver, 2007; Glennan, 2002; Kendler & Woodward, 2021; Woodward, 2003), or perhaps as a relationship that is itself underwritten by a mechanism (Glennan, 1996, 2017), then one can accommodate looping and high-level causal relationships (as between bar hours and alcoholism, gregariousness and alcohol exposure, liver enzymes and time of first drink). As this point is already adequately covered in the literature, I insist instead on distancing mechanism from another form of reduction: obsession with detail and a tendency to miss the forest for the trees.

If one associates mechanisms with tunneling inward and downward, it is but a small step to associate them with scientific strategies that lose sight of the whole in the process of trying to learn increasingly more about the parts. Thus, mechanism can sometimes be seen as an opponent to the need to find patterns in the organization of causes (or in addition to causes). For many philosophers, to embrace a mechanistic psychiatry is tantamount to embracing the thesis that piling on of lower-level details is always to be preferred, no matter how insignificant or irrelevant (see Batterman & Rice, 2014; Brigandt, 2013; Chirimuuta, 2014; Levy, 2014; Levy & Bechtel, 2013; Rice, 2015; Ross, 2015, 2021, 2022; Woodward, 2013). Here is a representative statement of the view:

> [According to mechanists], not only does veridical representation of the causal mechanism make a model explanatory, the more accurate and detailed that representation is, the more explanatory the model will be... [T]his view mistakenly implies that more accurate detail concerning mechanisms is always better. (Batterman & Rice, 2014, p. 352)[3]

This claim is typically conjoined with the effort to recognize diverse forms of explanation beyond mechanistic approaches in certain domains. Minimal model explanations, optimality explanations, dynamical

[3] In fact, mechanists are committed to the opposite of these claims. In a further twist of irony, basic requirements of the alternative views seem to be even more explicitly committed: the demand for ever more invariant generalizations requires the inclusion of every difference that makes a difference; the requirement of proportionality demands that variables adjust themselves to every splitting that improves their fit to the explanandum phenomenon. So, although the view is often used to criticize mechanistic approaches, it rather transparently applies to everyone in the explanation business who take a stand on issues such as the scope and proportionality of an explanation.

explanations, network explanations are to be required in such domains – not mechanistic explanations.

There is, in this discussion, an important lesson for psychiatrists, neuroscientists, and psychologists who prefer to think about their work in mechanistic terms: they should avoid the temptation of endless fascination over the smallest things. There is neither an explanatory nor a metaphysical, philosophical justification for the view that the most useful explanations or interventions are always to be found among molecules, cells, or any other level for that matter, or that the most useful explanations must be in this or that language. This message is, in my view, an important corrective against the often myopic focus of molecular and cellular scientists, let alone physicalists, who think that explanations in their domains are superior in some important respect to those offered by people who attend to variables at the levels of organisms or societies. The cast of mind attracted to mechanism might also include those who are prone to extreme forms of physicalism or reductionism, and for them, this is a useful corrective.

A helpful way to make this point about myopic attention to detail would be to look at examples of science where people are pursuing things in apparent conformity with this drive for detail, and then to show how the unbridled drive for detail is leading people to miss important causal factors essential to the aims of psychiatry. If the complaint is about GWAS, and that perhaps the grain or causal distance involved in the mechanisms (relating SNPs to symptoms) is inappropriate, then the task is to provide arguments for that conclusion and perhaps to begin to suggest higher-level causal structures that have gone missing and that might serve the objectives of the psychiatrist just as well or better. This is precisely what our research group proposed for the purposes of forward-chaining from GWAS (Craver et al., 2020; Dozmorov et al., 2020; Reimers et al., 2019).

Another context in which discussions of this sort would be fruitful is in the recent fascination with personalized approaches to health care more generally (Tabery, 2023). The drive for genetic mechanisms can crowd out higher-level sciences due to an unjustified belief in the superiority of lower-level explanations or, worse, the illegitimacy of higher-level explanations. This is an important point and one that, in fact, receives considerable support from recent work in mechanistic philosophy of science.

To be clear, however, the embrace of mechanistic approaches to psychiatry need not be saddled with reductionism. The resurgence of philosophical interest in mechanism since 2000 was born in part as a response to austere forms of reductionism and physicalism, as an effort to show why knowledge of higher-level causes is often crucial for explaining things. It was formulated also in explicit contrast to physicalist ideas of Phil Dowe (2000) and Wesley Salmon (1984) and in response to John Bickle's "new wave reductionism" (Bickle, 1998) and direct psychophysical connections (Bickle, 2003). In the hands of Bechtel and Richardson, Glennan, Wimsatt, Darden, and myself, among others, it emerged as an explicit effort to argue that contemporary science and philosophy, viewed through the proper lens, offer no sanctuary for the would-be reductionist. We argued, all of us, that mechanism does not entail reduction and (following Lycan) indeed could help make sense of the existence of causes at higher levels, or causes described more abstractly than the most detailed description would provide (Craver, 2007; Glennan, 2009).

But what, again, about the detail obsession of mechanism? The much discussed model-to-mechanism mapping requirement that we introduced to distinguish mechanistic explanations from phenomenal models (3M; see Kaplan 2011; see also Craver & Kaplan, 2020) requires only that a mechanistic explanation (as opposed to a mere re-description of the phenomenon in a different language) must contain at least some details about how the mechanism works. It does not require that an adequate explanation must contain all the details. Nor should it require that knowing more of the details always makes an explanation better.[4] Knowing more relevant details might make a description more complete, in some obvious sense of completeness, but some details matter more than others, and make more of a difference to how the mechanism behaves, than do others. Nothing in 3M entails commitment to a "more details, better" thesis (see Kaplan & Craver, 2011).

To come at this from another angle, it is useful to distinguish the mechanism from the model. The mechanism is that portion of the causal structure of the world we seek to understand. The model is a representation, depiction, sketch of the thing. All models of mechanisms involve abstraction, for surely part of what it is to be a representation is to have an aspectual character. So, commitment to the idea that psychiatry can be usefully organized around a search for mechanisms need not commit one to the idea that there is one or even a handful of legitimate ways of representing those mechanisms. Anatomical diagrams might display spatial arrangements; dynamical models might explain the choreography of parts; network models might be useful in visualizing and detecting modular

[4] Some expressive sentences in Kaplan (2011) do appear to evince such a conviction but, read in context, reveal an altogether different interpretation.

subsystems. The significant differences in what these models represent and how they represent it should not blind us to the fact that they can all be used to represent different aspects of one and the same mechanism. Differences in model format do not always indicate a difference in explanatory objectives; for example, a pathway diagram might well be used to represent how the stages of a mechanism are possibly arranged with respect to one another (contra Ross, 2015). (For more on explanatory and representational pluralism, see Glennan, 2017; Hochstein, 2016).

Despite the semantic association of mechanism with knowing details of the causal structure of a system, to embrace a mechanistic approach to psychiatry is to embrace the importance of causally relevant details wherever one finds them. This is the opposite of a manic drive for detail and is, instead, an insistence on causes at many levels, organized so that the outcome we want to understand comes about or is maintained.

20.6 Looking Forward

If the philosophy of science is to contribute something of relevance to psychiatry and science in general – and I count myself among the chief supporters of the idea that it is relevant, even essential – it will be by promoting and delivering sustained reflection on the aims and practices of science, on the problems scientists themselves confront, on the assumptions that can be tweaked and abandoned, on the inferences that should be guarded, on the norms of community governance that promote collective progress.

We can perhaps find a common core of agreement with various criticisms of mechanistic approaches discussed earlier: That things (such as people and symptoms) change, and that those changes can be described at multiple levels or scales; That changes at one level often have explanations at other levels; That sometimes those explanations work by looking down, revealing more internal changes; That sometimes they work by looking out and up, by situating the change to be explained in a wider context, or by looking back to an etiology; That real things in the "middle range" are acted on simultaneously by myriad of forces, only some of which we deem relevant in the case at hand; That in systems of such complexity, there inevitably will be different perspectives (as in Dupré, 1993), each of which foregrounds the causally relevant parts and activities that stand out from that perspective and backgrounds the rest. One can be a mechanist and at the same time grasp that often many kinds of models are required to reveal how the mechanism works.

Suppose everyone agrees on all that while we disagree about the appropriate extension of the word "mechanism," "level," "reduction," or what have you. If so, there is good work to be done to think about how scientists do and should go about discovering causal structures of that sort. Darden and I participated in that discussion together (Craver & Darden, 2013), and we suggested at that time that there should be more fruitful engagement with the literature on causal modeling and automated approaches to causal inference (e.g., Pearl, 2009; Spirtes, 2000). In many ways, this has been borne out in the work of Illari and of Russo and Williamson (Clarke et al., 2013, 2014; Illari, 2011; Illari & Russo, 2014; Russo & Williamson, 2007; Williamson, 2011). It has recently become more apparent that new mechanistic views of constitutive relevance dovetail with the work on inference about causal mediation (Pearl, 2014; Weinberger 2019) – a connection most worthy of continued articulation.

The project of linking a qualitative understanding of the implied worldview of the workaday scientist with quantitative and automatable methods would be most useful in psychiatry. In the use of GWAS, it might help to resolve the persistent challenge that we do not know the mechanism that links relevant SNPs (or combinations of those), perhaps via environmental factors, to the expression of the psychiatric disorder in question. It might help us say when neuroscience is, and is not, likely to be helpful in answering questions about a given complex of symptoms. It might help us direct our attention at different portions of the causal nexus to recognize choke points and places of intervention into complex causal systems.

Another path forward is to recognize the futility of a bottom–up approach to the improvement of psychiatric taxonomy and to understand the dynamic interplay between our understanding of the disorders and of their underlying mechanisms. As I suggested earlier, this taxonomy is likely to be use dependent, grouping like with like in different ways depending on one's aims (e.g., prognosis, prevention, or cure). These different uses will direct scientists to altogether distinct portions of the causal structure of the world, or at least will emphasize different aspects of that causal structure as reflects the needs of their own vantage point. There is a need to understand the kind of co-evolutionary negotiation that happens at the intersection of psychiatry and mechanism (see Feest [2025] for experimental psychology; Francken, Slors, & Craver [2021] for cognitive ontology). There is also a need to recognize that the causal context of a mechanism is often just as or more important as its interior for understanding many phenomena. That is precisely why looking up and out is so important (Bechtel, 2009). There are further questions about whether psychiatric disorders can themselves be fruitfully conceived as mechanisms (in whole or in part), or whether they are better conceived as affecting many neurocognitive mechanisms at once, or as something else entirely. These are questions that arise within a philosophy that takes the idea of organized mechanisms more or less for granted and then asks questions about whether those can be known and, if so, how they might be known most efficiently.

Finally, the effort to characterize diversity in the causal-mechanical structure of the world (as exemplified in, e.g., Craver & Darden, 2013; Glennan, 2017; Glennan & Illari, 2017; Ross, 2022) promises to shed light on differences relevant to discovery and control. Different kinds of mechanism (e.g., a cascade versus a linear, feed-forward process) have different implications for where to direct one's interventions (early, in the case of cascades), and how one schematizes the explanation can make important differences in how one thinks about it. Rather than seeing these forms of causal arrangements (cascades, pathways, etc.) as contrasts to mechanisms, enshrining more stipulative definitions of rather loose-in-practice constructs, it seems more helpful to not engage in what might primarily be a dispute about words and turn to what matters: how different ways of organizing causes together change what scientists need to do to discover them, provide evidence about them, explain them, predict them, or what have you. The effort to draw a dividing line between those causal structures that count as mechanisms and those that do not will always seem to be arbitrary. The focus should rather be on how these different structures call out for different scientific approaches, different kinds of experiments, and different forms of inference (see Craver & Darden, 2013; Glennan & Illari, 2017).

If philosophy of psychiatry is to be useful, not merely as a new intellectual playground for sparring about age-old issues but rather as a participant in the discussion about how psychiatry can best achieve its objectives, it will be because it provides new tools for thinking about what psychiatry is trying to accomplish and how best we can accomplish it. A mechanistic approach, suitably liberalized, seems to me indispensable in that endeavor and a useful starting place for taking on the important challenges the science seems to face.

Acknowledgments

Special thanks to Becko Copenhaver, Lindley Darden, Phyllis Illari, William Newsome, Federica Russo, Stuart Glennan, and Peter Zachar for comments on an earlier draft.

REFERENCES

Alon, U. (2006) *An introduction to systems biology*. Chapman and Hall/CRC Press.

Batterman, R. W., & Rice, C. C. (2014). Minimal model explanations. *Philosophy of Science, 81*(3), 349–376.

Bechtel, W. (2006). *Discovering cell mechanisms: The creation of modern cell biology*. Cambridge University Press.

(2007). Biological mechanisms: Organized to maintain autonomy. In F. C. Boogerd, F. J. Bruggeman, J.-H. S. Hofmeyr, & H. V. Westerhoff (Eds.), Systems biology (pp. 269–302). Elsevier. https://doi.org/10.1016/B978-044452085-2/50014-0

(2009). Looking down, around, and up: Mechanistic explanation in psychology. *Philosophical Psychology, 22*(5), 543–564.

(2013). Addressing the vitalist's challenge to mechanistic science: Dynamic mechanistic explanation. In S. Normandin & C. T. Wolfe (Eds.), *Vitalism and the scientific image in post-Enlightenment life science, 1800–2010* (pp. 345–370). Springer.

Bechtel, W., & Abrahamsen, A. (2011). Complex biological mechanisms: Cyclic, oscillatory, and autonomous. In C. Hooker (Ed.), *Philosophy of complex systems* (Vol. 10, pp. 257–285). North-Holland. https://doi.org/10.1016/B978-0-444-52076-0.50009-2

Bechtel, W., & Abrahamsen, A. (2013). Thinking dynamically about biological mechanisms: Networks of coupled oscillators. *Foundations of Science, 18*(4), 707–723.

Bechtel, W., & Richardson, R. C. (2010). *Discovering complexity: Decomposition and localization as strategies in scientific research*. MIT press.

Bickle, J. (1998). *Psychoneural reduction: The new wave*. MIT Press.

(2003). *Philosophy and neuroscience: A ruthlessly reductive account* (Vol. 2). Springer Science & Business Media.

Boas, M. (1952). The establishment of the mechanical philosophy. *Osiris, 10*, 412–541.

Brigandt, I. (2013). Systems biology and the integration of mechanistic explanation and mathematical explanation. *Studies in History and Philosophy of Science Part C: Studies in History and Philosophy of Biological and Biomedical Sciences, 44*(4, Part A), 477–492. https://doi.org/10.1016/j.shpsc.2013.06.002

Chirimuuta, M. (2014). Minimal models and canonical neural computations: The distinctness of computational explanation in neuroscience. *Synthese, 191*(2), 127–153.

Clarke, B., Gillies, D., Illari, P., Russo, F., & Williamson, J. (2013). The evidence that evidence-based medicine omits. *Preventive Medicine, 57*, 745–747.

(2014). Mechanisms and the evidence hierarchy. *Topoi, 33*, 339–360.

Craver, C. F. (2007). *Explaining the brain: Mechanisms and the mosaic unity of neuroscience*. Oxford University Press.

(2015). Levels. In T. Metzinger & J. M. Windt (Eds.), *Open MIND*: 8(T). https://open-mind.net/papers/levels

Craver, C. F., & Bechtel, W. M. (2007). Top-down causation without top-down causes. *Biology and Philosophy, 22*, 547–563.

Craver, C. F., & Darden, L. (2013). *In search of mechanisms: Discoveries across the life sciences*. University of Chicago Press.

Craver, C. F., Dozmorov, M., Reimers, M., & Kendler, K. S. (2020). Gloomy prospects and roller coasters: Finding coherence in genome-wide association studies. *Philosophy of Science, 87*(5), 1084–1095.

Craver, C. F., Glennan, S., & Povich, M. (2021). Constitutive relevance & mutual manipulability revisited. *Synthese, 199*(3), 8807–8828.

Craver, C. F., & Kaplan, D. M. (2020). Are more details better? On the norms of completeness for mechanistic explanations. *The British Journal for the Philosophy of Science, 71*, 287–319.

Craver, C. F., Tabery, J., & Illari, P. (2024). Mechanisms in science. In E. N. Zalta & U. Nodelman (Eds.), *Stanford encyclopedia of philosophy* (Fall 2024 ed.). https://plato.stanford.edu/archives/fall2024/entries/science-mechanisms

Darden, L. (2006). *Reasoning in biological discoveries: Mechanism, interfield relations, and anomaly resolution*. Cambridge University Press.

Des Chene, D. (2000). *Physiologia: Natural philosophy in late Aristotelian and Cartesian thought*. Cornell University Press.

Des Chene, D. (2005). Mechanisms of life in the seventeenth century: Borelli, Perrault, Régis. *Studies in History and Philosophy of Science, Part C: Studies in History and Philosophy of Biological and Biomedical Sciences, 36*(2), 245–260.

Dijksterhuis, E. J. (1961). *The mechanization of the world picture* (Vol. 184). JSTOR.

Dowe, P. (2000). *Physical causation*. Cambridge University Press.

Dozmorov, M. G., Cresswell, K. G., Bacanu, S.-A., Craver, C., Reimers, M., & Kendler, K. S. (2020). A method for estimating coherence of molecular mechanisms in major human disease and traits. *BMC Bioinformatics, 21*(1), 473.

Dupré, J. (1993). *The disorder of things: Metaphysical foundations of the disunity of science*. Harvard University Press. https://books.google.com/books?hl=en&lr=&id=Ev3HvgSjb1EC&oi=fnd&pg=PA1&dq=info:yMfV3yopQNkJ:scholar.google.com&ots=a1GjA1OBMv&sig=zxbY4VgySkAqjoEFmXM7EP8NKaM

Dupré, J. A. (2013). Living causes. *Proceedings of the Aristotelian Society, 87*, 19–35.

Dupré, J. A., & Nicholson, D. J. (2018). A manifesto for a processual philosophy of biology. In D. J. Nicholson & J. A. Dupré (Eds.), *Everything flows: Towards a processual philosophy of biology* (pp. 3–48). Oxford University Press. https://library.oapen.org/handle/20.500.12657/29752

Feest, U. (2025). *Operationism in psychology: An epistemology of exploration*. University of Chicago Press. https://press.uchicago.edu/ucp/books/book/chicago/O/bo240967636.html

Francken, J. C., Slors, M., & Craver, C. F. (2022). Cognitive ontology and the search for neural mechanisms: Three foundational problems. *Synthese, 200*(5), 378.

Fritsche, L. G., Fariss, R. N., Stambolian, D., Abecasis, G. R., Curcio, C. A., & Swaroop, A. (2014). Age-related macular degeneration: Genetics and biology coming together. *Annual Review of Genomics and Human Genetics, 15*(1), 151–171.

Garber, D., & Roux, S. (Eds.). (2013). *The mechanization of natural philosophy*. Springer.

Glennan, S. S. (1996). Mechanisms and the nature of causation. *Erkenntnis, 44*, 49–71.

(2002). Rethinking mechanistic explanation. *Philosophy of Science, 69*(S3), S342–S353.

(2009). Productivity, relevance and natural selection. *Biology & Philosophy, 24*(3), 325–339.

(2010). Mechanisms, causes, and the layered model of the world. *Philosophy and Phenomenological Research, 81*(2), 362–381.

(2017). *The new mechanical philosophy*. Oxford University Press.

Glennan, S. S., & Illari, P. (2017). Varieties of mechanisms. In S. Glennan & P. Illari (Eds.), *The Routledge handbook of mechanisms and mechanical philosophy* (pp. 91–103). Taylor & Francis.

Glennan, S. S., Illari, P., & Weber, E. (2022). Six theses on mechanisms and mechanistic science. *Journal for General Philosophy of Science, 53*(2), 143–161.

Harrington, A. (2019). *Mind fixers: Psychiatry's troubled search for the biology of mental illness*. W.W. Norton.

Hochstein, E. (2016). One mechanism, many models: A distributed theory of mechanistic explanation. *Synthese, 193*(5), 1387–1407.

Illari, P., & Russo, F. (2014). *Causality: Philosophical theory meets scientific practice*. Oxford University Press.

Illari, P. M. (2011). Mechanistic evidence: Disambiguating the Russo–Williamson thesis. *International Studies in the Philosophy of Science, 25*(2), 139–157.

(2013). Mechanistic explanation: Integrating the ontic and epistemic. *Erkenntnis, 78*(2), 237–255.

Kaplan, D. M. (2011). Explanation and description in computational neuroscience. *Synthese, 183*(3), 339–373.

Kaplan, D. M., & Bechtel, W. (2011). Dynamical models: An alternative or complement to mechanistic explanations? *Topics in Cognitive Science, 3*(2), 438–444.

Kaplan, D. M., & Craver, C. F. (2011). The explanatory force of dynamical and mathematical models in neuroscience: A mechanistic perspective. *Philosophy of Science, 78*(4), 601–627.

Kendler, K. S., & Woodward, J. (2021). Top-down causation in psychiatric disorders: A clinical-philosophical inquiry. *Psychological Medicine, 51*(11), 1783–1788. https://doi.org/10.1017/S0033291721001811

Kendler, K. S., Zachar, P., & Craver, C. (2011). What kinds of things are psychiatric disorders? *Psychological Medicine, 41*(6), 1143–1150.

Krakauer, J. W., Ghazanfar, A. A., Gomez-Marin, A., MacIver, M. A., & Poeppel, D. (2017). Neuroscience needs behavior: Correcting a reductionist bias. *Neuron, 93*(3), 480–490.
Krickel, B. (2014). *The mechanical world: The metaphysical commitments of the new mechanistic approach* (Vol. 13). Springer International Publishing.
Levy, A. (2014). What was Hodgkin and Huxley's achievement? *The British Journal for the Philosophy of Science*, 65(3), 469–492.
Levy, A., & Bechtel, W. (2013). Abstraction and the organization of mechanisms. *Philosophy of Science, 80*(2), 241–261.
Machamer, P., Darden, L., & Craver, C. F. (2000). Thinking about mechanisms. *Philosophy of Science, 67*, 1–25.
Maturana, H. R., & Varela, F. J. (1991). *Autopoiesis and cognition: The realization of the living* (Vol. 42). Springer Science & Business Media.
Nicholson, D. J. (2013). Organisms do not equal machines. *Studies in History and Philosophy of Science Part C: Studies in History and Philosophy of Biological and Biomedical Sciences, 44*(4), 669–678.
Pearl, J. (2009). *Causality*. Cambridge University Press.
(2014). Interpretation and identification of causal mediation. *Psychological Methods, 19*(4), 459.
Povich, M., & Craver, C. F. (2017). Mechanistic levels, reduction, and emergence 1. In *The Routledge handbook of mechanisms and mechanical philosophy* (pp. 185–197). Routledge.
Reimers, M. A., Craver, C., Dozmorov, M., Bacanu, S.-A., & Kendler, K. S. (2019). The coherence problem: Finding meaning in GWAS complexity. *Behavior Genetics, 49*(2), 187–195.
Rice, C. (2015). Moving beyond causes: Optimality models and scientific explanation. *Noûs, 49*(3), 589–615. https://doi.org/10.1111/nous.12042
Ross, L. N. (2015). Dynamical models and explanation in neuroscience. *Philosophy of Science, 82*(1), 32–54.
(2021). Causal concepts in biology: How pathways differ from mechanisms and why it matters. *British Journal for the Philosophy of Science, 72*(1), 131–158.
(2022). Cascade versus mechanism: The diversity of causal structure in science. *The British Journal for the Philosophy of Science*, 723623.
Ross, L. N., & Bassett, D. S. (2024). Causation in neuroscience: Keeping mechanism meaningful. *Nature Reviews Neuroscience, 25*(2), 81–90. https://doi.org/10.1038/s41583-023-00778-7
Roux, S. (2017). From the mechanical philosophy to early modern mechanisms. In S. Glennan & P. Illari (Eds.), *The Routledge handbook of mechanisms and mechanical philosophy* (pp. 26–45). Routledge.
Russo F. (2022). *Techno-scientific practices: An informational approach.* Rowman & Littlefield International.
Russo, F., & Williamson, J. (2007). Interpreting causality in the health sciences. *International Studies in the Philosophy of Science, 21*(2), 157–170. https://doi.org/10.1080/02698590701498084

Salmon, W. (1984). *Scientific explanation and the causal structure of the world.* Princeton University Press.
Spirtes, P., Spirtes, P., Glymour, C. N., & Scheines, R. (2000). *Causation, prediction, and search.* MIT Press.
Steel, D. (2007). *Across the boundaries: Extrapolation in biology and social science.* Oxford University Press.
Tabery, J. (2023). *Tyranny of the gene: Personalized medicine and its threat to public health.* Knopf.
Turkheimer, E. (2012). Genome wide association studies of behavior are social science. In K. S. Plaisance & T. A. C. Reydon (Eds.), *Philosophy of behavioral biology* (pp. 43–64). Springer Science + Business Media. https://doi.org/10.1007/978-94-007-1951-4_3
Weaver, R. M. (2022 [1953]). *The ethics of rhetoric.* Henry Regnery. www.gutenberg.org/ebooks/68421
Weinberger, N. (2019). Mechanisms without mechanistic explanation. *Synthese, 196*, 2323–2340.
Westfall, R. S. (1977). *The construction of modern science: Mechanisms and mechanics.* Cambridge University Press.
Williamson, J. (2011). Mechanistic theories of causality, part 1. *Philosophy Compass, 6*, 421–432.
Woodward, J. (2003). *Making things happen: A theory of causal explanation.* Oxford University Press.
(2013). Mechanistic explanation: Its scope and limits. *Aristotelian Society Supplementary, 87*(1), 39–65.
(2017). Explanation in neurobiology. In D. M. Kaplan (Ed.), *Explanation and integration in mind and brain science* (pp. 70–100). Oxford University Press.

CHAPTER 21

Commentary on Craver's "Mechanistic Psychiatry"

Lauren N. Ross

Craver's chapter engages with the mechanism concept in psychiatry and the field's goals of explaining, understanding, and ultimately improving psychiatric diseases and disorders. The mechanism concept has received significant attention in philosophical work, especially over the past two decades and in discussions of biology, neuroscience, medicine, and other life sciences. Craver's work has contributed significantly to contemporary "new mechanist" views, which maintain that explanatory practice in the life sciences involves uncovering the mechanisms responsible for various outcomes of interest. (While philosophers have proposed numerous frameworks for capturing scientific explanation – frameworks that appeal to laws of nature, causes and causal systems, unifying patterns, and mathematical necessities – the new mechanist approach suggests that many explanations involve appealing to mechanisms.) On this framework, a natural phenomenon is explained when one identifies and cites the mechanism that produces the phenomenon in question.

A significant advantage of Craver's analysis is its practice-oriented perspective, which focuses on how scientists actually provide explanations, what methods underlie their work, and what goals their research aims to serve (Craver, 2007). Indeed, such a perspective is shared by many mechanist accounts, which are motivated by the fact that the mechanism term is "so ubiquitous in scientific writing," as is seen in discussions of genetic mechanisms, a drug's mechanism of action, the mechanisms of neuron signaling, and so on (Craver, Chapter 20 in this volume). Even when etiology is unknown, psychiatrists and medical researchers often state that their goal is to identify the mechanisms underlying behaviors, traits, and disorders of interest.

In taking such a practice-first approach, Craver outlines how the mechanism concept is understood in much of the philosophical literature by outlining various features characteristic of mechanisms. First, mechanisms are causal systems that specify particular "entities" and "activities" that produce and are responsible for the phenomenon of interest. Entities can be understood as causal factors (such as neurotransmitters, enzymes, and genes), while activities capture types of causal relationships (including binding, splicing, activating, etc.). The mechanism includes some set of entities and activities that together produce the phenomenon of interest. A second feature of mechanisms is that they have some organization, such as how the causal steps in the mechanism are arranged. This feature captures how some mechanisms contain steps organized in a linear chain, or a feedback loop, or some other configuration. Third, Craver suggests that mechanism explanations do not follow a "more details, the better" approach, and that models of mechanisms can be abstract, nonreductive, and capture macro-scale causal relationships.

How exactly does mechanism relate to the topics of causation and causal explanation? Accounts of scientific explanation aim to identify the central aspects and logical structure of genuine scientific explanations; such features can help distinguish explanations that are better, worse, or failed, but also to capture important scientific projects that are nonexplanatory (such as prediction, description, and classification). In the last four decades of work on scientific explanation, much of the philosophical community has identified *causation* and *causal relationships* as crucial elements of most scientific explanations, especially in the life sciences. While earlier accounts viewed explanations as dependent on laws of nature, unifying frameworks, or statistical relationships, these have been largely dropped in favor of causal accounts of explanation, and for a good reason. Causation helps capture the directionality of explanation and the control that explanatory factors provide over their targets (both of which earlier accounts struggled to accommodate). Additionally, accounts of causal explanation – such as the well-known interventionist account (Woodward, 2003) – well capture the many explanations scientists provide, the specialized methods they use for identifying explanatory causal structures, and the goals that these explanations support. In this manner, many explanations in the life sciences fit the mantra that "causes explain their effects," and extensive literature on causal explanation supports and studies this.

Accounts of causal explanation require many components. In particular, these accounts should specify how causation is defined and understood, how explanatorily relevant causes are selected, what "levels" or "scales" explanatory causes reside on, and what types of causal structures or systems figure in such explanations. In the context of psychiatry, this work can help capture when something is causally relevant to a psychiatric outcome; can compare different causal investigative strategies; and can identify different types of causal systems in this domain, such as causes that differ with respect to their stability and specificity (Kendler, 2005; Woodward, 2010).

If causal explanation has advantages over previous accounts of scientific explanation and captures well the scientific work, what exactly does mechanism add here? If mechanism is a type of causal structure, this suggests that mechanism is dependent on our understanding of causation, methods for identifying causality, and strategies for engaging in causal reasoning. In fact, many mechanistic philosophers, including Craver, rely on an interventionist account of causation to elucidate the notion of mechanism, yet the difference between causation and mechanism is not always appreciated or clear (Craver, 2007). This is seen in cases where the insights and guidance provided by accounts of causation and causal explanation are inappropriately credited to mechanistic approaches, which themselves depend on such causal frameworks. Slippage and lack of clarity between causal explanation and mechanistic explanation are often the culprit here.

One way to address this – and to make the mechanism concept clear – is to specify exactly what type of causal structure mechanism refers to. In the philosophical literature, two main approaches to characterizing mechanism are common. In the first, mechanism is defined narrowly, such that it refers to a causal structure with particular features. This first approach stems from original uses of mechanism in the 17th century, where it captured living systems that were analogized to simple machines and understood reductively in terms of lower-level component parts. This use of mechanism remains prevalent today and typically refers to causal systems that are hierarchical, finely detailed, and described in terms of mechanical interactions. This is seen in reference to enzyme mechanisms, a drug's mechanism of action, and mechanisms of cell signaling, as all involve reference to molecular causal components that underlie some effect of interest. These mechanisms are often described in fine-grained detail (often molecular detail) and involve causal relationships described in terms of mechanical interactions (force, action, and motion) (Ross, 2021). One implication of this notion of mechanism is that there are other causal structures that are not mechanisms, as there are a huge variety of diverse causal systems with different features than those identified in the narrow notion of mechanism. For example, unlike the notion of mechanism, some systems have interacting causes from both higher and lower scales (such as explanations involving biological and social-environmental factors), and some explanations cite macro-scale causal systems that lack appeals to lower-level causal components. It is along these lines that others have grown interested in other causal systems that are nonmechanistic, as seen in appeals to notions of causal pathways, processes, cascades, circuits, triggers, and so on (Dupre, 2013; Ross, 2021, 2022; Ross & Bassett, 2024).

In the second notion, mechanism is defined broadly, such that it refers to nearly any type of causal system and is often used synonymously with "causal system." While many philosophical accounts of mechanism began with narrower conceptions, a large number have broadened their definitions to include increasingly more causal systems in the mechanism framework. Some view this as an "imperialistic" strategy to engulf all causal systems and causal explanation within the mechanism framework (Kaplan, 2017). This view does not deny that there are diverse types of causal system and causal explanation in the life sciences; it just classifies them all as mechanisms. A main worry with this broad notion is that mechanism is so expansive that it loses any clear meaning beyond "causal system." This has led new mechanists to cite fairly generic features as characteristic of mechanisms – such as the features mentioned earlier – where these features are less illuminating because they are present in all causal systems. For example, it is suggested that mechanisms have some organization of their causal factors, but as all causal systems have this feature, it does not highlight anything unique to mechanisms, but instead a necessary presence in any causal system. Further indication of this expansive notion is seen when new mechanists specify "what are not mechanisms" and all examples are noncausal systems (mere correlations, relations of mathematical dependency, etc.) (Craver & Tabery, 2015). This reinforces conflation of mechanism and causation while making it unclear what an account of mechanism provides above and beyond accounts of causation and causal explanation (which do the hard work of distinguishing cause from correlation, etc.). One wonders what would change if we simply replaced "mechanism" with "causal system" in these accounts; would they tell us anything more about causal explanation, reasoning, and understanding that causal frameworks fail to provide?

Whether one adopts a narrow or a broad notion of mechanism, there should be one point we can all agree on: the importance of capturing different types of causes and causal systems that are present in the world and that scientists cite in their explanations. These are seen in references to causal diversity in psychiatry – systems with causes that are specific, stable, proximal, distal, and so on (Ross and Kendler, Chapter 8 in this volume). This suggests that it is more important to capture causal varieties in science than to pin down which types of causal systems are (or are not) mechanisms. As Craver states, "The effort to draw a dividing line between those causal structures that count as mechanisms and those that do not will always seem to be arbitrary" (Craver, Chapter 20 in this volume).

Can we sideline issues of what mechanism means and focus on causal varieties? One challenge for this is that the term "mechanism" remains a status and gatekeeper concept in many life science fields. This is seen in top science journals and competitive grants (National Science Foundation, National Institute of Health, National Institute of Mental Health) that explicitly state that they will support the work that identifies mechanisms and provides "mechanistic insights" (Ross & Bassett, 2024). This situation is complicated by the fact that researchers in the fields of biology and neuroscience use the mechanism concept in differing ways and engage in much debate (as seen in peer review) over whether or not a given paper has provided mechanistic insights. Journal editors face serious challenges, as their journal guidelines state that papers should present "mechanistic research" but struggle to provide a clear definition of how mechanism should be understood (Ross & Bassett, 2024).

Thus, while the main focus should be on the causal varieties found in the world and that are needed to provide scientific understanding, we also need to grapple with what mechanism means and how it is used. To prevent crosstalk and properly guide the field, discussions of mechanism should be further clarified because at the moment they remain unclear and unhelpful to many. Promising ways forward – and that are impactful for psychiatry – will clarify what types of causal systems matter for the field, different types of methods that support identifying causal structure, what mechanism means (or should mean) in scientific and clinical discussions, and what types of causal reasoning will help the field address its main goals.

REFERENCES

Craver, C. (2007). *Explaining the brain.* Oxford University Press.

Craver, C., & Tabery, J. (2015). Mechanisms in science. *Stanford Encyclopedia of Philosophy (SEP).* Retrieved August 10, 2025 from https://plato.stanford.edu/entries/science-mechanisms/

Dupré, J. A. (2013). Living causes. *Proceedings of the Aristotelian Society, 87,* 19–35.

Kaplan, D. M. (2017). *Integrating mind and brain science: Explanation and integration in mind and brain science.* Oxford University Press.

Kendler, K. S. (2005). "A gene for...": The nature of gene action in psychiatric disorders. *American Journal of Psychiatry, 162*(7), 1243–1252. https://doi.org/10.1176/appi.ajp.162.7.1243

Ross, L. N. (2021). Causal concepts in biology: How pathways differ from mechanisms and why it matters. *The British Journal for the Philosophy of Science, 72*(1), 131–158.

(2022). Cascade versus mechanism: The diversity of causal structure in science. *The British Journal for the Philosophy of Science.* https://doi.org/10.1086/723623

(2024). Explanation in contexts of causal complexity: Lessons from psychiatric genetics. In W. C. Bausman, J. K. Baxter, & O. M. Lean (Eds.), *From biological practice to scientific metaphysics* (pp. 209–235). Publishers Minnesota Studies.

Ross, L. N., & Bassett, D. S. (2024). Causation in neuroscience: Keeping mechanism meaningful. *Nature Reviews Neuroscience, 25*(2), 81–90. https://doi.org/10.1038/s41583-023-00778-7

Woodward, J. F. (2003). *Making things happen.* Oxford University Press.

(2010). Causation in biology: Stability, specificity, and the choice of levels of explanation. *Biology & Philosophy, 25*, 287–318.

Section 8

CHAPTER 22

Introduction to Hyman's "Mechanism Matters"

Peter Zachar

In his chapter Steven Hyman describes several paths forward for a more mechanistic understanding of psychiatric disorder, articulating the promise of such an approach as well as illustrating how it encompasses a variety of projects.

He begins by discussing the disappointing levels of success that can be attributed to the treatment of psychiatric disorders. Although many people benefit from treatment, relief is often partial, temporary, or even nonexistent. It is unlikely, he notes, that treatments will be able to have high success rates at reducing symptoms, minimize unwanted side effects, and prevent relapses and disease progression unless they target underlying mechanisms.

Also troubling, writes Hyman, is that there have been very few new treatments introduced since the middle of the 20th century, and most of those were based on serendipity rather than basic research. Even though the potential market for new treatments is extensive, lack of information about which underlying mechanisms to target has led industry to reduce its investment in psychiatric research.

To some extent, Hyman lays the blame for this stagnation on psychiatry's reliance on the descriptive psychopathology of the DSM and the ICD, which, as he notes, is blind to underlying mechanisms – or as he says, for a psychiatry based on surface phenomenology only, mechanistic heterogeneity is cryptic. He acknowledges that this is not a psychiatry-specific problem, noting that for diseases such as type 2 diabetes, treatments may be effective only for a subset of patients who appear clinically indistinguishable from other people with the same diagnosis.

One way to make progress, he suggests, is to use biomarkers to stratify DSM-ICD categories into more mechanistically tractable subclasses. He offers several examples of biomarkers, noting that "biomarker" is itself a broad class encompassing diagnostic, stratification, disease progression tracking, and treatment biomarkers – all of which can reside across multiple levels of analysis. The point here is that psychiatry has treatments that work some of the time, but it is not always clear why. It would be better to know when they work and why – with "when" and "why" being closely related. Mechanistic biomarkers potentially make "when" more predictable and promote the formulation of hypotheses regarding "why."

Throughout the chapter Hyman describes some successful applications of biomarkers in medicine. These include driver mutations that span different kinds of cancer (lung, liver, etc.), which predict treatment prognosis better than the type of cancer. Another example is new drugs to target excessive amyloid beta and tau levels that can be prescribed for Alzheimer's disease before symptoms manifest but only after the excessive levels of these proteins have been confirmed.

Hyman is particularly critical of the categorical model used in the DSM-ICD, which, in addition to being blind to mechanistic heterogeneity, has created over-specified categories. The negative consequences of this approach include exaggerated comorbidity relative to those categories, heterotypic discontinuity between categories over time, and the use of rigid diagnostic thresholds in a one-size-fits-all manner that cannot be adjusted to respond to variation in age, disease stage, family history, and so on.

This is not to say that making progress is simply a matter of prioritizing the discovery of mechanisms. As Hyman acknowledges, psychopathology is incredibly complex, with causes existing across different spatial and temporal scales. Psychopathology involves behavior and multiple layers of perception as influenced by personal history, cognitive capacities, personality traits, and sociocultural environment all in the context of being embodied biological organisms. Furthermore, the manifestation of psychopathology can be described in a wide variety of overlapping ways.

There have been, Hyman notes, many false dawns in the science of psychopathology. He is not claiming that the field is out of the dark yet, but he does believe that many new technologies in genomics, computer science, and data science have begun to emanate tangible sparks of progress, and he expects they will increasingly light the way to a more causation-based and successful psychiatry.

In his response, Kenneth Kendler defends a continuing role for descriptive psychopathology in psychiatric science. He notes how close attention to clinical description has contributed to his own work in psychiatric genetics. In his view, it is incorrect to blame descriptive psychopathology/taxonomy (and the DSM-ICD) for the lack of progress in developing new treatments. As Kraepelin realized, it is hard to go very far without an accurate description of what you are seeking biomarkers for even if those descriptions need further iteration and refinement.

Psychiatric disorders, no matter how they are taxonomized, are causally complex and difficult to figure out. Using the paradigm of validators, the DSM workgroups could and would readily incorporate biomarkers into the classification if they were available, but except for narcolepsy, none have not been forthcoming. Kendler notes that in the 1940s there was a realization that discovering biomarkers for rheumatic fever was being obstructed because the specialists each had their own favored description of the disorder – so shared criteria were proposed. When important biomarkers for rheumatic fever were later discovered, they were added to the consensus description of the disease that had proven useful; they did not replace it. Furthermore, notes Kendler, the biomarkers did not eliminate casual heterogeneity; they tracked it.

The interchange between Hyman and Kendler show how contrasting views on the relationship between the search for diagnostically useful biomarkers and the description of clinical phenomenology have important implications for one's view about the future trajectory of psychiatric science, including for funding priorities. For those who have devoted their careers to the advancement of the science, different visions for where to go next are also imbued with great passion.

Because we value the interactive nature of these Copenhagen volumes, commentaries on the main chapters are shared with the chapters' authors to invite feedback – which sometimes takes the form of clarifications of the arguments and occasionally suggestions for improvement. When Steve Hyman received Ken Kendler's commentary, he took this process a step further and penned a written response. As volume editors, we thought this commentary-phase exchange was articulating some core issues and wanted to include it in this volume, but I also suggested that Ken be given a chance to respond briefly.

In his rejoinder, Hyman argues that the problem is that clinical description in psychiatry does not yield scientific kinds that can lead to the discovery and/or be augmented with information about biomarkers. He agrees that careful clinical description is important to understanding patient's distress and dysfunction, but those descriptions are typically based on surface features. They are causally heterogenous, partial descriptions demarcated by arbitrary thresholds – and thus cannot ground a progressive psychiatric science. Furthermore, as they are taken literally, they more likely represent an obstacle to progress. What psychiatry needs is what Hyman calls ground truth – for example, the ability of amyloid deposits to stratify Alzheimer's disease from other clinically indistinguishable dementias. Without such anchoring, the selection of biological correlates would be ungrounded and speculative. With such anchoring, a more principled identification of biological correlates of things like treatment response could reduce the reliance on clinical description in decisions-making. In Hyman's view, rapidly advancing technology, computational methods, and large-scale genetic studies could help lead the way.

In his rejoinder, Kendler agrees that striking advances in basic science offer exciting new possibilities for insight into the etiology and pathology of psychiatric disorders. He reiterates that the continued reliance on clinical description in the DSM is the result of the inability to discover diagnostically useful biomarkers, not the cause. He continues to disagree with Hyman about the scientific value of some descriptive categories – about which much has been learned. For example, the DSM-III distinctions between panic disorder and generalized anxiety disorder and between major depression and bipolar disorder have been shown to have substantial validity even though these categories are also unlikely to carve nature at the joints in the way dictated by traditional notions of natural kinds. There could of course be some rapid progress with sudden shifts in our understanding (akin to a Kuhnian revolution), but in Kendler's view, in the iteration of constructs, small cumulative improvements also represent the kind of hard work that can produce progress.

CHAPTER 23

Mechanism Matters

Advancing Beyond Descriptive Psychiatry?

Steven E. Hyman

Current psychotherapies, medications, and neuromodulatory interventions have significant benefits for people with mental illness, but too often these treatments fall short. Existing treatments may provide only partial or temporary relief of symptoms and sometimes no benefit at all. Several highly morbid and disabling symptom clusters lack effective treatments altogether, including the highly disabling cognitive symptoms of schizophrenia (Green et al., 2000) and the social communication difficulties of autism (Hyman, 2012). With very few exceptions (e.g., brexanolone for postpartum depression), current pharmacologic treatment represents chemical modifications of serendipitously discovered 1950s prototypes. Even xanomeline-trospium, a new mechanism antipsychotic drug approved by the US Food and Drug Administration (FDA) in 2024, was identified serendipitously when its antipsychotic properties were observed during a failed clinical trial attempting to enhance cognition in individuals with Alzheimer's disease (Yohn et al., 2022). Lack of insight into the mechanisms underlying psychiatric disorders has not only driven reliance on serendipity but has also stalled advances in efficacy. Clozapine, the antipsychotic drug that is most effective – for reasons that remain a mystery – was first synthesized in 1959. Even when effective, existing treatments act on symptoms but not underlying disease mechanisms, thus failing to slow conditions that are progressive or reliably prevent relapses. Treatment-limiting side effects – not only for medications such as antipsychotic drugs or neuromodulatory treatments such as ECT but even for some psychotherapies such as some exposure therapies – highlight the need for greater safety and tolerability as well as greater efficacy.

Treatments that are effective are often beyond the reach of people suffering from mental illness. Insurance is inadequate in many countries; well-trained practitioners are in short supply in many countries, and formularies in many low- and middle-income countries fail to stock an adequate range of cost-effective drugs to treat mental illness (Institute of

Medicine, 2014; National Academies of Sciences, Engineering, and Medicine, 2016). Widespread marginalization of people with mental illness has contributed to many shortsighted policies. In the United States, for example, deinstitutionalization of the seriously mentally ill was not accompanied by provision of financial resources, facilities, or personnel needed to provide adequate care resulting in dire outcomes such as widespread homelessness and incarceration in jails and prisons (Ransom, 2023). Given the ubiquity of stigmatization and "othering" of people with serious mental illness and given the lessons of history, it seems improbable that policymakers will allocate the funding and resources needed to improve conditions significantly. This perilous situation for people with mental illness underscores the need for scientists in academia and industry to develop treatments directed at underlying mechanisms to halt disease onset and progression and the deterioration that contributes powerfully to stigma and marginalization. Unmet need for safer and more effective treatments is widely recognized.

Combined with the high prevalence and global burden of mental disorders (Hjorthøj et al., 2017; Whiteford et al., 2013), investment by industry could produce significant commercial opportunities. Yet the pharmaceutical industry has spent the last two decades progressively and substantially decreasing its investment in research and development for mental illness (Bell, 2020; Geils & Riley, 2022; Kesselheim, 2015; Pankevitch, 2014). According to investors, industry leaders, regulators, and other stakeholders (National Academies of Sciences, Engineering, and Medicine, 2017; Paul & Potter, 2024), leading obstacles to investment are the lack of insight into mechanisms of mental illness and the absence of biomarkers to match patients with treatment and monitor efficacy. The lure of potentially lucrative markets cannot overcome experience and strong predictors of failure. Without insights into disease mechanisms, attempts to identify pathways and molecular targets for psychiatric treatment development remains tied to informed speculation (National Academies of Sciences, Engineering, and Medicine, 2017). Without robust quantitative biomarkers, investigators are left to rely on the descriptive diagnoses of the DSM system to select patients for clinical trials; in that case the probability of demonstrating efficacy is low (Krainc, 2023; National Academies of Sciences, Engineering, and Medicine, 2023; Paul & Potter, 2024). It is thus unsurprising that psychiatric drugs have the highest failure rates among all therapeutic areas in costly late-stage clinical trials. Worse, these failures occur disproportionately for lack of efficacy (rather than toxicity), indicating the falsification of therapeutic hypotheses (e.g., the wrong target or pathway for patients' conditions) and an inability to identify appropriate, potentially treatment-responsive patients (Krainc et al., 2023; Pankevitch et al., 2014).

Why has psychiatric therapeutics proven so difficult despite recognition of the profound limitations of current treatments? It can be stated without exaggerated defensiveness that nature has placed high hurdles in the way of understanding and treating mental illness. The complexity of human brains is both staggering and humbling. At every scale from the genetic and molecular to the circuits and computations that give rise to sensation, cognition, emotion, behavioral control – and to symptoms of mental illness – complex dynamical interactions, stochasticity, and emergent properties are the rule. Thus, reductionist approaches, while absolutely necessary for the design of interpretable neurobiological experiments, fall short in their predictive and explanatory power when questions demand integrative answers or attempts are made to follow causation – for example, a high impact genetic mutation – across levels of analysis. Further, we must recognize significant diversity of brain structure and function, cognition, and behavior across approximately 8 billion members of our species, harboring tens of millions of genetic differences and developing in vastly different environments and cultures. In this chapter, I intend to keep the complexity and heterogeneity of human brains and mental illness front of mind but will not dwell on a scientific exposition. Rather, in the spirit of the symposium from which this chapter is derived, my plan is to examine the epistemic obstacles to understanding and treatment of mental illness. The obstacles to which I refer are not imposed by nature but result from our field's dogged unwillingness to grapple with neural complexity and the hidden diversity of underlying mechanisms characteristic of biology and medicine. The result has been decades of research designs foredoomed to failure – my focus here – and a disservice to people with mental illness through the imposition of a nosology rife with shifting diagnoses, such as in children or after a first psychotic episode, an incredible frequency of comorbidity, poor prediction of treatment needs, and a categorical structure (Hyman 2010, 2021, 2023) that readily takes on the characteristics of an identity. Psychiatry lags most other fields of medicine in elucidation of disease mechanisms and in therapeutics partly because the brain and its outputs represent humanity's greatest scientific challenge. However, as alluded to earlier, human cognitive biases have made the scientific challenges much harder. A bias toward essentializing, and thus the often-unconscious formation of generalizations based on a few salient representative features (Kahneman & Tversky, 1972), often has utility, even survival value, in everyday life by simplifying complex situations to permit faster processing and responses to novelty, rewards, and threats. For successful science, however, investigators must surmount such automatic heuristics biases. Unfortunately, a central theme in descriptive psychiatry (Robins & Guze, 1970) has been to embrace such biases in the form for discontinuous categories. In Procrustean fashion, Spitzer and the DSM-III Task Force molded and stretched complex data (when there was data) into a uniform set of boxes, the discontinuous categories defined by criteria that had been selected for interrater reliability. Despite a disavowal of claims to validity in the DSM volumes, the forced categorical structure fits with human tendencies to essentialize complex phenomena and reify named abstractions. In this way the DSM converts complex, heterogeneous observations – including self-observations in the case of those with mental illness – into simple, uniform entities treated as etiologically uniform that can be thought of as having independent existence (Pisl et al., 2025).Of course, in human biology, there are a limited number of disease mechanisms and psychiatry, like the rest of medicine, must justifiably cluster patients into a limited number of classes based on mechanism for the purposes of diagnosis and treatment. Treatment development would be impossible if residual heterogeneity beyond shared mechanisms caused each patient to be treated as unique. Indeed, insight into disease mechanisms identifies those aspects of variability that matter for disease course altering as opposed to symptomatic treatment or reassurance. Recognition of human uniqueness retains an important role, however, in forming the relationships of professionals and diverse caregivers with those suffering from illness, as there is more to treatment and its reception than biomarkers and therapeutics. Progress in therapeutics requires that diagnostic groupings be treated as hypotheses to be tested as technology and measurement permit. Ultimately, the goal of what is aspirationally called precision medicine is to group patients based on well-validated biomarkers integrated with their evolving symptoms and impairments to match them with the treatments most likely to be beneficial at the relevant point in their illness.

Scientifically driven alterations in diagnoses and thresholds occur piecemeal across most of medicine, as new discoveries cannot be expected to synchronize. In the DSM system, in contrast, every disorder is formally conceptualized in the same way as a discontinuous category. Moreover, revisions of the DSM emerge in unitary fashion from a single organized process conducted under the guidance of a small group of people brought together by a single organization. That is a recipe for epistemic capture by the incumbent structure with rejection of outlier observations and new diagnostic approaches. Epistemic hegemony that strongly facilitates essentializing and reification is thus a critical impediment to progress, as is the continuing commitment to phenomenology. This commitment that was entirely rational and defensible during the mid-20th century as the edifice of psychoanalytic theory crumbled with no objective biological insights to replace it. Now, however, the prioritization of phenomenology is a monument to cognitive inertia and the pathologies of normal science described by Kuhn (1962).

To understand how DSM categories and commitment to phenomenology undercuts our field, consider the infirmities of ubiquitously used case–control research designs when employed in psychiatry research. If the individuals recruited into "case" cohorts are diagnosed by DSM or other descriptive psychiatry-based criteria, much evidence exists for variability that can vitiate research results. Notwithstanding the goal of making durable observations with meaningful effect sizes, scientists using such designs and hoping to find group mean differences are functionally blind to the underlying heterogeneity given the lack of biomarkers to stratify patients by underlying disease mechanisms. For those involved in treatment development, including clinical trialists, the few companies still meaningfully engaged in psychiatry research, and regulators, there is little choice but to rely on entrenched DSM criteria or other surface descriptions for patient selection and endpoints. The result is that even for drugs that are eventually approved by the FDA, there are multiple failed clinical trials in which the active drug is not significantly superior to placebo, and for many patients that improve there is no certainty about the relative contributions of the active drug, the placebo, or the natural waning of episodic symptoms (Khin et al., 2011; Krainc et al., 2023; Stone et al., 2022). The upshot is the recognition that the inability to stratify patients by disease mechanism in psychiatry is an important source of failure (Hyman, 2012; Krainc et al., 2023). Since companies cannot continue to spend on a failing proposition, they have, in large measure, reallocated their resources away from psychiatry – despite the unmet need – and into areas such as cancer, autoimmunity, and metabolism where mechanisms are increasingly understood and where mechanism-based biomarkers enhance the possibility of successful clinical trials.How can research on psychiatric therapeutics advance beyond serendipity toward more systematic approaches that will ultimately match the right patients with the right treatment at the right time (precision medicine)? Psychiatry must work with all due speed toward retiring the DSM system from the realms of science and treatment development and advance toward discovering and validating biomarkers. Ordinary language terms such as "depression" or "lung cancer" create significant value in human discourse. But they are not scientific terms, and adding the modifier "major" to depression does not make it so.The limitations imposed by phenomenology extend to all diagnostic systems that rely on it including HiTOP (Kotov et al., 2017) and the International Classification of Disease (World Health Organization, 2019), despite their advantages over the DSM in embracing (HiTOP) and advancing toward (ICD-11) dimensional diagnoses. At the same time, I must confess that my central argument focused on cryptic mechanistic heterogeneity within psychiatric diagnoses suffers from a serious empirical hole. Although polygenicity and the failures of case–control designs are consistent with such heterogeneity, neither I nor anyone else has insight into the number of mechanisms that might underlie psychiatric symptoms or the degree to which multiple mechanisms jointly contribute to any person's mental illness. While awaiting the discovery of disease mechanisms in psychiatry, there is no reason to imagine that psychiatry is exempt from a central challenge of medicine: recognition that different underlying disease mechanisms (and thus different treatment needs) often give rise to clinically indistinguishable syndromes. Across medicine the history of unacceptable variability of treatment responses despite shared clinical presentations has contributed to a goal of "precision medicine" in which mechanism-based biomarkers match patients with the right treatment at the right point in their illness.

A significant challenge for psychiatry research, including imaging, physiology, genome-wide association studies (GWAS), and rare variant association studies (RVAS) in genetics, lies in low-quality case definitions in case–control study designs. In psychiatric case–control studies, affected individuals are typically selected by DSM or other descriptive diagnostic criteria and thus, among other infirmities, suffer from mechanistic heterogeneity and arbitrary boundaries with health and other diagnosed conditions. Within diagnosis heterogeneity means that "cases" in case–control studies are comprised of individuals with an unknown number of distinct and overlapping disease mechanisms. While ordinary language terms such as "depression" or "lung cancer" are useful signifiers in the context of popular discourse, they are not scientific terms. Scientists and clinicians should not fall into the cognitive trap laid by reification of DSM categories. Named DSM disorders such as schizophrenia or major depression do not identify internally coherent natural kinds like elements in the periodic table (Hyman, 2021).The Diagnostic and Statistical Manual of Mental Disorders of the American Psychiatric Association beginning with its paradigm-setting third edition (DSM-III; American Psychiatric

Association, 1980) was promulgated with the goal of maximizing interrater reliability – achieving only middling success in that regard (Clarke et al., 2013) – while making no claims to validity. The DSM-III and its successor volumes have gained widespread influence in clinical practice, research, and diverse administrative uses. The scholar and psychiatrist Kenneth S. Kendler might argue that my concerns about the DSM system are misplaced because in his view DSM criteria are better understood as indexical (fallible indices of a hypothetical diagnostic construct) than as constitutive of the disorders they describe (Kendler et al., 2017). While a theoretically attractive position, there is little evidence that the world's diverse scientists, clinicians, epidemiologists, insurance adjusters, litigators, and policymakers construe DSM criteria as fallible indices, but employ them rather as constitutive of psychiatric disorders (Hyman, 2010, 2021). One telling example is the reliance on DSM criteria by the US Food and Drug Administration (FDA) as the basis for psychiatric clinical trials required for new drug approvals. FDA examiners do not use DSM criteria in the belief that they identify homogeneous patient cohorts, but because they represent the psychiatry community's consensus and compelling alternatives have not been forthcoming. The resulting drug approvals are highly consequential and result in marketing and prescription of medications for such conditions as major depression or schizophrenia as if they were coherent entities with respect to treatment needs. When patients respond poorly to several mechanistically similar antidepressants, they are described as having treatment-resistant depression. How odd. If a prescribed antibiotic failed to treat a cough caused by smoke inhalation or cancer, we would not describe the patient as treatment resistant; we would say we got the diagnosis wrong. Further evidence for reified, constitutive use of DSM criteria is their widespread employment for medical records, insurance reimbursement, determinations of disability, and many legal and administrative matters. DSM diagnoses are often required to apply for research grants or publish studies, and their prominent role in licensing examinations across mental health professions forces trainees to memorize them, surely a step toward reification (Hyman, 2010, 2021).

As alluded to earlier, the initial reliance on phenomenology by the descriptive psychiatry forerunners of the DSM-III (Robins & Guze, 1979) was historically justified as a disciplined, empirically grounded alternative to psychoanalytic theories, which in any case had largely eschewed making diagnoses. In the decades since DSM-III was published, however, significant advances in relevant science and technology should have brought to the fore scientifically rigorous alternatives to descriptive psychiatry, especially as implemented by the DSM system. Unfortunately, epistemic blinders created by the broad embrace of the by the DSM system combined with pessimism about alternatives to phenomenology have stunted programs of research attempting to find alternatives (Hyman, 2010, 2023). The impact of such blinders has proven terribly damaging to psychiatry research. For example, as alluded to previously, widely used case–control research designs in which "cases" are defined by DSM criteria smuggle implicit blindness to underlying patient heterogeneity into many studies. The result is that psychiatry research is plagued by small effect sizes and nonreplications (Lawrie, 2025; Marek & Laumann, 2025). A very troubling example comes from case–control studies based on structural or functional magnetic resonance imaging (MRI); despite more than 30 years of enormous expenditure of funds, effort, and human subject participation, despite more than 50,000 publications in PubMed yielded by searching for magnetic resonance imaging and mental disorders (as of August 30, 2025), MRI has failed to deliver diagnostic utility. In current clinical practice, there is no reason to obtain an MRI study for a new patient except to rule out a structural neurologic lesion. While the situation could partly represent shortcomings of the technology, far more likely it reflects the problem of unexamined heterogeneity that has not been overcome by increasing sample size (Greene et al., 2022; Marek & Laumann, 2025; Marek et al., 2022; Segal et al., 2023). Only in the last several years have imaging researchers recognized the fundamental infirmity of case–control designs for a field that lacks tools to account for the background variability of human brains, the computational heterogeneity and many unknowns related to cognition and symptom formation (Nour et al., 2022), or the biomarkers needed to stratify patients by mechanism. A recently described experimental approach to MRI imaging "precision functional mapping" uses individuals as their own controls in place of cohort-based case–control designs (Demeter & Greene, 2025). In a recent study employing this methodology, individuals with symptoms of depression were studied for 18 months with densely repeated fMRI examinations (Lynch et al., 2024). The study reported a nearly twofold expansion of the brain's salience network – a large effect size. It is an open question whether this alternative to case–control designs will stand up across studies, but it exemplifies and attempt to confront interindividual heterogeneity despite the continuing lack of biomarkers or other tools to stratify patients. Approaches using individuals as their own controls will have to address such questions as to whether results can be usefully generalized to subsets of patients without falling prey to overfitting.

Reliance on phenomenology is not the only significant intellectual weakness of the DSM system. As previously described (Hyman, 2007, 2010, 2021), major concepts have been propagated through the modest revisions of DSM diagnostic criteria without serious attention to much needed structural reforms, such as the need to begin incorporating quantitative dimensions. The paradigm-setting DSM-III (1980) is a product of the descriptive psychiatry of the 1960s and 1970s and thus antedated the development of modern human population and molecular genetics, molecular biology, epigenomics and proteomics, the coalescence of neurobiology into a coherent field (including its first graduate programs), modern computers and computational tools, data sciences, magnetic resonance imaging, and much else. Its foundations lay in the need for diagnoses that would help match patients with the newly emerging drugs of the 1950s pharmacologic revolution (Hyman 2012). A group of psychiatrists at Washington University, St. Louis created a bold and then largely sensible departure from the diagnostic approaches of the time (e.g., Robins & Guze, 1970). These self-styled descriptive psychiatrists eschewed the theoretical phantasms of psychoanalysis and hewed to such empirical data as was available, with enough discipline that they limited themselves to a small number of well-studied disorders, unlike the 265 disorders included in the DSM-III. Unfortunately, they chose discontinuous categories rather than quantitative dimensions as their conceptual representation of psychiatric disorders. This choice was partly influenced by their reverence for the 19th- and early 20th-century psychiatrist Emil Kraepelin, a careful empirical observer who had attempted – albeit not to his ultimate satisfaction – to distinguish dementia praecox (schizophrenia) from the manic-depressive insanity (bipolar disorder), and who believed furthermore that psychiatric disorders would ultimately be shown to be biological natural kinds that would, for example, "breed true" across generations. The choice of a categorical nosology was also partly a rejoinder to the antipsychiatry movement. Robert Spitzer (1975), the architect of DSM-III, argued with concern about the contentions of David Rosenhan (1973), questioning whether psychiatrists could distinguish well from ill, let alone make meaningful diagnoses. While Rosenhan's work was later shown to be fraudulent (Cahalan 2019; Scull, 2023), it captured a deep anxiety in psychiatry that exerted significant influence. Perhaps categorical diagnoses seemed to create a stronger intellectual stake in the ground than concepts of mental illness as quantitative deviations from health requiring normative decisions to set thresholds of illness. But the decision to treat mental disorders as discontinuous categories meant that schizophrenia or depression would share a conceptual framework with conditions like smallpox – either you have it or you don't – rather than type 2 diabetes mellitus or hypertension, conditions understood to be dimensional, which appeared, even contemporaneously, to be better models for depression and other psychiatric disorders. The arbitrary and rigid nature of disease thresholds based on symptom counts in the DSM categorical system has troubling consequences for prevention and early intervention, especially if insurance companies are involved. For dimensionally represented conditions such as type 2 diabetes and hypertension, thresholds require policy decisions, but these can be made based on empirical data of risk or harm and can be revised as new information emerges. Moreover, flexible categories such as prediabetes and subtyping based on quantitative clustering can be superimposed on quantitative data such as glucose tolerance, hemoglobin A1C, age of onset, body mass index, and the like for treatment decisions, epidemiologic studies, and other purposes.

In recent decades further evidence has accrued that strongly favors quantitative dimensions for psychiatric disorder. Evidence from shared genetic risk factors (Brainstorm Consortium, 2018; Grotzinger et al., 2022), overlapping polygenic risk in healthy and affected individuals (International Schizophrenia Consortium, 2009), epidemiology of environmental exposures, symptom distribution, and comorbidity (McGrath et al., 2020), molecular biology (Gandal et al., 2018), and neuroscience (reviewed in Hyman, 2021) demonstrate that individual symptoms and genetic risk alleles are normally distributed in human populations with no evidence of discontinuities in data distribution that would support a categorical distinction from health or between disease categories (Barch et al., 2013; Riglin et al., 2016; Riglin et al., 2017; Robinson et al., 2011; Robinson et al., 2016). In a system with nearly 300 poorly drawn discontinuous categories, symptoms associated with distinct disorders are not understood as the products of one or more mechanisms constitutive of that person's illness but are diagnosed as the co-occurrence of multiple distinct illnesses, comorbidity. When putative comorbidity results in sequentially changing diagnoses, as frequently occurs early in the course of psychotic illnesses (McGorry et al., 2018), an affected person might hypothetically participate in an imaging study, genetics study, or clinical trial with an initial diagnosis that is superseded by a different diagnosis a few months or years later. There are no clear protocols by which to annotate the initial study with the result of adding additional confounding to an already troubled literature. Moreover, shifting diagnoses and accrual of comorbid diagnoses create significant problems in clinical care, exacerbated in fragmented mental health care systems as exist in the United States where an affected person might be passed among multiple practitioners and institutions lacking clarity into the person's diagnostic trajectory.

While there is much that is amiss with the DSM system, we will not soon have a satisfactory replacement that can serve the clinical and administrative needs to which the DSM and related nosologies are put. My central contention is that the research community must retire this epistemically damaging approach to diagnosis and work assiduously to end *complete* reliance on phenomenology in psychiatric diagnosis. The operative consideration for the foreseeable future is termination of *complete* reliance. Unlike cancer and Alzheimer's disease, where diagnosis and staging are moving entirely to objective biomarkers that have implications for treatment (Jack et al., 2024; Veitch et al., 2021), psychiatry will continue, at least for many years, to rely on clinical description in conjunction with objective biomarkers as they are discovered and validated. For many cancers, treatment is dictated by somatic driver mutations. Alzheimer's disease appears to have biomarkers unique to the broad diagnosis (there are significant subtypes) as well as those shared with other forms of neurodegeneration and psychosis spectrum disorders (Jack et al., 2024; Johnson & Hyman, 2022). Moreover, once symptoms of cognitive decline emerge, treatments aimed at underlying mechanisms lose their efficacy. In contrast, at least at this stage of our knowledge, different clinical syndromes such as DSM-5-TR (2022) schizophrenia and bipolar 1 disorder or bipolar 2 disorder, major depression, and anxiety disorders share DNA risk variants (Brainstorm Consortium, 2018; Grotzinger et al., 2022) and patterns of brain gene expression (Gandal et al., 2017; Ling et al., 2024). As a result, candidate molecular and proteomic biomarkers as well as circuit-based biomarkers currently under investigation in psychiatry must be integrated with clinical information to be interpretable.

Studies aimed at discovering mechanism-based biomarkers for psychiatric disorders are early stages. These studies include molecular and cellar markers of excessive or inappropriate synapse elimination for psychosis spectrum disorders (Johnson & Hyman, 2022) and abnormalities in circuit function in mood and anxiety disorders (Scangos et al., 2022; Sheth & Mayberg, 2023). Such research will extend over many years, likely with the successes and failures characteristic of early clinical investigation. Beyond the challenges inherent in the science, it is important to focus on epistemic issues that bear on design of studies and their interpretation. Because DSM categories are so flawed and such poor mirrors of nature resulting *inter alia* from cryptic heterogeneity of mechanisms and transdiagnostic sharing of risk factors and symptoms (Hyman, 2010, 2021, 2023), their use in research designs for biomarker discovery or validation could very well prove lethal to these efforts. DSM criteria are not a "gold standard" for any biological measure. Warning flags abound, including the very limited success of case–control studies in which patient cohorts have been selected by DSM criteria. Because discovery and interpretation of biomarkers to be used for diagnosis, within diagnosis stratification, transdiagnostic predictors of treatment response, staging of diseases, and interpretation of treatment effect versus placebos are highly biased by the criteria used to select them, new strategies are necessary. To foreshadow my recommendations (in alignment with my own current research efforts), I would argue for a strategy in which DSM diagnoses are entirely ignored. Instead, attempts at biomarker discovery seem most likely to succeed insofar as designs can minimize antecedent diagnostic bias, without becoming entirely impractical. This goal can be approached by retreating from narrow diagnoses such as schizophrenia or bipolar 1 disorder to broad spectra such as a psychosis spectrum or a mood and anxiety spectrum that might then be reanalyzed from the bottom up. Spectra can be selected by such factors as shared genetics, comorbidity, shared symptoms and treatment response. I have encouraged such attempts (Andrews et al., 2009; Hyman, 2007). Given the heterogeneity and complexity of human brains, cognition, behavior, and mental disorders, it is unsurprising that even when one "zooms out" to a larger grouping, selection criteria do not converge on unitary, fully coherent constructs. However, these are reasonable starting points for scientific reanalysis, far more defensible than the narrow, arbitrarily bounded categories of the DSM system. As different research consortia select categories for reanalysis, there will surely be overlap among them. It could not be otherwise.

As I have emphasized, when patient cohorts are selected using DSM or other phenomenologically based diagnostic criteria for case–control studies the typical outcomes of which are null results, or studies described as positive based on p values and small effect sizes followed by frequent non-replications (Khin et al., 2011; Marek & Laumann, 2024; Nour et al., 2022; Stone et al., 2022), one must ask why the reliance on DSM categories continues. While descriptive psychiatry began as a liberating rejoinder to psychoanalytic theory and practice, it has congealed into a poster child for Thomas Kuhn's (1962) concept of normal science, constituting a deeply ingrained cognitive structure for psychopathology enforced by training and entrenched community norms. Observations that should call the basic structure and assumptions of the DSM and closely related nosologies into question – such as the plague of comorbidity – are instead explained within the DSM structure. The remarkable level of cross-disorder genetic correlation identified by GWAS (e.g., a genetic correlation of 0.7 between DSM schizophrenia and bipolar disorder) has produced relatively few papers questioning disorder boundaries (Smoller, 2013), few proposals to jettison the categorical structure (Hyman, 2021, 2023), or recognition that shared and unshared mechanisms lurk unexpectedly beneath the surface of clinical description. For the most part, cross-disorder genetic correlation is treated as interesting, has generated many papers in high-profile journals, but has not generated a clarion call to action. Anomalous findings such as these generate more research within the paradigm but not a deeper questioning of assumption. Within the bounds of community-tolerance characteristic of normal science (i.e., agreement, *inter alia*, on good questions, acceptable methods, permissible interpretations, and desirable meetings and journals), DSM criteria continue to be used to structure scientific questions and design studies and to serve as the standards by which candidate biological mechanisms are measured. When such mechanisms transgress the boundaries of a DSM category, alternative explanations are created or the measure is discarded. It is interesting to reflect on the fate of dexamethasone suppression test (DST). It is a moot question whether the DST might have found utility as a treatment response biomarker to compliment the rating scales based on self-report. Individuals with abnormal results in the DST did not conform to the boundaries of DSM major depression, and the test is long forgotten. Whether or not the DST could have been a useful objective biological marker, the story of its proposal and demise is a remarkable illustration of power of cognitive distortion within the psychiatry research community. An arbitrarily constructed box, the DSM category of major depression, has been elevated to the gold-standard status by which to judge the significance and utility of a well-defined biologic measure. De facto, the DSM system has achieved the goal of being an influential common language for psychopathology underwritten by the poorly supported belief that its operationalized diagnostic criteria provide interrater reliability. Beginning with the DSM-III, selected sets of criteria have been field-tested for interrater reliability at a modest number of chosen academic and clinical centers (Regier et al., 2013). Interrater reliability for psychiatric disorders is measured by Cohen's kappa coefficient where a kappa value of 1 represents perfect agreement and a kappa coefficient of 0 indicates agreement at the level of chance. More than 50 years ago, Robins and Guze (1970) argued reliability of criteria would lead to diagnostic validity; certainly, without diagnostic agreement, investigations of the scientific underpinnings of a given diagnosis would not be possible. However, their optimism has not been borne out. In field tests for the DSM-5, Regier et al. (2013) reported that the kappa coefficient for major depression, where there had been no change in the diagnostic criteria, was 0.2 – an unacceptable level – and that among the diagnoses examined, five were in a range described as "very good" (kappa = 0.60–0.79), nine were accounted as good (kappa = 0.2–0.59), six were accounted as questionable (kappa = 0.2–0.39), and three were unacceptable (kappa values less than 0.2). These results are particularly terrible given that most psychiatric diagnoses and treatments are made by non-psychiatrists, who can order standard laboratory tests for general medical diagnoses. For objectives tests in medicine, the best results for the DSM and accounted by Regier et al. (2013) as "very good" would be considered intolerable and dangerous.With no claims to validity and such disappointing results for reliability, it is unfortunate that the influence of descriptive psychiatric diagnoses has, if anything, expanded in recent years. This is because investigators have increasingly undertaken studies based on mining data from psychiatric electronic medical records (EMRs), increasingly in combination with artificial intelligence (AI). Unlike most of medicine where EMRs contain objective laboratory measures (such as fasting glucose, hemoglobin $A1_C$, BMI, age of onset, presence of antibodies against insulin, and measures of end organ damage for a patient with suspected or established diabetes mellitus), EMRs in psychiatry contain a congeries of surface-level observations and descriptive DSM and ICD diagnoses (and ICD codes). Imaging results may be included but, as discussed, they do not provide meaningful clinical information concerning psychiatric disorder per se. When AI uses psychiatric EMRs as training data, it ingests the problematic biases of descriptive psychiatry and lack anything akin to ground truth against which the data can be measured, such as biopsy results for cancer, CSF levels of A-beta or tau levels, or their anatomic distribution by PET scanning for Alzheimer's disease. The enthusiasm in psychiatry for the combination of EMRs and AI in the absence of biomarkers or anything approximating ground truth is highly disconcerting because once again it leads the field into an intellectual *cul de sac*, no matter how trendy.For psychiatry, paths to the discovery of disease mechanisms and mechanism-based biomarkers are proving to be extremely difficult, with piecemeal successes and many rejected hypotheses. However, glimmers of success in identifying CSF fluid biomarkers of PET biomarkers for psychosis spectrum disorders (Gracias et at., 2022; Onwardi et al., 2020) and personalized biomarkers to guide deep brain stimulation for depression (Scangos et al., 2021) indicate that success is possible. A terrible misstep, however, that would long delay mechanism-based biomarker discovery would be the continued embrace of the DSM system and related nosologies dependent on phenomenology whether in newly designed studies or in EMRs.If psychiatry can emerge intellectually from its long, normal science, epistemic commitment to phenomenology, how then best to proceed in the quest for disease mechanisms and biomarkers thereof? To minimize biases retained, even unconsciously, from the long dominance of descriptive psychiatry and DSM categories psychiatry, a fresh reanalysis of psychopathology is most likely to succeed if it begins with the broadest possible diagnostic frameworks that remain scientifically tractable. I believe (Hyman, 2007, 2023) that a reanalysis of psychopathology based on etiology (e.g., Dalmau et al., 2008) and pathophysiological mechanisms should begin with broad disease spectra (Andrews et al., 2009) that can rest of the data – but not the conclusions – of recent studies of comorbidities and genetics (e.g., Grotzinger et al., 2022; McGrath et al., 2020). Such analyses justify beginning with a psychosis spectrum, a spectrum comprised of mood and anxiety pathology, and others. None of these spectra will be perfect, some will overlap, and some may turn out to be misleading, but the recruitment of patients into recontactable cohorts should prove possible. Analysis of patient cohorts with such spectrum conditions should include complementary interdisciplinary approaches such as reasonably deep phenotyping consistent with retention of participants in cohorts, genotyping, collection and analysis of cerebrospinal fluid (CSF) and plasma, and well-considered imaging or physiology, again consistent with longitudinal recall. A critical error in psychiatric research, recently repeated by the Psychiatric Genomics Consortium (PGC), is the failure to create sample and phenotype data repositories for data sharing and in recognition that new technologies and new hypotheses will arise. Deeper phenotyping and biobanking is costly and has thus been left out of most psychiatric genetics, but the result is hundreds of statistically significant DNA variants that cannot be assigned with any confidence to a meaningful patient grouping. The Alzheimer's Disease Neuroimaging Initiative (ADNI; Veitch et al., 2022) took a different tack over the last 20 years, and after a period of trial and error has produced biomarkers that are revolutionizing Alzheimer's disease treatment development and its clinical applications. In fairness to psychiatric researchers, unlike neurodegenerative disorders, psychiatric disorders lack pathognomonic findings including ground truth-like diagnostic anchors such as amyloid, tau, alpha-synuclein, or TDP-43. The lack of any salient pathologic anchors for patient grouping or anything approximating diagnostic ground truth, a psychiatric equivalent of ADNI would have been impossible until the last decade. Perforce it would have been an undisciplined, costly fishing expedition. What has changed is success of psychiatric genetics, notwithstanding its reliance on very shallow phenotyping (Mullins et al., 2022; Trubetskoy et al., 2023). While shallow phenotyping, cross-sectional designs, and lack of biobanking means that the scientific value of risk-associated DNA variants is far less then they might have been, the phenotypic associations are "good enough" to confer meaningful scientific traction and, when integrated with multiomics and neurobiology, generate fruitful hypotheses, some of which, limited by technology and the ethics that limit human experimentation, are already being tested in patient cohorts. Several reasonable approaches to discovery of circuit-level biomarkers have been initiated for depression and obsessive-compulsive disorder based on physiological recordings from patients undergoing deep brain stimulation (Scangos et al., 2022; Sheth & Mayberg, 2023) and for schizophrenia spectrum and other psychotic disorders through biochemical investigation of cerebrospinal fluid and positron emission tomography (PET) (Dalmau et al., 2008; Gracias et al., 2021, Onwordi et al., 2020) following upon the successful example of ADNI (Veitch et al., 2022).

Because psychiatry lacks access to human biopsy samples from affected tissue of the sort available to almost all other areas of disease research, it must rely on inferences from genetics, cerebrospinal fluid postmortem samples, and more recently from human cellular models derived from induced pluripotent stem cells (iPSCs) for clues to molecular mechanisms of mental illness. As alluded to earlier, the development of genomic technologies, computational tools, and data-sharing consortia during the first decade of the 21st century made it possible to successfully conduct unbiased large-scale studies of human genetics such as genome-wide association studies (GWAS) in which psychiatry and psychology have been both leaders and beneficiaries (Abdellaoui et al., 2023). Although there is a long way to go, both in gene discovery and interpretation, GWAS has yielded hundreds of genome-wide significant loci associated with mental disorders including schizophrenia (Trubetskoy et al., 2022), bipolar disorder (Mullins et al., 2021), major depressive disorder (Adams et al., 2024) and others. The next step, which is to extract clues to biological mechanisms from GWAS results is extremely difficult. GWAS loci do not directly yield causal variants associated with risk of psychiatric disorders (or any other phenotype.) Rather, GWAS loci represent haplotype blocks, a sequence of contiguous genetic markers found together within a particular population; these markers are inherited together because they are physically linked on a section of a chromosome. A variety of approaches are needed to identify the variant, typically a single nucleotide polymorphism (SNP) that most likely exerts a causal effect on the phenotype. The next challenge comes from the small effect size exerted by each genome-wide significant locus and the fact that the vast majority of significant GWAS loci (more than 90%) occur in the noncoding genome. Noncoding sequences typically have roles in gene regulation but are less well understood than sequences that code for proteins. In addition to GWAS, advances in DNA sequencing, including cost reductions, have made it possible to sequence all protein coding regions of the genome (whole exome sequencing) from tens of thousands of individuals affected by mental disorder and controls. These studies have yielded ultra-rare high-impact protein truncating variants – resulting in hemizygous null mutations – that have so far been associated with schizophrenia (Singh et al., 2022) and bipolar disorder (Palmer et al., 2022). Such high-impact variants are useful experimentally because they can be used in generate transgenic animals (mouse and nonhuman primates) and induced human pluripotent cell (iPSC) lines derived from patients or controls to interrogate the function of protein coding genes associated with mental illness. Technologies for sequencing the RNAs in a single cell (yielding that cell's transcriptome) and identifying the complete pattern of chromatin modification in a single cell (yielding its epigenome) have become so efficient (Jain et al., 2023; Russell et al., 2024; Tian et al., 2023) that it is now possible to systematically study millions of individual neurons and glia derived from postmortem human brains donated by people who had mental disorders as well as unaffected controls. Integrated with results from genetics studies, transcriptomes and epigenomes from postmortem human brains provide early glimpses into disease mechanisms (Ling et al., 2024). The goal is to exploit knowledge of mechanisms to nominate therapeutic targets and biomarkers that will supplement and partially displace phenomenology in diagnosis and stratification. Fluid biomarker studies of schizophrenia spectrum and mood disorders are currently planned or under way (Hyman, 2023; Johnson & Hyman, 2022; Krainc et al.,, 2023; Paul & Potter, 2024), but these will move the field forward if prosecuted in the types of broad diagnostic spectra described previously, and not in cohorts selected by artificially bounded and internally heterogeneous DSM disorders. Continued use of DSM disorders as a basis for research, especially when cognitive distortions lead them to be treated as if they are natural kinds with an independent existence, will vitiate the efforts to analyze and interpret genetics, phenotyping, and analysis of patient-donated biological fluids, tissues, and postmortem brains. No matter how advanced the technologies used for the study of research participants or applied to the analysis of donated fluids, tissues, or cell lines, continuing reliance on descriptive diagnoses especially if made at a single point in time, fundamentally degrades the interpretability of research findings. It would be far better if funding agencies were to invest in globally diverse, recontactable cohorts analogous to the well-functioning UK biobank, albeit younger, smaller and more focused. To advance research on severe mental disorders such as the schizophrenia spectrum or bipolar disorder, relevant participants at high risk or with early symptoms would have to be oversampled. Such populations tend to be undersampled in existing general-purpose cohorts, although more common and often less severe conditions such as depression and anxiety are well represented. As in the UK biobank, individuals would be asked to consent to genetics studies, recontact for repeated phenotyping and biomarker collection over time, and biobanking of samples (Allen et al., 2024).

23.1 Mechanism

Not only genetically complex chronic diseases but even some rare monogenic disorders such as amyotrophic lateral sclerosis (ALS), once considered single biological entities based on their clinical presentations, are now recognized as distinct conditions. Despite similar or even indistinguishable clinical presentations, they may have different underlying genetics, different pathophysiological mechanisms, or both and, most importantly, respond to different mechanism-based treatments. Monogenic forms of ALS can be caused by mutations in different genes that may cause different, albeit often overlapping, rates of progression. The importance of objective biological markers to distinguish among these symptomatically similar conditions is their markedly different responses to treatment. We are in an era in which gene therapies, which target DNA, and antisense oligonucleotides (ASOs) and small interfering RNAs (siRNAs), which target RNA, are approved for a growing number of conditions and becoming the standard of care for some. In the example of ALS, only a rare familial form caused by mutation of the SOD1 gene responds to tofersen, an antisense oligonucleotide targeted to its gene product. From early reports, tofersen appears to halt disease progression in what otherwise is a uniformly fatal illness, and for some patients permits modest recovery of function. Patients with other forms of ALS, for the most part indistinguishable by symptoms, still await the discovery of disease-altering treatments. Among neuropsychiatric disorders, the severe neurodevelopmental disorders (NDDs), lumped into autism spectrum disorder in DSM-5-TR (American Psychiatric Association, 2022) and associated with autism, intellectual disability, and seizure risk, result from *de novo* mutations in more than 200 genes (SFARI, 2024). These NDDs are the disorders within the DSM that should be broken out, likely into separate categories based on causative mutations. Each will have one or more distinct treatments that target specific DNA or RNA sequences; several such treatments are currently in clinical trials. Thus, the phenomenologically defined DSM-5-TR autism spectrum disorder is an outmoded diagnosis that has no relationship to modern genetics or targeted treatment development for the most severely affected individuals in the spectrum, those with penetrant *de novo* mutations. Dementias with similar clinical presentations and age of onset may result from different proteinopathies (amyloid, tau, alpha-synuclein, or TDP-43). These are diagnosable with increasing precision using fluid biomarkers and positron emission tomography (PET) scans, and have strikingly different implications for prognosis and treatment – none discernable with the outmoded phenomenological approach of the DSM-5-TR, which lumps distinctly different pathophysiologies into major and minor neurocognitive disorders (American Psychiatric Association, 2022).

For highly polygenic but significantly genetically influenced conditions such as schizophrenia, bipolar disorder, major depression, and other mental disorders, affected status is associated with loading for genetic risk alleles. However, given polygenicity, the pleiotropic effects of genes, chance development influences (ranging from somatic mutations in dividing brain cells to the wiring of complex networks), and environmental exposures, affected individuals likely have a nearly unique stochastic grab bag of risk alleles and other risk factors associated with mental disorder phenotypes. Much remains unknown about how genetic and nongenetic factors, including risk factors for mental illness, might converge on a smaller number of pathways involved in building the brain, maintaining it in the face of challenges to homeostasis, and mediating change (plasticity) in response to environmental and bodily stimuli. The resulting neural mechanisms, differently tuned according to a person's genetics and developmental influences, presumably give rise to the rich diversity of normal interindividual differences as well as risk of mental illness. The complex diversity of genetic, stochastic, and exposure-related etiologies and the likely diversity of disease mechanisms underlying phenomenologically defined common mental disorders are entirely consistent with currently unacceptable variability of treatment responses within any diagnosis.

I have used the terms "mechanism" and "disease mechanism" repeatedly in this essay. Having been reminded (Barack et al., 2022; Ross & Bassett, 2024) that neuroscientists and psychiatrists – myself included – often use such terminology to mean different things in different contexts, a clarification is in order. According to the Oxford English Dictionary online (accessed May 1, 2024), "mechanism" entered the English language in the 1660s as a borrowing from the postclassical Latin term *mechanismus*, which was used to refer to the structure of a machine, engine, or device for controlling natural forces. Seventeenth-century Cartesian philosophers used "mechanismus" to denote "the mechanical structure and action of nature" that Descartes had posited. Descartes's reductionist, mechanical ideas of nature and of human brain function – only a nonmaterial rational soul was exempted from this mechanistic picture – were based on machines constructed by humans, with well-defined components that interacted in understandable ways, like the meshing of gears. Clearly, Cartesian reductionism is no longer an apt basis for understanding the structure and function of human brains; at a minimum, such reductionism cannot cope with the ubiquity of emergent properties of brains and their outputs. That said, the 17th-century concept of *mechanismus* remains a thought-provoking metaphor for the circumscribed – albeit still often highly complex – biological mechanisms of disease that we seek out in order to gain understanding and, more pragmatically, to aid in the discovery of biomarkers and therapeutics.

Mechanisms in health and disease represent causal processes, based on biological substrates (metaphorically the machines or devices, such as an enzyme cascade, ion channel, or neurotransmitter-containing vesicle) that produce outputs (such as metabolites, action potentials hormone release, cognition, or behavior) or alterations in the structure or function of biological systems. Causal explanations are deeper and have greater explanatory power than classifications, descriptions, or correlations because meaningful causal explanations are grounded in experimental manipulation that can probe and potentially falsify models derived from observation alone. Ideally the scientific influence of causal explanations reflects the rigor and thoroughness with which they have been tested. There are always exceptions to such epistemic generalizations. Despite the lack of experimental manipulation, a statistically highly convincing genetic association can be described as causal because germline genetic sequences are established at fertilization, prior to any developmental processes or environmental exposures, and are thus not subject to reverse causation. That said, experimentally demonstrated causal mechanisms provide deeper insight that observation alone into how the brain works (based on its causal structure), how things can go wrong, and how we can intervene, ideally to put things right. In short, the utility of mechanisms in biology and medicine lies in the power they confer for incisive experimentation, explanation, and control: the ability to target interventions to the right structures in the brain to reduce distress, treat disease – or for nefarious purposes.

It is within this general rubric that the term "mechanism" takes on the different meanings among which scientists often slip. The most important distinction relates to complexity and predictability. The simpler and most basic use of "mechanism" (looking back to 17th-century machine metaphors) is that of causal mechanisms with well-defined lower-level components that interact predictably or, if more probabilistically, in a lawful and explicable manner. Examples include the interaction of an enzyme with its cofactors and substrates or the opening of an ion channel. Causal systems with emergent properties are more complex. With such mechanisms causal claims cannot be precise, and predictive power is diminished. Examples include many higher-level brain functions such as the relationship of synaptic networks to circuits, circuits to computations, and computations to cognition and behavior. The complexity of brains, the problem of understanding causation across scales, emergent properties, and the nondeterministic nature of many brain functions make reductionist, machine-like models inappropriate as explanations for much of what the brain does.

An additional situation that involves weaker claims of causality involves those processes or systems in which defined inputs statistically predict outputs in a significant fashion and with a reasonable effect size but in which many intervening steps are poorly understood or entirely unknown. Examples of such processes that produce weaker causal claims are clinical trials and transgenic (or pharmacologically treated) animal models. In both examples the input is well defined (a drug or a gene) and a statistically significant output is observed (albeit not always), but the intervening processes ("the machine") are largely a black box.

23.2 Biomarkers

Across all disease areas, unacceptable heterogeneity of treatment responses has given rise to an aspiration for what is described as "precision medicine" where the goal is to match the right patient with the right treatment at the right time. Precision medicine relies on use of objective, ideally quantitative biomarkers and well-targeted treatments to achieve this goal. A US National Institutes of Health (NIH) and Food and Drug Administration (FDA) working group defines a biomarker as a "characteristic that is measured as an indicator of normal biological processes, pathogenic processes, or responses to an exposure or intervention, including therapeutic interventions" (FDA-NIH Biomarker Working Group, 2016). A biomarker may be molecular, for example measured within a bodily fluid – a fluid biomarker – or perhaps measured using a selective ligand for PET. Alternatively, biomarkers can be cellular, physiological, structural, or cognitive, but in all cases the measurement must be well validated in each context of use and highly replicable so that drug developers and regulatory agencies throughout the world can rely on their utility. Examples of fluid biomarkers include biochemical assays of cerebrospinal fluid (CSF) to measure beta amyloid or pathologic forms of tau for AD, determination of viral titers in blood (as for human immunodeficiency virus), presence of pathogenic antibodies or immune cells in blood or synovial fluid for some autoimmune diseases, or in cerebrospinal fluid for the anti-NMDA receptor psychosis that may phenocopy schizophrenia (Dalmau, 2008). Imaging biomarkers include PET, such as measures of glucose uptake to follow progression or treatment response of a cancer or ligand-based PET to measure brain levels of amyloid or tau in AD. Physiological biomarkers include electroencephalography for sleep disorders or epilepsy. The context of use for biomarkers includes diagnostic biomarkers, patient stratification biomarkers (to separate clinical diagnoses into mechanistically different subgroups for prognosis or treatment), tracking biomarkers to stage disease progression, and treatment biomarkers that can demonstrate engagement of a drug with its intended molecular target or disease associated pathway or to objectively document a treatment response. Among fluid biomarkers, levels of low-density lipoprotein cholesterol measured in blood are used both in clinical trials of cardiovascular medicines and clinical practice to determine when a person has crossed a threshold at which treatment is recommended and to adjust doses of cholesterol-lowering drugs. Treatment biomarkers are particularly needed in clinical trials for conditions characterized by high placebo responses such as Parkinson's disease, where they are being developed, or major depression where they would prove very useful (Shin, 2016; Stone, 2022). As a result of the astronomical costs and complexity of the clinical trials needed to gain regulatory approvals coupled with recent advances in tools that facilitate biomarker discovery, industry today will almost never initiate a new drug discovery program in the absence of informative biomarkers (Krainc, 2023; Paul & Potter, 2024).

The most rapid advances toward precision medicine have occurred in medical oncology where excisional biopsies provide samples for analysis, including DNA sequencing to identify acquired somatic mutations in the cancer cells, often result of environmental exposures such as tobacco smoking or excessive hormonal stimulation. Based on DNA sequencing and characterization of thousands of biopsy samples, somatic mutations in cancer cells have been divided into drivers of pathogenesis and passengers. Identification of driver mutations or their protein products can be used as biomarkers for prognosis and treatment selection. Increasingly, the protein products of driver mutations can be therapeutically targeted by monoclonal antibodies or other drugs that carry therapeutic payloads into the cancer cells while sparing noncancerous cells. Identical driver mutations can occur in cancers that have begun in different tissues or organs; these mutations are more useful as defining features of a cancer and treatment selection than the tissue of origin. Alternatively, different driver mutations may occur in a given tissue or organ resulting in a different likelihood of metastasis or other prognostic feature and different treatment response. Thus, for example, a diagnosis of lung cancer provides far less information about prognosis or appropriate treatment than a diagnosis based on an informative biomarker. Among lung cancers, non–small cell lung cancers often acquire driver mutations in the gene encoding the epidermal growth factor receptor (EGFR). As is typical of cancer genetics, different EGFR mutations confer different clinical outcomes and respond to different treatments. Because the underlying disease mechanisms depend on precise driver mutation, older clinical trials that enrolled patients diagnosed simply with non–small cell lung cancers but did not stratify by driver mutation failed to detect the significant efficacy of gefitinib because the subset of patients for whom the drug worked was only a small fraction of the total (Lynch, 2004; Paez, 2004). Subsequent biomarker-based patient stratification made it possible to design efficient clinical trials to detect the efficacy of desirable – because well-targeted – therapies. The pairing of targeted treatments with companion biomarkers has decreased the need to rely on blunderbuss cytotoxic chemotherapies and increasingly to replace such older, poorly tolerated treatments entirely or in part. Increasingly, instead of the tissue in which a cancer is found, it is the biomarker that determines the medical treatment.

Because it is often characterized by penetrant somatic mutations, cancer therapeutics is not an ideal model for psychiatric disorders. Examples of successful use of biomarkers that is more relevant for psychiatry are their use to separate diverse causes of dementia. Indeed, many patients with dementias, such as AD, Lewy body dementia (LBD), various tauopathies, or vascular dementia, are treated by psychiatrists for disruptive behavioral or psychotic symptoms or depression. In fact, the previously mentioned positive allosteric modulators (PAMs) of M4 muscarinic receptors, recently approved as antipsychotic drugs for schizophrenia, were discovered when they failed to achieve significance in their originally intended indication of improving cognition AD but were observed to reduce the psychotic symptoms typical of AD in the clinical trials population (Yohn, 2022). Clinical trials to gain approval of M4 muscarinic receptor PAMs to treat psychosis in patients with neurodegenerative disorders are progressing.

A monoclonal antibody (lecanemab) that removes beta amyloid from the brains of patients with AD is the first mechanism-based drug for AD to receive FDA and European Medicines Agency (EMA) approval. While the safety and efficacy of lecanemab must be improved upon, it likely represents the dawn of AD therapeutics that can slow disease progression. Historically, the initial clinical trials that used monoclonal antibodies directed at beta amyloid were conducted prior to the development of fluid biomarkers (CSF amyloid beta peptides and phospho-tau levels) or PET that detect amyloid and tau in brain. The putative AD patients enrolled in these older clinical trials were therefore selected based on symptoms and clinical course by experts in dementia. The clinical trials failed uniformly, and when the patients who participated ultimately came to autopsy, approximately 30% were found not to have AD at all, meaning that they did not have excessive amyloid – the target of the experimental drugs being tested – in their brains. The most common cause of the non-AD dementia cases was LBD, but the important point is that clinical experts could not distinguish among causes of dementia based on phenomenology. The success of more recent clinical trials stems, in part, from early identification of patients with amyloid in their brains, indeed prior to the onset of symptoms after which treatments may no longer be effective. Given their specific mechanism of therapeutic action and an associated APOE-based safety risk, lecanemab will not be prescribed or covered by insurance unless the intended patients have biomarker-proven AD and a demonstrated lack of homozygotic APOE4 alleles. A similar set of requirements for biomarker-proven disease will likely accompany monoclonal antibodies directed against pathological forms of tau (which forms neurofibrillary tangles and causes cell death) now in clinical trials for AD and soon for inherited tauopathies. The DSM-5-TR (American Psychiatric Association, 2022) is, by intention, entirely descriptive, and thus excludes laboratory tests from its diagnostic criteria. As such, it divides dementia into major or mild neurocognitive disorders depending on symptom severity (American Psychiatric Association, 2022). Insofar as future editions of the DSM continue to embrace phenomenology alone, practitioners using this official manual will not be able to make diagnoses of specific causes of dementia (Veitch et al., 2022) that provide prognostic information and will be required for prescribing meaningful treatment. In that sense, reliance on a descriptive diagnostic schema such as the DSM-5-TR will marginalize the practitioners who rely on it fully and potentially harm their patients as the medical community at large is being trained on the use of biomarkers in medical school and residencies and moving rapidly toward reliance on them, especially as biomarkers become increasingly prominent in FDA drug approvals for brain disorders. In addition to the approval of lecanemab and pending judgments on other monoclonal antibodies directed against beta amyloid, an antisense oligonucleotide treatment of SOD-1 amyotrophic lateral sclerosis (ALS), also known as motor neuron disease, was recently awarded accelerated approval by FDA based on reduction in the neuronal injury biomarker, neurofilament light chain (NfL), which is well validated and responds more rapidly than slowing of disease progression can be observed clinically (Food and Drug Administration, 2024). In contrast, psychiatrists narrowly trained to rely only on the "official" DSM classification will not have the diagnostic tools to prescribe approved treatments for patients they currently treat; in particular, they will lack the diagnostic tools and may lack the training to make appropriate referrals at a presymptomatic stage (laboratory tests only) when patients are most likely to benefit (Veitch et al., 2022). A reader of this chapter might demur thinking that nothing blocks a referral. However, a realistic situation that arises is an older patient with a treatment-refractory mood disorder in which a presymptomatic neurodegenerative disorder might be playing a role. In a referral network in which insurance administrators question the expertise and standing of a psychiatrist to order an expensive test that is not included in an officially sanctioned disease classification a treatable cause of dementia might be missed.

An analogous situation already exists for sleep disorders, where some diagnoses have long depended on laboratory tests, such as polysomnography and the diagnosis of narcolepsy (CSF levels of orexin). With the appropriate abolition of the historical distinction between organic and nonorganic disorders in ICD-11 (Reed et al., 2019; World Health

Organization, 2021), all sleep disorders that were still listed under mental and behavioral disorders in ICD-10 were removed from ICD-11 chapter 6, Mental, Behavioral, or Neurodevelopmental disorders, and listed in a new unified chapter 7, Sleep-wake disorders (Reed, 2019). These examples serve as reminders that concerted pragmatic (i.e., not philosophical) efforts are under way to replace pure phenomenology in diagnosis (i.e., the exclusion of laboratory tests) in the service of matching appropriate patients with treatment. While the diagnosis of neurodegenerative disorders or sleep-wake disorders may be wrongly written off as marginal to the core interests of psychiatry and clinical psychology (perhaps by those who still harbor a fondness for the irrational organic-functional distinction), the demise of pure phenomenology does not end there. As noted earlier, promising efforts are advancing to discover therapeutically actionable, personalized physiological biomarkers to guide deep brain stimulation (DBS) for people with depressive symptoms unresponsive to psychotherapy or existing antidepressant drugs (Scangos et al., 2021; Sheth & Mayberg, 2023). For those tempted to write off DBS as a boutique treatment, it is worth recalling that it has become a standard, widely used treatment for patients with Parkinson's disease when L-dopa and dopamine agonist therapies have ceased to be beneficial. For the schizophrenia spectrum disorders, evidence of synapse loss based on small but internationally replicated research studies using biochemical assays in CSF or PET scanning for synaptic markers (Onwordi et al., 2020, Johnson & Hyman, 2022, Gracias et al., 2022) is being investigated for its utility as biomarkers for patient stratification, disease staging, and treatment (Krainc et al., 2023).

23.3 Depression, Antidepressant Drugs, and the Need for Biomarkers

The US Food and Drug Administration (FDA) and collaborators analyzed the data from all double-blind, placebo-controlled phase 3 antidepressant trials submitted to FDA for drug approval for patients diagnosed with major depression based on DSM criteria for all approved antidepressants prior to ketamine, which was approved later. The data for drug responses (drug–placebo difference on rating scales such as Hamilton or Madras) were analyzed at the individual patient level. Despite all of these drugs having been approved, the results of the clinical trials were disappointing. Only approximately 24% of patients with DSM major depression had a substantial and convincing therapeutic response to the active drug. Approximately 63% of patients had modest improvements based on the rating scales that FDA interpreted as nonspecific, a category that could not be deconvoluted but includes small drug effects, placebo responses, or course-dependent regression to the mean for patients' symptoms (Stone, 2022). These results from the phase 3 efficacy trials submitted to FDA are roughly consistent with findings from a differently designed "effectiveness" trial, the Star*D study, a large pragmatic clinical trial that excluded few participants (e.g., based on comorbid anxiety) than the efficacy trials submitted to FDA for drug approval. In Star*D, which was commissioned and overseen by the US National Institute of Mental Health, 28% of patients experienced a large clinical response (considered to be remission) when they received full doses of a selective serotonin reuptake inhibitor antidepressant for an adequate period of time (Rush, 2006; Trivedi, 2006). Over time, as additional drugs and pharmacologic add-ons were administered, the response rates rose, but it is difficult to be certain of the role that drugs, placebo, and time played in these eventual responses. These results have important similarities to studies of drugs that target cancers with EGFR mutations or used to treat AD. Major depression diagnosed by the purely descriptive DSM criteria would appear to identify heterogeneous patient groups, approximately a quarter of whom (albeit not necessarily mechanistically homogeneous) respond reasonably well to a monoaminergic antidepressant. Although the good responders tended to have somewhat more severe symptoms than did the nonspecific responders in the FDA analysis (Stone, 2022), they were not distinguishable *ex ante* from others enrolled in the clinical trials cohorts.

Cryptic heterogeneity of mechanisms in psychiatric disorders contributes to clinical trial failures not only for drugs but for other treatments as well, for example early termination after futility analyses in multisite clinical trials of DBS for depression prior to the application of individualized biomarkers (reviewed in Sheth & Mayberg, 2023). These failures motivated the research alluded to earlier to distinguish personalized biomarkers identified by intracranial physiological recordings that, with the help of machine learning, could guide the location and pattern of electrical stimulation (Scangos et al., 2021; Sheth & Mayberg, 2023).

Beyond clinical trials, as introduced in the earlier sections, costly and, for the field, rather embarrassing casualty of DSM diagnoses based in phenomenology are case–control studies that attempted to use noninvasive neuroimaging for diagnosis. Thirty years of research using magnetic resonance imaging (MRI) has failed to identify clinically useful case–control differences even when results from thousands of subjects are meta-analyzed (Marek, 2022; Thompson, 2020). It had been hoped that structural or functional MRI would become a useful diagnostic tool, but to date, the only clinical application of brain imaging is to follow up on suspicion of a structural lesion or other neurologic disorder. It is unlikely that the failure to identify case–control differences for DSM disorders results from technical limitations given the spatial resolution of the most advanced imaging technologies, for example 7 Tesla MRI. Rather, the heterogeneity of disease mechanisms in the absence of stratification biomarkers, superimposed on the background variability of human brain structure and function, creates a currently insuperable signal-to-noise problem (Greene, 2022; Marek, 2022). In sum, notwithstanding the compelling need for better psychiatric therapeutics and potential financial rewards for companies that produce them, years of clinical trial failures have led industry to reallocate capital and expertise away from psychiatry toward more mature areas of medicine such as cancer, autoimmunity, and metabolism, in which they are more likely to succeed. As noted, the inability to stratify patients by underlying mechanism affects not only clinical trials but all clinical research in psychiatry.

The argument is strong that psychiatry cannot effectively improve diagnosis and treatment unless it can move beyond its current full reliance on phenomenology. Without mechanistic insight, rational systematic approaches to nomination of therapeutic targets and discovery of biomarkers are not feasible, and the field will, of necessity, continue to rely on serendipity and guesswork. It is easier to find fault, however, than to find a solution. Research on the human brain is fiendishly difficult, and the aspects of brain function that go awry in mental illness are among the most complex and challenging of all. I am not advocating that the compelling need to reduce reliance on phenomenology makes the science faster or easier; indeed, psychiatry, driven by the unmet needs of our patients, has often gotten ahead of the evidence. However, here and elsewhere (Hyman, 2023), I have adduced evidence that meaningful and durable progress is being made that will lead scientists to the discovery of mechanisms underlying psychiatric disorders. Given this progress and the goals of advancing treatment discovery and development to provide more effective and well-targeted treatments, I would argue that a concerted effort is needed to improve psychiatric diagnosis, and that it is timely and possible.

REFERENCES

Abdellaoui, A., Yengo, L., Verweij, K. J. H., & Visscher, P. M. (2023). 15 years of GWAS discovery: Realizing the promise. *American Journal of Human Genetics, 110*, 179194. https://doi.org/10.1016/j.ajhg.2022.12.011

Adams, M. J., Psychiatric Genomics Consortium Major Depressive Disorder Working Group, Lewis, C. M., & McIntosh, A. M. (2024). Genome-wide study of major depression in 685,808 diverse individuals identifies 697 independent associations, infers causal neuronal subtypes and biological targets for novel pharmacotherapies. *medRxiv, 1*, 2024.04.29.24306535.

Allen, N. E., Lacey, B., Lawlor, D. A., Pell, J. P, Gallacher, J., et al. (2024). Prospective study design and data analysis in UK Biobank. *Science Translational Medicine, 16*(729), eadf4428. https://doi.org/a0.1126/scitranslmed.adf4428

American Psychiatric Association. (1980). *Diagnostic and statistical manual of mental disorders* (3rd ed.). American Psychiatric Association.

American Psychiatric Association. (2022). *Diagnostic and statistical manual of mental disorders* (5th ed., text rev.). American Psychiatric Association.

Andrews, G., Goldberg, D. P., Krueger, R. F., Carpenter, W. T., Hyman, S. E., at al. (2009). Exploring the feasibility of a meta-structure for DSM-V and ICD-11: could it improve utility and validity? *Psychological Medicine, 39*, 1993–2000.

Barack, D. L., Miller, E. K., Moore, C. I, Packer, A. M., et al. (2022). A call for more clarity around causality in neuroscience. *Trends in Neurosciences, 45*, 654–655. https://doi.org/10.1016/j.tins.2022.06.003

Barch, D. M., Bustillo, J., Gaebel, W., Gur, R., Heckers, S., Malaspina, D., et al. (2013). Logic and justification for dimensional assessment of symptoms and related clinical phenomena in psychosis: relevance to DSM-5. *Schizophrenia Research, 150*, 15–20. https://doi.org/10.1016/j.schres.2013.04.027

Bell, J. (2020). *Big pharma backed away from brain drugs. Is a return in sight?* BioPharma Dive. Retrieved February 10, 2024 from www.biopharmadive.com/news/pharma-neuroscience-retreat-return-brain-drugs/570250/

Brainstorm Consortium. (2018) Analysis of shared heritability in common disorders of the brain. *Science, 360*(6395), eaap8757. https://doi.org/10.1126/science.aap8757

Cahalan, S. (2019). *The great pretender*. Grand Central Publishers.

Dalmau, J., Gleichman, A. J., Hughes, E. G., Rossi, J. E, Peng, X., et al. (2008). Anti-NMDA-receptor encephalitis: A case series and analysis of the effects of antibodies. *Lancet Neurology, 7*, 1091–1098.

Demeter, D. V., & Greene, D. J. (2024). The promise of precision functional mapping for neuroimaging in psychiatry. *Neuropsychopharmacology, 50*, 16–28.

FDA-NIH Biomarker Working Group. (2016 [updated November 29, 2021]). *BEST (Biomarkers, EndpointS, and other Tools) Resource*. Food and Drug Administration; National Institutes of Health.

Food and Drug Administration. (2024). *FDA approves treatment of amyotropic lateral sclerosis associated with a mutation in the SOD1 gene*. Retrieved May 1, 2024 from https://www.fda.gov/drugs/news-events-human-drugs/fda-approves-treatment-amyotrophic-lateral-sclerosis-associated-mutation-sod1-gene

Gandal, M. J., Haney, J. R., Parikshak, N. N., Leppa, V., Ramaswami, G., et al. (2018). Shared molecular neuropathology across major psychiatric disorders parallels polygenic overlap. *Science, 359*, 693–697.

Geils, H., Riley, A., & Levelle T. A. (2022). Incentivizing drug development in serious mental illness. *Clinical Therapeutics, 44*(9), 1258–1267,

Gottesman, I. I., & Shields, J. (1967). A polygenic theory of schizophrenia. *Proceedings of the National Academy of Sciences, USA, 58*, 199–205. https://doi.org/10.1073/pnas.58.1.199

Gracias, J., Orhan, F., Holmén-Larsson, J., et al. (2022). Cerebrospinal fluid concentration of complement component 4A is increased in first episode schizophrenia. *Nature Communications, 13*(1), 6427. htps://doi.org/10.1038/s41467-022-33797-6

Green, M. F., Kern, R. S., Braff, D. L., & Mintz, J. (2000). Neurocognitive deficits and functional outcomes in schizophrenia: Are we measuring the "right stuff"? *Schizophrenia Bulletin, 26*, 119–136.

Greene, A. S., Shen, X., Noble, S., Horien, C., Hahn, C. A., et al. (2022). Brain-phenotype models fail for individuals who defy sample stereotypes. *Nature, 609*, 109–118. https://doi.org/10.1038/s41586-022-05118

Grotzinger, A. D., Mallard, T. T., Akingbuwa, W. A., Ip, H. F., Adams, M. J., et al. (2022). Genetic architecture of 11 major psychiatric disorders at the biobehavioral, functional genomic and molecular genetic levels of analysis. *Nature Genetics, 54*, 548–559.

Hjorthøj, C., Stürup, A. E., McGrath, J. J., & Nordentoft, Me. (2017). Years of potential life lost and life expectancy in schizophrenia: A systematic review and meta-analysis. *Lancet Psychiatry, 4*, 295–301. https://doi.org/10.1016/S2215–0366(17)30078-0

Hyman, S. E. (2007). Can neuroscience be integrated into the DSM-V? *Nature Reviews Neuroscience, 8*, 25–32.

(2010). The diagnosis of mental disorders: The problem of reification. *Annual Review of Clinical Psychology, 6*, 155–179.

(2012). Revolution stalled. *Science Translational Medicine, 4*, 155cm11. https://doi.org/10.1126/scitranslmed.3003142

(2021). Psychiatric disorders: Grounded in human biology but not natural kinds. *Perspectives in Biology and Medicine, 64*(1), 6–28. https://doi.org/10.1353/pbm.2021.0002

(2023). The biology of mental disorders: Progress at last. *Daedalus Fall, 2023*, 186–208.

Institute of Medicine. (2014). *Improving access to essential medicines for mental, neurological, and substance use disorders in sub-Saharan Africa: Workshop summary*. The National Academies Press. https://doi.org/10.17226/18380

International Schizophrenia Consortium, Purcell, S. M., Wray, N. R., Stone, J. L., Visscher, P. M., et al. (2009). Common polygenic variation contributes to risk of schizophrenia and bipolar disorder. *Nature, 460*, 748–752. https://doi.org/10.1038/nature08185

Jack, C. R., Andrews, J. S., Beach, T. G., Buracchio, T., Dunn, B., et al. (2024). Revised criteria for diagnosis and staging of Alzheimer's disease. *Nature Medicine*, 30, 2121–2124. https://doi.org/10.1038/s41591-024-02988-7

Jain, S., Pei, L., Spraggins, J. M., Angelo, M., Carson, J. P., et al. (2023). Advances and prospects for the Human Biomolecular Atlas Program (HuBMAP). *Nature Cell Biology, 25*, 1089–1100.

Johnson, M. B., & Hyman, S. E. (2022). A critical perspective on the synaptic pruning hypothesis of schizophrenia pathogenesis. *Biological Psychiatry, 92*, 440–442. https://doi.org/10.1016/j.biopsych.2021 12.014

Kahneman, D., & Tversky, A. (1972). Subjective probability: A judgment of representativeness. Cognitive Psychology, 3, 430–454.

Kendler, K. S. (2017). DSM disorders and their criteria: How should they inter-relate? *Psychological Medicine, 47*, 2054–2060. https://doi.org/10.1017/S0033291717000678

Kesselheim, A. S., Hwang, T. J., Franklin, J. M. (2015). Two decades of new drug development for central nervous system disorders. *Nature Reviews Drug Discovery, 14*, 815–816. https://doi.org/10.1038/nrd4793

Khin, N. A., Chen, Y.-F., Yang, Y., Pang, P., & Laughren, T. P. (2011). Exploratory analyses of efficacy data from major depressive disorder trials submitted to the US Food and Drug administration in support of new drug applications. *Journal of Clinical Psychiatry, 72*, 462–472.

Kotov, R., Krueger, R. F., Watson, D., Achenbach, T. M., Althoff, R. R., et al. (2017). The hierarchical taxonomy of psychopathology (HiTOP): A dimensional alternative to traditional nosologies. *Journal of Abnormal Psychology, 126*, 454–457.

Krainc, D., Martin, W. J., Casey, B., Jensen, F. E, et al. (2023). Shifting the trajectory of therapeutic development for neurological and psychiatric disorders. *Science Translational Medicine, 15*(720), eadg4775. https://doi.org/10.1126/scitranslmed.adg4775

Kuhn, T. S. (1962). *The structure of scientific revolutions* (2nd ed.). University of Chicago Press.

Ling, E., Nemesh, J., Goldman, M., Kamitaki, N., Reed, N., et al. (2024). A concerted neuron-astrocyte program declines in ageing and schizophrenia. *Nature, 627*, 604–611. https://doi.org/10.1038/s41586-024-07109-5

Lynch, C. J., Elbau, I. G., Ng, T., et al. (2024). Frontostriatal salience network expansion in individuals with depression. *Nature, 633*, 624–633.

Lynch, T. J., Bell, D. W., Sordella, R., Gurubhagavatula, S., Okimoto, R. A., et al. (2004). Activating mutations in the epidermal growth factor receptor underlying responsiveness of non-small-cell lung cancer to gefitinib. *New England Journal of Medicine, 350*, 2129–2139.

Marek, S., Tervo-Clemmens, B., Calabro, F. J., Montez, D. F., Kay, B. P., et al. (2022). Reproducible brain-wide association studies require thousands of individuals. *Nature, 603*, 654–660.

McGorry, P. D., Hartmann, J. A., Spooner, R., & Nelson, B. (2018). Beyond the "at risk mental state" concept: Transitioning to transdiagnostic psychiatry. *World Psychiatry, 17*, 133–142.

McGrath, J. J., Lim, C. C. W, Plana-Ripoll, O., Holtz, Y., & Agerbo, E. (2020). Comorbidity within mental disorders: A comprehensive analysis based on 145,990 survey respondents from 27 countries. *Epidemiology and Psychiatric Sciences, 29*, e153. https://doi.org/10.1017/S2045796020000633

Mullins, N., Forstner, A. J., O'Connell, K. S., Coombes, B., Coleman, J. R. I., et al. (2021). Genome-wide association study of more than 40,000 bipolar cases provides new insights into the underlying biology. *Nature Genetics, 53*, 817–829. https://doi.org/10.1038/s41588-021-00857-4

National Academies of Sciences, Engineering, and Medicine. (2016). *Providing sustainable mental and neurological health care in Ghana and Kenya: Workshop summary*. The National Academies Press. https://doi.org/10.17226/21793

National Academies of Sciences, Engineering, and Medicine. (2017). *Therapeutic development in the absence of predictive animal models of nervous system disorders: Proceedings of a workshop*. The National Academies Press. https://doi.org/10.17226/24672

National Academies of Sciences, Engineering, and Medicine. (2023). *Multimodal biomarkers for central nervous system disorders: Development, validation, and clinical integration: Proceedings of a workshop*. The National Academies Press. https://doi.org/10.17226/27208

Nour, M. M., Liu, Y., & Dolan, R. J. (2022). Functional neuroimaging in psychiatry and the case for failing better. *Neuron, 110*, 2524–2544. https//: doi.org/10.1016/j.neuron.2022.07.005

Onwordi, E. C., Halff, E. F., Whitehurst, T., Mansur, A., Cotel, M.-C., et al. (2020). Synaptic density marker SV2A is reduced in schizophrenia patients and unaffected by antipsychotics in rats. *Nature Communications, 11*, 246.

Oxford English Dictionary, s.v. mechanism (*n.*), Etymology. May 1, 2024. https://doi.org/10.1093/OED/5601535568

Paez, J. G., Jänne, P. A., Lee, J. C. Tracy, S., Greulich, H., et al. (2004). EGFR mutations in lung cancer: Correlation with clinical response to gefitinib therapy. *Science, 304*, 1497–1500.

Palmer, D. S., Howrigan, D. P., Chapman, S. B., Adolfsson, R., Bass, N., et al. (2022). Exome sequencing in bipolar disorder identifies AKAP11 as a risk gene shared with schizophrenia. *Nature Genetics, 54*, 541–547.

Pankevich, D. E., Altevogt, B. M., Dunlop, J., Gage, F. H., & Hyman, S. E. (2014). Improving and accelerating drug development for nervous system disorders. *Neuron, 84*, 546–553.

Paul, S. M., & Potter, W. Z. (2024). Finding new and better treatments for psychiatric disorders. *Neuropsychopharmacology, 49*, 3–9. https://doi.org/10.1038/s41386-023-01690-5

Pisl, V., Meerman, S. T., & Batstra, M. (2025). From suffering to disorders conceptual analysis of reification in psychiatry. *Philosophy, Psychiatry, and Psychology*. Online advanced publication. https://doi.org/10.1353/ppp.0.a967324

Ransom, J., & Harris, A. J. (2023). *How Rikers Island became New York's largest mental institution.* New York Times. December 29. Retrieved August 12, 2025 from www.nytimes.com/2023/12/29/nyregion/nyc-rikers-homeless-mental-illness.html

Reed, G. M., First, M. B., Kogan, C. S., Hyman, S. E., Gureje, O., et al. (2019). Innovations and changes in the ICD-11 classification of mental, behavioural and neurodevelopmental disorders. *World Psychiatry, 18*(1), 3–19. https://doi.org/10.1002/wps.20611

Regier, D. A., Narrow, W. E., Clarke, D. E., Kraemer, H. C., & Kuramoto, S. J. (2013). DSM-5 field trials in the United States and Canada, part II: Test-retest reliability of selected categorical diagnoses. *American Journal of Psychiatry, 170*, 59–70.

Riglin, L., Collishaw, S., Richards, A., Thapar, A. K., Maughan, B., O'Donovan, M. C., & Thapar, A. (2017). Schizophrenia risk alleles and neurodevelopmental outcomes in childhood: A population-based cohort study. *Lancet Psychiatry, 4*(1), 57–62. https://doi.org/10.1016/S2215-0366(16)30406-0

Riglin, L., Collishaw, S., Thapar, A. K., Dalsgaard, S., Langley, K., Smith, G. D., et al. (2016). Association of genetic risk variants with attention-deficit/hyperactivity disorder trajectories in the general population. *Journal of the American Medical Association Psychiatry, 73*(12), 1285–1292. https://doi.org/10.1001/jamapsychiatry.2016.2817

Robins, E., & Guze, S. B. (1970). Establishment of diagnostic validity in psychiatric illness: Its application to schizophrenia. *American Journal of Psychiatry, 126*, 983–987.

Robinson, E. B., Koenen, K. C., McCormick, M. C., et al. (2011). Evidence that autistic traits show the same etiology in the general population and at the quantitative extremes. *Archives of Genetic Psychiatry, 68*, 1113–1121.

Robinson, E. B., St. Pourcain, B., Anttila, V., et al. (2016). Genetic risk for autism spectrum disorders and neuropsychiatric variation in the general population. *Nature Genetics*, 48, 552–555.

Rosenhan, D. (1973). On being sane in insane places. *Science, 179*, 250–258. https://doi.org/10.1126/science.179.4070/250

Ross, L. N., & Bassett, D. S. (2024). Causation in neuroscience: Keeping mechanism meaningful. *Nature Reviews Neuroscience, 25*, 81–90.

Russell, A. J. C., Weir, J. A., Nadaf, N. M., Shabet, M., Kumar, V., et al. (2024). Slide-tags enables single-nucleus barcoding for multimodal spatial genomics. *Nature, 625*, 101109. https://doi.org/10.1038/s41586-023-06837-4

Rush, A. J., Trivedi, M. H., Nierenberg, A. A., Stewart, J. W., et al. (2006). Acute and longer-term outcome in depressed outpatients requiring one or several treatment steps: A STAR*D report. *American Journal of Psychiatry, 163*, 1905–1917.

Scangos, K. W, Makhoul, G. S., Sugure, L. P., Chang, E. F ., & Krystal, A. D. (2021). State-dependent responses to intracranial brain stimulation in a patient with depression. *Nature Medicine, 27*, 229–231.

Scull, A. (2023). Rosenhan revisited: Successful scientific fraud. *History of Psychiatry*, 34, 180–195. https://doi.org/10.1177/0957154221159878

Segal, A., Parkes, L., Aquino, K., Kia, S. M, Wolfers, T., et al. (2023). Regional, circuit and network heterogeneity of brain abnormalities in psychiatric disorders. *Nature Neuroscience, 26*, 1613–1629.

SFARI. (2024). *SFARI gene*. Retrieved May 1, 2024 from https://gene.sfari.org

Sheth, S. A., & Mayberg, H. S. (2023). Deep brain stimulation for obsessive-compulsive disorder and depression. *Annual Review of Neuroscience, 46*, 341–358. https://doi.org/10.1146annurev-neuro-110122-110434

Shin, C. W., Hahn, S., Park, B.-J., Kim, J.-M., Park, E. O., & Jeon, B. (2016). Predictors of the placebo response in clinical trials on Parkinson's disease: A meta-analysis. *Parkinsonism and Related Disorders, 28*, 83–89.

Singh, T., Poterba, T., Curtis, D., Akil, H., Al Eissa, M., et al. (2022). Rare coding variants in ten genes confer substantial risk for schizophrenia. *Nature, 604*, 509–516. https://doi.org/10.1038/s41586-022-04556-w

Smoller, J. W. (2013). Disorders and borders: Psychiatric genetics and nosology. American Journal of Medical Genetics B Neuropsychiatric Genetics, *162B*, 559–578.

Spitzer, R. (1975). On pseudoscience in science, logic in remission, and psychiatric diagnosis: A critique of Rosenhan's "On being sane in insane places". Journal of Abnormal Psychology, *84*, 442–452. https://doi.org/10.1037/h0077124

Stone, M. B., Yaseen, Z. S., Miller, B. J., Richardville, K., et al. (2022). Response to acute monotherapy for major depressive disorder in randomized, placebo controlled trials submitted to the US Food and Drug Administration: Individual participant data analysis. *British Medical Journal, 378*, e067606. https://doi.org/10.1136/bmj-2021-067606

Thompson, P. M., Jahanshad, N., Ching, C. R. K., et al. (2020). ENIGMA and global neuroscience: A decade of large-scale studies of the brain in health and disease across more than 40 countries. *Translational Psychiatry, 10*(1), 100.

Tian, L., Chen, F., & Macosko, E. Z. (2023). The expanding vistas of spatial transcriptomics. *Nature Biotechnology, 41*, 773–782. https://doi.org/10.1038/s41587-022-01448-2

Trivedi, M. H., Rush, A. J., Nierenberg, A. A., Warden, D., Ritz, L., et al. (2006). Evaluation of outcomes with citalopram for depression using measurement-based care in STAR*D: Implications for clinical practice. *American Journal of Psychiatry, 163*, 28–40.

Trubetskoy, V., Pardiñas, A. F., Qi, T., Panagiotaropoulou, G., et al. (2022). Mapping genomic loci implicates genes and synaptic biology in schizophrenia. *Nature, 604*, 502–508. https://doi.org/10.1038/s41586-022-04434-5.

Veitch, D. P., Weiner, M. W., Aisen, P. S., Beckett, L. A. DeCarli, C., et al. (2022). Using the Alzheimer's Disease Neuroimaging Initiative to improve early detection, diagnosis, and treatment of Alzheimer's disease. *Alzheimer's Dementia*, 18, 824–857.

Whiteford, H. A., Degenhardt, L., Rehm, J., Baster, A. J., Ferrari, A. J., et al. (2013). Global burden of disease attributable to mental and substance use disorders: Findings for the Global Burden of Disease Study 2010. *Lancet, 382*, 1575–1586. https://doi.org/10.1016/S0140-6736(13)61611-6

World Health Organization (WHO). (2018). *International classification of diseases* (11th rev.) WHO.

World Health Organization (WHO). (2021). *International Classification of Diseases, Eleventh Revision (ICD-11).* Retrieved August 12, 2025 from https://icd.who.int/browse11

Yohn, S. E., Weiden, P. J., Felder, C. C., & Stahl, S. M. (2022). Muscarinic acetylcholine receptors for psychotic disorders: Bench-side to clinic. *Trends in Pharmacological Sciences, 43*, 1098–1112.

CHAPTER 24

Commentary on Hyman's "Mechanism Matters"

Kenneth S. Kendler

24.1 A Response to Hyman

I have, for many decades, read widely and deeply within the rich corpus of descriptive psychopathology. It has enriched my appreciation of the variations of the syndromes in psychiatry that we diagnose, study, and attempt to treat. It has helped me develop interview assessments used in a wide variety of psychiatric genetic studies, from family to twin, high-density pedigree, and now Genome-Wide Association Study case–control studies. I have taught two generations of psychiatric residents on the importance of this tradition and our need to know our rich descriptive inheritance. My teachings have been met with substantial (but not universal) appreciation. I have served on various DSM committees from DSM-III-R onward and tried to use my psychopathological expertise to improve our nosology, in part by increasing the empirical rigor of the evaluation for change using the concept of validators.

It is therefore with some chagrin that I first read Dr. Hyman's chapter that deeply criticizes the role of descriptive psychiatry/phenomenology in modern psychiatry and especially in our diagnostic system. What I aim for in this chapter is to try to put Dr. Hyman's remarks in an historical and conceptual context, and redirect some of his substantial (and well-deserved) frustration with the slow pace of discovery of novel therapeutics in psychiatry away from the convenient but, I will argue, misplaced target of descriptive psychopathology. For background, I give two short historical sketches.

First, it is universally recognized that our current psychiatric nosology was substantially shaped by the writings of Emil Kraepelin (1856–1926). Stephan Heckers and I carefully reviewed the introductory chapters of the eight editions of his famous and highly influential textbook to describe the evolution of his nosological principles (Heckers & Kendler, 2020). It was clear to us that Kraepelin conceptualized a progressive framework for psychiatric nosology to be developed over what he felt would be decades. He rejected what he saw as the premature efforts to develop diagnostic categories from neuropathologic work that became quite popular in Europe in the last half of the 19th century. Instead, he saw the first stage as consisting of a careful study of clinical features of putative psychiatric syndromes: that is, signs, symptoms, and especially course of illness. Tentative diagnostic categories would emerge for that clinical research paradigm. He was, in this conceptualization, highly influenced by two of his predecessors: Kahlbaum and Heckers (Kendler & Engstrom, 2017). Next, he expected that the methods of neuropathology and etiologic studies, in particular genetics, would validate these clinical syndromes. He was optimistic that the psychiatric disorders thus identified would be natural kinds. He had faith that these three critical realms of psychiatric science – descriptive psychopathology, neuropathology, and etiology – would converge in identifying the true kinds of psychiatric illness, but that descriptive psychiatry would lead the way.

My second sketch is a short historical story from the field of rheumatology, the discipline in medicine that, after psychiatry, has had the greatest interest in the development of structured diagnoses. One of the first sets of criteria for this group of diseases was proposed by T. Duckett Jones in the *Journal of the American Medical Association* (*JAMA*):

> Despite our increase in knowledge of rheumatic fever, no specific diagnostic test has been forthcoming. This is a distinct deterrent to the advancement of the problem. From the study of the medical literature, it is obvious that each observer has his own diagnostic criteria and that these may differ widely. For several reasons the importance of rather strict diagnostic criteria would seem essential at this time, and these may be enumerated as follows. (Jones, 1944, p. 481)

Jones goes on to provide major and minor clinical manifestations of rheumatic fever, which include carditis, arthralgias (joint pain), nodules, rashes, fever, and so on – all signs and symptoms of rheumatic fever. No biomarkers (aka lab tests) were mentioned because, in 1944, no good lab measures existed to track the inflammatory changes that underlay rheumatic fever.

In 1992, an update of what were called the Jones criteria was published, also in *JAMA* (Dajani et al., 1992). Like the original Jones criteria, the updated version contained a nearly identical list of major and minor clinical manifestations on rheumatic fever. But now, three laboratory findings were also included. Two were elevated measures of acute-phase reactants (biochemical measures of immune activation measurable in blood) – erythrocyte sedimentation rate and C-reactive protein – and one finding that was electrocardiographic evidence of carditis – a prolonged interval of transmission of electrical signals in the hearth (the "PR interval").

What happened here? Advances in understanding the pathophysiology of rheumatic fever and developments in laboratory science produced robust indices of the underlying disease process that in clinical settings had proven their practical value in diagnosis. Rheumatologists did not abandon their descriptive clinical criteria. Rather, they added in "biomarkers" as they were developed. Also of note, these biomarkers were heterogeneous in etiology. Two of them reflected general immune activation by blood markers while the third detected an electrophysiological abnormality in heart conduction secondary to the carditis. This pattern is seen across the evolution of criteria sets for other rheumatic diseases such as rheumatoid arthritis and systemic lupus erythematosus.

Now let us turn to DSM. Hyman is incorrect when he states that no biomarkers are part of DSM-5 criteria. The exception is for the diagnosis of narcolepsy where criterion B2 reads, "Hypocretin deficiency as measured using cerebrospinal hypocretin-1 immunoreactivity values . . . less than or equal to 110 pg/ml" (American Psychiatric Association, 2013, p. 373). The criterion was developed because of the strong scientific evidence that narcolepsy is caused by a hypocretin deficiency (Mignot et al., 2021). Thus DSM-5 has dipped its toe in the biomarker water. But what has held up the developments in other areas? Is it the DSM workgroups (that review each criteria set every time a new edition of DSM is developed) that, in their fervent devotion to descriptive psychopathology, have ignored advances in the field that have identified valuable biomarkers that would be diagnostically useful? Or is it because for no other psychiatric disorder do we have, like we do in narcolepsy, a detailed understanding of the pathophysiology and a good biomarker that directly reflects that disease process?

Now another story. One of the many goals of DSM-5 (American Psychiatric Association, 2013) was to replace the descriptive nosology that dominated DSM-III and DSM-IV with an etiologically based system. That didn't work. In writing, with Peter Zachar, a history of these developments (Zachar et al., 2019), I had a chance to speak to several chairs of the DSM-5 workgroups who were asked to implement this goal. One of them, when I asked about how his group dealt with this charge, gave a belly laugh. He told me that at the first meeting of his workgroup – a distinguished group of nosologic and biological researchers – they took this up as a first order of business. It took less than 10 minutes, with much joking, to dispense with that idea. Then they got down to the real work of the committee. Everyone knew that the field was not close to being ready to make that leap. So much for high-quality biomarkers circa 2008.

There is a long history of failed biomarkers in psychiatry that I will not rehearse here. One example will suffice: the dexamethasone suppression test (DST) for melancholia (Carroll et al., 1981) – the key reference to which was cited 2,488 times as of May 22, 2024. As reviewed in detail by Schumacher and Santambrogio (2023), the first reports were quite positive with modest sample sizes. However, further testing revealed poor sensitivity and a general lack of specificity for melancholia. The conclusion: "A plethora of investigations by other research groups applying the DST yielded contradictory findings, which resulted in it finally being rejected" (Carroll et al., 1981, p. 14). This story could be told over and over again for many decades of the 20th and now 21st centuries.

Let's go back to the rheumatologists working to update the Jones criteria in 1992. I don't know the details of their decision-making approach to expand the Jones criteria with the laboratory tests for rheumatic fever. We know that they kept all the prior "descriptive" criteria: that is, signs and symptoms of the disorder. I doubt there was much gnashing of teeth over these "new-fangled" laboratory tests. I suspect they adopted these new measures with pleasure and enthusiasm, as it made them more accurate diagnosticians.

So, is the discipline of descriptive psychiatry or its representation in the DSM at fault for the lack of development of biomarkers and their sparsity in DSM criteria? The historical record does not support this claim. The position of DSM-5 on the historical arc of psychiatry was, alas, very much like Jones found the field of rheumatology in 1944. They had good clinical descriptions but no good biomarkers. Despite much effort, the field of psychiatry had not moved very far since DSM-5. That is a problem for all of us, but placing the blame for this either on descriptive psychiatry or on DSM seems misplaced. Indeed, the diverse field of psychiatric science needs to develop and begin to validate the biomarkers. Only then can the DSM process get to work and consider adding them to their clinical criteria as occurred for rheumatic fever.

Kraepelin was overly optimistic in his vision for advancement in psychiatric science. It is far from clear that our disorders are of natural kind. It is not at all certain that our multiple validators – outcome, neurobiology, response to treatment, genetics, and so forth – will all converge on the same syndromes (Kendler, 1990). But I do believe that Kraepelin was correct in suggesting that before biological psychiatry and genetics could profitably contribute to psychiatric science, the descriptive psychiatrists had to produce some semblance of a coherent diagnostic system. You have to start somewhere. This is clear in the very early psychiatric genetic investigation in the 19th century where most studies were done on the generic category of "insanity" (Kendler, 2021). The field clearly advanced with the widespread acceptance of Kraepelin's categories, not because those are necessarily correct, but because they provide some standardization so results could be compared across research groups, which marks the beginning of what we can all hope is an iterative process of data-driven improvement in psychiatric nosology over time.

Kraepelin was not averse to changing his diagnostic opinions in the face of new data, clearly shown by his initial decision to exclude involutional melancholy from his category of manic-depressive illness – which he reversed after an empirical study of the question by his student Dreyfus (Dreyfus, 1907; Kendler & Engstrom, 2020). Like Kraepelin, I believe the descriptive psychopathologists would endorse biomarkers enthusiastically, adding them to the criteria if they passed the test of improving diagnostic validity. Blaming them for the current state of psychiatric nosology is an example, I would suggest, of "shooting the messenger." As Hyman points out in this essay, the real problem is the extraordinary complexity of our psychiatric syndromes and the substantial limitations of our scientific tools. I do hope he is right that advances in molecular genetics and neuroscience will change this picture in the coming decades. This descriptive psychiatrist and, I predict, the large majority of my colleagues will be cheering this effort on.

REFERENCES

American Psychiatric Association. (2013). *Diagnostic and statistical manual of mental disorders: fifth edition, DSM-5*. American Psychiatric Association.

Carroll, B. J., Feinberg, M., Greden, J. F., Tarika, J., Albala, A. A., Haskett, R. F., James, N. M., Kronfol, Z., Lohr, N., & Steiner, M. (1981). A specific laboratory test for the diagnosis of melancholia: standardization, validation, and clinical utility. *Archives of General Psychiatry, 38*(1), 15–22.

Chang, H. (2004). *Inventing temperature: Measurement and scientific progress*. Oxford University Press.

Dajani, A. S., Ayoub, E., Bierman, F. Z., Bisno, A. L., Denny, F. W., Durack, D. T., Ferrieri, P., Freed, M., Gerber, M., & Kaplan, E. L. (1992). Guidelines for the diagnosis of rheumatic fever: Jones criteria, 1992 update. *Journal of the American Medical Association, 268*(15), 2069–2073.

Dreyfus, G. L. (1907). *Die Melancholie: Ein Zustandsbild des manisch-depressiven Irreseins*. Gustav Fischer.

Heckers, S., & Kendler, K. S. (2020). The evolution of Kraepelin's nosological principles. *World Psychiatry, 19*(3), 381–388. https://doi.org/10.1002/wps.20774

Jones, T. D. (1944). The diagnosis of rheumatic fever. *Journal of the American Medical Association, 126*(8), 481–484.

Kendler, K. S. (1990). Toward a scientific psychiatric nosology: Strengths and limitations. *Archives of General Psychiatry, 47*(10), 969–973, www.ncbi.nlm.nih.gov/pubmed/2222134

(>2012). Epistemic iteration as a historical model for psychiatric nosology: Promises and limitations. In K. S. Kendler & J. Parnas (Eds.), *Philosophical issues in psychiatry II: Nosology* (pp. 303–322). Oxford University Press.

(2021). The prehistory of psychiatric genetics: 1780-1910. *American Journal of Psychiatry, 178*(6), 490–508. https://doi.org/10.1176/appi.ajp.2020.20030326

Kendler, K. S., & Engstrom, E. J. (2017). Kahlbaum, Hecker, and Kraepelin and the transition from psychiatric symptom complexes to empirical disease forms. *American Journal of Psychiatry, 174*(2), 102–109. https://doi.org/10.1176/appi.ajp.2016.16030375

(2020). Dreyfus and the shift of melancholia in Kraepelin's textbooks from an involutional to a manic-depressive illness. *Journal of Affective Disorders, 270*, 42–50. https://doi.org/10.1016/j.jad.2020.03.094

Klein, D. F. (1964). Delineation of two drug-responsive anxiety syndromes. *Psychpharmacologia, 5*, 397–408.

Leonhard, K. (1959). *Aufteilung der Endogenen Psychosen* (2nd ed.). Akademie Verlag.

(1979). *The classification of endogenous psychoses: Translated from the German by Russell Berman* (E. Robins, Ed.). Irvington Publishers.

Mignot, E., Zeitzer, J., Pizza, F., & Plazzi, G. (2021). Sleep problems in narcolepsy and the role of hypocretin/orexin deficiency. In M. A. Steiner, M. Yanagisawa & M. Clozel (Eds.), *The Orexin System: Basic science and role in sleep pathology* (Vol. 45, pp. 103–116). S. Karger AG.

Schumacher, M. M., & Santambrogio, J. (2023). Cortisol and the dexamethasone suppression test as a biomarker for melancholic depression: A narrative review. *Journal of Personalized Medicine, 13*(5), 837. https://doi.org/ARTN/10.3390/jpm13050837

Zachar, P., Regier, D. A., & Kendler, K. S. (2019). The aspirations for a paradigm shift in DSM-5: An oral history. *Journal of Nervous and Mental Disorders, 207*(9), 778–784. https://doi.org/10.1097/NMD.0000000000001063

24.2 Hyman's Response to Kendler

On my reading of Ken Kendler's response to my essay, I fear that we are talking past each other. Kendler's discussion of the historical importance of phenomenology in psychiatric diagnosis and his choice of the dexamethasone suppression test (DST) to exemplify prior failures to identify biological diagnostic tests are quite telling. I have no argument with either example in isolation, but I do not think that either the important historical contributions of descriptive psychiatry or the problems with early, conceptually confused attempts to find biological correlates of arbitrarily drawn DSM categories (depression) or putative subtypes (melancholia) bear on modern efforts to complement clinical descriptions with objective, quantitative, mechanism-based biomarkers. I am aware that despite success in neurology in gaining approvals for novel therapeutics for Alzheimer's disease and SOD-1 amyotrophic lateral sclerosis based on stratification, disease progression, and treatment biomarkers, there are no guarantees that psychiatry will be able to follow quickly. The advantage with respect to those neurodegenerative disorders is ground truth, even if it initially required postmortem examinations to separate Alzheimer's disease (characterized by amyloid and tau in the brain) from clinically indistinguishable but mechanistically unrelated forms of dementia. Psychiatry still has no such ground truth data, at least not yet. It is, however, finally in possession of objective, if still probabilistic, connection to nature through genetic associations. The genomic and computational tools developed in this century have created an inflection point for psychiatric research by making possible unbiased, large-scale genetics and neurobiological follow-on studies at the necessary scale (Hyman, 2021, 2023). Psychiatrists and psychologists have long contributed foundational basic science studies, but without the statistically convincing associations between disorder phenotypes and biological observations, the selection of biological correlates remained ungrounded and speculative; there was no principled, transparent way of associating psychiatric disorders with underlying mechanisms. As noted, plausible measures, such as the DST, were connected in relatively small samples to mental disorders such as major depression, melancholia (however defined), mania, and mixed states. However, the methodologies of the day could not determine whether abnormalities of the hypothalamic–pituitary–adrenal axis acted in upstream causal chains or represented downstream adaptations to pathogenic processes. What Kendler describes correctly as a history of many failures antedated modern tools to investigate human biology.

The second way in which Kendler and I seem to be talking past each other is more important, even if hiding in plain sight: the lack of ground truth. Returning to the DST, neither DSM-defined depression nor melancholia are natural kinds, even if grounded in brain biology (Hyman,

2021). When Kendler notes that the DST had inadequate sensitivity and specificity, we must ask about the status of the diagnostic construct that represented the gold standard against which this test was being measured. Here precisely is an instance in which commitments to history and phenomenology have repeatedly waylaid psychiatry: descriptive psychiatry has no tools to identify mechanistically homogeneous patients, no more than neurologists could identify amyloid pathology within cohorts of patients with dementia. Statistical patterns of genetic loading from among an enormous number of risk alleles segregating in population and, more indirectly and inferentially, variability of treatment responses and the failure of structural neuroimaging to identify clinically robust case–control differences argue that nature has bequeathed us significant underlying heterogeneity. Short of a main effect grounded in known biology, like serum glucose in diabetes mellitus, there is no reason to expect the DST or any other biological test to correlate with diagnostic entities that are products of human consensus constructed with only surface characteristics to go on. Perhaps in genetically or otherwise stratified mood disorder cohorts, the DST might have shown greater utility, potentially as to be a disease course (prognostic) biomarker or a treatment biomarker. I am not suggesting that the DST is worth pursing; rather, I am illustrating why failures to develop diagnostic tests in the premodern era, using DSM disorders as a biological gold standard, have no bearing on how we should proceed today.

Medicine has long been in possession of some reasonably good diagnostic tests such as measurements, alluded to earlier, of glucose in blood or urine to diagnose forms of diabetes mellitus and measurement of hemoglobin and red cell counts to diagnose anemia or polycythemia. During the 1990s, partly in the context of the HIV epidemic and with new ideas about cancer therapeutics, the US National Institutes of Health (NIH) and the US Food and Drug Administration (FDA) recognized that such broad, high-level diagnostic tests fell well short of what was needed to modernize treatment development and clinical care. These agencies began serious joint efforts, which continue to this day (FDA-NIH Biomarker Working Group, 2021; National Academies of Sciences, Engineering, and Medicine, 2023), to consider the nature, criteria for validation, and applications of biomarkers with the goal of improving mechanism-based patient stratification, measurement of disease course, and measurement of treatment effects and toxicities (I discuss these different contexts of use for biomarkers in Chapter 23 in this volume. A useful example from the 1990s that illustrates the relationship between clinical description and biomarkers is focused on treatment development for HIV/AIDS. Clinical description played a critical role in biomarker discovery and validation by providing a connection to the status of the patients. With successful establishment of objective, ideally quantitative biomarker, however, clinical description was obviated, given that it is subject to patient and observer biases. For HIV/AIDS there were significant disagreements between drug developers and regulators over selection of biomarkers for disease progression and treatment efficacy with the goal of reducing morbidity and mortality as an endpoint for clinical trials. Regulators initially insisted on CD4/CD8 T-cell ratios (as HIV depleted CD4 cells, which correlated with clinical disease progression). Drug developers wanted to use viral titers in blood, as these were more rapidly responsive to interventions and easier to measure. Eventually, viral titers were validated as surrogate endpoints for HIV treatment development and clinical use. In cancer medicine, the early 21st century saw the development of the Cancer Genome Atlas, a large-scale genome-sequencing and molecular characterization project that examined thousands of cancer samples (https://www.cancer.gov/ccg/research/genome-sequencing/tcga) and represented a critical step toward cancer biomarkers that could be matched with targeted treatments. Critical differences between these HIV/AIDS and cancer efforts compared with psychiatry are that diagnoses in the former have solid biological anchors. The differences from psychiatric diagnosis are enormous, and yet genetics complemented by neurobiology and computational approaches give evidence of progress that I have detailed elsewhere (Hyman, 2023).

I have nothing but the greatest respect for careful clinical description in medicine and the important role it has played in the history in psychiatry. I consider the Washington University descriptive psychiatrists heroic for definitively breaking free of the dominant psychoanalytic approaches of their time and bringing sober empiricism-backed psychiatric diagnosis after a long absence. Notwithstanding the well-deserved respect, it is also true that Robins and Guze (1970) were entirely wrong in their assertion that reliable diagnoses grounded in empiricism would lead to convergence of external validators on categories that would approximate natural kinds (Hyman, 2021). Robins and colleagues might have done better had they read and internalized the work of Gottesman and Shields (1967) who proposed a polygenic model of schizophrenia. In the end, however, polygenicity and other sources of heterogeneity (chance and highly diverse exposomes) would be the intellectual undoing of their hopes of convergence. In contrast to their predictions, schizophrenia is not a stable diagnosis over the life course, especially in the critical early years of illness;

schizophrenia does not "breed true" in family studies (consistent with polygenicity) and it is not distinct (or delineated in Robins and Guze's terminology) from bipolar disorder in many important aspects. Careful clinical description is critically important to the understanding of patients, but it is limited in the depth of insight it can offer. Ultimately, mechanism-based stratification will be necessary if we are ever to treat the right patients with the right drugs at the right time.

Despite much criticism of the DSM system, calls for a deep examination of descriptive psychiatry have been rare, for three reasons. First, descriptive psychiatry has served psychiatry extremely well compared with psychoanalytic theory, which it displaced in the late 20th century. It is fair to state that different psychoanalytic and psychodynamic theorists and practitioners were relatively uninterested in diagnosis because, in their view, the conflicts lying at the root of a patient's symptoms would not be well encompassed by explicit diagnoses, and in any case would be expected to emerge in the context of treatment. From the sober vantage of descriptive psychiatry, moreover, psychoanalytic ideas about symptom pathogenesis were at best speculative, even fanciful, and untested by any meaningful scientific procedures. Second, despite caveats, descriptive psychiatry has seemed to serve psychiatry well enough for the half century since the publication of DSM-III (American Psychiatric Association, 1980). Third, and most important, there has been well-grounded pessimism about doing better given the limitations of the relevant science. I do endorse the view, however, that advances in technology, computation, and genetics are creating new scientific opportunity. If we are to exploit this moment in scientific history to the benefit of our patients, we must clear out the intellectual underbrush represented by the DSM system that has, *inter alia*, bequeathed us approximately 300 categorical disorders – enough to make Procrustes blush – now reified by human cognitive habit, arbitrary diagnostic thresholds based on symptom counts chosen by intuition, a plague of comorbidity for which the diagnostic system bears much responsibility, and many additional problems. I am aware that none of these intellectual infirmities were entailed by a descriptive approach to psychiatric diagnosis. However, the problems discussed in my essay are very real, and no one should take it personally that science and technology have given us an opportunity to do better.

REFERENCES

American Psychiatric Association. (1980). *Diagnostic and statistical manual of mental disorders* (3rd ed.). American Psychiatric Association.

FDA-NIH Biomarker Working Group. (2021 [2016]). *BEST (Biomarkers, EndpointS, and other Tools) Resource*. Food and Drug Administration/ National Institutes of Health.
Gottesman, I. I, & Shields, J. (1967). A polygenic theory of schizophrenia. *Proceedings of the National Academy of Sciences, USA, 58*, 199–205.
Hyman, S. E. (2010). The diagnosis of mental disorders: The problem of reification. *Annual Review of Clinical Psychology, 6*, 155–179.
(2021). Psychiatric disorders: Grounded in human biology but not natural kinds. *Perspectives in Biology and Medicine, 64*(1), 6–28. https://doi.org/10.1353/pbm.2021.0002
(2023). The biology of mental disorders: Progress at last. *Daedalus Fall, 2023*, 186–208.
McCarroll, S. A., Feng, G., & Hyman, S. E. (2014). Genome-scale neurogenetics: Methodology and meaning. *Nature Neuroscience, 17*, 746–763.
National Academies of Sciences, Engineering, and Medicine. (2023). *Multimodal biomarkers for central nervous system disorders: Development, validation, and clinical integration: Proceedings of a workshop*. The National Academies Press. https://doi.org/10.17226/27208
Robins, E., & Guze, S. B. (1970). Establishment of diagnostic validity in psychiatric illness: Its application to schizophrenia. *American Journal of Psychiatry, 126*, 983–987.

24.3 Kendler's Rejoinder to Hyman

I have been encouraged to pen a brief response to Dr. Hyman's rejoinder thereby producing a full back-and-forth exchange on his main chapter. We agree on much, and this is clearer than when we started. Hopefully, we are now talking more "to" rather than "past" each other. We are both deeply excited about the possibilities for etiological insight into psychiatric illness fueled by striking advances in molecular techniques coupled with the large-scale collaborative studies needed to collect informative samples. We both respect the important contributions made by descriptive psychiatry – which continue to form the basis of our nosology – to this effort. Dr. Hyman has, at least as it appeared to me, modified his earlier position where he argued that a major reason why our field has been unable to develop high-quality biomarkers is DSM. It is my position that this is due almost entirely to the slow development of our basic science in the face of the astounding complexity and likely heterogeneity of our disorders. The fact that DSM still uses clinical criteria is the *result* of the slowness of the development of good biomarkers and not, at least in a substantial degree, the *cause*.

There are two interrelated points of softer disagreement remaining, one about the past and another about the future. First, Hyman argues that,

"Notwithstanding the well-deserved respect, it is also true that Robins and Guze (1970) *were entirely wrong* in their assertion that reliable diagnoses grounded in empiricism would lead to convergence of external validators on categories that would approximate natural kinds." That claim is too strong and not well supported by traditional diagnostic validators. A large amount of evidence suggests that Kraepelin's two major categories of major mental illness – mood disorders and schizophrenia – differ meaningfully on a range of validators: course, patterns of familial aggregation, pharmacological response, and aspects of brain anatomy, among others. Have they produced clean natural kinds? Clearly not. But that is too much to expect given the great complexity of the nature of psychiatric illness. Importantly, in my view, they have provided a start for the difficult process of developing more homogenous clinical conditions. More than Hyman, likely because I have immersed myself in this literature for many years now, I have come to respect the aggregate clinical experience and wisdom represented in our historically informed nosology. We disregard these traditions at our peril, not because they deliver on "ground truths" or the promise of natural kinds, but rather because they provide *a place to start.* Furthermore, Hyman's claim that descriptive categories are, by their nature, blind with respect to causation is not sustained by an historical analysis. In addition to Kraepelin's distinction between mood disorders and schizophrenia, subsequent diagnostic proposals – for example, the separation of panic disorder from generalized anxiety disorder (Klein, 1964) and major depression from bipolar disorder (Leonhard, 1959, 1979) – have also been shown to have substantial validity including meaningful biological differences and treatment responses. While we cannot claim that these diagnostic differences led to the identification of accurate biomarkers, they reflect important progress nonetheless. If I might summarize my key position on DSM, it is that it serves many important roles in our field, and improving its grounding in empirical research is an important and ongoing task. Problems arise when it is asked to do something it was not designed to do – in this case, to produce true natural kinds of psychiatric disorders with distinct etiologies.

Second, I see neuroscience and psychiatric phenomenology as contributing to a long iterative discourse of continual refinement of our categories. Recall the progress seen in rheumatic fever in the early part of this dialogue. I doubt we will make the leap from our current syndromes to clean natural kinds in one step. What strikes me as the most plausible framework for this process is the concept of epistemic iteration as illustrated by the historian of science Hasok Chang in his *Inventing*

Temperature (Chang, 2004). I have previously explored aspects of the application of this framework in psychiatric nosology (Kendler, 2012). This framework suggests that, rather than one great discovery that will shift our nosology dramatically from its current clinical foundations to etiological entities, we should expect many small improvements, each driven by partial insights.

The diagnostic utility of those insights would need to be tested and likely reflect, as we saw for rheumatic fever, biological processes operating at many levels. We need to recall that psychiatric nosology is ultimately a pragmatic discipline seeking to find ways to better describe our disorders, which in turn improves our ability to study, diagnose, and treat them. The idea that biomarkers will do away with the need for traditional diagnostic criteria of signs, symptoms, and course of illness strikes me as unrealistic and not consistent with what we have seen in the evolution of diagnostic criteria for autoimmune disorders like rheumatic fever.

REFERENCES

Chang, H. (2004). *Inventing temperature: Measurement and scientific progress.* Oxford University Press.

Kendler, K. S. (2012). Epistemic iteration as a historical model for psychiatric nosology: Promises and limitations. In K. S. Kendler & J. Parnas (Eds.), *Philosophical issues in psychiatry II: Nosology* (pp. 303–322). Oxford University Press.

Klein, D. F. (1964). Delineation of two drug-responsive anxiety syndromes. *Psychpharmacologia, 5*, 397–408.

Leonhard, K. (1959). *Aufteilung der Endogenen Psychosen* (2nd ed.). Akademie Verlag.

(1979). *The classification of endogenous psychoses: Translated from the German by Russell Berman* (E. Robins, Ed.). Irvington Publishers.

PART III

Causality and Nosology

Section 9

CHAPTER 25

Introduction to Borsboom's "Between Correlation and Causality"

Kenneth S. Kendler

The author of the following chapter, Denny Borsboom, has played a leading role in the rise of the network model in psychopathology. This model has developed into a viable alternative to the older conventional common-factor model. These two models provide quite different explanations for why psychiatric disorders tend to cluster together in disorders. Let us illustrate this using two commonly co-occurring symptoms in individuals with major depression: insomnia and tiredness. The common-factor model assumes that the two symptoms co-occur because they are both caused by a latent construct: the psychobiological state of depression. By contrast, the network model implies a more common (and perhaps naïve) presentation, assuming a direct causal link between the two symptoms, especially in the direction of "I sleep poorly on night x" followed by "during day x + 1 I am tired."

In the chapter that follows, Borsboom appropriately criticizes this common view of the network model, specifically that the paths (aka edges) connecting the symptoms (nodes) in a network are causal in nature. He reviews, with plausible examples, six potential mechanisms whereby symptoms x and y might be correlated in affected individuals, but not because of a causal path from x → y or y → x. These mechanisms are (1) resource competition, (2) evidential overlap, (3) shared mechanisms, (4) consistency drives, (5) statistical processes, and (6) unobserved common causes. He notes that this list is not intended to be exhaustive.

Borsboom gives clear descriptions of each of these mechanisms, so I will not repeat those here. Rather, given that his claims are likely approximately true, I provide some thoughts about the implications of his position. I would suggest at least three reasons why the etiology of the associations between symptoms within psychiatric syndromes are likely to be heterogeneous. First, studies in psychiatric epidemiology have shown that it is quite challenging to determine whether the association between putative risk factors and risk for psychiatric disorders are causal or instead result from one of a wide variety of confounding factors (Ohlsson & Kendler, 2020). Should the association between symptoms of psychiatric illness be strikingly different? Second, at a higher level, a wide variety of models have been proposed for the observed comorbidity between disorders with a range of research suggesting that multiple mechanisms are almost certainly involved (Neale & Kendler, 1995). Again, would we expect the association between symptoms within disorders to be much more causally homogeneous? Third, recent research we have done shows that the causal factors, in particular psychiatric symptoms, are likely influenced by the symptomatic context in which they appear. In particular, in a population-based twin study of last-year major depression (MD) in which we measured the occurrence of all the DSM-IV symptoms of MD reported over the last year, we showed that depressive criteria occurring outside depressive episodes were substantially less heritable than those occurring within such episodes (Kendler & Aggen, 2023). More importantly, we showed that these criteria were not closely genetically related. This means that a common symptom like insomnia that can occur as a transient symptom of stress, pain, or a sick baby is not closely related to the insomnia that occurs in the context of a depressive episode. This adds further complexity to the efforts to track the causal relationship between individual symptoms.

In summary, there is little doubt that the network theory for psychiatric symptoms provides a viable and conceptually useful addition to the older common-factor model in no small part because it provides a different conceptual framework within which we can understand symptom associations. But Borsboom is also certainly correct that this model does not provide a definitive solution to the question of the causal relationship between individual symptoms. Indeed, much prior research suggests that this question will have no simple answer and will certainly involve a relatively wide variety of different causal and confounding mechanisms. His essay and these accompanying comments should leave us with a rich appreciation of the multiple mechanisms through which the structure of the symptoms of our psychiatric disorders might arise.

REFERENCES

Kendler, K. S., & Aggen, S. H. (2023). A population-based twin study of the symptomatic diagnostic criteria for major depression that occur within versus outside of major depressive episodes. *Psychological Medicine, 53*, 1–8. https://doi.org/10.1017/S0033291723001241

Neale, M. C., & Kendler, K. S. (1995). Models of comorbidity for multifactorial disorders. *American Journal of Human Genetics, 57*(4), 935–953. www.ncbi.nlm.nih.gov/pubmed/7573055

Ohlsson, H., & Kendler, K. S. (2020). Applying causal inference methods in psychiatric epidemiology: A review. *Journal of the American Medical Association Psychiatry, 77*(6), 637–644. https://doi.org/10.1001/jamapsychiatry.2019.3758

CHAPTER 26

Between Correlation and Causality

Perspectives on Symptom Interactions in Network Models of Psychopathology

Denny Borsboom

26.1 Introduction

The psychometric question of how mental disorders relate to their symptoms is central to research on psychopathology because it regulates the way constructs are operationalized and represented in statistical models used throughout the discipline. Traditionally, symptoms have been seen as observable indicators of disorders that are not themselves observable (i.e., are latent). Latent variable models have been used to implement this conceptualization statistically, as they implement with the notion that distinct symptoms (represented in the model as psychometric indicators) are a function of a common latent structure (Aggen, Neale, & Kendler, 2005; Krueger, 1999). Because latent variable models are interpretable as common cause models (Bollen & Pearl, 2013; Borsboom, 2005, 2022), they are naturally aligned with the substantive idea that the relation between symptoms and disorders is of a causal nature.

From this point of view, symptoms function as passive psychometric indicators of a latent construct, which means that the correlations between these symptoms are, in a nontrivial sense, spurious. Just like chest pain and shortness of breath may arise as a result of an abnormality in the functioning of the heart, depression symptoms such as insomnia and sad mood arise as a result of an abnormality in the functioning of the mind–brain, and this is why they are correlated. This is consistent with the core assumptions of the latent variable model, as this model typically represents correlations between indicators as arising solely from their common dependence of indicators on a latent construct; as a result, conditioning on this latent construct screens off the correlations between its indicators, a feature of latent variable models known as local independence (Borsboom, Mellenbergh, & Van Heerden, 2003).

However, in the past decade it has been argued that this theory does not sit well with the symptomatology of mental disorders. That is, symptoms of psychopathology are likely to stand in relatively direct relations to each other, and these relations may very well be causal (Borsboom & Cramer, 2013; Cramer et al., 2010). For example, a depression symptom such as insomnia may cause the symptoms of fatigue and concentration problems; the symptom of fear may cause the symptom of avoidance; the persecutory delusions may cause the symptom of anxiety. If such relations are indeed present, this implies that correlations between these symptoms are anything but spurious. Instead, it suggests that symptoms are not mere passive psychometric indicators but active causal agents; as such, increased understanding of the causal relations between them may be pivotal for improving our understanding of the question how mental disorders arise. In particular, the pattern of causal relations between symptoms can be represented as a network in which symptoms are nodes and direct relations are connections between nodes. It has been argued that if the relations between symptoms in such a symptom network are sufficiently strong, symptom activity can become self-sustaining, which leads to a stable state of symptom activation that we phenomenologically recognize as a mental disorder (Borsboom, 2017).

In recent methodological work, this theoretical perspective has been coupled with a systematic approach to identify the structure of these symptom networks from empirical data. This approach has become known as *network psychometrics* (Marsman & Rhemtulla, 2022). In network psychometrics, as applied to psychopathology, symptoms are represented as nodes, and connections between nodes represent nonzero conditional associations between variables (Borsboom et al., 2021; Epskamp et al., 2017; Epskamp & Fried, 2018; Haslbeck & Waldorp, 2020; Huth et al., 2023; Mohammadi & Wit, 2019; Van Borkulo et al., 2014). Although such networks can be constructed from a variety of data sources (e.g., $N = 1$ time series, cross-sectional data, multiple time series), in general edges have the same statistical interpretation: an edge between two symptoms in a network means that some portion of the variance in one symptom can be predicted from the other symptom while statistically controlling for all the other symptoms in the network.

The network analysis approach has been intensively used in psychopathology research over the past decade (Contreras et al., 2019; Guloksuz, Pries, & Van Os, 2017; Robinaugh et al., 2020; Wichers et al., 2021). The pattern of findings is that (1) such analyses return networks in which the majority of symptoms are connected directly or indirectly, (2) network structures extend beyond the border of traditional diagnoses, and (3) the great majority of symptoms exhibit positive conditional associations (e.g., see Boschloo et al., 2016; Fried et al., 2016). These findings are consistent with factor analytic approaches, in which this pattern is picked up by a hierarchical factor model with a general factor at the apex or, alternatively, by a bifactor model (Caspi et al., 2014).

What do these conditional associations represent? In early papers that advocated the network approach (Borsboom & Cramer, 2013; Cramer et al., 2010), the suggestion was that the correlation patterns in the data could be fully explained by networks of direct causal interactions between symptoms. This idea is also central in the network theory of mental disorders (Borsboom, 2017). However, network analysis approaches are merely statistical models that encode conditional associations; as such, they do not directly get us to causal interactions. In fact, the statistical analyses used to construct networks from empirical data solely aim to identify nonzero conditional associations; they are neutral with respect to the question of where these associations come from. In contrast to network theories (Borsboom, 2017), which explicitly propose the existence of direct causal relations, network models are purely statistical structures that do not utilize causal assumptions in model estimation (even if the researchers who use them may). This can also be clearly brought out by contrasting the undirected network approaches typically used in network psychometrics with techniques that do involve explicit causal assumptions in statistical modeling (Briganti, Scutari, & McNally, 2023).

Although some of the connections found in empirical analyses of symptom networks may be indicative of direct causal relations, there are typically also many connections with an unclear causal signature. Although the network theory may be attractive for some sets of symptoms that feature nonzero conditional associations (e.g., insomnia and fatigue), it is much less clear how other sets of symptoms become coupled (e.g., psychomotor retardation and suicidal ideation). For this reason, it is important to inquire which processes, both causal and noncausal, might create observed statistical associations between symptoms in empirical data. In this chapter, I suggest a number of mechanisms that may underlie the edges in networks as they are empirically estimated. In turn, I discuss competition for limited resources, overlapping evidence bases, shared mechanisms, consistency drives, marginalization and conditioning, and unobserved common causes.

26.2 Competition for Limited Resources

Many symptoms that play a role in psychopathology involve processes that operate on finite resources. The most common such resources are time and money. Time is an intrinsically finite resource: no matter how you look at it, our lives are finite, and there are only 24 hours in a day. For most of us, money is also a finite resource. However, in contrast to the case with time, there are situations in which money is practically infinite relative to processes that require it (e.g., the coffee at my university is practically free for employees, so no matter how much coffee I drink, I will never be able to go bankrupt as a result). Thus, while we all have the same amount of time, we do not all have the same amount of money, which can produce important contextual variation in the liability to develop certain symptoms.

Finite resources operate under a conservation principle. For instance, money spent on one activity cannot be spent on another, as spendings are constrained by the total budget. In cases where multiple processes depend on the same resource, this conservation principle implies that if one activity depletes the resource, then another activity is limited. In ecology, this process is well known (e.g., it occurs when two species eat the same food) and has been modeled extensively (Gavina et al., 2018; Goh, 1979; May, 1973).

It is evident that some of the processes implicated in psychopathology share finite resources. One example involves time and money spent on substance abuse. Time expenses in substance abuse are partly intrinsic to the psychological or physical effects of the drug (in the sense that intoxication limits one's ability to engage in other activities) and partly related to cultural factors (especially if the substance is illegal, acquiring it can take many hours a week). Time spent on substance abuse cannot be spent on competing activities, such as working or spending time with people who do not tolerate use the substance (in many cases, this includes partner and family). Hence, the symptom of drug abuse is likely to influence other areas of life through the common dependence on shared resources. In fact, this principle is of such paramount importance that the interference of excessive substance use with other activities due to time spent on use is formulated as a symptom itself (American Psychiatric Association, 2013).

Of course, substance abuse is also a clear example of how money can operate as a finite resource. Substances, especially illegal ones, cost sizeable amounts of money, and money spent on them cannot be spent on rent; as a result, the symptom of drug abuse increases the chance of adverse events such as losing one's house and problems that result from this – many of which are separately listed as symptoms in diagnostic manuals. Here, it is important to note the moderating effects of financial conditions with respect to the liability to develop certain symptoms. If a billionaire becomes addicted to slot machines, it may not be physically possible to spend the money quickly enough to reach the end of their bank account, while a poor person may end up broke within a day. Because financial problems are among the main triggers for many symptoms in the DSM-5 (including worry, anxiety, and stress) as well as other issues relevant to psychopathology (housing problems, relational problems), it is likely that poverty increases the activation of symptoms in psychopathology networks.

Although the effects of competition for the shared resources of time and money are most evidently prominent in substance abuse, they are by no means limited to this domain. In fact, most disorders cost significant amounts of time. Obsessive compulsive disorder, for instance, is characterized by an inability to control obsessions and compulsions, and compulsive behavior can come to take up most of the day. People in manic episodes have been known to spend large amounts of time focused on activities that directly compete with their family life, as they may become absorbed by grandiose plans. Autistic spectrum disorders include symptoms of hyperfocus, where people spend excessive amounts of time on highly limited activities. In general, it seems hard to even conceive of a mental disorder being a disorder if its symptoms did not require any time at all.

To the extent that mental disorders require so much time as to make it impossible for a person to hold a job, common resources of time and money become coupled, and symptoms that share these resources become coupled as well (De Ron et al., 2023). Of course, while time and money are important, many other finite resources are likely to be involved in psychopathology as well. For example, most of us have finite social resources (e.g., our closest circle of family and friends) that, if depleted (e.g., due to family falling-out), cannot be readily replenished; our physical constitution also has a role to play here (e.g., wearing out one's body makes it harder to engage in many positive activities).

Note that, while interventions on a finite resource can influence the processes that depend on it (e.g., giving a person more money implies they can pay rent longer and can buy more drugs), the situation is, in my opinion, not appropriately characterized as a common cause system because of the complicated dynamics of feedback between the resource and the activities that depend on it (see De Ron et al., 2023, for examples of formal characterizations that accurately represent this system). Through these feedback processes, competition for shared finite resources will produce systematic associations between processes that require those resources; symptoms that are defined on the state of these processes will therefore become structurally associated, which results in nonzero conditional associations in networks.

26.3 Overlapping Evidence Bases

Many of the symptoms in diagnostic manuals such as the DSM-5 and ICD-10 can only be assessed through self-report. In some cases, the reason for this is practical. Even for symptoms such as weight loss and sleep loss, which may be subject to direct physical measurement, the implementation of physical measurement procedures is typically too cumbersome. In other cases, the reason is principled. We have no objective procedures for assessing, say, whether a person feels worthless or whether they have been contemplating suicide. Ardent reductionists may consider science fiction scenarios in which some future brain reading machine would be able to assess such feelings and cognitions objectively, or in which we can achieve psychiatric diagnoses without asking people questions. However, apart from the fact that there are no good reasons to think that such procedures will ever materialize, objective measurements of feelings and thoughts are simply not on any scientific horizon, so from a practical point of view we must make do without them.

The questions asked in diagnostic interviews and questionnaires inquire whether or not a person has been or is in a given state. They do this by presenting the person (or people in their environment) with a hypothesis that the person is asked to confirm or disconfirm. That is, "Have you felt worthless in the past two weeks?" is framed as a factual question. The client is thus implicitly asked to evaluate the truth of a sentence, namely "I have felt worthless in the past two weeks." We do not know much about the cognitive processes that underlie the response process to such questions, but it seems reasonable to suppose that the person in question will search for pieces of evidence for the hypothesis put before them. Such evidence may involve the recollection of momentary mood states (i.e., episodes of feeling worthless), elements of schemas (i.e., enduring cognitive representations of the self – "I am a worthless person"), or things that other people have said (e.g., comments about a person's work that the person interpreted as signaling that they are worthless).

In cognitive psychology, processes in which people sample evidence from memory are often modeled with diffusion models (Ratcliff, 1978; Wagenmakers et al., 2007). In such models, accumulation of evidence happens over time through sequential sampling of information. By sequentially sampling information elements, the evidence for or against a hypothesis gradually rises. When the evidence hits a boundary (the evidence standard the person uses), the person responds. Although it is not my intention to suggest that this model is an adequate representation of the response processes that go on during a diagnostic interview, I do think that it is likely that something resembling this process is happening. A person must retrieve information about themselves to answer the question, and often the symptomatology explicitly targets recurrent states or states that consist of multiple elements, so some form of sampling from memory must occur.

Considering the response process in this way, it is evident that different diagnostic queries have overlapping evidence bases. That is, information elements used to arrive at a response to one question will also be used to answer another. For example, suppose that a person has just experienced an encounter in which their partner shouted at them that they were good for nothing. That information element may be used both to answer the question of whether the person has felt worthless and the question of how good their relationship to their partner is. As a result, the answers to these questions become entangled through their overlapping evidence bases. To the extent that this overlap in evidence bases is stable over time, the effect will lead to nonzero conditional associations between the answers to the questions in a time series model (e.g., on data as collected in Experience Sampling study); to the extent that it is invariant across individuals, it will lead to nonzero conditional associations in the individual differences model. Hence, overlapping evidence bases will produce structural connections between nodes in symptom networks.

A particularly interesting case of overlapping evidence bases occurs when symptoms are part of each other's evidence base. For example, it stands to reason that a person who endorses the statement that they are worthless may count this endorsement as evidence for the proposition that they would be better off dead. Thus, feelings of worthlessness may be an evidence base for the symptom of suicidal ideation. Similarly, the presence of symptoms that refer to unusual perceptual experiences (e.g., hearing voices) may be processed as evidence for delusions (e.g., being the chosen one). Clearly, in such cases one should not expect the symptoms to vary independently; thus, these evidential relations will ordinarily produce connections between the corresponding nodes in symptom networks.

In some cases, overlapping evidence bases result from overly high semantic overlap. This happens, for instance, if interview questions or psychometric items are formulated similarly. In this case, overlapping evidence bases can arise purely as a methodological artifact, and the problem may be solved by choosing a different way of framing the question or item (e.g., avoiding synonyms). However, in many other cases (such as the ones discussed earlier), the overlapping evidence base is not a methodological artifact but part and parcel of the way the symptom network operates. In such cases, overlapping evidence bases would ideally be modeled rather than eliminated.

26.4 Shared Mechanisms

In the formulation of the network theory of mental disorders (Borsboom, 2017), mental disorders are conceptualized as stable states of symptom networks that are able to sustain their own activity. In this formulation, the concept of a symptom is taken to be largely congruent with the formulation of symptoms in diagnostic manuals such as DSM-5 and ICD-10. Symptoms, as commonly formulated in these manuals, are sometimes seen as mere registrations of a mental state (i.e., the classic notion of an "observed variable" in psychometrics). In such a "thin" conception of symptoms, the encoding of the *presence* of a symptom in a dataset is equated to the symptom itself, and the network approach then borders on operationalism or behaviorism (e.g., Freund et al., 2022).

In my opinion, however, this conceptualization is too limited. The presence of, say, insomnia (as, say, encoded by the symbol '1' in a spreadsheet) is not identical to insomnia, just like the presence of an elephant is not identical to an elephant. For example, in contrast to the representation of its presence, insomnia itself is highly complex. It arises out of the interplay of a rich set of biological mechanisms (e.g., the biological clock), representational mental states (e.g., beliefs on how much sleep a human being needs), behaviors (e.g., taking a night cap as a coping mechanism), and external conditions (e.g., noise in the environment). At the level of an individual concrete case – that is, a person – each of these is instantiated in some way (i.e., John's biological clock is a set of neurons in his head, his night cap is a glass of whisky, noise in the environment is a siren). It is this *instantiation* of the condition at the level of the individual case that gives insomnia its causal powers, not the *representation* of the condition in a numerical symbol – just like an elephant can hurt you but the representation of the presence of an elephant cannot.

In such a "thick" conceptualization of symptoms, symptoms themselves are complex and involve the activity of various mechanisms. The biological clock is an excellent example of such a mechanism. The biological clock is a well-understood physical system (Deboer et al., 2007; Rijo-Ferreira et al., 2019) that aligns the behavioral state of an organism (wake versus sleep) with external conditions (day versus night). The system generates a biological pulse of coordinated patterns of neural activation, hormone production, and body temperature, which in turn regulates behavior. For instance, the biological pulse prepares the body for sleep in the evening, lowering the bodily temperature and secreting melatonin and, as such, enhancing the person's propensity to fall asleep.

The biological clock is clearly an evolutionary adaptation that serves to regulate behavior. Because the sleep state contrasts with practically all other activities, regulatory effects of the biological clock affect these other activities too. An important example is eating. The pulse generated by the biological clock, together with our cultural customs and behavioral habits, typically leads to a coordinated pattern of calorie intake, where people get hungry at predictable times of the day. This means that, usually, eating behavior has a rhythm too, and this rhythm is synced with the sleep pattern. In my country, for instance, if you represented sleeping and eating musically, you would get something that resembles quadruple time: sleep-eat-eat-eat; sleep-eat-eat-eat; sleep-eat-eat-eat. . .).

Because of the broad regulation of behavior the biological clock partly orchestrates, disruptions in behavioral patterns in different areas of the system will tend to be synced as well. So, if the biological clock is disrupted in some way, we should expect to find disruptions in various behaviors at the same time. We all have experience with such coordinated disruption. If we fly to a different time zone, we are out of phase with the day–night rhythm of our destination. Because of the importance we attach to sleep, the sleep disruptions are most noticeable. But other biological rhythms are out of sync as well. For instance, many of us also have the experience of waking up in the middle of the night with severe bouts of hunger.

Because sleeping and eating both depend on rhythms generated by the biological clock, disruptions in the synchronization of the biological clock with the external day–night conditions will propagate through the system. Now, returning to the domain of psychopathology symptoms, we should therefore expect that, if in depression such shared mechanisms are indeed affected, symptoms such as sleep problems and appetite problems in depression will, at least in part, be coordinated. Indeed, depression for many people involves a disruption of the rhythm of life; people with depression may be awake at night, sleep during the day, and eat at unusual times (Germain & Kupfer, 2008). If one represented the sleep-eat rhythm of such people musically, it is likely that rather than the orchestrated sleep-eat-eat-eat beat, we may get a result more reminiscent of the chaotic patterns of free jazz: sleep-eat-eat-eat-eat-sleep-eat-sleep-eat-eat. . .

The coordination between rhythms will produce nonzero conditional associations in symptom networks. These associations result, at least in part, from the fact that that symptoms like sleep problems and appetite *share a mechanism* (i.e., the biological clock). Given the high level of integration and synchronization between functions in the human system, such "mechanism sharing" may be widespread and as a result may be responsible for many other edges found in symptom networks.

Our scientific culture favors a mindset in which biological factors are more easily seen as causes, and some people tend to think of the above example as a common cause model more or less automatically. In such a conception, the biological clock causes both eating and sleeping behavior, and as result, loss of appetite and insomnia should be modeled as effects of a common biological cause. However, this conception is not consistent with what we know about the way these systems work (Deboer et al., 2007; Rijo-Ferreira et al., 2019). As noted, we can bring the biological clock out of phase (e.g., by traveling), which will lead to sleep problems and eating disruptions, and this surely instantiates a common causal effect. However, if for some reason we change our sleep patterns (e.g., by taking a job with shiftwork or because of factors causing insomnia), this will affect the biological clock, which may have an effect on appetite regulation. Because the biological clock is responsive to external conditions (after all, its function is to align our activity with the diurnal rhythm), it is also possible that changes in our eating patterns (e.g., not eating anymore or eating at irregular times) may influence the biological clock, which can in turn influence sleep. It should be noted that, relative to other animals, the capacity to change our environment through behavior adds a layer to this complexity by greatly expanding the possibility of human beings to get into trouble. Many animals can get jet lag, but they cannot inflict them on themselves; however, the insomniac who turns on the light and takes a night cap disrupts the biological clock, both through alcohol consumption and through light conditions, and as such creates the potential for a feedback loop of problems that can maintain each other.

Thus, the causal organization of this type of system does not seem to be described adequately in terms of a common cause model, but rather involves the synchronized development of different variables reminiscent of differential equation representations of dynamical systems. Psychological states, behavior, external conditions, and biological mechanisms are intertwined to such a degree that the system can be responsive to causal interventions at each of these levels. Inducing insomnia may disrupt the biological clock, which may cause changes in eating; inducing changes in eating may induce changes in sleep behavior, which may cause changes in the biological clock; interventions on the biological clock will lead to changes in both eating and sleeping patterns. Potentially, differential responses to stress may lead this type of integrated system to be pushed out of equilibrium in different directions (e.g., if some respond to stress by eating or sleeping more, rather than less), leading to distinct patterns of symptomatology as observed, for instance, in typical versus atypical depression (Lojko & Rybakowski, 2017).

26.5 Consistency Drives

Many symptoms require representational mental states to have a particular type of content. The most prominent cases occur when symptomatology phrased in terms of belief states. In such cases, the determination of whether a symptom is present usually depends in part on determining *what* the person believes – that is, what the content of the belief state is. Delusions are a prominent example; when a person is convinced that they are Napoleon, we judge that belief state as delusional at least in part because of its outlandish contents. Other examples concern representational states that are involved in post-traumatic stress (e.g., thoughts about the trauma) and obsessive-compulsive disorder (e.g., the belief that one is dirty – which may, in this case, be flanked by a meta-representation, namely the insight that the belief itself is irrational).

The content of mental states plays an interesting role in symptom networks. It has been noted, for instance, that one of the appeals of the network approach lies in the fact that many connections between symptoms "make sense" (Kalis & Borsboom, 2020). The reason many people find plausible a connection between, say, obsessions with being dirty and compulsive cleaning is that, in ordinary life, we clean things because they are dirty. Similarly, a connection between the conviction that one is a burden to one's environment and contemplating suicide "makes sense" because we often deal with a burden by removing it. Many safety behaviors satisfy similar relations at the content level. One avoids theaters to prevent an embarrassing public panic attack; one avoids cellars because one may encounter spiders there; one avoids going near the park where one was assaulted to prevent that from happening again. Arguably, it is the fact that such relations make sense that allows us to put ourselves in patients' shoes to some extent (Jaspers, 1963).

These and other cases suggest that much psychopathology satisfies a level of "basic rationality," in the sense that people justify their actions by giving reasons for them and adapt their belief states in view of what they perceive as evidence. Naturally, it is hallmark of psychopathology that such rationalizations of behavior are often maladaptive (e.g.., avoiding theaters is not a good way of dealing with panic attacks) and that the justification of belief states is sometimes inappropriate (e.g., that there are cameras in the mall does not imply that one is being spied on). However, this does not detract from the point that people who suffer from psychopathology, just like all other people, engage in rationalization of beliefs and behaviors, and that in doing so they typically are sensitive to the content of mental states (Borsboom, Cramer, & Kalis, 2019).

The rationalization of behavior is an extremely complicated topic that I cannot hope to address adequately in this chapter. Rather, I want to point to a relatively incontestable consequence of basic rationality, which is that in many cases people are driven to maintain consistency among their mental states (e.g., their beliefs, expectations, thoughts) and their actions. Of course, this drive toward consistency is a deeply studied topic throughout psychology; consider, for instance, research on cognitive dissonance (the aversion to inconsistency between attitudes and behaviors; Festinger, 1957) and confirmation bias (the tendency to search for evidence that is consistent with one's hypothesis; Wason, 1968).

If we consider cognitive, affective, and behavioral states to be nodes in a network that can take positive or negative values (Dalege et al., 2018), then the drive for consistency will result in aligned patterns for those states that are connected through their representational content. For instance, danger, fear, and avoidance are connected in our folk psychology: if something is dangerous, we fear it and therefore try to avoid it. An internal drive for consistency will therefore lead to states that are strongly connected, which will tend to align. This means that we will tend to see people who believe that spiders are dangerous, are afraid of spiders, and avoid them; and we will tend to see people who do not believe spiders are dangerous, are not afraid of them, and do not avoid them. We should see relatively fewer people who, say, are not afraid of spiders but still avoid them studiously, or who have other inconsistent patterns.

Of course, this is not to say that such inconsistent patterns do not exist; clearly, there are many people who know that spiders are not dangerous but are still afraid of them (the fact that people often shrug at confessing this is another testament to the importance we attach to consistency). The point is that, on average, the connections in question will lead to patterns of alignment, and these will lead to nonzero associations between variables that encode the relevant states. Thus, a drive for consistency will tend to lead to connections between nodes in symptom networks that involve representational mental states and behaviors that serve to align the state of the world to the person's preferences or desires.

Despite the basic rationality that is typically exhibited in psychopathology, the connections between representational mental states, the external world, and behavior are often, as the DSM-5 puts it, "inappropriate." For example, we identify persecutory beliefs partly through their content but also in part by judging that the person's evidential basis does not justify the belief state; one would commonly acknowledge that it is certainly possible that the "government" is spying on a person, but the fact that there are cameras in the mall is insufficient to conclude this. People who suffer from delusional states may see evidence where there is none, interpret events that are basically unconnected to their belief states as extremely important, and interpret random events as extremely meaningful. If this happens, belief states and perceived evidence can connect in a feedback system that can get stuck in a state where the belief and perceived evidence are aligned so firmly that nothing can break the connection. Such states have been designated "belief traps" (Scheffer et al., 2022).

26.6 Marginalization and Conditioning

The mechanisms inducing network connectivity that have been discussed so far reflect processes that are of substantive interest, and further investigation of how they induce connectivity is important. However, there are also purely statistical processes that can induce nonzero conditional associations. The most important of these are implicit marginalization and conditioning on common effects.

Marginalization is a statistical term that indicates that variables have been collapsed over – that is, they have been disregarded from the statistical model. An example is combining subsamples. Suppose that, say, one has data on smoking and cancer, and one has also assessed gender. If one computes the correlation between smoking and cancer without taking gender into account, one is marginalizing the distribution over gender by combining the data of males and females. Marginalization is the opposite of conditioning – the process by which one controls for variables in the data by computing statistics for each level of these variables separately.

The effects of marginalization are important in network analysis, because it captures what happens when we ignore part of a network by only looking at a subset of variables. In the standard psychometric network model, associations that make up the pairwise edges are conditioned on all other variables in the network. Now suppose that two nodes A and B are not directly connected in the network but do share a connection to node C. If we collapse the data over C, for instance by just deleting C from the data and running the network on the dataset with C excluded, the part of the association between A and B that was produced by their common statistical dependence on C will be absorbed in the relation between A and B. Thus, marginalizing over C produces an edge between A and B that in many contexts would be interpreted as "spurious" (Epskamp et al., 2018).

The point generalizes. For example, imagine that we have assessed all symptoms of the DSM-5 in a large sample and have computed the network structure of the symptoms using a standard network psychometrics model, such as the Ising model (van Borkulo et al., 2014). If we discard, say, all the data on externalizing disorders, then any dependencies between internalizing symptoms that were due to common connections with externalizing symptoms will produce edges among the symptoms that remain in the analysis. If we subsequently delete all symptoms except those of depression, all the edges that distinct depression symptoms had in common with, say, generalized anxiety or panic symptoms will be absorbed in the depression symptom network. In typical networks observed in psychopathology, the associations are such that this can be regarded as a general rule, because the system as a whole is relatively connected (Boschloo et al., 2016). The more variables one ignores, the more edges will be present in the network of the remaining variables. The converse is also true: adding additional nodes to the network will generally lead edges to vanish from the network of variables with which one started.

Now, in typical situations, researchers compute network on a set of symptoms that cannot reasonably be assumed to be the complete network (Neal & Neal, 2023). Thus, researchers only observe part of the symptom network. This means that all symptoms that have not been observed have been implicitly marginalized over. Due to the laws of statistics, this implies that the purely passive process of not observing parts of the symptom space will lead to network edges over and above any direct connections nodes may have. As a result, implicit marginalization is an important process that produces nonzero associations in symptom networks. While this not necessarily a problem, it is useful to be aware of it if one is interpreting empirically estimated networks.

The second statistical process that can induce nonzero conditional associations is implicit conditioning on common effects or, more generally, selection bias. The effect of this mechanism is best explained through an example. Suppose that two soldiers in a firing squad (B and C) have the order to shoot a prisoner (A). Both are nervous and may fail to fire their rifle with a nonzero probability. Suppose B and C fire completely independently, so that learning that B fired gives no information on whether C fired. Now imagine one is given the information that B did not fire. Then one has no information on whether C fired. B and C are thus uncorrelated. However, now suppose that one learns the prisoner is dead (conditioning on A). Upon inspecting the rifles of the soldiers, one also finds that B did not shoot. Then, one suddenly has information: for if B did not fire his rifle, but the prisoner is dead, then C must have done it. So, conditioning on a common effect (A) renders the causes of that common effect (B and C) correlated, even if they were originally independent.

The effect of implicit conditioning on a common effect has been interpreted as a variant of Berkson's bias (De Ron et al., 2021; but see Haslbeck et al., 2022), which arises through subgroup selection. In psychopathology networks, the effect can be seen if one includes a total score of the variables represented in a network and includes it in the network as well. The total score acts as a common effect of the constituent items, and as a result, conditioning on it changes the conditional associations between items. The effect arises in exactly the same way as in the firing squad example. Say we have a total score comprised of two dichotomous items. Then if we learn a person has a total score equal to 1, and we also know that one item has the value 0, then we know that the other item must have the value 1. The point generalizes to larger item sets, although the effect will become ever smaller as the number of items increases.[1]

There are also occasions where networks are created from data of individuals who are diagnosed with a disorder that is a function of the symptoms in a network. In this case, there may be implicit conditioning as well, to the extent that the diagnosis may be a causal effect of the item scores. Note that if the total score or diagnosis is a positive function of the item scores (no items are inversely weighted), the effects of this mechanism will be to lower existing conditional associations and possibly render them

[1] Note that, strictly speaking, this effect is not causal, as the item scores and total score are not distinct entities. The actual relation is one of supervenience (Markus & Borsboom, 2013); the total score supervenes on the item scores (differences in item scores are necessary but not sufficient for differences in total scores). However, statistical models cannot tell the difference between supervenience and common effect structures, so for the current presentation the distinction is immaterial.

negative. The effects of subgroup selection can be countered by simply advising not to create subgroups on symptom scores (De Ron et al., 2021 by adjusting one's interpretation to their presence (Haslbeck, Ryan, & Dablander, 2022) or by correcting the analysis statistically (Boot et al., 2023).

26.7 Unmeasured Common Causes

Psychopathology symptoms are likely to stand under the influence of a broad set of factors outside the symptom network. Insofar as these factors are shared among symptoms, so that they function as common causes, they will create associations between symptoms that cannot be explained away by conditioning on other symptoms. In these cases, symptoms will feature nonzero conditional associations, which leads to edges in the network. Three of the most obvious such features are adverse life events, personality dispositions, and shared genetic effects.

In research on depression, for instance, several life events that may have a joint effect on symptomatology have been documented to include romantic loss, stress, health problems, and interpersonal conflict (Keller et al., 2007). These are broad generalizations that subsume a set of events that are likely to impact several symptoms at the same time; for example, the category of "romantic loss" may include romantic breakups that cause sad mood and feelings of worthlessness; the category of "stress" may include severe financial problems that lead to concentration problems and suicidal ideation, among others. If such events are indeed common causes but are not accounted for in the analysis, they will lead to nonzero conditional associations.

Personality traits may encode behavioral tendencies and dispositions that facilitate symptom expression (Lunansky, van Borkulo, & Borsboom, 2020). It is remarkable that personality questionnaires often contain items with very similar wordings to DSM-5 symptoms. For instance, the DSM-5 diagnosis of depression involves the symptom of sad mood, which is required to be present most of the time, most of the days for at least two weeks; the NEO-PI contains the neuroticism item "I often feel lonely or sad"; similarly, the DSM-5 requires persistent feelings of worthlessness, while the NEO-PI includes the item "I have a low opinion of myself." There are many other such examples, both for depression and other disorders, where the personality questionnaire seems to address a stable disposition to develop (mild versions of) DSM symptomatology. In some cases, this may also be partly accounted for by overlapping evidence bases, as both the personality items and answers to clinical interview questions may be based on the same evidence. To the extent that such dispositions influence the liability to develop multiple symptoms at the same time, this will produce nonzero condition associations between these symptoms in the data.

Shared genetic effects have been widely suggested for different mental disorders (Grotzinger, 2021). Although genetic analyses are typically executed at the level of disorder diagnoses, so that the level of individual symptoms is less clearly documented, it seems likely that some of the genetic variance in mental disorders involves effects that are expressed via mechanisms that influence multiple symptoms at the same time. It is currently unclear to what extent such effects are channeled by the same types of mechanisms that I have discussed earlier, or whether they involve different, as yet unknown mechanisms.

As soon as an unmeasured event or disposition causes individual differences in various symptoms, it will create some amount of overlap between them that is picked up as a nonzero conditional association in a between-person network. It stands to reason that various such common causes influence various sets of symptoms. To the extent that such effects average out over symptoms but not over people, this will create a haze of positive correlations between symptoms. In an observational study, such correlations will behave as if a common latent variable has affected the symptoms. However, if one includes the actual causes in the model, one may see that they affect sets of symptoms rather than a common latent variable that channels the effects. For example, Cramer et al. (2012) found that the data contradict the hypothesis that effects of romantic loss, stress, interpersonal conflict, and health problems are channeled via a latent variable, and Fried et al. (2015) found the same for the effects of the death of people's spouses. However, in a situation where many such common causes are operative but none is measured, a latent variable model may describe the data well. In such cases, the latent variable encodes a sort of aggregate of everything that influences more than one symptom.

Unobserved common causes are typically modeled as exogenous – that is, they influence the network but are not influenced by it. For events that are entirely unconnected to symptomatology, like pandemics or economic crises, this is uncontroversial. However, many other events can arise partly under the influence of symptomatology; romantic breakup or loss of a job are examples for which this can be the case. In such situations, the external commonality could also be seen as part of the network, and the situation is analytically the same as the marginalization process discussed earlier.

26.8 Discussion

In this chapter, I have suggested several processes that may be responsible for the widely observed nonzero conditional associations between psychopathology symptoms. It is important to note that the processes in question are neither exhaustive (it is likely that more exist) nor mutually exclusive. For example, if one considers a pair of symptoms, like feelings of worthlessness and depressed mood, it is plausible that multiple processes are at work simultaneously; for instance, one can readily imagine that evidential overlap, consistency drives, and common causes are relevant to the conditional association between these variables. In my view, therefore, it is likely that in reality we are looking at a hodgepodge of these processes when we analyze a matrix of correlations in psychopathology.

The fact that the processes described in this chapter are not mutually exclusive frustrates standard hypothesis-testing strategies often used in psychology, where the leading idea is to pit different theories against each other by deriving differential predictions for the data. It would be easy to come up with an experiment to contrast, say, the hypothesis that conditional associations are entirely produced by consistency drives with the hypothesis that they are entirely produced by common causes. However, it is not clear that such an approach is viable if both processes are operative at the same time. In such cases, it may be more profitable to use a modeling approach that can incorporate the joint operation of multiple processes (Scheffer & Beets, 1994; Scheffer & Carpenter, 2003).

It is interesting to note that many of the processes listed need not necessarily be thought of as instances of direct causation. Of course, researchers can differ in their conceptualization of causal relations, and some readers may feel comfortable with the interpretation of all processes discussed in this chapter as being causal in nature. However, there may also be readers who object to such a characterization for a variety of reasons: for example, some of the processes concern the co-evolution of a set of systems that is coupled but not intrinsically directional (e.g., the example of the biological clock); the processes involve evidential relations rather than causal ones (e.g., when two symptoms are part of each other's evidence base); or alignment is driven by semantics (e.g., in consistency drives) (De Boer et al., 2021; Oude Maatman, 2020). It is not my ambition in this chapter to adjudicate between different interpretations of these processes, or to argue for or against a particular account of causation. The important point is that a wide range of processes can generate conditional associations, and that theorizing on these processes provides fertile ground for the interpretation of network modeling results.

For researchers who are not inclined to count the processes I have described in this chapter as causal, an alternative is to think of these relations as structural connections (Borsboom, 2022). In this conceptualization, two variables are structurally connected to the degree that it is hard to change one without changing the other. This can be the case even if a strictly causal interpretation is hard to substantiate (because cause and effect are not clearly separable, independently manipulable, modular, etc.; De Boer et al., 2021). Such a "soft" interpretation of network connections both matches the conditional independence relations that are the target of psychometric network analysis and offers a plausible backdrop to theorize about connections in symptom networks.

In addition, thinking about these processes can inform theory construction efforts. For example, one can interpret (patterns of) stable conditional associations between symptoms to play the role of empirical phenomena (Bogen & Woodward, 1988). Network modeling then essentially functions as a phenomena detection procedure (Haig, 2013). Theory construction efforts may subsequently focus on creating formalized theories to explain why we find certain edges in our empirically estimated networks to be robust (Borsboom et al., 2021; Olthof et al., 2023; Robinaugh et al., 2019). In such an interpretation, the existence of direct causal relations between symptoms is just one of the many possible explanatory theories that may be developed to explain these. More explicit theorizing on these relations can lead to better formal models that may provide a better understanding of how mental disorders arise and hopefully ultimately lead to better treatments (Robinaugh et al., 2019; Ryan, Haslbeck, & Robinaugh, 2023).

Importantly, the analysis also shows why network models do not map onto network theory in a straightforward way. Although statistical models are well suited to detect general connectivity patterns among symptoms, with respect to the explanatory potential of network theories, they deliver the *explanandum* rather than the *explanans*. It is useful to note that this is the case for any network, regardless of whether it is based on cross-sectional or time series data. The reason for this is simply that, despite any other virtues they might have, network models will not solve the problem of induction. Given a theoretical model, one can deductively work out what statistical model one would expect to hold, but given a statistical model, there are always multiple possible explanations for why that model holds.

If symptoms of mental disorders are indeed coupled because of a myriad of processes, such as the ones sketched in this chapter, what does that imply for the relation between symptoms and disorders from a conceptual standpoint? Several observations can be made on this topic. First, the fact that so many different types of processes are likely involved in sustaining mental disorders undercuts the idea that we should expect mental disorders to be identifiable with common causes of their symptoms. Second, given the fact that the interactions between symptoms involve many different levels of analysis (biological, psychological, social, financial, cultural), a good theoretical characterization of mental disorders should be able to accommodate this; this suggests that accounts of mental disorders that focus on only one of these levels should be interpreted with caution. Third, because many of the processes sketched piggyback on the subjective experience of patients and the folk psychological concepts they use to interpret that experience (e.g., consider the example of consistency drives and the rationalization), a successful analysis of mental disorders will have to involve some kind of integration of the first-person experiential perspective and the mind-independent physical realities of the human body and its environment.

Acknowledgments

I would like to thank Jonas Haslbeck and Karoline Huth for comments on an earlier draft of this chapter.

REFERENCES

Aggen, S. H., Neale, M. C., & Kendler, K. S. (2005). DSM criteria for major depression: Evaluating symptom patterns using latent-trait item response models. *Psychological Medicine, 35*, 475–487.

American Psychiatric Association. (2013). *Diagnostic and statistical manual of mental disorders* (5th ed.). American Psychiatric Publishing.

Bogen, J., & Woodward, J. (1988). Saving the phenomena. *The Philosophical Review, 97*, 303. https://doi.org/10.2307/2185445

Bollen, K. A., & Pearl, J. (2013). Eight myths about causality and structural equation models. In S. L. Morgan (Ed.), *Handbook of causal analysis for social research* (pp. 301–328). Springer Netherlands.

Boot, J., de Ron, J., Haslbeck, J. M. B., & Epskamp, S. (2023). Correcting for selection bias after conditioning on a sum score in the Ising model. Online publication ahead of print. https://doi.org/10.31219/osf.io/xq8ur_v1

Borsboom, D. (2005). *Measuring the mind: Conceptual issues in contemporary psychometrics*. Cambridge University Press.

Borsboom, D. (2017). A network theory of mental disorders. *World Psychiatry, 16*, 5–13.

(2023). Psychological constructs as organizing principles. In L. A. van der Ark, W. H. M. Emons, & R. R. Meijer (Eds.), *Essays on contemporary psychometrics: Methodology of educational measurement and assessment*. Springer. https://doi.org/10.1007/978-3-031-10370-4_5

Borsboom, D., & Cramer, A. (2013). Network analysis: An integrative approach to the structure of psychopathology. *Annual Review of Clinical Psychology, 9*, 91–121.

Borsboom, D., Cramer, A., & Kalis, A. (2019). Brain disorders? Not really: Why network structures block reductionism in psychopathology research. *Behavioral and Brain Sciences*, 42, E2. https://doi.org/10.1017/S0140525X17002266

Borsboom, D., Deserno, M. K., Rhemtulla, M., Epskamp, S., Fried, E. I., McNally, R. J., Robinaugh, D. J., Perugini, M., Dalege, J., Costantini, G., Isvoranu, A.-M., Wysocki, A. C., van Borkulo, C. D., van Bork, R., & Waldorp, L. J. (2021). Network analysis of multivariate data in psychological science. *Nature Reviews Methods Primers, 1*(1), 58.

Borsboom, D., Deserno, M. K., Rhemtulla, M., Epskamp, S., Fried, E. I., McNally, R. J., Robinaugh, D. J., Perugini, M., Dalege, J., & Constantini, G. (2022). Author correction: Network analysis of multivariate data in psychological science. *Nature Reviews Methods Primers, 2*(1), 1–2.

Borsboom, D., Mellenbergh, G. J., & Van Heerden, J. (2003). The theoretical status of latent variables. *Psychological Review, 110*, 203–219.

Boschloo, L., Schoevers, R. A., van Borkulo, C. D., Borsboom, D., & Oldehinkel, A. J. (2016). The network structure of psychopathology in a community sample of preadolescents. *Journal of Abnormal Psychology*. https://doi.org/10.1037/abn0000150

Briganti, G., Scutari, M., & McNally, R. J. (2023). A tutorial on Bayesian networks for psychopathology researchers. *Psychological Methods, 28*(4), 947–961. https://doi.org/10.1037/met0000479

Caspi, A., Houts, R. M., Belsky, D. W., Goldman-Mellor, S. J., Harrington, H., Israel, S., . . . & Moffitt, T. E. (2014). The p factor: One general psychopathology factor in the structure of psychiatric disorders? *Clinical Psychological Science, 2*, 119–137.

Contreras, A., Nieto, I., Valiente, C., Espinosa, R., & Vazquez, C. (2019). The study of psychopathology from the network analysis perspective: A systematic review. *Psychotherapy and Psychosomatics, 88*(2), 71–83. https://doi.org/10.1159/000497425

Cramer, A. O. J., Borsboom, D., Aggen, S. H., & Kendler, K. S. (2012). The pathoplasticity of major depression. *Psychological Medicine, 42*, 957–965. https://doi.org/10.1017/S003329171100211X

Cramer, A. O. J., Waldorp, L. J., van der Maas, H., & Borsboom, D. (2010). Comorbidity: A network perspective. *Behavioral and Brain Sciences, 33*, 137–150.

Dalege, J., Borsboom, D., van Harreveld, F., & van der Maas, H. L. J. (2018). The Attitudinal Entropy (AE) framework as a general theory of individual attitudes. *Psychological Inquiry, 29*(4), 175–193.

de Boer, N. S., de Bruin, L. C., Geurts, J. J. G., & Glas, G. (2021). The network theory of psychiatric disorders: A critical assessment of the inclusion of environmental factors. *Frontiers in Psychology, 12*. Online-only publication. https://doi.org/10.3389/fpsyg.2021.623970

de Ron, J., Deserno, M., Robinaugh, D., Borsboom, D., & van der Maas, H. L. J. (2023). Towards a general modeling framework of resource competition in cognitive development. *Child Development, 94*, 1–22.

de Ron, J., Fried, E. I., & Epskamp, S. (2021). Psychological networks in clinical populations: Investigating the consequences of Berkson's bias. *Psychological Medicine, 51*(1), 168–176. https://doi.org/10.1017/S0033291719003209

Deboer, T., Détári, L., & Meijer, J. H. (2007). Long term effects of sleep deprivation on the mammalian circadian pacemaker. *Sleep, 30*, 257–262.

Epskamp, S., & Fried, E. I. (2018). A tutorial on regularized partial correlation networks. *Psychological Methods, 23*, 617–634.

Epskamp, S., Maris, G., Waldorp, L. J., & Borsboom, D. (2018). Network psychometrics. In P. Irwing, D. Hughes, & T. Booth (Eds.), *The Wiley handbook of psychometric testing: A multidisciplinary reference on survey, scale and test development* (pp. 953–986). Wiley.

Epskamp, S., Rhemtulla, M. T., & Borsboom, D. (2017). Generalized network psychometrics: Combining network and latent variable models. *Psychometrika, 82*, 904–927. https://doi.org/10.1007/s11336-017-9557

Festinger, L. (1957). *A theory of cognitive dissonance*. Stanford University Press. https://doi.org/10.1515/9781503620766

Freund, I. M., Arntz, A., Visser, R. M., & Kindt, M. (2022). Jumping back onto the giants' shoulders: Why mental representations deserve a place in a network perspective of psychopathology. *Behaviour Research and Therapy, 156*, 104154. https://doi.org/10.1016/j.brat.2025.104154

Fried, E. I., Bockting, C., Arjadi, R., Borsboom, D., Amshoff, M., Cramer, A. O. J., Epskamp, S., Tuerlinckx, F., Carr, D. & Stroebe, M. (2015). From loss to loneliness: The relationship between bereavement and depressive symptoms. *Journal of Abnormal Psychology, 124*, 256–265. https://doi.org/10.1037/abn0000028

Fried, E. I., Epskamp, S., Nesse, R. M, Tuerlinckx, F., & Borsboom, D. (2016). What are 'good' depression symptoms? Comparing the centrality of DSM and non-DSM symptoms of depression in a network analysis. *Journal of Affective Disorders, 189*, 314–320.

Gavina, M. K. A., Tahara, T., Tainaka, K.-i., Ito, H., Morita, S., Ichinose, G., Okabe, T., Togashi, T., Nagatani, T., & Yoshimura, J. (2018). Multi-species coexistence in Lotka-Volterra competitive systems with crowding effects. *Scientific Reports*, 8, 1–8.

Germain, A., & Kupfer, D. J. (2008). Circadian rhythm disturbances in depression. *Human Psychopharmacology, 23*(7), 571–585. https://doi.org/10.1002/hup.964

Goh, B. (1979). Stability in models of mutualism. *The American Naturalist, 113*, 261–275.

Guloksuz, S., Pries, L. K., & van Os, J. (2017). Application of network methods for understanding mental disorders: pitfalls and promise. *Psychological Medicine, 47*(16), 2743–2752. https://doi.org/10.1017/S0033291717001350

Grotzinger A. D. (2021). Shared genetic architecture across psychiatric disorders. *Psychological Medicine, 51*(13), 2210–2216. https://doi.org/10.1017/S0033291721000829

Haig, B. D. (2013). Detecting psychological phenomena: Taking bottom-up research seriously. *The American Journal of Psychology, 126*(2), 135–153. https://doi.org/10.5406/amerjpsyc.126.2.0135

Haslbeck, J. M. B., Ryan, O., & Dablander, F. (2022). The sum of all fears: Comparing networks based on symptom sum-scores. *Psychological Methods, 27*(6), 1061–1068. https://doi.org/10.1037/met0000418

Haslbeck, J. M. B., & Waldorp, L. J. (2020). MGM: Estimating time-varying mixed graphical models in high-dimensional data. *Journal of Statistical Software, 93*(8 SE-Articles), 1–46. https://doi.org/10.18637/jss.v093.i08

Huth, K. B. S., de Ron, J., Goudriaan, A. E., Luigjes, J., Mohammadi, R., van Holst, R. J., Wagenmakers, E.-J., & Marsman, M. (2023). Bayesian analysis of cross-sectional networks: a tutorial in R and JASP. *Advances in Methods and Practices in Psychological Science, 6*(4), 25152459231193336. https://doi.org/10.1177/25152459231193334

Jaspers, K. (1963 [1923]). *General psychopathology*. Manchester University Press.

Kalis, A., & Borsboom, D. (2020). Folk psychology as a causal language. *Theory & Psychology, 30*(5), 723–728.

Keller, M. C., Neale, M. C., & Kendler, K. S. (2007). Association of different adverse life events with distinct patterns of depressive symptoms. *The American Journal of Psychiatry, 164*(10), 1521–1622. https://doi.org/10.1176/appi.ajp.2007.06091564

Krueger, R. F. (1999). The structure of common mental disorders. *Archives of General Psychiatry*, 56(10), 921–926. https://doi.org/10.1001/archpsyc.56.10.921

Łojko, D., & Rybakowski, J. K. (2017). Atypical depression: Current perspectives. *Neuropsychiatric Disease and Treatment, 13*, 2447–2456. https://doi.org/10.2147/NDT.S147317

Lunansky, G., van Borkulo, C. D., & Borsboom, D. (2020). Personality, resilience, and psychopathology: A model for the interaction between slow and fast network processes in the context of mental health. *European Journal of Personality, 34*(6), 969–987. https://doi.org/10.1002/per.2263

Markus, K., & Borsboom, D. (2013). *Frontiers of validity theory: Measurement, causation, and meaning.* Routledge.

Marsman, M., & Rhemtulla, M. (2022). Guest editors' introduction to the special issue "Network Psychometrics in Action": Methodological innovations inspired by empirical problems. *Psychometrika, 87*, 1–11. https://doi.org/10.1007/s11336-022-09861-x

May, R. M. (1973). *Stability and complexity in model ecosystems*. Princeton University Press.

Mohammadi, R., & Wit, E. C. (2019). BDgraph: An R package for Bayesian structure learning in graphical models. *Journal of Statistical Software, 89*(3 SE-Articles), 1–30. https://doi.org/10.18637/jss.v089.i03

Neal, Z. P., & Neal, J. W. (2023). Out of bounds? The boundary specification problem for centrality in psychological networks. *Psychological Methods, 28*(1), 179–188. https://doi.org/10.1037/met0000426

Olthof, M., Hasselman, F., Oude Maatman, F., Bosman, A. M. T., & Lichtwarck-Aschoff, A. (2023). Complexity theory of psychopathology. *Journal of Psychopathology and Clinical Science, 132*(3), 314–323. https://doi.org/10.1037/abn0000740

Oude Maatman, F. (2020). Reformulating the network theory of mental disorders: Folk psychology as a factor, not a fact. *Theory & Psychology,* 30(5), 703–722. https://doi.org/10.1177/0959354320921464

Ratcliff, R. (1978). A theory of memory retrieval. *Psychological Review, 85*, 59–108.

Rijo-Ferreira, F., & Takahashi, J. S. (2019). Genomics of circadian rhythms in health and disease. *Genome Medicine, 11*(1), 82. https://doi.org/10.1186/s13073-019-0704-0

Robinaugh, D., Haslbeck, J. M. B., Waldorp, L., Kossakowski, J. J., Fried, E. I., Millner, A., … Borsboom, D. (2019). Advancing the network theory of mental disorders: A computational model of panic disorder. *Psychological Review, 131*(6), 1482–1508. https://doi.org/10.31234/osf.io/km37w

Robinaugh, D. J., Hoekstra, R. H. A., Toner, E. R., & Borsboom, D. (2020). The network approach to psychopathology: A review of the literature 2008–2018 and an agenda for future research. *Psychological Medicine, 50*(3), 353–366.

Ryan, O., Haslbeck, J. M. B., & Robinaugh, D. (2023). Improving treatments for mental disorders using computational models. *Behaviour Research and Therapy, 189*, 104706. https://doi.org/10.1016/j.brat.2025.104706

Scheffer, M., & Beets, J. (1994). Ecological models and the pitfalls of causality. *Hydrobiologia, 275*, 115–124. https://doi.org/10.1007/BF00026704

Scheffer, M., Borsboom, D., Nieuwenhuis, S., & Westley, F. (2022). Belief traps: Tackling the inertia of harmful beliefs. *Proceedings of the National Academy of Sciences of the United States of America, 119*(32), e2203149119. https://doi.org/10.1073/pnas.2203149119

Scheffer, M., & Carpenter, S. R. (2003). Catastrophic regime shifts in ecosystems: linking theory to observation. *Trends in Ecology & Evolution, 18*(12), 648–656. https://doi.org/https://doi.org/10.1016/j.tree.2003.09.002

van Borkulo, C. D., Borsboom, D., Epskamp, S., Blanken, T. F., Boschloo, L., Schoevers, R. A., & Waldorp, L. J. (2014). A new method for constructing networks from binary data. *Scientific Reports, 4*, 5918.

Wagenmakers, E. J., Van Der Maas, H. L. J., & Grasman, R. P. P. P. (2007). An EZ-diffusion model for response time and accuracy. *Psychonomic Bulletin & Review, 14*(1), 3–22. https://doi.org/10.3758/BF03194023

Wason, P. C. (1968). Reasoning about a rule. *Quarterly Journal of Experimental Psychology, 20*, 273–281.

Wichers, M., Riese, H., Hodges, T. M., Snippe, E., & Bos, F. M. (2021). A narrative review of network studies in depression: What different methodological approaches tell us about depression. *Frontiers in Psychiatry, 12*, 719490. https://doi.org/10.3389/fpsyt.2021.719490

CHAPTER 27

Commentary of Borsboom's "Between Correlation and Causality"

Eric Turkheimer

The Descent of Man sparked many scientific revolutions, but none were more intellectually profound or ethically challenging than the exposure of human behavior to the bright light of natural science. Before Darwin, people could still hold out some hope that we were separated from the rest of nature by our souls, our creation in the image of God. Human behavior had always been in the domain of theology, or, among skeptics, philosophy; "behavioral science" didn't exist. After Darwin, scientifically clear-eyed people had to recognize that behavior – personality, intellect, family, culture – evolved just as surely as our bipedal posture. No one was more attuned to this revolution than Darwin's cousin, Francis Galton. Galton made the application of Darwin's new science to human behavior, in all its diversity, his life's work. Human anatomy had been naturalized once scientific dissection of cadavers was permitted; the psychologist Wilhelm Wundt was already naturalizing human perception; Galton possessed unwavering confidence that the rest of human behavior was not far behind.

Galton was wrong about this – tragically wrong. A century and half later, human behavior still resists natural scientific explanation. The theological obstacles to human science have indeed been brushed aside, but ethically based methodological obstacles remain. We can dissect cadavers but not live humans. We can't raise humans under controlled conditions. Most importantly – and here lies Galton's tragic error – we can't breed them. Galton's proclamations about the inevitable application of natural science to people were made in the interest of eugenics, which he saw as the practical technology of evolutionary theory, as bridge building is to theoretical physics, or medical therapeutics to human biology.

Human science turns out to be a limited enterprise, not because people are possessed of extra-biological capabilities, but because humans have *chosen* to limit the methodological tools we are allowed to apply to each other. Galton knew this, at least implicitly, when he was not blinded by his mania for eugenic programs to improve the "race." The statistics he and his followers invented, still the basis of quantitative work in the behavioral sciences, amounted to a concerted effort to conduct science without the experiments that are prohibited in humans. Galton's famous admonition, "Whenever you can, count," was the beginning of the effort: behaviors can be counted when they can't be manipulated. But more was required: counting isn't science any more than hammering is architecture. So, Galton invented the concept of variation to quantify differences among the things he counted. Along with his student Karl Pearson, he invented covariation to quantify relations among multiple counts. After Galton's death, statisticians in his lineage, like Charles Spearman and L. L. Thurstone, extended the concept of covariation to the development of factor analysis, allowing large collections of counts to be analyzed simultaneously.

Finally, in 1963, Raymond Cattell, arguably the last of the great Galtonians (great in their generativity, their arrogance, and their greatly regressive politics), came up with a provocative title for the statistically based scientific tradition Galton founded: multivariate experimental psychology (Cattell, 1963). The name is an oxymoron. Although factor analysis and its adjacent methods are certainly multivariate, they are not, by intentional design, experimental. Indeed, that is the whole point. Calling the methods experimental is an assertion that sufficiently sophisticated statistics can replace randomized manipulation as a tool of scientific inference. It is a denial of the famous quote from R. A. Fisher (1938): "To consult the statistician after an experiment is finished is often merely to ask him to conduct a *post mortem* examination. He can perhaps say what the experiment died of."

Although network analysis is a statistical heir to this Galtonian multivariate legacy, I hasten to add that the beauty of Borsboom's contribution lies in its explicit rejection of the hyperrealist arrogance that was so easily transformed into eugenics by Galton and Cattell. In fact, a key feature of network analysis is its rejection of the "latent variables" that were posited by factor analysis. Properly understood, latent variables are statistical contrivances, not entities residing in people's heads or genomes. The temptation to reify them into human essences like IQ has proven impossible for theorists to resist, even for those with better intentions than Galton or Cattell. I have noted in a previous volume of this series (Turkheimer, 2017) that the perennial hope that mental disorders will finally turn out to be real entities in the brain or genome is rooted just as surely as is IQ in essentialist statistics. Network analysis offers a way out.

It replaces the invisible hand of shadowy latent variables with real phenotypes bumping into other real phenotypes. Lack of sleep causes irritability, which causes poor spousal relations, which cause sleep disturbance.

This is a much more plausible model of the way things might actually work, but it does not overcome the fundamental problem of causal underdetermination, as Borsboom so generously recognizes. Multivariate statistical models are doubly indeterminate. First, simply as a matter of statistics, any given model can be transformed, rotated in factor analytic language, into statistically equivalent models that have exactly the same fit to the data. Second, closer to Borsboom's concerns, even after a rotation has been selected, there are many causal scenarios that might generate the observed structure of the data. This state of affairs is no one's fault: not Galton's, not Cattell's, not Borsboom's; rather, it is the epistemic price we pay for treating our fellow humans decently, refusing to breed them or to manipulate their environments in ways not permitted by our institutional review board (IRB).

The most refreshing aspect of Borsboom's chapter, ironically, does not augur well for the future success of multivariate experimental psychology. Often, when people think about the causal processes underlying statistical models, they imagine very simple causal relations, the classic one being, "Is genetic variant X a cause of psychiatric syndrome Y?" Scientists have fared poorly enough on questions like these, but Borsboom reminds us that human causation, especially human behavioral causation, doesn't work that way. Human causal systems are reciprocal, dynamic, and intertwined with the always limited assessment procedures we can bring to bear on them. Can network analysis do a better job than factor analysis at elucidating this kind of causal complexity? Sure, and to some extent it already has, but it is worth noting that Borsboom resists Cattellian overreach and doesn't make any promises. His humility is admirable but sobering.

What can be done? The intricate detail of the causal processes Borsboom outlines suggests that successful causal explanations of psychiatric disorders may need to be more local than has generally been imagined. The search for the causes of depression writ large may be hopeless, but small-scale experimentation may be able to combine with large-scale modeling to make progress in more limited ways that could nonetheless be productive, especially for treatment. Two models for this idea make use of the word "experimental" in a less grandiose way than Cattell, working within the boundaries set by the IRB. Experimental social psychology has a rich history of working with constructs like emotion, anxiety, and identity, which constitute the *psyche* of psychopathology. Another version of the same idea is experimental psychopathology, as embodied in the (largely psychology-based) professional society bearing that name. The mark of these approaches is that they search for the causes of behavioral entities in the interactions of other behavioral entities, manipulating them experimentally where they can. The science produced by these methods will almost never provide the burst of insight produced by successful reductions in the physical sciences, or the decisive therapeutic triumphs achieved when basic human biology "translates" into effective medicine. The results often seem descriptive as much as they are explanatory, but a richly measured and carefully modeled description may be the best that can be achieved by human science that respects personal autonomy in all the ways Galton did not.

REFERENCES

Cattell, R. B. (1963). Concepts of personality growing from multivariate experiment. In J. M. Wepman & R. W. Heine (Eds.), *Concepts of personality* (pp. 413–448). Aldine Publishing Company.

Fisher, R. A. (1938). Presidential address. *Sankhya: The Indian Journal of Statistics, 4*(1), 14–17.

Turkheimer, E. (2017). The hard question in psychiatric nosology. In K. S. Kendler & J. Parnas (Eds.), *Philosophical issues in psychiatry IV: Psychiatric nosology* (pp. 27–44). Oxford University Press.

Section 10

CHAPTER 28

Introduction to Campbell's "What Is the Role of Generalizations in Psychiatry?"

Kenneth S. Kendler

John Campbell reviews for us how to think about the causal processes that might be at work in psychiatry. The laws of physics cannot be a plausible model because it deals with matter – particles, planets, and the like. In psychiatry, we deal with patients who are both brained and minded. The brain is a physical system but one of staggering complexity. The mind is a whole different kind of thing, and it is here that empathic understanding must come into play. Given now important our interactions with our conspecifics are – our spouses, children, friends, and particularly enemies – evolution has likely tuned our emphatic understanding for accuracy to help us intuit the motivations and internal emotional states of our fellow humans.

How does this all impact psychiatric science? How do we balance this funny mix of kinds of knowing, clearly articulated by Jaspers: of explanation and understanding. I would like to give an illustration of how these kinds of approaches might impact one subject of substantial clinical and scientific interest in the field of psychiatry: how experienced stressful life events relate to the risk for subsequent episodes of depression. This is not a new idea. In his famous "Treatise on Insanity" published in 1845, the French alienist Esquirol gives a table of the 12 leading moral (aka psychological) causes of insanity. Domestic troubles top the list, second is "misery and reverses of fortune," with "disappointed affection" ranking number three (Esquirol, 1845, p. 47).

The science of stressful life event (SLEs) assessments got started in the 1960s (Holmes & Rahe, 1967), and was substantially influenced by the British sociologists George Brown in the 1970s–1980s (Brown & Harris, 1978). This included many studies showing that several kinds of SLEs substantially raised the risk for an episode of major depression (MD) over the subsequent few months. Many studies examined the features of the SLE that were most depressogenic (those that feature loss and humiliation) and that had the highest risk (those that produced a high "long-term contextual threat"). I played a central role in more than a decade of studies at the Virginia Twin Registry where we interviewed thousands of twins, rating the occurrence of a large number of such SLEs (28 of them at one stage) and how those related to the risk for subsequent onset of MD (Kendler & Prescott, 2006; Kendler et al., 1998, 1999). For example, following more than three yearly interviews of approximately 2,000 female twins, we found that in the month of the SLE occurrence, the risk for MD increased 17.9-fold if the interviewee reported being assaulted, 7.1-fold if she had been divorced, and 6.2-fold if a close relative had died (Kendler et al., 1998). This was done in a scientific way, utilizing explanation to give us insight into one aspect of psychopathology.

But it was not quite that simple. Our interviewers often got to know the twins well. I paraphrase the story one of them told me:

> I interviewed a woman in her late 40s, single, never married, an identical twin. She was an accountant, seemed quite well put together but reported a bad depression in the last year – the only one she ever had. She met every single symptom except for suicidal ideas. To my surprise, as we went through the long list of stressful events, she didn't report any of them in the months before this episode. After we finished the interview while I was collecting my papers, she said, "All those bad things you asked me about . . . you missed the thing that set off my depression." I perked up and asked if she might describe that. The story was very touching. She had never married and lived with her mother all her adult life. Her mother had been quite ill for some years. They obviously had a close relationship. Some five years ago, a few months before she died, her mother bought her daughter a parrot, saying something about her being afraid that she might get lonely after her death, which she knew was coming. Well, a few weeks before her depression started, the parrot died. Even in telling this this story she teared up a bit, and so did I.

You don't have to be a psychoanalyst for your emphatic understanding to kick in hearing this story. In a very human way, the parrot had become a symbol for her mother and, in its death, re-raising her deep sadness at the passing of her mother. I have remembered it all these years. I recall thinking that there is a part of human experience – the idiosyncratic ways in which we attach importance, value, and meaning to the events and experiences around us – that will forever be untouchable by the scientific method. Perhaps that is a good thing.

I did not rush out and add "Death of a parrot" to our life event inventory, because this story was too unique – we couldn't detect it by our methods. But I would consider adding an item about death of close pets. Another time in our study, when the husband was dosing off in a nearby chair in the living room, the female twin, who had a dog sitting at her feet for the entire visit, said to our interviewer while walking out, "Why didn't you ask us about the death of our pets [pointing to her dog]? I would be much more upset with that than the death of him [pointing rather derisively at the sleeping husband]."

So, speaking as a clinical psychiatric researcher, I would say there are broad trends of human behavior, involving processes largely shared among the diversity of our species, that we can examine via explanatory scientific methods. We can and have made a lot of progress with such methods. And we can study brains using whatever tools we have. But lurking underneath that there are processes we cannot get to that reflect an idiosyncratic and important part of lived, "minded" humanhood that can sometimes be accessible to us only through empathic understanding.

REFERENCES

Brown, G. W., & Harris, T. O. (1978). *Social origins of depression: A study of psychiatric disorder in women*. Tavistock.

Esquirol, E. (1845). *Mental maladies: A treatise on insanity*. Lea and Blanchard.

Holmes, T. H., & Rahe, R. H. (1967). The social readjustment rating scale. *Journal of Psychosomatic Research, 11*(2), 213–218. www.ncbi.nlm.nih.gov/pubmed/6059863

Kendler, K. S., Karkowski, L. M., & Prescott, C. A. (1998). Stressful life events and major depression: Risk period, long-term contextual threat, and diagnostic specificity. *Journal of Nervous and Mental Disease, 186*(11), 661–669. www.ncbi.nlm.nih.gov/pubmed/9824167

(1999). Causal relationship between stressful life events and the onset of major depression. *American Journal of Psychiatry, 156*(6), 837–841. www.ncbi.nlm.nih.gov/pubmed/10360120

Kendler, K. S., & Prescott, C. A. (2006). *Genes, environment, and psychopathology: Understanding the causes of psychiatric and substance use disorders*. Guilford Press.

CHAPTER 29

What Is the Role of Generalizations in Psychiatry?

John Campbell

29.1 The Relation between Laws and Singular Causal Statements

It seems to be definitional of "science" that it involves a quest for generalizations. Physics and biology, for example, are largely occupied with finding laws that govern the behavior of things. On the other hand, we do not usually think of history as a science, even if we respect the attempts of historians to find out what actually happened in the past, and in that sense regard history as a factual investigation. The reason we do not think of history as a science is that historians are not, usually, attempting to find generalizations governing the behavior of human groups.

Research in psychiatry today often takes the form of a search for generalizations. We don't just want the history of what happened to one patient or another; we want to understand the general principles in play so that we can bring our findings to bear on the treatment of further patients. We think of psychiatry as scientific because we think of it as attempting to find the general principles underlying the generation of mental illness in particular patients.

In physics, we have generalizations like Newton's "force = mass times acceleration." In psychiatry, we have proposals such as "irregularities in the firing of dopamine neurons cause attentional deficits" or "humiliation causes major depression." I say "proposals" somewhat cautiously because, rightly or wrongly, people often regard the generalizations of physics as having stronger evidence supporting them than do the generalizations of psychiatry. Perhaps that is just a matter of psychiatry being a younger science than physics. Nonetheless, the natural, perhaps the default view is that laws play the same kind of role in psychiatry as they do in physics, even if at the moment they are not on the same evidential footing.

In particular, we can look at the role of laws in constituting the truth of singular causal statements, such as "the striking of this match caused the fire" or "this patient's ingestion of LSD caused their psychosis." These are "singular" in the sense that they are statements about the causal relation between two concrete happenings, such as a particular ingestion of LSD and the contraction of psychoses. (In contrast, there are general causal statements, such as "smoking causes cancer," which do not relate concrete happenings but rather characteristics of objects.) On what we might call Hempel's classical view, laws are required to bridge the gap between the initial conditions that cause the outcome and the outcome itself. To substantiate a true singular causal statement, we must have general laws from which, together with a statement of the initial conditions, the occurrence of the outcome can be derived.

In particular, there is a background heuristic of determinism that we usually take to apply in both domains. Suppose we have two physical processes, the striking of one match in the wind and the striking of another match in the wind. If one match goes out immediately while the other burns on, we assume that there must have been some characteristic that was different in the two cases – maybe the wind blew in a somewhat different direction, with a somewhat different strength, in one case compared with the other. Similarly, suppose we have two psychiatric patients who seem to have very similar backgrounds and who present very similarly in interview. One goes on to contract one specific set of delusions; the other does not. We tend to assume that there must be some difference between the initial conditions in the two cases that would explain that difference in outcome, even if the laws involved are very complex.

Nevertheless, the picture of psychiatry that this suggests is hard to believe. A "completed" psychiatry, on this account, would be a comprehensive set of laws that we could use to derive confident predictions about who would develop which disorder when, and what they will be thinking and feeling, given only enough knowledge of the initial conditions. Such a "completed" psychiatry seems a long way off. If that kind of knowledge of laws is required for us to have knowledge of which concrete happenings are causing which in the psychological life of an individual patient, then it seems impossible, at least in the short term, for us to have any knowledge at all of concrete causes and effects in psychiatric cases.

You might argue that this kind of picture is only relevant, if ever, at most in such cases as physics. It doesn't really apply to psychiatry. Hempel's classical view should be applied, if at all, only to physics and other basic sciences. The trouble is that this leaves us with no analysis of the place of specifically psychiatric generalizations in addressing individual cases. If a role for the interplay between general laws and individual cases is found only at the level of physics, then we have, as yet, no role for an interplay between general laws and individual cases within psychiatry itself. Yet surely there is such a role. If someone proposes that certain serotonin irregularities are implicated in depression, surely that ought to bear on the analysis of the individual patient before one. If we've given up on the idea of a "complete" set of psychiatric laws bridging past and future, then what are we to say about how psychiatric generalizations bear on our causal analyses of individual patients? And what are we to say about the sense in which psychiatry aims to be a science, if it isn't aiming to find a complete set of laws governing its subject matter?

The great thing about Hempel's classical analysis is that it gives us a sharp picture of the relation between general laws and singular causal claims. If it is indeed true, the singular causal claim is such by virtue of the existence of laws connecting cause and effect. Suppose, though, that we shift to more recent counterfactual or probabilistic analyses of causation. We might, for example, say:

> *X* causes *Y* if and only if, were there to be an intervention on *X*, there would be a difference in the values of *Y*.

Or:

> *X* causes *Y* if and only if the probability of *Y* given *X* is greater than the base-rate probability of *Y*.

These analyses are both stated at the level of general causation, at which we make claims such as "Smoking causes cancer," which connect two general variables such as "number of cigarettes smoked per day" and "risk of contracting cancer." Both types of analysis require, and have been given, considerable supplementation, of course (see, e.g., Hitchcock, 2018; Woodward, 2003). But the point I am making here is that these approaches do not immediately explain the relation between general and singular causation.

As they are usually developed, these approaches do not have anything like the straightforward simplicity of Hempel's account of the relation between laws and singular causation. If we ask how a proponent of a counterfactual or probabilistic analysis would explain singular causation, the natural starting point is to apply the analysis directly to singular causal statements. So, we would have:

> Concrete happening *a* causes concrete happening *b* if and only if, had there been an intervention on *a*, there would have been a difference in whether *b* happened.

Or:

> Concrete happening *a* causes concrete happening *b* if and only if the probability of *b* given *a* is greater than the probability of *b*.

(Again, these two approaches require, and have been given, a great deal of supplementation.)

There's evidently a marked difference between this kind of approach and Hempel's to singular causation. Hempel's explanation of what it is for one concrete happening to cause another appeals directly to the notion of law. Thus, an account of the relation between generalizations and singular causation is built in immediately to the explanation. On counterfactual or probabilistic approaches, however, no such analysis of the relation between generalizations and singular causation can be read off immediately. We are thus left casting about for an account of the relation between general causal claims in psychiatry and singular causal claims in psychiatry: between "insomnia causes major depression," for example, and "Sally's insomnia caused her to contract major depression."

Indeed, Ellery Eels, developing a probabilistic approach to causation, argued that singular causation should be given a different type of probabilistic analysis to general causation. According to him, "very little (if anything) about what happens [at the level of singular causation] can be inferred from [general] causal claims, and . . . very little (if anything) about [general] causal relations can be inferred from [singular] causal claims" (Eells 1991, p. 6). This kind of view is at the other end of the scale from Hempel's. This suggests we need a model of singular causation in psychiatry that would explain (1) how we can determine singular causal relations without appealing to a Hempelian background of laws allowing us to infer effect from cause and (2) what the role might be of generalizations in psychiatry when finding the causal connection between one concrete happening and another.

I'll sketch a positive picture that seems to meet these conditions.

29.2 Singular Causation

In Hempel's classical picture, the relation between an earlier event and a later event it causes is bridged by laws. So, in this picture, if psychiatry is to address causal relations between individual events in the life of a patient, it has to find a collection of laws that bridge past and future.

You might argue that a metaphysical demand that causation requires laws connecting the causing event to the outcome does not mean that one must know the laws to know of the existence of the causal relation. While this seems correct as an abstract statement, it is a bit difficult to see how it could be of help here. Because how are we supposed to find out about the singular causal relation without knowledge of laws? Let's say that this works by finding out about **X**, where finding out about **X** does not require knowledge of laws connecting the cause event and the outcome event. Suppose we say that spotting **X** relating *c* and *e* is enough for one to have evidence that *c* caused *e*, without requiring to find laws connecting *c* and *e*. Then, since we (supposedly) know that the existence of a causal connection is enough to imply the existence of laws connecting cause and effect, we can conclude from spotting **X** connecting *c* and *e* that there are laws connecting *c* and *e*. But what on earth could **X** be, if it doesn't itself involve the identification of laws connecting cause and effect, for it to have this evidential force? There really seems to be no way of answering this. We seem to be dealing with a certain sleight of hand involving the word "cause" if we announce that one can have the right to claim that *c* caused *e* even without knowing of the existence of laws connecting *c* and *e*, but that somehow, once one has reached the claim, "*c* caused *e*," one does have evidence for the existence of such laws.

There is, however, another way to think of singular causation: that is, by thinking not in terms of laws but in terms of persisting objects and processes connecting earlier events to later events. The distinction here is easy to miss because it is natural to suppose that the objects and processes are themselves law-governed, so that what we have is merely a species of Hempelian causal explanation rather than a fundamentally different type of causation. But consider the example shown in Figure 29.1.

Here we have a steel ball being heated at place p1 at time t1. The ball then travels to place p2 at time t2. But we assume that its trajectory is indeterminate. Perhaps it must be a spatiotemporally continuous path traveled at a finite speed, but that's all – the ball may go in any direction. In particular, there are no laws affecting specifically where the ball winds up. Thus, we cannot give a Hempelian explanation for why, at the end of the exercise, it is hotter at place p2, at t2, than it is in the surrounding atmosphere. The laws together with the initial conditions do not imply that there will be heat at p2, t2. Nevertheless, we do know the causal explanation for why it's hot at p2, t2. The cause of that outcome was the application of heat to the steel ball at p1, t1.

In this example, it's not exclusively laws that are bridging the gap between *c* and *e*. It's the persisting object, the steel ball itself, that is transmitting causal influence from earlier to later. We can't give the causal

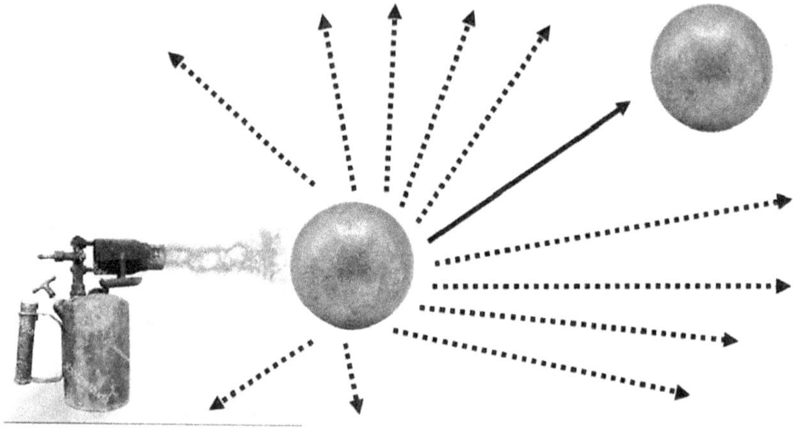

Figure 29.1 Heated steel ball taking an indeterministic trajectory from place p1 to place p2. There are no laws governing the path of the ball. Still, it is evident that the cause of the later heat at p2 is the earlier application of heat at p1. The causation is transmitted not by laws and initial conditions, but by the movement of the persisting ball.

explanation here without appealing to the identity of the steel ball over time. In this picture, the role of persisting objects or processes in causal explanation is at least as fundamental as any role for laws. Let's now look at how this picture may apply in psychiatry.

29.3 Singular Causation in Psychiatry

Karl Birnbaum famously drew a distinction between pathogenic and pathoplastic features of a disorder. He contrasted the defining, or essential, features of a disorder – the pathogenic aspects – which are common to all who suffer the disorder, with its pathoplastic aspects, which may vary from individual to individual, or from culture to culture (Birnbaum, 1974). As Ken Kendler (2015, p. 1951) put it, "In more modern terms, pathogenic features would reflect neurobiological processes while pathoplastic features would arise largely from cultural and psychological influences. For example, Birnbaum would likely argue that delusions in schizophrenia reflect pathogenic processes, but the content of the delusions typically arise from pathoplastic influences." We could diagram the idea here as in Figure 29.2.

Here the analogue of the heated steel ball is the progression of the disorder over time. There may be generalizations governing this

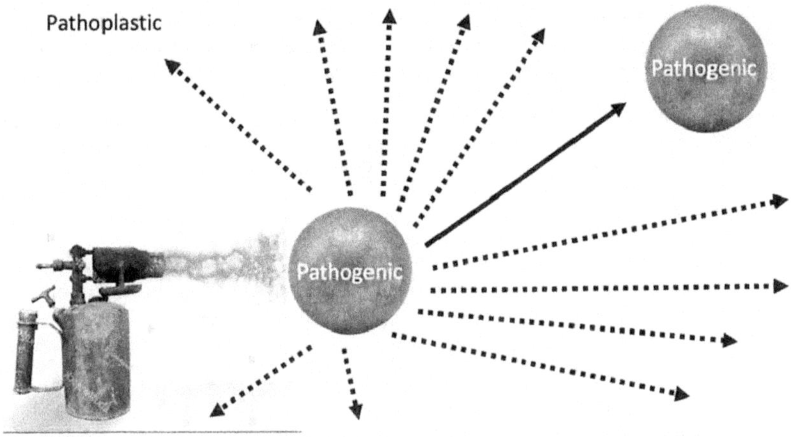

Figure 29.2 In this model, the pathogenic aspects of the disorder are thought to constitute a stable structure transmitting causal influence over time. The pathoplastic aspect of the disorder may vary indeterministically over time.

progression. Similarly, in the case of the steel ball, there may be regularities governing how such ball conducts, retains, and loses heat, which are required for the causal explanation. But these generalizations, together with statements of the initial conditions, cannot of themselves explain why the outcome is heat at place p2 and time t2. For that, we must look at the actual trajectory of the ball itself, from the initial application of heat to the coming to rest at p2, t2, to give the causal explanation of why it's hot at p2, t2. Similarly, in the progression of a mental disorder, there may be regularities governing how the disorder unfolds. But there will also be significant indeterminacy in the content and color of the disorder, which develops in different ways across different patients.

Shitij Kapur (2003, p. 17) has proposed that "Psychosis is seen as a dynamic interaction between a bottom-up neurochemical drive and a top-down psychological process . . . not as an inescapably determined outcome of a biology." Here the causal explanation of psychosis in an individual patient is not being seen as on the Hempelian model; there is no suggestion that the "top–down psychological process" implicated is subject to laws. In this picture, a dopamine vigilance system is ordinarily implicated in our finding particular stimuli salient, in some things rather than others gaining our attention. If, for example, you are walking through a bad part of town late at night, your vigilance system may be going into overdrive, drawing your attention to every passing shadow or movement in every alleyway. In Kapur's picture, in psychosis there is an irregularity in the vigilance system that leads to random releases of dopamine, so that even in broad daylight, in an ordinary and safe environment, one's attributions of salience to particular random stimuli may be greatly enhanced, so that one finds oneself greatly alarmed – or cheered – by perceived aspects of the world that do not in fact merit any such reaction. Kapur sums up his view like this:

> Delusions in this framework are a "top-down" cognitive explanation that the individual imposes on these experiences of aberrant salience in an effort to make sense of them. Since delusions are constructed by the individual, they are imbued with the psychodynamic themes relevant to the individual and are embedded in the cultural context of the individual. This explains how the same neurochemical dysregulation leads to variable phenomenological expression: a patient in Africa struggling to make sense of aberrant saliences in much more likely to accord them to the evil ministrations of a shaman, while the one living in Toronto is is more likely to see them as the machinations of the Royal Canadian Mounted Police. (Kapur, 2003, p. 15)

Kapur's picture has no demand of determinism about the specific contents of the delusions to which a psychotic patient is subject. In a particular case the content of a delusion might relate to the ministrations of a shaman, or to the machinations of the Royal Canadian Mounted Police, but there may be no laws from which we could have predicted the delusions would take just these forms, rather than relating to the ministrations of one's next-door neighbor, or the machinations of the local hospital board. The patient is navigating their way through a space of possible contents for their delusions, and just as in the case of our heated steel ball, their path through this space may be indeterminate, in principle not predictable in advance.

29.4 Jaspers on Singular versus General Causation

Karl Jaspers famously drew a distinction between two types of approach a therapist can take to a patient. On the one hand, there is a "subjective" approach, in which the therapist tries to understand the patient "from the inside," achieving an understanding of the patient's perspective on the world. On the other hand, the therapist may view the patient "objectively": to put it roughly, the therapist here may simply note the symptoms the patient is displaying and use them to reach a diagnosis and recommendation for treatment. As Jaspers put it, the two types of pathology here are: "1. We sink ourselves into the psychic situation and understand genetically by empathy how one psychic event emerges from another. 2. We find by repeated experience that a number of phenomena are regularly linked together, and on this basis we explain causally" (Jaspers, 1959, p. 301). Now notice that these two types of approach both seem to involve causal insight. In the first, "subjective" approach, the therapist aims to determine "how one psychic event emerges from another"; in the second, "objective" approach, the aim is to find generalizations on the basis of which we can "explain causally."

One would naturally expect that a proficient therapist will be routinely switching back and forth between these two approaches to a patient, wherever possible. For all that Jaspers says to the contrary, however, these two approaches to psychopathology might be quite independent of one another. That is, it might be that developing insight into the patient's perspective, and imaginatively understanding the patient, does not at all depend on one's knowledge of generalizations governing the psychological life of the patient. A therapist developing this type of imaginative understanding of a patient might be like a historian working up a chronicle of events leading to a major happening, such as the First World War. An historian developing an understanding of the timeline leading to the War will certainly be interested in causality: for example, what was the role of the German Kaiser in igniting the conflict? But the historian will not be developing knowledge of general laws governing the onset of wars, and will not be relying on any such laws, for there may be none. (Of course, some laws will be relevant to the inquiry: What was the maximum speed military shipping could reach at that time? What were the general constraints on the speed at which an army could cross a particular region? But the historian will typically not be looking for laws governing the ignition of the particular historical events in which they are interested.) Thus, the historian, in Jaspers's sense, is understanding how one event "emerges from" another, without depending on laws governing the relations between those events. Similarly, a "subjective" therapist engaged with a patient over a course of years might develop a "history" of the emergence of one psychological event from another in the patient, without relying on general laws governing those psychological events. On the other hand, it might be possible to develop an austerely "objective" understanding of patients that looks only for generalizations governing symptoms, diagnosis, and treatment, without leaning on a "subjective," imaginative understanding of the patient. (Here again there might be *some* reliance on the alternative approach: for example, in developing an "objective" approach, you might need to rely on a subjective understanding of the patient to determine whether they are experiencing a symptom such as "suicidal ideation." But the law-governed packages of symptoms, diagnosis, and treatment will not themselves rely on subjective understanding to develop knowledge of which symptoms should be bundled together as indicative of a particular diagnosis, for example.)

If we leave it like this, it might seem that Jaspers is proposing a dichotomy between (1) a "historical" approach to the patient that is all about one singular event emerging from another and (2) a Hempelian approach to psychiatry, in which all explanation ultimately derives from knowledge of laws. It might seem that these are two quite different approaches. The first is not really "scientific" at all; it is humanistic and does not depend on generalizations. The second is scientific: it is all about the search for generalizations and the application of them.

29.5 Traveling through an Indeterminate Space

Our discussion to this point, however, suggests that a quite different analysis is possible. Recall our discussion of the heated steel ball traveling through an indeterminate space. We had the ball traveling to place p2 at time t2, and causally explained the heat at p2, t2 by the ball having been heated at t1 and then traveling to p2, t2. But we could not explain in terms of initial conditions and laws why the ball traveled to p2, t2 rather than some other destination. Its travel through the space was truly indeterministic.

Nevertheless, there is plainly a significant role here for generalizations governing the internal dynamics of the steel ball itself. There are, we can suppose, laws governing exactly how the application of heat affects the temperature of the ball, how well the ball retains heat, and how much heat it radiates. Having this understanding of generalizations governing the persisting steel ball itself is essential to one's causal understanding of the outcome.

Now consider a schizophrenic patient, in the light of Kapur's analysis of psychosis. We can consider the phenomenon of schizophrenia in the patient based on the model of the heated steel ball: the schizophrenia is a persisting process, with some characteristic patterns of development over time. Of course, schizophrenia itself has somewhat more complexity than the heat regulation of a steel ball. But in this way of thinking of it, there is similarly a *single thing* here: the persisting disorder itself, which unfolds in a relatively law-governed way over time. And while the generalizations here are not nearly so well understood as in the case of the steel ball, psychiatry certainly has a strong investment in finding the generalizations that indicate someone is at low risk or high risk for developing schizophrenia, what the early symptoms of psychosis look like, and what prognosis to give for how the disorder can be expected to develop over time. There may be a lot of complexity in the articulation of the laws here, but insofar as we really do have a diagnosis here, we expect there to be a single thing, the disorder, changing predictably.

Nonetheless, in this approach, the laws and initial conditions will not enable one to predict or explain the specific contents of the delusions of a particular subject. Whether the subject's delusions will concern an evil shaman or the activities of the RCMP may not be predictable on the basis of our knowledge of the characteristic patterns of development of psychosis. Thus, we will not be able to explain the specific contents of the delusions of the subject on the basis of our hard-won knowledge of the general patterns governing the disorder.

This is why we need imaginative understanding of the patient. Imaginative understanding of a patient is from the outset concerned with the specific details of the delusions the patient develops. It is imaginative understanding, not general laws, that allows us to find what is causing what in the elaboration of the patient's delusions. Of course, the psychiatrist following the patient's paths of thought and feeling may come to recognize that they exhibit the structural features associated with a particular disorder, such as schizophrenia. And the knowledge from generalizations as to what kind of developments to expect in the patient, such as delusions of being controlled or having thoughts inserted into one's mind, may well be helpful in informing the therapist what to look for. But they will not extend to the actual details of the patient's specific delusions. Here there is no substitute for imaginative understanding in allowing one to understand which psychic phenomena are emerging from which in the life of the patient.

The proposal here then is that the model of the heated steel ball traveling through an indeterminate space of possibilities provides us with an alternative model to the Hempelian idea of a completed set of laws governing all the phenomena science seeks to understand. Such a complete set of laws for psychiatry seems a far-off dream, and adhering to that picture of what one is about in psychiatric research is likely to result only in pessimism about delivering what is "scientifically" required. If we use the model of the heated steel ball, though, we can see how there can be a more modest role for generalizations in psychiatry: in characterizing general patterns relating to particular disorders, so that we can understand a disorder as a single thing unfolding over time, even though it may not, even in principle, ever be possible to explain, in terms of those laws, why one specific psychic event is emerging from another in the psychological life of the patient. For that, it may be that imaginative understanding will always be needed.

REFERENCES

Birnbaum, K. (1974 [1923]). The making of a psychosis (H. Marshall, Transl.). In S. R. Hirsch & M. Shepherd (Eds.), *Themes and variations in european psychiatry* (pp. 197–238). John Wright.

Eells, E. (1991). *Probabilistic causality*. Cambridge University Press.

Hempel, C. G. (1942). The function of general laws in history. *Journal of Philosophy, 39*, 35–48.

Hitchcock, C. (2018). Probabilistic causation. *Stanford Encyclopedia of Philosophy*. Retrieved September 11, 2025 from https://seop.illc.uva.nl/entries/causation-probabilistic

Jaspers, K. (1959 [1913]). *General psychopathology*. Manchester University Press.

Kapur, S. (2003). Psychosis as a state of aberrant salience: A framework linking biology, phenomenology, and pharmacology in schizophrenia. *American Journal of Psychiatry, 160*, 13–23.

Kendler, K. S., Aggen, S. H., Li, Y., Lewis, C. M., Breen, G., Boomsma, D. I., Bot, M., Penninx, B. W. J. H., & Flint, J. (2015). The similarity of the structure of DSM-IV criteria for major depression in depressed women from China, the United States and Europe. *Psychological Medicine, 45*, 1945–1954.

Woodward, J. (2003). *Making things happen: A theory of causal explanation*. Oxford University Press.

CHAPTER 30

Commentary on Campbell's "What Is the Role of Generalization in Psychiatry?"

Denny Borsboom

Campbell's contribution investigates the possible function of scientific laws in psychopathology, specifically the idea that the standard notion of scientific law could function in the way it has traditionally done in scientific explanation. An important way of thinking about this, as outlined by Campbell, is to introduce scientific laws as general axioms that act as premises in a deductive argument through a covering law. Properties of an individual case then feature as the *explanandum*. Variants on this approach generally emulate Aristotle's well-known *modus ponens* argument scheme that deduces the mortality of Socrates from the premises that all men are mortal and that Socrates is a man. Although many different theories of explanation have been produced over the past century, I think it is fair to say that most working scientists have something like this model in mind when they think about explanations of individual cases.

Campbell identifies two problems with the notion that something like a scientific law could be applied in psychiatry. First, scientific laws that function in deductive arguments generally have a deterministic character, at least in the sense that in their idealized forms they are exceptionless. Explanations of individual cases in psychiatry, however, typically involve haphazard etiological trajectories, and it is next to impossible to imagine how these could fall under general scientific laws. Second, the explanation of individual cases generally involves some form of empathic understanding. Campbell likens the formulation of explanations of an individual case to the task of a historian who tries to reconstruct how one event led to another. Campbell notes that to understand how certain events cause each other in the person's individual trajectory, we will typically employ our ability for empathic understanding; we put ourselves in the person's shoes (Jaspers, 1968).

Much of traditional 20th-century philosophy of science was erected on the basis of logical reconstructions of physics, and this is particularly true for the covering law model and its relatives, which play an important role in Campbell's discussion. Through the influence of the hypothetico-deductive account of scientific method, the idea that psychology and psychiatry should search for general laws has been highly influential in the discipline, and many remnants of this dominance remain. I fully agree with Campbell's supposition that the applicability of such models in psychology and psychiatry is likely to be limited. Individual cases are too idiosyncratic to expect covering law models to hold, and there is no doubt in my mind that considering the subjective experience of the person and using empathic abilities to access that experience are not relics of a prescientific age that will become obsolescent as soon as we dig deep enough in genetics, neuroscience, or the behavioral sciences. Rather, we need to develop new models of scientific explanation to accommodate their role.

In support of Campbell's attempt to reconcile the scientific outlook with the haphazard idiosyncrasy of the individual person's condition, it may be useful to consider alternative styles of explanation. In the past few years, a tradition I have found remarkably fruitful is one based on systems-based thinking (Meadows, 2008), especially as utilized in the literature on ecosystems (Scheffer, 2009). The ecosystems literature offers powerful metaphors and analogies for thinking about individual cases, causality, and the role of empathy in our understanding of cases (Lunansky et al., 2021). I will discuss this analogy in terms of two properties that match Campbell's concerns: how we should think of individual trajectories and their causal analysis, and how we may embed empathic understanding in our analyses of systems.

Using the systems approach, the individual is characterized as a system of interacting elements (thoughts, affect states, behaviors, environmental features, etc.). The healthy system can be thought of as analogous to a stable, flourishing ecosystem, in which myriads of interactions between species and environment maintain a stable state (e.g., a healthy rainforest) that is able to process perturbations that are typically modeled as random events (periods of draught, population shocks through epidemic outbreaks, forest fires, etc.).

In the ecosystems literature, it is well known that through internal dynamics (e.g., a species evolving to a highly dominant state) or through external interventions (e.g., erosion due to externally forced processes, like humans cultivating land) the system can lose resilience and become unstable (Scheffer, 2009). In this situation, a random shock can lead to problems that multiply faster than the system can repair them, and as a result the system can go through a sudden transition that incurs drastic changes until it settles into a new stable regime (e.g., a desert).

In mental health, one can imagine an analogous mechanism to be operative: environmental conditions (e.g., enduring financial stress) can cause problems (e.g., worry) that the system is not able to resolve in time (e.g., because it employs maladaptive coping mechanisms like drug or alcohol use), which will then tend to cause other problems (e.g., insomnia) that may form reinforcing feedback loops with existing problems (e.g., worry). Such interactions make the system less resilient to perturbations, so that if a random shock hits the system (e.g., the loss of loved one), the system can spiral out of control until the it settles into a new stable regime in which the problems ecology has itself become stable. We would phenomenologically recognize such a state as a mental disorder.

How does such an account fare with respect to Campbell's analysis? One important consequence of this type of model is that it minimizes the role of incidental triggering causes in explanation. For instance, if a system is unstable, a minor perturbation can lead it to collapse. However, what the minor perturbation is, exactly, does not really matter. If it has lost resilience, a forest may collapse because of a fire, a draught, or a butterfly flapping its wings in the wrong direction. In other words, these perturbations can be thought of as being random (in fact, that is also how they are typically modeled: as noise). The same may hold for the perturbations that trigger disorders. If so, even if one could identify "the cause" of the onset of a mental disorder, that identification might not buy one much in terms of advancing our understanding of the system. If this type of theory is true, it does not predict specific causes to have specific effects, and individual etiologies should be expected to vary greatly.

One may alternatively expect to find definite causes in the elements of the system, particularly in the causal relations that characterize it. However, even here we should expect significant heterogeneity. Even the simplest network model I know (the so-called Ising model; Finneman et al., 2021) has, for p nodes, p threshold parameters and $p(p - 1)/2$ interactions. There are many configurations of these parameters that can lead the model to be vulnerable to shocks. Also, it is often impossible to reduce instability to any one of these parameters: the system is vulnerable because of the way all of them act together. Thus, different people can have vulnerable systems for different reasons. Surely one can say that if certain patterns of interaction obtain, the system will be less stable (in fact, that is the essence of the network theory of mental disorders; Borsboom, 2017). However, one can only say that when considering the system as a whole; in other words, it is the *pattern* that matters, not the features that make up the pattern. In this sense, resilience is very similar to classic dispositional concepts in the philosophy of science, such as fragility (Choi & Fara, 2021).

Thus, in this case, we should expect significant heterogeneity: if individual people are thought of as systems, it is unavoidable that some of the system elements and relations will be idiosyncratic. Of course, there will be some aspects of the system that involve robust mechanisms that support generalizations. For instance, if a person uses alcohol as a coping mechanism, this may interfere with the operation of the biological clock to cause bad or insufficient sleep, and that is a type of causal relation that may be relatively general, so that it can function as a sort of scientific law. However, other relations may be highly dependent on the particular system under consideration; for instance, whether a person does or does not use drugs as a coping mechanism depends on whether drugs are available (a physical condition of the environment), whether the person knows that they can be used (a mental knowledge state dependent on their learning history), whether other people around them use drugs (a social state involving the behavior of neighboring individuals), and a host of other features. As Campbell notes, some such conditions and pathways may be highly unique, or "pathoplastic." For instance, drug consumption may lead to delusional states, but the content of these states will influence behaviors differentially: a person who forms the delusion that they are manipulated by a shaman will likely act differently (and thus manipulate their environment differently) from a person who forms the delusion that others can hear their thoughts.

Finally, people will change the architecture of the system based on its state; for instance, if a person is doing badly, they may seek out a therapist, who may actively change connections in the person's mental health ecosystem. For example, the therapist may teach the person alternative coping styles (e.g., dealing with stress through physical exercise rather than through drug consumption). This means that mental health systems are *adaptive complex systems* – that is, complex systems that change their architecture as a function of their state, just like food web structures in ecology can change as a function of the density of animal populations (e.g., foxes eat rabbits but will resort to eating squirrels if there are few rabbits, which means the network structure of the food web changes as a function of its state).

The fact that people do this routinely makes them moving targets. Typically, concerns about generalizability are framed in terms of whether findings of one person can be generalized to others, but the question whether finding about you, as you exist today, can be generalized to future versions of yourself is far from moot. In Campbell's analogy, you may consider yourself a steel ball, heated at some point and carrying the heat with you across some idiosyncratic trajectory to exert its causal effects there. However, in humans, it's quite possible the very laws of their functioning change along that trajectory as well, so that the laws that govern heat at Campbell's p2, t2 are not the same as those at p1, t1.

If one thinks about the analysis of complex systems in this way, it seems unavoidable that to understand individual cases, one will need to tailor one's systems analysis to them. That is, in forming an explanation of why a person is in a given condition, one needs to be sensitive to idiosyncrasies; one needs to build up a person-specific theory that somehow describes the system architecture of the person and derives the likely consequences of that architecture. After all, to explain a phenomenon is to present an analysis of the world that makes the phenomenon unsurprising.

Currently, we have no scientific theories that are sufficiently flexible to accommodate the many subtle context dependencies we have to rely on when making sense of an individual case, and therefore one should marvel at the fact that humans are actually quite good at understanding, explaining, and predicting each other's behavior. Despite the fact that "folk psychology" is sometimes mocked, it is quite staggering how successful it really is when it comes to explaining and predicting behavior in our ordinary lives. How is this possible? Well, we may lack scientific theory, covering laws, and mechanistic knowledge, but we do have some very powerful computational machinery under the hood to navigate the social world: the human brain. Somehow, this allows us to employ that mysterious technique of mentally simulating what it would be like if we stood "in the other person's shoes": empathic understanding. When we mentally simulate what it would be like to, say, suffer from arachnophobia, we see "in our mind" that a likely response to this would be to avoid spiders, and as such this mental simulation gives us a means of epistemic access to parts of the network structure of the person: if you are afraid of spiders, you will avoid them (Kalis & Borsboom, 2020).

In this view, therefore, empathic understanding can be viewed as a methodological technique. It is one of the many techniques we use to chart other people's systems architecture of thoughts, feelings, and behavior; one that is particularly useful in assessing connections between different mental states (e.g., different beliefs that support each other, in the way that the belief "shamans have magical powers" facilitates having the belief

"I have been cursed by a shaman") and between mental states and behavior (e.g., believing that one has been cursed motivates seeking a magical cure to lift the curse).

In sum, in psychiatry we deal with a complex, adaptive system that is in part accessible only through an assessment technique that has no parallel or precedent in the classical sciences. It may be that this system turns out to be amenable to classical explanations such as those investigated by Campbell in ways we cannot currently fathom, but there is an equally good chance that no such analysis is forthcoming. In the latter case, it may be fruitful to investigate alternative explanatory models, such as those afforded by complexity science and systems thinking.

REFERENCES

Borsboom, D. (2017). A network theory of mental disorders. *World Psychiatry, 16*, 5–13.

Choi, S., & Fara, M. (2021). Dispositions. In E. N. Zalta (Ed.), The Stanford encyclopedia of philosophy (Spring 2021). Metaphysics Research Lab, Stanford University.

Finnemann, A., Borsboom, D., Epskamp, S., & van der Maas, H. L. J. (2021). The theoretical and statistical ising model: A practical guide in R. *Psych, 3*(4), 594–618. https://doi.org/10.3390/psych3040039

Kalis, A., & Borsboom, D. (2020). Folk psychology as a causal language. *Theory & Psychology, 30*(5), 723–728.

Lunansky, G., van Borkulo, C. D., Haslbeck, J. M. B., van der Linden, M. A., Garay, C. J., Etchevers, M. J., & Borsboom, D. (2021). The mental health ecosystem: Extending Symptom networks with risk and protective factors. *Frontiers in Psychiatry, 12*, 640658. https://doi.org/10.3389/fpsyt.2021.640658

Jaspers, K. (1963 [1923]). *General psychopathology*. Manchester University Press.

Meadows, D. H. (2008). *Thinking in systems: A primer*. Chelsea Green.

Norton, J. D. (2008). The dome: An unexpectedly simple failure of determinism. *Philosophy of Science, 75*(5), 786–798. https://doi.org/10.1086/594524

Scheffer, M. (2009). *Critical transitions in nature and society*. Princeton University Press. https://doi.org/10.2307/j.ctv173f1g1

Section 11

CHAPTER 31

Introduction to Zachar's "Versions of Disorders We Aspire to Explain"

Kenneth S. Kendler

In a thoughtful essay that follows, Peter Zachar interweaves several philosophical issues that relate to classification in general and psychiatric classifications specifically. I think it will be most useful to interested readers if, in this introduction, I steer away from a largely conceptual/philosophical critique of Zachar's essay and rather comment from the perspective of a working clinician and psychiatric nosologist who has, for better or worse, spend several decades working on various versions of the DSM – the accepted nosology for American psychiatry.

I will therefore enumerate several perspectives to place the following chapter in context. Let me begin with the history of medicine and, even more importantly, psychiatry. DSM-III did not begin in an historical vacuum but in fact was substantially shaped by multiple short- and long-time historical trends within these fields. These in turn impacted many conceptual decisions made about the nature and goal of the criteria. The field was, therefore, not entirely open to all the choices that Zachar raises with respect to classificatory practices. For example, at its origin, it was decided that DSM-III would be a descriptive document that took no position with respect to the etiology of psychiatric disorders. Despite much publicity that this was going to change in DSM-5, the field was not even close to ready to make a transition from descriptive to etiologic-based diagnoses (Zachar et al., 2019).

The DSM-III, published in 1980, was based, in the broadest possible terms, on the history of psychiatric nosology dating back to around 1800. By 1980, the major concepts of schizophrenia, melancholia/depression, and mania/bipolar illness had already been formed and well established, not to mention, autism, anorexia, anxiety neurosis, and many more. No one considered the option to abandoning these major categories. With respect to criteria sets, two were already in existence that were impactful on most of the relevant work groups in DSM-III: the Feighner criteria (Feighner et al., 1972) and Research Diagnostic Criteria (RDC)

(Spitzer et al., 1975). Given that Spitzer, the head of the DSM-III effort, was also in charge of the RDC, it was widely expected that the RDC criteria for a number of the key psychiatric nosologic categories would heavily influence those proposed for DSM-III. Not only did these two criteria sets contain specific diagnostic criteria, but they also contained thresholds (e.g., the number of criteria needed to meet a diagnostic threshold). With respect to specific criteria sets, a careful study of relevant textbooks of psychiatry reveal that the individual signs and symptoms of melancholia/depression (Kendler, 2016a), mania (Kendler, 2017), and schizophrenia (Kendler, 2016b) were all relatively stable over the course of the 20th century and closely related to those adopted for DSM-III. So, many of the specific decisions made by the designers of the DSM-III and the subsequent editions have been historically constrained.

Another constraint on the DSM process has been a series of changes introduced gradually in the course of the transitions from DSM-III to DSM-IIIR to DSM-IV and eventually to DSM-5. The revision process moved from an exercise in expert consensus to an empirically informed, validator-based process. This was an informal shift of emphasis from DSM-III to DSM-IV, which was accelerated during the DSM revision by the Scientific Review Committee appointed by the American Psychiatric Association (Kendler, 2013) and the subsequent formation of the DSM Steering Committee. In essence, this process now requires, for any change in diagnostic criteria, that empirical evidence be presented to support the greater validity, reliability, and/or utility of the revised version versus the criteria it will replace. For new diagnoses, evidence for substantial validity, reliability, and utility are required. Given the many negative consequences of diagnostic change, the DSM systems struggle to find the right threshold for evidence for change that does not retard progress in the field but prevents changes that produce only minimal improvement in the performance of the diagnostic manual. A nosologic system can, on the one hand, generate so much inertia that it feels frozen and prevents progress. But given the historical investments in complex nosologies, opening it up for rapid, only modestly supported change risks the integrity of the entire enterprise.

I hope this more pragmatic view of the nuts and bolts of the DSM revision process can help frame Zachar's more philosophical views. These contrasting approaches reflects, for me, one of the more challenging aspects of psychiatric nosologic work: specifically, the need to keep one's head straight about the many conceptual issues involved while at the same time grappling with the messy business of a living nosologic document – how to establish it and when and how to change it.

REFERENCES

Feighner, J. P., Robins, E., Guze, S. B., Woodruff, Jr., R. A., Winokur, G., & Munoz, R. (1972). Diagnostic criteria for use in psychiatric research. *Archives of General Psychiatry, 26*(1), 57–63. https://doi.org/doi:10.1001/archpsyc.1972.01750190059011.

Kendler, K. S. (2013). A history of the DSM-5 Scientific Review Committee. *Psychological Medicine, 43*(9), 1793–1800. https://doi.org/S0033291713001578

(2016a). The phenomenology of major depression and the representativeness and nature of DSM criteria. *American Journal of Psychiatry, 173*(8), 771–780. https://doi.org/10.1176/appi.ajp.2016.15121509

(2016b). Phenomenology of schizophrenia and the representativeness of modern diagnostic criteria. *Journal of the American Medical Association Psychiatry, 73*(10), 1082–1092. https://doi.org/10.1001/jamapsychiatry.2016.1976

(2017). The clinical features of mania and their representation in modern diagnostic criteria. *Psychological Medicine, 47*(6), 1013–1029. https://doi.org/doi:10.1017/S0033291716003238

Spitzer, R. L., Endicott, J., & Robins, E. (1975). *Research diagnostic criteria for a selected group of functional disorders* (2nd ed.). New York Psychiatric Institute.

Zachar, P., Regier, D. A., & Kendler, K. S. (2019). The aspirations for a paradigm shift in DSM-5: An oral history. *Journal of Nervous and Mental Disorders, 207*(9), 778–784. https://doi.org/10.1097/NMD.0000000000001063

CHAPTER 32

Versions of Disorders We Aspire to Explain
Nominal, Conventional, and Factual Features

Peter Zachar

32.1 Causal Relationships

As a descriptive term, causation refers to a variety of relationships between before and after. For instance, the cause – or the "before" part – can be producing, sustaining, or changing. Let me illustrate each option with respect to anxiety. Events experienced as highly traumatic can *produce* stress and anxiety. Continual and intrusive memories of the traumatic event can then *sustain* the anxiety for longer periods of time or *change* mildly disruptive anxiety into something more debilitating.

Other kinds of causal relationships that have been discussed include causation being irreversible or reversable and distal or proximal (Krieger, 2008; Ross & Woodward, 2022). The loss of a romantic relationship might precipitate a depressive episode, which can be *reversed* with the formation of a new relationship. Some would say that for a depressive episode to be an actual psychiatric disorder, there should be a degree of *irreversibility* where the depression persists even if the person finds a replacement relationship. Lauren Ross and Kenneth Kendler (Chapter 8 in this volume) explore the distal versus proximal distinction. An example of a proximal cause is ingesting a psychedelic drug leading to the experience of hallucinations. Childhood adversity, such as physical and sexual abuse, is considered a distal cause of various disorders in adulthood.

These differences largely emphasize variation in the causes, but causal relationships are made complex not only by variation in the before part but also by variation in the after. For instance, with *multifinality*, the same risk profile can have many different outcomes (Nolen-Hoeksema & Watkins, 2011).

In classification theory, nonessentialist approaches emphasize variation in the after, or variation in what we aspire to explain. Variation in what we want to explain will be the primary focus of this chapter.

In what follows, adopting a nominalist perspective, I will review some current ideas about the protean or changeable nature of psychopathology. I will then discuss the interplay of decisions and discovery in classification by focusing on classificatory choices as understood from the perspective of scientific conventionalism. More specifically, I will examine the importance of classificatory choice points that cannot be settled once and for all by reference to facts alone, but that also promote the discovery of facts. The resulting disorders that we aspire to explain are not privileged or inevitably destined to be discovered, but neither are they mere theoretical fictions. When I return to causation, I will suggest that implementing diagnostic conventions generates different versions of what we want to study, and some of those versions might not be causally interchangeable.

32.2 Multiple Options for Lumping and Splitting Classifications

In the classification of psychopathology, diagnostic criteria can be categorized as sensitive, specific, and nonspecific. A sensitive criterion is one which indicates the presence of a disorder. A specific criterion is one that distinguishes the disorder from other disorders. A nonspecific (transdiagnostic) criterion occurs across disorders. Forbes et al. (2023) show that about 63% of the criteria in the DSM are disorder specific and about 37% are disorder nonspecific. Interestingly Forbes et al. report that of the top 15 most nonspecific criteria in the DSM, 10 (or 67%) are DSM depression criteria.

Looking at major depressive disorders, the following might be considered prototypical depression criteria:

Little pleasure in doing things
Feeling down or hopeless
Feeling bad about yourself
Recurrent suicidal ideation

At one time or another, the following have been considered sensitive to depression, but they are also nonspecific for depression:

Anxiety
Headaches
Gastrointestinal distress
Depersonalization

In addition, we could list a number of auxiliary psychiatric criteria that could be incorporated into a depression symptom[1] network. These might include

Identity instability
Disturbances in the sense of self
Fear of going 'crazy'
Ideas of reference

Thus, the population of potential diagnostic criteria for depression is larger than the circumscribed list of nine criteria included in the DSM.

Van Os and Reininghaus (2016) discuss what they term the *extended psychosis phenotype*, or a collection of psychotic experiences that do not indicate the presence of a psychotic disorder. This implies that the domain of psychosis is broader than what is included in DSM criteria sets. By analogy, an *extended depression phenotype* could incorporate additional features beyond those listed in the DSM diagnostic criterion set.

In writing about emotions, Faucher and Tappolet (2008) distinguish an avocado-pear metaphor and a wax metaphor. In the United States, avocado-pears are just called avocados. An avocado is a fruit with a hard pit at its center. Applied to psychiatric disorders, in the avocado metaphor, depressive disorder would possess a deep hard core that defines the stable nature of disorder, but individual differences can lead to slight variations in expression on the surface. For example, the pattern of depressive symptoms can vary across different precipitating stressful events (Keller et al., 2007).

Wax, on the other hand, is malleable all the way through. When warmed up it, can take many different forms. It can cool down and maintain a specific shape, but it also can be rewarmed and morph again in larger and smaller ways. The wax metaphor suggests a more malleable depression concept. For instance, one can add and subtract symptoms to create different kinds of depression such as melancholia and postpartum depression, but also make the concept fluid enough to incorporate "masked depression," which includes inexplicable pain and impulsivity but not sadness or anhedonia (Wender & Klein, 1981).

One feature to which I would like to call attention is that in classifying and measuring, there is some *choice* regarding how we lump and split features. As suggested earlier, DSM descriptive definitions are partial

[1] To be technically precise, symptoms are reported and signs are observed. This distinction is not always followed, and I use *symptoms* loosely to refer to both.

representations of disorders – and in a hypothetical extended symptom network we can foreground and background different features. For example, with depression, we could choose to foreground anxiety and identity instability, which would result in an agitated, poor-prognosis depression.

Let me also note that the population of potentially relevant diagnostic criteria should not be limited to those that happen to be classified in the DSM-ICD, which Berrios (2003) claims is largely based on the descriptive psychopathology of the late 19th century. Were the list of potential specific and nonspecific criteria to become more extensive, the potential classificatory options available for selection would expand. Furthermore, in addition to symptoms, other validating criteria such as past psychiatric history, prognosis, and risk factors are relevant considerations.

32.3 Nominalism and the Protean Nature of Psychopathology

Previously, I have argued that a nominalist (versus an essentialist) view of emotion offers an informative analogy with psychopathology (Zachar, 2022) For instance, an emotion such as fear is constituted by characteristic precipitants, cognitions, behaviors, subjective feelings, and physiological responses. Basic emotion theorists contend that the patterning of cognitions, behaviors, and feelings that define fear is the result of the activation of an affect program for fear (Ekman, 1992; Griffiths, 1997). In basic emotion theory, affect programs are the essences of emotions.

In contrast, according to the theory of psychological construction, there is no specialized affect program for fear (Barrett, 2006; Russell, 2003). Over time, different and varied patterns of cognitions, behaviors, and feelings occur in our emotional lives. Adopting a nominalist view, psychological constructionists argue that occasionally a pattern occurs that resembles what a local language names fear, but many patterns occur that are not named.[2]

The nominalism of the psychological constructionists closely resembles the nominalism of John Locke. According to Locke, we do not have a specific name for the killing of an old man, but we do for the killing of one's father – patricide. Locke claims that it would be impractical to specifically name every combination of features that can occur if we are not likely to use these names with some regularity. In addition, according

[2] One important difference between psychiatric disorders and emotions is that disorders are not typically transient and thus closer to moods than emotions.

to Locke, those combinations of features that by convention are assigned names *gain* some perceived privilege over those that are not.

Like the shifting components of emotions, different combinations of symptoms (and other validators) can ebb and flow throughout our lives in a protean or changeable manner (Caspi et al., 2020; Hartmann et al., 2021).[3] Classification systems such as the DSM give some of them specific names – and perhaps the act of assigning specific names confers some perceived importance to those patterns. Many other patterns occur that are not named, but any actually occurring combination of features could be foregrounded and named if doing so were deemed useful.

Nominalism emphasizes both the view discussed in the last section that DSM definitions are partial representations of disorders and the view discussed in this section that many other symptom patterns occur that are not named. With that as a background framework, let us now turn to scientific conventionalism.

32.4 Psychiatric Classification and Scientific Conventionalism

In the philosophy of science, conventionalism represents a rejection of a priori necessities, absolutes, and self-evident foundations. Scientific conventionalism holds that if what we discover is contingent on previous choice points, things can be otherwise – but not be any way we want them to be.

For example, in Euclidean geometry the three interior angles of a triangle add to 180 degrees – a logical necessity based on the parallel postulate. Euclid proposed five postulates that were assumed to be true, but no one was ever able to prove #5, the parallel postulate. In the 19th century geometricians discovered that if they chose to assume certain postulates were false, they can work out alternative geometries. In one alternative geometry based on rejecting the parallel postulate, the interior angles of a triangle add to less than 180 degrees. In another alternative based on rejecting the second postulate, the interior angles add to more than 180 degrees. These alternative geometries are as deductively rigorous as Euclidean geometry.

A leading advocate for scientific conventionalism, Henri Poincare (2001), argued that some geometric axioms are conventions, not absolutely

[3] Historically the notion that a single disorder can manifest differently over time was associated with the notion of "unitary psychosis," which is often contrasted with a Kraepelinian model of distinct categories (Dakar, 2021).

true or false but more or less convenient for certain purposes. Such conventions are established by decisions and agreement at choice points.

Debates about alternative geometries ceased to be armchair exercises when Einstein used one of the alternatives to formulate the general theory of relativity. For various reasons, however, conventionalism fell out of favor in the philosophy of science.[4] Nevertheless, it lives on in other guises such as the partial nature of operational definitions, the underdetermination of theory by evidence, the theory-ladenness of observation, and the role of nonempirical factors in classification. Different versions of conventionalism straddle the scientific realist–anti-realist divide in various ways. I am interested in scientific conventionalism because it can highlight the importance of practical decisions without viewing the outcomes of those decisions as theoretical fictions or constructions we just make up.

Poincare claimed that scientific conventions are freely chosen, but he did not believe that they are merely arbitrary or random. Consider the dimensions of blood pressure and mood. There are clear differences between low blood pressure and a hypertensive crisis or between a euthymic mood and a melancholic depression. Between these categorically labeled endpoints, there is typically a region in which things are vague.

The classic example of vagueness in philosophy is the paradox of the heap. Sand scattered on the floor and a heap of sand can be viewed as distinct categories. If you slowly drop grains of sand one after another on the floor, eventually you will end up with a heap of sand, but there is no fixed point or threshold at which adding one more grain of sand transforms scattered sand into a heap. Thus, between the scattered sand and a heap there is a region for which there is no fact of the matter as to whether the sand forms a heap. These quantities of sand are called borderline cases.

There are also borderline cases for high blood pressure and disordered mood. For both, risk for negative consequences increases with increasing values. It is thus reasonable to target the setting of thresholds in regions that are transitional between normal and abnormal.

Let us look more specifically at major depressive disorder. In the DSM, a person must meet five of nine criteria to be diagnosed with depression. Consider two different approaches to setting diagnostic thresholds – cautious and bold. Cautious classifiers argue that thresholds should be set high

[4] One reason scientific conventionalism fell out of favor is that some people construed conventions to be like analytic statements – true by definition alone not true because of the facts. Quine's argument against the analytic versus synthetic distinction showed that analytic statements were not forever isolated from factual considerations. This argument also undermined scientific conventionalism, so construed.

to avoid false positives (Horwitz & Wakefield, 2012; Wakefield & First, 2003). Bolder classifiers argue that thresholds should be lowered to encourage early interventions when problems are milder – an approach known as the staging model (McGorry et al., 2006).

There is no absolute fact of the matter as to where the diagnostic threshold should be for all purposes, but setting it to either minimize false positives or track a greater range of risk is not arbitrary. Once the relevant conventions are in place, false-positive and false-negative rates are factual matters. A diagnostic threshold, however, remains a classificatory decision or a convention. It does not establish the true measure of depression any more than Euclidean geometry establishes the true measure of space or than a meter establishes the true measure of length.

Situations that lack decisive facts of the matter about how to best classify something raise the question of the relationship between conventions and facts. As noted earlier, there is no absolute fact of the matter whether the diagnostic threshold for depression should be four, five, or six (of the nine).

In thinking about this feature of conventions, the philosopher Leszek Kolakowsi (1969) described scientific conventionalism as the destruction of the concept of fact. The notion that scientific conventions are definitions that are radically isolated from a world of facts, however, begets misunderstanding about how some scientific conventions work. With that in mind, let us examine the convention–fact relationship.

32.5 Conventionalism and Factual Constraints

As noted, a commonly discussed feature of scientific conventions is that they are neither true nor false.[5] The claim that conventions are neither true nor false does not require that classificatory choices be isolated from facts absolutely. Indeed, the empiricist philosophers such as Carnap and Reichenbach who advocated for some forms of scientific conventionalism argued that conventions (such as operational definitions) promote the discovery of facts by bridging theoretical constructs with empirical reality (van Loo & Romejin, 2015). An easy-to-understand example of this is that if we want to discover the point prevalence of major depressive disorder in

[5] Some conventions are what Poincare called definitions disguised as descriptions, e.g., "depression occurs when someone has 5 or more DSM symptoms." Other conventions, e.g., "classifications should be etiologically based," are decisions contingent on normative judgments.

Table 32.1 *Depression–anxiety comorbidity.*

D1 = Depression + Insomnia D2 = Anxiety + Concentration problems	D1 and D2 comorbidity = 15.3%
D1 = Depression + Insomnia D2 = Anxiety + Concentration problems or Anxiety + Insomnia or Anxiety + Concentration Problems and Insomnia	D1 and D2 comorbidity = 20.8%

a population, we need to select a convention for distinguishing between depressed and not depressed (e.g., five of nine DSM criteria).

Particularly in domains such as psychopathology, when there is an abundance of facts, how the facts sort can be influenced by decisions made at choice points, but that does not mean the decisions make the facts. The resulting classifications are subject to constraints.

van Loo and Romeijn (2015) illustrate such factual constraints with respect to comorbidity. The DSM-III had diagnostic exclusions rules where a disorder lower in a diagnostic hierarchy (e.g., dysthymia) would not be diagnosed if it could be associated with a symptomatically broader disorder higher in the hierarchy (e.g., schizophrenia). In a sense, what the DSM-III said was that nonspecific symptoms of schizophrenia such as social withdrawal and concentration problems should not be used to make an additional diagnosis. The DSM-IV eliminated many exclusion rules leading to an explosion of comorbidity. Using the DSM-IV, a person who meets criteria for dysthymia and schizophrenia would be diagnosed with two disorders. Some thinkers claim this comorbidity is artificial/arbitrary, based primarily on classification choices.

Using a large epidemiological sample and brief operational definitions of depressed mood and anxiety, van Loo and Romeijn examined all possible combinations of symptoms, finding that in the largest combination, 33.8% of the sample report no symptoms ever meeting clinically relevant duration criteria to be considered present. The most common combination of symptoms was 15.3% of the sample reporting all depressed mood and anxiety symptoms present. Furthermore, starting with two categories, depression and insomnia (D1) and anxiety and concentration problems (D2), they were able to modify the comorbidity rates by altering symptom overlap. As shown in Table 32.1, by adding the overlapping symptom of insomnia to anxiety, they were able to increase depression–anxiety comorbidity from 15.5% to 20.8% of the

Table 32.2 *Mania and OCD comorbidity*

D1 = Mania + Drug use D2 = Compulsions + Obsessions	D1 and D2 comorbidity = .0007%
D1 = Mania + Drug use D2 = Compulsions + Obsessions or Drug use	D1 and D2 comorbidity = .0007%

cases.[6] In this example comorbidity rates were partly dependent on classification choices.

In contrast, when looking at combinations of manic mood, compulsions, obsessions, and drug use, 83.2% of the sample reported no symptoms ever meeting criteria to be considered present. The most common symptom profile was drug use alone, reported by 9.7% of the sample. Many possible combinations were rare or nonexistent. In this example D1 was mania and drug use and D2 was compulsions and obsessions. As seen in Table 32.2, unlike for the depression and anxiety, adding the overlapping symptom of drug abuse to compulsions and obsessions did not raise comorbidity with mania because none of the new possible combinations actually occurred. In this example, comorbidity rates were dependent on empirical population characteristics.

The point here is that if we sent out to explain comorbidity rates, those rates could vary across different classificatory decisions. van Loo and Romeijn claim that these rates, however, are not just artifacts of classificatory choices, but neither are they independent of classification choices. We make classificatory decisions, but once they are in place, we do not then make further choices about what the facts are.

32.6 Conventions: Constituting What We Measure but Not Making It Up

Counting the number of people in a population who are depressed requires having a measure of depression. For instance, when epidemiologists agree to diagnose depression if a person meets at least five criteria on the *Patient Health Questionnaire-8* (PHQ-8) for two weeks or more, they are both establishing a way to measure depression and defining depression. van Loo and Romeijn (2015) refer to this as doing double duty. As a

6 This measure of the rise in comorbidity was not reported in the article. Thank you to Jan-Willem Romeijn for calculating it for me.

measurement device, the PHQ-8 *indexes* or detects the presence of depression. When the choices we make in defining disorders are written into how we measure them, the definitions also partly *constitute* what is measured. As stated by van Loo and Romeijn, what counts as a measure of depression and what depression is cannot be answered independently of each other.

What should we make of the claim that there is no absolute fact of the matter as to whether something like gastrointestinal distress should be included in our measure of depression, but when those choices are written into our measure, they partly constitute what the measure indexes?

Kenneth Kendler (2017) describes the constituting position as one that claims there is nothing to a disorder beyond the methods used to measure it. One problem with the constituting view, he notes, is that if the definitional criteria constitute the disorder, any change in the definition changes the nature of the disorder. In addition, if you meet the diagnostic criteria, you have the disorder and there is nothing more to it. The concept is closed.

This view is reminiscent of Bridgman's (1927) early views on operational definitions. According to Bridgman, "the concept is synonymous with the corresponding set of operations" (p. 5) and "If we have more than one set of operations, we have more than once concept," and "strictly there should be a separate name to correspond to each different set of operations" (p. 10).

In contrast, if diagnostic criteria are fallible indicators of a disorder and only index its likely presence as argued by Kendler, the criteria could be mistaken. Considered this way, false-positive and false-negative diagnoses make sense according to the indexical view but not to the constituting view.

I agree with Kendler's wariness of taking DSM definitions literally and treating them as fixed but suggest that in a scientific conventionalist framework, classificatory choices do not close off concepts. As Zachar, Schaffner, and Turkheimer (2020) claimed in their description of operational definitions as open concepts, such definitions are contingent on classificatory choices and thus are revisable in the light of further factual considerations.

Considered as open concepts, the constituting function of scientific conventions is not limited to an initial anointing event that is then fixed. As Poincare held, conventions are not arbitrary but more or less convenient for certain purposes. Convenient means they must work for those purposes. We can examine this further with some contrasts.

Thomas Edison invented the light bulb.
George Lucas made up light sabers, but he did not invent them.

To actually invent a working light saber is more involved than making one up. Making things up are not subject to the practical and empirical constraints of actual inventions. For example, a working light saber needs to visibly luminesce as red, green, or white. It needs to cut through objects and deflect laser beams. It needs to be balanced for use in battle. It needs a power source.

It is interesting to notice that Hasok Chang's (2004) book about the development of thermometers is not titled *Inventing the Thermometer* but *Inventing Temperature*. In Chang's view, how we understand the nature of temperature is partly constituted by our thermometry. Chang states that one goal of thermometry was to devise a workable temperature scale that does not refer to the properties of any specific material substance. This was no small feat. As with light sabers, to say that such a measure of temperature was invented does not mean it was made up. Inventions have to work and are subject to empirical and practical constraints.

One can also use some engineering terminology and speak of measures being *designed*. To become a successful invention, designs have to be implemented, tested out, and iterated over time. During iteration, decisions made at choice points can make a difference in what is measured. Let me give two brief examples.

First, when the Minnesota Multiphasic Personality Inventory (MMPI) depression scale was originally designed, items were placed on the scale if they differentiated between a group of visitors to the University of Minnesota Hospitals who were not being treated for any illness and people in the depressive phase of a manic-depressive illness (Hathaway & McKinley, 1940). As suggested by Tellegen et al. (2003), one result of this approach was that the resulting depression scale included depression-specific items but was also boosted by nonspecific markers of general psychiatric distress such as "sometimes feeling useless" and "not being as content as others." Many clinicians value this scale for being a sensitive indicator of psychiatric distress that has a depressive dimension. MMPI depression was not made up, but what the scale indexed and modeled was influenced by design choices.

My second example is highly speculative. In psychological testing, some test developers have decided that a symptom such as crying nearly every day is not an adequate depression scale item because it is related to indicators of depression for women but not men – and may bias the prevalence rates (Morey, 2003). When psychologists construct tests, they try to assure that the test has desirable psychometric properties such as high internal consistency and temporal stability. They do so with multiple iterations over which they select items that support these features and delete those that do not. In theory, test developers could set out to construct a depression scale that had the feature of being gender neutral. Indeed, such a goal has some precedent in measuring vocational interests, work on the validity of ADHD, and the development a scale to measure prolonged grief disorder (Diamond, 1975; Morse et al., 2024; Prigerson et al., 2009). I am not saying this is a good idea or that it could developed, but let's assume that after successive iterations the attempt is successful.

The gender-neutral standard is clearly a convention. All the same, if such a measure were developed, we might even say that gender-neutral depression was out there before we measured it. We did not make it up like someone made up conventions for "real bourbon," as in, real bourbon must have at least 51% corn in the mash and be aged at least 2 years in new charred oak barrels. It is possible that there was no "real bourbon" in the world until this recipe was implemented. We probably wouldn't say that no one manifested the gender-neutral depression pattern until the first person took the test, even though gender-neutral depression notion has strong conventional elements.

From a more essentialist perspective, "true depression" is predefined by the world, and all our measures should seek to represent that phenomenon. Nominalism allows for alternatives based on the idea that the world contains more than any measure or construct can represent. The differences between those who hold these perspectives can be seen in their likely reactions to Fried (2020) showing that different measures of depression (BDI, HAM-D, etc.) are not simply interchangeable indices of the same thing. An essentialist might say one or more of these measures are flawed indicators. A nominalist would be more comfortable with variation across measures as long as it is recognized. Rather than seeking to bootstrap our way to the correct description and true measure of depression, nominalists would allow that some of the choices we make along the way become a part of what we measure and what is indexed.

32.7 Bringing It Back to Causal Relationships: Explaining Versions

One of most popular comic book characters ever created, Batman, has been depicted as many different yet overlapping versions over the years. There is the heroic Batman of the 1950s who has crime-fighting adventures, the campy Batman of the 1960s television show, Batman the detective, Batman the dark knight, obsessed and angry, and so on.

Consider also the many possible versions of a song such as *Amazing Grace*, including standard gospel versions, jazz versions, country versions, alt-rock versions, hip-hop versions, and reggae versions. I can readily imagine hearing a new and creative version of *Amazing Grace* and thinking something like, "it is the same song but completely different!"

Complex psychological states are also version rich. For instance, there are many versions of love and friendship. Queen Elizabeth and Prince Phillip or Atticus Finch and Scout are different versions of love. Matt Damon and Ben Affleck or Walter Sobchak and The Dude are different versions of friendship.

According to Nelson Goodman (1978), it makes no sense to talk about a world outside of any version – we only have access to versions. He goes so as far as to say that versions make our worlds. Goodman does not use the term "constituting," but he does talk about versions as designing worlds – that is, differences between versions are partly dependent on choices. Goodman does not want to say that versions can be true by means of corresponding to the actual world because that claim would seem to posit a neutral something (undescribed, undepicted, unperceived) that a version is true of.[7] This harkens back to the claim we saw earlier from van Loo and Romeijn that what counts as a measure of depression and what depression is cannot be answered independently of each other. Putnam (1996) also puts it nicely:

> Our language cannot be divided up into two parts, a part that describes the world "as it is anyway" and a part that describes our conceptual contribution. (p. 190)

Goodman does, however, say that versions can be right or wrong. Right versions are consistent with what else we know and pay their way in William James's sense: they are useful by helping us deepen knowledge, connect things up, see new things, increase what we can control, and so on. From this perspective, the neurodevelopmental disorder version of autism is a "right" version, the version of autism as a reaction to cold parenting is not.

Goodman could be seen as taking it too far by talking about *worldmaking*, particularly given recent developments in American culture. Social media has made it easier for people to be exposed primarily to claims about the way things are that correspond to how they want things to be. This has

[7] Goodman accepts that statements such as "Montgomery is the capital city of Alabama" can be true or false, but in his view van Gogh's *Starry Night* painting is neither true nor false.

not revealed anything new about human psychology. Work in cognitive and social psychology on cognitive mechanisms such as the frequency bias and motivated reasoning makes this recent development unsurprising but disappointing, nevertheless.

This unfortunate state of affairs has focused philosophical attention on the notion that, often, the world is not the way we want it to be or think it should be. We cannot just make it up, but notions such as *worldmaking* and *right versions making worlds* seem to go beyond the deflationary claim that there is no master version of the world to which all accurate versions can be reduced. Because Goodman believes that true versus false and actual versus fictional are important distinctions, he likely does not take it too far, but emphasizing world*making* makes that hard to see.

Batman and *Amazing Grace* are made up – you can generate as many versions of them as you can imagine. Movie versions of depression such as Conrad in *Ordinary People*, musical versions of depression such as *Like the Weather* by 10,000 Maniacs, and pictorial versions of depression such as *Melancholy* by Edvard Munch are made up, but they are also made up out of other versions that are not fictional.

Because the DSM, ICD, and MMPI operational definitions are partial representations of depression, they are also versions. As noted earlier, one can generate different versions of depression depending on what features one chooses to foreground and background by convention. For example, a more melancholic version of depression would foreground an incapacity to experience pleasure and a despondency that is qualitatively distinct from depressed mood. A version of depression that is akin to general psychiatric distress would foreground nonspecific depression symptoms. To be an actual version of depression, however, a pattern has to occur and cannot be made up. To be useful, a pattern should also occur with high enough frequencies to support generalizations.

With respect to classification, the view that classifications should be etiologically based is a convention. Up until this point in the chapter, I have portrayed versions as descriptively distinct – focusing on the descriptive or definitional features of measurement. Lurking in the background was the possibility that two descriptively distinct versions such as MMPI depression and gender-neutral depression are produced by different causal scenarios. Indeed, another possible way to demarcate versions would be to say that two versions of psychopathology are different if they require somewhat different causal explanations (even if they are descriptively similar). That is also assuming that different causes would require different interventions.

The causal explanation of psychopathology is complicated by how many different versions of what we attempt to study can be articulated. There are many reasons for there being a plurality of versions of psychopathology. The reason emphasized in this chapter is that in developing ways to measure psychopathology, conventions introduced at diagnostic choice points can generate different versions. This is consistent with the nominalist idea that the object eludes the concept, thus concepts cannot be more than versions of objects. The multiplicity of versions is another reason why diagnostic literalism, the reification of concepts and seeking privileged classification, is problematic. Being contingent on a convention, however, does not mean that what is discovered is made up.

32.8 Conclusions

Human behavior is causally complex, involving events at multiple levels of analysis that span across different spatial and temporal scales in a way that is hard to integrate. Unlike remote galaxies and hard-to-imagine subatomic particles, human behavior is familiar and accessible to us, and it seems it should be easier to get a hold on – but it has not been. Rather than conceptualizing the study of human behavior as an immature science in comparison to physics and chemistry, however, it may be more accurate to see the study of human behavior as the more difficult science.

In the past, I have argued against essentialist approaches to psychopathology, largely emphasizing the importance of variation in what can be included in depression (Aftab, 2020; Zachar, 2014). An equally strong non-essentialism about diagnostic categories can be gleaned in Hyman's (2021) intimation that some categories could be considered chance conjunctions of symptoms that can dissipate and reassort over a lifetime (i.e., consistent with the wax metaphor mentioned earlier).

I do not know if there is a continuum of psychopathology with more random events on one end and determined events on the other, but if so, complex psychopathology (and psychology) would probably fall somewhere in between. Some versions might even be borderline cases where it is hard to parse out chance and causation, but others will be marginally closer to the determined end and others marginally closer to the random end. If understanding causality is a priority, we should focus on defining versions that are closer to the determined end. But if causality is the only priority, then the versions we include in our etiologic-based classifications may also underrepresent the psychopathology that is there.

REFERENCES

Aftab, A. (2020). Psychiatric disorders as an imperfect community: interview with Peter Zachar, PhD. *Psychiatric Times*. Retrieved August 17, 2025 from www.psychiatrictimes.com/view/psychiatric-disorders-imperfect-community-peter-zachar-phd

Barrett, L. F. (2006). Are emotions natural kinds? *Perspectives on Psychological Science, 1*(1), 28–58. https://doi.org/10.1111/j.1745-6916.2006.00003.x

Berrios, G. E. (2003). The language of psychiatry and its history. In T. Hamanaka & G. E. Berrios (Eds.), *Two millennia of psychiatry in west and east* (pp. 81–91). Gakuju Shoin.

Bridgman, P. W. (1927). *The logic of modern physics*. Macmillan.

Caspi, A., Houts, R. M., Ambler, A., Danese, A., Elliott, M. L., Hariri, A., Harrington, H., Hogan, S., Poulton, R., Ramrakha, S., Rasmussen, L. J. H., Reuben, A., Richmond-Rakerd, L., Sugden, K., Wertz, J., Williams, B. S., & Moffitt, T. E. (2020). Longitudinal assessment of mental health disorders and comorbidities across 4 decades among participants in the dunedin birth cohort study. *Journal of the American Medical Association Network Open, 3*(4), e203221. https://doi.org/10.1001/jamanetworkopen.2020.3221

Chang, H. (2004). *Inventing temperature: Measurement and scientific progress*. Oxford University Press.

Daker, M. V. (2021). *The continuum of mental disorders and unitary psychosis*. Cambridge Scholars Publishing.

Diamond, E. E. (Ed.). (1975). *Issues of sex bias and sex fairness in career interest measurement*. U.S. Department of Health, Education, & Welfare.

Ekman, P. (1992). Are there basic emotions? *Psychological Review, 99*(3), 550–553. https://doi.org/10.1037/0033-295X.99.3.550

Faucher, L., & Tappolet, C. (2008). Facts and values in emotional plasticity. In L. C. Charland & P. Zachar (Eds.), *Fact and value in emotion* (pp. 101–137). John Benjamins.

Forbes, M. K., Neo, B., Nezami, O. M., Fried, E. I., Faure, K., Michelsen, B., Twose, M., & Dras, M. (2023). Elemental psychopathology: Distilling constituent symptoms and patterns of repetition in the diagnostic criteria of the DSM-5. *Psychological Medicine*, 1–9. Epub ahead of print. https://doi.org/10.1017/s0033291723002544

Fried, E. I. (2020). The 52 symptoms of major depression: Lack of content overlap among seven common depression scales: Corrigendum. *Journal of Affective Disorders, 260*, 744. https://doi.org/10.1016/j.jad.2019.05.029

Goodman, N. (1978). *Ways of worldmaking*. Hackett Publishing Company.

Griffiths, P. E. (1997). *What emotions really are*. University of Chicago Press.

Hartmann, J. A., McGorry, P. D., Destree, L., Amminger, G. P., Chanen, A. M., Davey, C. G., Ghieh, R., Polari, A., Ratheesh, A., Yuen, H. P., & Nelson, B. (2021). Pluripotential risk and clinical staging: Theoretical considerations and preliminary data from a transdiagnostic risk identification approach. *Frontiers in Psychiatry, 11*, 553578. https://doi.org/10.3389/fpsyt.2020.553578

Hathaway, S. R., & McKinley, J. C. (1940). A multiphasic personality schedule (Minnesota): I. Construction of the schedule. *Journal of Psychology, 10*(2), 249–254.

Horwitz, A. V., & Wakefield, J. C. (2012). *All we have to fear: Psychiatry's transformation of natural anxieties into mental disorders.* Oxford University Press.

Hyman, S. E. (2021). Psychiatric disorders: Grounded in human biology but not natural kinds. *Perspectives in Biology and Medicine, 64*, 6–28.

Keller, M. C., Neale, M. C., & Kendler, K. S. (2007). Association of different adverse life events with distinct patterns of depressive symptoms. *American Journal of Psychiatry, 164*(10), 1521–1529.

Kendler, K. S. (2017). DSM disorders and their criteria: How should they interrelate? *Psychological Medicine, 47*(12), 2054–2060. https://doi.org/10.1017/s0033291717000678

Kolakowski, L. (1969). *The alienation of reason: A history of positivist thought* (N. Guterman, Transl.). Doubleday.

Krieger, N. (2008). Proximal, distal, and the politics of causation: What's level got to do with it? *American Journal of Public Health, 98*(2), 221–230. https://doi.org/10.2105/ajph.2007.111278

McGorry, P. D., Hickie, I. B., Yung, A. R., Pantelis, C., & Jackson, H. J. (2006). Clinical staging of psychiatric disorders: A heuristic framework for choosing earlier, safer and more effective interventions. *Australian & New Zealand Journal of Psychiatry, 40*(8), 616–622. https://doi.org/10.1080/j.1440-1614.2006.01860.x

Morey, L. C. (2003). *Essentials of PAI assessment.* John Wiley & Sons.

Morse, M., Marzouqa, N., & Kim, A. (2024). *'Gender-equatable' can be a diagnostic validator for ADHD.* Poster presented at the American Professional Society of ADHD and Related Disorders, Orlando, Florida, January 20.

Nolen-Hoeksema, S., & Watkins, E. R. (2011). A heuristic for developing transdiagnostic models of psychopathology: Explaining multifinality and divergent trajectories. *Perspectives on Psychological Science, 6*(6), 589–609. https://doi.org/10.1177/1745691611419672

Poincaré, H. (2001 [1905]). Science and hypothesis. In S. J. Gould (Ed.), *The value of science: Essential writings of Henri Poincaré* (pp. 1–178). The Modern Library.

Prigerson, H. G., Horowitz, M. J., Jacobs, S. C., Parkes, C. M., Aslan, M., Goodkin, K., Raphael, B., Marwit, S. J., Wortman, C., Neimeyer, R. A., Bonanno, G. A., Block, S. D., Kissane, D., Boelen, P., Maercker, A., Litz, B. T., Johnson, J. G., First, M. B., & Maciejewski, P. K. (2009). Prolonged grief disorder: Psychometric validation of criteria proposed for DSM-V and ICD-11. *PLoS Medicine, 6*(8), e1000121. https://doi.org/10.1371/annotation/a1d1e0d-981f-4674-926c-0fbd2463b5ea.

Putnam, H. (1996). Irrealism and deconstruction. In P. J. McCormick (Ed.), *Starmaking: Realism, anti-realism, and irrealism* (pp. 179–200). Bradford Books.

Ross, L. N., & Woodward, J. F. (2022). Irreversible (one-hit) and reversible (sustaining) causation. *Philosophy of Science, 89*(5), 889–898. https://doi.org/10.1017/psa.2022.70

Russell, J. A. (2003). Core affect and the psychological construction of emotion. *Psychological Review, 110*(1), 145–172. https://doi.org/10.1037/0033-295x.110.1.145

Tellegen, A., Ben-Porath, Y. S., McNulty, J. L., Arbisi, P. A., Graham, J. R., & Kaemmer, B. (2003). *The MMPI-2 restructured clinical scales: Development, validation, and interpretation.* University of Minnesota Press.

van Loo, H. M., & Romejin, J.-W. (2015). Psychiatric comorbidity: Fact or artifact. *Theoretical Medicine and Bioethics, 36*, 41–60.

van Os, J., & Reininghaus, U. (2016). Psychosis as a transdiagnostic and extended phenotype in the general population. *World Psychiatry, 15*(2), 118–124. https://doi.org/10.1002/wps.20310

Wakefield, J. C., & First, M. B. (2003). Clarifying the distinction between disorder and nondisorder: Confronting the overdiagnosis (false-positives) problem in DSM-V. In K. A. Phillips, M. B. First, & H. A. Pincus (Eds.), *Advancing DSM: Dilemmas in psychiatric diagnosis* (pp. 23–55). American Psychiatric Association.

Wender, P. H., & Klein, D. F. (1981). *Mind, mood, and medicine.* Farrar Straus Giroux.

Zachar, P. (2014). *A metaphysics of psychopathology.* MIT Press. https://mitpress.mit.edu/books/metaphysics-psychopathology

(2022). The psychological construction of emotion: A non-essentialist philosophy of science. *Emotion Review, 14*(1), 3–14. https://doi.org/10.1177/17540739211058715

Zachar, P., Turkheimer, E., & Schaffner, K. F. (2020). Defining and redefining phenotypes: Operational definitions as open concepts. In A. G. C. Wright & M. Hallquist (Eds.), *Handbook of research methods in clinical psychology* (pp. 5–17). Cambridge University Press.

CHAPTER 33

Commentary on Zachar's "Versions of Disorders We Aspire to Explain"

James Woodward

The subject of Peter Zachar's chapter is classification, with a focus on psychiatry (of course). He suggests that classificatory choices should be "understood from the perspective of scientific conventionalism." I agree that there is an important conventional element in current systems for the classification of mental disorders.[1] Rather than seeing this as necessarily a limitation that needs to be overcome, my view is that many scientific theories, including very successful ones, contain conventional elements. (I take Zachar to agree.) In what follows I try to distinguish or disentangle different ways in which a scientific theory can contain conventional elements and to assess the implications of the presence of conventions in psychiatry.

I begin by suggesting that it may be fruitful to think in terms of a hierarchy of conventionality, going from weaker to stronger forms or from forms of conventionality that are relatively untroubling to forms that seem more problematic. I will follow Zachar in using some illustrations from spacetime physics (a major source of conventionalist ideas in science and philosophy) as well as psychiatry.

Suppose that the adoption of a classificatory scheme, operationalization or definition, and so forth (hereafter I will just say "definition") represents a "choice" such that its correctness is not a straightforward empirical matter. As we'll see, this is consistent with the usefulness of the definition depending in some more indirect way on empirical facts. The presence of

[1] As Zachar notes, claims about the role of convention in science were once popular, both among philosophers of science (e.g., Reichenbach) and among scientists themselves (Poincare, Einstein). In philosophy, claims about the presence of conventional elements have largely fallen into disfavor, in part because of arguments from Quine and others that all claims in science face the "tribunal of experience" in pretty much the same way. It seems to me, however, that Quine and other anti-conventionalists are mistaken about this. The various examples from spacetime physics mentioned earlier involve "conventional" choices that are not straightforwardly empirical. So, conventions (in the sense of definitional conventions or classificatory schemes that are conventional) are certainly present in successful science. I also think that Zachar is right about their presence in psychiatry.

such a choice of course implies that there are, in some sense, alternatives to choose among. But this possibility of choice can vary a lot in how significant or consequential or "arbitrary" it is. One possibility, presented in (1) below, is that, although arbitrary, the choice does not matter much. Another possibility is that facts about the world fail to support certain possible conventions and make others extremely natural and fruitful as in (2) below. Yet another possibility, presented in (3) below, is that there are a number nonequivalent alternative conventions and no obvious grounds for preferring one to the alternatives.

(1) One way in which choices may be non-consequential is that the alternative choices may be inter-translatable or at least make no empirical difference to any outcome we can recognize. In such a case, although we may need to choose some alternative to, so to speak, get on with things, it will not matter in terms of empirical consequences which one we choose, although one choice rather than another may be more pragmatically useful or convenient. To take a trivial example from spacetime physics, the choice of some particular coordinate system in which to do physical calculations is clearly a matter of convention. Given a set of frames that are in inertial motion with respect to one another, one may choose one as the rest frame to do calculations, but there is no fact of the matter about which frame is "really" at rest, although one choice or another may be more convenient. One way in which this choice clearly does not matter is that there are straightforward ways of translating results in one reference frame to another. Another way of bringing out that such a choice does not matter in any meaningful way is to note that it is always possible to formulate the physics in a frame-independent way, making it clear that choices of reference frames are not dictated by nature.

(2) Another, more interesting possibility is that although we have a choice of several alternatives to adopt, just one of these "works" or can be applied or used in the sense that the structure of the domain in which we are interested "supports" only that choice. Put differently, it may be that there is not enough of the right kind of structure in nature to support other choices.

One of the best-known physical illustrations of this possibility has to do with the notion of absolute (independent of a reference frame) simultaneity at a distance. Newtonian physics, at least in the version developed by Newton, assumes that this notion is well defined. One of Einstein's achievements in his formulation of the theory of special relativity was to recognize that the facts about spacetime structure and the behavior of light (in particular its constant velocity in all inertial frames) imply that the notion of absolute simultaneity at a distance has no empirical content; the facts about nature are such that there is nothing "out there" to support such a notion. There is a sense in which it is nonetheless possible to "define" a notion of absolute simultaneity (and in fact some physicists have done this), but such a definition will be in terms of spacetime structures that we have no reason to think exist and do not seem to be needed to do physics. (A reference frame–independent notion of absolute simultaneity at a distance thus has no "operationally meaningful" definition.) Einstein replaces the notion of simultaneity at a distance with a local notion that is empirically meaningful. There is a sense in which he rejects one definition of simultaneity and adopts another – another convention if you like. This is not fruitfully viewed as replacing one claim about an empirical fact with another, but at the same time the redefinition is empirically supported or motivated in the way I described. In this case there are empirical facts that make one choice of convention useful and another not useful, but the conventions themselves are not straightforward empirical claims.

(3) Finally, it may be that we have choices that are not inconsequential in the sense of (1) but where it is also not the case that among our possible choices just one is singled out as supported by nature as in (2). Here we seem to have a kind of conventionality that is "stronger" and arguably more worrisome than what is present in (1) or (2). I take that it is this possibility that concerns Zachar when he discusses the criteria for major depression (MD) and other mental disorders. It isn't just that the choice about which criteria for depression to adopt, and the claim that the satisfaction of five out of nine of these is sufficient for depression is a convention, although it obviously is. It is also the case, as Zachar illustrates, that different choices will have different empirical consequences – different estimates for the incidence of MD, and its comorbidity with other mental disorders, so this is different than possibility (1). In addition, with different choices of criteria for MD, we don't have anything like the inter-translatability between different coordinate systems that supports the judgment that it does not really matter which one we choose. Note also that the fact that different criteria for MD have different consequences is itself an empirical fact of considerable importance. As an abstract possibility, it might have turned out the structure of mental disorders was such that a very large number of reasonable sets of criteria for MD lead to largely the same results regarding who has MD, patterns of comorbidity with other disorders, and so on. However, as it happens, this is not the case.

Moreover, at present there are no known empirical facts (having to do with the structure of mental disorders, the brain, genetics, environmental causes of MD) that support the choice of these particular criteria rather than others, as in possibility (2). (Of course, "known" is important here – maybe there will be new discoveries that support some particular set of diagnostic categories, but, as observed below, these categories are not likely to coincide with current DSM categories.)

The kinds of conventionality present in systems of psychiatric classification thus seem different from those in the physics examples mentioned earlier. What should we make of those differences?

Before turning to this question, I want to consider another of Zachar's examples. This concerns the appropriate threshold for high blood pressure (or mood disorder). Of course, the main reason why we care about this is its implications for patient treatment. As Zachar notes, setting the threshold involves a trade-off between two competing considerations. On the one hand, if the threshold is set too high, patients who would benefit will not be treated. On the other hand, if the threshold is set too low, patients will receive unnecessary treatment, which may have costs. It seems clear that "nature" or "physiology" is not going to tell us which is the uniquely correct trade-off between these two considerations; instead, a "value judgment" about the relative importance of these two kinds of errors is required. In this sense a choice of "convention" is involved, but since the convention involves a judgment about values, it again seems rather different from the physics conventions described previously, where no such value judgments are involved. I will leave it to those who know more than I do about the bases of psychiatric classification to determine whether similar value judgments about the trade-off between the costs and benefits of under- and overdiagnosis are at work when criteria are chosen for disorders like MD and schizophrenia, but it seems plausible that this is and perhaps ought to be the case.

Once we recognize the role of value judgments in examples of this sort, we should also recognize that it would be wrong-headed to suppose that if we decide to set the threshold for high blood pressure at, say, 140/90, there must be some underlying physiological story that singles this out as the uniquely correct threshold. Arguably, for the purposes of biology or physiology (or causal understanding more generally), we should treat blood pressure as a continuous variable that is distributed in whatever way it in fact is and try to understand the factors affecting that. Similarly for mood disorder: if, as Zachar suggests, this varies continuously but we need to set a threshold for treatment, we should recognize the value judgments involved in the latter and take the continuous variable and not the threshold as the proper target for scientific explanation.

Of course, one might imagine a world in which the empirical facts about blood pressure and medical risk are very different than they in fact are – a hypothetical world in which everyone with blood pressure below 140/90 is uniformly at very low risk and everyone above 140/90 is uniformly at very high risk, so that the blood pressure–risk relation is represented by a step function that is horizontal to the y-axis everywhere (except the two levels corresponding to low and high risk) except at 140/90, where it is vertical or at least has a very high gradient. Here nature is such that the choice of 140/90 makes sense as the uniquely appropriate threshold; however, as I see it, there is still a choice involved in making this selection. This is another illustration of the way in which empirical facts might support a choice of a particular convention, even though the convention itself does not describe an empirical fact. Note also that in this case it would make sense to ask why the 140/90 threshold is special in this way. In the real world the gradient of the curve relating blood pressure to risk is presumably not so different at different points along the curve, and this makes the choice of a threshold look more arbitrary.

This example illustrates that classificatory schemes (and the adoption of conventions) can have very different goals, which can legitimately be used to motivate different choices. Goals having to do with patient health may require a threshold and, if so, may support some trade-offs over others. If we are interested in a scientific understanding of the causes of high blood pressure, the goal is different, and there is likely no reason to assign that threshold any particular significance.

Putting aside the role of conventions involving value judgments in classificatory schemes, what can we say about cases in which deep conventionality in the sense of category 3 is present – that is, cases in which alternative choices of conventions are consequential and in which we cannot point to some worldly structure that picks out one such choice as obviously the most appropriate one (as in our example of a step function for blood pressure)? One thing that can be done in such cases is to explore the consequences of different choices of conventions. How much of a difference does it make (and in what ways) if we adopt different criteria for MD? Such an exploration may not tell us that one choice of convention is superior to another, but it will at least tell us what follows from one choice rather than another. If we find, say, that conclusions about the incidence of MD or its comorbidity or the efficacy of various treatments are highly sensitive to the criteria used to characterize MD, this is at least something we should be aware of. If we find that many different choices lead to similar results but that a few choices are outliers in the sense that they lead to very different results, this may be, at least in the absence of countervailing considerations, an argument for using the former.

A second consideration is this: often the construction of a good *causal* theory for a range of outcomes and the choice of descriptive or classificatory characterizations of those outcomes go hand in hand. We aim at adopting characterizations of *explananda* that fit well with the causal theories we try to construct, and we also aim at building our theories in such a way that they fit well with these characterizations, so that each mutually constrains the other. In cases in which we can find causal theories and characterizations in which this sort of mutual constraint is present, the arbitrariness of our classifications seems considerably reduced. The introduction of Koch's postulates for bacterial diseases provides one illustration of this general point. Obviously, it is not true in general that every disease has one and only one bacterial cause, but it is true for some diseases, and to that extent, a scheme in which diseases are classified by their causes seems to have a kind of objectivity that is not (or may not be) present in other classificatory schemes.[2] A more complex example is the introduction of cladistic methods as a basis for biological classification. Such methods are based on a well-established causal theory – natural selection – and arguably provide a more objective basis (more objective in the sense that there is less of a role for nonequivalent arbitrary choices) for biological classification than do alternative methods such as phenetics. In the physics examples mentioned earlier we have very strong causal or explanatory theories, and it is arguably because of this that the conventional choices present seem less troubling than they are in some psychiatric cases.

I think it is plausible that a similar conclusion holds for mental disorders. To the extent that we have good causal theories about the etiology of depression (or perhaps more likely different etiologies for different varieties of depression), there will be a lot less arbitrariness in how depression or different varieties of it are identified and classified (although the point about the role of value judgments in setting therapeutic thresholds remains).

[2] For discussion, see Ross and Woodward (2016). In my view, adoption of a classificatory scheme in which certain diseases are individuated in terms of their causes amounts to adoption of a convention, but when we have reliable information about these causes, this is a good or fruitful or nonarbitrary convention. This contrasts with a characterization of a disease in terms of its symptoms, which was common in pre-Kochian biology as well as in contemporary psychiatry. Here there is usually less objectivity because there is some arbitrariness in what is included in the list of symptoms and different diseases may have the same symptoms.

However, if the cases of Koch's postulates and cladism are any guide, the schemes that result from strong causal theories are likely to be significantly revisionary – for example, some people currently classified as depressed may not be regarded so for the purposes of theory construction or may be regarded as suffering from other kinds of illnesses; some distinctions among kinds of depression may be recognized that are not currently recognized; categorial classification may be replaced by something more graded; and so on.

I said earlier that having good causal theories about the etiology of various mental disorders will reduce the arbitrariness (and other unsatisfactory features) of current classificatory schemes. It would be an understatement, however, to say that discovering such theories will not be easy and success is not guaranteed. If discoverable, the causal theories in question are presumably going to come largely from genetics and neurobiology. The genetic and neurobiological structures involved in mental illness are immensely complex and, in this respect, very different from, say, the biological facts that ground disease classification based on Koch's postulates. What I do claim is that *if* progress in classification occurs, this will very likely come from increased causal understanding.

Finally, a note about "realism." There is some tendency to suppose that if the criteria adopted for the mental disorders are regarded as conventions, it follows that we should not be "realists" about the existence of those disorders. I don't see how this follows. If we agree that the claim that five out of a list of nine criteria are sufficient for depression is a convention, it does follow that this is not a straightforward empirical claim. But it doesn't follow from this that we are committed to "anti-realism" or "instrumentalism" about depression (whatever exactly that means). Similarly, agreeing that the 140/90 cutoff for high blood pressure is a convention does not mean that there is no such thing as high blood pressure or that high blood pressure is not "real." On the contrary, adopting this convention means that we agree to understand high blood pressure in such a way that it is *true* that if your blood pressure measurement is higher than 140/90, you have high blood pressure.

I conjecture that the real concern about "realism" in connection with psychiatric disorders is something different: that the worldly correlates of the categories (variables, etc.) with which psychiatrists work do not enter into a sufficiently rich web of causal and predictive relationships – that they are not "good" variables from the point of view of causal or predictive analysis and fail to stand in robust connections with other variables, particularly those from the biological sciences. To take an extreme possibility,[3] suppose that satisfaction of the five out of nine criteria for MD does not correlate particularly well with responsiveness to various sorts of treatment, does not predict future mental health developments in patients satisfying the criteria, does not correlate with neural or genetic or other biological features, and so on. That would be a good reason to be dissatisfied with the five-out-of-nine classification theme and to look for an alternative. But in this case the problem with the criteria is not that they involve a convention, but rather that the convention leads to the failures of integration just described. Similarly, in this scenario, I don't think it would be helpful to conclude that MD (as specified by the standard criteria) is not "real" unless this is just a way of talking about lack of integration. But then why not talk directly about the integration issue and drop the worries about whether psychiatric categories are "real"? Lots of things belong to categories that are not particularly useful for predictive and explanatory purposes, do not fit smoothly with the rest of science, and are conventional in some respects, but this does not imply that the things so classified are "unreal." Consider "gothic novels," "paintings by da Vinci," "rocks that a person can comfortably sit on," etc.

Finally, let me note that the issue of the therapeutic usefulness for a classification is in principle rather different from the issue of the extent to which the classification is well integrated with the rest of science. A threshold of 140/90 for high blood pressure may be a good choice for therapeutic purposes even if the underlying biology does not pick this choice out as uniquely appropriate. Therapy and treatment are different goals, involving different choices and trade-offs, from constructing causal theories, even if the two are not completely independent of each other.

REFERENCES

Ross, L., & Woodward, J. (2016). Koch's postulates: An interventionist interpretation. *Studies in History and Philosophy of Science Part C: Studies in the History and Philosophy of Biological and Biomedical Sciences, 59*, 35–46. https://doi.org/10.1016/j.shpsc.2016.06.001

[3] This is for illustration purposes only. I don't claim that this is necessarily the actual situation with respect to depression.

PART IV

Causality and Phenomenology

Section 12

CHAPTER 34

Introduction to Roskies, Busch, and Walton's "Agency as a Framework for Thinking about Neuropsychiatric Disease"

Peter Zachar

The interventionist approach to causation has become a dominant perspective in the philosophy of science, for many reasons. One reason is that it can be generalized to causation across the physical sciences, biological sciences, psychological sciences, and social sciences without losing plausibility; in other words, in an interventionist framework, causality is not "softer" in psychology than it is in the physical sciences. That is not to say that the applications work the same way across sciences. For instance, in their chapter, Roskies, Busch, and Walton note that applying a neuroscientific intervention directly to the interconnected causal network that constitutes the brain is laden with complications.

One recent advance in neuroscience, deep brain stimulation, is stoutly interventionist. The potential efficacy of such interventions, however, has raised ethical questions regarding the effects of the intervention, namely that in addition to treating the symptoms of a disorder, the intervention might also change the person with the disorder.

Roskies and colleagues report that in the neuroethics literature, a number of concerns about deep brain stimulation interventions changing the person focus on its potential effects on agency. Indeed, they note that the role of agency is a recognized feature in several psychiatric disorders, including depression and obsessive-compulsive disorder. Furthermore, if agency plays a mediating role in psychiatric disorder or, even stronger, if there are disorders of agency, interventions on agency itself might be possible. To understand how agency might be altered in various interventions, it is important to characterize and measure it. As a first step, they describe the initial development of a self-report inventory they name the Agency Assessment Test (AAT).

They begin by comprehensively characterizing agency conceptually. They propose that the concept of agency refers to a multidimensional set of capacities that support effective and autonomous actions. Their conceptual analysis resulted in nine dimensions, among them capacity for action, attentional capacities, and emotional regulation. They then wrote items to measure these capacities. An important reason for adopting a capacitarian approach, in their view, is that a capacitarian view of agency is broadly held, at least implicitly, because it is arguably the foundation of our concepts of moral and legal responsibility.

The first result they report is a factor analysis. They extracted three interpretable factors, rotated to be correlated with each other. This was a bit surprising, as they anticipated that many more factors would emerge (per their nine dimensions). The three factors are named positive agency (e.g., I usually take measures to achieve my goals), negative agency (e.g., I have trouble functioning due to anxiety), and risk taking (e.g., I take risks that could harm me). They report that the first two factors were able to separate people scoring high and low on depression and high and low on anxiety but not those scoring high and low on obsessive-compulsivity.

The second result they report is a network analysis. To run this analysis, they created 16 facets of the AAT by grouping conceptually related items together and added measures of depression, anxiety, and obsessive-compulsivity as nodes. In the resulting network analysis, the disorder nodes were highly connected, with anxiety and depression being most connected. Interestingly, each disorder also had a different agency profile. Depression was correlated with problems in motivation and goal pursuit, anxiety with emotional regulation issues, and obsessive-compulsivity with loss of control of thoughts.

After speculating about why, according to these results, agency seems to be less multidimensional than they predicted, Roskies and colleagues return to the animating themes of the book, focusing on network analysis. They note that correlational data cannot itself establish causal relationships. According to these results, variations in disorders do covary with variations in agency, but whether developing a disorder causes changes in agency or the changes in agency alter a disorder is not clear.

They note, however, that from an interventionist perspective, these questions can potentially be answered. If disorders have different agentic profiles, and an intervention on profile-specific features of agency alters the symptoms of a disorder, that is causally relevant information. There are many possible ways to intervene on agency. A more reductive approach might look to see if a surgical intervention in the form of deep brain stimulation that altered one's agentic profile is followed by symptomatic improvement. Particularly with respect to a construct as psychological as agency is, if direct intervention experiments do not work, that does rule out a possible causal role for agency, but they propose it might suggest adopting a less reductive view of agency. Open questions for future work include getting more specific regarding the relationship between agency and mental health and illness and evaluating how well the AAT characterizes agency.

In his commentary, Josef Parnas wholeheartedly agrees that agency is a complex concept, which he illustrates by briefly describing some phenomenologically based ideas of Heidegger and Sartre, for example the importance of intentional directedness to human existence. With respect to psychopathology, Parnas claims that something like depression is always a disorder of agency. In his view, the nature of actual depression is deeper than the counting-of-symptoms approach utilized in this chapter – a thin view of the nature of depression that, Parnas claims, also characterizes most self-report inventories and ratings scales.

CHAPTER 35

Agency as a Framework for Thinking about Neuropsychiatric Disease

A Prelude to Asking Causal Questions

Adina L. Roskies, Erica Busch, and Ashley Walton

The notion of causation has been of central interest to philosophy of science, and it has seen a flourishing since the introduction of the interventionist framework of causation (Woodward, 2003) and causal explanation (Woodward & Hitchcock, 2003). Briefly, the interventionist framework holds that given two variables X and Y, X causes Y if a particular intervention on X would lead to a change in Y.[1] The interventionist framework has been used to identify causal structure and to elucidate the nature of scientific explanation. A number of theorists defend an interventionist approach to psychological explanation (e.g., Campbell, 2007; Rescorla, 2018), arguing that interventionism maintains the virtues of other leading theories of causal explanation such as nomological and mechanistic theories, and it comports better with scientific practice in psychology. For example, Rescorla argues that interventionism better characterizes practices in perceptual psychology, in which external stimuli are manipulated to determine the change in percept (Rescorla, 2018). We are fans of the interventionist approach, realizing, however, that while an interventionist approach is relatively easy to implement in perceptual psychology, where the relevant variables include perceptual stimulus parameters and verbal or behavioral report, it remains more difficult to employ in other areas of psychology and in psychiatry, where the variables involved may be more abstract, more difficult to assess or influence, and may involve central mechanisms whose causal structure remains opaque to us. Nonetheless, one of the most promising ways to get a handle on causal structure is through interventions, and although it is difficult to intervene on the brain, and even more difficult to do it through the types of

[1] This is overly simplified. The intervention or change in X must be "surgical," which has a technical definition but roughly means controls the value of the variable (Woodward, 2003) while other variables in the causal system are held fixed. There is a literature about broadening to include nonsurgical or soft interventions, and the limitations of both of these methods.

interventions called on by interventionist views of causation, developments in neuroscience and engineering make it increasingly possible to intervene in brain function, whether for therapeutic purposes or for more ethically questionable ones, such as for enhancement or entertainment.

As an example of novel techniques for neural intervention, consider deep brain stimulation (DBS), which chronically electrically modulates targeted subcortical regions, and is currently being used in more than 160,000 patients to treat the symptoms of recalcitrant Parkinson disease and a few other neurological and psychiatric disorders (Lozano et al., 2019). In general, DBS for Parkinson disease is highly effective, but worries have been raised in the neuroethics literature that DBS and other new methods of brain intervention that aim to treat diseases will have effects beyond those intended. The concern is that they will not only treat the disease or ameliorate its symptoms but also threaten to change the person being treated (e.g., Gilbert et al., 2017; Kraemer, 2013; Schermer, 2011; Witt et al., 2013). Many of the worries expressed are related to changes to a patient's agency: changes that affect the patient's autonomy, authenticity, self-control, or other aspects of the person he or she is (Gilbert & Viana, 2018; Lewis et al., 2014; Roskies, 2015). To adequately respond to such worries, we need to first understand the nature of the presumed threat (Bluhm, 2019; Gilbert et al., 2017, 2019). Do our neurointervention methods in fact affect agency? In what way? And if they do, are these changes problematic?

How can we answer or even begin to address these questions without methods of measuring agency? Here we begin to develop methods for characterizing agency, with the thought that they can be used in the future to assess whether neurointerventions affect agency, and if so, how. These assessments aim to characterize both changes in agency that correct for the agentive effects of neuropsychiatric disorders due to positive therapeutic value and those that alter the agent in unforeseen or noncompensatory ways. We note that the data described here are preliminary and for illustrative purposes only. We hope to present the data fully in future scientific publications.

In this chapter we describe a project aimed at developing a broad-based self-report instrument to "measure" agency, the Agency Assessment Test (AAT). First, we motivate the idea that treatments aimed at ameliorating neuropsychiatric disorders will plausibly affect agency. After all, many of these disorders are considered disorders, and not merely expressions of individual variability, precisely because they seem to affect agency in particular and recognizable ways that impede the flourishing of the individual both independently and in social contexts. For example, although depression is commonly referred to as a mood disorder, in addition to depressed affect, patients experience diminished motivation (an aspect of agency), irritability, rumination, and decreased self-control. All of these are or reflect aspects of agency. For example, motivation is what spurs us to act or exercise our agency, and lowered motivation leads to a lessening of our exercise of agency; irritability is an expression of negative affect, but may also affect aspects of agency such as impulsivity and control: whether one is able to ignore or overlook unwanted stimuli and whether ones is able to suppress certain, often maladaptive responses to them; rumination implies the inability to control unwanted thoughts; and self-control is executive control over one's actions. Several studies have shown that measures of agency are affected in depression (e.g., Corrigan & Schutte, 2023; Ehrenberg et al., 1991; Hobbs et al., 2009; Scott et al, 2022; Tapal et al., 2017). Moreover, several studies have suggested that increasing perceived agency may lessen the severity of depressive symptoms (Blazer, 2002; Cherewick et al., 2023; Hobbs et al., 2009; de Mol et al., 2018). Similar observations can be made for other neuropsychiatric disorders, albeit in different ways. For example, anxiety disorders often result from perceived lack of control over one's environment and over one's own responses to it (Gallagher & Trigg, 2016; Hoehn-Saric & McLeod, 1985); obsessive-compulsive disorder (OCD) appears to have other connections to agency, with patients prone to intruding thoughts and driven to compensate for the resulting anxiety with ritualistic actions (Fradkin & Huppert, 2018; Fradkin et al., 2019; Gentsch et al., 2012; Szalai, 2019). OCD symptom severity also correlates with agency scores on some measures (Tapal et al., 2017), and some treatments for OCD focus on reestablishing the patient's sense of control over the disruptive thoughts and emotions (Szalai, 2019). If we can sketch the ways in which agency are implicated and impacted by these disorders, they might be usefully conceptualized as disorders of agency, each with its own fingerprint or signature (Malik et al., 2022; Roskies, 2015).

In what follows, we describe the design and deployment of the AAT, the preliminary results from our dataset, and subsequent ideas for thinking about causation in psychiatry. We start with conceptual foundations and assumptions.

35.1 Agency: Foundational Assumptions

To evaluate whether neuropsychiatric diseases and effective treatment affect agency, we need to have a way of characterizing and measuring agency. Such a task is daunting, for the simple reason that there is no agreed-on definition of agency, and the concept seems singularly broad and ill-defined. The project must start with conceptual foundations (Goffin, 2000).

35.1.1 A Dimensional Approach

What is agency, and how can we answer this question without already knowing the answer? At its foundation, all agree that agency involves the capacity to act. But this agreement does not get us far, nor can it without a nuanced view of action. Do simple organisms act? Do machines? A clear view of action could lead to a conception of agency that is binary: something either is or is not an agent. However, even this would seem too simplistic a framework to be useful, for there are many things we may agree are agents, yet they differ so greatly in their capacities that it still would be important to be able to make distinctions among them. Better would be to hold that agentive things may have more or less agency (see, e.g., Petrolini, 2020 for a view of an agency spectrum). However, especially when one thinks of human agency, it seems that there are many aspects to agency, and it would be difficult to ordinally rank individuals. Is an agent with more motivation but less self-control more or less of an agent than one with the opposite profile? We assume that agency is not a binary category, or even a scalar one. To capture the richness of agency we think humans exhibit, we postulate that agency is a concept that can be characterized as having multiple dimensions. In other words, there is a multidimensional agency space. However, precisely what those dimensions are remains unclear. We aim to develop a test that can sample a broad agency space, to see how populations vary along these dimensions, and to use this to better characterize agency space. Developing such an assay should allow us to characterize the agency signatures of different neuropsychiatric conditions and enable us to describe the nature of agentive changes resulting from various interventions, including neurointerventions, treating these conditions.

Whether or not neuropsychiatric conditions can be effectively characterized through the lens of agency is an empirical question. However, if neuropsychiatric diseases are usefully conceptualized as disorders of agency, then it follows effective treatment of those diseases will lead to changes in agency as part of symptom relief, and we should be able to see changes in agency pre- and post-treatment. Moreover, if agency is a mediating factor in depression, then plausibly effective treatment of depression could involve interventions on deficits in agency. That is, in addition to seeing the manifestation of treatment for these disorders in shifts in a person's location in "agency space," it may be the case that aspects of agency are themselves levers for treatment. Thus, understanding the nature of agency in more detail may suggest ways to intervene for therapeutic purposes. These questions and others can best be explored once we have developed assays for agency.

35.1.2 Capacitarianism about Agency

In conceiving of agency, we take a capacitarian approach. That is, we posit that agency is comprised of a set of capacities that enable an organism to act effectively and autonomously in its environment. These range from motor capacities that are required for physical action to capacities for motivation, planning, and control (i.e., executive functions). The capacities of an individual may vary over time and may be affected by a variety of factors, including age, health, environment, and so on. Capacities may vary across individuals and may be impacted by, or reflect, psychological and social factors. Although the label "capacitarianism" may not be familiar to the average reader, the capacitarian notion of agency implicitly underlies familiar social frameworks such as the foundations of moral and legal responsibility (Vincent, 2013). In our intuitive grasp of morality, agents are held morally responsible for their actions only when they had the capacity to act appropriately and failed to do so; young children are not blamed for misdeeds in the same way that older children and adults are. Similarly, legal responsibility presupposes a variety of cognitive and control capacities. The insanity defense and juvenile justice systems are both reflective of the way our notions of legal responsibility are responsive to the lesser capacities of the mentally impaired or cognitively immature. As it is exercises of our agency that are subject to moral and legal assessment, we adopt the approach that agency can be characterized by a collection of capacities for control and self-determination.

35.2 The AAT

Our main aim, to develop an assay of agency, or the AAT, was pursued by developing a self-report instrument that could be administered online via platforms such as Mechanical Turk and Prolific. The hope is that an online test will be easy to administer to multiple patient groups. In designing the AAT we drew broadly from philosophical literature on agency, from work in clinical and cognitive psychology, from clinical case studies and the medical literature, and from extant psychological tests for things like personality, self-control, self-efficacy, and so on to broadly sample agency space (i.e., to assure content validity). From these sources we tried to identify the sorts of factors that might be important to agency and to develop questions to probe these. We did not work from any particular conception of agency but did try to identify aspects of particular views that we could query to see how various aspects of agency might cohere, and if there were patterns of answers that could bear on particular views or theories. We were mindful of the pressing practical need to keep the questionnaire short enough that people would complete it and do so honestly and attentively.

The numbers of questions phrased pro-agentively (e.g., "I'm confident in my own abilities") and those phrased negatively (e.g., "I don't have a lot of self-respect") were approximately matched. We asked people to rank how strongly they agreed or disagreed with statements regarding these aspects of agency, using a Likert scale from 1–7, with 1 being *strongly agree*, 4 being *neutral*, and 7 being *strongly disagree*. We embedded in the AAT a number of data checks to be able to exclude participants who were pushing buttons quickly or randomly, such as asking the same question more than once or asking questions designed to be answered in opposite ways. Duplicate questions had to be answered within two Likert ratings, and questions that were reverse-polarity had to be within two ratings after reverse-coding, in order to pass the data checks.

In designing the AAT questions, we identified several aspects of agency that seem conceptually distinct and at least plausibly somewhat independent. Then we wrote questions aimed at probing these dimensions. Many of these intuitive dimensions were clearly related to agentive efficacy, and questions probed the extent to which the subjects felt they were or failed to be agentive in a particular respect. Other questions explored characteristics that have been postulated to be relevant to or indicative of agency, such as willingness to take or attribute responsibility, belief in free will or in higher powers, cognitive style, and so on. Mindful of framing effects and response bias, we framed questions in both positive and negative ways. While we won't detail here every aspect that we included, the following is a representative but not exhaustive chart of broad categories explored by the AAT.

> **Motor control.** Acting on the world is perhaps the most fundamental aspect of agency. Being able to act physically on the world is a central aspect of agency, and hampering one's ability to act leads to diminution in agency. That said, motor abilities enable an expression of agency but do not exhaust it, and some human agents lose the ability to move most of their

bodies yet retain other aspects of agency. (Example : I have the ability to carry out fine motor movements [i.e., writing, grooming, folding or buttoning clothing].)

Decision-making. Another essential aspect of agency is the ability to make rational decisions and to take steps to implement them. Related aspects of agency to decision-making are capacities to set goals and plan for the future. (Example: I can choose between options that are presented to me without much difficulty.)

Thought control. The ability to attend to what one wants to attend to, to break ruminative cycles and otherwise control aspects of one's cognitive life. (Example: I am satisfied with my ability to maintain focused attention.)

Emotional control. Human agents experience emotions and are affected by them to differing extents. How one acts is affected by what emotional states characterize our experience and the ability to control emotions that are nonadaptive or that impinge on our goals. (Example: Even when I'm fearful, I'm capable of calming myself down or pushing through it.)

Social embeddedness or relational agency. It has been increasingly recognized that people are essentially social creatures, and that one's agency is affected by the way in which they interact with others. Thus, relational agency is argued to be an important aspect of human agency. The AAT includes questions about social embeddedness and the way in which it influences aspects of agency. (Example: Most people in my life respect my ability to make my own choices.)

Cognitive style. Questions probed need for cognition, relative reliance on reason versus emotion. (Example: I prefer to reason out my decisions rather than relying on intuition or emotion.)

Philosophical worldview. Including beliefs about free will, religion, fate, and the like. (Example: Free will is a basic part of human nature.)

Life control and authorship. Questions concerning how much a person felt in control of the direction their lives took. (Example: I am the author of my life's story, at least to a considerable extent.)

Temporal continuity. The extent to which a person identified with past and future selves. (Example: I am fundamentally the same person that I was three years ago.)

We soon discovered that none of the online platforms guarantee or validate self-reported medical or mental health conditions, necessitating that we embed assessment scales in the AAT test session. Once we included diagnostic screening questions in the survey, it became apparent that the survey was too long: subjects failed to finish the survey and/or the data suggested that they were no longer thinking about their answer. Thus, we realized that the questions had to be winnowed to acquire useful datasets. We thus condensed the AAT to 144 questions both on conceptual grounds and based on strong correlations among thematically related questions.

We were interested in assessing both objective aspects of agency, such as whether individuals have motor deficits or problems with response inhibition, and the subjective sense of agency (SoA), which concerns the subjects' experience of their own agency, which has figured prominently in some recent discussions in neuroscience and psychology. However, since we were restricted to collecting data online, even objective aspects of agency as probed by the AAT questions are still reported by the subject and thus may be colored by their own self-conception, memory effects, and so forth. We therefore implemented several behavioral tests to administer online alongside the survey with the thought that these may more objectively corroborate some of the self-report items. For example, we implemented Stop-signal and go/no-go tasks to measure inhibitory capacities. However, despite piloting seven tasks, we soon determined that the data from these tasks, when implemented on an online platform, required more time on task than subjects were willing to give, and/or results were too noisy to be of much use in corroborating the AAT. Consequently, we will not be discussing those results here. However, we acknowledge that even AAT questions designed to ask about objective matters may elicit answers that are inaccurate for a number of reasons, not the least of which that they may be affected by a subject's agentive profile, so all we report are subjective measures. In addition, we note that the AAT was designed to assess decontextualized or non-situational agency, or agency beliefs that are general and not tied to a specific action performance (see also Tapal et al., 2017). Non-situational agency is postulated to be more stable and trait related than more variable measures of contextual agency that are known to fluctuate on short timescales and can be affected by reward and punishment information related to task-related agentive success and other factors (Dewey & Knoblich, 2014; Kumar & Srinivasan, 2013).

Finally, we recognized that in trying to characterize agency space we faced the Scylla and Charibdis of two opposing pitfalls: first, the pitfall of failing to recognize or sample parts of agency space that were important to agency (that is, being blind to aspects of agency); and second, including as part of the agency characterization aspects or capacities that are in fact not relevant to agency at all. These questions will be important to come back to, but ultimately they are philosophical questions without definitive empirical answers. Keeping in mind the fact that both these dangers exist, and concordant with the history of science showing that theoretical constructs are not borne whole-cloth but are iteratively refined with the interplay of theory and measurement (see Chang, 2004), we moved forward with a preliminary collection of 221 questions in the AAT.

35.3 AAT Methods and Results

The AAT was administered online via Amazon Mechanical Turk, Qualtrics, and Prolific, and recruitment was done within those platforms. For the results we discuss here, a total of 2,466 adults who reported no history of reading disability and a minimum eighth-grade reading level took the questionnaire. Of this population, 56% were female, 42% male, and 2% gender nonconforming/other. There was a broad spread of ages (18–24: 12%; 25–34: 26%; 35–49: 34%; 50–64; 19%; 65 and older: 9%) and race and ethnicity (white: 75%; black: 9%; other: 16%; 21% reported Hispanic or Latino ethnicity). In addition to the AAT itself, participants were asked about any past or active diagnosis of a mental condition, and as part of the survey they filled out self-assessments for neuropsychiatric symptoms. All 2,466 participants filled out the Generalized Anxiety Disorder-7 (GAD7; Spitzer et al., 2006) and the Patient Health Questionnaire-9 (PHQ9; Kroenke et al., 1999) as measures of the severity of their anxiety and depression. While all 2,468 participants filled out the PHQ9 and the GAD7, only 1,878 participants filled out the self-report Yale-Brown Obsessive-Compulsive Scale (YBOC; Goodman et al., 1989) as a measure for OCD symptom experience.

Assessment scores on the PHQ9 range from 0 to 27, where scores of 1–4 indicate minimal depression, 5–9 mild depression, 10–14 moderate depression, 15–19 moderately severe depression, and 20–27 severe depression. Assessment scores on the GAD7 range from 0 to 21, where scores of 1–4 indicate minimal anxiety, 5–9 mild anxiety, 10–14 moderate anxiety, and 15–21 severe anxiety. Assessment scores on the YBOC Checklist range from 0 to 40, where scores of 0–7 indicate subclinical symptoms, 8–15 mild, 16–23 moderate, 24–31 severe, and 32–40 extreme OCD symptoms.

As is common with these conditions, there were significant comorbidities, with only a small number of participants scoring highly on only the anxiety, depression, or OCD assessments. To best visualize the overall impact of neuropsychiatric symptoms on agency, we ran a factor analysis on a sample that included both "control" participants whose scores on the self-assessments indicated no symptom experiences related to anxiety, depression, or OCD (less than 5 on GAD7 and PHQ-9 and less than 8 on YBOC) and participants whose scores indicated symptom experiences of all three conditions (greater than 5 on GAD7 and PHQ-9 and greater than 8 on YBOC). For this analysis, we excluded individuals that scored highly on only one or two of the GAD7, PHQ9, or YBOC. This yielded results from 268 control subjects and 977 anxiety/depression/OCD subjects.

35.4 Analysis and Preliminary Results

35.4.1 Factor Analysis

We ran a scree plot on the data, which indicated that four factors account for approximately 35% of the variance. We ran a factor analysis with four components using an oblique rotation. This non-orthogonal rotation was chosen because it allows for factors to be correlated. We think it implausible that dimensions of agency will all be independent. Since none of the questions loaded on the fourth factor above a level of .5, we discuss the first three factors.

Figure 35.1 shows participants' loadings on the first three factors, plotted in three-dimensional space. Separation between the groups was observed across the different factors, indicating that they occupied different regions in the multidimensional "agency" space. Figure 35.1(a) shows individual participants grayscale-coded by their GAD7 scores. Figure 35.1 (b) shows individual participants grayscale-coded by their PHQ-9 scores. Figure 35.1(c) shows individual participants grayscale-coded by their YBOCS scores. The relatively smooth variation in shade shows that the factor loadings in agency space predict diagnostic scores fairly well, especially for GAD7 and PHQ-9. To understand the nature of the factors identified, we looked at factor loadings. The questions that loaded onto one of the factors with greater than or equal to a value of .5 are shown in Figure 35.2.

Analysis of the content of the highly loading questions reveals that the first factor is associated with questions concerning self-efficacy, confidence, self-identification, and other positive, intuitively pro-agentive characteristics. In contrast, the questions that weighed most heavily on the second factor were questions pertaining mainly to emotional regulation. Questions weighing heavily on the third factor were almost all concerned with risk and novelty, and although they accounted for variance in the population, they did not help separate the different clinical populations

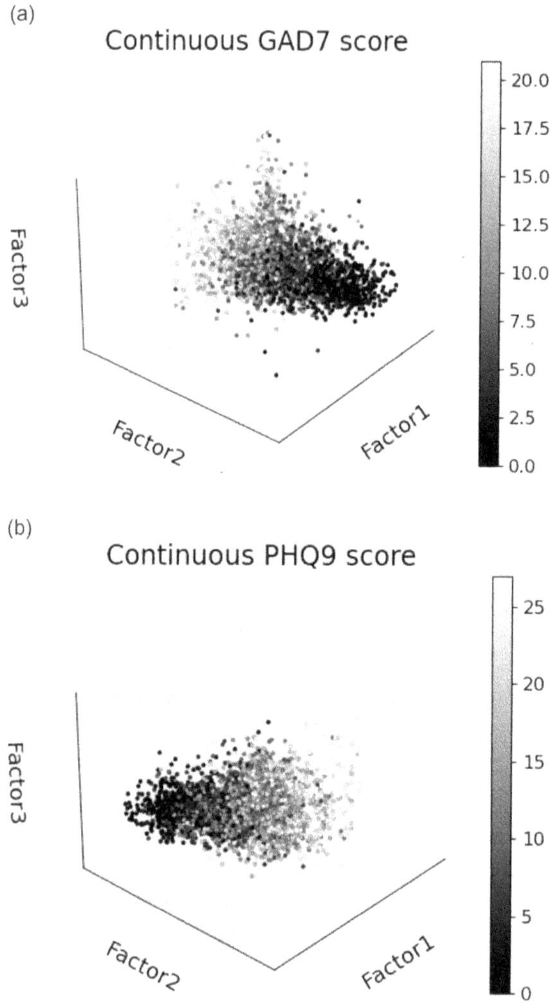

Figure 35.1 Plot of individual participants' on the first three factors coded by their scores on the diagnostic tests. Plots show that scores vary fairly smoothly will location in this agency space. (a) GAD7 scores; (b) PHQ-9 scores; (c) YBOCS scores.

(c)

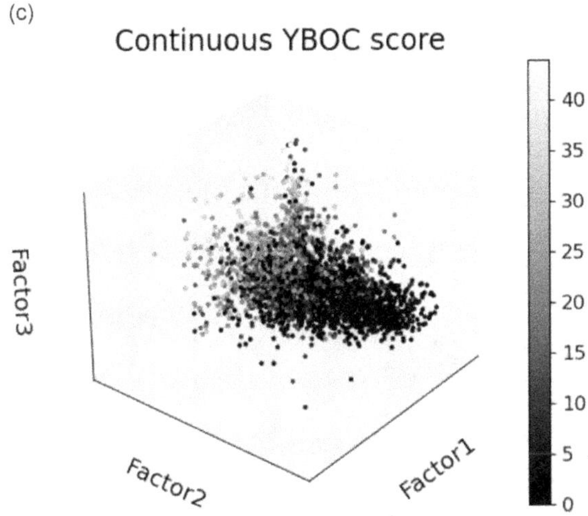

Figure 35.1 (*cont.*)

from controls. The fact that most of the variance was captured by the first two factors was surprising to us, as we expected more structure in the data.

35.4.2 Network Analysis

To further explore structure in the data, we ran a network analysis of the participant responses and their scores on the GAD7, PHQ9, and YBOC. We used EBICglasso to estimate a network of partial correlation coefficients or conditional independence associations between nodes and constructed graphical models of the results. Network analysis was run in JASP (JASP Team [2023] Version 0.18.1). The network graphs that JASP produces are based on the R package qgraph (Epskamp et al., 2012).

We initially ran each question as an individual node in the network, but the resulting network was too big to be interpretable. To reduce the number of nodes, we grouped the questions into conceptually similar groups. We extracted 16 different groups of conceptually related questions (mostly the same as identified earlier): motor control, life control, emotional control, thought control, impulse control, authenticity, motivation and goal pursuit, self-trust and optimism, relational agency, need for cognition, cognitive style (reason versus emotion), attitudes to novelty

Factor 1 – "Positive" Agency

Loading	AAT Question
.75	I live in accordance with my values and beliefs.
.71	Most of my decisions are consistent with my deep commitments.
.69	I have the ability to form my own character.
.66	I have free will.
.66	I usually take measures to achieve my goals.
.66	When faced with a touch decision, I carefully consider the pros and cons.
.64	Free will is a basic part of human nature.
.63	I try to use the same moral criteria to judge myself as I use to judge others.
.63	I am who I am due to my own choices.
.63	I am still an author of my story, even if others play a role.
.62	I generally feel very present in my life.
.61	Every person is responsible for their own actions.
.60	Even when I'm fearful, I'm capable of calming myself down or pushing through it.
.60	I trust my own perceptions of the world.
.59	I see my life as an ongoing project that is continuous and coherent.
.59	I am able to negotiate boundaries of my private spaces in a way that is comfortable to me.
.59	I try to identify and do what makes me happy.
.59	I am the author of my life's story, at least to a considerable extent.
.58	I know how to look at my emotions from a more objective perspective.
.57	The skills I've developed and my abilities are central to who I am.
.56	I have ability to initiate gross motor movements (walking, running, throwing, ect.).
.55	My actions align with my beliefs.
.55	The shape of my life so far informs my choices today.
.55	I am in full control of what I do.
.55	I have the ability to carry out fine motor movements (writing, grooming, folding or buttoning clothes, ect.).
.54	Even though I've grown and changed, who I am at my core stays constant.
.54	Most people in my life respect my ability to make my own choices.
.54	I take responsibility for my mistakes.
.53	When faced with a moral choice, I will do the right thing even if it is the more difficult course of action.
.52	I have control over my body.

Factor 2: "Negative" Agency

Loading	AAT Question
.62	Fear keeps me from doing projects that are important to me.
.61	I have trouble functioning due to anxiety.
.60	I find myself in emotional ruts that I don't know how to get out of.
.59	There are thoughts that won't go away even when I try to get rid of them.
.58	I sometimes do things and I don't understand why I'm doing them.
.57	I feel like I'm just going through the motions.
.57	I can become overwhelmed by sadness.
.57	My behavior sometimes doesn't make sense to me.
.55	I have trouble motivating myself.
.54	I feel like I'm trapped in my life and have very little ability to change anything.
.52	I find myself doing things without really willing them.
.51	I feel alienated from myself.
.51	I lost interest partway through projects.
.50	I worry too much.

Factor 3: Risk-taking

Loading	AAT Question
.80	I take risks that could have harmful physical consequences.
.79	I take risks that could harm me.
.69	I engage in dangerous social behaviors.
.68	I take risks that could harm others.
.64	I take risks that could have legal consequences.
.62	I take risks that could have financial consequences.

Factor 4

No questions loaded onto Factor four with a value of equal to or greater than .5

Figure 35.2 Questions that loaded onto one of the factors with greater than or equal to a value of .5.

and risk, temporal continuity, attitudes to morality, responsibility attribution, and belief in free will. Likert scores for questions pertaining to each of the groups were averaged together (and appropriately reverse-coded). We then recoded the Likert scores to range from +3 to −3, with 0 being neutral. In addition to 16 groups of questions, three other nodes were supplied by the average GAD7, PHQ9, and YBOC scores.

When questions were grouped according to themes reflecting the 16 different categories, a structure emerged that showed a core set of highly positively connected nodes that contribute to self-efficacy, and then other nodes with fewer or less strong connections that appear more peripheral, including relational agency, belief in free will, and cognitive style (Figure 35.3). There seem to be two subnetworks that are more strongly connected with each other than with most nodes in the other subnetwork: one consisting of the self-efficacy nodes mentioned, and the other involving authenticity and impulse control as well as attitudes toward morality and responsibility attribution. The main negative connections are seen between the nodes and the scores on the diagnostic tests, although some negative connections are seen in the main network.

The central nodes related to self-efficacy were life control, motor control, thought control, emotional control, self-trust, motivation, and goal pursuit, all strongly interconnected. Life control and self-trust/optimism emerged as having the highest expected influence. Less central were other nodes, including relational agency, and attitudes to novelty and risk. Attitudes to morality and responsibility also emerged as having high expected influence, forming the core of what seems to be a loosely connected subnetwork.

We also found that when we included nodes for overall score on the diagnostic tests (GAD7, PHQ9, YBOC), we found that those clustered together, with GAD7 and PHQ9 being most closely apposed, as would be expected given the overlap in the population. Moreover, the agency nodes aligned in ways that would be expected with these clinical scores: PHQ9 scores (indicating depression) were most strongly negatively associated with motivation and goal pursuit; GAD7 scores (indicating anxiety) were most strongly negatively associated with scores on emotional control; YBOC scores (reflecting OCD symptoms) were most strongly negatively associated with scores on thought control. The fact that the diagnostic scores covaried most strongly with the putative dimensions of agency known to be affected in the diseases they are used to diagnose suggests that the network structures that emerge from this analysis describe real relationships. This provides reason to think that some of the more

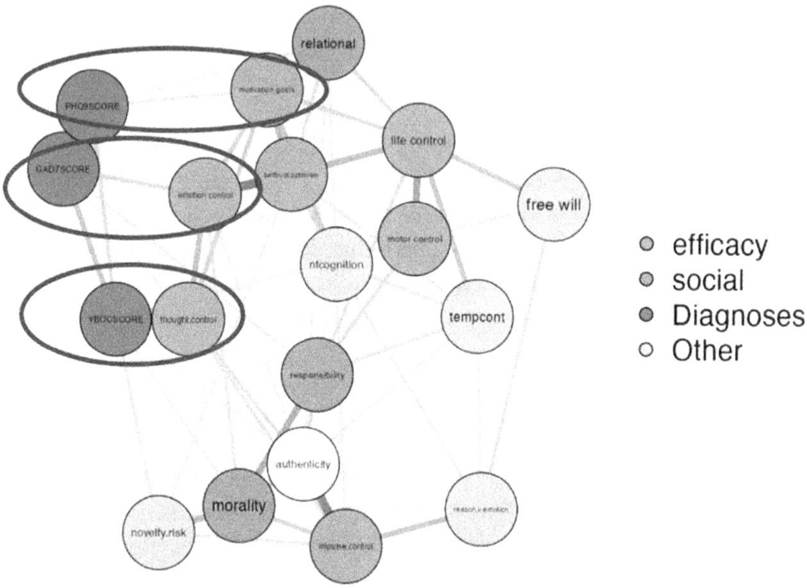

Figure 35.3 A network analysis was done on the averaged scores for 16 different groups of conceptually related questions: motor control, life control, emotional control, thought control, impulse control, authenticity, motivation and goal pursuit, self-trust and optimism, relational agency, need for cognition, cognitive style (reason versus emotion), attitudes to novelty and risk, temporal continuity, attitudes to morality, responsibility attribution, and belief in free will. Particularly strong connections were seen between the scores on the diagnostic tests and categories that make sense, such as a negative connection between anxiety measures and (positive) emotional control; between depression scores and (positive) motivation and goal setting/pursuit; and between OCD measures and thought control. A set of positively connected categories that broadly involve control across various domains is central to this network.

surprising structural features of the networks may be signal and not noise. What we report here is merely preliminary and requires more analysis and confirmation in additional datasets, but we think it is suggestive.

35.5 Discussion

Results of administering the AAT to subjects through an online platform show that different neuropsychiatric populations can be roughly classified on the basis of their responses to the AAT. This suggests that agency is impacted in particular ways by different disorders, as hypothesized. The items that weighed heavily on the first factor included a variety of questions that intuitively were related to personal efficacy and autonomy along a number of different intuitive dimensions (negative items were reverse-coded). Items weighing heavily on the second factor were primarily related to emotional regulation. The third factor included items related to attitudes toward risk. Interestingly, although risk attitudes accounted for a significant percentage of variance in the total population, they did not significantly help separate the different clinical populations: knowing which clinical group someone was in did not help predict what their answers would be to the risk questions, or vice versa. Upon reflection, this is perhaps not surprising: it is difficult to assess how self-report of risky behavior and attitudes should be interpreted. For example, one might expect that people suffering from anxiety disorders or OCD would engage in less risky behavior than populations unaffected by extreme anxiety. On the other hand, these same populations might assess the riskiness of their behaviors on a different scale or in a different way than unaffected populations, so their self-reports of risky behavior could be exaggerated. Indeed, even in populations that do not manifest mental health challenges, people vary widely in their tolerance to risk and may differ greatly in the ways they do or do not engage in risky behaviors. For example, some people may thrive on physical risk associated with adventure sports yet have little appetite for financial risk, while others may show a reverse pattern. Our data suggest these self-report measures are unreliable for characterizing different clinical populations.

The results of the factor analysis on our initial dataset are consonant with the results of Tapal et al. (2017), who reported two dimensions of variation on a limited 11-item survey regarding agency (or self-efficacy). They identified their dimensions as a positive sense of agency (PsoA) and a negative sense of agency (NsoA). Because the items from their survey were limited and did not explore many potential aspects of agency, they did not identify the NSoA items in a more fine-grained way, and thus did not identify the dimension with emotional regulation. In addition, as they did not include risk questions in their 11 items, they did not see the other component of variance that we observed.

The concordance with their study provides additional evidence about the robustness of our results. However, given our more ampliative view of the concept of agency, and our much more fine-grained method of assessing it, it was a surprise to us that factor analysis showed that just three factors were sufficient to capture 35% of the variance in the population. After all, we constructed the AAT with a variety of intuitive dimensions of agency in mind, and one might expect that those dimensions, or other less intuitive ones, would become evident in the analysis. Why is there not more structure in the data? Several possibilities come to mind. First, that agency really is comprised of two factors, one related to self-efficacy and control and the other to aspects of emotional control and self-regulation that are not merely inverted in sign but occupy another axis in agency space. If that is the case, and if our results track with the results of Tapal and colleagues (this is something that we are currently testing), perhaps agency is a less complex construct than we initially imagined, and a much more abbreviated measure of agency than we are using is sufficient to capture agency, something along the lines suggested by Tapal et al. However, there are a few reasons that lead us to resist this interpretation, at least for the present.

First, we were hampered in our ability to collect data with subjects drawn from a wide variety of clinical populations from which we initially wanted to collect data. Instead, we only were able to recruit significant numbers of subjects with high scores on measures of anxiety, depression, and OCD, and even then with significant overlap among these populations. Thus, if the agency signatures provide the fault lines along which the factor analysis would identify structure, there may not be enough diversity in our populations to discern further structure in agency space. For this reason, additional data with different clinical populations could lead to a quite different picture of agency than we get with this limited sample. Second, as originally conceived, this project would ideally incorporate data from clinical neurointervention studies. The project was begun just prior to the COVID-19 pandemic, just as clinicians suspended in-person work with clinical populations and DBS surgeries were indefinitely postponed. These pandemic-related disruptions prevented us from collecting data about the agentive effects of neurointerventions. We suspect that the differences in agency profiles prior to and after treatment interventions could potentially provide additional levers for discerning structure in agency space. A third reason to suppose that there is more structure in agency space than the two factors found is that we used some conceptual agentive dimensions in constructing the AAT. After all, many of the questions were devised to explore specific dimension-like constructs, such as aspects of self-control, motivation and persistence, and cognitive style issues like need for cognition. Despite being conceptually related, conceptual clusters did not clearly emerge from the factor analysis (other than risk-related questions). We were nonetheless curious about whether such conceptual dimensions had any signature in the data at all.

We performed a network analysis to assess this question, and we found good reason to think there is further structure in the data. The fact that our analysis yielded expected relations among some of the postulated conceptual dimensions of agency and clinical diagnoses suggests that agency can be usefully fractionated, and that this might yield important clinical insights. Moreover, some of our expectations were violated by the emergent network structure. For example, two of the nodes initially postulated to be part of the core self-efficacy group – impulse control and authenticity – are not as central as the others just mentioned, and seem more closely related to the second subnetwork anchored by morality and responsibility and to cognitive style (reason versus emotion) than to the rest of the self-efficacy network. Also interesting is that belief in free will is associated with life control and cognitive style but also appears peripheral compared to the core network. Again, we stress that these are preliminary results and more needs to be done to understand and verify their relationships.

Let us now return to the animating question of this book and this resulting collection of chapters: the question of causation in psychiatry and philosophy. While there is not much here that leads directly to causal inferences, the methods described here could provide a rich source of data to test ideas about causation. As has been discussed previously in the literature regarding mental disorders and network modeling, network analysis itself does not imply, though it may suggest, direction of influence or causation. Are people depressed because of low motivation and low sense of self-efficacy, self-trust, and so forth, or do they have lower scores on related questions in the AAT because they are depressed? All we have here thus far is correlation, but even on conceptual grounds alone we may think the arrow of causation plausibly goes in both directions: low motivation may lead to depressive mood, and depression could in turn lessen motivation. Indeed, the idea that these factors may be mutually influential motivates much of the push for network analysis and level-free thinking in psychiatry. However, part of the reason that causation may seem to be difficult to discern in these analyses is that we are eliding temporal information in these kinds of studies, information that could provide more of a handle on underlying causal processes. In addition, by looking at aggregate scores on diagnostic tests we may be missing particular causal levers in our analysis. We note that additional analyses with our dataset may be able to address this. Thus, we should be thinking not just in terms of levels of analysis but in terms of temporal and spatial scales.

While our analysis only raises but does not settle any questions about causation, as the interventionist framework of causation suggests, if we could intervene on this network, we may be able to see patterns of change that give us insight into the causal structures at work. It would be of particular interest to compare networks of AAT results from the same cohort before and after a particular type of intervention, such as DBS or transcranial magnetic stimulation (TMS) treatment (another neurointervention, and one being explored as a treatment for depression), or to compare networks after two similar neurointerventions, such as two different DBS treatments for Parkinson's, one in the globus pallidus and one targeting the subthalamic nucleus. Do both types of DBS treatments lead to similar agency network changes, or do they affect the network in different ways? Using these methods, we could begin to dissect the kinds of changes that lead to improvements in mental health. Perhaps, for instance, a particular intervention would affect one or several nodes in the self-efficacy collection. One might see (or fail to see) a corresponding change in the PHQ9 scores, giving us some reason to think that type of control or efficacy did (or did not affect) depressive symptoms. One could also do a more granular analysis of how depression is affected by particular interventions by including in the network analysis scores on individual diagnostic questions rather than using a summed score, as is done here. In addition, although neuropsychiatric disorders and dimensions of agency may mutually interact, they may do so at different timescales: for instance, we could find that measures of agency change due to intervention prior to observing changes in diagnostic scores on the screening tests, which may lag behind for days or weeks; this temporal asymmetry would also be suggestive of causal influence. On the other hand, we might find that even after successful treatment, network structure is barely changed by a manipulation, even though scores on both AAT tests and mental health assessments improve across the board, suggesting a more nonspecific relation between agency nodes and mental health. Would finding that DBS in a particular location (modulo individual neuroanatomy) led to noticeable movement in agency space and/or scores on diagnostic tests lead us to adopt a more reductionist framework than would, for example, the same results seen with cognitive behavioral therapy? All this remains to be determined, but with the AAT we have a tool for exploring these kinds of questions.

We close with the question of how to think about agency space and its relation to mental illness. Suppose our initial hypothesis about agentive signatures of mental disorders is borne out. What does an association with a position in agency space and a mental disorder signify? One of the advantages of thinking in terms of agentive profiles is that they can reflect both internal (biological and psychological) and external (social and environmental) influences, allowing a move away from purely reductionist thinking. Is it fruitful to conceptualize mental illness as signaled by regions in agency space? Do agentive profiles of these illnesses merely reflect the hidden, possibly reductive factors that are the primary causes? Does it matter which of these views is correct? We think these are open questions of considerable interest, and we look forward to continued discussions on the role of causation in psychiatry.

REFERENCES

Blazer, D. G. (2002). Self-efficacy and depression in late life: A primary prevention proposal. *Aging and Mental Health, 6*(4):315–324. https://doi.org/10.1080/1360786021000006938

Bluhm, R., Cabrera, L., & McKenzie, R. (2019). What we (should) talk about when we talk about deep brain stimulation and personal identity. *Neuroethics, 13*(3), 289–301. https://doi.org/10.1007/s12152-019-09396-6

Campbell, J. (2007). An interventionist approach to causation in psychology. In A. Gopnik & L. Schulz (Eds.), *Causal learning: Psychology, philosophy, and computation* (pp. 58–66). Oxford University Press. https://doi.org/10.1093/acprof:oso/9780195176803.003.0005

Chang, H. (2004). *Inventing temperature: Measurement and scientific progress.* Oxford University Press.

Cherewick, M., Hipp, E., Njau, P., & Dahl, R. E. (2023). Growth mindset, persistence, and self-efficacy in early adolescents: Associations with depression, anxiety, and externalising behaviours. *Global Public Health, 1*, 2213300. https://doi.org/10.1080/17441692.2023.2213300

Corrigan, J. A., & Schutte, N. S. (2023). The relationships between the hope dimensions of agency thinking and pathways thinking with depression and anxiety: A meta-analysis. *International Journal of Applied Positional Psychology, 8*, 211–255. https://doi.org/10.1007/s41042–023-00099-1

De Mol, J., D'Alcantara, A., & Cresti, B. (2018). Agency of depressed adolescents: Embodiment and social representations. *International Journal of Qualitative Studies on Health and Well-being, 13*(Suppl. 1),1564516. https://doi.org/10.1080/17482631.2018.1564516

Dewey, J. A., & Knoblich, G. (2014). Do implicit and explicit measures of the sense of agency measure the same thing? *PLoS One, 9*, E110118. https://doi.org/10.1371/journal.pone.0110118

Ehrenberg, M. F., Cox, D. N., & Koopman, R. F. (1991). The relationship between self-efficacy and depression in adolescents. *Adolescence, 26*, 361.

Epskamp, S., Borsboom, D., & Fried, E. I. (2018). Estimating psychological networks and their accuracy: A tutorial paper. *Behavior Research Methods, 50*(1), 195–212.

Epskamp, S., Cramer, A. O., Waldorp, L. J., Schmittmann, V. D., & Borsboom, D. (2012). qgraph: Network visualizations of relationships in psychometric data. *Journal of Statistical Software, 48*(4), 1–18.

Fradkin, I., Eitam, B., Strauss, A. Y., & Huppert, J. D. (2019). Thoughts as unexpected intruders: Context, obsessive-compulsive symptoms, and the sense of agency over thoughts. *Clinical Psychological Science, 7*(1), 162–180.

Fradkin, I., & Huppert, J. D. (2018). When our train of thought goes off track: The different facets of out-of-context thoughts in obsessive compulsive disorder. *Journal of Obsessive-Compulsive and Related Disorders, 18*, 31–39.

Galang, C. M., Malik, R., Kinley, I., & Obhi, S. S. (2021). Studying sense of agency online: Can intentional binding be observed in uncontrolled online settings? *Conscious Cognition, 95*, 103217. https://doi.org/10.1016/j.concog.2021.103217

Gallagher, S., & Trigg, D. (2016). Agency and anxiety: Delusions of control and loss of control in schizophrenia and agoraphobia. *Frontiers in Human Neuroscience, 10*, 459. https://doi.org/10.3389/fnhum.2016.00459

Gentsch, A., Schütz-Bosbach, S., Endrass, T., & Kathmann, N. (2012). Dysfunctional forward model mechanisms and aberrant sense of agency in obsessive-compulsive disorder. *Biological Psychiatry, 71*(7), 652–659.

Gentsch, A., & Synofzik, M. (2014). Affective coding: The emotional dimension of agency. *Frontiers in Human Neuroscience, 12*(8), 608. https://doi.org/10.3389/fnhum.2014.00608

Gilbert, F., Brown, Dasgupta, Martens, Klein, & Goering. (2019). An instrument to capture the phenomenology of implantable brain device use. *Neuroethics, 14*(Suppl. 3), S333–S340. https://doi.org/10.1007/s12152-019-09422-7

Gilbert, F., & Viana, J. N. (2018). A personal narrative on living and dealing with psychiatric symptoms after DBS surgery. *Narrative Inquiry in Bioethics, 8*(1), 67–77.

Gilbert, F., Goddard, E., Viaña, J. N. M., Carter, A., & Horne, M. (2017). I miss being me: Phenomenological effects of deep brain stimulation. *AJOB Neuroscience, 8*(2), 96–109. https://doi.org/10.1080/21507740.2017.1320319

Goffin, R. D., & Helmes, E. (Eds.). (2000). *Problems and solutions in human assessment: Honoring Douglas N. Jackson at seventy.* Kluwer Academic/Plenum Publishers. https://doi.org/10.1007/978-1-4615-4397-8

Goodman, W. K., Price, L. H., Rasmussen, S. A., Mazure, C., Fleischmann, R. L., Hill, C. L., Heninger, G. R., & Charney, D. S. (1989). *Yale-Brown Obsessive Compulsive Scale (YBOCS).* APA PsycTests.

Hirsch, J. K., Sirois, F. M., & Lyness, J. M. (2011). Functional impairment and depressive symptoms in older adults: Mitigating effects of hope. *British Journal of Health Psychology, 16*(4), 744–760. https://doi.org/10.1111/j.2044-8287.2010.02012.x

Hobbs, M., & McLaren, S. (2009). The interrelations of agency, depression, and suicidal ideation among older adults. *Suicide and Life-Threatening Behavior, 39*(2), 161–171. https://doi.org/10.1521/suli.2009.39.2.161

Hoehn-Saric, R., & McLeod, D. R. (1985). Locus of control in chronic anxiety disorders. *Acta Psychiatrica Scandinavica, 72*(6), 529–535. https://doi.org/10.1111/j.1600-0447.1985.tb02650.x

Kaiser, J., Buciuman, M., Gigl, S., Gentsch, A., & Schütz-Bosbach, S. (2021). The interplay between affective processing and sense of agency during action regulation: A review. *Frontiers in Psychology, 16*(12), 716220. https://doi.org/10.3389/fpsyg.2021.716220

Karsh, N., Eitam, B., Mark, I., & Higgins, E. T. (2016). Bootstrapping agency: How control-relevant information affects motivation. *Journal of Experimental Psychology and Genetics, 145*, 1333–1350. https://doi.org/10.1037/xge0000212

Kraemer, F. (2013). Authenticity or autonomy? When deep brain stimulation causes a dilemma. *Journal of Medical Ethics, 39*(12), 757–760. https://doi.org/10.1136/medethics-2011-100427

Kroenke, K., Spitzer, R. L., & Williams, J. B. W. (1999). *Patient Health Questionnaire-9 (PHQ-9)*. APA PsycTests.

Kumar, D., & Srinivasan, N. (2013). Hierarchical control and sense of agency: Differential effects of control on implicit and explicit measures of agency. In *Proceedings of 35th Annual Meeting of the Cognitive Science Society* (Vol. 35, pp. 2790–2795). Cognitive Science Society.

Lewis, C. J., Maier, F., Horstkotter, N., et al. (2014). Subjectively perceived personality and mood changes associated with subthalamic stimulation in patients with Parkinson's disease. *Psychological Medicine, 45*(1), 73–85.

Lozano, A. M., Lipsman, N., Bergman, H., Brown, P., Chabardes, S., Chang, J. W., Matthews, K., McIntyre, C. C., Schlaepfer, T. E., Schulder, M., Temel, Y., Volkmann, J., & Krauss, J. K. (2019). Deep brain stimulation: Current challenges and future directions. *Nature Reviews Neurology, 15*(3), 148–160. https://doi.org/10.1038/s41582-018-0128-2

Malik, R. A., Galang, C. M., & Finger, E. (2022). The sense of agency for brain disorders: A comprehensive review and proposed framework. *Neuroscience Biobehavioral Reviews, 139*, 104759. https://doi.org/10.1016/j.neubiorev.2022.104759

Mehta, M. M., Na, S., Gu, X., Murrough, J. W., & Morris, L. S. (2023). Reward-related self-agency is disturbed in depression and anxiety. *PLoS One, 18*(3), e0282727. https://doi.org/10.1371/journal.pone.0282727

Petrolini, V. (2020). Too much or too little? Disorders of agency on a spectrum. *European Journal of Analytic Philosophy, 16*(2), 79–99.

Rescorla, M. (2018). An interventionist approach to psychological explanation. *Synthese, 195*, 1909–1940.

Roskies, A. L. (2015). Agency and intervention. *Philosophical Transactions of the Royal Society B, 370*(1677), 20140215. https://doi.org/10.1098/rstb.2014.0215

Schermer, M. (2011). Ethical issues in deep brain stimulation. *Frontiers in Integrative Neuroscience, 5*. https://doi.org/10.3389/fnint.2011.00017

Scott, N. J., Ghanem, M., Beck, B., & Martin, A. K. (2022). Depressive traits are associated with a reduced effect of choice on intentional binding. *Conscious Cognition, 105*, 103412. https://doi.org/10.1016/j.concog.2022.103412

Slaby, J., Paskaleva, A., & Stephan, A. (2013). Enactive emotion and impaired agency in depression. *Journal of Consciousness Studies, 20*, 7–8.

Spitzer, R. L., Kroenke, K., Williams, J. B. W., & Löwe, B. (2006). A brief measure for assessing generalized anxiety disorder: the GAD-7. *Archives of Internal Medicine, 166*(10), 1092–1097.

Szalai, J. (2019). The sense of agency in OCD. *Review of Philosophy and Psychology, 10*(2), 363–380. https://doi.org/10.1007/s13164-017-0371-2

Tapal, A., Oren, E., Dar, R., & Eitam, B. (2017). The sense of agency scale: A measure of consciously perceived control over one's mind, body, and the immediate environment. *Frontiers in Psychology, 12*(8), 1552. https://doi.org/10.3389/fpsyg.2017.01552

Vincent, N. (2013). *Neuroscience and legal responsibility*. Oxford University Press.

Witt, K., Kuhn, J., Timmermann, L., Zurowski, M., & Woopen, C. (2013). Deep brain stimulation and the search for identity. *Neuroethics, 6*(3), 499–511. https://doi.org/10.1007/s12152-011-9100-1

Woodward, J. (2003). *Making things happen: A theory of causal explanation.* Oxford University Press.

Woodward, J., & Hitchcock, C. (2003). Explanatory generalizations, part I: A counterfactual account. *Noûs, 37*(1), 1–24. https://doi.org/10.1111/1468-0068.00426

CHAPTER 36

Commentary on Roskies, Busch, and Walton's "Agency as a Framework for Thinking about Neuropsychiatric Disease"

Josef Parnas

In their chapter, Roskies, Busch, and Walton present the first phase of a very ambitious project aiming at examination of the causal role of agency in mental disorders. The project is daunting because there are several unknowns. First, there is an issue of making a definition of agency and its variants. Next, it would be necessary to examine those variants across different clinical populations. Finally, there is a need to see whether modulating agency through brain stimulation leads to changes in the psychiatric condition. The authors frame their project within the model of interventionist approach. It is a complex project because this approach requires that all confounding and correlated influences and effects are kept under control. Moreover, it is not clear that the efficacy of deep brain stimulation, which is so successful in the treatment of chronic dystonia, Parkinson's disease, and some forms of epilepsy, is equally effective in treating mental disorders such as depressive disorder, schizophrenia, or obsessive-compulsive disorder (OCD).

Agency is indeed a very polysemic concept. Recently I encountered a paper about agency in pastoral tribes in the Sahel region where the concept was obviously used on a sociopolitical level. The authors propose a capacitarian view of agency that in their description is close to a description of a human being and their existence. These issues have been extensively dealt with in a fundamental ontology of the human being (Heidegger, 1953). According to Heidegger, a human being is Dasein (from the German: *Da* = there and *Sein* = being) – that is "being there." It signifies that a human being cannot be thought of apart from the world. Dasein is always already situated, and this situatedness is to a large extent not of their own doing. Dasein's own being is a matter of concern. Thus, Dasein is futuristically oriented, and human existence is framed by intentional directedness (*Sicht*). Dasein is always involved in projecting itself ahead of itself. This projection is determined by a coordination of affordances and desire. Phenomenology considers agency at different levels of ontological thickness. At the most basic level our self-awareness is characterized by a sense of spontaneity. This a very old philosophical term, and although we are all familiar with its meaning, it is very difficult to define. According to Sartre (2018), spontaneity of consciousness is consciousness of spontaneity. This agentive background is transformed to an agentive action through desire (Bernet, 2020). However, desire is never something exclusively subjective but very much context dependent, where affordances or obstacles modulate the desire. Thus, the world entices us to act. It is therefore conceptually very difficult to make distinctions between "objective agency" and "subjective agency" as the authors do at some places without clearly explaining the meaning of the terms. It is also dubious to talk about variance of agency that are relational or context independent.

The authors argue for the possibility that the affection of agency may play a crucial role in mental disorders. For example, they claim that "in depression there is a depressive affect, decreased motivation, irritability, ruminations and decreased self-control." All these features are considered as being expressive of specific changes in agency. Each one disturbs agency in its own peculiar way. It seems that the authors are inspired by diagrams from network analyses. From a clinical point of view, however, to say that depression involves a depressed mood as well as decreased motivation does not make a lot of sense. A truly depressed patient – that is, a patient with a clinical depression – is always characterized by a disorder of agency, and this feature is an integral part of the very meaning of the word "depression." The authors are very wise not to consider agency as a real kind, but rather a vague entity with multiple aspects, which they call dimensions.

The chapter describes in detail the development of agency assessment tests. Psychiatry has so far produced more psychometric scales than there are psychiatric patients on this planet, without a substantial effect on clinical practice or scientific progress. The authors use an internet approach, and psychopathology is assessed through scales, for example a scale for depression. When Max Hamilton developed his Hamilton Depression Scale, he was adamant that one could not arrive at a diagnosis of depression by using his scale. The purpose of his scale was to measure a change during treatment. Unfortunately, Hamilton's scale became incorporated into many other scales of diagnostic kind as well as entered the diagnostic manuals, where a sufficient number of depressive symptoms results in a diagnosis of depression. Today we are confronted with a situation where many patients have this diagnosis without being clinically considered to be in a depressed state. These people are frustrated for one reason or another. Something similar can be said about scales for anxiety.

OCD is even more complicated because many of the patients so diagnosed today actually suffer from a schizophrenia spectrum disorder (Rasmussen & Parnas, 2022). Perhaps it would be fruitful to conduct in-depth personal interviews with patients diagnosed by expert clinicians and extract from such interviews the modes in which agency appears to be affected. Two very interesting potential candidates for the study of agency are schizophrenia and melancholic depression. In the former there are multiple features affecting agency, such as diminished desire and interest, disorders of selfhood including ownership and agency, and a very peculiar psychological state of ambivalence. In the latter, there is an "inhibition" that is widely misunderstood today, but which refers to a temporal slowing of mental and motor processes. In addition, there is a clinically very significant feature of a profound insufficiency (*Unvermöglichkeit*).

In sum, the authors have a long and difficult but perhaps ultimately fruitful journey ahead of them.

REFERENCES

Bernet, R. (2020). *Force, drive, desire: A philosophy of psychoanalysis*. Northwestern University Press.

Heidegger, M. (1996 [1953]). *Being and time* (J. Stambaugh, Transl.). State University of New York Press.

Rasmussen, A. R., & Parnas, J. (2022). What is obsession? Differentiating obsessive-compulsive disorder and the schizophrenia spectrum. *Schizophrenia Research, 243*, 1–8. https://doi.org/10.1016/j.schres.2022.02.014

Sartre, J. P. (2018). *Being and nothingness*. Routledge.

Section 13

CHAPTER 37

Introduction to Gallagher's "Causal Interaction and Heterogeneous Integration in Level-Free Psychiatry"

Peter Zachar

Shaun Gallagher in his chapter argues that those who study psychopathology can adopt a level-free vocabulary without having to give up the explanatory virtues of levels of analysis thinking. In doing so, they can potentially make new contributions to our knowledge of psychopathology.

He begins by examining several deflationary accounts of levels that view different levels not as segregated from each other but as in interaction with each other. Each level is continually modified by and continually modifying the others. Gallagher also articulates something similar to this view, partly stemming from his prior commitment to enactivism. One idea behind enactivism is that rather than cognition being an abstract information-processing activity, it is both embodied and extended out into the world. Instead of the brain, body, and external world being distinct levels of analysis, cognition is constituted by processes that span across the brain, body, and external world.

One deflationary view examined by Gallagher is a box-free perspective. When levels are depicted visually, they are often segregated into separate boxes. Eliminating the boxes better represents how fluid and changeable the relationships between levels can be. Gallagher disputes this particular box-free view because it continues to use hierarchical, levels-oriented terms such *higher*, and *lower*, *underlying*, and *top-down* and *bottom-up*.

Another deflationary account examined by Gallagher is an emergent account in which different levels become fused into a greater whole that has new features not possessed by any of the component levels. Rather than levels being higher and lower relative to each other, they become different features of how the whole is organized. Gallagher also articulates something similar to this view, but he rejects the fusion idea. Rather than saying that levels such as processes of frontal lobe anatomy and attention disappear when they become fused into a single emergent phenomenon such as working memory, Gallagher argues that they can be integrated without having to lose their specific character: in other words, we can still distinguish between heterogenous, interacting biologic, psychological, and social processes and be level free.

Gallagher writes about processes rather than levels, focusing on the diverse and heterogenous processes that produce patterns. A pattern – or gestalt – is a stable organization of processes that are dynamically related to each other. None of these processes has ontological priority over any of the others. Such processes operate at different scales such as faster and slower, and larger and smaller. For example, action potentials in the brain are relatively fast processes, social interactions are relatively slow processes, but insofar as they causally interact, one is not necessarily more basic or on a more basic level than the other, and they can be viewed as organized in a single dynamic gestalt.

To give one example of how this might work, Gallagher looks to Woodward's interventionist notion of causality for inspiration, specifically Woodward's idea of conditional independence. Let's say we can explain something like the melting of ice with references to changes in temperature and volume. If we want to explain such a thermodynamic pattern, we do not need to give a fine-grained account of the motions of individual molecules because they would be reflected in the coarser-grained interaction of temperature and volume. Woodward would say that the explanation of the motions of the individual molecules is independent of the explanation of the melting of the ice, conditional on temperature and volume.

Woodward claims that it is useful to talk about temperature and volume interacting as a unique thermodynamic level. Because we can ignore details about the motions of individual molecules, they are not parts of the thermodynamic level. They are on another level. In response, Gallagher argues that if an explanation in terms of temperature and volume does not require reference to different levels, it's not clear what work levels talk is doing. Instead of saying that the motions of the individual molecules are on a different level, why not, he asks, just say they are not relevant to understanding a thermodynamic pattern of interaction or understanding a thermodynamic causal system? The task is to understand the different dynamic process that contribute to the emergence of various causal systems. Dividing relevant and nonrelevant processes up into "levels" does not add anything to the explanation.

For psychopathology, among the different interacting processes Gallagher mentions are behavioral, cognitive, interpersonal, and narrative processes. When integrated in a causal system, intervening on one of the processes can alter the pattern of activity in other processes.

In her commentary, Adina Roskies questions the aspiration to seek a level-free account. For one, so many different kinds of distinctions between levels can be made that lumping them all together as "levels talk" is muddled at best. She understands the advantages of a "level-neutral" account that does not give priority to one level above others, but in her view, refusing to talk about levels does not mean that they do not exist, or are not useful, or that the orderings between levels are limited to the strict hierarchies emphasized by Gallagher.

CHAPTER 38

Causal Interaction and Heterogeneous Integration in Level-Free Psychiatry

Shaun Gallagher

A number of theorists have pushed against the idea that scientific explanation requires that we think in terms of levels. For good reason much of this push has been motivated by considerations in psychiatry (see Kendler, Parnas, & Zachar, 2020). Despite some degree of skepticism about levels, many of the theorists who raise this issue nonetheless end up providing explanations that employ the concept of levels.[1] This concept clearly has a strong hold on our way of looking at things. Is it even possible to set it aside? In this chapter I'll explore this idea with the help of several of the theorists just mentioned. I'll suggest that we may be able to formulate a level-free account by appealing to James Woodward's interventionist concept of causality. This kind of account will appeal to two other notions: interaction and dynamical gestalt.

38.1 Box-Free Cognitive Science

In a recent article, Michael Spivey (2023) argued that over the past few decades interdisciplinary cognitive science has made important advances by turning from classic cognitivist views to a more "interactive framework." Much of this, in his view, has to do with embodied and extended cognition, neural networks, and dynamical systems theory. He calls it a "paradigm drift," indicating something of a slow transformation, in contrast to a paradigm shift. As a heuristic to substantiate his claim, he compares box-like diagrams of perceptual and linguistic explanations where recursive feedback arrows have been introduced over the years (from the 1980s to the 1990s) (see Figure 38.1).

More recent work in embodied cognition, broadly construed, led to more dramatic diagrammatic changes. As Spivey (2023, p. 232) explains,

[1] These theorists include Markus Eronen, Thomas Fuchs, Phillip Gerrans, Scott Kelso, Louis Sass, and James Woodward, to mention a few that I reference later.

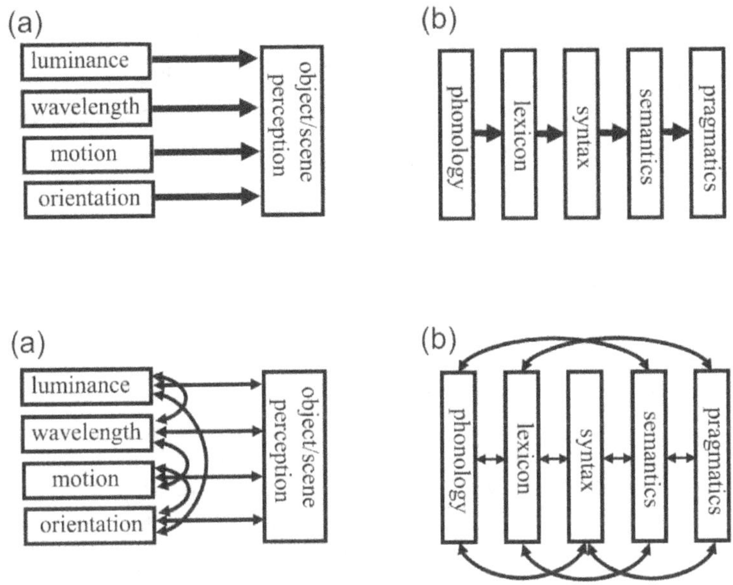

Figure 38.1 (Top) early sequential stage-based models of (a) vision and (b) language; (bottom) more interactive, feedback and context-rich models of (a) vision and (b) language. (From Spivey, 2023. CC BY-NC 4.0 Deed, https://creativecommons.org/licenses/by-nc/4.0/.)

> Language, vision, and action processes (as well as other cognitive processes) appear to share information with each other in a continuous bidirectional information flow, not delivering discrete completed packages of symbolic computation to each other at specific temporal instants but instead constantly exerting their fluid informational influences on each other in a "cascade". As a result of this observation, it begins to appear as if the arrows in the box-and-arrow diagram are doing most of the work and the boxes are not as isolable as once thought. Perhaps the diagram could be further improved by simply removing the boxes. (See Figure 38.2.)

Spivey calls his review a "pictorial essay" and offers numerous diagrams that are quite helpful and intuitive. For example, he suggests we could modify Figure 38.2 to represent a more action-rich activity (playing football) versus a more language-rich activity (reading).

> By removing the boxes in the schematic diagram [Figure 38.3], it may become easier to imagine how the cognitive system can softly reassemble

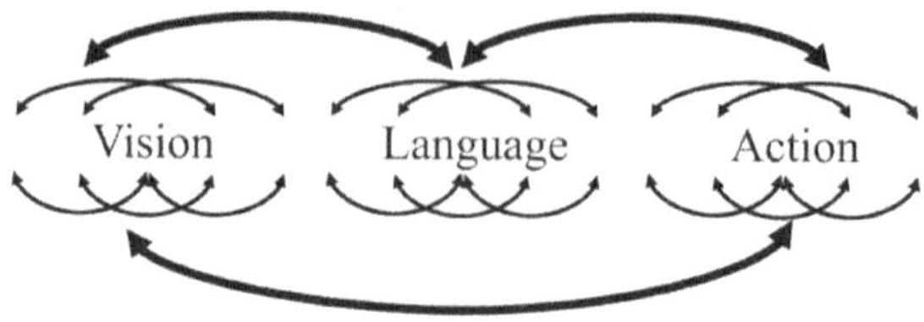

Figure 38.2 In place of a box-and-arrow diagram, this integrated "arrows-and-arrows" vision-language-action diagram may better depict the flexibility with which various cognitive processes can not only interact with each other but also reshape themselves. (From Spivey, 2023. CC BY-NC 4.0 Deed, https://creativecommons.org/licenses/by-nc/4.0/.)

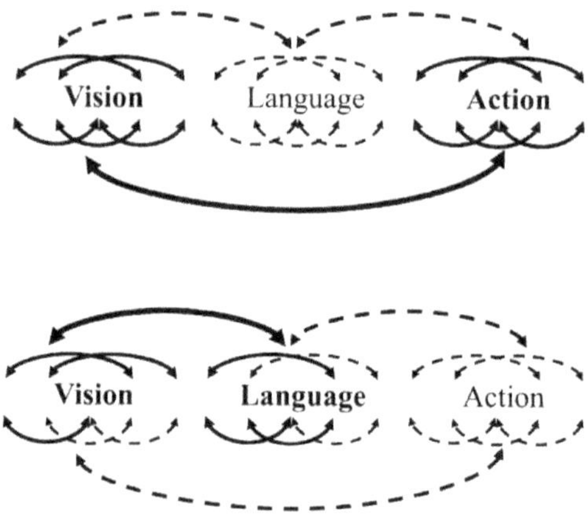

Figure 38.3 Football (top) versus reading (bottom). (From Spivey, 2023. CC BY-NC 4.0 Deed, https://creativecommons.org/licenses/by-nc/4.0/.)

> itself for a wide variety of spontaneous and creative behaviors—not simply being limited to the capabilities that might be "hard-wired" inside a vision component or inside an action component. (Spivey, 2023, p. 233)

Spivey suggests that these developments advance our understanding. As far as it goes, as someone who has defended embodied-enactive models, I tend to agree. Spivey goes on to suggest, optimistically, that Bayesian models, dynamical systems theory, and artificial neural networks capture much of the interaction concept, and with some work these different approaches could be made consistent. The consistency he is looking for supposedly comes along with thinking that the different approaches could be mapped out as operating on different levels. We know that Bayesian models, like predictive processing, endorse an analysis of processes arranged in a hierarchical set of levels. Spivey also points to work by Kelso, Dumas, and Tognoli (2013) who, as he says, "eloquently chart a multilevel research perspective that tries to understand the relationship between different levels while all the time respecting the autonomy of each. Rather than having to choose between a dynamical systems framework or a neural network framework, cognitive scientists can now embrace their coexistence and even their coextension" (Spivey, 2023, p. 240).

The argument here is about levels of analysis or explanation. On this view, interdisciplinary work in cognitive science requires an approach that is not satisfied with analysis of lateral relations at the same level of analysis; it requires looking vertically to underlying levels of analysis (psychology should look to neuroscience) and overlaying levels of analysis (e.g., social sciences). Different levels operate as constraints, or "reality checks." If claims made in psychology are incompatible with the claims of neuroscience or the social sciences, then there is a problem.

Here is one last diagram from Spivey (Figure 38.4). At the top, individual minds (pentagonal shapes) fit together to form a social group. In the middle, mental constructs form an individual mind. At the bottom, neural systems (the hexagons) work together to form a single cognitive construct.

To be sure, Spivey specifies that these are levels of explanation, and that in such interdisciplinary explanations psychology will be autonomous from neuroscience, and social sciences from psychology. That is, we can say some things about social phenomena that can't be said about psychological phenomena, and we can say some things about psychological phenomena that can't be reduced to neuronal processes.

At the same time, there is a clear supposition, evidenced by both the diagram and the description, that one level is more basic than another, and that explanations go top-down or bottom-up whenever appropriate. Furthermore, there is a clear segregation of phenomena – one finds pentagons at the top level but not puzzle pieces or hexagons. There are disciplinary lines, and crossing those lines can result in category mistakes or mereological fallacies. In this respect there is heterogeneity, but at the same time there has to be some sort of isomorphism. "[S]ome degree of isomorphism should be available to make sure that the model shapes proposed at one level are not categorically incapable of combining to produce the shapes at the next level above" (Spivey, 2023, p. 242).

Spivey doesn't mention new mechanist models, but his diagrams and descriptions start to resemble those in the new mechanist literature (e.g.,

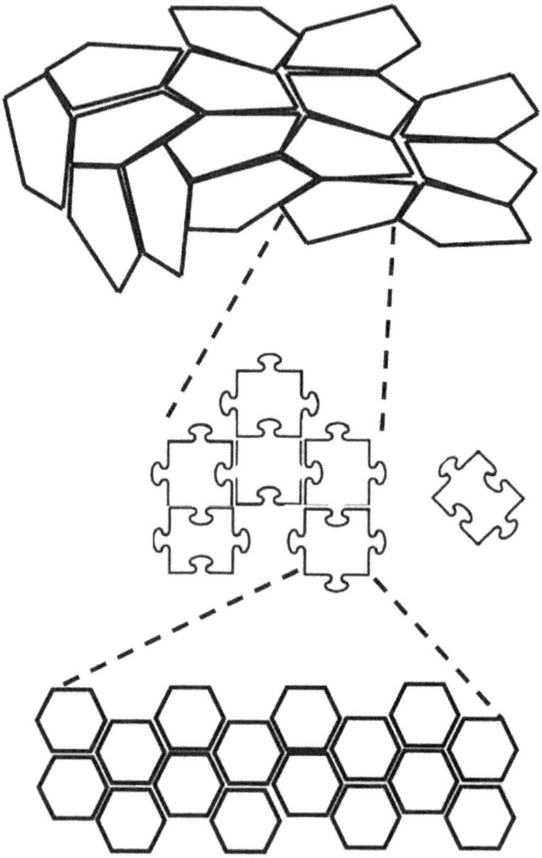

Figure 38.4 An abstract depiction of the relationship between higher-level, midlevel, and lower-level theoretical frameworks. (From Spivey, 2023. CC BY-NC 4.0 Deed, https://creativecommons.org/licenses/by-nc/4.0/.)

Craver, 2007). He makes one last suggestion that may be disruptive to that idea. He's happy to get rid of the boxes even in this diagram. We should note that the boxes (pentagons, puzzle pieces, and hexagons in this case) are not of the same sort as the earlier boxes; the latter seem more functional, while those in Figure 38.4 seem more compositional as he describes them. Still, the suggestion may be considered radical: get rid of the boxes and replace with arrows. We should shift (or drift) from stable representational units inside a brain to "information-bearing processes that emerge in the interaction between an organism and its environment"

(Spivey, 2023, p. 242). Let's just say processes and relations rather than states and representations. Box-free analysis is pictured as cutting-edge, state-of-the-art, cognitive science.

38.2 Leveling the Playing Field

Despite the emancipation from boxes, Spivey still insists on levels. The cutting edge doesn't cut through the lines that define the multistoried analytic framework. The following sections, which I intend as exploratory rather than as a set of grounded claims, consider what it would look like if we gave up the notion of levels. Is that even possible in cognitive science, or in psychiatry? I'll be appealing to some enactivist ideas here, and to some specific notions of causality.

On the enactive conception, an active cognitive (or biological) system is constituted through processes of dynamical coupling, involving some set of causal interactions among processes that extend over brain, body, and environment, and may include elements, properties, relations, and processes that are not internal to the organism or reducible to just the organism.[2] It's important to understand the nature of this causality. It has been variously called reciprocal causality, circular causality (Fuchs, 2012, 2020; Kelso, 1995; Varela & Goguen, 1978), or organizational causality (de Haan, 2020). Although there may be reciprocal (two-way) causal processes involved in cognition, this is not a complete characterization of the causality involved, since more than two elements may be involved in a more complex pattern of causality that can be circular, but can also involve multiple, nonlinear, or indirect interactions across different timescales.

[2] One controversial issue concerns the relation between causality and constitution. In some views there is a fallacy lurking in extended and enactive conceptions of cognition to the extent that they confuse causality and constitution, which are (and should be) distinguished (Adams and Aizawa [2008] and Aizawa [2010, 2014]). According to this criticism, extended and enactive approaches mistake some causal relations for constitutive (compositional) ones, understood as synchronic parts that make up a whole. For example, a notebook may facilitate my memory (causally), but it is not a constitutive part of my memory, as claimed by proponents of extended mind (Clark & Chalmers, 1998). For enactivists, constitution is not necessarily compositional; it can be understood as a dynamical relational process rather than a synchronic compositional relation. That is, on the enactive and extended views, the embodied reciprocal causal interactions involved in using a notebook (or some other aspect of the environment) may be partially constitutive of the cognitive process. I don't try to resolve this complex debate here. Rather, I'll just stake out my position as accepting the enactivist response, which is that a specific kind of causality *just is* constitutive of the cognitive process (see Gallagher, 2017, 2024; Kirchhoff, 2017; Krickel, 2017, 2018).

One characterization of circular causality retains the concept of levels. For example, Thomas Fuchs (2012, p. 331) writes: "mental illnesses are marked by a disruption of vertical circular causality; that is, the interplay between lower-level processes and higher faculties of the organism." One of his examples is the relation between genes and the organism. There is an "upward" causality in which genetic structure governs the production of specialized cellular organs and functions, and "downward" causation where the configurations and functions of the entire organism determine the genes that are more relevant to regulation of a certain individual cell. In this view, circular causality is just a form of reciprocal, downward and upward relations between parts and whole (Fuchs, 2020).

The concept of "organizational causality," suggested by Sanneke de Haan (2020, p. 119), might be more appropriate to the integrative perspective. De Haan develops the notion of organizational causality as a way to address psychiatry's integration problem, which involves explaining not just how physiological processes are related to experiential processes but, more generally, how different processes or theoretical perspectives (biopsychosocial) can be integrated (De Haan, 2020). As an example, she notes that we should not think of amygdala activation as part of a linear causal factor in my annoyance about a specific situation; we should rather think of amygdala activation as part of the phenomenon we call annoyance. Following Paul Humphreys (1996), De Haan suggests that organizational causality allows us to move away from the idea of levels or hierarchical arrangements.

In this respect, de Haan defends a concept of emergence that she defines in mereological terms: the whole is more than the sum of its parts. This whole is a gestalt in which the global processes can have characteristics that are different from the local processes. The global–local distinction, however, is not meant as a distinction of levels. On the one hand, according to this rejection of levels and hierarchies, the causal relations are neither bottom-up nor top-down. On the other hand, however, de Haan associates organizational causality with Humphreys' idea of emergence as fusion. To explain emergence as fusion, de Haan offers the analogy of a cake, where all ingredients, even if they start out as differentiated, once baked, become fused in such a way that one can no longer distinguish sugar from flour from flavorings, and so forth. In this regard she quotes Humphreys, who seemingly needs to refer to levels to explain the disappearance of levels: "when emergence occurs the lower-level property instances go out of existence in producing the higher-level emergent instances" (de Haan, 2020, p. 118; see Humphreys, 1996).

The fusion metaphor, however, is unhelpful. If, in the context of psychiatry, one is attempting to understand the contributions of physical, psychological, and social processes, it is not helpful to say that these dimensions are indistinguishably fused. Even if we bracket the talk of "levels," however, as de Haan wants to do, it's not clear that the various factors that constitute a human system go out of existence, or fuse to the point where we cannot discriminate among processes that are clearly affective, or clearly cognitive, or clearly intersubjective, and so forth, even if such processes are dynamically integrated. In psychiatric practice we need a model of integration that does not subvert useful distinctions among the neurobiological, the phenomenological, the social, and the existential, to use de Haan's own list of perspectives.

The notion of fusion, then, is not commensurable with the idea of a *differentiated integration* – that is, an integration of elements that continue to maintain their heterogeneity. Even if a system is constituted in some sense in the dynamical causal relations among its various factors and processes, those factors and processes remain distinct, albeit, in some cases, difficult to pull apart. Emergence as a confectionary fusion is too strong a characterization.

Instead, we can think of organizational causality as involving dynamical transformations. When one factor is dynamically related to another factor, both factors are transformed or changed, but they do not disappear or lose their specific character in the process. Neural processes do not become something other than neural; social processes do not become something other than social. In regard to human existence, for example, we can still discriminate physical, psychological, and social, as well as affective, cognitive, or intersubjective processes, even if we do not want to think of them as operating on different levels, and even if they are in some way causally integrated or meshed and transformed in the process. Even if an individual's affective life changes because of some neurological disturbance or environmental change, or through a practice of narrative, bodily, or cognitive therapy, affect, neurological processes, environmental factors, and narrative practices do not disappear. We can acknowledge that these processes may change as they mesh with other changing processes, but they are not fused into indistinguishable processes. Indeed, when de Haan (2020) discusses psychiatric diagnosis and treatment, she reverts to the concept of complex patterns of factors, framed in terms of network models.

Although the term *organizational causality* works well here, to avoid the idea of emergence as fusion, I'll refer to the idea of dynamical causality, where in some cases relations are nonlinear and transformational on both sides of the relation. The challenge is to think this through without appealing to either a hierarchy of levels or a deflationary fusion.

38.3 Levels of Disagreement

The question, then, is how heterogeneous factors or processes can be coherently integrated. Neurophysiological, experiential, affective, behavioral, cognitive, social, and normative factors, among others, form a motley diversity. Are these diverse factors necessarily integrated in a hierarchical scheme of levels? Does the idea that all these factors involve *processes* provide a common denominator? As Scott Kelso (1995, p. 3) puts it, "Everybody knows that the world is made up of processes from which patterns emerge." Should we talk about an emerging dynamical pattern rather than a fusion? In trying to work out how patterns emerge from heterogeneous processes, Kelso comes close to giving up on the idea that we need to think in terms of levels.

> Understanding will be sought in terms of essential variables that characterize patterns of behavior regardless of what elements are involved in producing the patterns or at what level these patterns are studied or observed . . . I will try to avoid dualities such as top-down versus bottom-up and macro versus micro because I think they can be misleading. What is macro at one level, after all, can be micro at another. (Kelso, 1995, p. 2)

He nonetheless retains the notion of different levels of explanation. "Mind you, no value is meant to be assigned to the words 'higher' and 'lower' as if one level is better or more fundamental than the other. I simply mean the levels above and below where the cooperativity (pattern, structure) is observed" (Kelso, 1995, p. 18). At the same time his account involves the complexity of self-organizing dynamical systems. "Often mechanisms for a given phenomenon are sought on lower levels, in the interior workings of the system. That view may be flawed if lower levels also turn out to be governed by the same kinds of self-organized dynamical principles or generic mechanisms shown to be at work [at higher levels]" (Kelso, 1995, p. 134). The closer you look at the elements, the more you see processes and patterns: dynamical relations rather than discrete elements or levels.

The problems to be solved in such a system concern *integration* (of the many and different kinds of processes or factors), *adaptation* ("how patterns are produced to accommodate different circumstances" or how they adjust to changing conditions [Kelso, 1995, p. 5]), and *persistence* or stability. This latter issue is critical for a self-organizing system in which, according to Kelso, there is no set of instructions to follow, no "self," "no agent inside the system doing the organizing' (p. 8). Principles of self-organization must solve these problems. We'll return to this idea, and to the kinds of principles required, later in the chapter.

Kelso indicates that "the precise patterns that form may differ from one scale of observation to another, but the basic pattern-forming principles are the same" (p. 25). I think this concept of patterns across different scales is not far from Merleau-Ponty's notion of gestalt, in which the "genesis of the whole by composition of the parts is fictitious. It arbitrarily breaks the chain of reciprocal determinations" (Merleau-Ponty, 1963, p. 50).[3] As Kelso argues, these reciprocal determinations – or, as specified earlier, dynamical causal relations – are not reducible to simple feedback loops or comparator models, since "there is no reference state [in a dynamic pattern] with which feedback can be compared and no place where comparison operations are performed" (Kelso, 1995, p. 9). If this is right, it would clearly be disruptive to the hierarchical arrangement of levels in predictive processing models that apparently depend on such comparator mechanisms, specifically mechanisms that allow comparisons between the expected and the actual sensory input.

All of this leads to the following question: What would an account of patterns or systems that did not appeal to hierarchical levels look like? The answer is necessarily complicated. One reason is that, as many agree, explanations framed in terms of different levels have been very productive in science; talk of levels is ubiquitous, according to Craver and Bechtel (2007). Eronen (2021) agrees, despite the fact that in an earlier paper he cited evidence contesting this ubiquity (Eronen, 2015). It is also the case that different conceptions of levels operate in many approaches to psychiatry. Philip Gerrans, for example, even as he attempts to integrate predictive processing with a mechanist approach in the psychiatric context, acknowledges something of a mishmash of levels.

[3] See, e.g., Jaspers (2017, pp. 28–29, 504). "All research differentiates, separates, and studies individual particulars in which it tries to discover certain general laws. Yet all these individual particulars are taken out from what is in reality a complex unity. In grasping particulars, we make a mistake if we forget the comprehensive whole in which and through which they exist. This never becomes the direct object of our study, but only does so *via* the particulars. . . . We can state the following in relation to it: the whole comes before its parts; the whole is not the sum of its parts . . . it is form."

> The notion of levels is ubiquitous, but not everyone uses it in the same way. It can refer to ordering relationships between theories. . .; the objects of theories ordered by size or complexity, e.g., cells are smaller and less complex than the organs they make up; functional analyses, e.g., vision is a higher-level property than edge detection; or levels of mereological containment, e.g., parts are at a lower level than wholes. These uses can overlap. The notion of level relevant to [Gerrran's analysis] is that of mechanism. Higher levels correspond to the organization of components, lower levels to components. (Gerrans, 2014, pp. 229–230)

In other words, he prefers a mereological conception. Yet, this would not be consistent with his appeal to predictive processing, where levels are not at all mereological, but include interlevel causal relations and reference state comparators between higher and lower levels.

In psychiatry, levels proliferate. Kenneth Schaffner (2020) lists levels of "abstraction, analysis, aggregation, behavior, complexity, function, perspective, organization, generality, and processes – as well as causation and control – as well as description and explanation, and more" (p. 384). Appeals are made to the concept of levels in the biopsychosocial model, where Engel (1981) considers the bio, the psycho, and the social as different levels organized in a "hierarchically arranged continuum" (p. 536); likewise in the network model of psychiatry that attempts to integrate across "different levels of explanation (biological, psychological, sociological)" (Borsboom, 2017, p. 11); likewise in the Hierarchical Taxonomy of Psychopathology (HiTOP) model (Kotov et al., 2017), which attempts to identify psychiatric phenomena based on patterns of symptom covariation spanning broader and narrower constructs (e.g., internalizing pathology versus distress) (Williams & Simms, 2020). Likewise, again, in phenomenological approaches (Fuchs, 2012). Louis Sass, for example, worries about how to explain the relations among the various "component processes" that make up human existence – whether they should be thought of as hierarchical, causal, or constitutive. As he puts it, "these questions pertain to theoretical issues that are difficult or even impossible to settle, such as overall attitudes toward holistic explanation or the enigmatic mind/body problem (generally viewed as utterly insoluble)" (Sass et al., 2018, p. 725). Even if we acknowledge that the concept of hierarchical levels has been productive in discussions of diagnosis and treatment in psychiatry (see e.g., Holmes et al., 2021), there is still no consensus on the dimensions to be included, or how general or specific they should be.

The proliferation of different levels is enough to motivate even theorists who often employ the notion of levels to add some qualifications and to move away from the concept of hierarchy, especially in the context of understanding psychiatric disorders (e.g., Eronen, 2021). Thus, for example, William Bechtel (2020) develops a mechanistic view that favors a heterarchical set of neural control mechanisms, rejecting a hierarchical organization in favor of lateral constraints within a network.

> Control mechanisms do not have to conform to a hierarchy, and the hierarchical perspective is especially misleading in the case of organisms. Control mechanisms are added to organisms opportunistically in the course of evolution when they serve to facilitate the ability of the organism to maintain and replicate itself as an autonomous system. This does not impose any requirement of hierarchical organization. (Bechtel, 2020, p. 31)

Likewise, Woodward (2020) notes that "levels eliminativism" – "the thought that we would be better off avoiding level talk entirely" – is motivated by the fact that researchers operate with different conceptions of levels without always distinguishing them. Nonetheless, Woodward endorses the concept of levels because it continues to do some useful work in science. After discussing several different types of levels, he focuses on an interactionist conception of level, characterized by conditional independence. Conditional independence concerns explanation. It relates to what we earlier called disciplinary autonomy: if we can explain a phenomenon in terms of a higher-level variable, we don't need to explain it as depending on a lower variable.

> For example, if we are interested in the relation between thermodynamic variables, we don't need a detailed description of the behavior of individual molecules; their aggregate impact as expressed in terms of variables like temperature or volume is all that is needed. (Woodward, 2020, p. 428)

That is, if I can explain a particular phenomenon in terms of temperature changes, there is no need to provide an account of subtending molecular changes. The explanation requires reference to only one level where relevant interactions take place. Woodward goes on to suggest that the interaction conception of level is closely tied to the role of different spatial, temporal, or energetic scales in constructing causal models. Different scales matter specifically as they relate to the "strength and nature" of causal interactions. The concept of scales, however, is different from the concept of levels. Eronen (2021, p. 929) notes that

> differences in time scales could be used to define levels, but scales are continuous, where the boundary between levels should be drawn may not have a clear answer ... The upshot is that defining levels in psychopathology is far from straightforward. The exact levels and their significance can vary strongly from context to context. In psychology, it is often unclear how

> part-whole or scale-based levels should be understood in the first place. This suggests that levels in psychopathology are best seen as heuristic idealizations that are helpful in making rough distinctions, but do not mark deep ontological features of the world.[4]

Craver and Darden (2013), for example, assume the distinction between levels and scales in their discussion of integration. They distinguish between levels of products, levels of units, levels of causation, levels of composition, levels of mechanisms, among others. Differences in timescales, in contrast, involve differences in how we measure processes (Eronen, 2015). Craver and Darden do discuss different temporal scales and intertemporal integration, indicating that "mechanisms often operate at and across different time scales' (p. 182), although they would deny causal relations across different levels. They focus on relatively large timescales (evolutionary, developmental) and downplay the role of feedback by dividing processes into stages (p. 172). Ladyman et al. (2007) call this "scale relativity," which they define as "the idea that which terms of description and principles of individuation we use to track the world vary with the scale at which the world is measured" (p. 199). The fact that some process is observable/measurable only at a specific scale (e.g., X), however, doesn't mean that if it is not observable/measurable at a different scale (e.g., Y), it is not operating or having some effect at Y. Priming and masking effects are examples.

In attempts to understand psychiatric disorders, Woodward (2020) notes, neat distinctions between levels or scales are complicated, because "the list of possible explanatory factors for some set of explananda may be very open ended and at different levels [by one or more different criteria]" (p. 432).

> Arguably, this is the case for many explananda in psychiatry: many different causal factors – social or environmental factors, factors having to do with

[4] Still, explanatory levels come with implicit (if not explicit) ontological commitments. Levels of explanation seemingly imply something about the levels of the *explananda*. For example, when one says that a theory about molecules is of lower level than a theory of neurons, that's because molecules are thought to be at a lower level. Oppenheim and Putnam (1958) clearly had both explanatory and ontological commitments. Thus, Eronen (2015, p. 48) writes: "The levels of Oppenheim and Putnam are not just an ordering of branches of science or theories; they involve 'things'. Oppenheim and Putnam assume that at each level there are certain types of things: elementary particles at the lowest level, atoms at the next higher level, and so on. In this sense, the levels of organization are not just reflecting features of theories and sciences, but also features of the world." In this regard, even if one thinks of levels as metaphorical (Craver, 2007), or as a heuristic, it doesn't mean that they are ontologically neutral. Implicitly, if not explicitly, they reflect, as William Wimsatt (2007, p. 203) suggests, "the ontological architecture of our natural world."

> personality type, as well as genes and brain structure – are relevant to paradigmatic mental illnesses such as depression .... (Woodward, 2020, pp. 432–433)

38.4 Causal Interaction and Dynamical Gestalt

My own view is that we should think of a system or pattern (to use Kelso's term) as an irreducible dynamical gestalt where processes are organized in nonlinear dynamical relations across different timescales. Kelso (1995). considers this perspective to be opposed to what he calls the 'machine stance' (p. 35), although, as Bich and Bechtel (2021) have argued, there may be productive ways to integrate mechanistic and dynamical (autopoietic) explanations. Indeed, the dynamical gestalt view is close to an enactive process view, most closely associated with Francisco Varela and a growing number of others (Di Paolo, 2005, 2021; Gallagher, 2017; Hutto & Myin, 2017; Thompson, 2007; Varela, Thompson, & Rosch, 1991; and in the context of psychopathology, de Haan, 2020; Fuchs, 2017, 2020). Evan Thompson (2007, p. 441) expresses an important insight in this regard:

> In the process view, "up" and "down" are contextual-relative terms used to describe phenomena of various scales and complexity. There is no base level of elementary entities to serve as the ultimate 'emergence base' on which to ground everything. Phenomena at all scales are not entities or substances but relatively stable processes, and since processes achieve stability at different [scales], while still interacting with processes at other [scales], all are equally real and none has absolute ontological primacy (Thompson slips back into levels vocabulary where I have placed "scales" in brackets).

I think we can go further. I think we can endorse what Woodward (2020, p. 436) calls "level neutrality." In his view, however, level neutrality allows us to talk about causal relations among variables across different levels; in my view, with respect to just these relations, it allows us to bracket talk about levels altogether, without explanatory loss. To justify the use of the enactivist concept of a level-free pattern as dynamical gestalt, I propose the following strategy.

1. Examine each of the different types of levels identified, for example, by Gerrans, Schaffner, and Woodward, and show how the level-free vocabulary of time or spatial scales and dynamical gestalts can substitute (or transform the account) without explanatory loss.

2. Ask whether we gain anything by making this substitution – for example, do we uncover a different but productive way of explaining psychiatric disorders or gain insights into therapeutic practices?

Clearly, I won't be able to pursue this strategy to completion here.[5] But we could make a start by considering one type of level explanation. Given where we started, with Spivey's suggestion that interactive models are gaining traction in cognitive science, I'll conclude by taking a close look at Woodward's interactionist conception of level.

Although raising doubts about the usefulness of various conceptions of levels, Woodward offers his own conception of level based on interaction, which is also tied to the concept of scales and conditional independence, as we mentioned earlier. The idea is that a unique level is defined by all processes that causally interact. Explanation can be confined to that level and can ignore other levels that are not part of the interaction.

> [T]his basis for level talk (which interactions are important and which can be ignored) is conceptually distinct from the issues about composition or size . . . Whether one object X is part of another object Y is obviously a distinct question from whether one can safely ignore features of X in explaining the behavior of Y. (Woodward, 2020, p. 431)

Specifically, interaction (of variables) is not the same as composition (of things that form parts and wholes). A unique level is defined by the strong interaction of variables with one another such that an explanation of such interactions can ignore the details about what is going on at other levels. In the best-case scenario, we can model a separable set of interactions in a restricted set of variables or factors. Woodward (2020) proposes that when we are in this sort of situation, "level-based considerations can be very heuristically useful in guiding judgments about which causal factors can be safely ignored" (p. 432). It is not clear why that is the case, however. Woodward does not rule out the idea that little things can interact with big things, or vice versa; "after all[,] viruses can destroy armies" (p. 429). In the context of psychopathology, social factors can play a causal role in depression, for example, and so can genes and neuronal processes. If we characterize the situation in terms of causal interaction, where all these factors, albeit at different temporal and spatial scales, interact, then in the

[5] Eronen (2015) offers a similar strategy in regard to mechanistic levels, translating the mechanistic analysis into terms that involve composition and different scales. He still thinks of composition in terms of levels and doesn't endorse a full-scale elimination of levels. He does argue that we can eliminate levels in the context of theory reduction and functional reduction. In Eronen (2021), however, he seems to retreat from his critique of levels and even refers to differences in scales as differences in levels.

interaction view they are all, by definition, on the same level. There is no reason to think that social factors are on a higher level than neuronal processes, or that neural processes are more basic than social factors in the etiology of depression, unless one is adopting different criteria for defining levels. And if other factors, such as the orbits of the celestial planets, do not play a causal role, then they are not part of the pattern of interaction. But why should that mean that they are on a different level?

Just here one can ask whether the notion of level is really doing any work. If we can say that this set of variables are interacting in a way that calls for explanation but some other set of variables are not part of this interaction, and we have a way of testing this (e.g., via causal intervention), then we can ignore the latter set. Why isn't that enough? Why say that the variables that are not interacting must be on a different level? What does it add to our explanation? If we are setting aside considerations about composition or size, for example, then what is the justification for characterizing this situation in terms of levels? It is clear that planets are different from neurons, just as, in another of Woodward's examples, gravity is different from strong or weak nuclear forces, and that they operate on different scales – but why say that planets are on a different level than neurons? Why not be deflationist and say simply that they are not interacting in a relevant way with neurons?

As Woodward points out, nature does not always provide the best-case scenario; often "the list of possible explanatory factors for some set of explananda may be very open-ended . . . Arguably, this is the case for many explananda in psychiatry: many different causal factors – social or environmental factors, factors having to do with personality type, as well as genes and brain structure – are relevant to paradigmatic mental illnesses such as depression" (Woodward, 2020, pp. 432–433). He argues, however, that in the interaction model, these different factors can be considered on the same level, and he cautions against introducing other level criteria that would confuse the issue. I think that's right, and that in effect this strategy totally discounts the notion of level, so that one does not even have to say, as Woodward goes on to say, "On my view, there is no problem in principle with the notion of interlevel causation" (p. 434). One can rather say, "What interlevel causation?"

Setting aside the concept of levels, which I think is implied by what Woodward calls "the simple version of the interactionist conception," does not undermine Woodward's interventionist test for causality. Indeed, it makes for a cleaner definition of intervention, since, for example, one does not have to worry about how one can do a top-down intervention that does not change the phenomenon being tested. One might think that the aforementioned phrase ("the simple version") is something like a caution from

Woodward that things are more complicated. But things can be more complicated without necessarily introducing the complications of levels. The notion of a dynamical gestalt allows for level-free complications, and not only does it work well with interventionist conceptions of causality, but the concept of dynamical gestalt can be defined in just such terms. The idea is that a variety of factors or processes and their dynamical causal interactions form a pattern or gestalt that defines a particular system that may be characterized by a psychiatric disorder such as depression. These factors may include bodily, experiential, affective, behavioral, cognitive, interpersonal, sociocultural, narratival, and normative processes dynamically organized in their causal (including nonlinear and recursive) relations. An intervention on any one process, above a specific threshold, for example in an experimental or therapeutic context, will have an effect on some or all of the other processes, and on the system as a whole. The whole is not a higher-level phenomenon – it's just the system or pattern of factors and their causal relations.

A dynamical gestalt, then, involves relational criteria that can help capture psychiatric disorders, which tend to be multifactorial. To the extent that we think of such disorders as a gestalt arrangement of factors, each individual case of a particular disorder may show different patterns of dynamical relations among the various factors. Different factors may involve different weights in different individuals. For example, anorexia presents differently in a disciplined person with a high degree of self-control than in an impulsive individual (Zachar, 2008, p. 334). Likewise, variations in the amount of social support or different cultural contexts may determine how a disorder develops. Yet, we can expect to see typical patterns associated with different disorders. Schizophrenia, for example, may affect multiple aspects of experience, cognition, mood, and agency in somewhat typical ways (Nekovarova et al., 2014) while panic disorder will be more aspect limited in its impact (Murphy, 2008).

One can study and provide an explanation of such a system by adopting principles like those set out by Kelso (1995) for the study of dynamical patterns. These are principles of self-organization. They are, as I understand them, as follows:

1. Interactions among the different factors are nonlinear: "the whole is not only greater than, but different than the sum of the motions of its parts" (p. 16).
2. Energy in the system is not uniformly distributed; it dissipates via those structures that tend to be efficient, reducing the degrees of freedom that contribute to behavior.

3. This leads to an emerging pattern organized by order parameters (collective variables), created by the coordination between processes, but in turn influencing the behavior of the processes. This is dynamical causality (Kelso refers to it as circular causality).
4. Order parameters around nonequilibrium phase transitions may lead to loss of stability giving rise to new or different patterns, but this is balanced by some degree of stability due to order parameters that are not as near to transitions.
5. Perturbations continually test the system, "allowing it to feel its stability" or to move toward new patterns.
6. Control parameters (external constraints) or boundary conditions influence the development of new patterns. (And if control parameters do constrain the system, there is no need to consider them as being on different levels).
7. Order parameters may be simple or complicated, giving rise to behavioral complexity.

Kelso indicates that "the precise patterns that form may differ from one scale of observation to another, but the basic pattern-forming principles are the same" (1995, p. 25).

I think the concept of a gestalt formation across a heterogeneous collection of interacting variables/factors/processes (including biopsychosocial factors), distributed across different scales, justifies the claim that psychology "is not just applied physics, or for that matter, applied biology" (Kelso, 1995, p. 25). Moreover, I think its combination with the model of interventionist causality in the context of psychiatry points in a direction that may allow us to uncover a different but productive way of explaining psychiatric disorders or gain insights into therapeutic practices. A box-free, level-free explanation in terms of dynamical–causal interaction may help us explain why in some cases movement or dance therapy, or narrative therapy, or cognitive-behavioral therapy, or group therapy, or changing some environmental features, or reeducating normative expectations, or some combination of such treatments may be just as effective (or more or less effective) than medication, deep brain stimulation, and so forth.

REFERENCES

Adams, F., & Aizawa, K. (2008). *The bounds of cognition*. Blackwell.

Aizawa, K. (2010). The coupling-constitution fallacy revisited. *Cognitive Systems Research, 11*, 332–342.

(2014). The enactivist revolution. *Avant, 5*(2), 19–42.

Bechtel, W. (2020). Rethinking psychiatric disorders in terms of heterarchical networks of control mechanisms. In K. S. Kendler, J. Parnas, & P. Zachar (Eds.), *Levels of analysis in psychopathology: Cross-disciplinary perspectives* (pp. 24–46). Cambridge University Press.
Bich, L., & Bechtel, W. (2021). Mechanism, autonomy and biological explanation. *Biology and Philosophy, 36*(6), 53.
Borsboom, D. (2017). A network theory of mental disorders. *World Psychiatry, 16*(1), 5–13.
Clark, A., & Chalmers, D. (1998). The extended mind. *Analysis, 58*(1), 7–19.
Craver, C. F. 2007. *Explaining the brain: Mechanisms and the mosaic unity of neuroscience.* Oxford University Press.
Craver, C. F., & Bechtel, W. (2007). Top-down causation without top-down causes. *Biology and Philosophy, 22*, 547–563.
Craver, C. F., & Darden, L. (2013). *In search of mechanisms: Discoveries across the life sciences.* University of Chicago Press.
de Haan, S. (2020). *Enactive psychiatry.* Cambridge University Press.
Di Paolo, E. (2005). Autopoiesis, adaptivity, teleology, agency. *Phenomenology and the Cognitive Sciences, 4*(4), 429–452.
(2021). Enactive becoming. *Phenomenology and the Cognitive Sciences, 20*(5), 783–809.
Engel, G. L. (1981). The clinical application of the biopsychosocial model. *The Journal of Medicine and Philosophy, 6*(2), 101–124.
Eronen, M. I. (2015). Levels of organization: A deflationary account. *Biology and Philosophy, 30*(1), 39–58.
(2021). The levels problem in psychopathology. *Psychological Medicine, 51*(6), 927–933.
Fuchs, T. (2012). Are mental illnesses diseases of the brain. In S. Choudhury & J. Slaby (Eds.), *Critical neuroscience: A handbook of the social and cultural contexts of neuroscience* (pp. 331–344). John Wiley & Sons.
(2017). Self across time: The diachronic unity of bodily existence. *Phenomenology and the Cognitive Sciences, 16*(2), 291–315.
(2020). The circularity of the embodied mind. *Frontiers in Psychology, 11*, 1707.
Gallagher, S. (2017). *Enactivist interventions: Rethinking the mind.* Oxford University Press.
(2024). *The self and its disorders.* Oxford University Press.
Gerrans, P. (2014). *The measure of madness: Philosophy of mind, cognitive neuroscience, and delusional thought.* MIT Press.
Holmes, J., Mareva, S., Bennett, M. P., Black, M. J., & Guy, J. (2021). Higher-order dimensions of psychopathology in a neurodevelopmental transdiagnostic sample. *Journal of Abnormal Psychology, 130*(8), 909–922.
Humphreys, P. (1996). Aspects of emergence. *Philosophical Topics, 24*(1), 53–70.
Hutto, D., & Myin, E. (2017). *Evolving enactivism.* MIT Press.
Jaspers, K. (2017). *General psychopathology.* Johns Hopkins University Press.
Kelso, J. A. S. (1995). *Dynamic patterns: The self-organization of brain and behavior.* MIT Press.

Kelso, J. A. S., Dumas, G., & Tognoli, E. (2013). Outline of a general theory of behavior and brain coordination. *Neural Networks, 37*, 120–131.

Kendler, K. S., Parnas, J., & Zachar, P. (Eds.). (2020). *Levels of analysis in psychopathology: Cross-disciplinary perspectives.* Cambridge University Press.

Kirchhoff, M. (2017). From mutual manipulation to cognitive extension: Challenges and implications." *Phenomenology and the Cognitive Sciences, 16*, 862–878.

Kotov, R., Krueger, R. F., Watson, D., Achenbach, T. M., Althoff, R. R., Bagby, R. M., Brown, T. A., et al. (2017). The Hierarchical Taxonomy of Psychopathology (HiTOP): A dimensional alternative to traditional nosologies. *Journal of Abnormal Psychology, 126*(4), 454–477.

Krickel, B. (2017). Making sense of interlevel causation in mechanisms from a metaphysical perspective. *Journal for General Philosophy of Science / Zeitschrift für Allgemeine Wissenschaftstheorie, 48*(3), 453–468.

(2018). Saving the mutual manipulability account of constitutive relevance. *Studies in History and Philosophy of Science, Part A, 68*, 58–67.

Ladyman, J., & Ross, D. (2007). *Everything must go: Metaphysics naturalized.* Oxford University Press.

Merleau-Ponty, M. (1963). *The structure of behavior* (A. Fisher, Transl.). Beacon.

Murphy, D. (2008). Levels of explanation in psychiatry. In K. S. Kendler & J. Parnas (Eds.), *Philosophical issues in psychiatry* (pp. 99–124). Johns Hopkins Press.

Nekovarova, T., Fajnerova, I., Horacek, J., & Spaniel, F. (2014). Bridging disparate symptoms of schizophrenia: A triple network dysfunction theory. *Frontiers in Behavioral Neuroscience, 8*, 171.

Oppenheim, P., & Putnam, H. (1958). Unity of science as a working hypothesis. *Minnesota Studies in the Philosophy of Science, 2*, 3–36.

Sass, L.,Borda J. P., Madeira, L., Pienkos, E., & Nelson, B. (2018). Varieties of self disorder: A bio-pheno-social model of schizophrenia. *Schizophrenia Bulletin, 44*(4), 720–727.

Schaffner, K. (2020). Approaches to multilevel models of fear: The what, where, why, how, and how much?" In K. S. Kendler, J. Parnas, & P. Zachar (Eds.), *Levels of analysis in psychopathology: Cross-disciplinary perspectives* (pp. 384–409). Cambridge University Press.

Spivey, M. J. (2023). Cognitive science progresses toward interactive frameworks. *Topics in Cognitive Science, 15*(2), 219–254.

Thompson, E. (2007). *Mind in life: Biology, phenomenology, and the sciences of mind.* Harvard University Press.

Varela, F., & Goguen, J. A. (1978). The arithmetic of closure. *Journal of Cybernetics, 8*(3–4), 291–324.

Varela, F., Thompson, E., & Rosch, E. (1991). *The embodied mind: Cognitive science and human experience.* MIT Press.

Williams, T. F., & Simms, L. J. (2020). The conceptual foundations of descriptive psychopathology. In A. G. C. Wright & M. N. Hallquist (Eds.), *The*

Cambridge handbook of research methods in clinical psychology (pp. 33–44). Cambridge University Press.

Wimsatt, W. C. (2007). The ontology of complex systems: Levels of organization, perspectives, and causal thickets. In W. C. Wimsatt (Eds.), *Re-engineering philosophy for limited beings: Piecewise approximations to reality* (pp. 193–240). Harvard University Press.

Woodward, J. (2020). Levels: What are they and what are they good for? In K. S. Kendler, J. Parnas, & P. Zachar (Eds.), *Levels of analysis in psychopathology: Cross-disciplinary perspectives* (pp. 424–449). Cambridge University Press.

Zachar, P. (2008). Real kinds but no true taxonomy: An essay in psychiatric systematics. In K. S. Kendler & J. Parnas (Eds.), *Philosophical issues in psychiatry* (pp. 327–354). Johns Hopkins University Press.

CHAPTER 39

Commentary on Gallagher's "Causal Interaction and Heterogeneous Integration in Level-Free Psychiatry"

Adina L. Roskies

There has been a lot of interest lately in the possibility of downward causation, the idea that higher-level processes or events can cause lower-level ones. Downward causation, if it could be made sense of, is seen by some as a way to approach the philosophical problem of free will naturalistically, while others have heralded it as a promising way to explain aspects of the pathogenesis or treatment of psychiatric conditions. But the possibility of downward causation has been called into question because it is claimed to require causation across levels, and interlevel causation has been viewed as problematic. Reductionist accounts, for example, hold that entities or processes at higher levels can be reduced to entities or processes at lower levels, and that causal relations only "really" occur at the most fundamental level. On this basis, Kim's (1998) causal exclusion argument holds that mental states do not enter causal relations and are merely epiphenomenal. Alternatively, the New Mechanist account holds that neuroscientific explanation is mechanistic explanation, and that the relationship between mechanisms at different levels is one of constitution (part/whole). Because constitution relations are not causal relations, interlevel causation does not exist: causation can only occur within a level (see, e.g., Bechtel & Craver, 2007; Craver, 2007). Several thinkers have suggested that if we can rid ourselves of levels, these problems and others would disappear (Eronen, 2013).

In his chapter, Gallagher promotes a level-free account of cognitive science, or at least he charts a course toward such an account.[1] He cites approvingly Spivey's interactionist picture of cognitive science but criticizes it for embracing the notion of levels. Gallagher's view of cognition is a

[1] We should distinguish here between "level-free" and "level-neutral" accounts. A level-free account does not make reference to levels at all, while a level-neutral account does not prioritize one level over another. Thus, Woodward's account of causal relevance is level neutral in that it is applicable to phenomena at any level, yet it is not level free, for one of its claimed virtues is that it can explain how interlevel causation is possible.

dynamical and enactivist one, according to which a cognitive or biological system is constituted through dynamical coupling between processes that range over brain, body, and environment and that may include elements, properties, relations, and processes that are neither internal nor reducible to the organism. As such, any account of the workings of the cognitive or biological system will make reference to entities and phenomena that are identifiable at diverse temporal and/or spatial scales, of varying complexity and so on. *Dynamical*, *circular*, *reciprocal*, or *organizational* causality are terms that have variously been used to refer to the ways in which a mesh of causal interactions among different phenomena lead to the formation of enmeshed systems that are reciprocally determined by their elements. This web of interconnected relations also makes difficult the demarcation of levels, especially if levels imply a strict hierarchical structure. Gallagher uses the term "irreducible dynamical gestalt" to characterize his picture of a level-free and interactionist-friendly explanation of psychiatric disorders. The relevant factors, regardless of temporal and spatial scale, are delineated (or, as he says, "defined") by their causal interactions. Thinking of things as a gestalt is meant to obviate the notion of levels – no causal factor is more or less basic than another. His approach to a level-free explanation is to examine the use of levels and see if they can be replaced by other terms such as scale or dynamical gestalt "without explanatory loss," and then to see what might be gained with the result.

Aside from worries I have that dynamical gestalt and related notions like dynamical causality are not well suited to explanatory clarity, I find the drive for a level-free science to be undermotivated. To be sure, levels talk in science is ubiquitous, has multiple meanings, and is often confusing and frequently confused. But that is not news. Many philosophers (e.g., Gerrans and Schaffner, Craver and Darden, Eronon, Woodward) have commented on the fact that there are many ways in which levels are used in psychiatry and in science more generally: differences of spatial scale, differences of disciplinary interest, differences in composition or constitution, in complexity, and so on. Sometimes levels talk is used to imply a strict hierarchy, and other times it is used loosely. Confusion can result from lack of explicitness about what is meant or implied by "level," and from sliding between different notions of levels. But often the meaning is clear, and merely the fact that people use them differently does not provide reasons to do away with levels talk – being clearer about what one means and what useful work they do would be sufficient. One worries that merely replacing terms like "level" with other terms like "scale" and "gestalt" will be a wash; there is no clear explanatory gain.

Gallagher's chapter is frustratingly unclear about what he means by level: What exactly are we being asked to do without? And what is implied by the term "level" that it is so problematic? Does Gallagher assume that levels talk implies reductionism? Is it that it is unclear what the relevant mechanisms are that could support interactions between levels? Gallagher himself asks how heterogeneous factors or processes can be coherently integrated. Although he doesn't say so explicitly, the best reconstruction I can muster is that by "level" he means an ordering relation that implies a strict hierarchy. And he is likely correct that much of the natural world does not easily conform to such strictness. But it does not seem to me that notions of levels need to obey such strict ordering, nor that using levels to gesture at less-than-strict orderings is not useful. For example, we know that brain architecture is very complicated, and that in the cortex there are, in addition to feed-forward connections, also feedback and lateral connections. Indeed, there are numerous connections that disrupt a strict hierarchy. Nonetheless, it is possible to discern some organization in the mess: we have been able to identify canonical cortical microcircuits and other repetitive structural motifs, different brain areas that – although there is more going on there than early physiology suggested – can usefully be seen as involved in processing increasingly complex features. The simplifications or idealizations reflected in levels talk imposes (and allows us to see) structure on the complex mess that the brain presents to us, which can be fruitful in the generation of theory and the pursuit of scientific explanation and understanding. Although we are still bootstrapping ourselves to a more nuanced view of, say, visual processing than that suggested by early work in the neurophysiology of the visual cortex, it is not clear what we would have achieved had Hubel and Weisel embraced the dynamical gestalt of the cortex on day one.

Gallagher notes that interventionist theories of causation are friendly to level neutrality. However, interventionists such as Woodward don't advocate a level-free account. Why not? Woodward (2020) mentions but does not fully endorse the possibility of defining levels in interactionist terms: in terms of processes that causally interact, where causal interaction is indicated by the conditional dependence between their variables. Given an interactionist view of levels, causal explanations are necessarily intralevel, since to be at a level is simply to be causally relevant. Woodward cautions, however, that when this interactionist view and differing conceptions of levels are mixed, "confusion can occur." Where Gallagher thinks this is a reason to prefer doing away with levels entirely, Woodward does not (more on this below) and seems to distance himself from an interactionist view.

Woodward instead argues that retaining the notion of levels is important to adequately describe scientific practice and to effectively deal with scale-related invariances found in science. He is cognizant of the many ways in which scientists and philosophers employ the term "level." He believes that interlevel causation occurs, and in fact that causal explanations can be better (more simple, compact, general, etc.) when higher-level variables can substitute for collections of lower ones based on the conditional independence of the lower variables from the upper. That is, when the causal impact of the lower-level variables on the effect can be fully represented or captured by the impact of the higher-level variables on it, the explanation need not advert to the lower-level variables. (Here the notion of levels is used to discusses differences of scale.)

Charting relations of conditional independence may be possible without levels talk, but determining causal relevance is not all that matters to scientific understanding of a phenomenon. We want to understand how the elements constituted, what are the mechanisms at work, what tools to employ to change them, what law-like relations they take part in, and so on. Many of the ways levels talk is used reflect these interests.

For example, Woodward explains how we can simplify scientific explanations by ignoring variables that an *explanandum* is conditionally independent of given an intervention on variables that are coarser or less fine-grained: we don't need to describe causes at a lower level if we can at a higher level. But notice, to understand why the explanation is more simple, attractive, and so forth, one needs to make reference, implicitly or explicitly, to some notion of level. Thus, the interventionist can unproblematically countenance (excuse the phrase) "higher-level phenomena" being causally relevant to phenomena at a lower level.

Woodward concludes his discussion of levels talk thus:

> [W]hat legitimate work does it [levels-talk] do? In addition to the role played by compositional considerations, we can think of claims about levels as encoding information about what factors it is permissible to ignore in modeling and causal analysis – either because these factors are unconditionally irrelevant to some effect of interest or (more commonly) because, they are irrelevant, conditional on information represented by other variables. (2020, p. 448)

Thus, while Woodward's interventionist approach to causation is "level neutral" in that it is applicable to phenomena at many different levels, it is not "level free," for one of its strengths is its ability to account for interlevel causation. This is indeed an asset, for it is unlikely that thinking and talking in terms of levels would be so widespread in science if it did not capture important features of the way the world and our way of interacting with it is organized. Failing to acknowledge the structure implied by levels and treating everything as if it were on par clearly misses something important to scientific understanding. In the examples Woodward discusses, we can account for some of the virtues of the interventionist account by levels talk: we note that it can make sense of interlevel causation, including downward causation. This is a big win, for as mentioned earlier, downward causation is a potential solution to several thorny philosophical problems.

Ultimately, I think the problem with doing away with levels in the way that Gallagher promotes is that if we achieve this, it is only because we refuse to talk about them, and in so doing we may be less attuned to potentially relevant information. The old joke about the dog is apt here: "If you call a tail a leg, how many legs does a dog have? Answer: 4. Calling a tail a leg doesn't make it one." Denying levels talk does not obviate the need to somehow think about ordering things, simplifying things, or highlighting the sorts of things our levels talk highlights. Gallagher seems to appreciate this general point, for he criticizes de Haan's method of doing away with levels by fusion. He sees the virtue in retaining distinctions that are useful:

> In regard to human existence, for example, we can still discriminate physical, psychological, and social, as well as affective, cognitive or intersubjective processes, even if we do not want to think of them as operating on different levels, and even if they are in some way causally integrated or meshed and transformed in the process. Even if an individual's affective life changes because of some neurological disturbance, or because of some environmental change, or through a practice of narrative, or bodily, or cognitive therapy, for example, neither affect, nor neurological processes, nor environmental factors, nor narrative practices go out of existence. (Gallagher, Chapter 39 in this volume, p. 417)

I agree with Gallagher that the causal interaction of many factors – biological, psychological, social, and environmental – together leads to psychiatric disease (or health).

These distinctions are useful, and many of them appeal to differences that are sometimes characterized as differences in level. Gallagher wants us to try to develop a level-free science where we can eschew talk of levels "without explanatory loss." But what do we leave out in a level-neutral account other than the word *level*? And what do we gain by refusing to talk about levels? The answer remains unclear.

REFERENCES

Craver, C. F. (2007). *Explaining the brain: Mechanisms and the mosaic unity of neuroscience*. Oxford University Press.

Craver, C. F., & Bechtel, W. (2007). Top-down causation without top-down causes. *Biology and Philosophy, 22*, 547–563.

Eronen, M. I. (2013). No levels, no problems: Downward causation in neuroscience. *Philosophy of Science, 80*(5), 1042–1052. https://doi.org/10.1086/673898

Eronen, M. I. (2021). The levels problem in psychopathology. *Psychological Medicine, 51*(6), 927–933.

Kim, J. (1998). *Mind in a physical world: An essay on the mind-body problem and mental causation*. MIT Press.

Krickel, B. (2017). Making sense of interlevel causation in mechanisms from a metaphysical perspective. *Journal for General Philosophy of Science / Zeitschrift für Allgemeine Wissenschaftstheorie, 48*(3), 453–468.

Wimsatt, W. C. (2007). The ontology of complex systems: Levels of organization, perspectives, and causal thickets. *Canadian Journal of Philosophy, S20*, 207–274.

Woodward, J. (2020). Levels: What are they and what are they good for? In K. S. Kendler, J. Parnas, & P. Zachar (Eds.), *Levels of analysis in psychopathology: Cross-disciplinary perspectives* (pp. 424–449). Cambridge University Press.

Section 14

CHAPTER 40

Introduction to Parnas and Zandersen's "A Disease Like No Other"

Peter Zachar

In their chapter, Josef Parnas and Maja Zandersen critically examine the etiological claim that schizophrenia is a brain disease. They are not arguing against a claim that it is a confirmed brain disease, but rather against some implications that follow from the inference that schizophrenia is a disease even though the biopathology is not yet mapped out. To focus the discussion, Parnas and Zandersen describe what they consider a folk psychological definition of disease in medicine. A disease is an unwanted affliction caused by a biopathological process. It has a characteristic pattern of onset, time course, and outcome – including the potential death of the patient. As unwanted afflictions, diseases are experienced as deserving of treatment.

They then proceed to challenge, in several ways, the extent to which schizophrenia can be understood using this commonsense disease framework. With respect to onset, Parnas and Zandersen question the notion of "converting" from a prodromal stage to schizophrenia, because important features of the disorder can manifest early in development, albeit in attenuated forms. If "schizophrenia" is not identified with the full DSM syndrome, onset is difficult to pin down with precision. Certainly there are differences between early-stage and late-stage manifestations of the schizophrenia, but the progression is often gradual and lacking in sudden leaps.

They also examine the experience of having an affliction. Schizophrenia consists in a disturbance of selfhood or the basic experience of subjectivity. This is sometimes characterized as a disturbance of "ipseity," which is the manifestation of experience as "my experience," something that is normally understood pre-reflectively. Disturbances of ipsety alter people's very sense of existence, agency, and individuality. Unlike for other diseases, this disturbance is not something clearly seen by the patient as extraneous to one's sense of me-ness because the me–versus–not-me distinction is fuzzy. Clinicians may look at patients and interpret schizophrenia as an affliction, but for any patient, experiencing an unwanted affliction requires encountering something that is happening to them, but not them. Because the disturbance in schizophrenia affects one's pre-reflective sense of me-ness, the distancing required to experience the disturbance as an affliction imposed on me is compromised.

Exploring another aspect of a patient being unable to gain a first-person, reflective distance from a disturbance of selfhood, they describe the phenomenon of double bookkeeping. In one sense the patient is immersed in and not separate from their disturbed subjectivity, and in another sense they track shared features of the social world – which Parnas and Zandersen describe as a coexistence of attitudes. The example they give is a woman hearing her mother's voice talking negatively about her and then confronting her mother about it. In one sense, this woman knew that when she was hearing the voices, her mother was miles away in her own apartment. In the self-contained world of the psychosis, there is no reflection on the contradiction. Rather than seeking to establish shared reality testing and insight into the private world of a disturbed subjectivity, a more pressing goal, according to Parnas and Zandersen, is to reduce the extent to which the two experiential realities interfere with each other.

Finally, with respect to a disease-related course and outcome, Parnas and Zandersen note the evidence is mixed. As for typical diseases, many patients have chronic unremitting courses that are associated with intense suffering for them and their families. Other people recover to greater or lesser extents. For example, in some cases people continue to have an altered subjectivity but report a decent quality of life. Some patients continue to identify with their private subjective worlds and are reluctant to give them up – learning to live with these alterations or, in some cases, feeling some sense of loss if they "improve."

The title of the chapter is "A Disease Like No Other" – suggesting that for schizophrenia, the disease–versus–not disease distinction cannot be made so strictly. In the view of Parnas and Zandersen, even when it is conceptualized as illness or disease, schizophrenia should not be put in the same box as other neurological diseases, somatic diseases, and psychiatric disorders. To do so would mischaracterize its nature.

In his commentary Shaun Gallagher describes the distinction between the older term *personalized medicine* and the more recent term *precision medicine.* He notes that rather than developing interventions personalized for individuals, precision medicine seeks increased technological exactness and detail, with the goal of reshuffling diagnostic categories into many subgroups and matching individual to the best subgroup. Gallagher introduces Aristotle's claim that a science can only be as precise as its subject matter allows and then expands on Parnas and Zandersen's reasons for claiming that there are important limits to precision in a science of persons – although he suggests that their focus on self-disturbance alone is itself overly precise.

CHAPTER 41

A Disease Like No Other
Phenomenology of Schizophrenia and Its Pathogenetic Consequences

Josef Parnas and Maja Zandersen

41.1 Introduction

We begin with a brief anecdote containing two events from the professional life of the first author:

> I started as an intern in psychiatry in 1974 at a state hospital (a classic asylum) 100 kilometers from Copenhagen. When I arrived at the hospital, a group of patients supervised by a nurse were passing by. The nurse offered help in carrying my boxes into the apartment. The group consisted of male catatonic patients that moved like automatons without saying anything, and the orderly instructed them how to carry the boxes. At that moment, I was thinking that schizophrenia must be a brain disease because such a bizarre behavior could not possibly be caused by psychological factors. However, we know now that such severe catatonia was iatrogenic, caused by institutionalization.
>
> Some years later, as a resident at a university hospital in Copenhagen, I followed as an outpatient a young female librarian with schizophrenia, who was for the most part completely mute and who refused antipsychotic treatment. She had a complicated system of pathological experiences and their delusional elaborations. At each session, I tried to persuade her to start antipsychotic medication. One day, she turned to me and said "you understand nothing. My world is as delicate as a spider net. You cannot remove one corner without causing a total collapse". Certainly, this statement did not sound organic in origin. I have been thinking about it for several years and below we will address the intricate issue of insight into psychosis.

Despite intensive research over the past hundred years, the pathogenesis of schizophrenia remains largely unknown. Kraepelin (1899), Bleuler (1911), and Schneider (1959) all believed that there is some unknown organic factor causing the syndrome. This view of schizophrenia as a cognitive deficit has survived to our time as indicated by the title of Nancy Andreasen's book, *The Broken Brain* (1984).

In an exalted paper on the future of psychiatry as a branch of precision medicine, Insel and Cuthberg (2015) declared that mental disorders are brain diseases. They do not explain what exactly they mean by the term "brain disease." It has gradually become a standard assumption that schizophrenia must be caused by some pathological process in the brain that we have not yet identified. The hope for a biological solution to the enigma of schizophrenia is kept alive by an anticipation of future breakthroughs in technology and neuroscience.

The assumption of a cognitive deficit goes hand in hand with the notion of schizophrenia as a *disease*. In the present chapter, we will discuss this conceptualization of schizophrenia as a disease. Here, we maintain a commonsense folk psychological perspective on the notion of disease. In this perspective, a disease is an affliction of the individual organism associated with a change in one of the tissues. The disease affects the well-being and function of the subject and may result in death. Typically, it has an onset, undertakes a certain course, and has a characteristic outcome. The affected person considers their disease as something disagreeable and unwanted – that is, considering the affliction as an affliction. The patient typically has an awareness of the need of treatment and of the risks associated with the illness if it remains untreated.

In this chapter, we present examples of phenomenological characteristics of schizophrenia that question its status as a typical disease. We begin with a brief description of schizophrenia as a disorder in the basic sense of self and thus not exclusively as something alien to the subject. We then discuss the question of how to define the onset of schizophrenia in an individual, followed by a discussion of the insight into illness and the so-called "double bookkeeping." Finally, we will address some issues pertaining to course and outcome. Throughout the chapter we will present brief vignettes from patients with schizophrenia that illustrate the points in question.

41.2 Selfhood

Our mental life is characterized by two closely interdependent features: subjectivity and individuality. All our experiences, such as perceptions, thoughts, or sensations, are permeated by a sense of subjectivity or, phrased differently, all experiences are immediately felt as mine without any need for reflective effort. This form of first personal giveness of our mental life is designated as "first-person perspective" or "ipseity" (from Latin: *ipse* = self). At the same time, this sense of for-me-ness entails a very basic individuality implying that my experiences are felt as uniquely mine and therefore in opposition to what is not me. In phenomenology, these very primitive basic features are designated as the "minimal self" and in psychopathology sometimes as the "basic self" or "core self."

In schizophrenia, this very basic sense of ipseity is unstable. The patient may feel ephemeral, not fully existing, not properly awake, or having a disturbed sense of self-coincidence, a difficulty "catching up" with oneself. The basic disorder of subjectivity may be reflected in several dimensions of selfhood described by, among others, Jaspers (1997) and Scharffeter (1980) as a sense of existing and being alive (vitality), of being an agent, of ownership, of embodiment, of temporal persistence, of cohesion, of demarcation from the world. In other words, we are not dealing with the issue of personality understood as a sophisticated individuality characterized by temperament and cognitive abilities, habits, personality traits, personal history, and so forth.

In schizophrenia, we are dealing with a disturbance of the very basic sense of subjectivity, which remains fully intact in other brain disorders (Parnas & Henriksen, 2014; Parnas & Zandersen, 2018; Raballo et al. 2021). This was already pointed out by the French psychiatrist Eugène Minkowski in 1927 stating that a severely organically demented patient asked the deictic question, "Who are you and where are you?" would answer, "I am me and I am here," whereas a patient with schizophrenia may say, "I am energy in the cosmos" (Minkowski, 1927).

The following vignette from one of our patients illustrates the disorder of subjecthood in schizophrenia:

> This dissolved self . . . It is a truly dissolved self. I feel that I am everywhere and nowhere at the same time. It is like a dream in which I am not present. It is like a sea where you can see fishes and plants and there is a current of water. It is in such a way that I feel that I am present. Not as a fish or a plant but as a current of water. My life feels like a manuscript written by someone else. I am open to the idea that my childhood was not my own. That my childhood is somebody else's and that I have taken it over in some way. If you said to me that what I am telling you actually is about my friend instead of me, then I would be open to this suggestion. That my ideas stem from a movie or from another person. (Parnas & Zandersen, 2021, p. 23)

In sum, schizophrenia is characterized by a disorder of the sense of subjecthood not found in any other mental or somatic illness. This has implications for schizophrenia as a disease concept. It is clear that the disorder is not something alien or extraneous to the subject. It is afflicting the subject in a very fundamental way, and the disorder cannot clearly be separated from the self. From a phenomenological perspective, the disorder of ipseity or selfhood can be considered as a basic generative level of psychopathology in schizophrenia that is implicated in the development of delusions, hallucinations, and influence phenomena (Parnas & Henriksen, 2016; Parnas et al., 2021; Parnas et al., 2023). Phenomena at the level of selfhood are not necessarily associated with the development of psychosis but may be observed in schizotypal disorders as well as in biological relatives of schizophrenia probants (Raballo & Parnas 2011; Raballo et al., 2011).

41.3 The Question of the Onset of Schizophrenia

Contemporary psychiatry often pictures schizophrenia as a well-defined disease with an easily datable onset. The onset is defined as (1) a full articulation of at least one psychotic symptom, (2) the emergence of the entire schizophrenic syndrome, or (3) a crossing of a psychometric threshold on a scale used in clinical high-risk research. In such studies, the median age of onset is approximately 25 years. However, in more classical literature, schizophrenia was considered a rather insidious disorder with difficulties of pinpointing the exact onset. In the 1970s and 1980s, during the longitudinal prospective high-risk studies (Parnas, 1999), the issue of onset was considered a conceptual rather than an empirical or technical issue. These studies uniformly indicate that schizophrenia is a developmental disorder with deviation in developmental patterns of psychomotor milestones, affectivity and cognition. During the school years, girls with pre-schizophrenia may exhibit tendencies to introversion whereas boys exhibit a mixture of introversion and acting-out behavior (Tyrka et al., 1995). The Copenhagen High-Risk study demonstrated a decreased emotional rapport in adolescents who subsequently develop schizophrenia spectrum disorder (Parnas et al., 2016). Two studies indicate that self-disorders in adolescence predict the subsequent onset of schizophrenia spectrum disorder in adult age (Koren et al., 2020; Parnas et al., 2016).

One of the early features of schizophrenia is a strange feeling of being different from others, often present since very early childhood (Parnas et al., 2021; Stephensen et al., 2024a; Stephensen et al., 2024b). One of our patients described this feeling in the following way:

> I feel like I'm not a natural human being or a proper human being or something like that. I have always tried so much to be a real human being, but I have the feeling that I'm not. (Henriksen & Nordgaard, 2016, p. 266)

When patients report this feeling of being different, they may thematize it as feeling alien on the earth, as not being the child of their biological parents and being extraterrestrial or being some sort of fantasy figure.

In a recently published self-report, a patient describes her childhood in the following way.

> I have always had this feeling that there was something deviating from the norm or different about me. As a child, I had a distinct feeling that my parents were not my parents. I was sure that I was adopted. Looking at my parents, I could not see myself in them. Back then, I did not like talking and especially to my parents. Not because I did not like them, but I was very aware that what I had inside of me, I could not talk to anyone about. I felt that I had another way of being in the world than the one I saw around me. I was seeing it with different eyes. I could not recognize myself in other children. I was quiet and thought a lot about things, and I was wondering why other children could be happy all the time. I really did not understand it. I could not just play. (Mørch, 2021, p. 1)

The Japanese psychiatrist Mari Nagai in her study of pathologies of introspection in schizophrenia uses the term "Anderssein" to label this phenomenon (Motobayashi et al., 2016). She writes that an abnormal or "neurotic" feeling of difference from peers presupposes a worldly, ontic dimension of comparison. Thus, one can feel fatter than others, tiny compared to others, coming from a poor family, and so forth. Nagai argues that in schizophrenia it is the very dimension of comparison that the patient cannot articulate, because the issue of difference pertains to the very ontological structure of being in the world. Consequently, the worldly characteristics to which the patient points are simply attempts to articulate a prior and ineffable feeling of profound difference. The altered ontological structure is of course linked to the disorders of selfhood, which become manifest in the patients' relation to the world and others.

One of our patients came to treatment with a list of all her faults.

I am stupid
I am ugly
I walk wrongly
I sing wrongly
I am too slow
I am too fast
My head is ugly
Etc…

This seemingly endless list testifies to the difficulty the patient experiences in providing a concrete self-description. Instead, we are presented with an array of adjectives that cover an ineffable feeling of being "wrong" or different. *Forkert*, the Danish word for "wrong," points etymologically to something that is composed in a skewed way (Henriksen & Parnas, 2014).

During the adolescence, which is the age of maximal self-reflection, many patients experience solipsistic feelings, feelings of radical alienation from other people and interest in existential or philosophical issues, and they may have a sense of being able to penetrate into deeper layers of reality than others can. Such experiences may acquire a delusional quality, which is only rarely detectable during a psychiatric interview.

In sum, it is most often impossible to date the onset of schizophrenia. This is not due to a "lack of data" but because the notion of onset is not properly conceptualized. We must assume that the nature and range of psychopathology will be heavily age dependent. The available phenomenological data indicate that schizophrenia is a very gradual process with antecedents in very early childhood, and we cannot expect a full DSM-5 syndrome to emerge at the age of 5 years.

41.4 Lack of Insight and Double Bookkeeping

The DSM-5 considers impaired insight into illness as an intrinsic feature of schizophrenia along its other symptoms. The DSM compares the impaired insight with the neurological disorder of anosognosia. The medical definition of insight comprises awareness of suffering from an illness, its potential consequences and risk factors, and the need of treatment. A somatic patient with an insight into her illness is in a reflective position; she looks at her symptoms and makes a judgment that these symptoms are unwanted and indicate the disease. Such reflection presupposes a subject–object experiential distance, where the intact "reflecting self" judges its own body part, organ, or a part of her own mental life as being ill. However, in schizophrenia there is no actual possibility of such a distance. Since schizophrenia is an affliction of subjectivity, the subject cannot coil upon oneself and judge the objectified subject as being ill (Henriksen & Parnas, 2014). In other words, the affected subjectivity cannot reflect on itself in any "impartial" manner. Professor Saks describes this lack of insight in schizophrenia from a first personal perspective:

> I completely recognized that the things I was saying and doing and feeling would be thought to amount to a diagnosis of schizophrenia; but I thought that it was not true – I did not really have the illness (. . .) So, my thinking went, I looked like I had schizophrenia (. . .) but if we knew enough, we would see that I really did not. (Saks, 2009, p. 972)

What we understand from this vignette is that despite all her symptoms of schizophrenia, Saks still believed that at the deepest level she was not sick, but rather had an insight and knowledge that surpassed the current status of science. This vignette brings us to the issue of a very characteristic feature of the schizophrenic psychosis, namely "double bookkeeping." This term was coined by Bleuler, but was already described at the beginning of modern psychiatry by Pinel and Esquirol (Parnas et al., 2021). The patient lives in two realities: one that is our shared common reality of the social world with all its demands and difficulties; and another that is not of this world, but rather linked to some hidden transcendent dimension. To Saks, this transcendent dimension was a layer of the world not yet discovered by science. It is important not to conflate double bookkeeping with the obvious fact that all psychotic patients live their psychoses in our shared common reality. In the case of organic psychosis or delusional disorder (paranoia), the patient's psychosis is attempted to be integrated in our shared social world, whereas in schizophrenia, psychosis happens, so to say, in another world – that is, outside our social reality.

A comparison of delusional disorder and schizophrenia is illustrated by the following cases. One of our patients (Parnas et al., 2021) suffering from delusional disorder was convinced that the tap water was toxic and caused her skin problems and a general malaise. She contacted her own general practitioner several times. There were several inspections by the technical authorities from the municipality, which failed to detect anything wrong with the water. The patient ended up believing there was a conspiracy among her own doctor, the technical authorities, and the mayor of the municipality.

Another patient of ours, who suffered from schizophrenia, had a similar belief about the toxicity of water. He did not contact any public authorities but, after some experimentation, found the solution himself: he stored water in containers on his balcony to detoxify it in the fresh air and then used it for cooking.

In a phenomenological perspective, the kernel of double bookkeeping and of the articulation of the psychotic world is connected to a fragmentation of the self. A part of the subject becomes an Alter (another), and this "otherness" in the midst of subjectivity becomes a kernel on which further alienation may be articulated in terms of delusions, hallucinations, or phenomena of influence (Parnas et al., 2024; Sandsten et al., 2022). In other words, double bookkeeping implies a modification of the private subjective space into a private psychotic world, where the physical loss of nature and the principle of non-contradiction do not apply.

Because the psychotic affliction happens in the midst of the subjectivity as a revelation, there is no possibility of inner reflective distance. The affliction possesses a value and status of truth and validity, which cannot be contradicted by empirical arguments. One of Esquirol's patients said to him, "you are completely right, but you cannot convince me" (Parnas et al., 2021). For the patient, an empirical counterargument is in principle irrelevant and does not apply to his private world. In a similar way, we cannot talk somebody out of having a toothache. The two worlds are incommensurable in their mode of being.

Thus, in double bookkeeping there is a strange coexistence of attitudes. During an interview, a female patient mentioned that she heard her mother's voice talking negatively about her while her mother was miles away in her own apartment. The patient confronted her mother with the hallucinatory content, and the mother of course denied having said anything like that. The patient turned to the interviewer and said, "and then I do not know what to believe." It did not occur to the patient that it was physically impossible to hear her mother talking from several miles away, and apparently she expected that this impossibility would also not strike the psychiatrist.

It is important to emphasize that the condition of double bookkeeping is rather persistent, and the usual distinction between remissions and relapses becomes problematic in this perspective (Jones & Shattell, 2016). However, the condition of double bookkeeping may occasionally collapse, and the patient may act out their psychotic experiences in the shared social world. It is also important not to consider the psychotic experience as a fictive product of imagination, because to the patient it possesses a meaningful value of truth. Thus, the therapeutic goal should not be simply to remove delusions and hallucinations assuming that a healthy person is left behind. Rather, it is important to treat the patient in a way that allows them to establish a meaningful existence in which the two realities of the double bookkeeping do not interfere with each other.

41.5 The Course and Outcome of Schizophrenia

At the societal level, schizophrenia is a very expensive illness, only surpassed by cardiovascular diseases. Schizophrenia is associated with increased premature mortality due to suicide and to somatic illness. Patients with schizophrenia have an increased risk of drug and alcohol abuse and criminal behavior. Long-term follow-up studies find that approximately one-third of the patients have a chronic unremitting course whereas the remainder either recover or have only mild to moderate symptoms (Molstrom et al., 2022). However, such research employs rather gross measurement tools and cannot address neither the issue of double bookkeeping nor the current movement of "recovery." Finally, it must be stressed that schizophrenia is very often associated with immense suffering in the affected individuals and their relatives. In this respect, schizophrenia displays many features also pertaining to the standard notion of disease.

However, also with respect to course and outcome, schizophrenia displays paradoxical features, some of which we have already mentioned in the preceding section. In addition, we will point out the somewhat paradoxical findings in some studies (Katschnik, 2000; Larsen & Gerlach, 1996) that patients with schizophrenia do not differ markedly from control populations on the quality of life as measured by psychometric scales. Some patients with schizophrenia become doctors, faculty members, or professors and lead a seemingly normal life despite their symptoms. With respect to "recovery," many patients are in fact not willing to give up their contact with the transcendent dimensions, their ability to hyper-reflect, or even their auditory verbal hallucinations. The symptoms are an integrated part of their subjectivity, and removing the symptoms may, in some patients, correspond to turning off a part of themselves and results in a painful feeling of emptiness.

> One day I felt a strange and peculiar sensation but could not figure out what was different until I realized that my mind was silent for the first time in my life; it was strange. I had to understand this silence; what was it? That day I thought I had had a stroke since there were no sounds. [. . .] The first couple of months, I missed the voices; they had been part of me for so long; what was I to do without them?" (Mørck, 2023, p. 2)

Although Mørck (2023) manages to find her way without the voices and feels relieved, she also felt like having to "reconnect" with her mind again.

There are empirical studies showing that schizophrenia may be associated with increased creativity among biological relatives (Kyaga et al., 2011). The relationship between creativity and psychopathology is often portrayed as an inverse u-curve (Acar et al., 2018; Karlsson, 1970). Thus, minor levels of psychopathology increase creativity until a certain threshold, and thereafter, with increasing psychopathology, there is a dramatic decline in creative abilities. In light of our preceding discussion, the increased creativity in some patients and their relatives may be viewed as part of their fundamental psychopathology. The person is not constrained by the dogmas of prevailing common sense and may have access to the ontological dimensions of human existence. Such access is characteristic for many of the valuable cultural productions. Thus, with respect to creativity, schizophrenia deviates dramatically from the standard notion of disease.

41.6 Conclusion

Schizophrenia has continuously been regarded as a brain disease with some form of chains in the neuron substrate. At the time of Kraepelin, an entrance ticket to the academic career in psychiatry was a neuroanatomic publication. Today, this entrance ticket frequently consists in fMRI studies. Despite the concerted effort in this research paradigm, we still have no clear idea about the pathogenesis of schizophrenia.

It seems that on several dimensions, schizophrenia deviates from a typical notion of a disease. All these deviations are linked to the psychopathological nature of schizophrenia. However, the level of psychopathological knowledge among psychiatrists has declined dramatically because the DSM and ICD manuals function as textbooks. It is also clear that scientists working with schizophrenia have a quite limited familiarity with its clinical picture.

We have arrived at our depiction of schizophrenia through a combination of clinical work with schizophrenia patients, longitudinal studies of offspring of schizophrenic mothers, psychopathological interviews in the Copenhagen linkage study, and systematic research on self disorders in the schizophrenia spectrum over the last thirty years. The depiction we have presented is certainly different from the standard portrayal of schizophrenia and will probably strike many readers as quite exotic. However, it is compatible with the foundational descriptions of schizophrenia and especially with the contributions of phenomenological psychiatry (Blankenburg, 1971; Minkowski, 1927; Tatossian, 1978).

In our view, schizophrenia deviates markedly on several points from the standard notion of a brain disease. Schizophrenia is basically an expression of altered structures of subjectivity that have no analog either in somatic medicine or among other psychiatric disorders. Unless we have a profound understanding of the fundamental psychological mechanisms operating in schizophrenia spectrum disorders, the likelihood of an empirical breakthrough seems to us quite meager.

REFERENCES

Acar, S., Chen, X., & Cayirdag, N. (2018). Schizophrenia and creativity: A meta-analytic review. *Schizophrenia Research, 195*, 23–31.

Andreasen, N. C. (1984). *The broken brain: The biological revolution in psychiatry.* Harper & Row.

Blankenburg, W. (1971). *Der Verlust Der Natürlichen Selbstverständlichkeit: Ein Beitrag Zur Psychopathologie Symptomarmer Schizophrenien.* Enke.

Bleuler, E. (1950 [1911]). *Dementia praecox or the group of schizophrenias* (J. Zinkin, Transl.). International Universities Press.

Henriksen, M. G., & Parnas, J. (2014). Self-disorders and schizophrenia: A phenomenological reappraisal of poor insight and noncompliance. *Schizophrenia Bulletin, 40*(3), 542–547. https://doi.org/10.1093/schbul/sbt087

Henriksen, M. G., & Nordgaard, J. (2016). Self-disorders in schizophrenia. In G. Stanghellini & M. Aragona (Eds.), *An experiential approach to psychopathology: What is it like to suffer from mental disorders?* (pp. 265–280). Springer.

Insel, T. R., & Cuthbert, B. N. (2015). Medicine. Brain disorders? Precisely. *Science, 348*(6234), 499–500. https://doi.org/10.1126/science.aab2358

Jaspers, K. (1997 [1959]). *General psychopathology* (J. Hoenig & M. W. Hamilton, Transl.). John Hopkins.

Jones, N., & Shattell, M. (2016). Not what the textbooks describe: Challenging clinical conventions about psychosis. *Issues of Mental Health in Nursing, 37*(10), 769–772. https://doi.org/10.1080/01612840.2016.1180725

Karlsson, J. L. (1970). Genetic association of giftedness and creativity with schizophrenia. *Hereditas, 66* (2), 177–182. https://doi.org/10.1111/j.1601-5223.1970.tb02343.x

Katschnig, H. (2000). Schizophrenia and quality of life. *Acta Psychiatrica Scandinavica Supplement, 407*, 33–37. https://doi.org/10.1034/j.1600-0447.2000.00006.x

Koren, D., Tzivoni, Y., Schalit, L., Adres, M., Reznik, N., Apter, A., & Parnas, J. (2020). Basic self-disorders in adolescence predict schizophrenia spectrum disorders in young adulthood: A 7-year follow-up study among non-psychotic help-seeking adolescents. *Schizophrenia Research, 216*, 97–103. https://doi.org/10.1016/j.schres.2019.12.022

Kraepelin, E. (1899). *Lehrbuch Der Psychiatrie* (6th ed.). Johann Ambrosius Barth.

Kyaga, S., Lichtenstein, P., Boman, M., Hultman, C., Långström, N., & Landén, M. (2011). Creativity and mental disorder: Family study of 300,000 people with severe mental disorder. *British Journal of Psychiatry, 199*(5), 373–379. https://doi.org/10.1192/bjp.bp.110.085316

Larsen, E. B., & Gerlach, J. (1996). Subjective experience of treatment, side-effects, mental state and quality of life in chronic schizophrenic out-patients treated with depot neuroleptics. *Acta Psychiatrica Scandinavica, 93*(5), 381–388. https://doi.org/10.1111/j.1600-0447.1996.tb10664.x

Minkowski, E. (1927). *La Schizophrénie. Psychopathologie Des Schizoides Et Des Schizophrènes*. Payot.

Molstrom, I. M., Nordgaard, J., Urfer-Parnas, A., Handest, R., Berge, J., & Henriksen, M. G. (2022). The prognosis of schizophrenia: A systematic review and meta-analysis with meta-regression of 20-year follow-up studies. *Schizophrenia Research, 250*, 152–163. https://doi.org/10.1016/j.schres.2022.11.010

Motobayashi, Y., Parnas, J., Kimura, B., & Toda, D. L. (2016). "The 'Schizophrenic' in the Self-Consciousness of Schizophrenic Patients", by Mari Nagai (1990). *History of Psychiatry, 27*(4), 493–503. https://doi.org/10.1177/0957154x16660457

Mørck, C. H. (2023). Awakening from schizophrenia. *Schizophrenia Bulletin*, sbad051. https://doi.org/10.1093/schbul/sbad051

Mørck, H. C. (2021). To see with closed eyes. *Schizophrenia Bulletin, 47* (2), 273–274. https://doi.org/10.1093/schbul/sbaa108

Parnas, J. (1999). From predisposition to psychosis: Progression of symptoms in schizophrenia. *Acta Psychiatrica Scandinavica Supplement, 395*, 20–29. https://doi.org/10.1111/j.1600-0447.1999.tb05979.x

Parnas, J., Carter, J., & Nordgaard, J. (2016). Premorbid self-disorders and lifetime diagnosis in the schizophrenia spectrum: A prospective high-risk study. *Early Interventional Psychiatry, 10*(1), 45–53. https://doi.org/10.1111/eip.12140

Parnas, J., & Henriksen, M. G. (2014). Disordered self in the schizophrenia spectrum: A clinical and research perspective. *Harvard Review Psychiatry, 22*(5), 251–265. https://doi.org/10.1097/hrp.0000000000000040

(2016). Mysticism and schizophrenia: A phenomenological exploration of the structure of consciousness in the schizophrenia spectrum disorders. *Consciousness and Cognition, 43*, 75–88.

Parnas, J., Raballo, A., Handest, P., Jansson, L., Vollmer-Larsen, A., & Saebye, D. (2011). Self-experience in the early phases of schizophrenia: 5-year follow-up of the Copenhagen Prodromal Study. *World Psychiatry, 10*(3), 200–204. https://doi.org/10.1002/j.2051-5545.2011.tb00057.x

Parnas, J., Urfer-Parnas, A., & Stephensen, H. (2021). Double bookkeeping and schizophrenia spectrum: Divided unified phenomenal consciousness. *European Archives of Psychiatry and Clinical Neuroscience, 271*(8), 1513–1523. https://doi.org/10.1007/s00406-020-01185-0

Parnas, J., Yttri, J. E., & Urfer-Parnas, A. (2024). Phenomenology of auditory verbal hallucination in schizophrenia: An erroneous perception or something else? *Schizophrenia Research, 265*, 83–88. https://doi.org/10.1016/j.schres.2023.03.045

Parnas, J., & Zandersen, M. (2018). Self and schizophrenia: Current status and diagnostic implications. *World Psychiatry, 17*(2), 220–221. https://doi.org/10.1002/wps.20528

(2021). Talking to patients and rediscovering disordered selfhood in schizophrenia. *Psychiatric Times, 38*(1), 23–26.

Raballo, A., & Parnas, J. (2011). The silent side of the spectrum: Schizotypy and the schizotaxic self. *Schizophrenia Bulletin, 37*(5), 1017–1026. https://doi.org/10.1093/schbul/sbq008

Raballo, A., Poletti, M., Preti, A., & Parnas, J. (2021). The self in the spectrum: A meta-analysis of the evidence linking basic self-disorders and schizophrenia. *Schizophrenia Bulletin, 47*(4), 1007–1017. https://doi.org/10.1093/schbul/sbaa201

Raballo, A., Sæbye, D., & Parnas, J. (2011). Looking at the schizophrenia spectrum through the prism of self-disorders: An empirical study. *Schizophrenia Bulletin, 37*(2), 344–351. https://doi.org/10.1093/schbul/sbp056

Saks, E. R. (2009). Some thoughts on denial of mental illness. *American Journal of Psychiatry, 166*(9), 972–973. https://doi.org/10.1176/appi.ajp.2009.09030409

Sandsten, K. E., Zahavi, D., & Parnas, J. (2022). Disorder of selfhood in schizophrenia: A symptom or a gestalt? *Psychopathology, 55*(5), 273–281. https://doi.org/10.1159/000524100

Scharfetter, C. (1980). *General psychopathology: An introduction*. Cambridge University Press.

Schneider, K. (1959). *Clinical psychopathology* (M. W. Hamilton, Transl.). Grune & Stratton.

Stephensen, H., Urfer-Parnas, A., & Parnas, J. (2024a). Double bookkeeping in schizophrenia spectrum disorder: An empirical-phenomenological study. *European Archives of Psychiatry and Clinical Neuroscience, 274*(6), 1405–1415. https://doi.org/10.1007/s00406-023-01609-7

(2024b). An empirical-phenomenological exploration of anderssein ("feeling different") in schizophrenia: Being in-between particular and universal. *Psychopathology,* 57(6), 245–269.

Tatossian, A. (1978). *La Phénoménologie Des Psychoses.* Masson.

Tyrka, A. R., Cannon, T. D., Haslam, N., Mednick, S. A., Schulsinger, F., Schulsinger, H., & Parnas, J. (1995). The latent structure of schizotypy: I. Premorbid Indicators of a taxon of individuals at risk for schizophrenia-spectrum disorders. *Journal of Abnormal Psychology, 104*(1), 173–183. https://doi.org/10.1037//0021-843x.104.1.173

CHAPTER 42

Commentary on Parnas and Zandersen's "A Disease Like No Other"

Shaun Gallagher

Precision psychiatry, as part of precision medicine, centers its analysis on biomarkers (genes), environment, and lifestyle.[1] In descriptions of precision psychiatry, however, the roles played by environmental factors, lifestyle, and subjective experience are quickly downplayed, especially if such things cannot be easily translated into computational data. This is very clear in the following characterization.

> The endeavour of bringing precision medicine to psychiatry rests on, and simultaneously contributes to, the evolving knowledge of the biological pathways involved in the major mental illnesses. It builds on the aims of the Research Domain Criteria by the National Institute of Mental Health ... which has initiated a research approach to generating a neurobiologically valid framework for classifying mental illness and for generating novel interventions related to neurobiological underpinnings. (Fernandes et al., 2017, p. 2)

In this view, precision psychiatry searches for "a simply definable pathological mechanism" and is therefore centered on brain research, primarily concerned with "data from physiological recordings, brain imaging, 'omics' biomarkers" (Fernandes et al., 2017, p. 2; also Insel & Cuthberg, 2015). Added, almost as an afterthought, are "environmental exposures and self-reported experience," which are understood as data points that ultimately translate to neural activations – aiming for an "integrative understanding of mental illness as disorders of the brain" (Fernandes et al., 2017, p. 2). Essential to the project of precision psychiatry is the integration of information across a massive amount of data to be framed in terms of systems biology and modeled by "computational psychiatry tools to produce a

[1] *Toward Precision Medicine. Building a Knowledge Network for Biomedical Research and a New Taxonomy of Disease. National Research Council Committee on a Framework for Developing a New Taxonomy of Disease.* Washington, DC: National Academies Press; 2011. Cited in Fernandes et al. (2017).

biosignature – a set of biomarkers – that, when applied to individuals and populations, will produce better diagnosis, endophenotypes (measurable components unseen by the unaided eye along the pathway between disease and distal genotype), classifications and prognosis, as well as tailored interventions for better outcomes" (Fernandes, 2017, p. 3).[2]

Explaining the origin of the term "precision psychiatry," Fernandes et al. write:

> The original term, personalised medicine, was changed to precision medicine to emphasise that its technologies and treatments are not developed for each individual patient, as the term personalised suggests, but rather that a high level of exactness in measurement will be achieved such that, eventually, it will be personalised. (2017, p. 3)

This change of terminology signals a complete change in direction, away from personalized psychiatry and orthogonal to where clinicians aim to arrive. The roundabout idea is that to attain a personalized psychiatry we need to make it as impersonal and as mathematically measurable as possible. If there is a hint of the personal in the environmental and experiential dimensions, we need to translate them into more computational friendly terms.

Furthermore, again signaling the opposite of a personalized psychiatry, precision psychiatry does not abandon classification systems, but claims to improve them, creating a "highly sophisticated and intricate classification system, where infinitesimal categories will, ideally, attain perfection in a detailed multidimensional classification" (Fernandes et al., 2017, p. 4). Again, this promises to ultimately lead to more individualized, albeit not precisely personalized, treatment. Rather, "In precision psychiatry . . . a given patient would receive an existent treatment pre-established according to the patient's disease class, and not a medication that would be specifically created for that individual following consideration of their unique features, as would be the case in 'personalised psychiatry'" (Fernandez et al., 2017, p. 4). There is some disagreement in this respect, however. Passos et al. (2022, p. 24) claims that the endpoint of precision psychiatry is the "unique person," the "real patient." But one important question is how one conceives of that unique person, and in one reading, that person is defined with precision by a big set of impersonal data points that determine the classification in which he or she falls.

[2] Passos et al. (2022, p. 22), in an article entitled "Precision psychiatry: The future is now," seemingly admit that it not yet now, since "the use of treatment response calculators in the clinic has not yet been validated, and its independent use has not been showed to surpass the ability of clinicians."

Fernandez et al. conceive of precision psychiatry as an advance beyond Aristotelian science, which they portray as "normal" science, using Thomas Kuhn's phrase. In contrast, their paradigm-changing non-Aristotelian science is more Marxist in the sense that its aim is not to just describe the world but to change it, by teaming up with advanced technology. Whether this is a precise characterization of the Aristotelian/non-Aristotelian contrast, there is one principle that derives from Aristotle that may be disruptive to the massive project of precision psychiatry, namely Aristotle's contention that each science can only be as precise as its subject matter allows, or "as the nature of the subject permits" (Aristotle, 2014, p. 1094b). Since the subject of psychiatry is precisely the human subject or person, the idea of associating precision in psychiatry with the impersonal seems counterintuitive.

Parnas and Zandersen offer an alternative. Specifically, in regard to schizophrenia, they offer a phenomenological precision, which is to say, only as much precision as the subject permits. For the person with schizophrenia the self disorder involves a blind spot in their experience – it's "an affliction that prevents a full insight into illness" (Parnas & Zandersen, Chapter 41 in this volume). But a subjective blind spot is not the only thing that disrupts precision.[3] The difficulty also concerns the phenomenological status of the subject's *world* (rather than environment), and the package that we encounter in the subject's experience. The subject's experience is a package because it includes a mix of reflective and prereflective processes that are not easily pulled apart. Parnas and Zandersen call it the "self," which includes ipseity, a very basic sense of self. It is difficult to provide precise measurements of self and world, I suggest, because they are co-constituted in dynamical, nonlinear relational processes.[4]

What we find on both sides of this co-constitution, in the case of schizophrenia, is an immeasurable instability that leads to a double counting or double bookkeeping. Parnas and Zandersen attempt to be as precise as possible in their description of the self disorder: the "very basic sense of ipseity is unstable. The patient may feel ephemeral, not fully existing, not properly awake, or having a problematic sense of self-coincidence, i.e. a difficulty 'catching up' with herself." Their focus on

[3] What Parnas and Zandersen say about the indeterminacy of the time of onset for schizophrenia fits here: "[I]t is most often impossible to date the onset of schizophrenia. This is not due to a 'lack of data,' but because the notion of onset is not properly conceptualized" (Chapter 41 in this volume).

[4] In precision psychiatry such nonlinear patterns are said to be addressed by machine learning and big data techniques (Passos et al., 2022).

ipseity, however, may be too sharp, and seemingly somewhat surgical. Although there may be several dimensions involved in ipseity, including "a sense of existing and being alive (vitality), a sense of being an agent, a sense of ownership, embodiment, a sense of temporal persistence, a sense of cohesion, a sense of demarcation from the world," it is not clear that this means that "we are not dealing with the issue of personality understood as a sophisticated individuality characterized by temperament and cognitive abilities, habits, personality traits, personal history, etc." Over time all of these aspects of self (or what I have elsewhere called a "self-pattern"; Gallagher, 2024) may be affected by disruptions of prereflective ipseity, and may then loop around to modulate basic ipseity in further interactions. We can think here about the different timescales involved in ipseic processes and their relation to additional and perhaps more complex processes that involve reflection, memory, and a narrative time frame. Thus, the patient with schizophrenia quoted by Parnas and Zandersen indicates a difficulty in just that autobiographical narrative dimension: "My life feels like a manuscript written by someone else. I am open to the idea that my childhood was not my own." In this context, to be precise is not to make a surgical incision that would cut these processes (ipseic versus self-narrative) off from one another, but to recognize how they dynamically interact, and how those interactions come as part of the package called self.

Likewise, the sense of "demarcation from the world" is not so clear-cut. As Parnas and Zandersen suggest, in schizophrenia, the "very ontological structure of being in the world" is altered, and this is "manifest in the patients' relation to the world and others" (Chapter 41 in this volume). We can think of this in terms of what the phenomenologist Alfred Schutz (1974) called "multiple realities." In the case of schizophrenic delusions, the everyday "paramount" reality seemingly exists side by side with a delusional reality (Morales & Gallagher, 2023). As Parnas and Zandersen put it, "The patient lives in two realities: one reality which is our shared common reality of the social world with all its demands and difficulties, and another reality, which is not of this world, but is rather linked to some hidden transcendent dimension." Accordingly, the experiencing subject does not live in one unified world of meaning that can be measured objectively in a view from nowhere; rather, that person lives in multiple realities that exist in an ambiguous relation to one another. Importantly, in different realities I may not be my everyday self, and I may thus experience myself differently. Additionally, what is a true belief that could be measured in one reality (the delusion) may be classified as a false belief in the other (shared world), just as in one reality (of the theatrical play) it is true to say that Hamlet killed Polonius but in the other reality (of everyday life) this is not true, since Hamlet and Polonius are mere fictional characters. World differences lead to double bookkeeping, a schizophrenic accounting where 1 in the delusional world is 0 in everyday reality. The ambiguity involved in double bookkeeping is not something we can resolve once we have the correct data; it is part of the phenomenon of schizophrenia; it is an irregular bit that cannot be made precise by finding the right algorithm or measure.[5]

Even if precision psychiatry followed the model of precision medicine to consider lifestyle in addition to biomarkers and environment, according to some studies (Katschnik, 2000; Larsen & Gerlach, 1996), as Parnas and Zandersen point out, "patients with schizophrenia do not differ markedly from control populations on the quality of life as measured by psychometric scales."

> Some patients with schizophrenia become doctors, faculty members, or professors and lead a seemingly normal life despite their symptoms. With respect to "recovery", many patients are in fact not willing to give up their contact to the transcendent dimensions, their ability to hyper-reflect or even their auditory verbal hallucinations. The symptoms are an integrated part of their subjectivity and removing the symptoms may in some patients correspond to turning off a part of themselves and resolves in a painful feeling of emptiness. (Parnas & Zandersen, Chapter 41 in this volume)

In this respect, it is difficult to know precisely what counts as recovery. Should recovery be measured as changing a molecular biosignature, righting the "omics" network, or normalizing the patient's fMRI results?

The precision in phenomenology is to recognize that experiences of self and world are not precise; they are full of ambiguities, uncertainties, imperfect processes, and multiple timescales that extend over multiple realities that may be more or often less integrated. The starting point for phenomenology is the imprecision of the person rather than the supposed precision of categorizations, genes, brain images, and individualized medication routines. This is not to say that we should dismiss the project of precision psychiatry and its advanced tool set. We should not, however, assume that precision can be fully defined in strict objectivist,

[5] There is more to say about the unpredictability of transitions between these worlds – what, following Maria Lugones, we can call "world traveling," which is sometimes voluntary and sometimes involuntary. In either case such transitions are not necessarily individually pathological, and in some cases they may reflect social pathologies (see Morales & Gallagher, 2023).

mathematical, computational terms without losing sight of the subject. The unique person should not be viewed as the endpoint, a technologically classified subject ready for the cure, but rather the beginning point of a unique encounter.

REFERENCES

Aristotle. (2014). *Nicomachean ethics* (R. Crisp, Ed. and Transl.). Cambridge University Press.

Fernandes, B. S., Williams, L. M., Steiner, J., Leboyer, M., Carvalho, A. F., & Berk, M. (2017). The new field of "precision psychiatry." *BMC Medicine, 15*(1), 1–7. https://doi.org/10.1186/s12916-017-0849-x

Gallagher, S.. (2024). *The self and its disorders.* Oxford University Press.

Insel, T. R., & Cuthbert, B. N. (2015). Brain disorders? Precisely. *Science, 348*(6234), 499–500.

Katschnig, H. (2000). Schizophrenia and quality of life. *Acta Psychiatrica Scandinavica, 102*, 33–37.

Larsen, E. B., & Gerlach, J. (1996). Subjective experience of treatment, side-effects, mental state and quality of life in chronic schizophrenic out-patients treated with depot neuroleptics. *Acta Psychiatrica Scandinavica, 93*(5), 381–388.

Morales, A., & Gallagher, S. (2023). Delusional realities, world traveling and transitional objects. In A. Falcato & J. Gonçalves (Eds.), *The philosophy and psychology of delusions: Historical and contemporary perspectives* (pp. 112–126). Routledge.

Passos, I. C., Ballester, P., Rabelo-da-Ponte, F. D., & Kapczinski, F. (2022). Precision psychiatry: The future is now. *The Canadian Journal of Psychiatry, 67*(1), 21–25.

Index

For EU product safety concerns, contact us at Calle de José Abascal, 56–1°,
28003 Madrid, Spain or eugpsr@cambridge.org.

www.ingramcontent.com/pod-product-compliance
Lightning Source LLC
LaVergne TN
LVHW011657200926
848484LV00004B/966

* 9 7 8 1 0 0 9 3 9 0 6 3 7 *